A-Z GREATER GLASGOW

REFERENCE

Motorway	**M8**		Car Park (selected)	P
A Road	**A77**		Church or Chapel	†
B Road	**B812**		Cycleway (selected)	🚲
Dual Carriageway				■
Tunnel	**A739**			H
One-way Street	Traffic flow on A Roads is also indicated by a heavy line on the driver's left.	→		13 8
Road Under Construction	Opening dates are correct at the time of publication.		Information Centre	i
Proposed Road			National Grid Reference	⁶60
Junction Name	TOWNHEAD INTERCHANGE		Park and Ride	Kelvinbridge **P+R**
Restricted Access			Police Station	▲
Pedestrianized Road			Post Office	★
Track / Footpath			Toilet	▽
Residential Walkway			Viewpoint	☀
Clean Air Zone	Zone edge. Within Zone.		Educational Establishment	▢
Railway	Level Crossing / Station / Tunnel		Hospital or Healthcare Building	▢
Subway (SPT) Station	Ⓢ		Industrial Building	▢
Built-up Area	MILL ST.		Leisure or Recreational Facility	▢
Local Authority Boundary	▬ · ▬ · ▬		Place of Interest	▢
Postcode Boundary	▬ ▬ ▬		Public Building	▢
Map Continuation	40 Large Scale City Centre 4		Shopping Centre or Market	▢
			Other Selected Buildings	▢

Barcode: T0340404

SCALE

Map Pages 4-7 1:5,855

0	⅛	¼ Mile
0 100 200	200	400 Metres

10.82 inches (27.49cm) to 1 mile 17.08cm to 1km

Map Page 6-165 1:11,733

0	¼	½ Mile
0 250	500	500 Metres

5.4 inches (13.728cm) to 1 mile 8.52cm to 1km

EDITION 7 2023

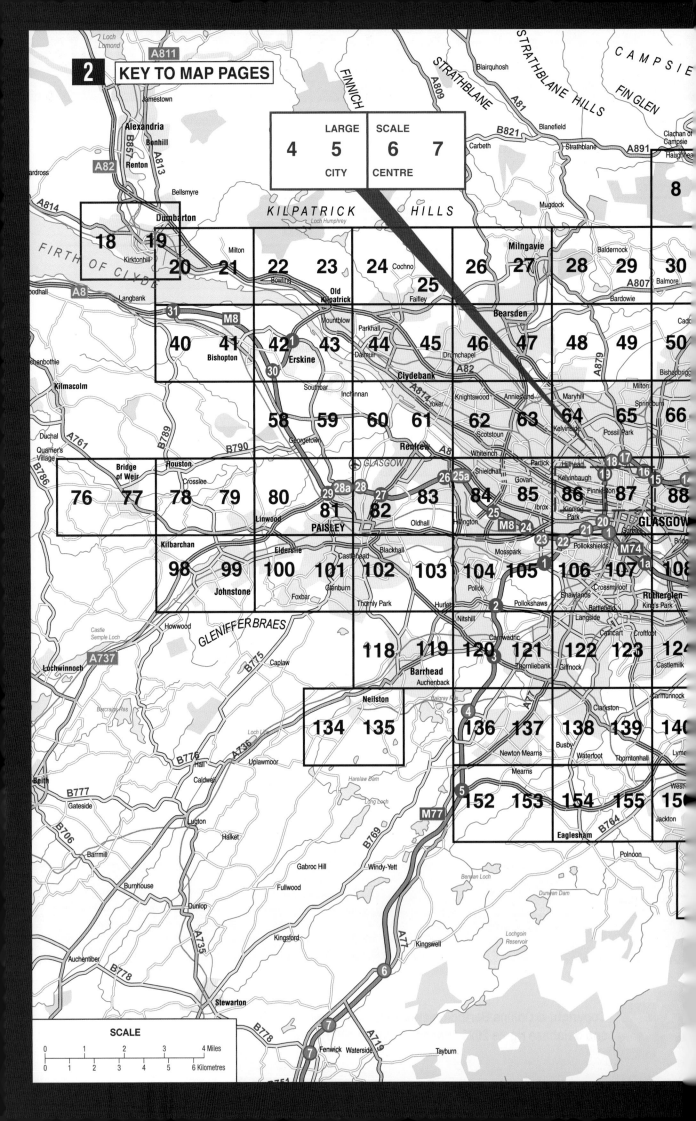

2 KEY TO MAP PAGES

	LARGE	SCALE	
4	**5**	**6**	**7**
	CITY	CENTRE	

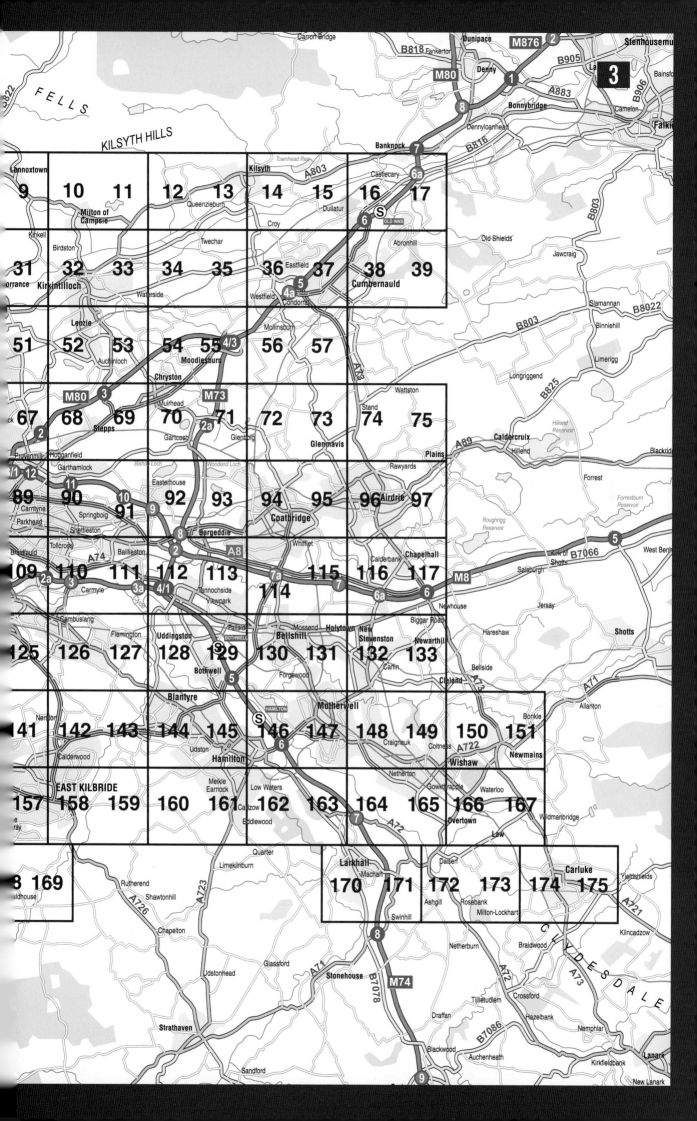

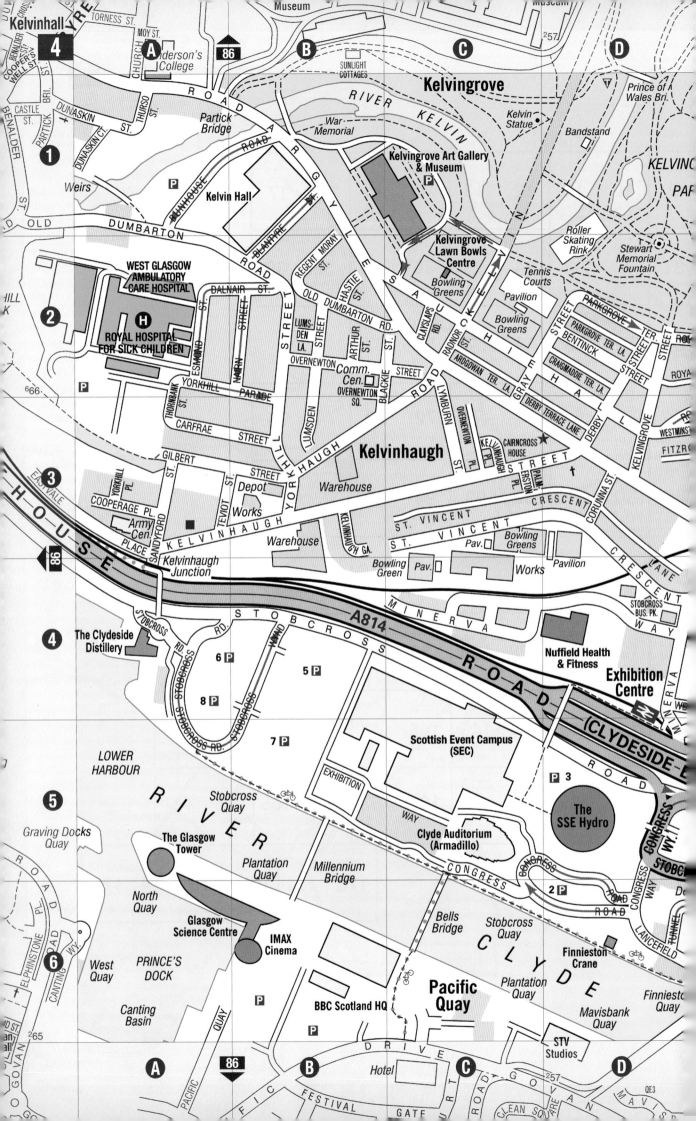

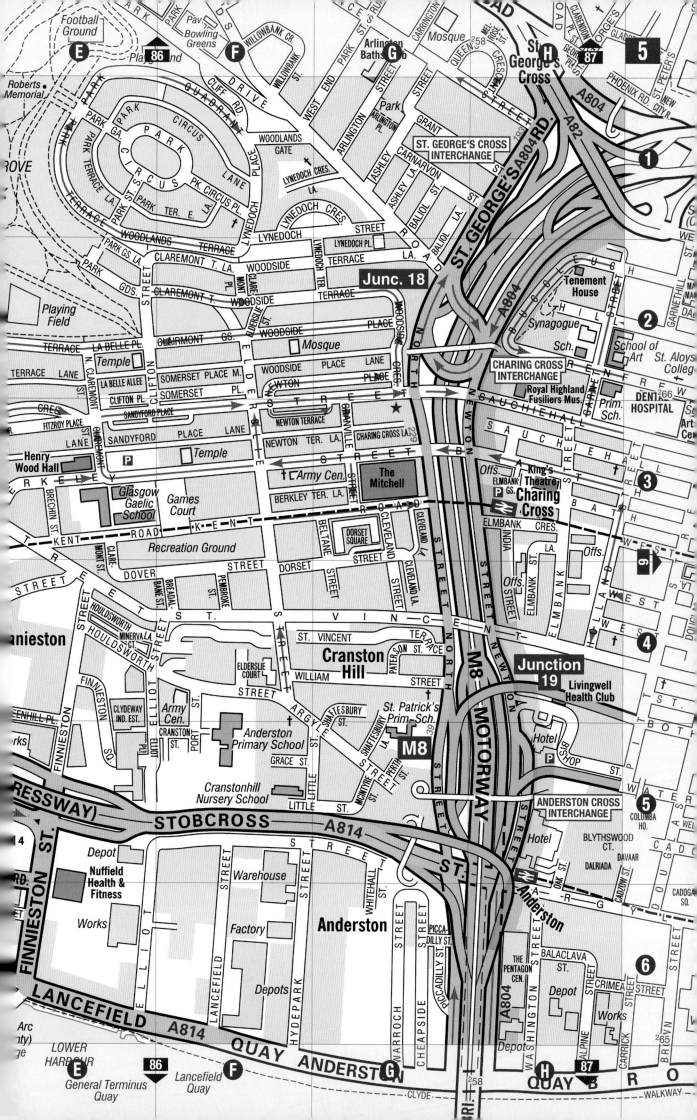

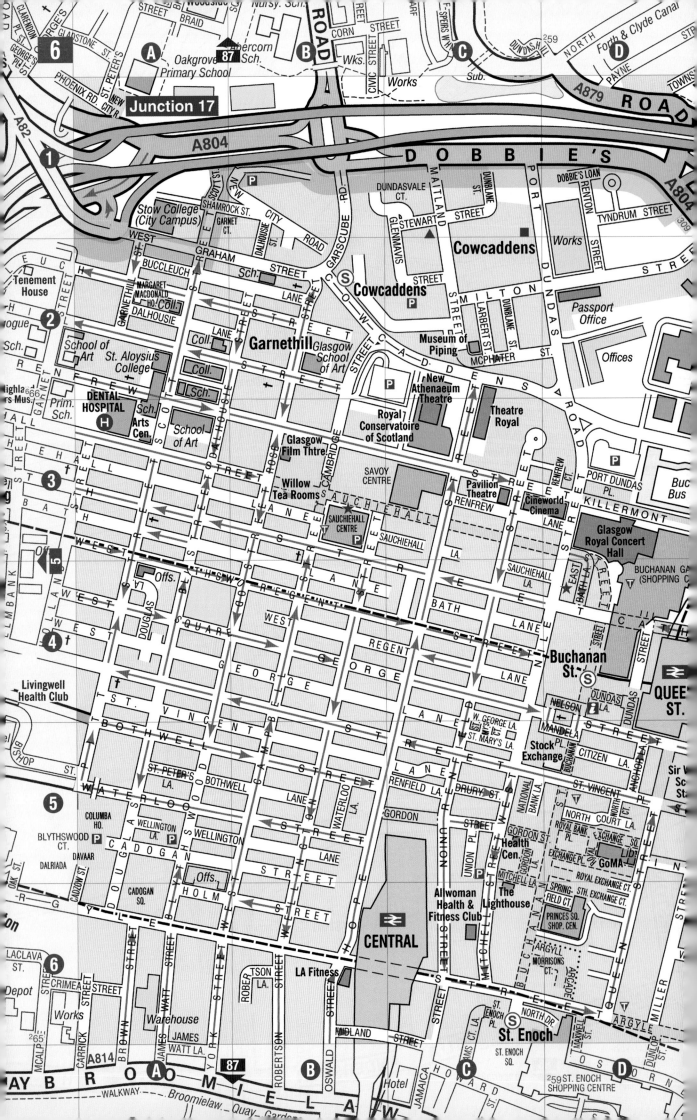

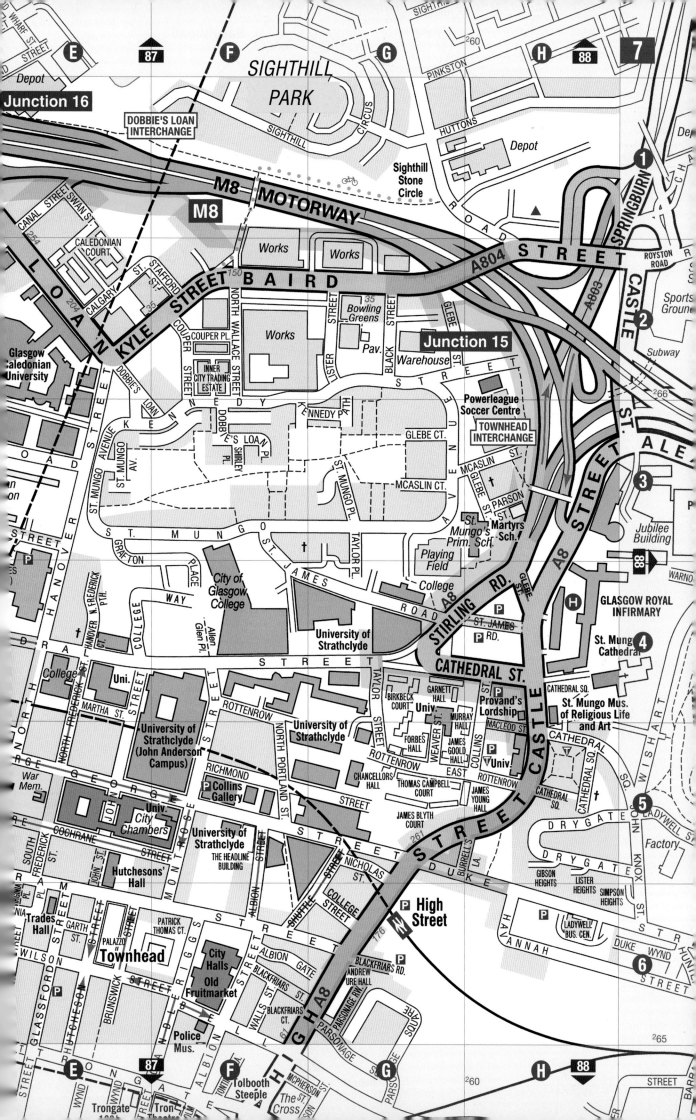

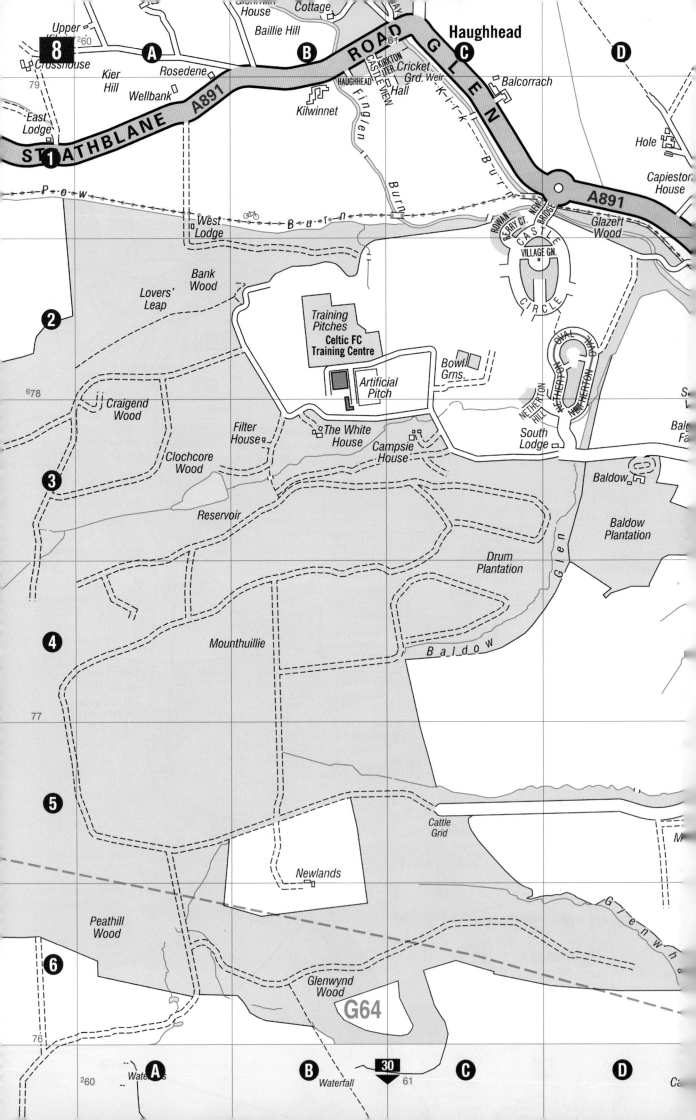

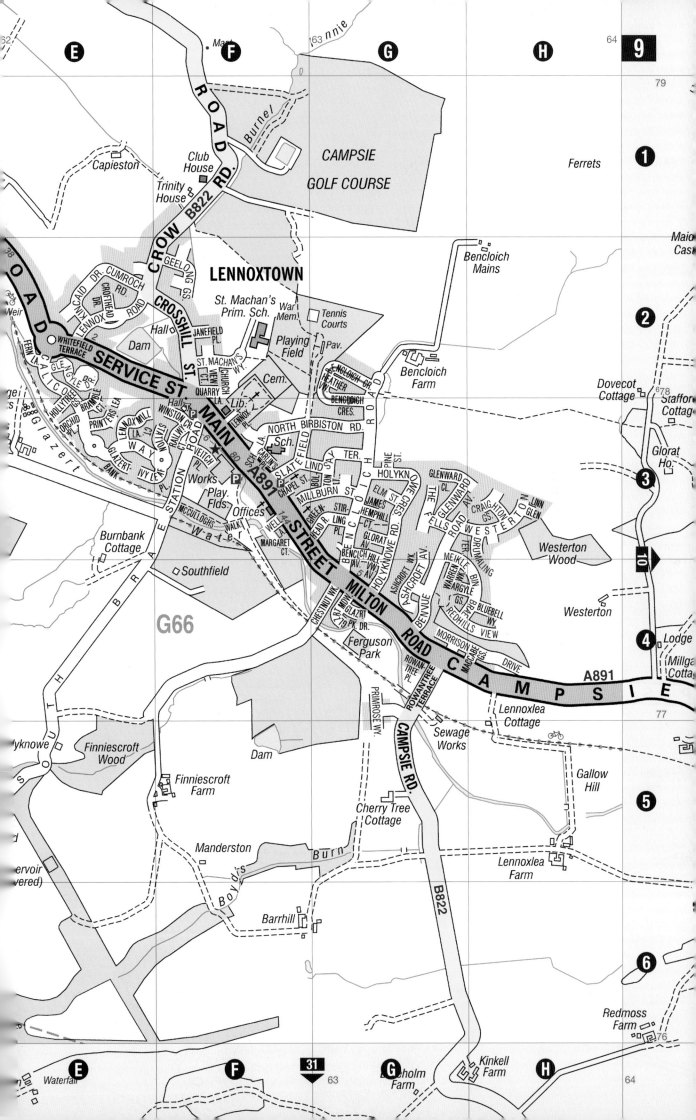

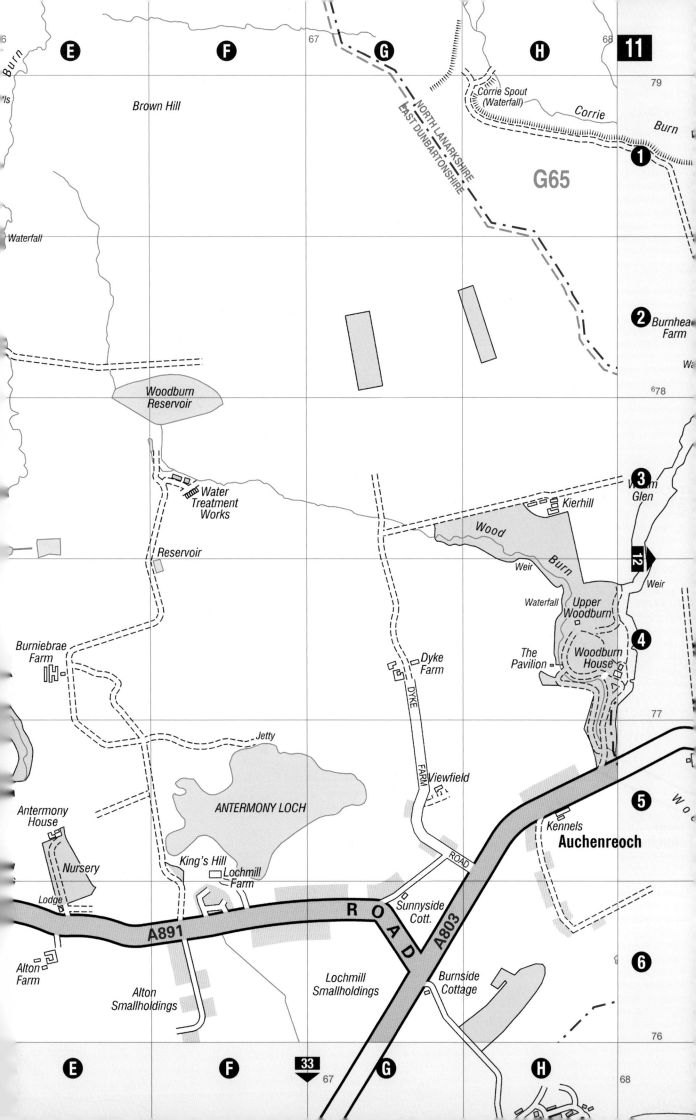

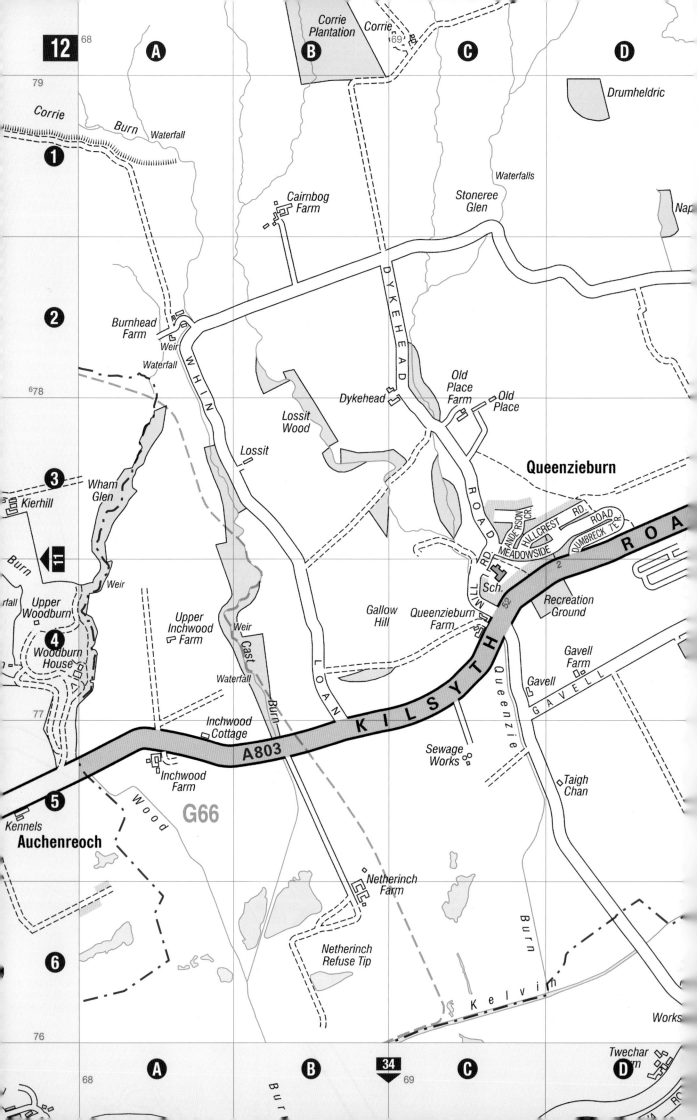

A   B   C   D

79

Corrie

Corrie
Plantation

Corrie

69

Drumheldric

Burn   Waterfall

Waterfalls

1

Nap

Cairnbog
Farm

Stoneree
Glen

DYKEHEAD

2

Burnhead
Farm

Weir

Waterfall

WHIN

Lossit
Wood

Dykehead

Old
Place
Farm

Old
Place

678

Queenzieburn

3

Wham
Glen

Kierhill

Lossit

ROAD

ANDERSON
CR.

HILLCREST

RD.

ROAD

ROAD

MEADOWSIDE

DUMBRECK TER.

Burn

rfall

Upper
Woodburn

Weir

MILL RD.

2

Sch.

52

ROA

4

Woodburn
House

Upper
Inchwood
Farm

Weir

Gallow
Hill

Queenzieburn
Farm

Recreation
Ground

Gavell
Farm

Gavell

GAVELL

Cast

Waterfall

KILSYTH

Queenzie

Inchwood
Cottage

A803

Burn

Sewage
Works

Taigh
Chan

5

Kennels

Auchenreoch

Wood

Inchwood
Farm

LOAN

G66

Netherinch
Farm

6

Netherinch
Refuse Tip

Burn

Kelvin

Works

76

Twechar

A   B

69   C   D

68

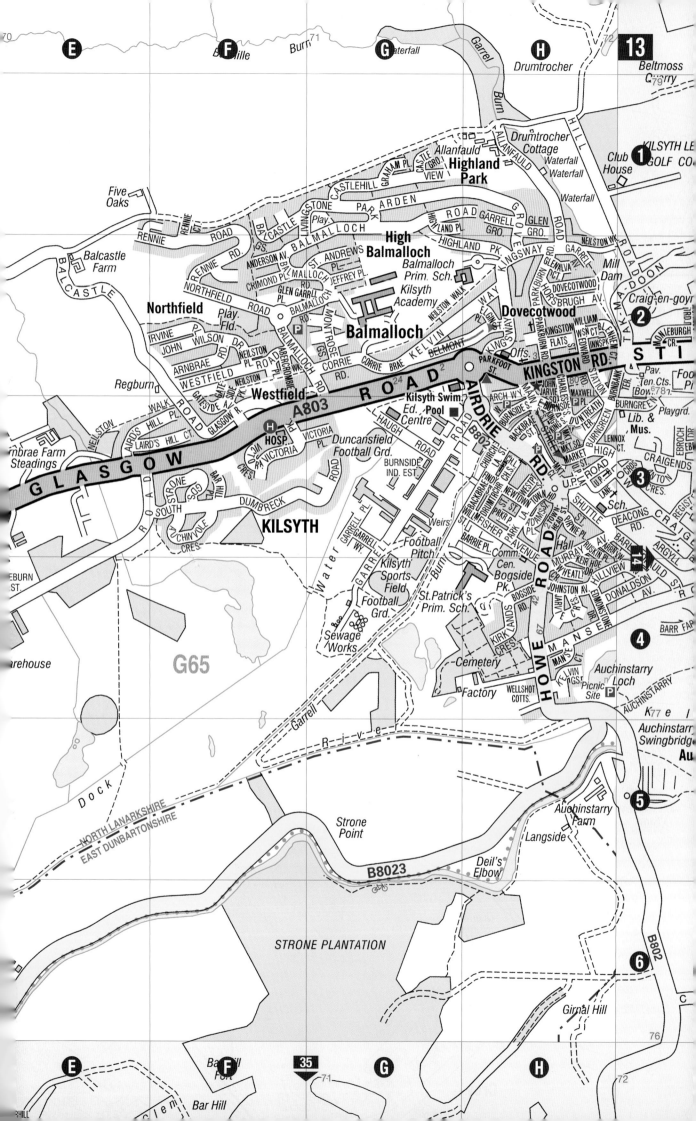

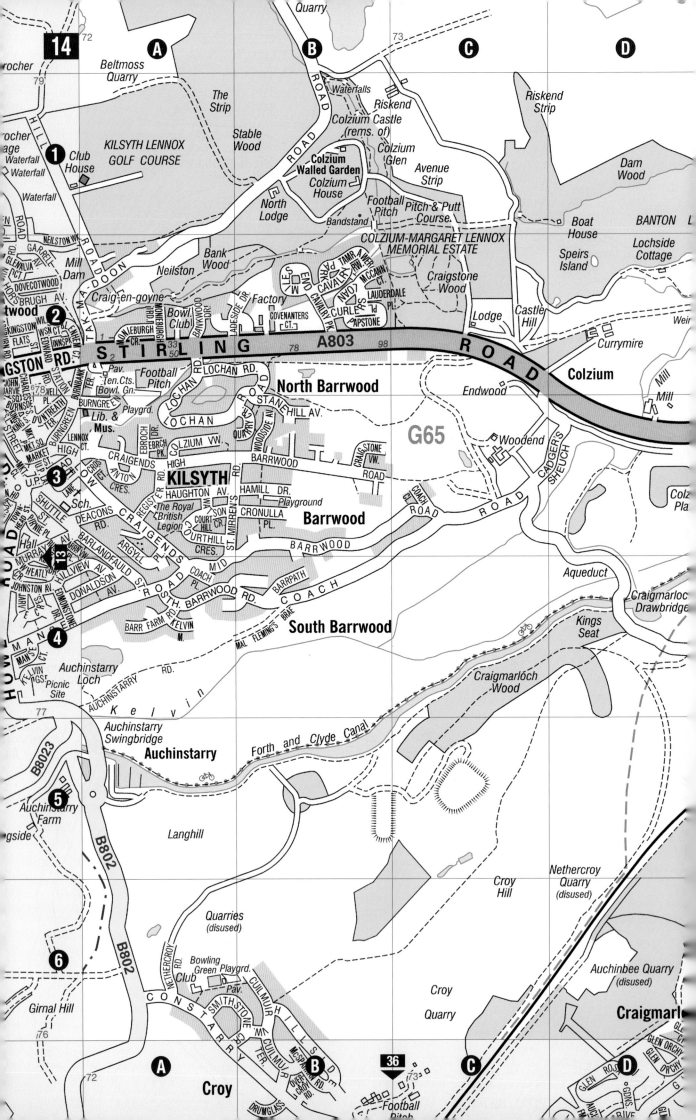

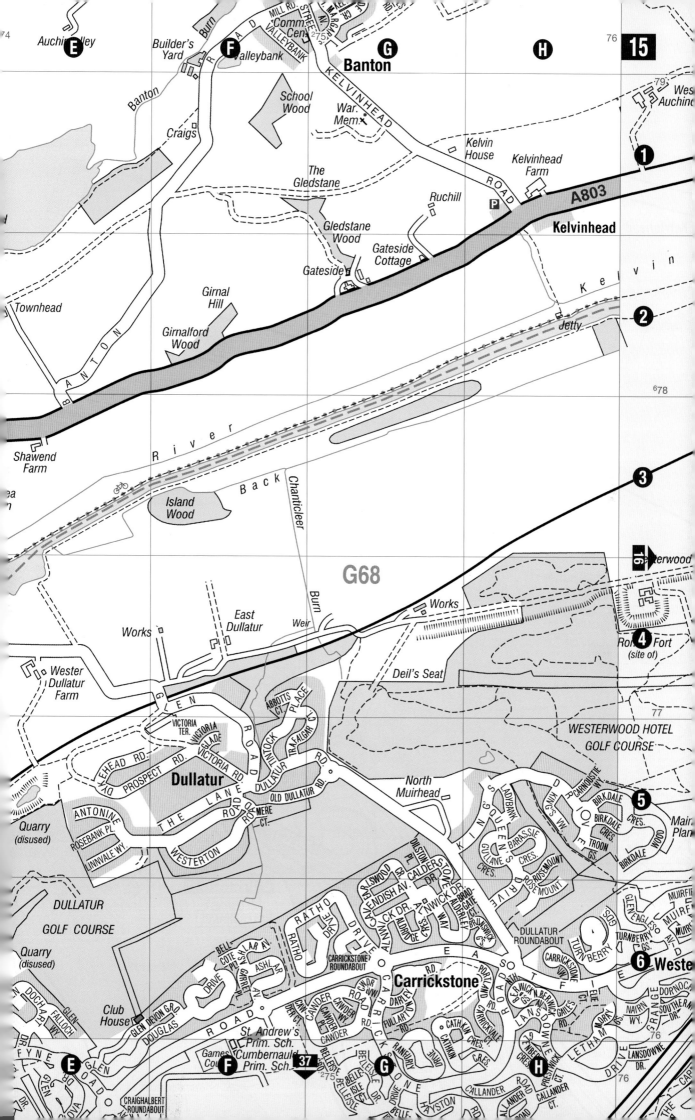

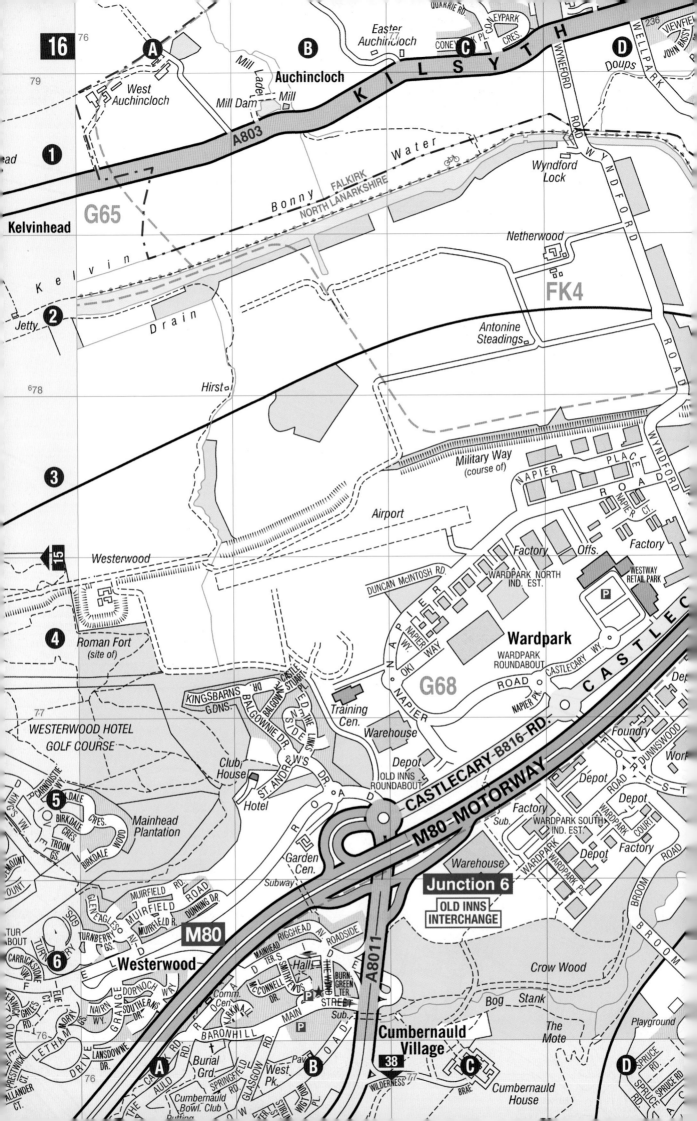

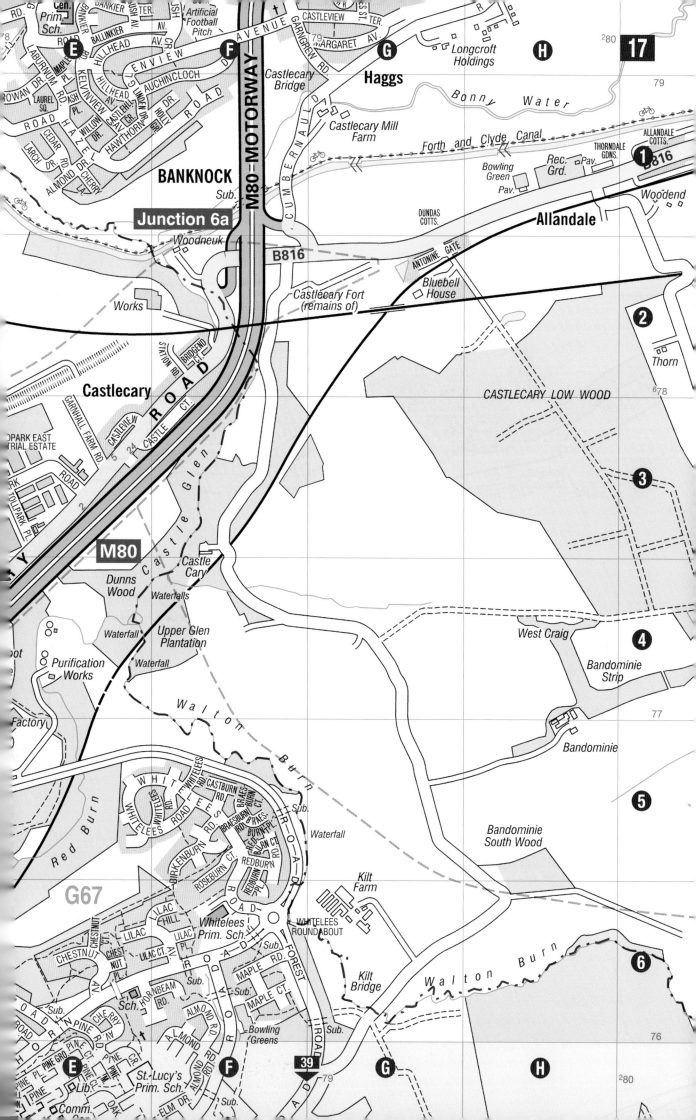

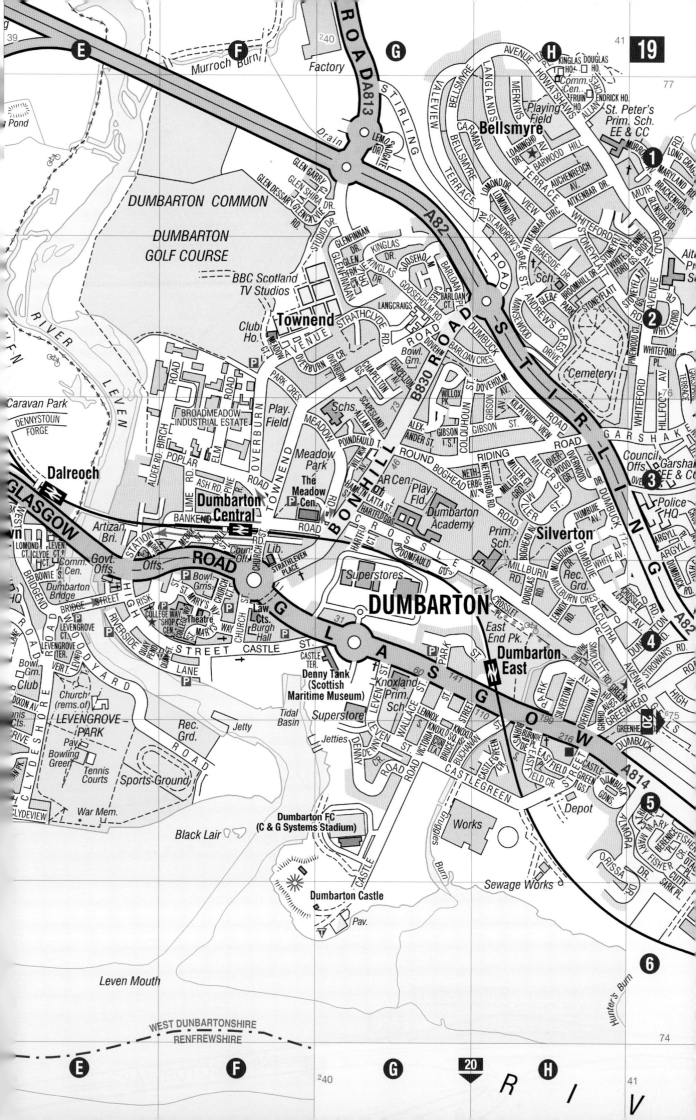

Waterfall

Waterfall

Spardie Linn

E Overtoun

Overtoun

F

G

H

Grouse
Butts

Greenland
Reservoir No.2

Overflow

76

Raven's Crag

Lang Craigs

1

Greenland
Reservoir No.

ood Hill

Barnhill

TOM'S SEAT

Ford

Dumbar

Treedom Cottage

Sluice

Carnoch
House

Middleton

Waterfall

Rigangower

Craignair

Waterfall

Middleton Wood

Mast

2

Boat House

Loch
Bowie

Milton Burn

umbowie

Boat House

Old Chapel of Colquhoun
(remains of)

675

Northwood

Waterfall

Greenland

Mattockhill

Old Mill
House

Riggengower

Waterfalls

Milton House

Craigunnock

Quarry
(Stone)

3

G82

Milton

EVANS
MILTON
CT.

King
George's
Field

PARKVIEW

MILTON HL

Auchentorlie Wood

Auchentorlie
Burn

22

ck Hill

Dumbuck

LENNOX

COLQUHOUN
RD.

HILLVIEW

WHYTE CNR.

Fort
SHEEP HILL

T Wood

Dumbuck
Farm

CRANNOG
CT.

CRANNOG

4

OAD

DUMBARTON

A82

ROAD

Auchentorlie
House

Dam
74

Animal Welfare
Centre

GRE

G60

Au
Waterfa

Milton Island

Weir

A82

DUMB

5

Works

WEST DUNBARTONSHIRE
RENFREWSHIRE

Dunglass Castle
(remains of)

C L Y D E

6

73

LONGHAUGH POINT

E

F

41
43

G

H

44

A   B   245   C   D

No.2   76
Overflow

LOCH HUMPHREY
(Reservoir)

Boat Shed

Ford

1

G r o u s e   B u t t s

Greenland
Reservoir No.3

Dam

Sluice

C R A I G A R E S T I E

K I L P A

Rigangower

2

675

Bow Linn

Waterfalls

Waterfall

Reservoir

Waterfall

Quarry (Disused)

3

McKellar's
Wood

Auchentorlie Burn

Auchentorlie Glen

G
l
e
n
a
r
b
u
c
k

21

Lonendale
Wood

T Wood

4

Hill of Dun

Haw Craig

K I L P A

Auchentorlie
Cottage

Auchentorlie
House

74

Dam

High
Auchentorlie

East Wood

Gavinburn C

Waterfall

Bowling

Torwood Villa

Lodge

Weir

Waterfalls

Glenarbuck House

G R E A T   **A82**   **W E S T E R N**

Dunarbuck
Cottage

MANSE

SCOTT   AVENUE

Weir

U B A R T O N

5

LITTLE MILL

LA

LITTLE MILL

CLYDE VW CT

R O A D   **D U M**

Bowling

A814

P

Lodge

Gavinbu

Little
Mill Pl.

Works

P

Basin

HELENSLEA

Gavi
Lib. Prim
EE S

s Castle
(of)

Jetty

Frisky
Wharf

Bowling Harbour

Pier

WEST DUNBARTONSHIRE

RENFREWSHIRE

ROMAN CRESCENT

ROMAN

Chapel Hill

Depo

GA

R I V E R

CRESCENT

PORTPATRICK

C L Y D E

6

73

A   B   **42**   245   C   Donald's Quay
Light
Navigation Beacon   D

MAR HALL
GOLF COURSE

E F 47 G Dirty Loch H 48 **23**

76

1

C

TRICK HILLS

Loch Humphrey Burn

GREENSIDE RESERVOIR

G82

2

OGAIROCH

THE SLACKS

G81

675

Loch

3

Humphrey Burn

24

74

RICK BRAES

Ford

Waterfall

4

attle Grid

es

Craigleith

Blackmailing

Blackmailing
Reservoir
(covered)

G60

Filter
Beds

Waterfall

5

Drums

Lodge

Hole
Cottage

Mount
Pleasant

Netherclose

Carleith

6

73

North Dalnottar
Cemetery

A82 ROAD

Cemy.

CRESCENT

KIRKTON

GAVINBURN
PL

GAVINBURN

ROAD

A814

N.SEFIELD

THISTLENEUK

MOUNT PLEASANT

Halls

GLEBE
CT.

KILPATRICK

CH'RCH

HILLVIEW

DR.

43

47

G

GREAT

Clydebank
Crematorium

Carleith
Prim. Sc

Old
Kilpatrick

E

STATION Kilpatrick

F

STATION

Rec. Grd.

ASHTREE

LISSET
RD.

G

H

48

A

B COCHNO LOCH 49
(Reservoir)

C

D

Overflow
Boat House

J A W · R E S E R V O I R

Dam

1

COCHNO HILL

2

675

Bog Wood

Lo

3

Auchenduich
Wood

Waterfall

Humphrey

23

Burn

Adam's Well

Dam

Ford

Waterfalls

Sheepfold

Cochnohill

4

C O C H N O

Cochno

Waterfall

Wester Cochno

74

G81

Cochno Filters

R O A D

Tanks

C O C H N

5

Waterfalls

WESTER COCHNO
HOLDINGS

Cave

Waterfalls

COCHNO

BRAE

Dam

Duntiglennan
Farm

DUNCOMBE AV.

GREENSIDE

Cochno

COCHNO

Cochno Burn

6

Cochno
TER.

MIRREN

DRIVE

FARM

CRAIGHIRST DR.

HEATHER AV.

GLENHEAD

BIRNIEHILL
CT.

CRESCENT

Playing
Fld.

WESTBURN CR.

CRESCENT

ROMAN

HILL

RD.

RD.

COCHNO

CRS.

SPINNERS

JAMESON

AUCHINLECK

Carleith

RUSSELL RD.

ANTYRE

CRESCENT

GIELEA

DUNTOCHER

R O A D

BREVAL

BRAEHEAD AV.

HILLCRES

DUNELLAN DR. PL.

CROFTPARK RD.

INVLECK

73

RUSSELL

PL.

RD.

BD.

CRAIGI

DAVIDSN

REDMOSS

HILLEND

CRES.

BRAEHEAD

CR.

Weir

BRNSIDE

CR.

ottar

A

Carle
Prim. Sch.

MO

STARK

B E E C H E S

DALGLEISH

BISSETT CR.

CARLEITH

BEECHES AV.

DUNN S.

HOGAN

MOS

B

St.
Mary's
Sch. EE
& CC

HELENA

DUNTIGLENN

44 49

R O A D

ROAD

Pav. Football
Pk.

ANTONINE

VEITCHES
CT.

C

GARDENS

WAULKMILL

BRAEHEAD

ROAD

D

VICTORIA
PL.

GLASGOW

ebank
atorium

48

CARLEITH

MOS

St.

Lib

ROMAN

CT.

HELENA

ROAD

Golden Hill

Golden Hill

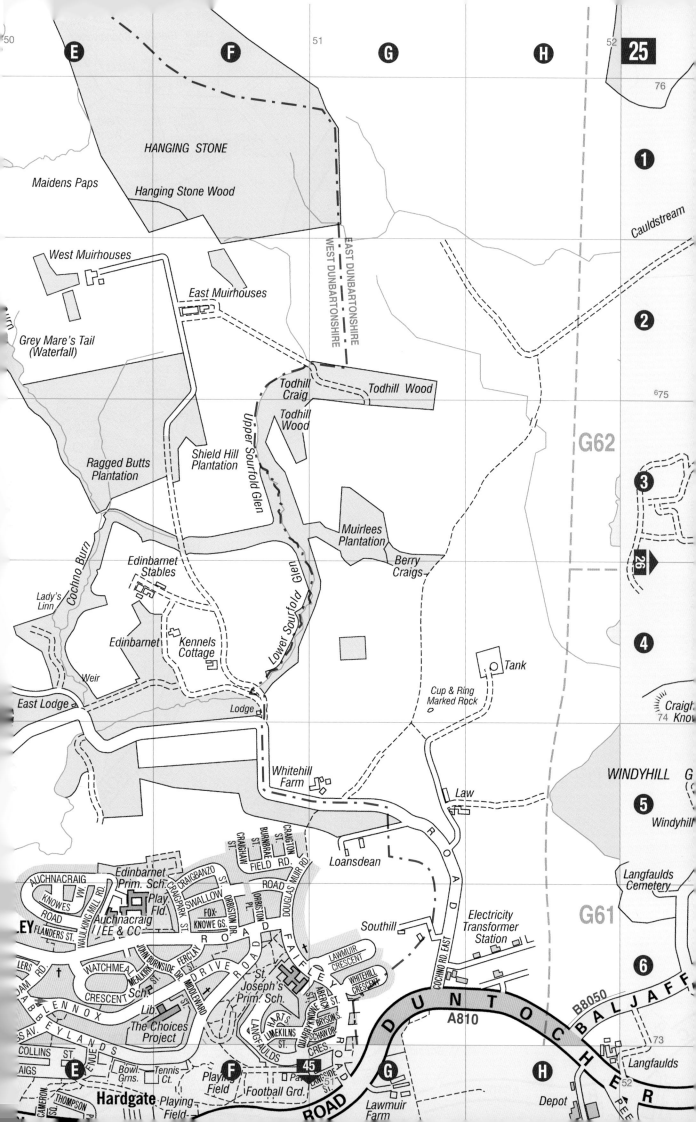

E   F   51   G   H   52

76

1

Cauldstream

HANGING STONE

Maidens Paps

Hanging Stone Wood

West Muirhouses

East Muirhouses

2

675

Grey Mare's Tail (Waterfall)

EAST DUNBARTONSHIRE
WEST DUNBARTONSHIRE

Todhill Craig

Todhill Wood

Todhill Wood

G62

Ragged Butts Plantation

Shield Hill Plantation

Upper Sourfold Glen

3

Muirlees Plantation

Edinbarnet Stables

Lady's Linn

Cochno Burn

Lower Sourfold Glen

Berry Craigs

26

Edinbarnet

Kennels Cottage

4

Tank

Weir

Cup & Ring Marked Rock

Craig Know
74

East Lodge

Lodge

WINDYHILL G

Whitehill Farm

Law

5

Windyhill

CRAIGTON ST.

BURNBRAE ST.

CRAIGHAW FIELD RD.

Loansdean

R
O
A
D

Langfaulds Cemetery

G61

CRAIGBANZO ST.

ROAD

Edinbarnet Prim. Sch.

Play Fld.

SWALLOW

CRAIGPARK ST.

ORBISTON DR.

ORBISTON PL.

Douglas Muir Rd.

Southill

Electricity Transformer Station

6

AUCHNACRAIG

KNOWES ROAD

VW.

FLANDERS ST.

Auchnacraig EE & CC

FOX-KNOWE GS

JOHN BURNSIDE DR.

FERGLAY

DRIVE

ROAD

FAIFLEY

LAWMUIR CRESCENT

WHITEHILL CRESCENT

COCHNO RD. EAST

B8050

BALJAFF

WATCHMEAL

MEALKIRK ST.

Sch.

CRESCENT

LENNOX

MIDDLEWARD ST.

St. Joseph's Prim. Sch.

ABERCH

QUARRYKNOWE CRES.

73

The Choices Project

Lib.

EYLANDS

HARTS ST.

LANGFAULDS

LIMEKILNS ST.

BRYSON'S

SCHAW DR.

D
U
N
T
O
C
H
E
R

A810

ROAD

52

Langfaulds

COLLINS ST.

AV.

THOMPSON

CAMERON SQ.

AIGS

E

Bowl. Grns.

Tennis Ct.

45

F

Playing Field

Football Grd.

Pa

LANE

51

ROAD

G

Lawmuir Farm

DUNTOCHER

H

Depot

PEE

R

Hardgate   Playing Field

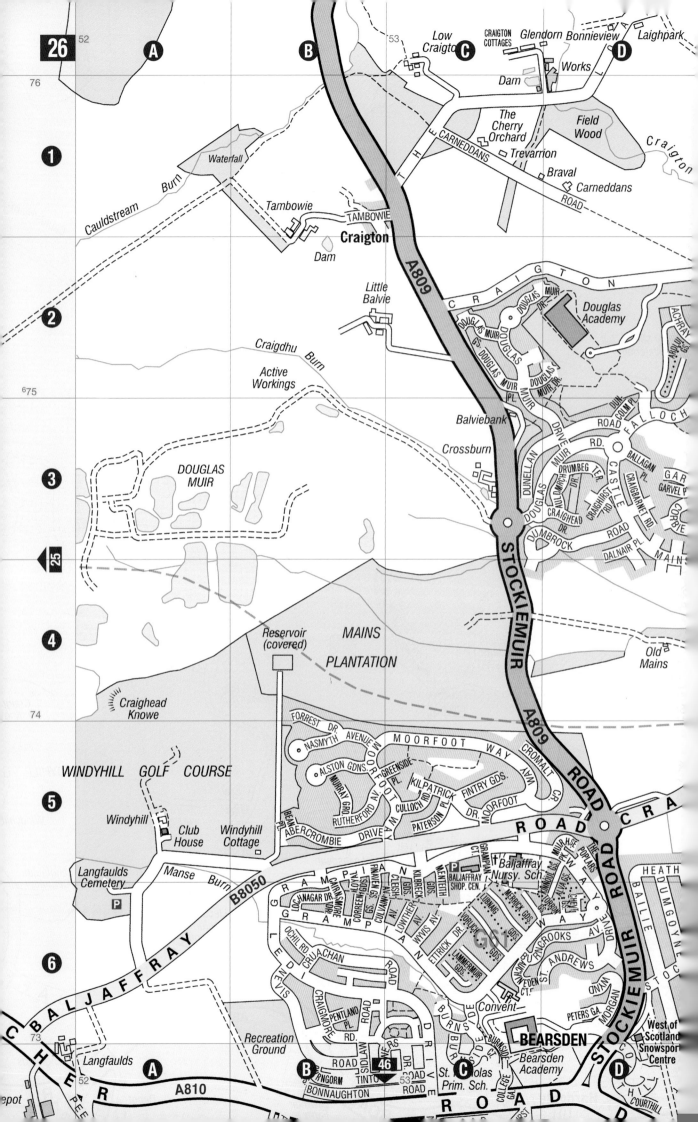

76

A   **B**   **C**   **D**

1

Cauldstream   Burn   Waterfall   Tambowie
The Cherry Orchard
Low Craigto   CRAIGTON COTTAGES   Glendorn   Bonnieview   Laighpark
Dam   Works
Field Wood
Trevarrion
Braval
Carneddans
Craigton
TAMBOWIE
Craigton
Dam

2

Little Balvie
Craigdhu   Burn
Active Workings
Balviebank
CRAIGTON
Douglas Academy
ACHRAY
DOUGLAS MUIR GS.
DOUGLAS MUIR PL.
DOUGLAS MUIR DR.

675

3

DOUGLAS MUIR
Crossburn
DUN. COLM PL.
DUNELLAN DRIVE
DOUGLAS MUIR
DRUMBEG TER.
CASTLE
BALLAGAN PL.
CRAIGBARNET RD.
GAR. GARVEL P.
CRAIGHEAD DR.
CRAIGHIRST RD.
ROAD
CORBIE
DUMBROCK
DALNAIR PL.
MAIN

◀ 25

4

Reservoir (covered)
MAINS   PLANTATION
STOCKIEMUIR   A809   ROAD
Old Mains

74

Craighead Knowe

5

WINDYHILL   GOLF   COURSE
FORREST DR.
NASMYTH   AVENUE   MOORFOOT   WAY   CROMALT CR.
ALSTON GDNS.
MOORFOOT
GREENSIDE PL.
KILPATRICK RD.
FINTRY GDS.
MOORFOOT DR.
ROAD   ROAD   CRA
Windyhill   Club House   Windyhill Cottage
MURRAY GRO.
RUTHERFORD AV.
CULLOCH RD.
PATERSON PL.
ABERCROMBIE   DRIVE
MUIR   HSE.
THE POPLARS
Langfaulds Cemetery
Manse   Burn   B8050
GRAMPIAN CT.
BALJAFFRAY SHOP. CEN.
Baljaffray Nursy. Sch.
HEATH
DUMGOYNE

6

BALJAFFRAY
LOCHNAGAR DR.
CAIRNSMORE DR.
CORREEN GDS.
RNNEN GDS.
CLESH
KILBRECK GDS.
MENTEITH GDS.
VORLICH DR.
URNAG
NEVROCK GDS.
BURNCROOKS AV.
ST. ANDREWS
BAILIE
STOC
GRAMPIAN   ROAD
OCHIL RD.
CRUACHAN
LOWTHER   AV.
WYVIS AV.
LAMMERMUIR GDS.
EDEN   CT.
Convent
MORGAN   WIND
PETERS GA.
West of Scotland Snowspor Centre
NEVIS
CRAIGMORE
PENTLAND PL.
SIDLAW ROAD
WERS
TINTO
ROAD
BURNSIDE
BURNSIDE   DR.
St. Nicholas Prim. Sch.
COLLEGE
BEARSDEN
Bearsden Academy
COURTHILL

73

Langfaulds   Recreation Ground
A   RNGORM   ROAD   **B**   46   BONNAUGHTON   ROAD   **C**   **D**
CHER   EE   R   A810   ROAD   ROAD
pot   53

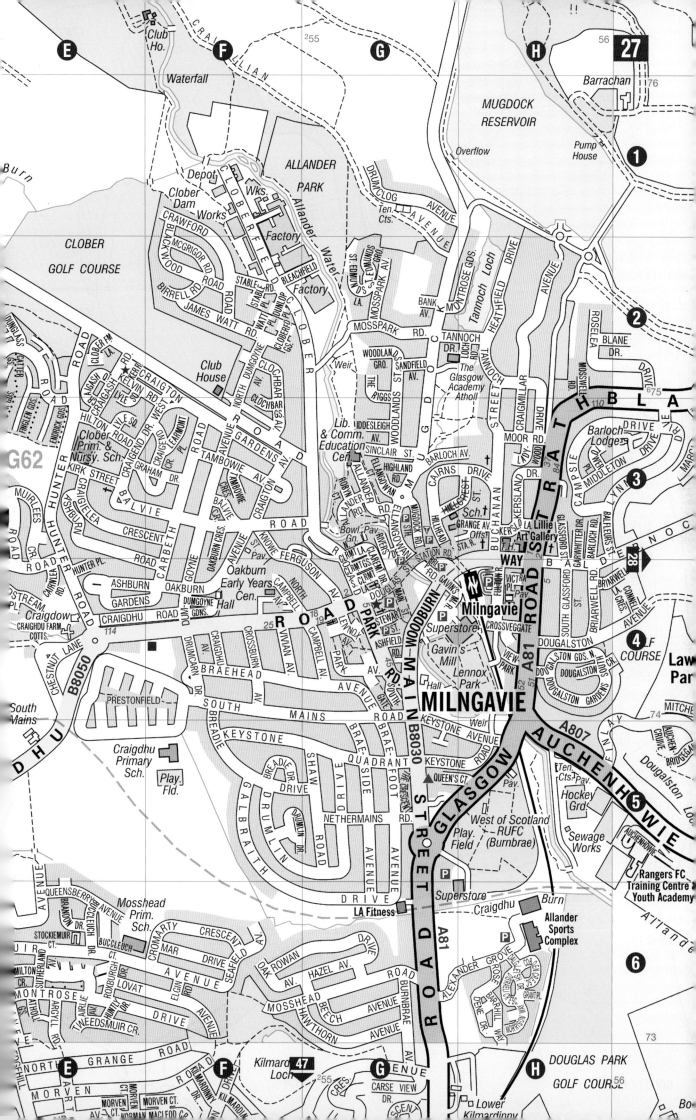

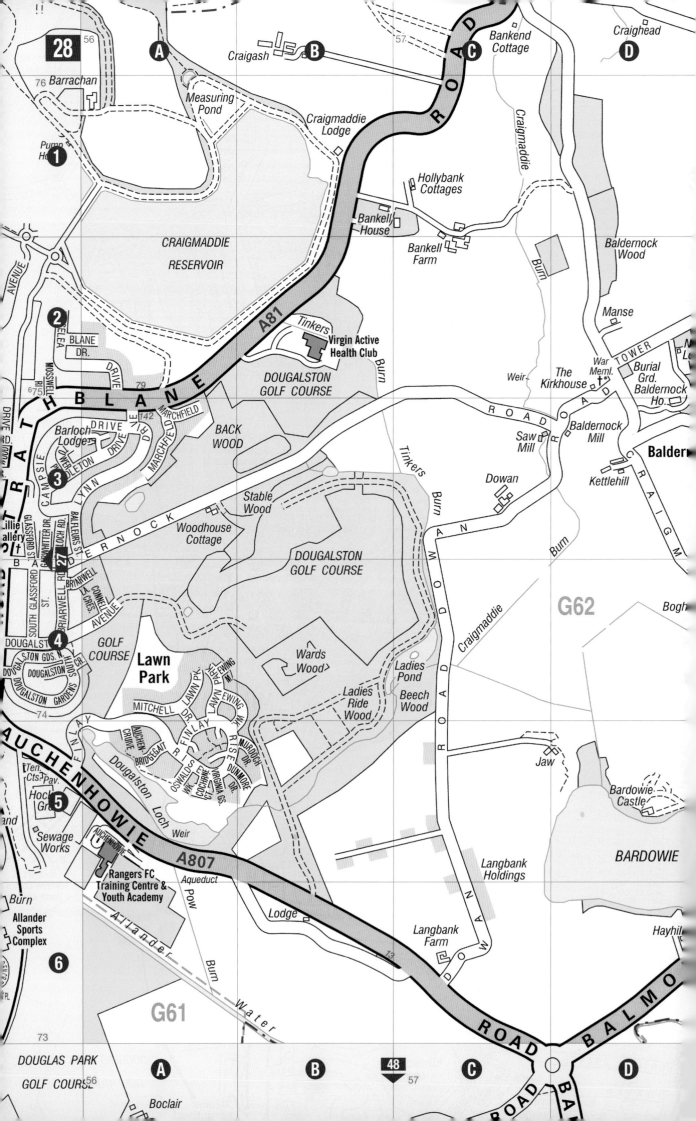

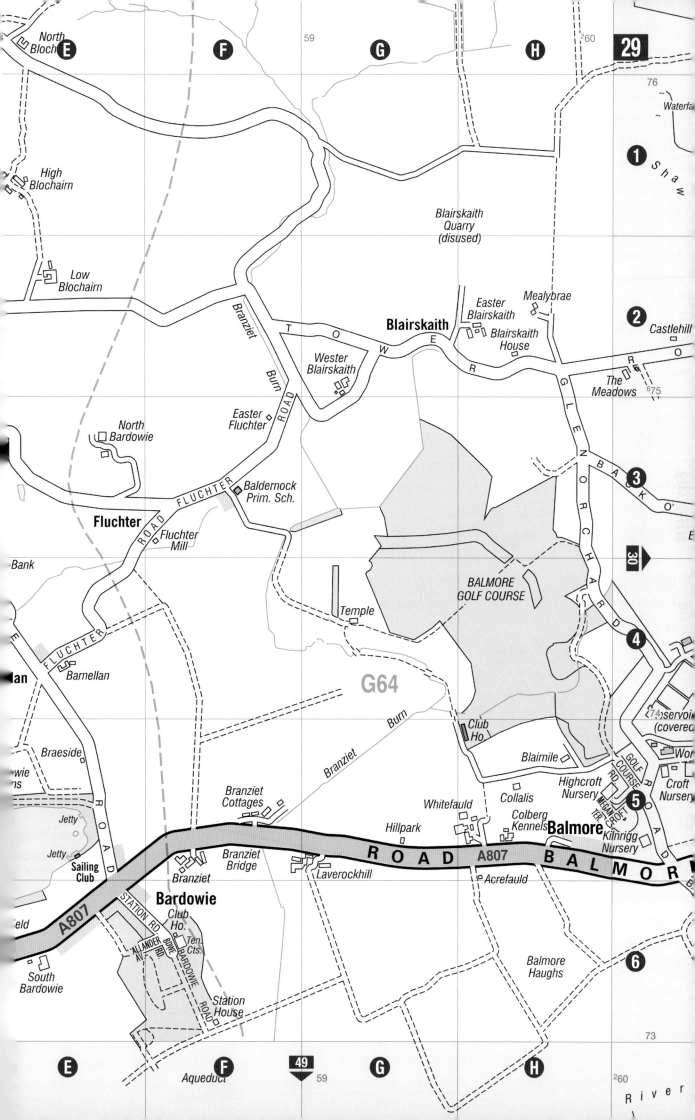

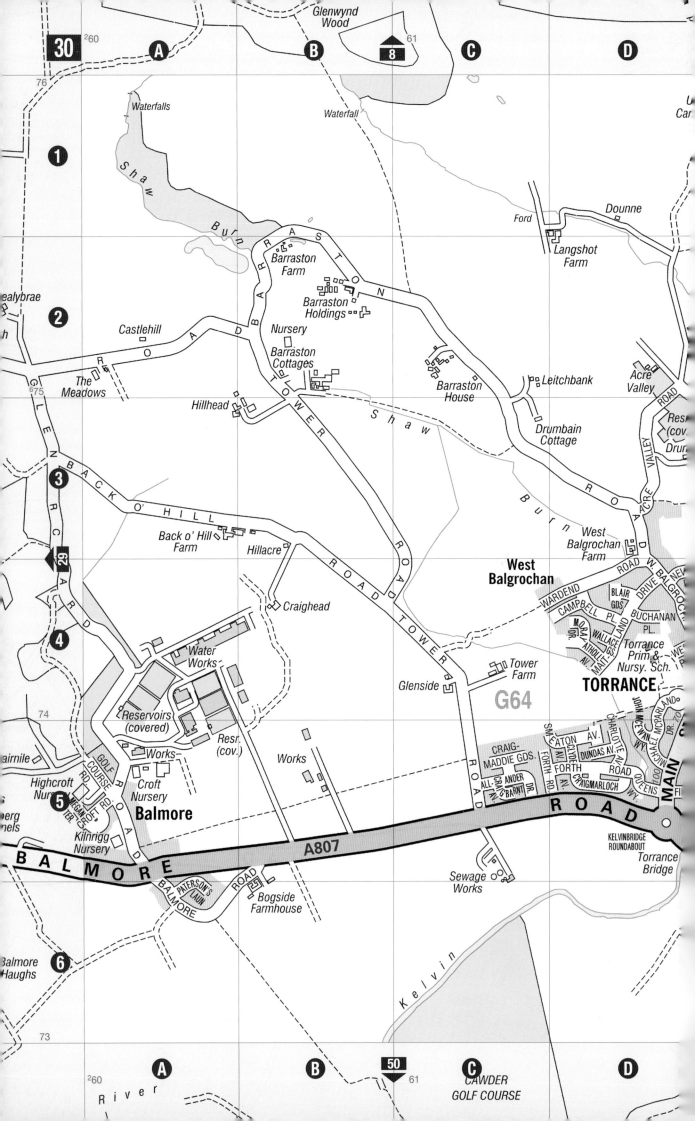

E   **F**   63   9   **G**   **H**   64 Redl Farm **31**

76

Waterfall

Waterfall

Kinkell Farm

Braeholm Farm

1

dbank

B822

Wetsho

Whitehill

Balquharrage Cottages

2

Balquharrage

R O A D

K I R K I N T I L L O C H

675

East Balgrochan Farm

Weir

Craigen Glen Cottage

ROAD

Carlston Cottages

CARLSTON STEADINGS

Carlston

3

Hay Cot

EASTERTON COTTAGES

East Balgrochan

MCGILLIVRAY AV.

B822

Red

32

FERGUSLEA TERRACE

West Carlestoun

ROAD

Hayston

Ferrymill House

Balgrochan House

KING'S PK

WOWL

CRES

WOODMILL DR.

PARK CRES

Playing Field

Burn

HAYSTON GOLF COURSE

4

A M P S I E

KELVINDALE

Wardhill

Meadowbank Farm

G66

River

74

Hays

CORMACK AV.

HAW

THORNA DR.

DALRIADA DR.

ST.

GUTHRIE

ROAD

HILL

KELVIN VIEW

Meadowbank House

KELVIN BRAY

PARK CL.

MOR. PL.

KELVIN WAY

KELVIN

ADAMSLIE

ADAMSLIE CR.

5

Sewage Works

Sandy Knowes

Easter Cadder

A803   G L A S G O

GLASGOW BRI. COTTS.

EASTER CADDER COTTAGES

6

ANCE

A807

Hungryside Bridge (Drawbridge)

Slipway Glasgow Bri.

Glasgow Bri.

Forth and Clyde Canal

73

E   ROAD   **F**   51   63   **G** ROAD   **H**   64

KIRKINTILLOCH

Leafield

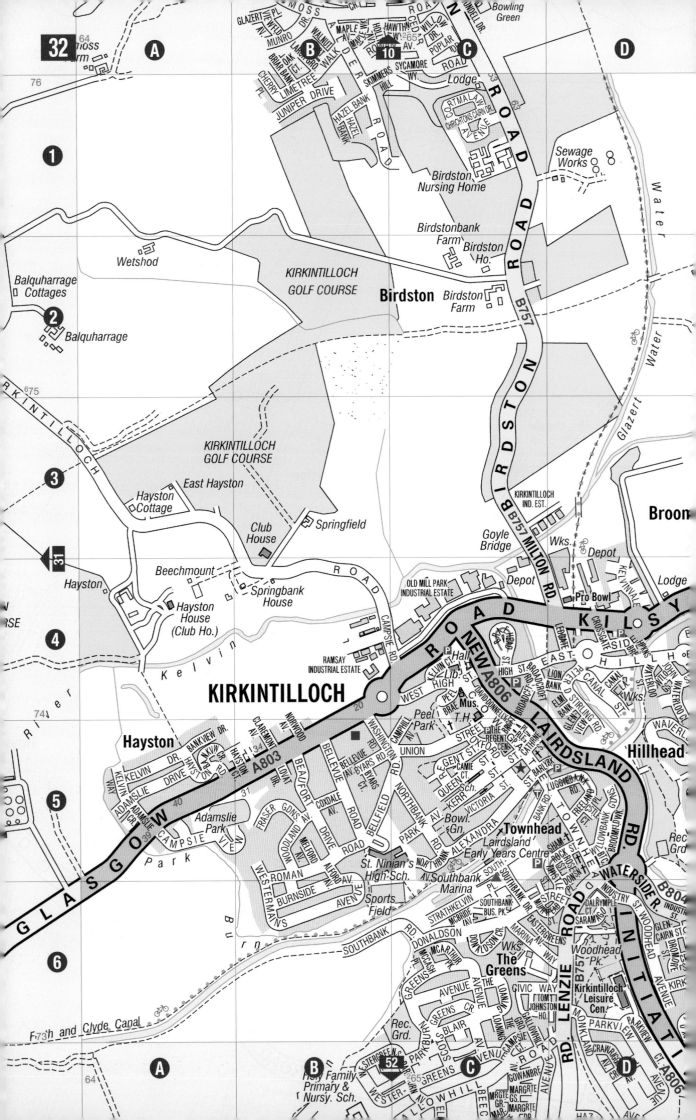

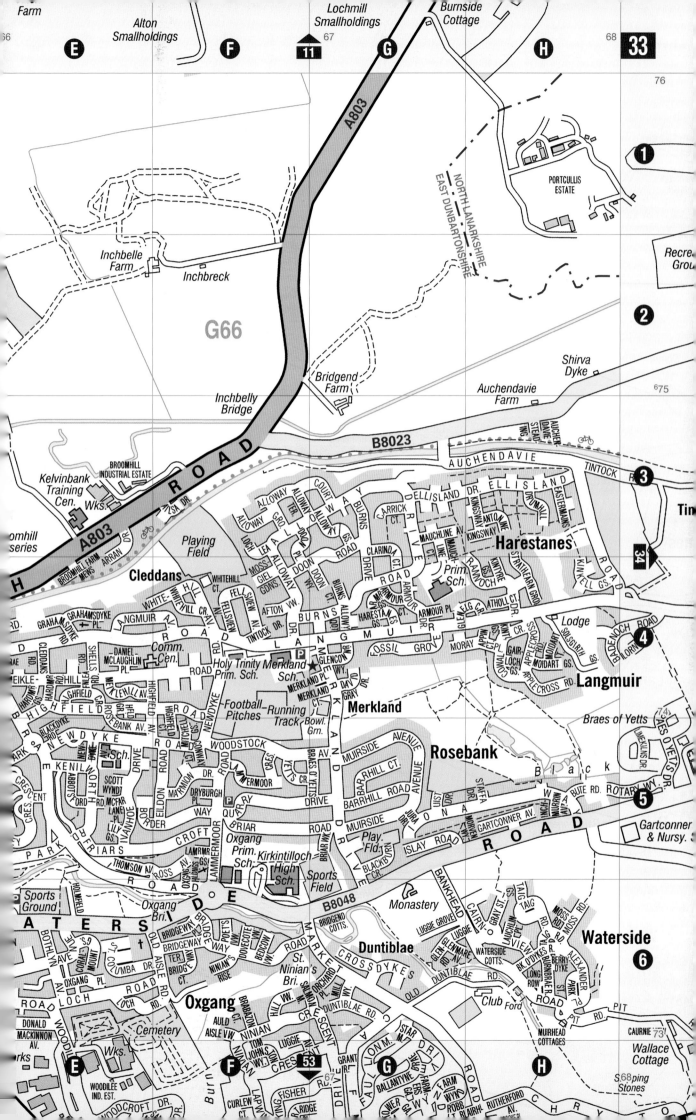

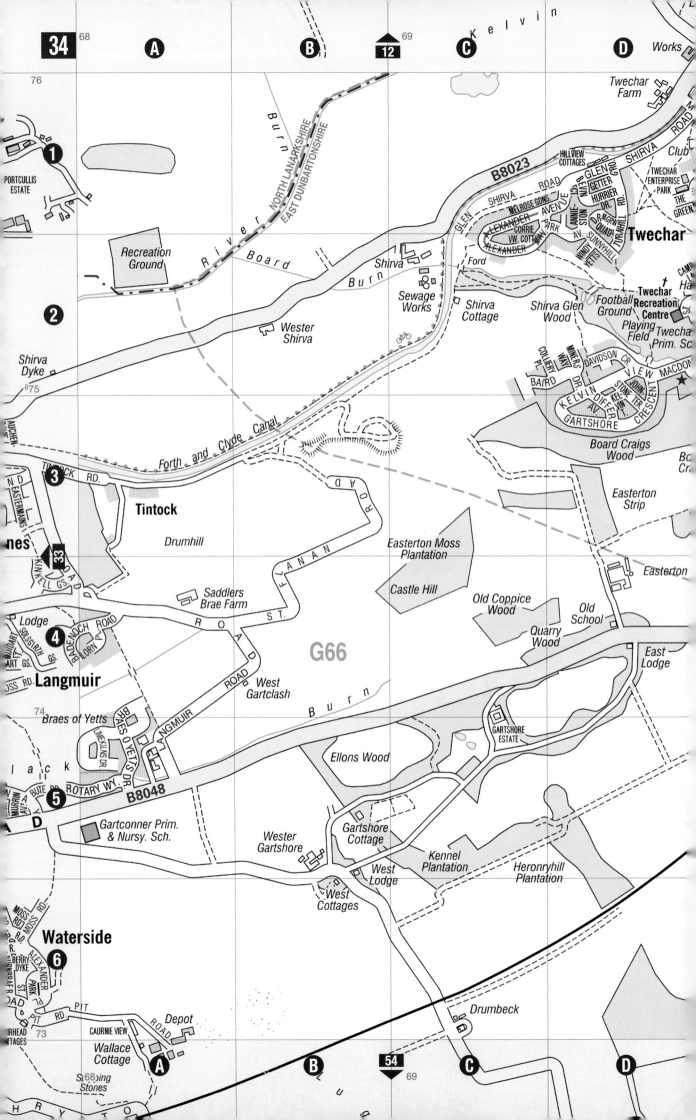

A · B · 12 · 69 · C · D

Works

Kelvin

Twechar Farm

1

PORTCULLIS ESTATE

76

NORTH LANARKSHIRE
EAST DUNBARTONSHIRE

Burn

B8023

HILLVIEW COTTAGES

SHIRVA ROAD

TWECHAR ENTERPRISE PARK

THE GREEN

Club

SHIRVA ROAD

MELROSE GDNS.
ALEXANDER
CORRIE VW. COTTS.
ALEXANDER

GLEN
SHIRVA AVENUE
PARK
ANNIE-STON
GETTER
HURRIER DR.
DR.MGRW
QUAD!
GLEN KELVIN GRO.
TURNHILL RD.

Twechar

Recreation Ground

Shirva Burn

Sewage Works

Shirva

Ford

WINDY YETTS
SUNNYHILL

Wester Shirva

Shirva Cottage

Shirva Glen Wood

Football Ground
Playing Field

† Twechar Recreation Centre

Twechar Prim. Sc.

2

Shirva Dyke

675

AUCHEN-

MINERS WAY
COLLIER
BAIRD
POL.

DAVIDSON CR.
STONE TER.

JOHN
KEL-
VIN
T.

VIEW

MACDON

Board Craigs Wood

KELVIN
GARTSHORE
AV.
DIFFER
CRESCENT

Bo
Cr

Forth and Clyde Canal

Easterton Strip

ND
EASTERMAINS'

3

TINTOCK RD.

Tintock

Drumhill

ROAD

FLANAN

Easterton Moss Plantation

Castle Hill

Old Coppice Wood

Easterton

Old School

33

KINKELL GS.

Saddlers Brae Farm

ROAD ST.

Quarry Wood

East Lodge

nes

Lodge
SOLSGIRTH
ART GS.
LORN P.
MUDDART
BADENOCH ROAD

4

G66

West Gartclash

West Burn

GARTSHORE ESTATE

JSS RD. Langmuir

74 Braes of Yetts

LANGMUIR ROAD
LIMEKILNS DR.
BRAES O YETTS DR.

Ellons Wood

lack

MURRIN

BUTE RD.
ROTARY WY.
B8048

5

D

Gartconner Prim. & Nursy. Sch.

Wester Gartshore

Gartshore Cottage

West Lodge

Kennel Plantation

Heronryhill Plantation

MOSS RD.
MOSS RD.

Waterside

BERRY DYKE

6

ALEXANDER PARK
ST.

West Cottages

Drumbeck

PIT RD.
IRHEAD TAGES

73

PIT ROAD

Depot

CAURNIE VIEW

Wallace Cottage

A · B · 54 · 69 · C · D

68

S 68ing Stones

HRYTO

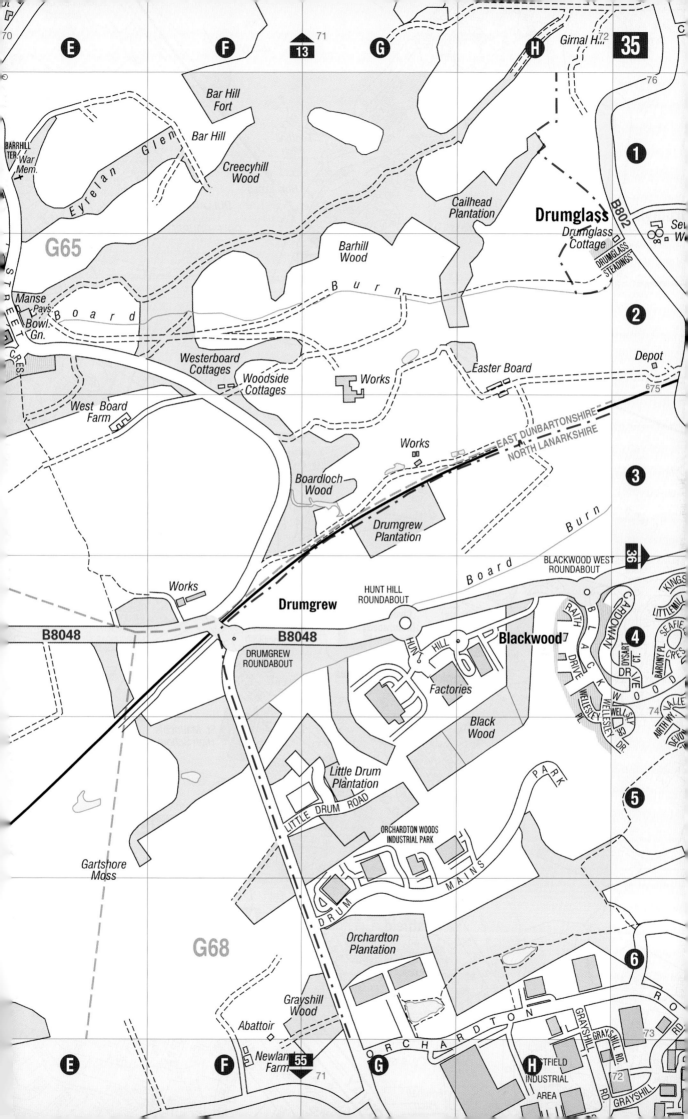

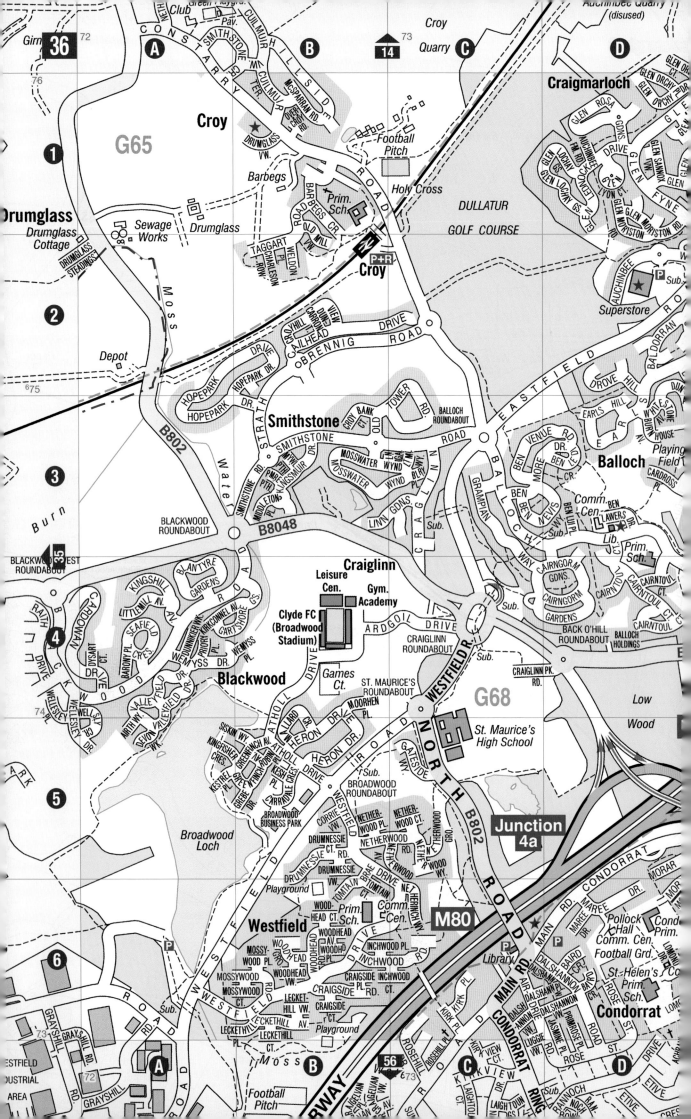

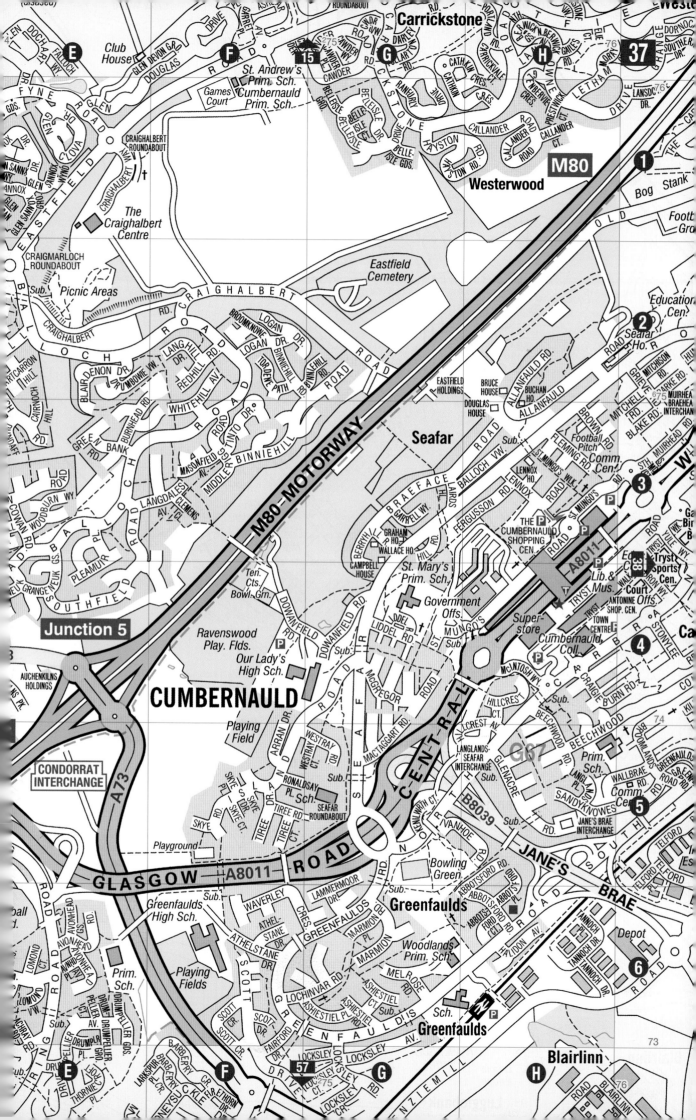

E **F** **17** **G** **H**

Walton

Kilt Bridge

280

76

ROAD PL.

MAPLE

Sub.

Sch. HORNBEAM RD.

MAPLE CT.

79

Sub.

Sub.

Crowbank **1**

ROAD HOLLY

PINE AV.

CHERRY AV.

ALMOND RD.

Bowling Greens

Sub.

ROAD

PINE GRO.

PINE PL.

PINE CT.

PINE RD.

PINE CR.

St. Lucy's Prim. Sch.

ALMOND RD.

Glenhead Wood

Glenhead

PINE RD.

PINE

Lib.

OAK RD.

ELM DR.

Sub.

2

Comm. Cen.

RONHILL OP. CEN.

HAWTHORN RD.

675

Abronhill High Sch.

OAK ROAD

GEAN CT.

Sub.

Glenhead Wood

3

Abronhill

BIRCH RD.

BIRCH RD.

ROAD

Football Grd.

Comm. Cen.

Tennis Cts.

LIME CRES.

CRESCENT

FANNYSIDE

Sub.

LIME

MUIR

ROAD

FORTH ST.

Sub.

4

Subs.

BLACKTHORN ROUNDABOUT

ROAD

AULD

74

Mid Forest

Forest Plantation

Forest Plantation

Forest Plantation

5

Glencryan Burn

FANNYSIDE

PALACERIGG COUNTRY PARK

LOCHS

Palacerigg Cottage

PALACERIGG GOLF COURSE

6

Cattle Grid

Palacerigg House

Visitor Cen.

Club House

Picnic Area

P House

73

E **F** **G** **H**

79

Cherrybank Nurseries

Herd's Hill

280

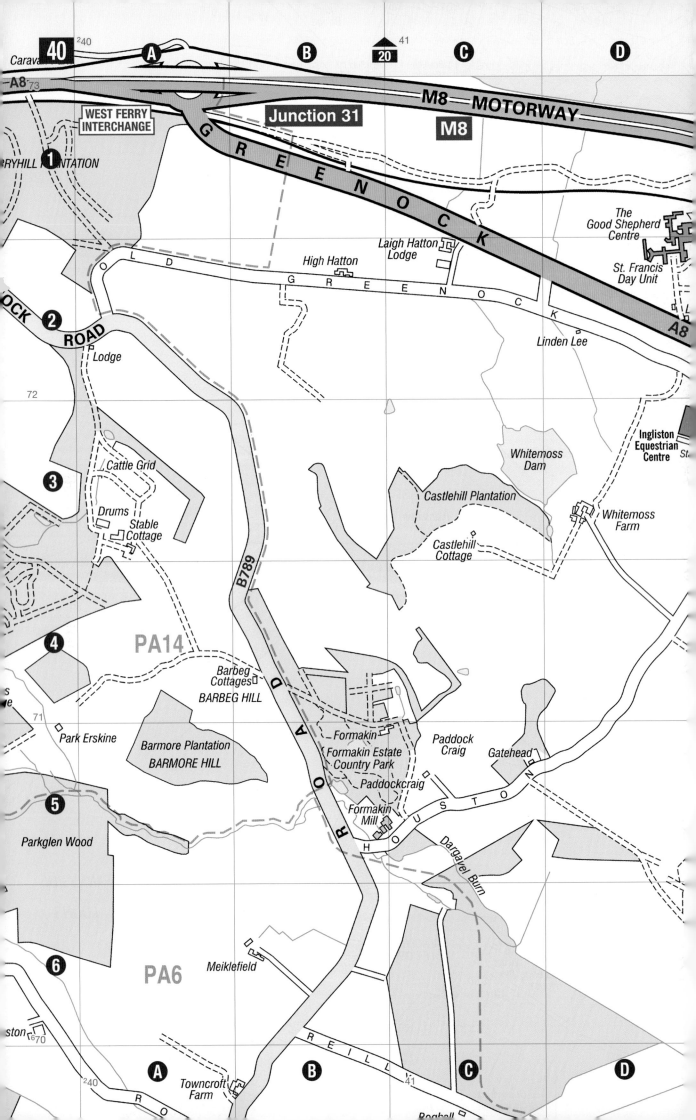

40 240
A
B
▲ 41
20
C
D

Caravan
A8 73
M8 MOTORWAY
WEST FERRY INTERCHANGE
Junction 31
M8

G
R
E
E
N
O
C
K

The Good Shepherd Centre
St. Francis Day Unit

1
RRYHILL PLANTATION

O   L   D   G   R   E   E   N   O   C   K
High Hatton
Laigh Hatton Lodge

A8

OCK
2 ROAD
Lodge
Linden Lee

72

3
Cattle Grid

Ingliston Equestrian Centre   St.

Whitemoss Dam

Castlehill Plantation

Drums
Stable Cottage

Whitemoss Farm

Castlehill Cottage

4
PA14

B789

Barbeg Cottages
BARBEG HILL

Formakin

Paddock Craig

Gatehead

71
Park Erskine

Barmore Plantation
BARMORE HILL

H
O
U
S
T
O
N

Formakin Estate Country Park

Paddockcraig

5

Parkglen Wood

Formakin Mill

Dargavel Burn

6
PA6

Meiklefield

ston
670

240

A
Towncroft Farm

B
R   E   I   L   L   41

C

D

Roghall

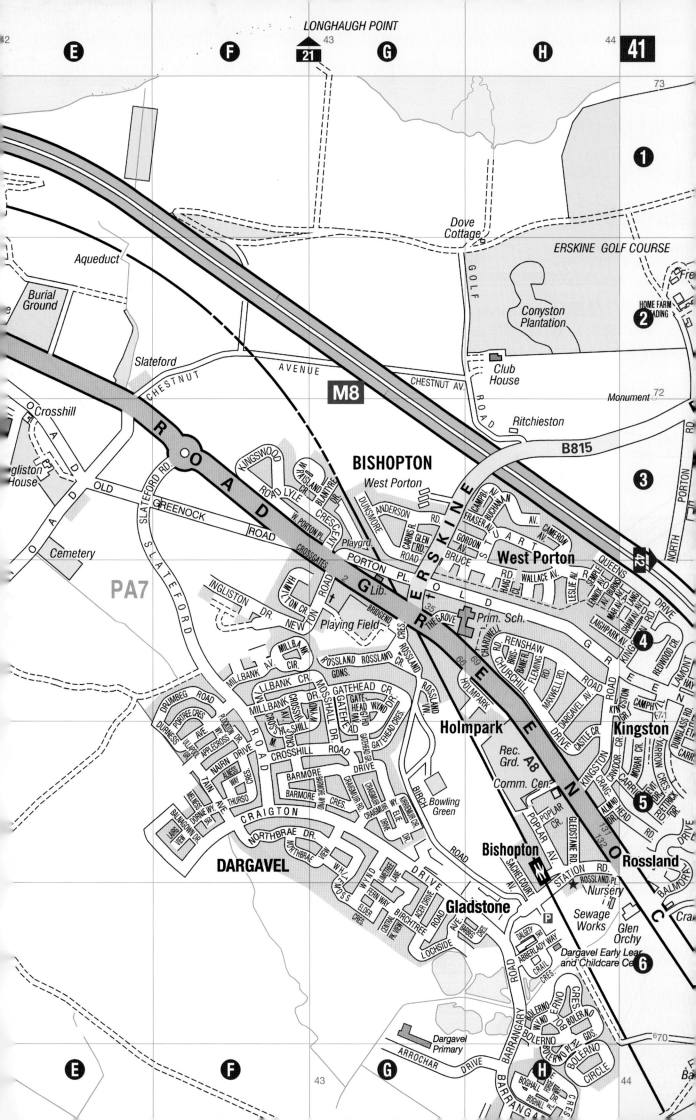

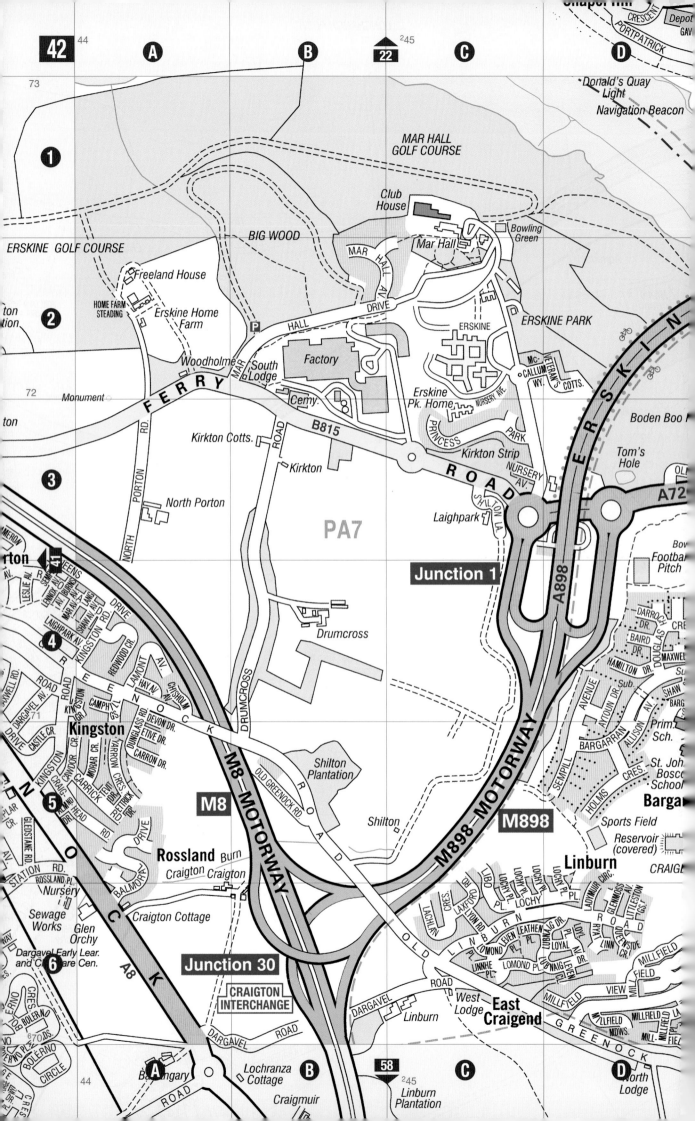

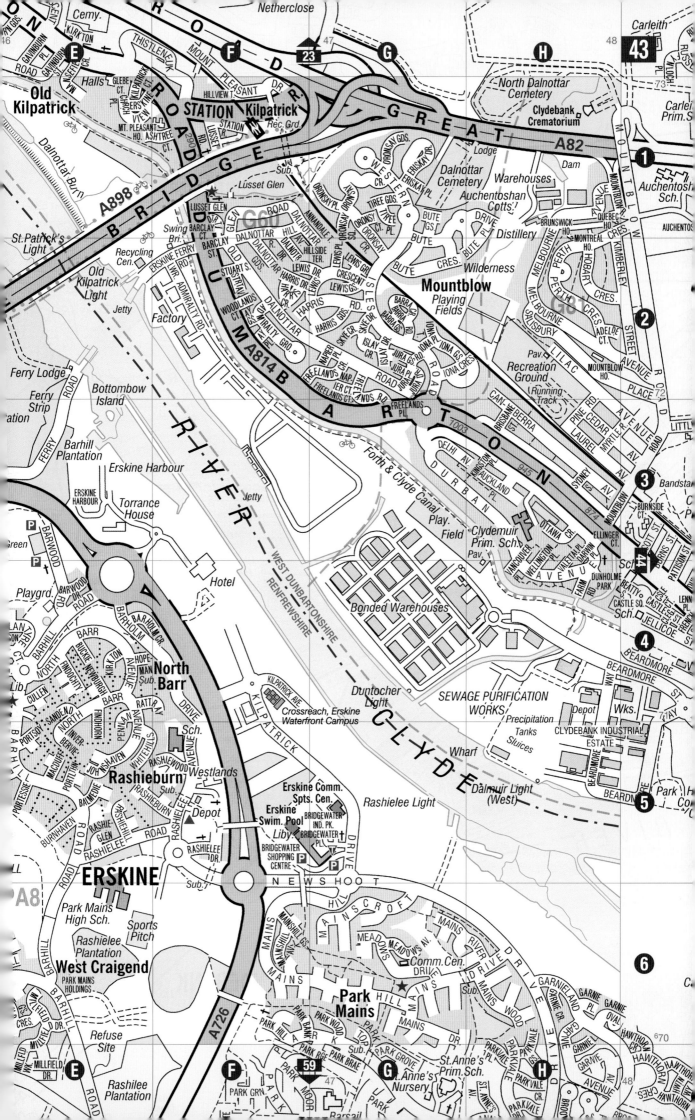

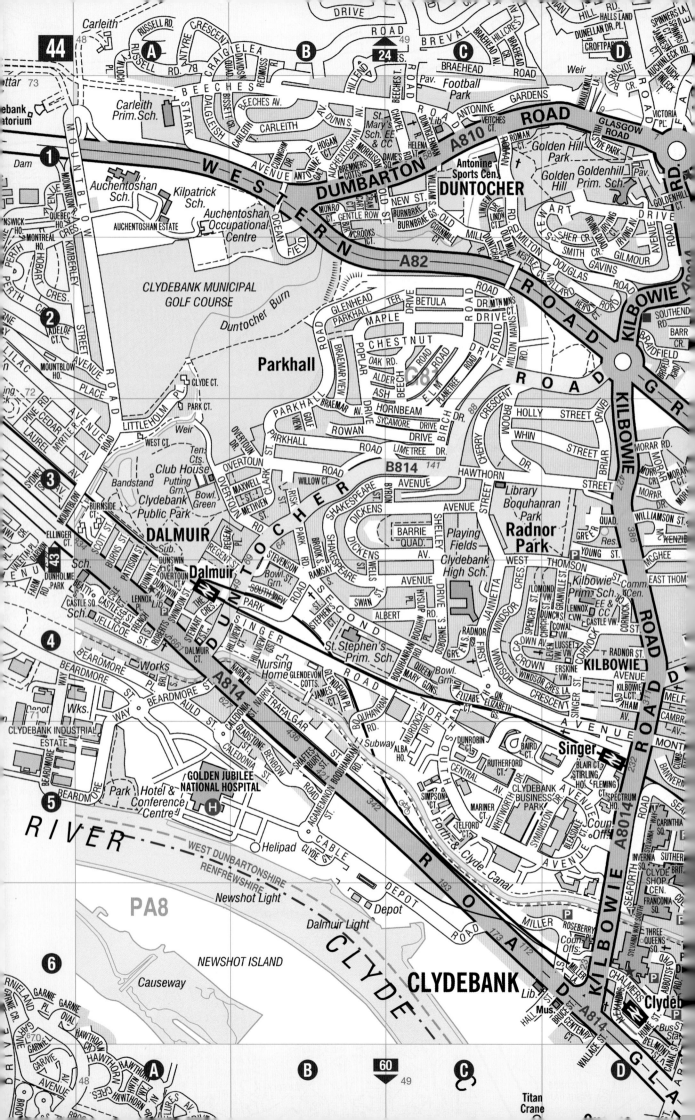

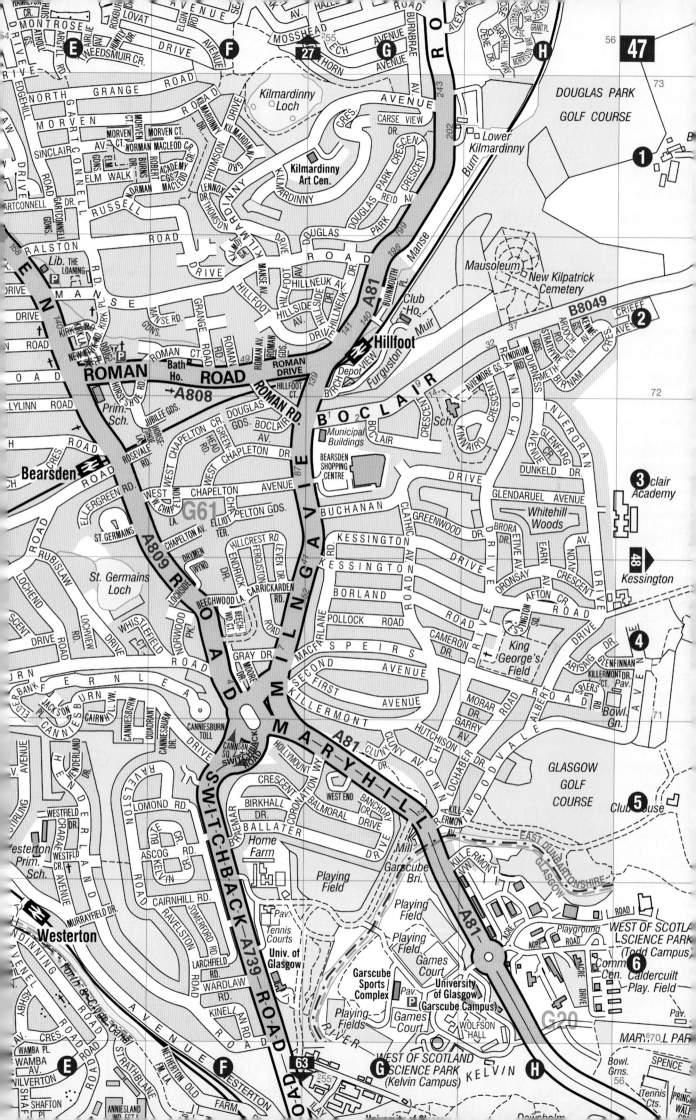

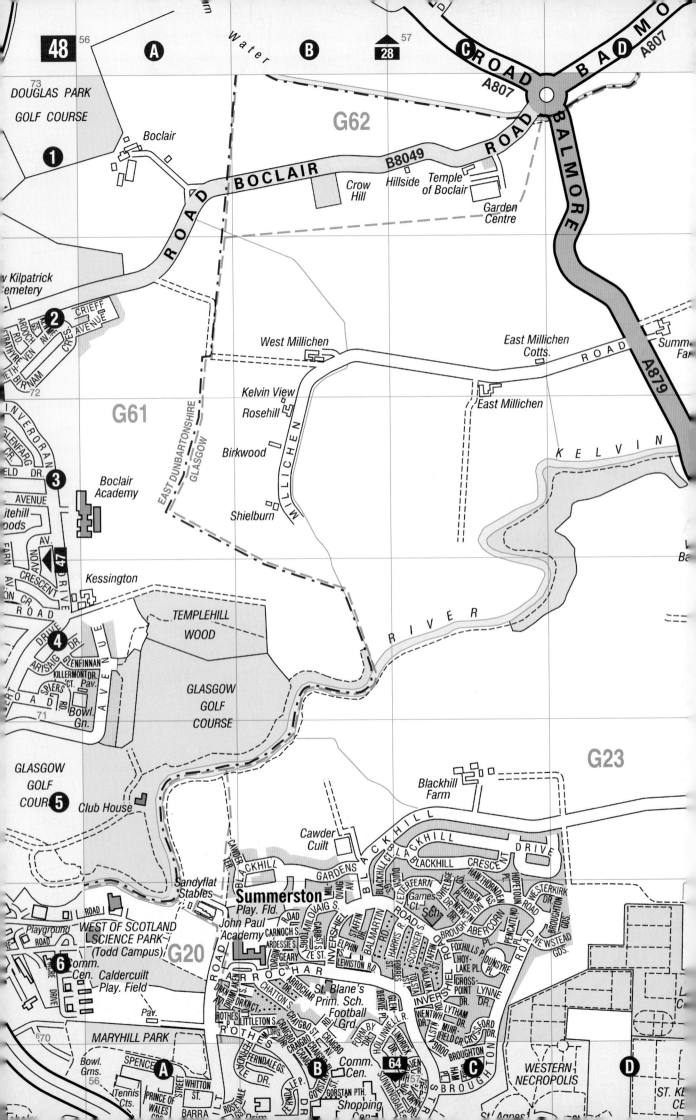

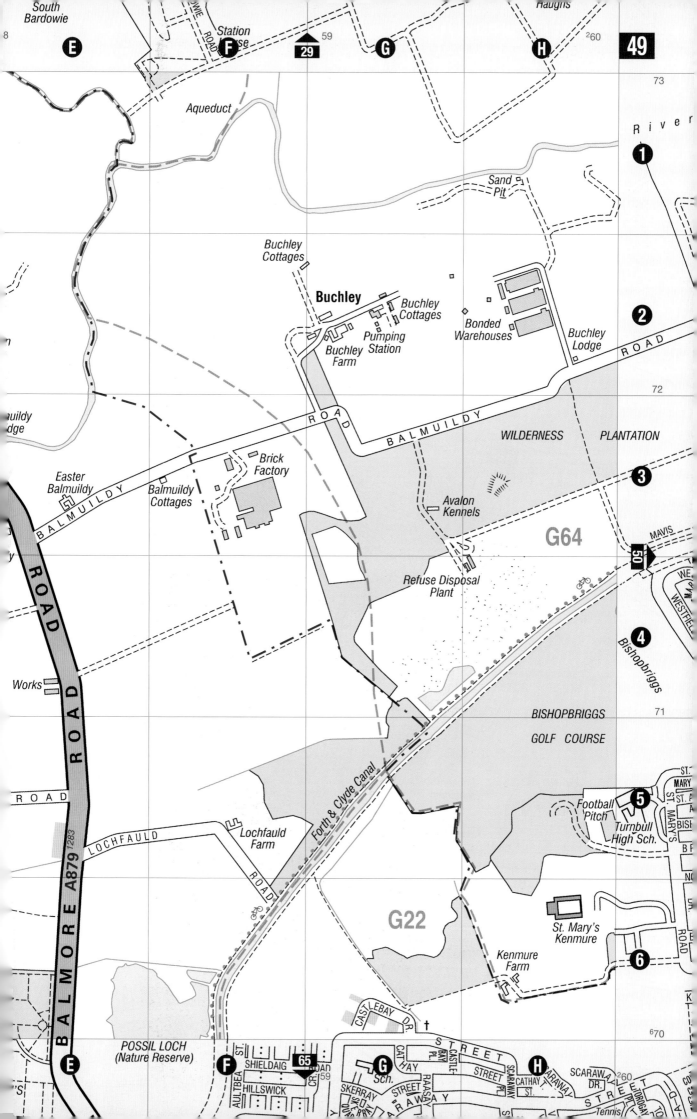

South Bardowie

E

Station House

F

29 · 59

G

260

H

73

Aqueduct

River

1

Sand Pit

Buchley Cottages

Buchley

Buchley Cottages

Bonded Warehouses

2

Pumping Station

Buchley Lodge

ROAD

Buchley Farm

72

BALMUILDY

ROAD

WILDERNESS PLANTATION

muildy dge

Easter Balmuildy

Brick Factory

Balmuildy Cottages

BALMUILDY

Avalon Kennels

3

G64

MAVIS

50

WE

WESTFIELD

Refuse Disposal Plant

4

Bishopbriggs

71

Works

ROAD

BALMORE

A879 1283

LOCHFAULD

Lochfauld Farm

Forth & Clyde Canal

BISHOPBRIGGS GOLF COURSE

ST. MARY

ST. A

ST. MARY'S

BISH

Football Pitch

5

Turnbull High Sch.

BF

NO

ROAD

G22

St. Mary's Kenmure

6

Kenmure Farm

ROAD

KT

670

CASTLEBAY DR.

†

POSSIL LOCH (Nature Reserve)

E

F

SHIELDAIG

65 · 59

G

Sch.

CASTLE-

BAY PL.

STREET

STREET

SCARAWAY DR.

260

H

AULTBEA ST.

HILLSWICK

SKERRAY ST.

CRES

CATHAY

RAASAY ST.

SCARAWAY ST.

CATHAY ST.

STREET

ARAWAY

Tennis

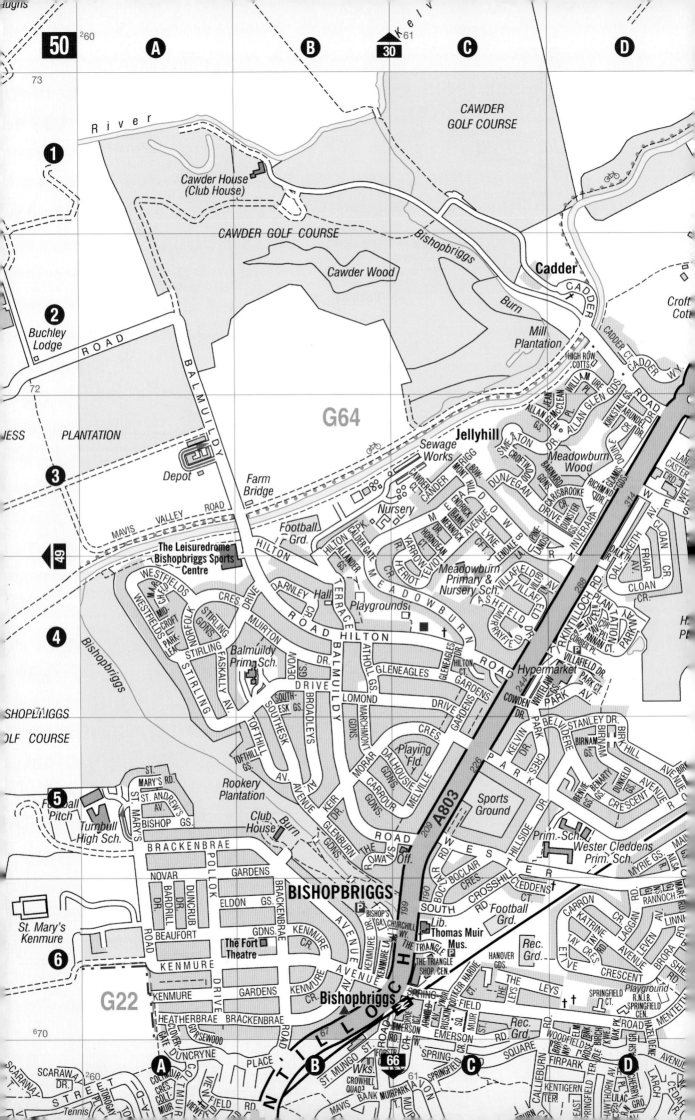

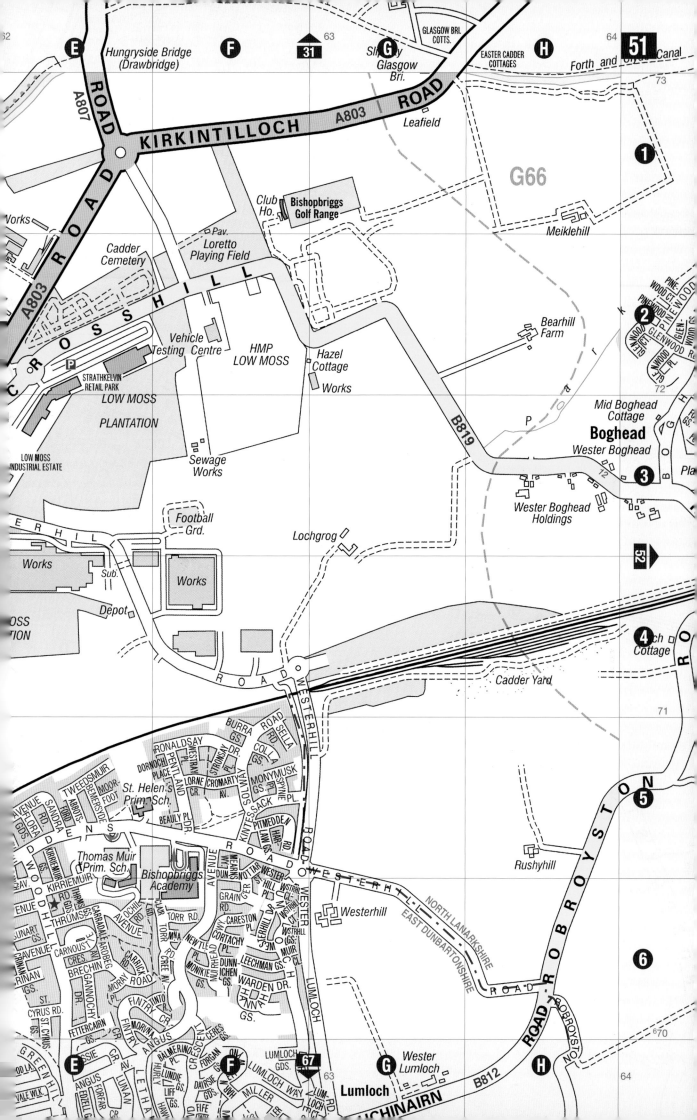

E Hungryside Bridge (Drawbridge) F 31 63 Sh y Glasgow Bri. G GLASGOW BRL. COTTS. EASTER CADDER COTTAGES H Forth and Clyde Canal 51

KIRKINTILLOCH ROAD

A807

A803 ROAD

A803

Leafield

G66

73

1

Club Ho. Bishopbriggs Golf Range

Meiklehill

Pav. Loretto Playing Field

Cadder Cemetery

CROSSHILL

Bearhill Farm

k

2

PINE WOOD CT. PINEWOOD GLEN WOOD GS. GLENWOOD RD. GLEN WOOD PL. GLE WOOD

72

P Vehicle Testing Centre

HMP LOW MOSS

Hazel Cottage

Works

B819

r a l P

Mid Boghead Cottage

Boghead Wester Boghead

BOG GS. H GS. Pla

3

STRATHKELVIN RETAIL PARK

LOW MOSS PLANTATION

Sewage Works

Works

Wester Boghead Holdings

12

LOW MOSS INDUSTRIAL ESTATE

Football Grd.

Lochgrog

52

ERHIL D

Works Sub.

Works

Lo ch Cottage R

4

OSS TION

Depot

Cadder Yard

71

ROAD

WESTERHILL

5

BURRA GS. ROAD SELLA RD. COLLA GS. ROAD

RONALDSAY PLACE SWESTRAY STRONSAY PL. MONYMUSK GS. SPYNIE PL.

DORNOCH PENTLAND LORNE CROMARTY AV.

TWEEDSMUIR MOOR FOOT BEMERSYDE ABBOTS FORD St. Helen's Prim. Sch. BEAULY PL. KINTESSACK HAR PITMEDDEN RD. ANN GS.

AVENUE FLORA RD. SANDRA GDS.

WOOD KIRRIEMUIR KIRRIEMUIR RD. THRUMS OCHIL RD. Thomas Muir Prim. Sch. Bishopbriggs Academy AVENUE ROAD NOTTAR GRAINGER RD. DUN MEARNS WESTER HILL PL. WSTRHILL WESTER WSTHLL WCTRLL Westerhill NORTH LANARKSHIRE EAST DUNBARTONSHIRE

Rushyhill

ROBROYSTON

6

AVE LINAN PAV ENUE RINAN GS. CARNOUST CRES BRECHIN CARRADALE ARDBEG GANNOCHY DR. TORR RD. TORR PL. CARRICK MORN ROAD CREE AV. NEWTLE PL. MUIRHEAD DUNN ICHEN MONIKIE GS. WARDEN DR. LEECHMAN GS. HANNAH GS. MUIR GL. WESTERHILL LUMLOCH ROAD

ROBROYSTON ROBROYSTON

SUNART AVENUE CRINAN GS. ST. CYRUS RD. FETTERCAIRN FINTRY FINTRY CR. TINTO RD. ANGUS MORVNA GS. CERES CRESCENT FORGAN LUMLOCH GDS. LUM LUMLOCH CT.

GREENHILL OD LA ESSIE CR ANGUS FORFAR AV. LUNAN LETHA BALMERINO PL. HURLY LUNDIE GS. DAIRSIE GS. LIFF GS. FIFE GS. MALLER LUMLOCH WAY 67 63 Lumloch G Wester Lumloch B812 H

E VALE WLK. EDELL CR F UCHINAIRN 64 670

KIRKINTILLOCH A803

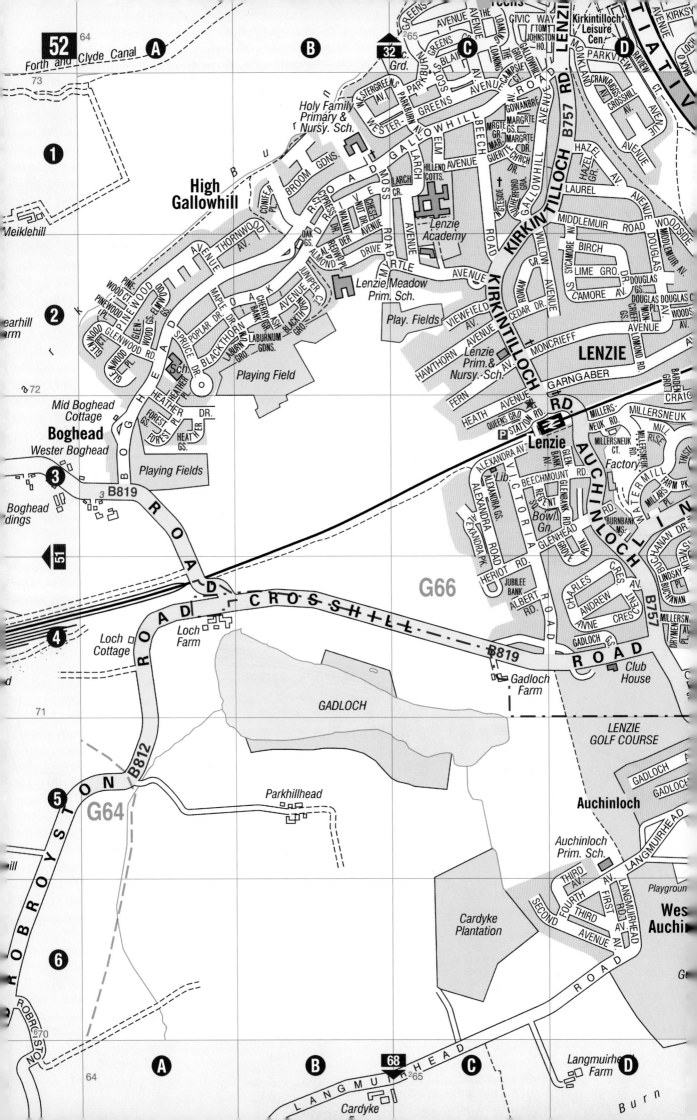

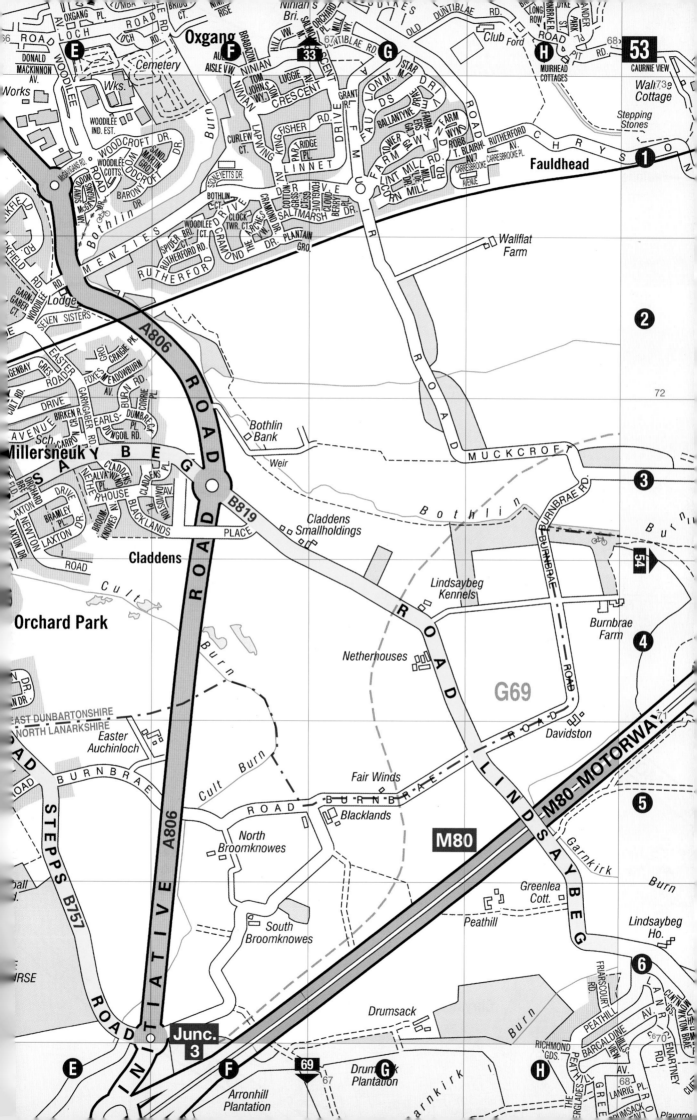

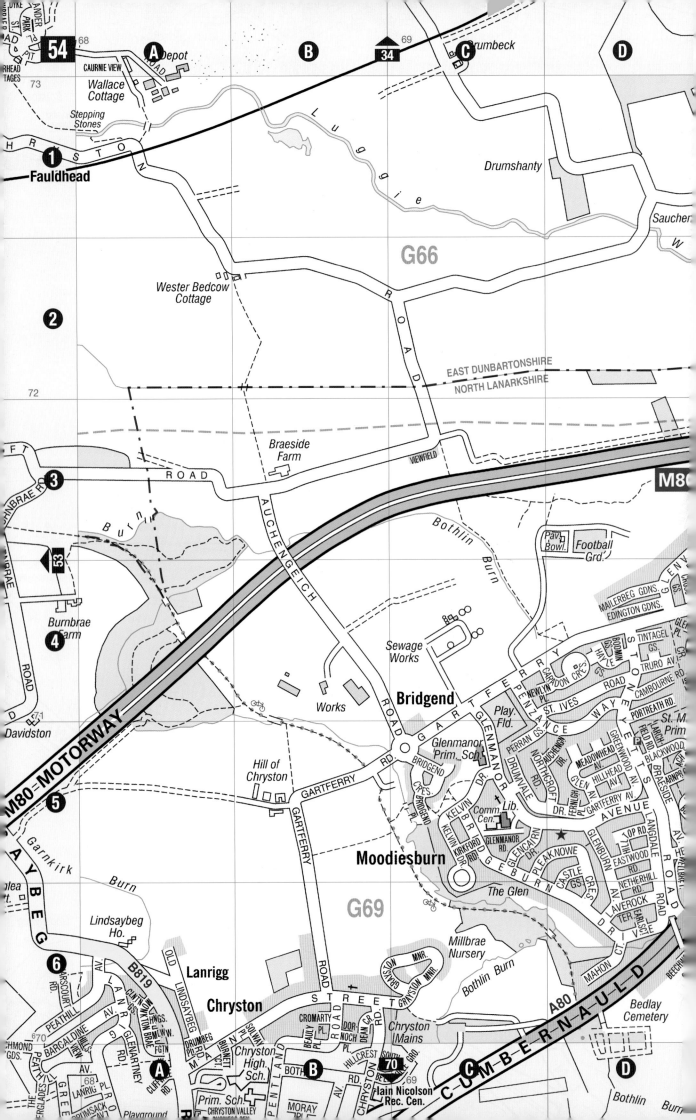

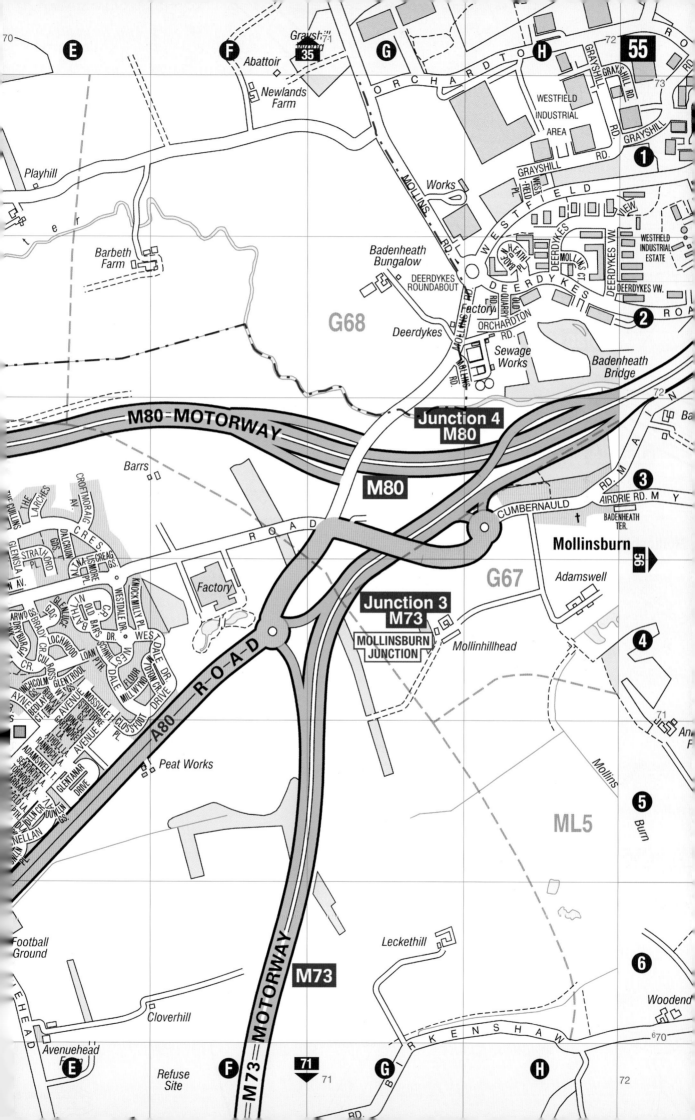

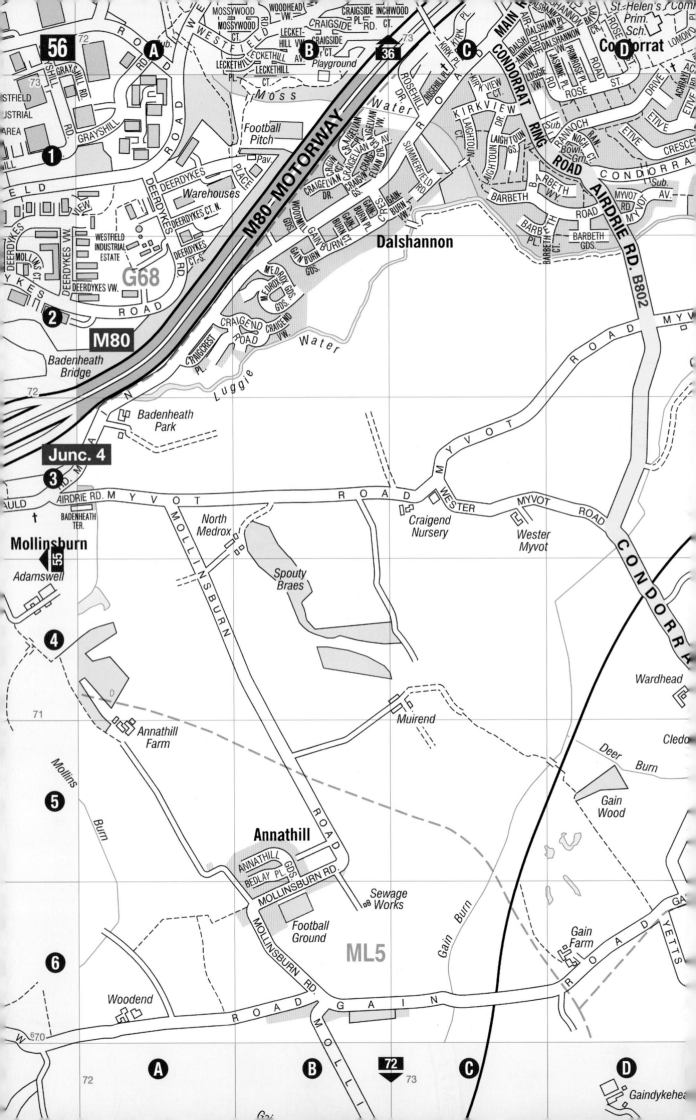

E

F 37

G Greenfaulds

H 57

73

Blairlinn

76

1

B8039

BLAIRLINN IND. EST.

2

72

3 Lochside Cottage

Garngibboch

Wester Blairlinn

Millcroft Corn Mill

Milncroft Farm

Madgiscroft Quarry

Cragside

Milncroft Wood

SPAIRDRUM

North Bellstane Plantation

South Myvot

Hallbrae

Loanhead

G67

Summerhill

Broomlee Strip

Summerhill Strips

B802

Summerfield Strip

4 Bellstane Lodge

Mill Lade

Shank Burn

Clay Pit

ML6

71

Bellstane

5 South Bellstane Plantation

Shank Bridge

CULLOCHRIG

BLACKBOG

Mossywood

Mossywood Clumps

Douglas Glen

6 Cullochrig Plantation

North Myvot

Cumbernauld Rugby Football Club Playing Field

Playing Field

Auchenkilns Holdings

CHAPELTON ROAD

AUCHENKILNS ROAD

A73

LENZIEMILL

MILLCROFT ROAD

COBBLEBRAE ROAD

GARNGIBBOCH ROAD

MILLCROFT ROAD

SHANKBURN ROAD

GAIN AND SHANKBURN ROAD

SHANKBURN

The Gains

Blackcraig Wood

Black Craig

Heatherfield Wood

Cleddans

East Lodge

West Lodge

New West Lodge

Hairstanes Cottage

East Lodge Wood

CONDORRAT

B802

Douglas Plantation

Mosshouse

670

Cullochrig

E

F 73 275

G

H

76

ROAD

CULLOCH

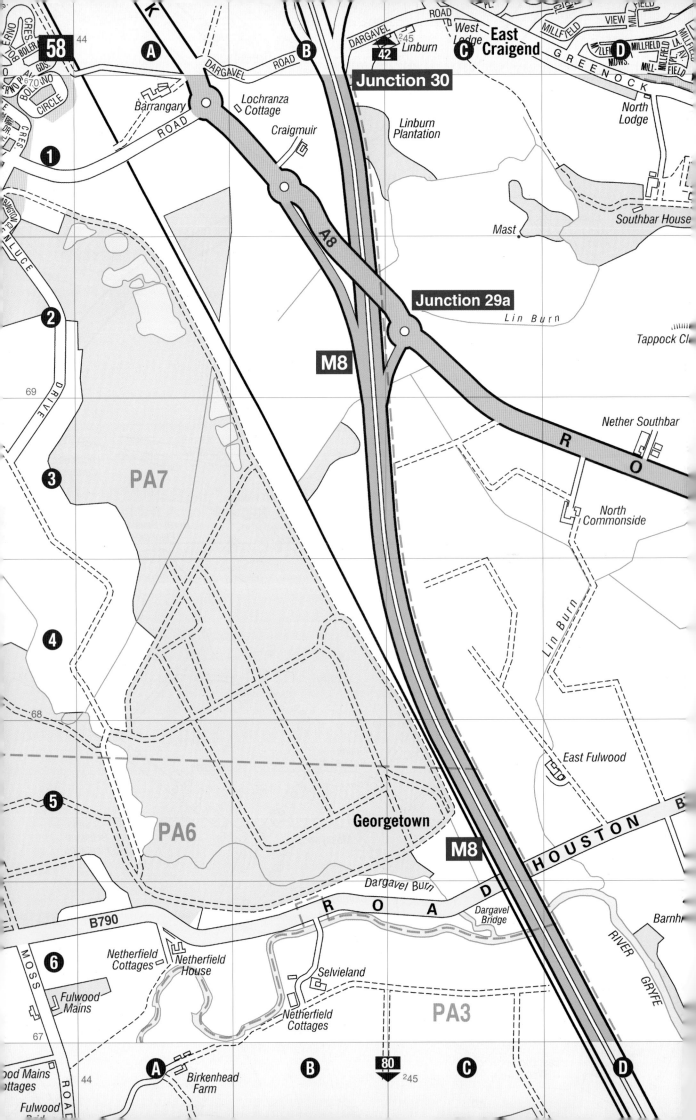

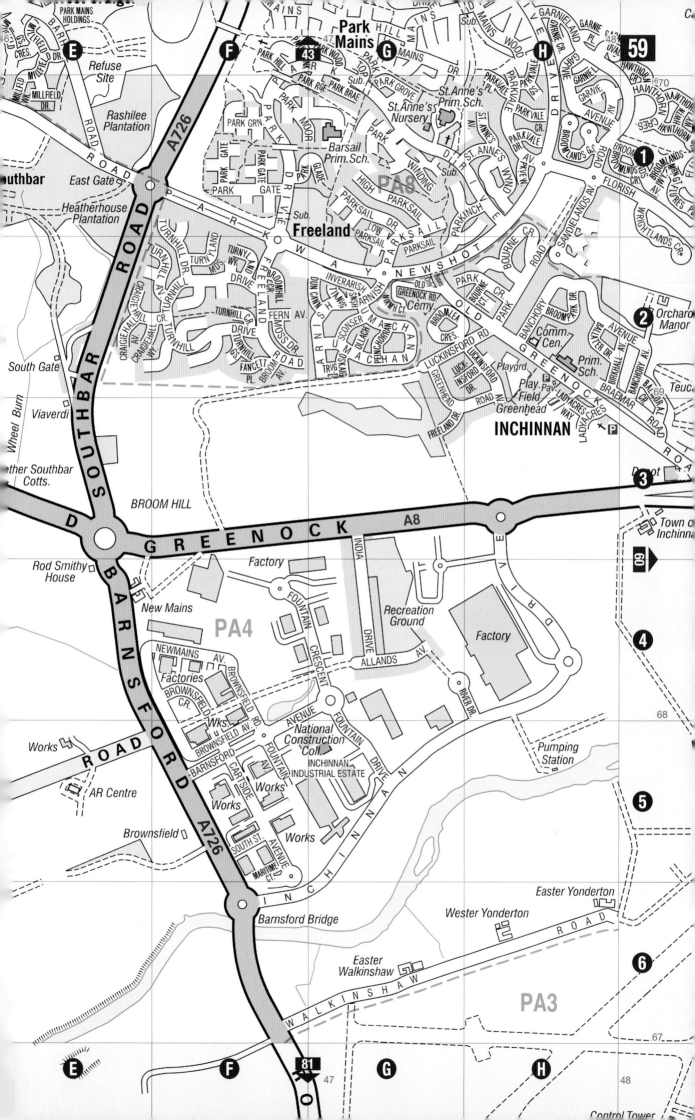

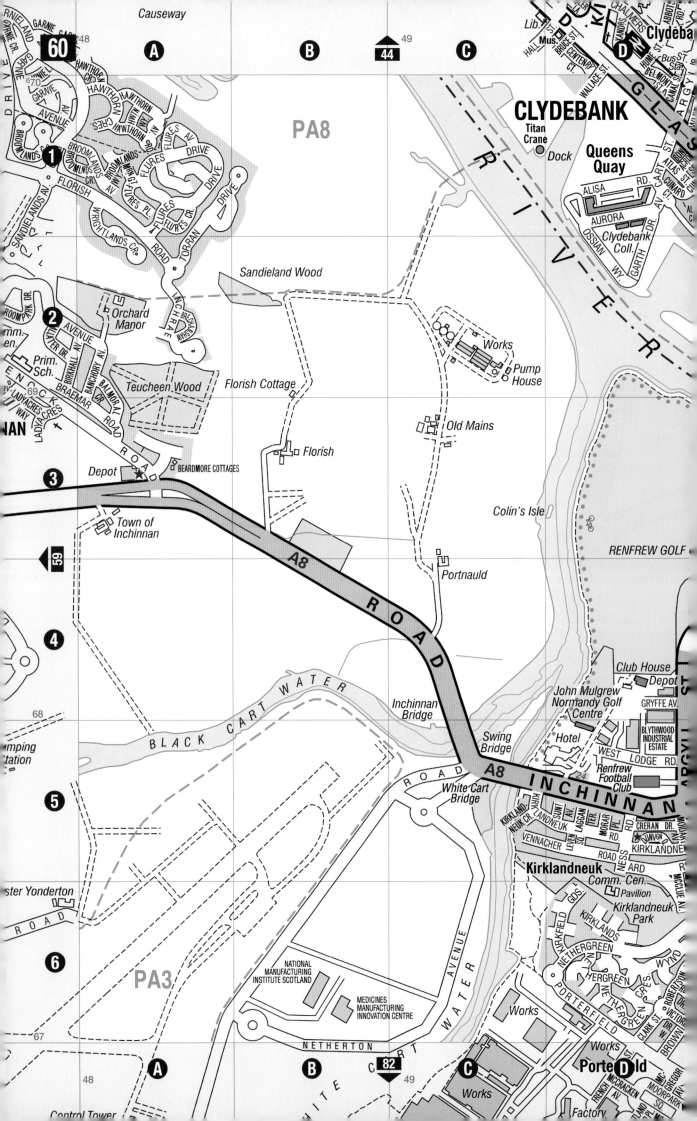

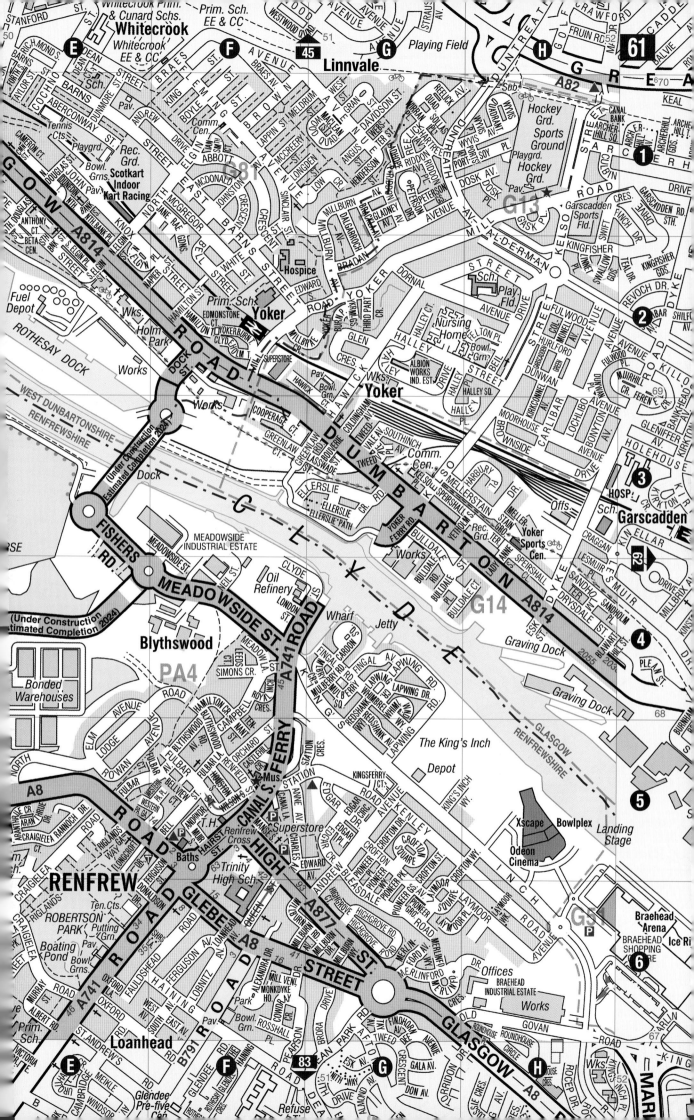

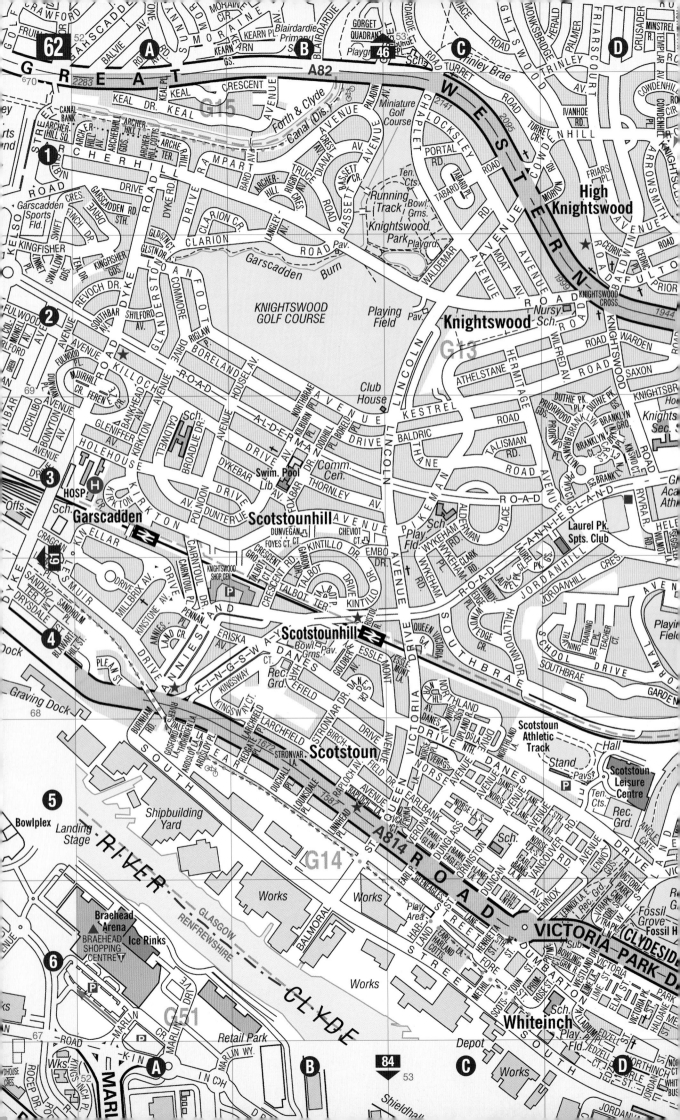

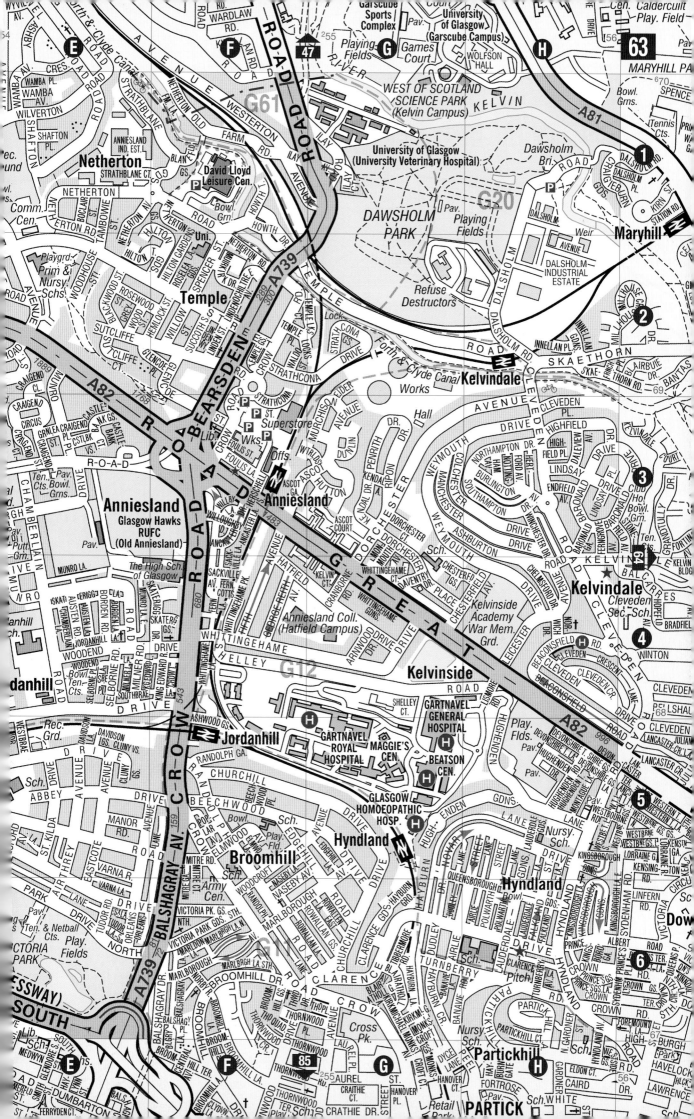

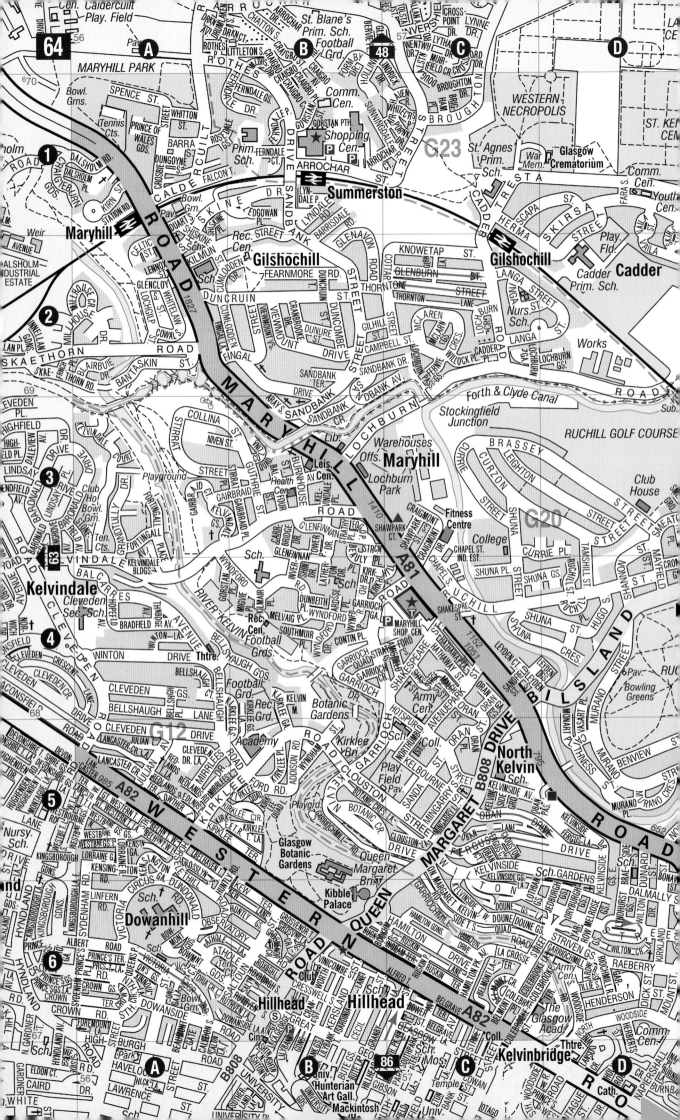

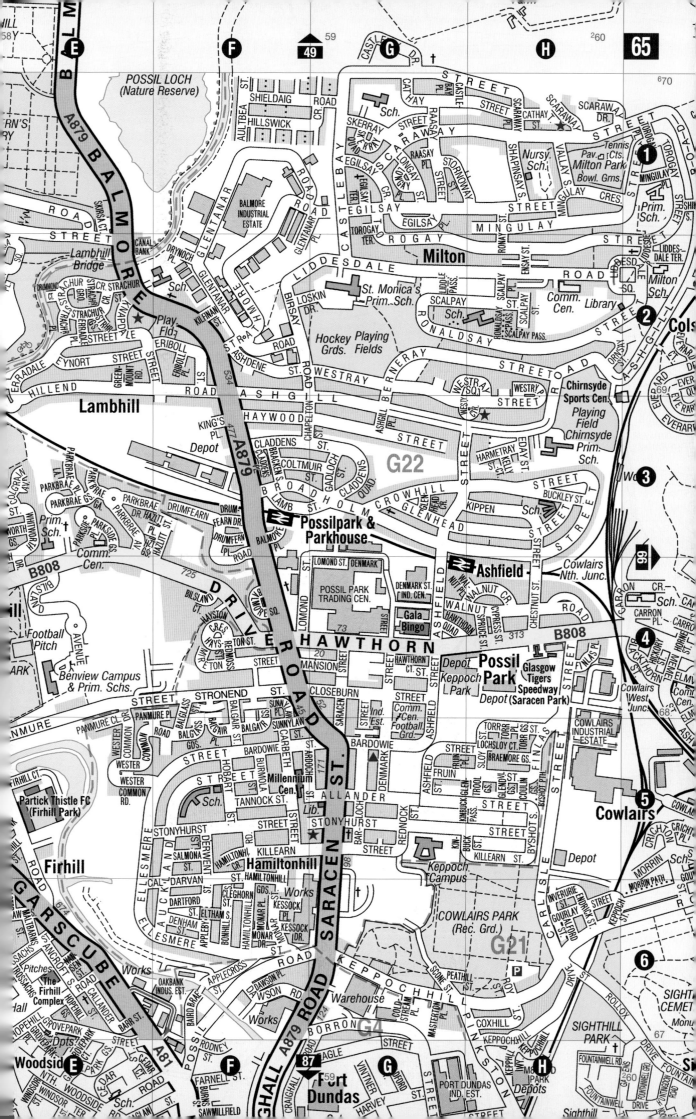

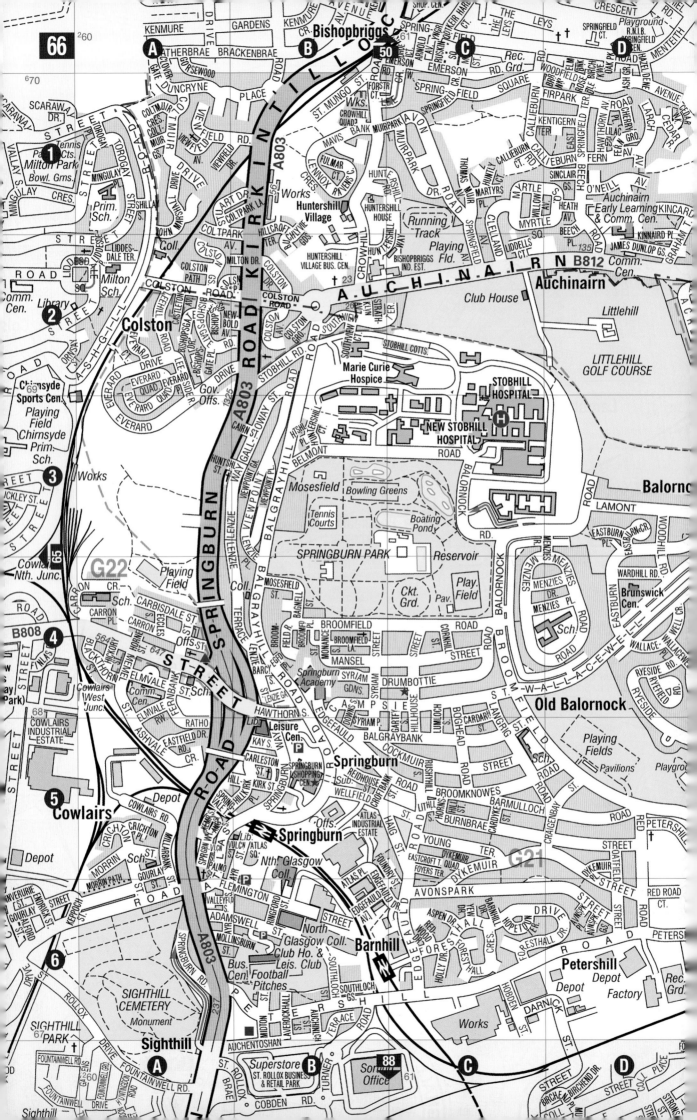

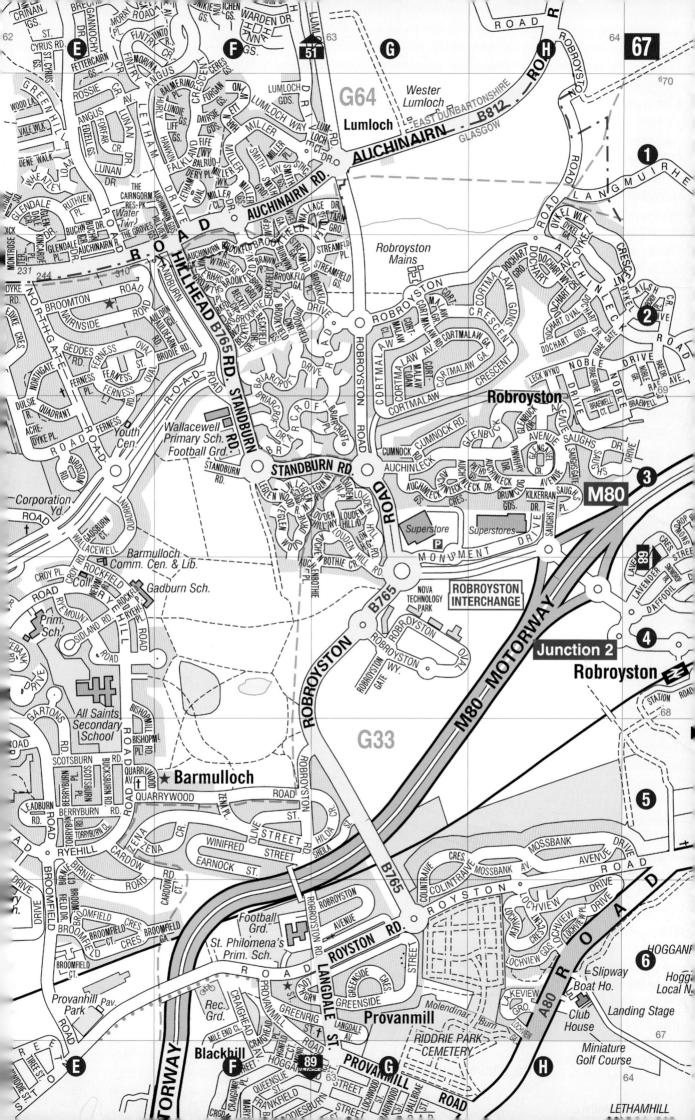

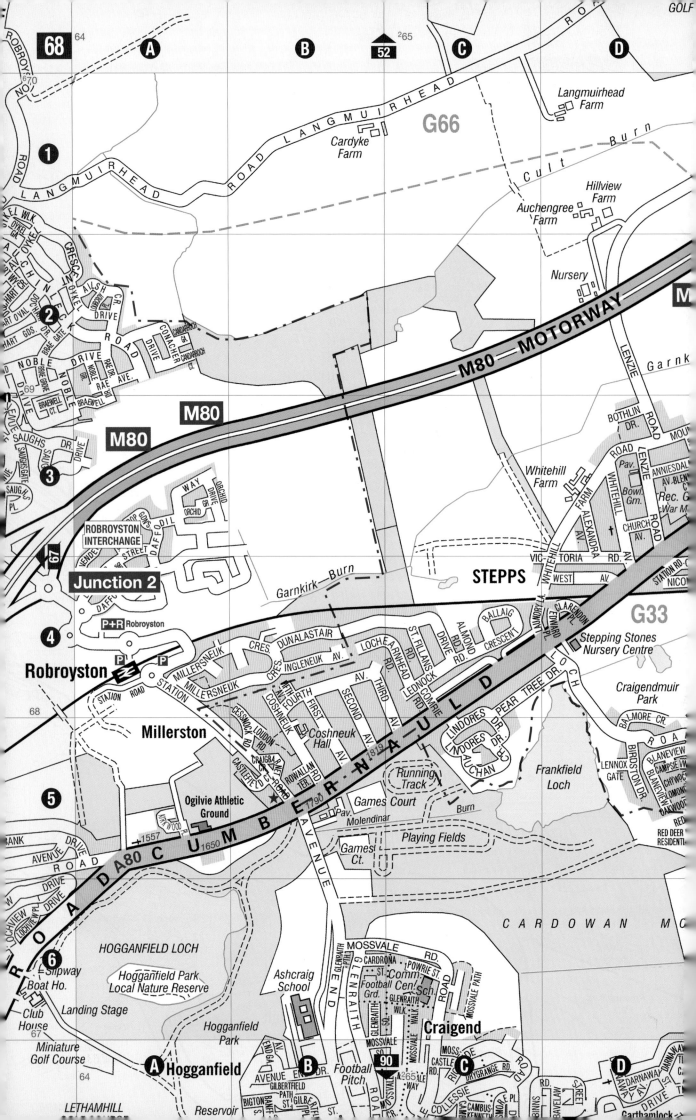

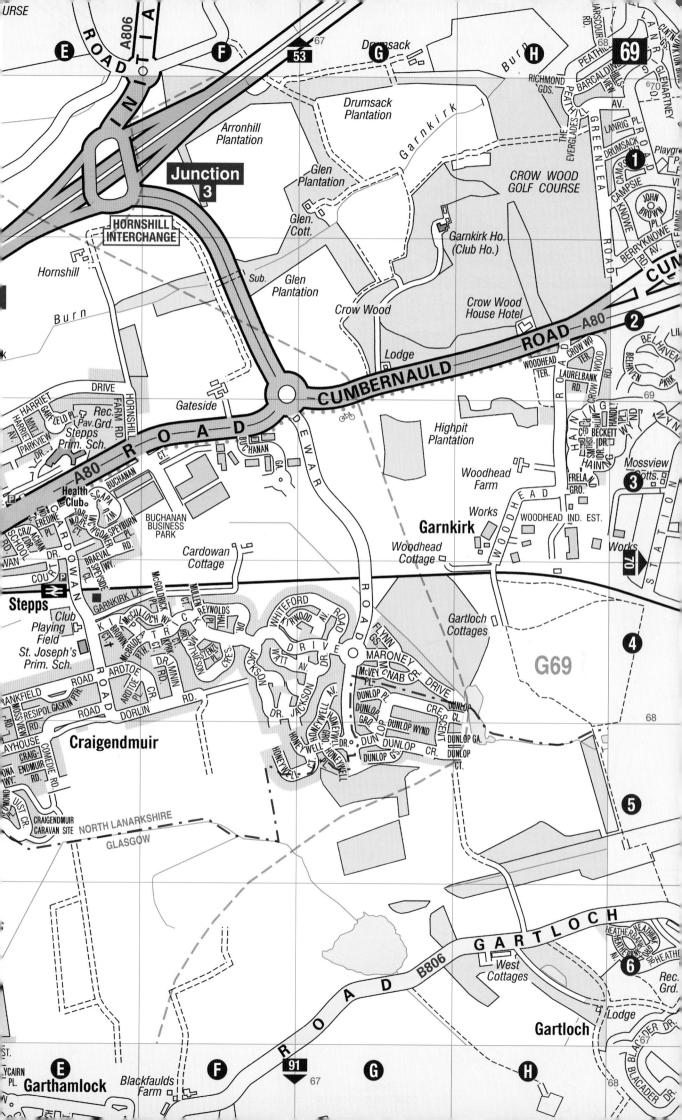

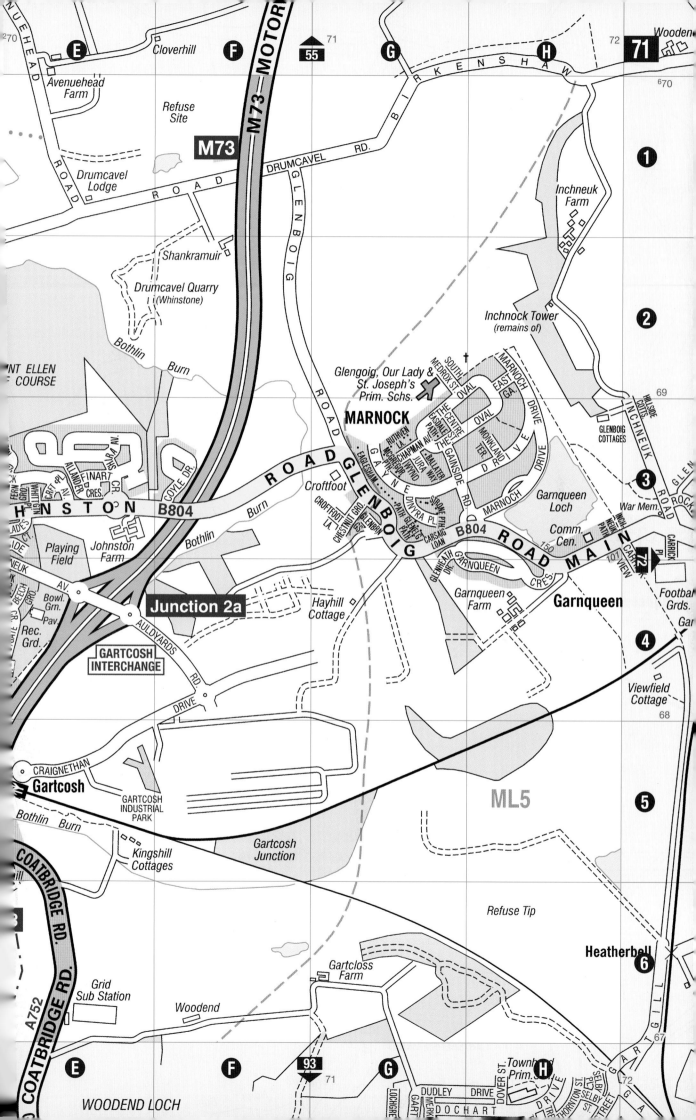

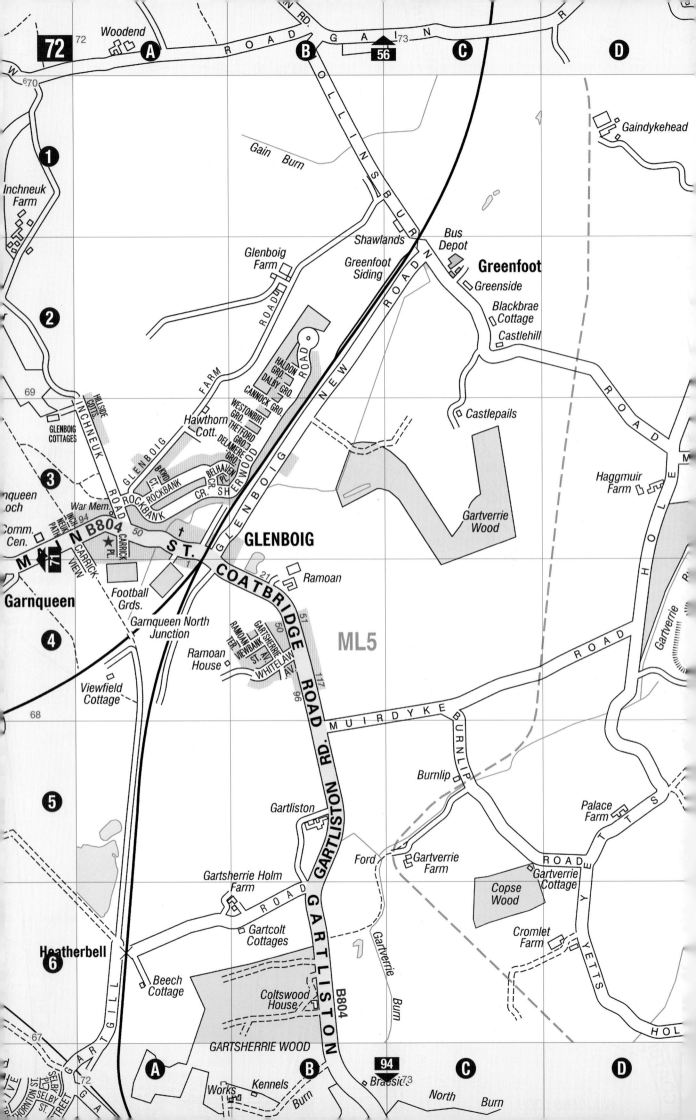

Woodend **A**

B **56** 73 **C** **D**

ROAD GAIN N

COLLINSBURN

W 670

Gaindykehead

1

Gain Burn

Inchneuk Farm

Shawlands

Bus Depot

Greenfoot

Glenboig Farm

Greenfoot Siding

Greenside

2

69

Blackbrae Cottage

Castlehill

HILLSIDE COTTS.

NEW ROAD

INCHNEUK

GLENBOIG COTTAGES

FARM ROAD

Castlepails

ROAD

3

nqueen och

Hawthorn Cott.

WESTONBIRT GRO.

THETFORD GRO.

DELAMERE GRO.

HALDON GRO.

DALBY GRO.

CANNOCK GRO.

Haggmuir Farm

GLENBOIG ROAD

BKWD. ST.

ROCKBANK

BELHAVEN CR.

SHERWOOD

GLENBOIG ROAD

Gartverrie Wood

INCHNEUK ROAD

War Mem.

94

M N B804

50

Comm. Cen.

INCHNEUK PATH

CARRICK VIEW

71

CARRICK PL.

†

ST.

GLENBOIG

21

Ramoan

Garnqueen

Football Grds.

COATBRIDGE

ROAD

ML5

ROAD

Gartverrie

4

Garnqueen North Junction

Ramoan House

RAMOAN TER.

VIEWBANK ST.

GARTSHERRIE AV.

WHITELAW AV.

50

51

117

96

HOLE ROAD

68

Viewfield Cottage

MUIRDYKE

BURNLIP

ROAD

Burnlip

Palace Farm

5

Gartliston

GARTLISTON ROAD RD.

Ford

Gartverrie Farm

Gartverrie Cottage

ROAD

YETTS

Gartsherrie Holm Farm

Copse Wood

Cromlet Farm

Heatherbell

6

Gartcolt Cottages

B804

Gartverrie Burn

YETTS

HOL

Beech Cottage

GARTLIGILL

GARTLISTON ROAD

Coltswood House

67

GA

SELBY ST.

THORNTON ST.

SELBY STREET

72

A

GARTSHERRIE WOOD

Works

Kennels

Burn

B

94 73

Braeside

North Burn

C

D

74 76
Mosshouse **A**
Riggend **B**
C
Wattston **D**

Monveda

Laigh Riggend

1
670

Brackenhirst Plantation

BRACKENHIRST ROAD
ROAD

MILL
A73
STIRLING ROAD

GREENGAIRS

2

69

MEIKLE
GLENBURN CT.
ROADSIDE PL.
MEIKLE CR.
B803

Meik.
Drumg.
Farm

3

73

Laverock Knowe

B803
ROAD

4
68

Drumshangie Moss

Depot

ARRAN DR.
NEIL GDNS.
STRTYRE GRAN TON
DUNNET
BANCHORY AV.
TREE AV.
HAWKWD.

Dalmacoulter Reservoir (covered)

5 Crowhill Plantation

wood

hsoles

A73

ROAD BALLO

AIRDRIE GOLF COURSE

Dykehead Farm

Airdriehill Farm

ROAD

6 Roughcraig Glen

CRESCENT
STRATHSPEY CRES.
STRATHLANE CR.
STRATHCAIRN CRES.
STRATHMRE
STRTHGO CR.
STRATHPEFFER
STAINEY
BRAH
BLUEBELL WAY
BOOMHOLM PL.
RINGHOLM WAY
DYKH
STRATH

STRATH-NAVER CR.
STRGL CR.
BROOMPARK
ARDBEG CR.
LOCHSIDE
ARDMORE CR.
SPEYBURN PL.
BALBLAIR RD.
TOBERMORY RD.

FETTERCAIRN PL.
DALWHINNIE PL.
LINKWOOD
BOWMORE PL.
TALISKER CR.
LINKWOOD RD.
CRES.

DYKEHEAD ROAD

North Burn

Airdriehill Quarry (dis)

ROAD
DRIEHILL

A
Ceme
CHEVIOT CT. PENTLAND CT.
MERRICK CT.
THRASHBISH
FERGUSON
HOLEHILLS DRIVE
WAY

Holehills
B
DALMACOULTER RD.
LAVEROCK RD.
Works

96 STIRLING RD.
INDUSTRIAL ESTATE
62

C

D
Airdriehill Quarry (dis)

hill

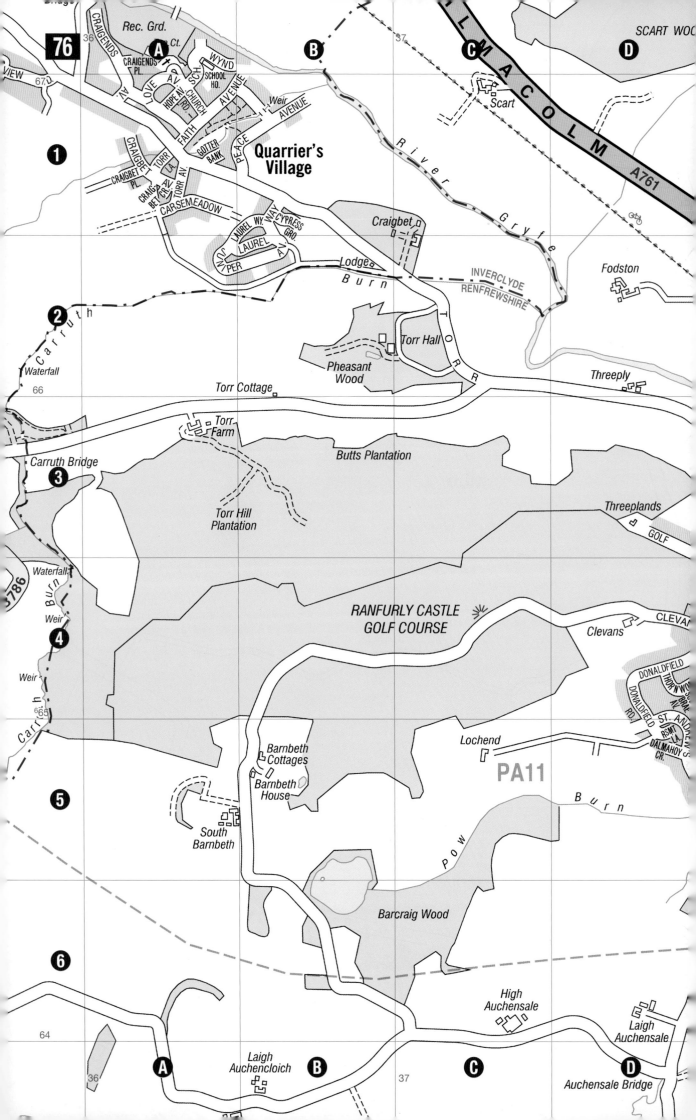

36
670
VIEW
66
65
64

37

Rec. Grd.

CRAIGENDS

A

Ct.
CRAIGENDS
PL.

WYND
SCH.
SCHOOL
HQ.

LOVE
AV.
HOPE AV.
CHURCH RD.
FAITH
SCH.
AV.
AVENUE
Weir
AVENUE

PEACE
GOTTER
BANK

B

1

CRAIGBET
PL.
TORR
LA.
CRAIGBET CR.
TORR AV.

CARSEMEADOW

LAUREL WY.
WAY
CYPRESS
GRO.
LAUREL
AV.
PER

**Quarrier's
Village**

Craigbet

Lodge
Burn

C

L M A C O L M
A761

Scart

SCART WOO

D

River
Gryfe

INVERCLYDE
RENFREWSHIRE

Fodston

2

Carruth
Waterfall

Pheasant
Wood

Torr Hall

Torr Cottage

T
O
R
R

Threeply

3
Carruth Bridge

Torr
Farm

Butts Plantation

Torr Hill
Plantation

Threeplands

GOLF

786
Waterfall
Burn
Weir

4

Weir

Carruth

**RANFURLY CASTLE
GOLF COURSE**

Clevans
CLEVAN

DONALDFIELD
THORN WO
BRAE
AV.
DONALDFIELD
RD.
ST. ANDREW'S
RSMT
LA.
DALMAHOY
CR.

Lochend

PA11

5

Barnbeth
Cottages
Barnbeth
House

South
Barnbeth

Pow
Burn

Barcraig Wood

6

36
64

A

Laigh
Auchencloich

B

High
Auchensale

C

Laigh
Auchensale

D
Auchensale Bridge

37

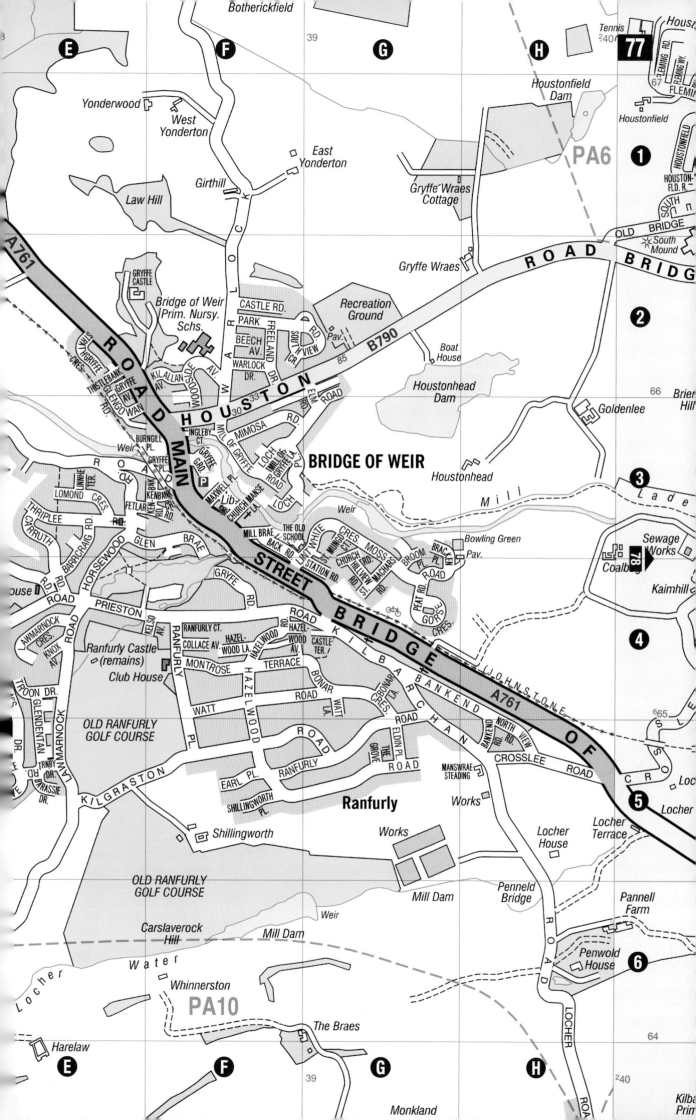

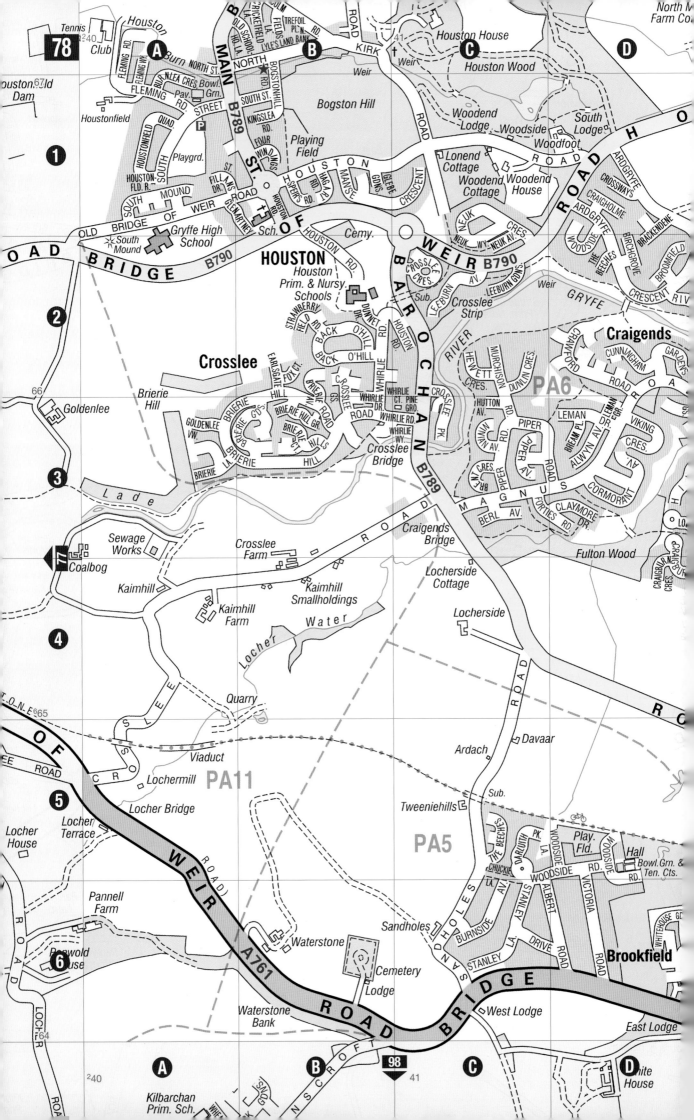

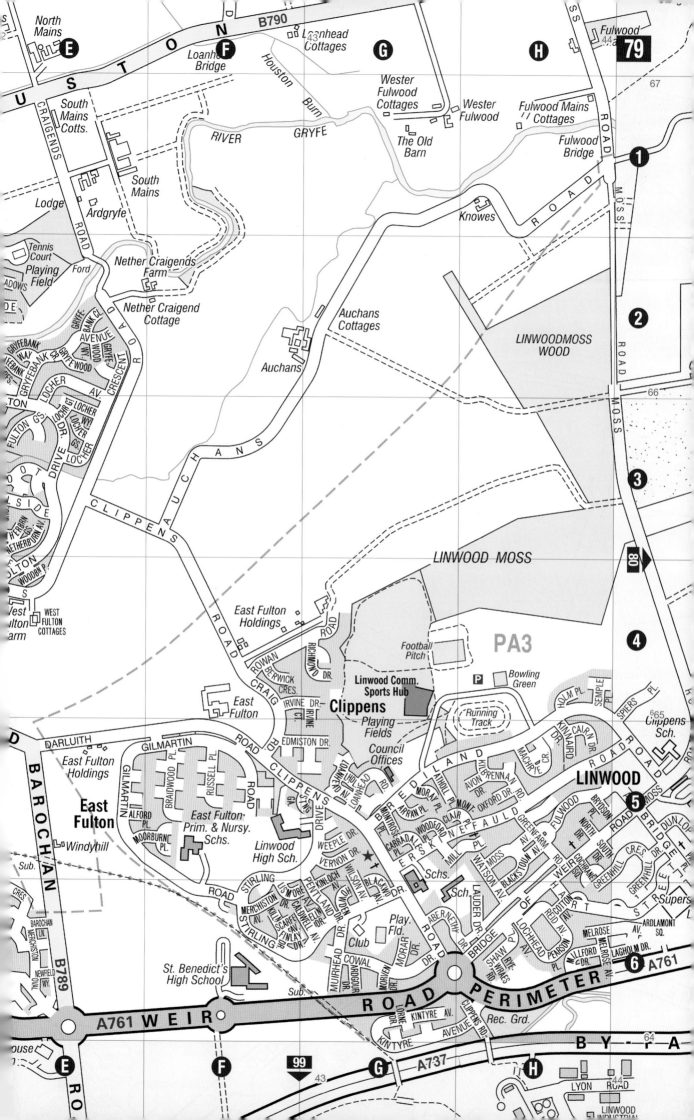

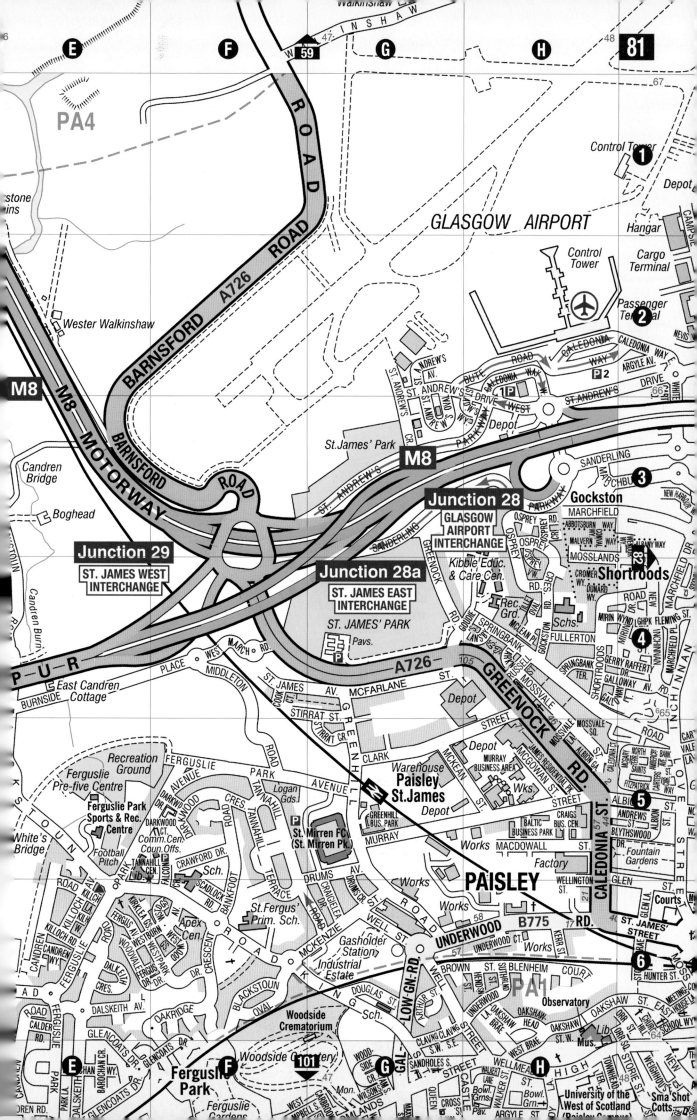

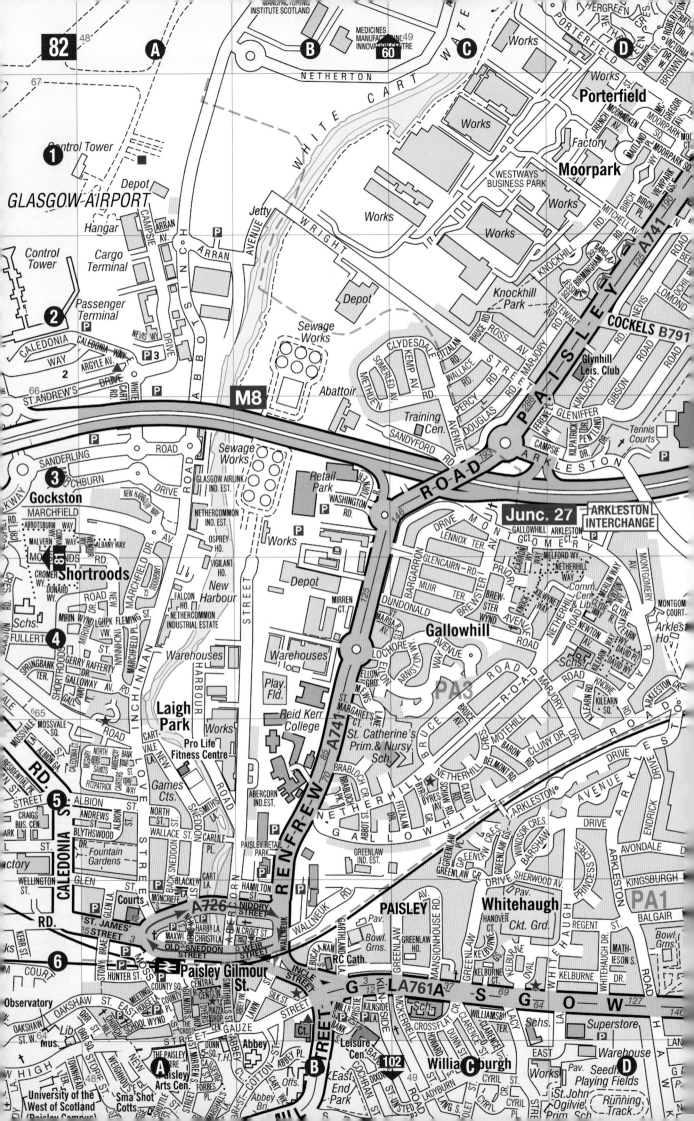

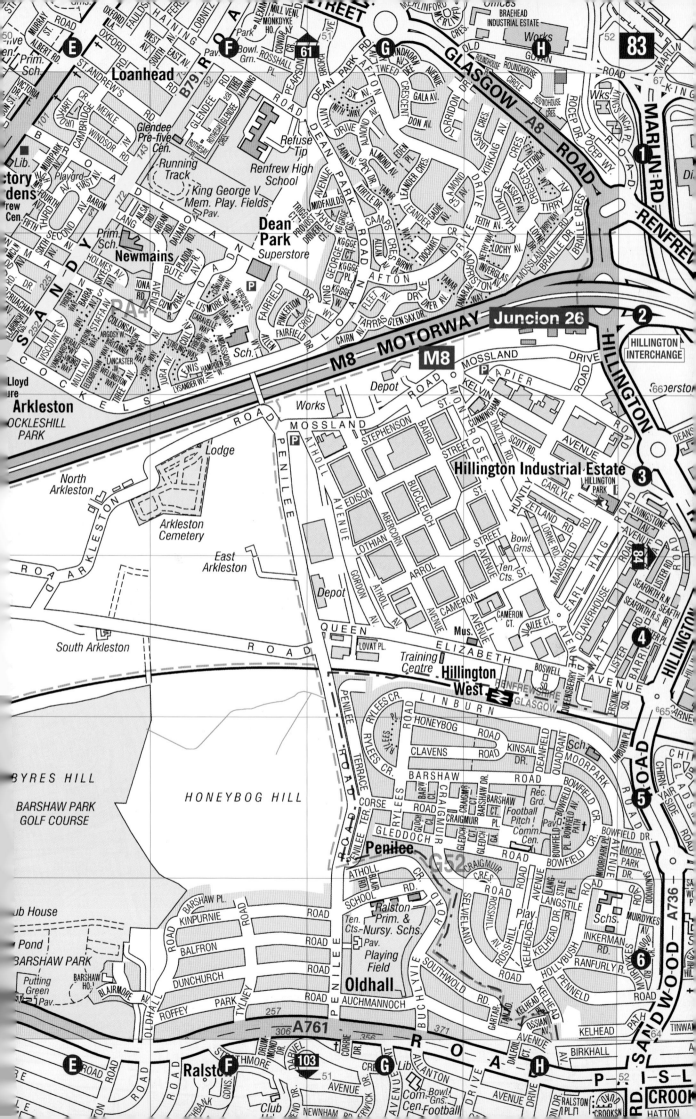

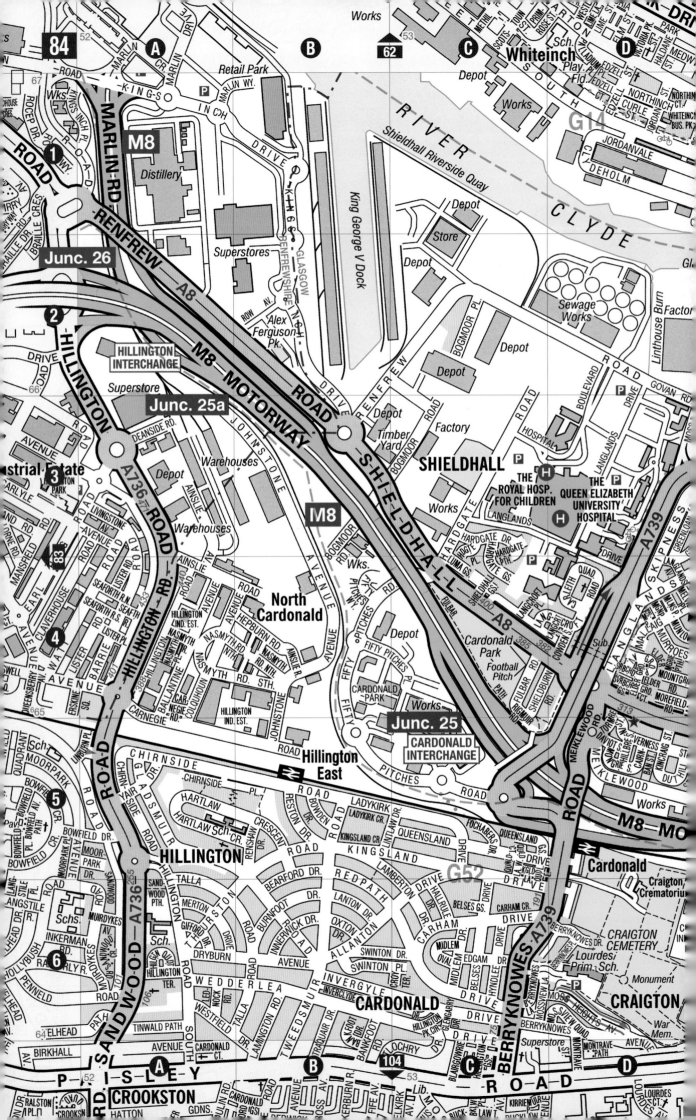

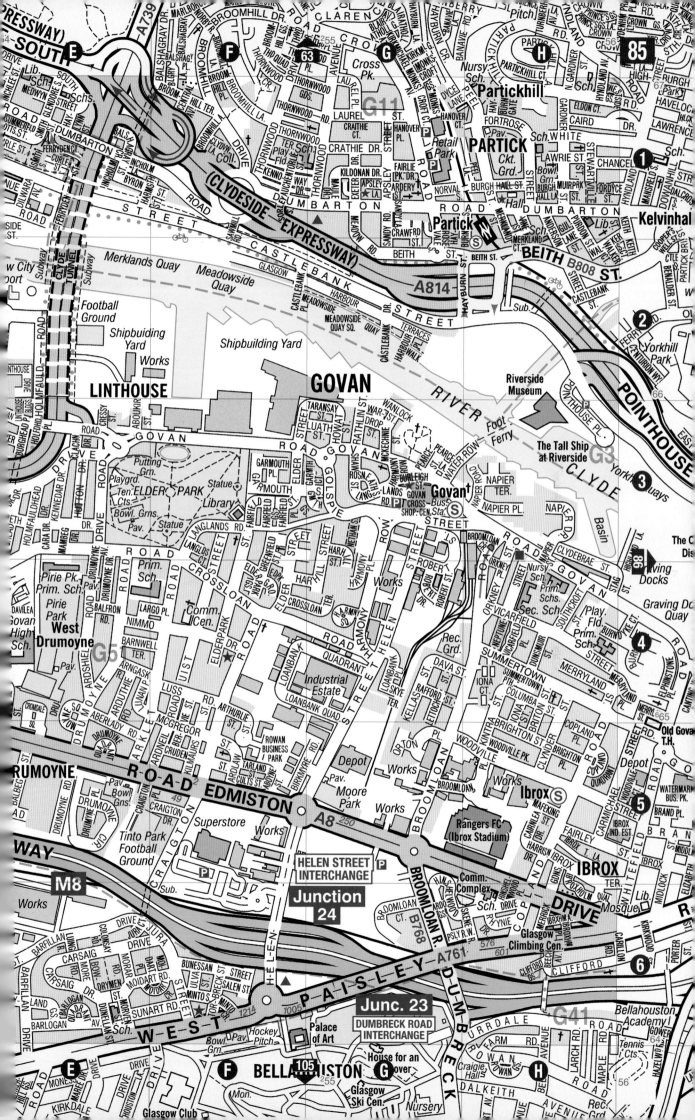

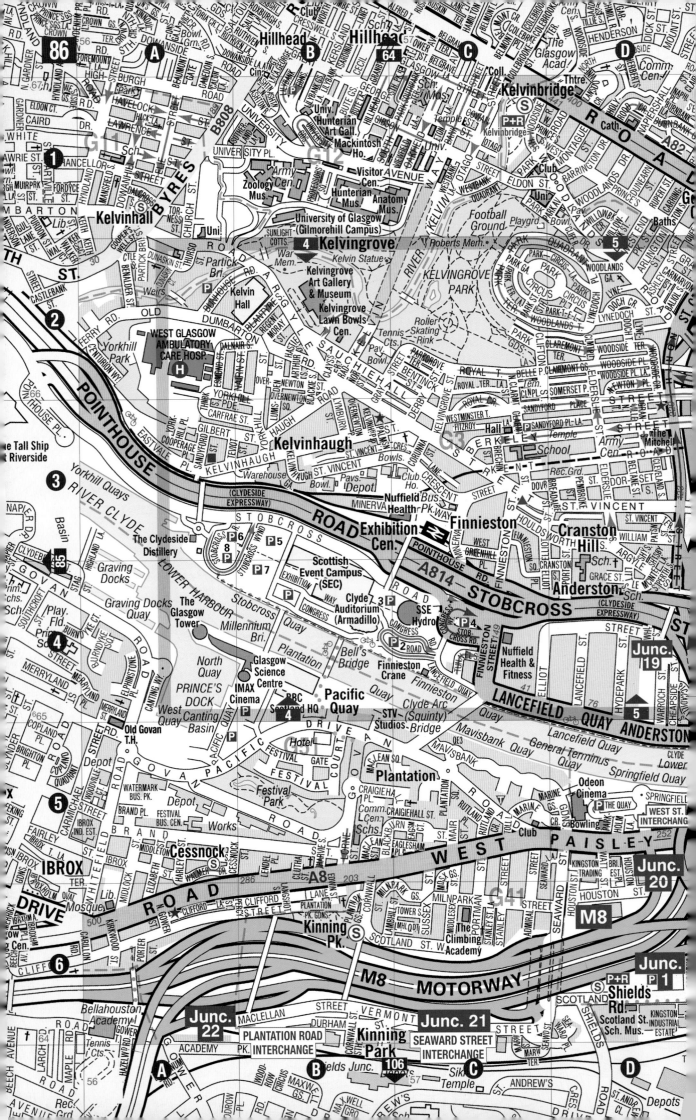

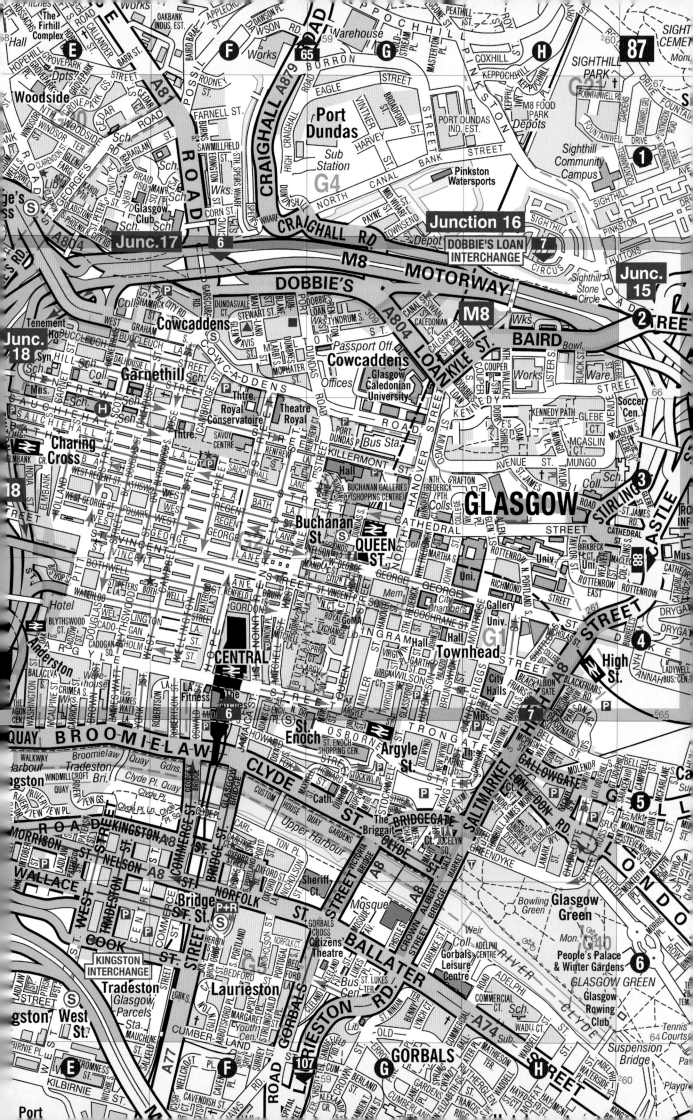

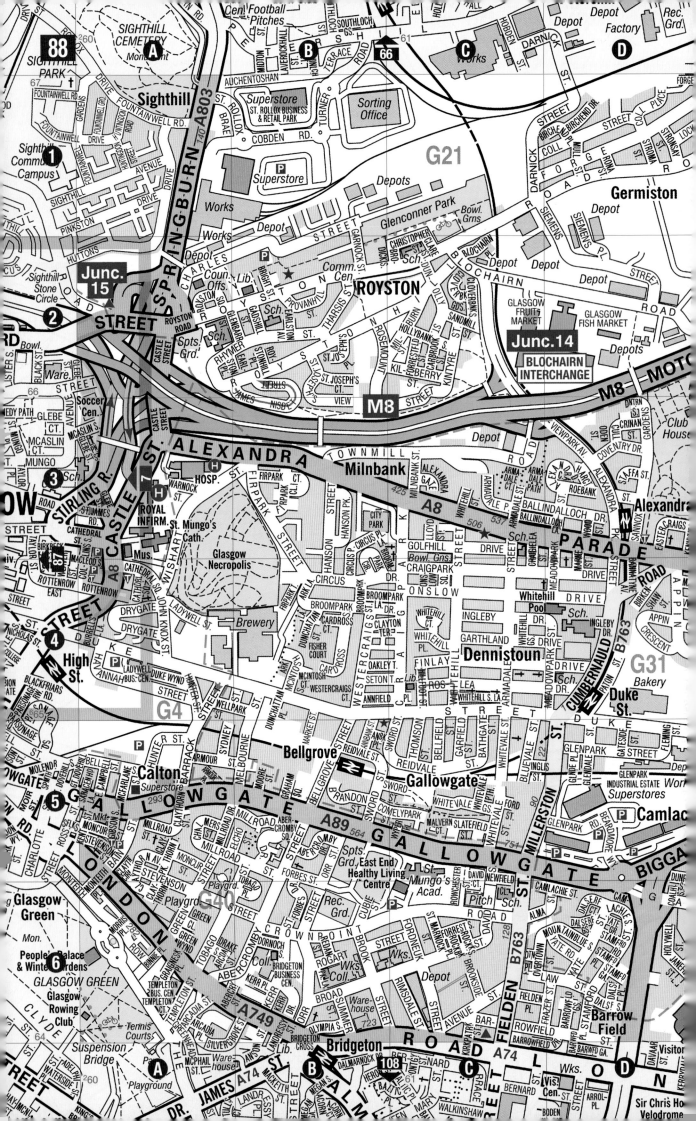

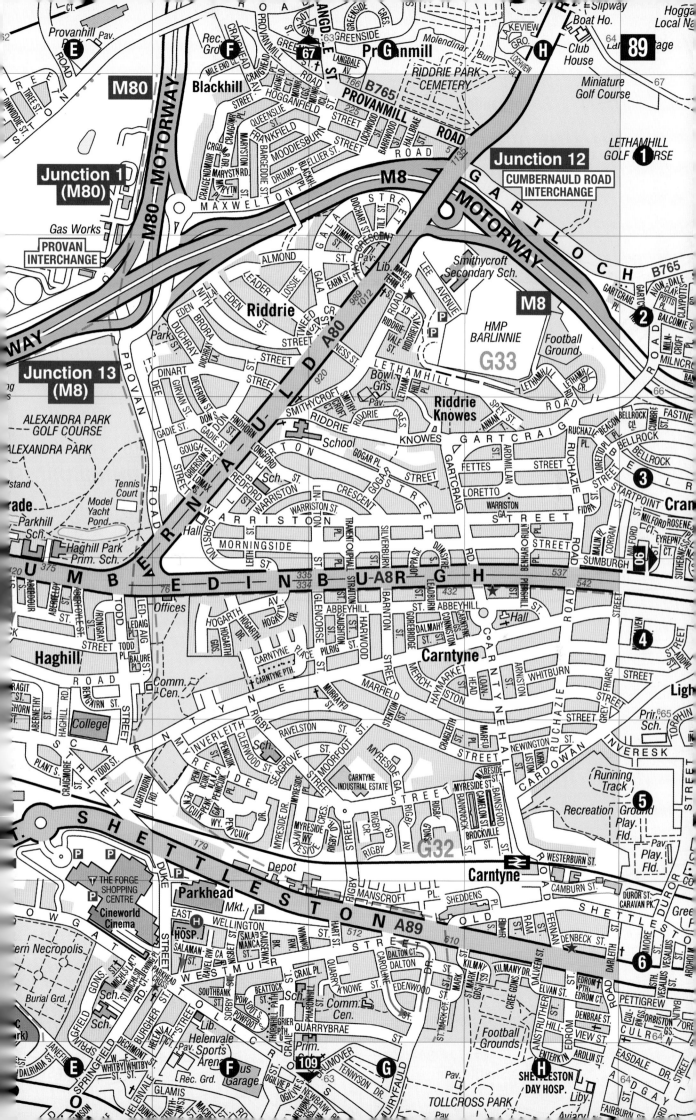

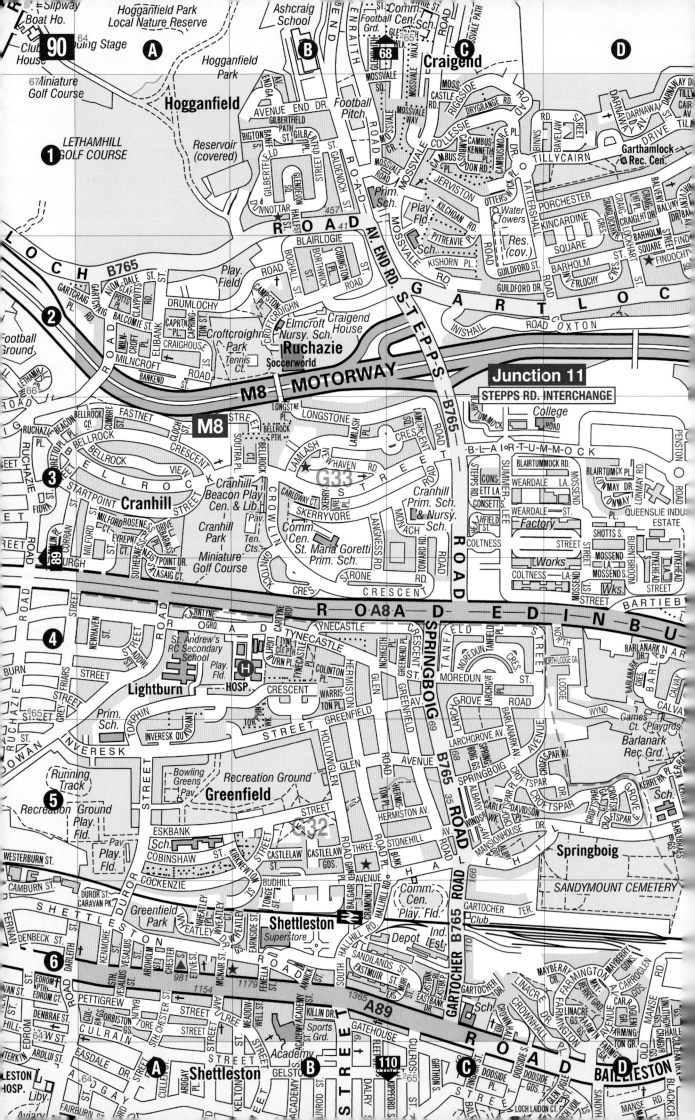

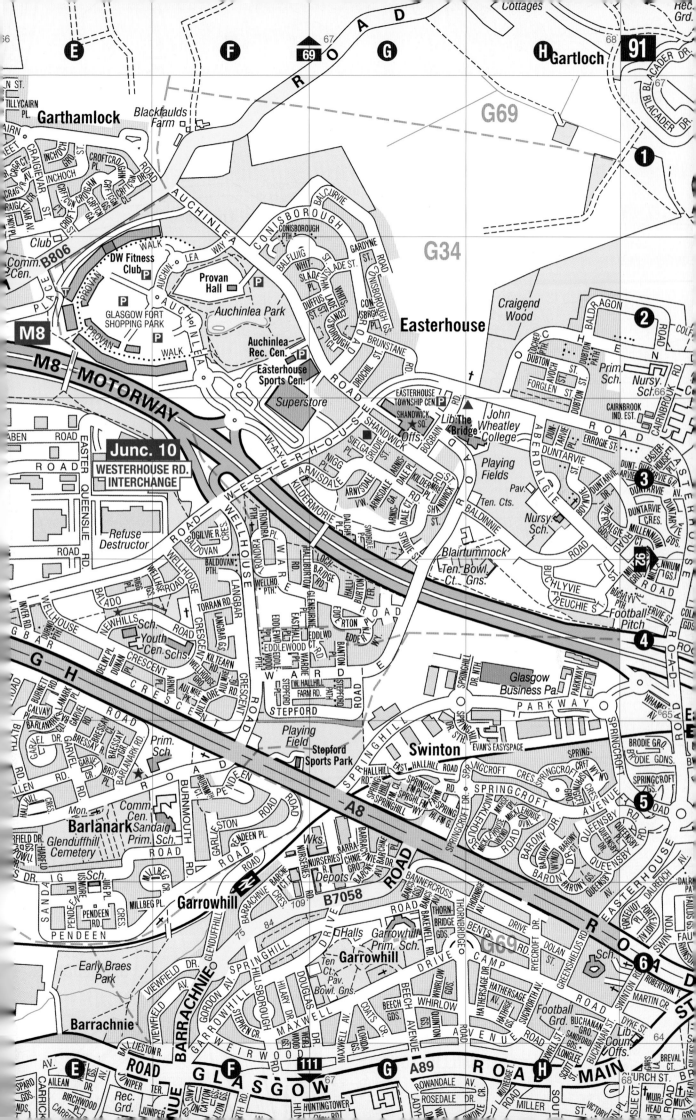

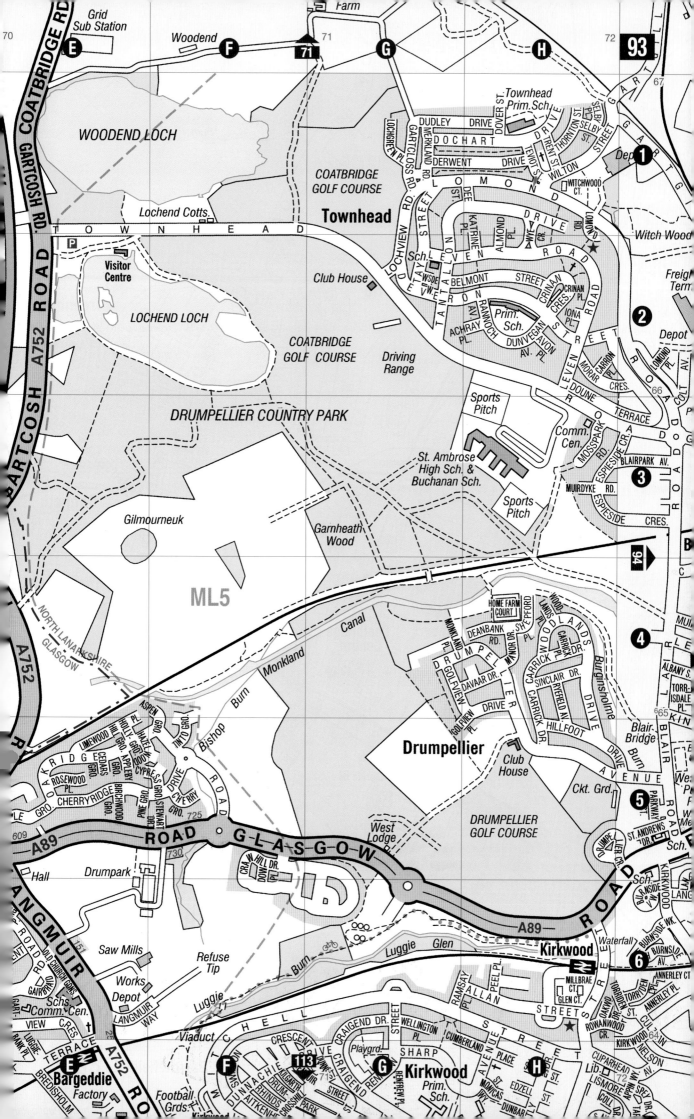

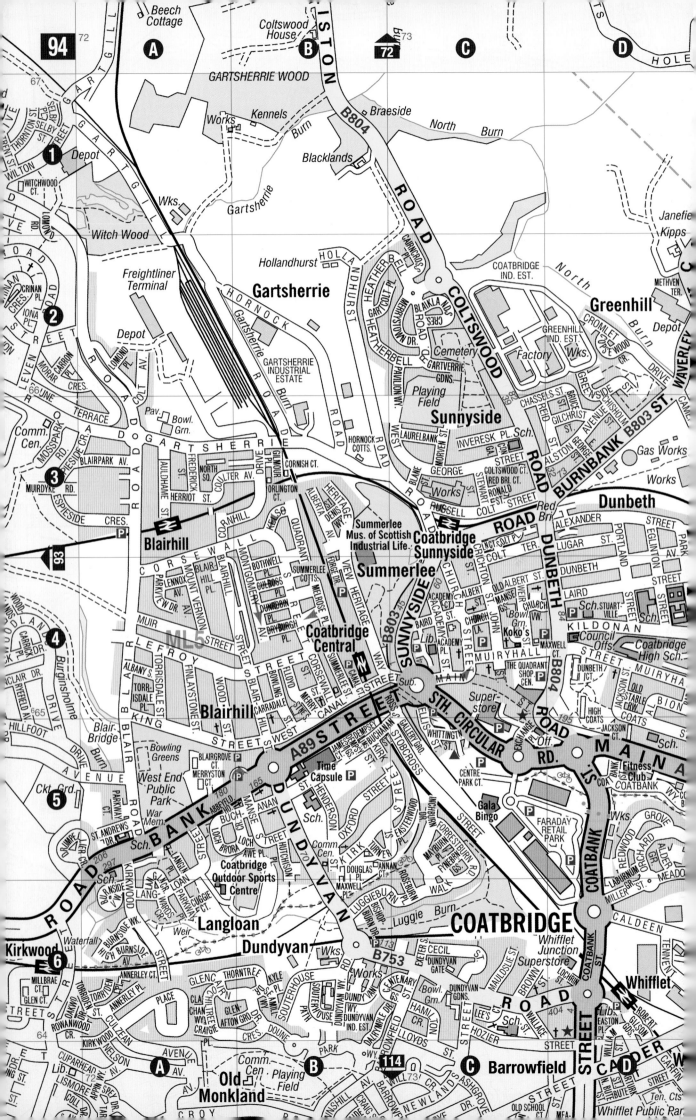

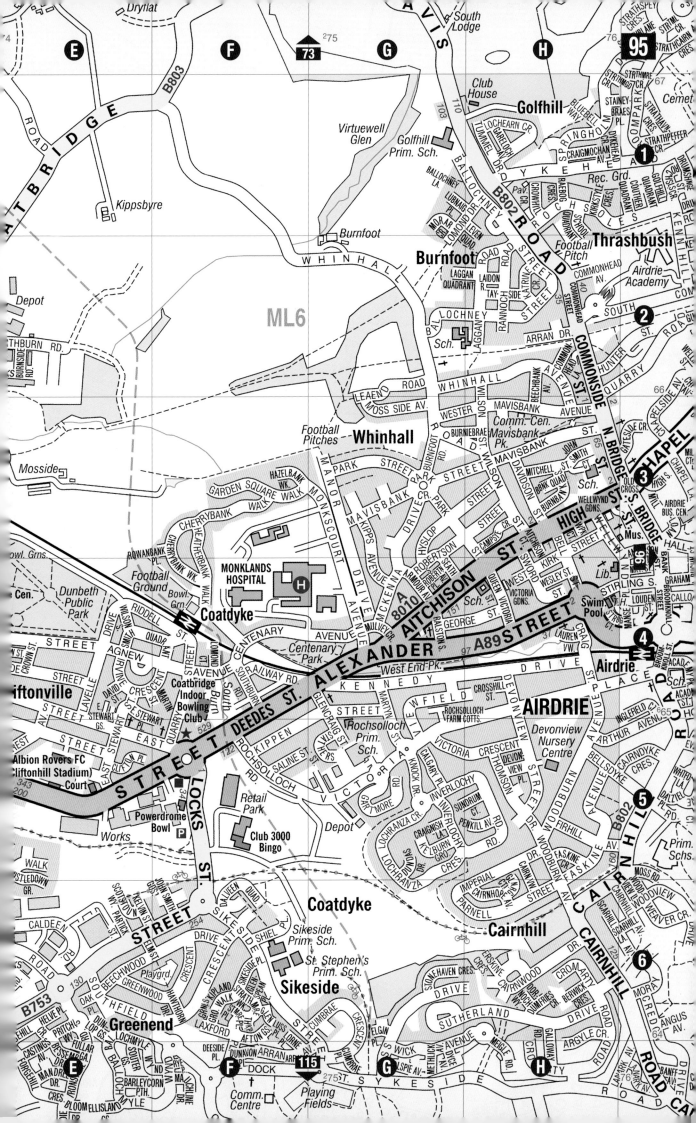

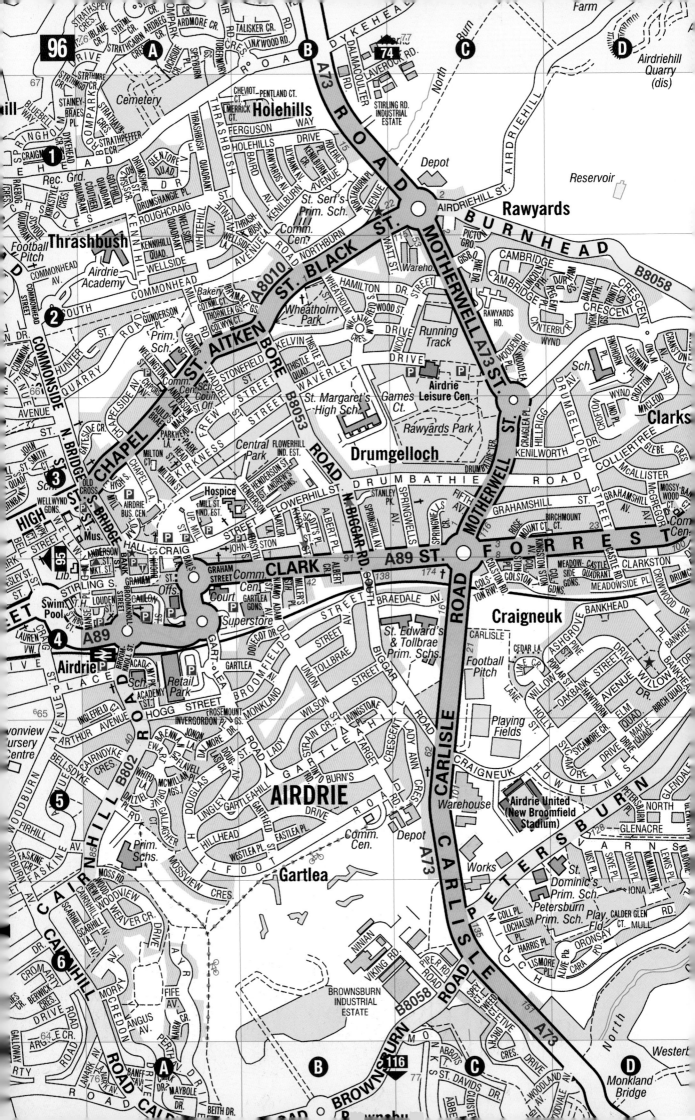

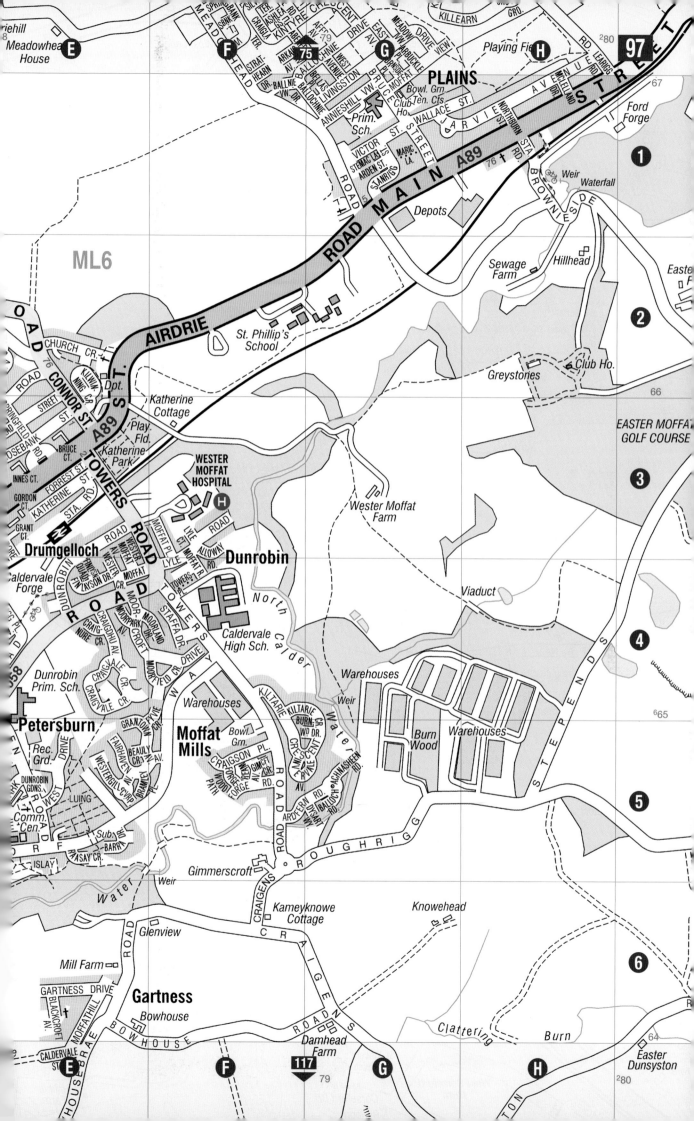

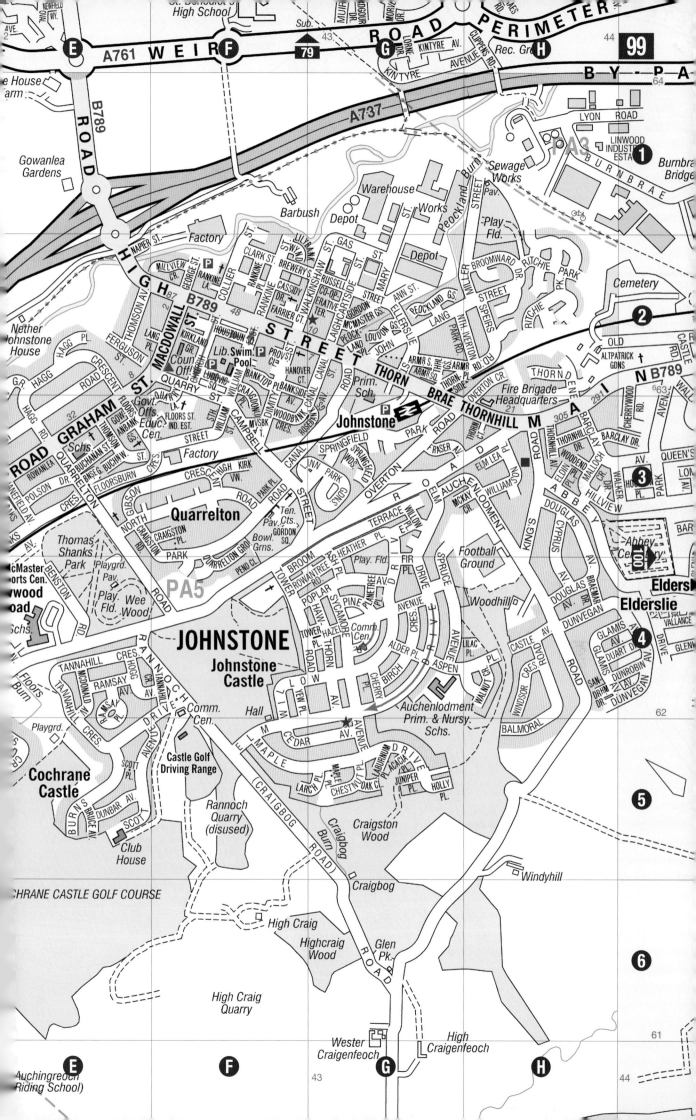

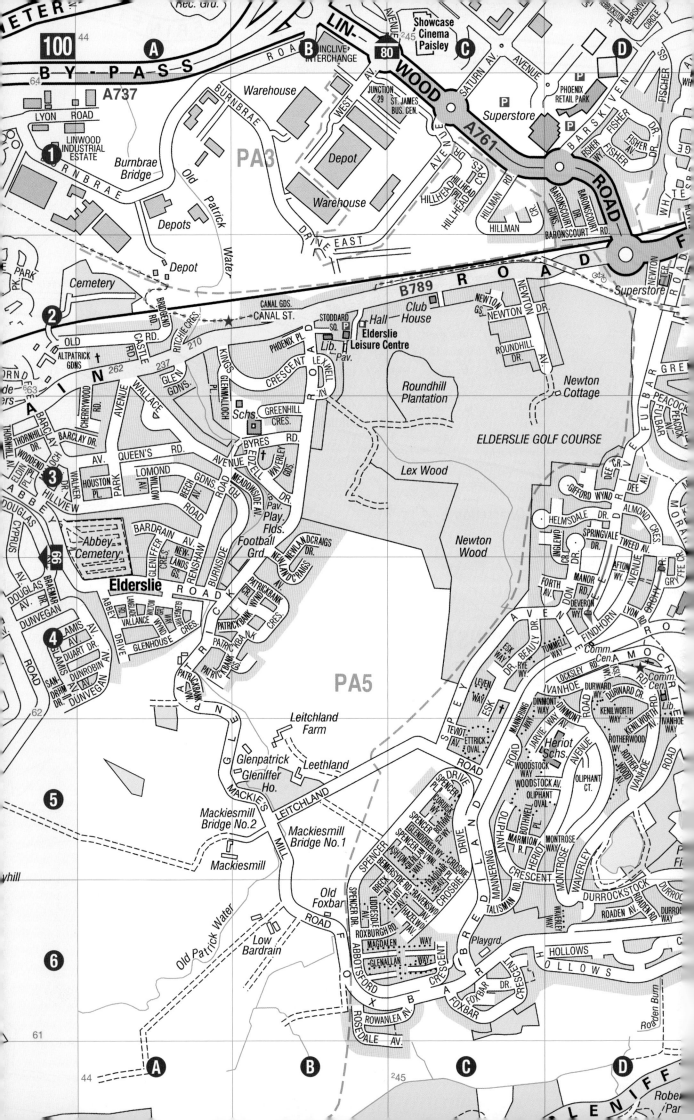

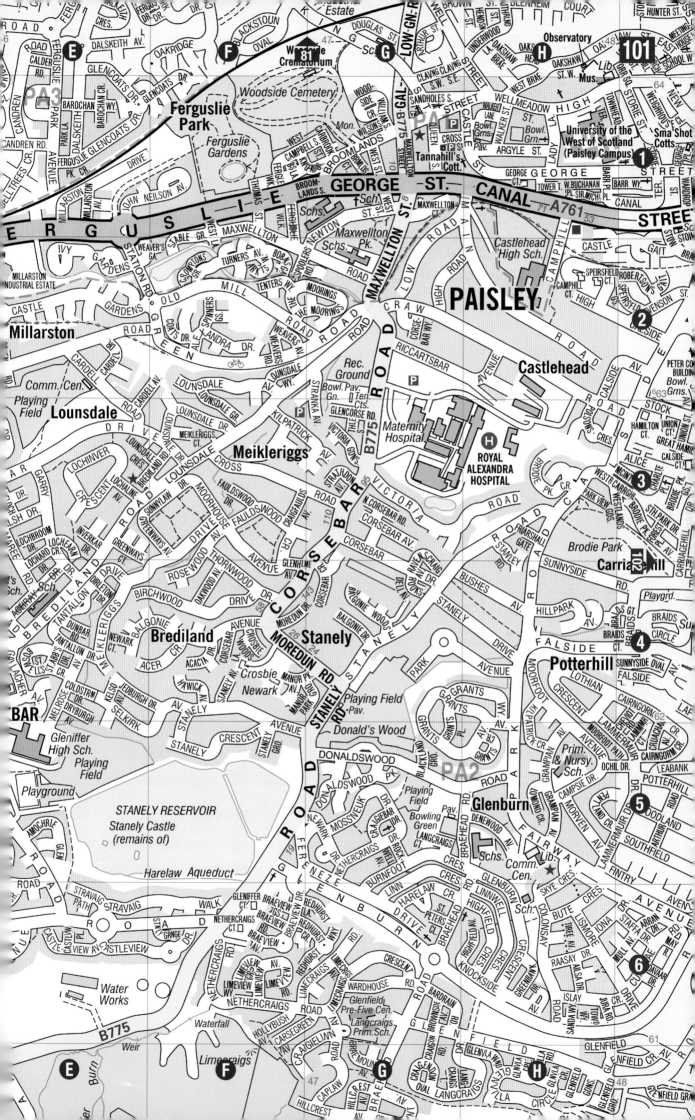

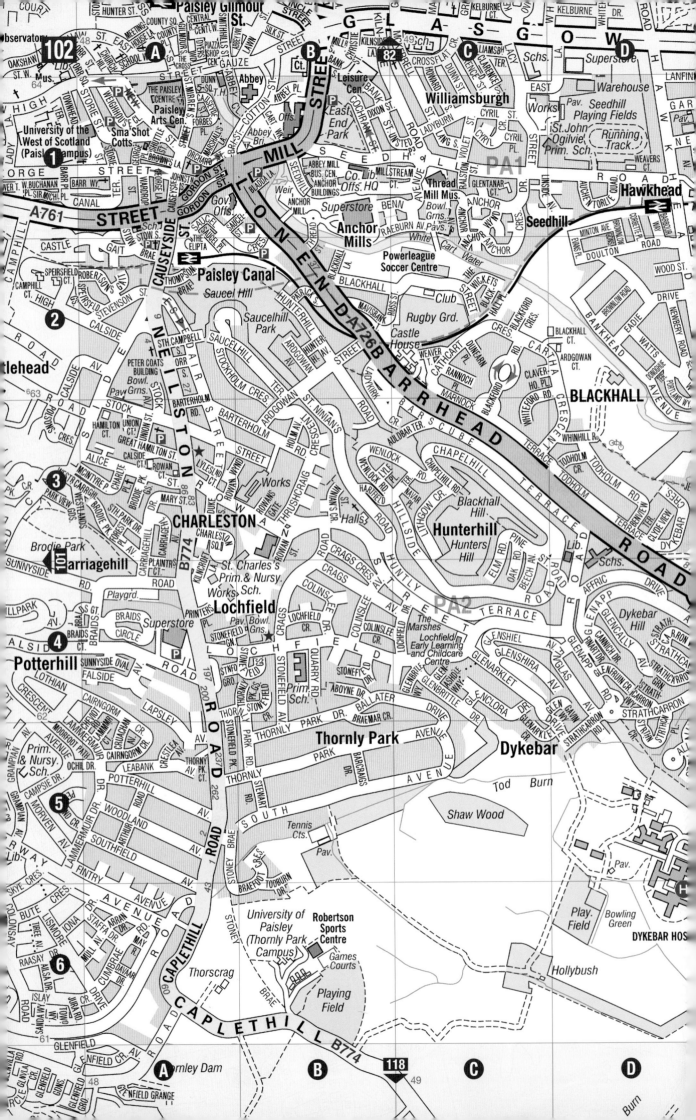

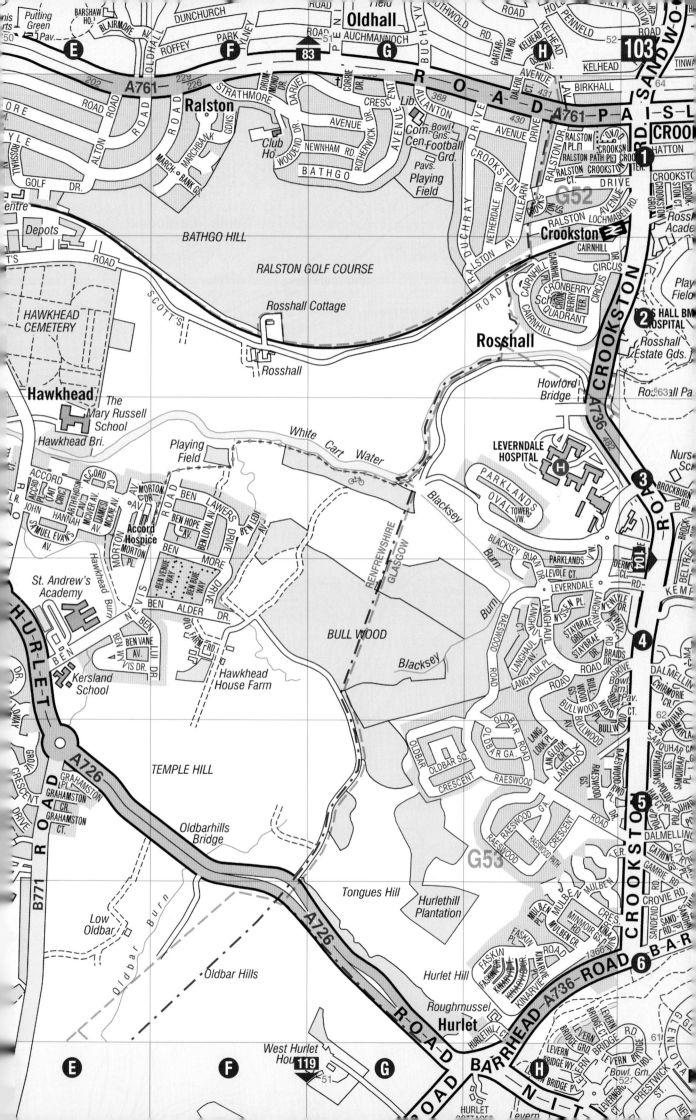

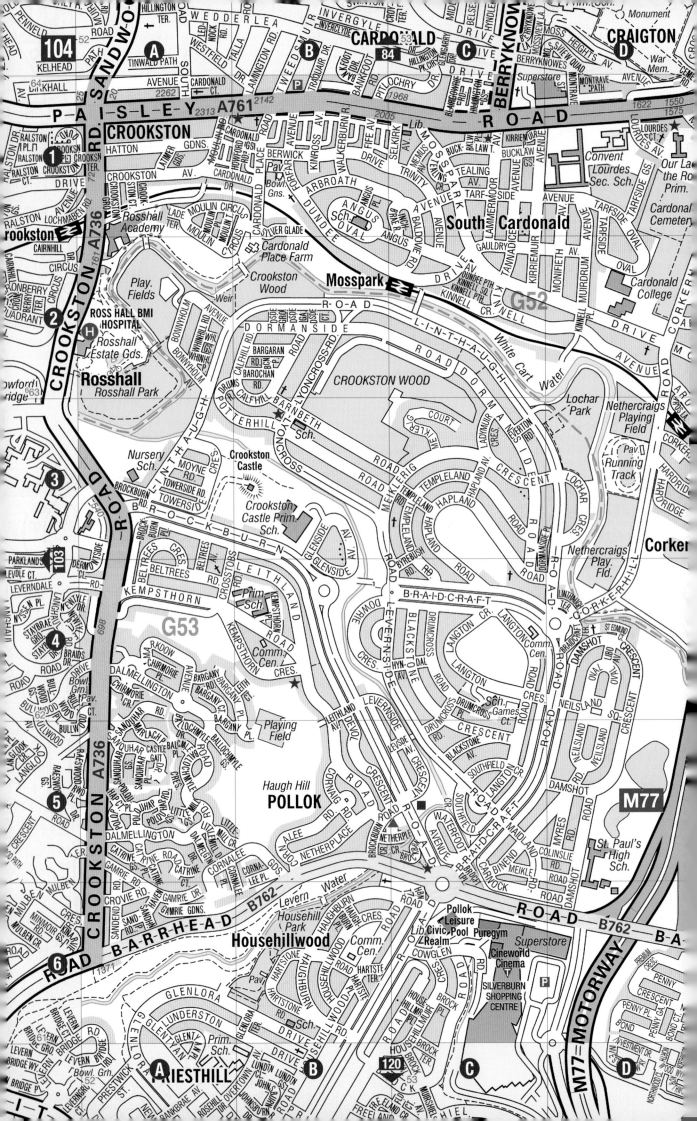

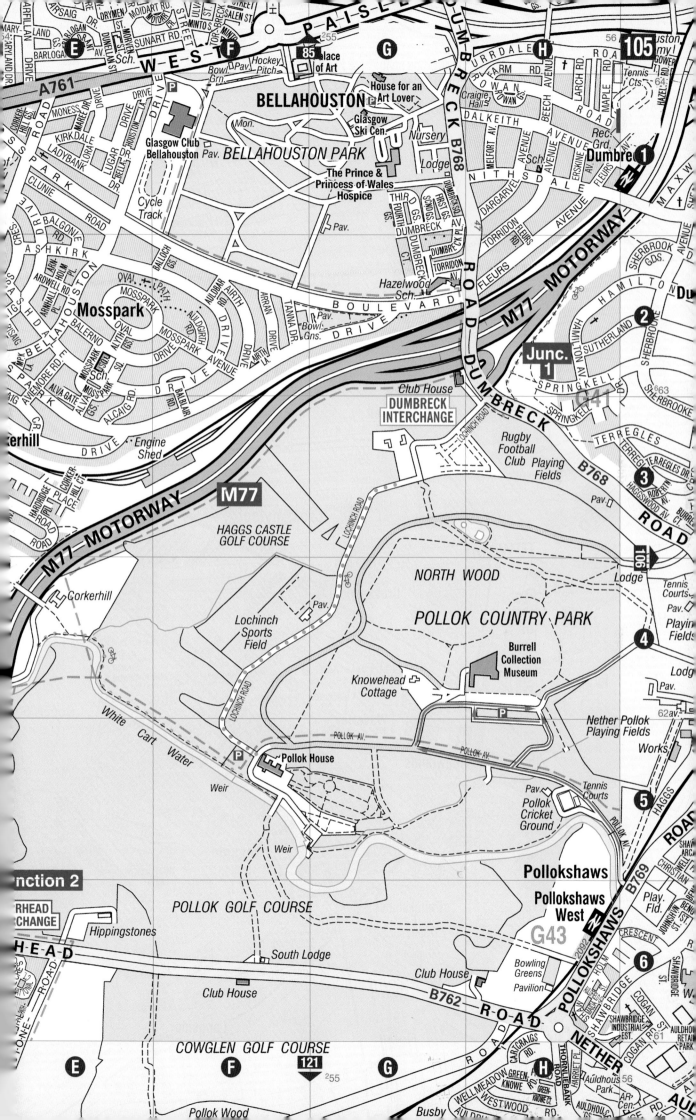

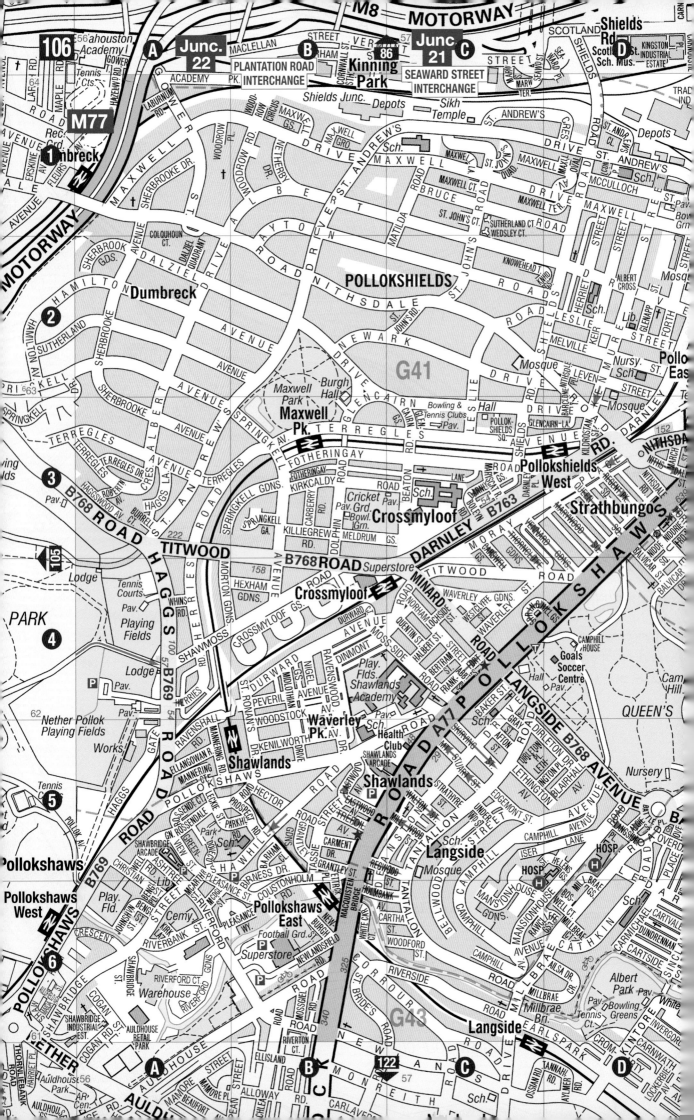

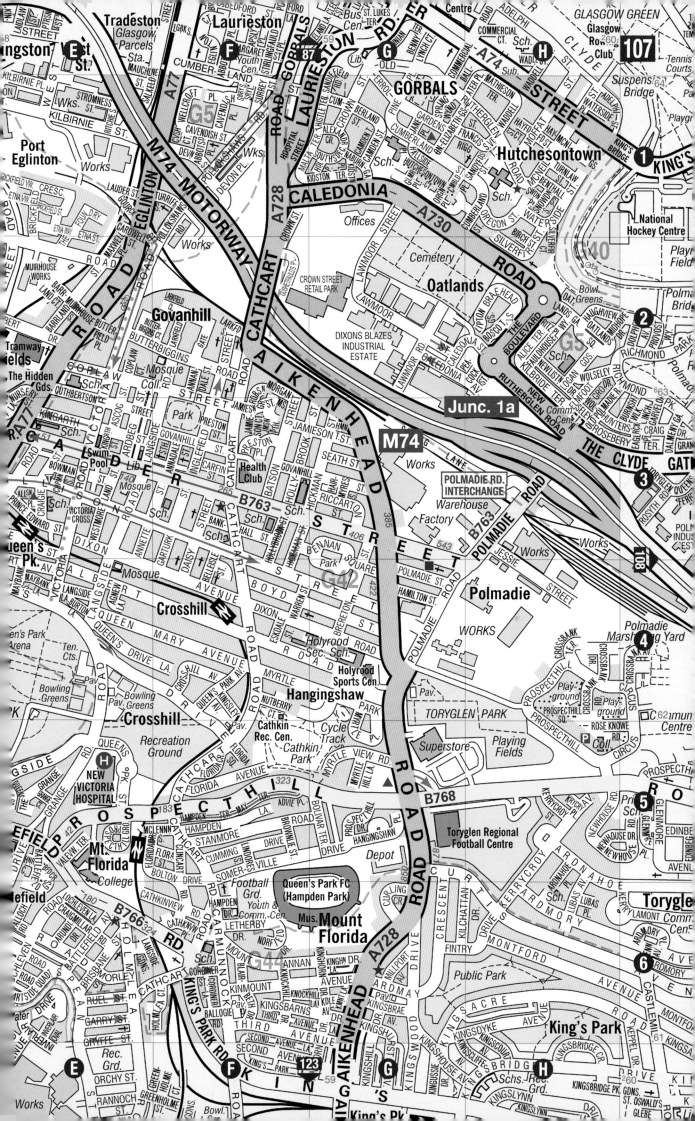

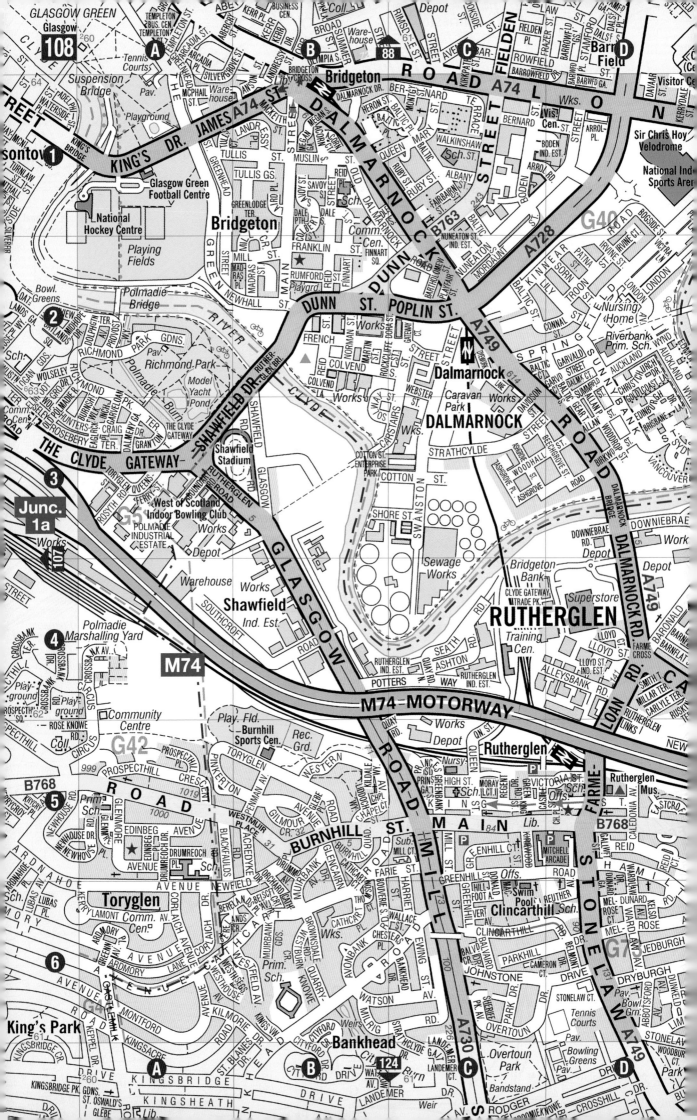

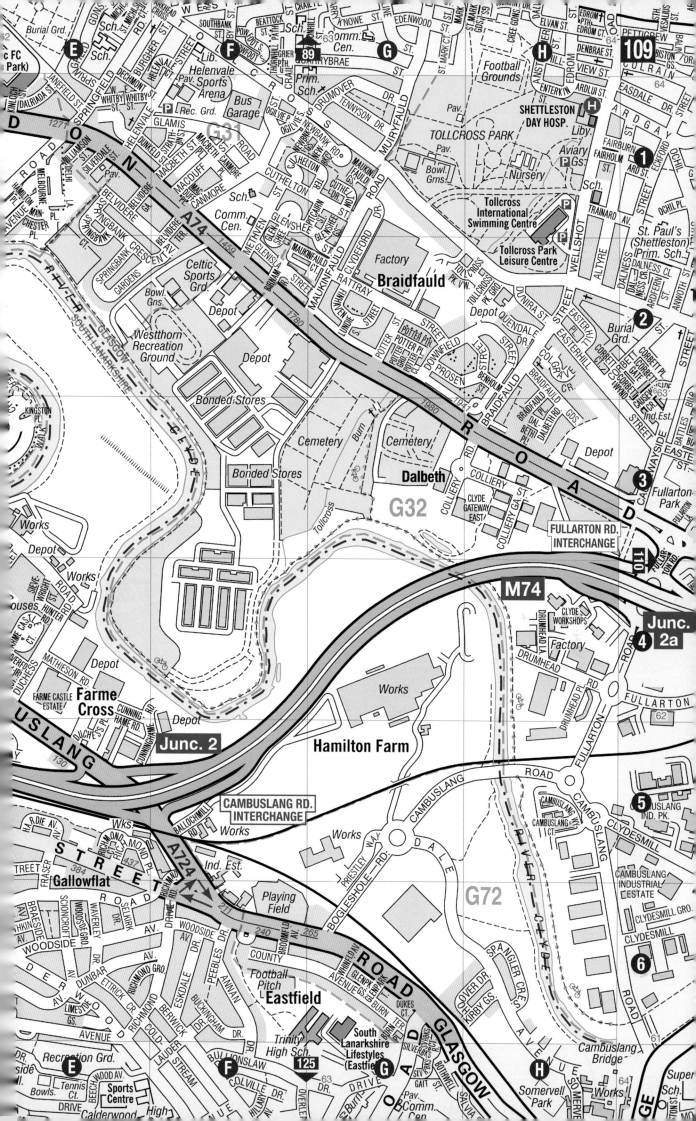

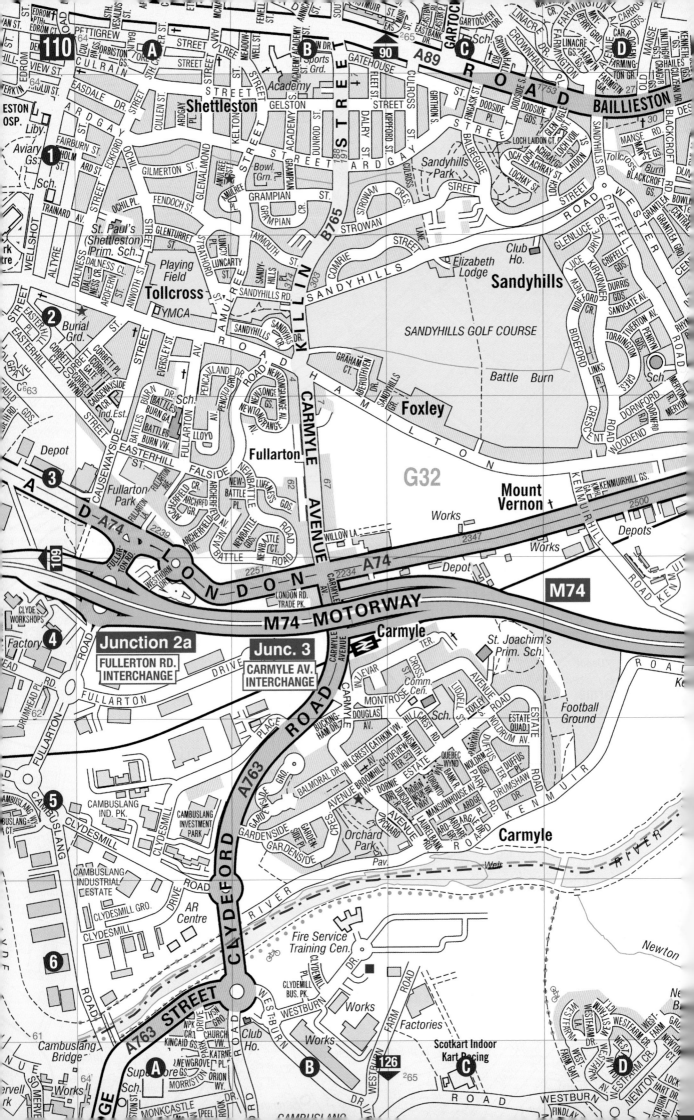

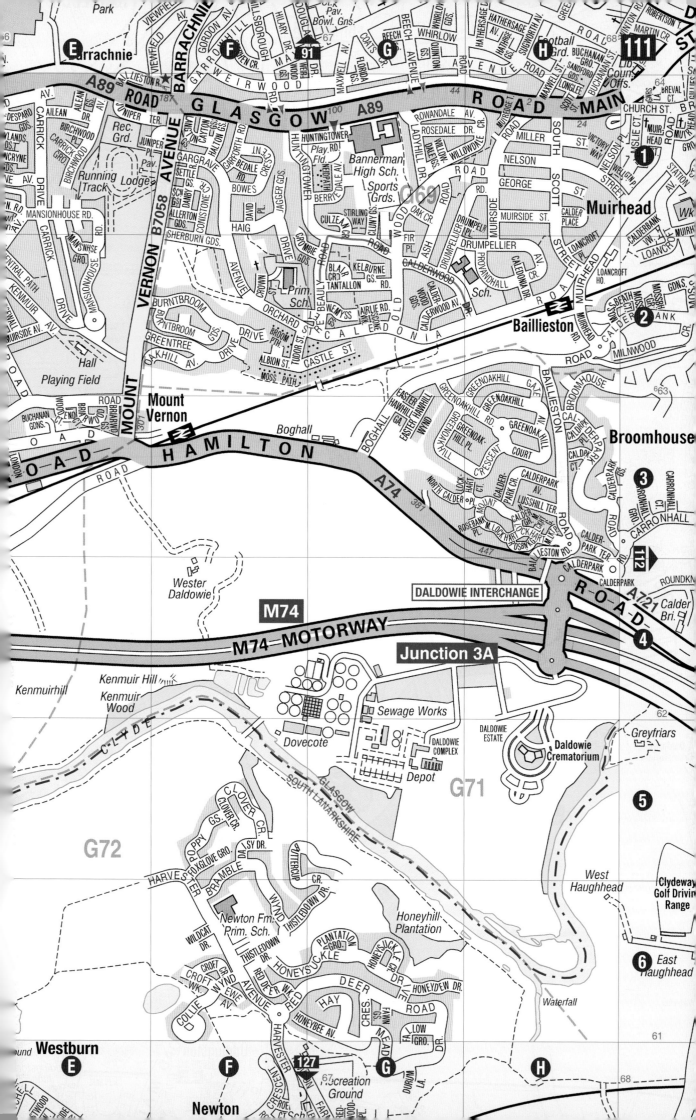

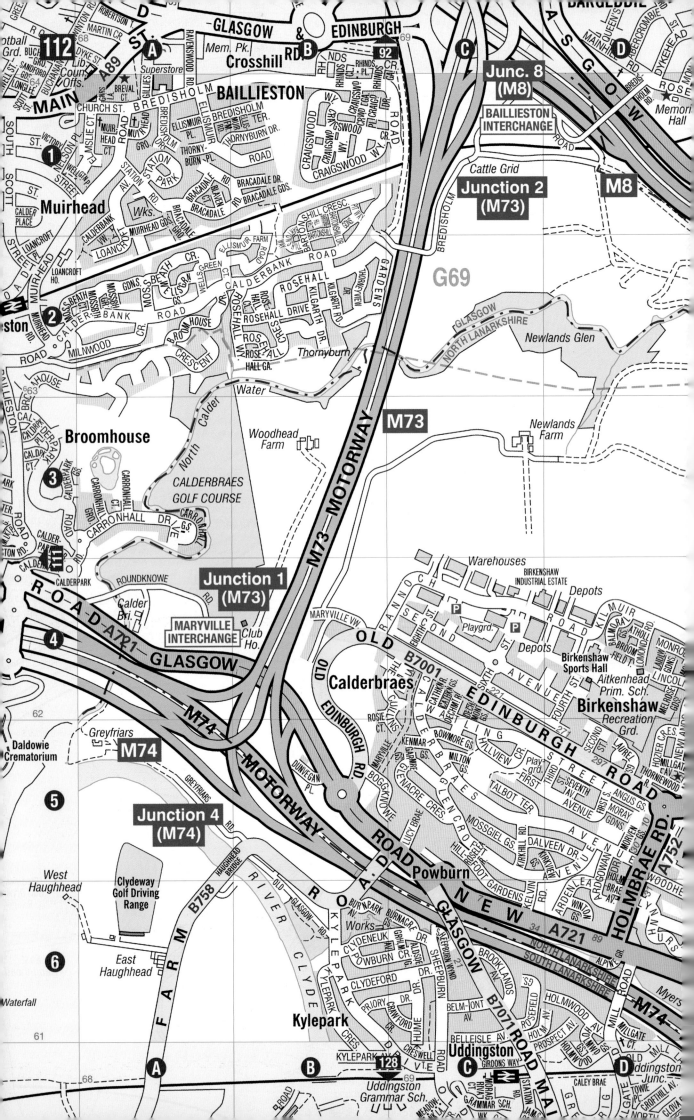

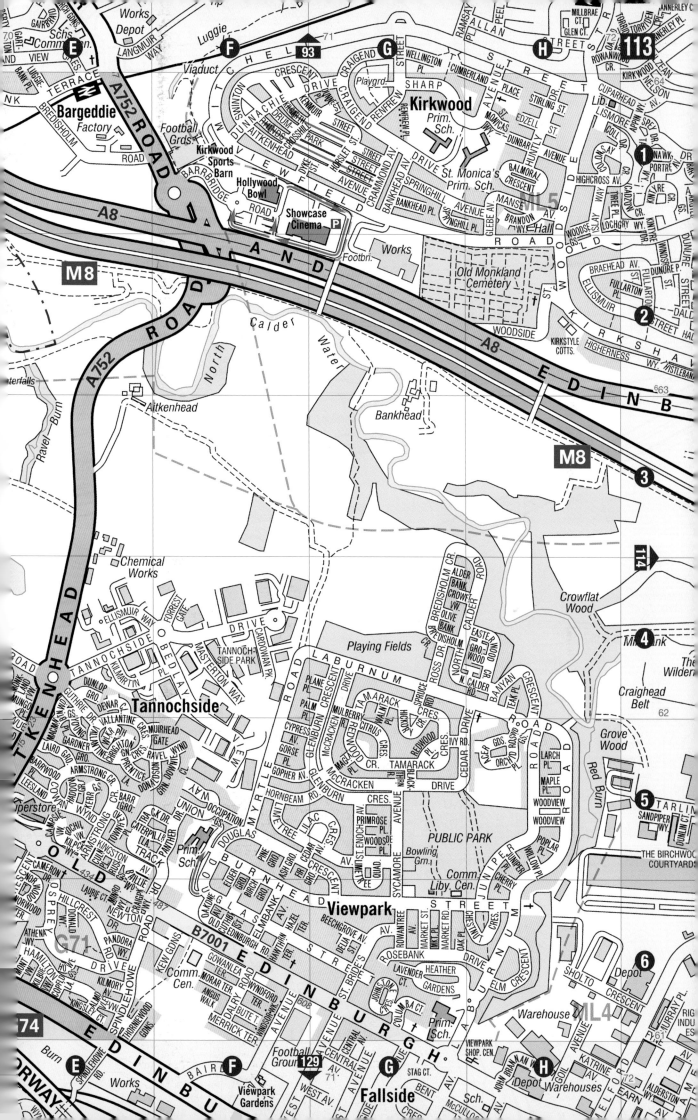

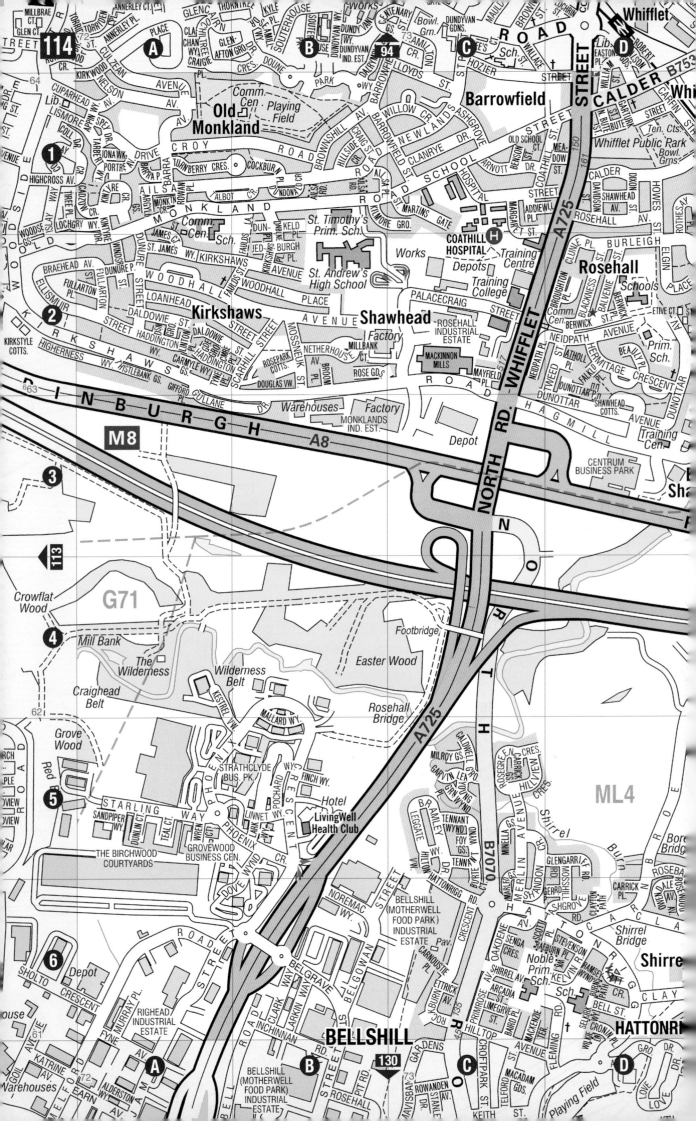

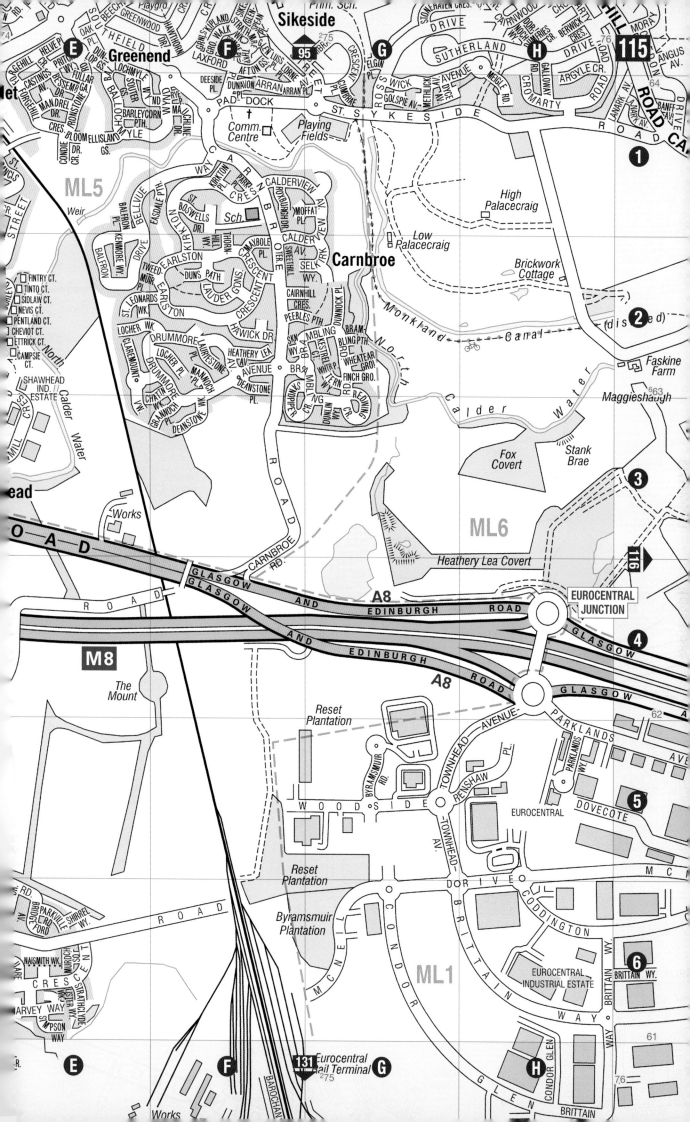

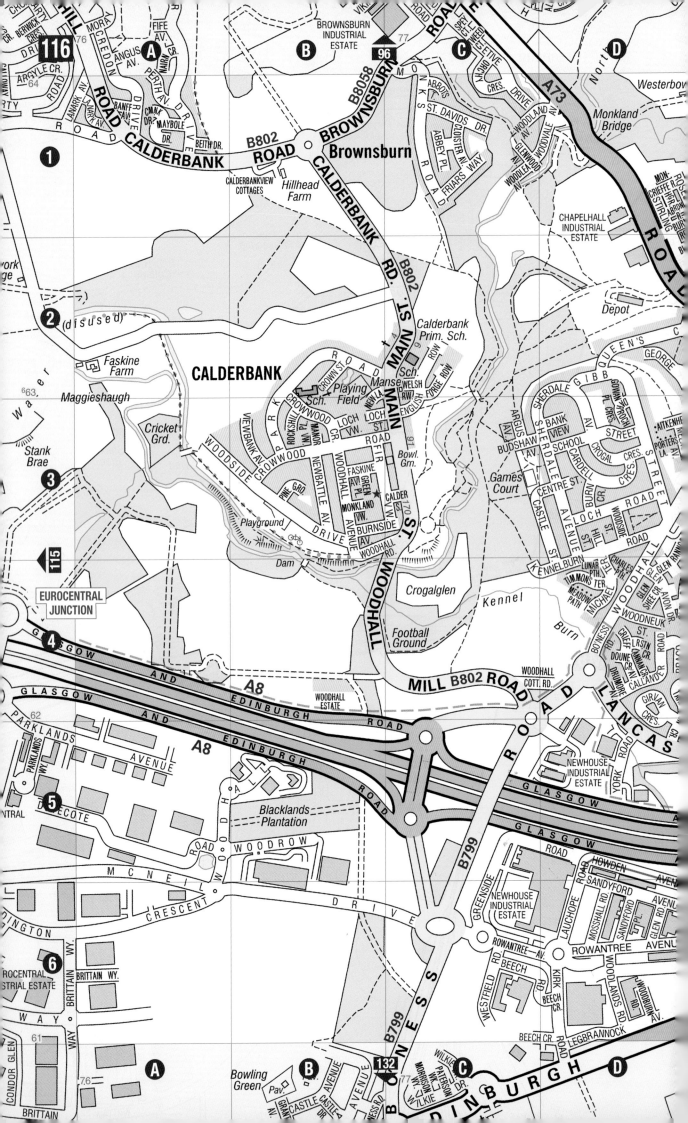

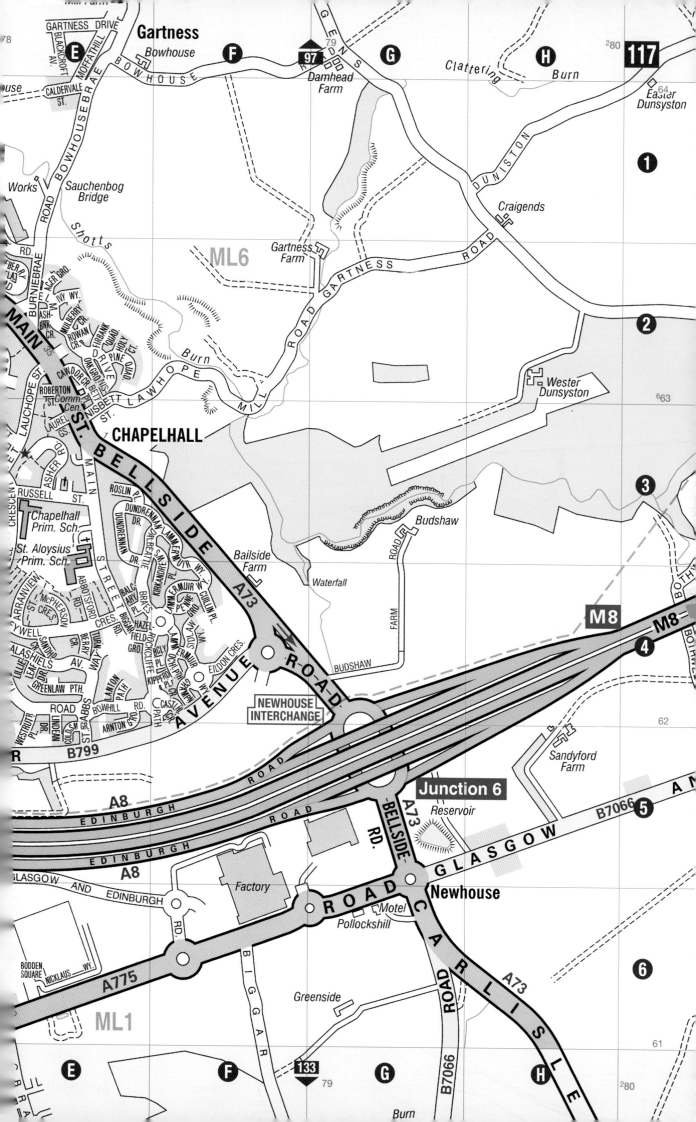

Mill Farm

Gartness

GARTNESS DRIVE
BLACKCROFT AV.
CALDERVALE ST.
BOWHOUSE BRAE
MOFFATHILL
BOWHOUSE

Bowhouse

E **F** **97** **G** **H** **1**

Clattering Burn

²80

Easter Dunsyston ⁶⁴

Damhead Farm

Works

Sauchenbog Bridge

Shotts

DUNISTON ROAD

Craigends

ML6

Gartness Farm

GARTNESS ROAD

2 ⁶⁶³

Wester Dunsyston

BURNIEBRAE
LAUCHOPE ST.
ROBERTON ST.
Comm. Cen.
CAWDOR CR.
NISBETT ST.
LAUREL GS.
ASHER RD.
RUSSELL ST.
ACER GRO.
IVY WY.
ASH-BNK. CR.
MULBERRY CR.
ROWAN CR.
FIRBANK DRIVE
OAKGRO.
PINE QUAD
HOLLY TGT.
NISBETT

MAIN ST.

Burn

ROAD GARTNESS

LAWHOPE MILL

³⁶²

3

Budshaw

Waterfall

CHAPELHALL

ST. BELLSIDE

Chapelhall Prim. Sch.
St. Aloysius' Prim. Sch.

ROSLIN PL.
DUNDRENNAN DR.
DUNDRENNAN DR.
LAMMERMUIR
DALBEATTIE
ABBOTSFORD RD.
McPHERSON RD.
CRES.
ARRANVIEW
LILLIE
LEAF
GREENLAW PTH.
SANDHO
BERRY WAY
AV.
GALASHIELS
WESTRUTH
LINDEN
DR.
BALG. ARY PL.
BIGGAR RD.
HAZEL GRO.
ROCKCLIFFE PL.
TURN-WAY
LANTON PATH
BOWHILL RD.
ARNTON GRO.
LAMMERMUIR W.
BRAES
LAMMERMUIR
KIPPERDI PL.
CASTL. PATH
PENE GRO.
SOLAS YM.
OCHIL PL.
WY.
CULLIN PL.
EILDON CRES.

AVENUE
A73
ROAD

Bailside Farm

FARM

BUDSHAW

ROAD

M8 **M8** **M8**

4 ³⁶²

Sandyford Farm

B799

A8

EDINBURGH ROAD

EDINBURGH ROAD

A8

NEWHOUSE INTERCHANGE

BELLSIDE RD.

Junction 6

A73

Reservoir

B7066

GLASGOW

5

GLASGOW AND EDINBURGH

Factory

BIGGAR RD.

ROAD

CARLISLE ROAD

A73

Newhouse

Motel
Pollockshill

6

BODDEN SQUARE
NICKLAUS WY.
A775

ML1

Greenside

E **F** **133** ⁷⁹ **G** **B7066 H** ²⁸⁰

Burn

³⁶¹

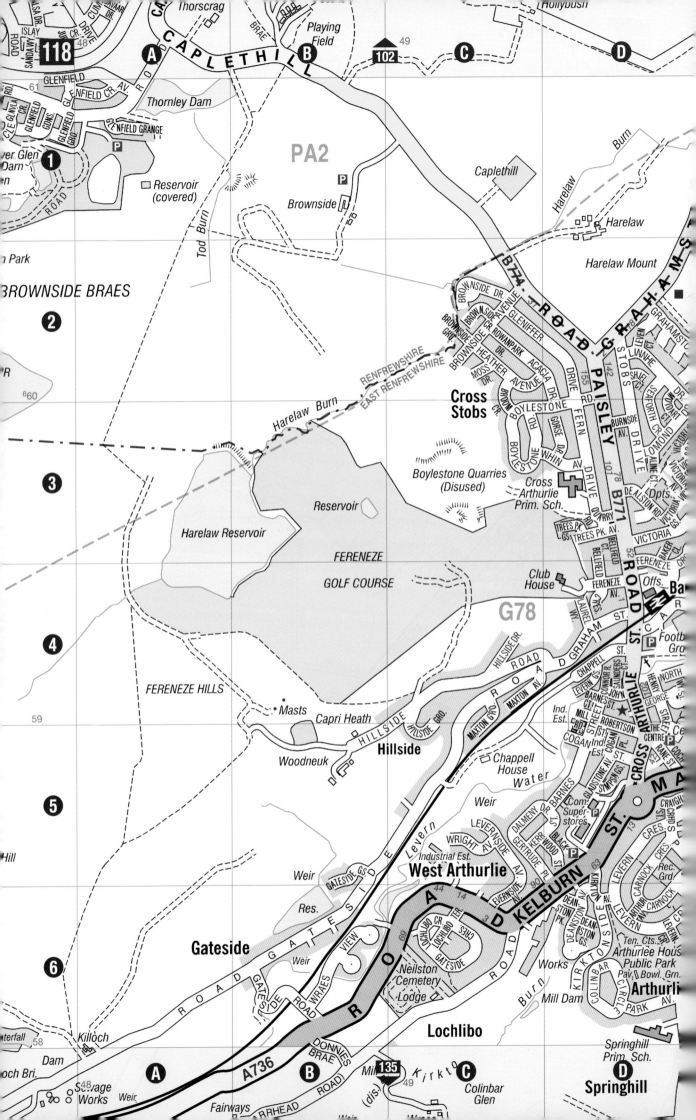

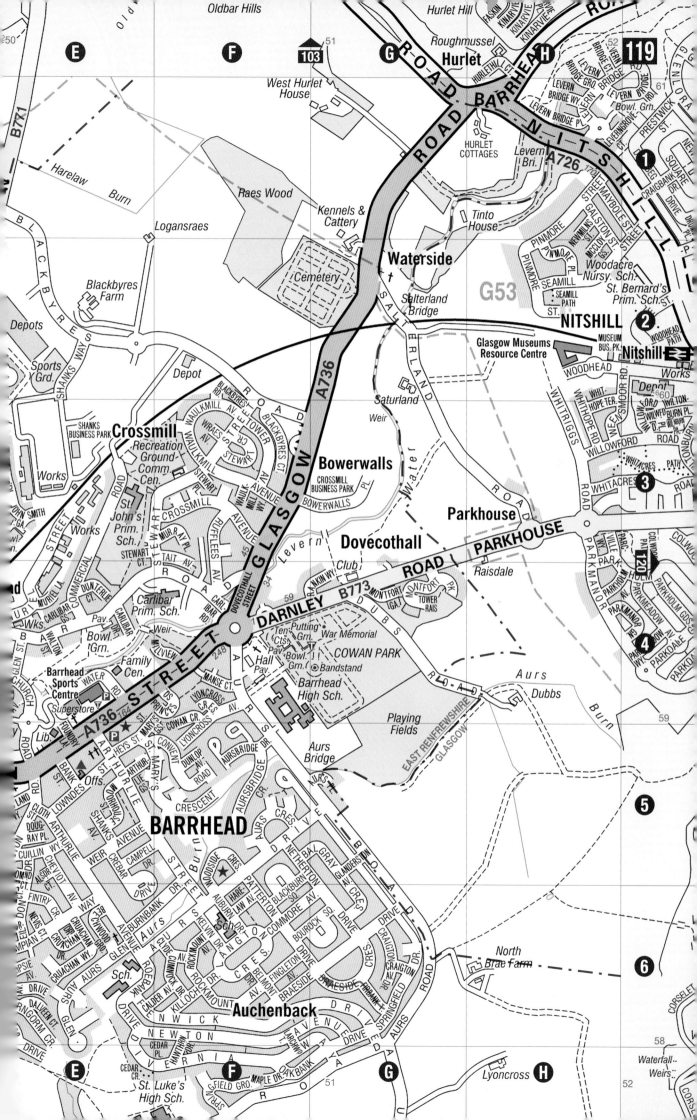

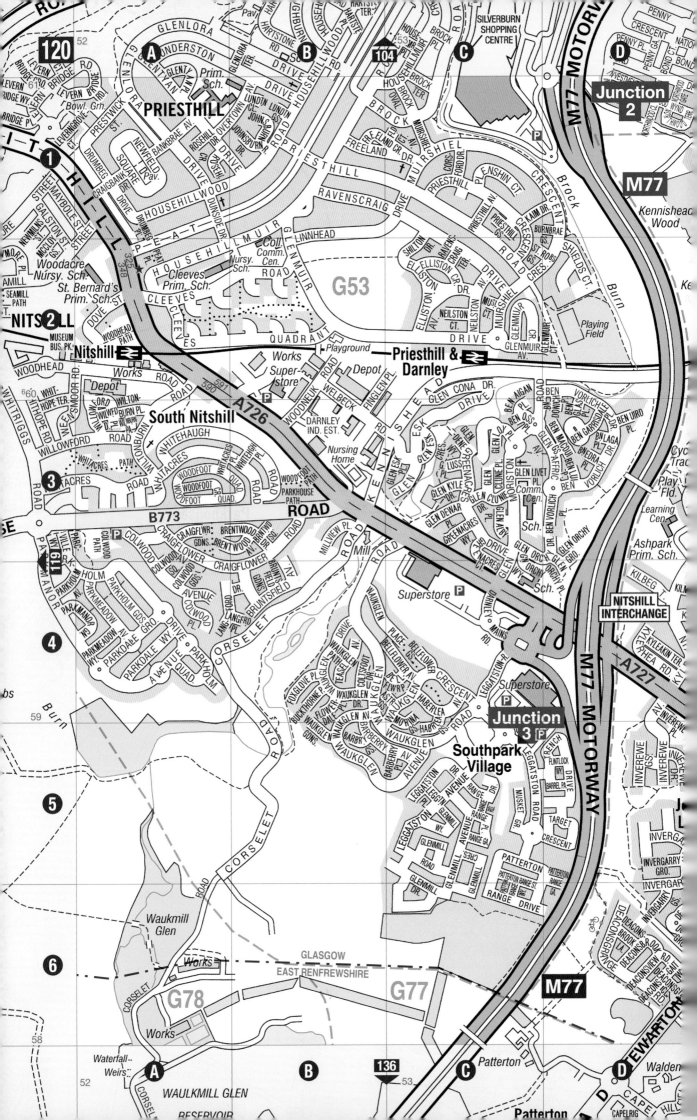

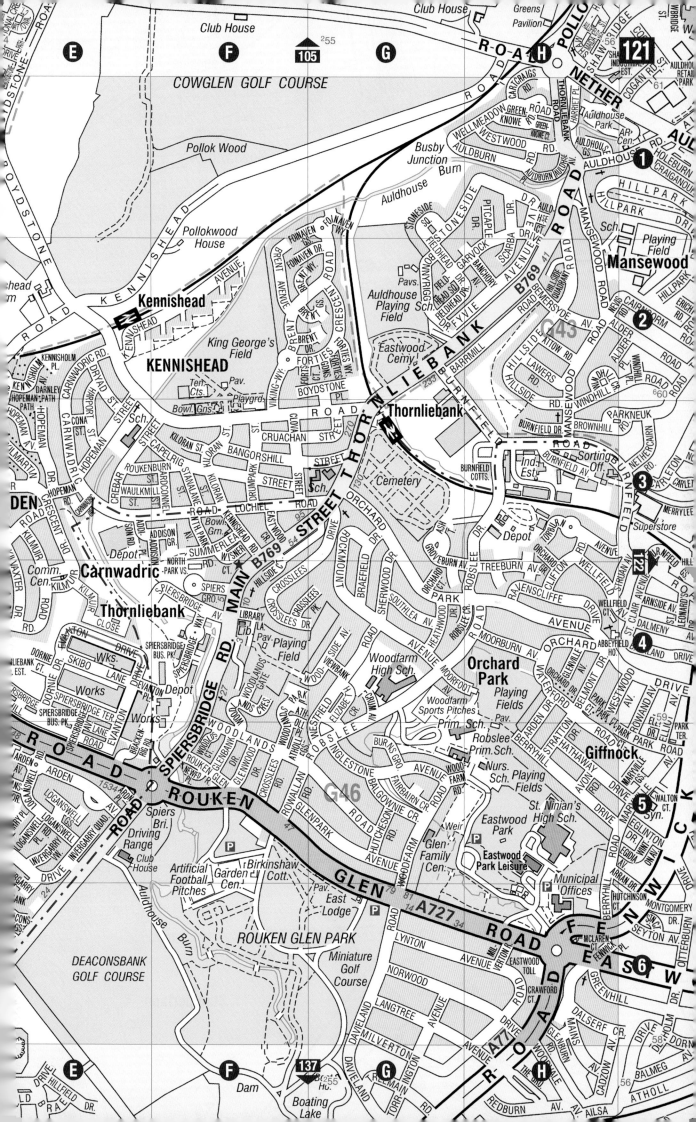

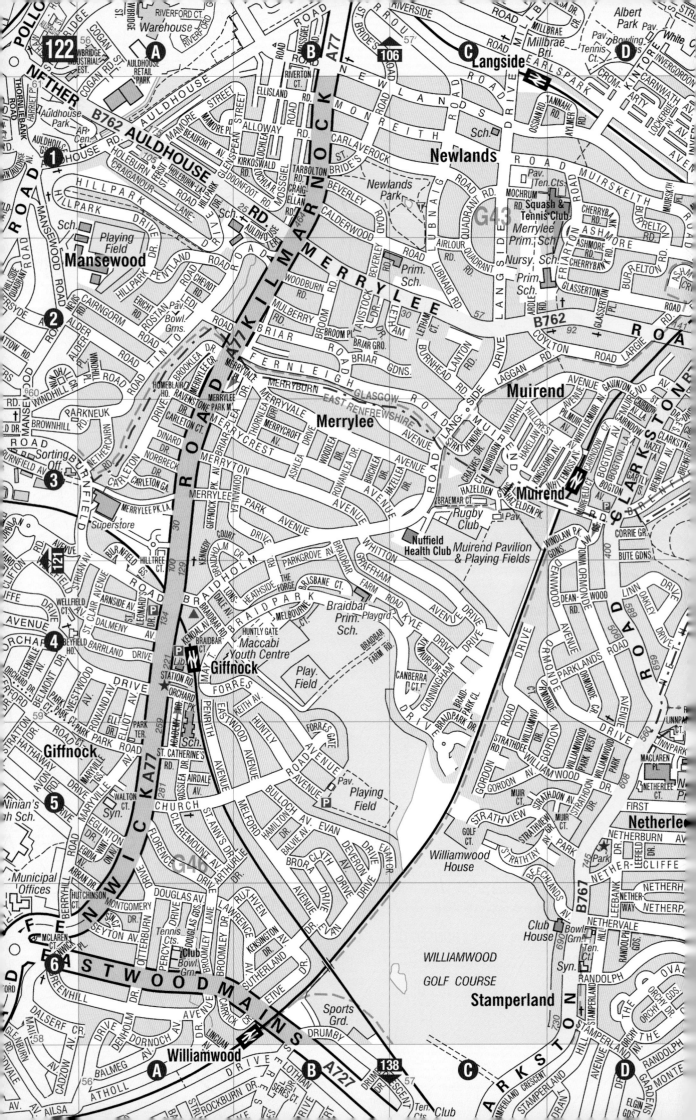

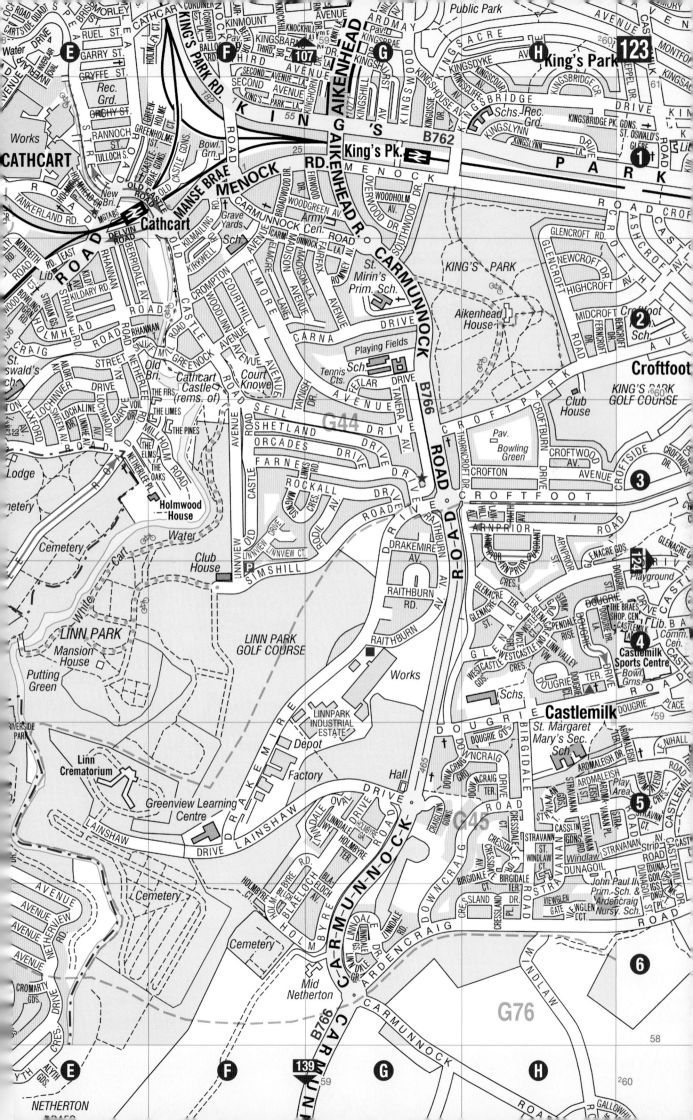

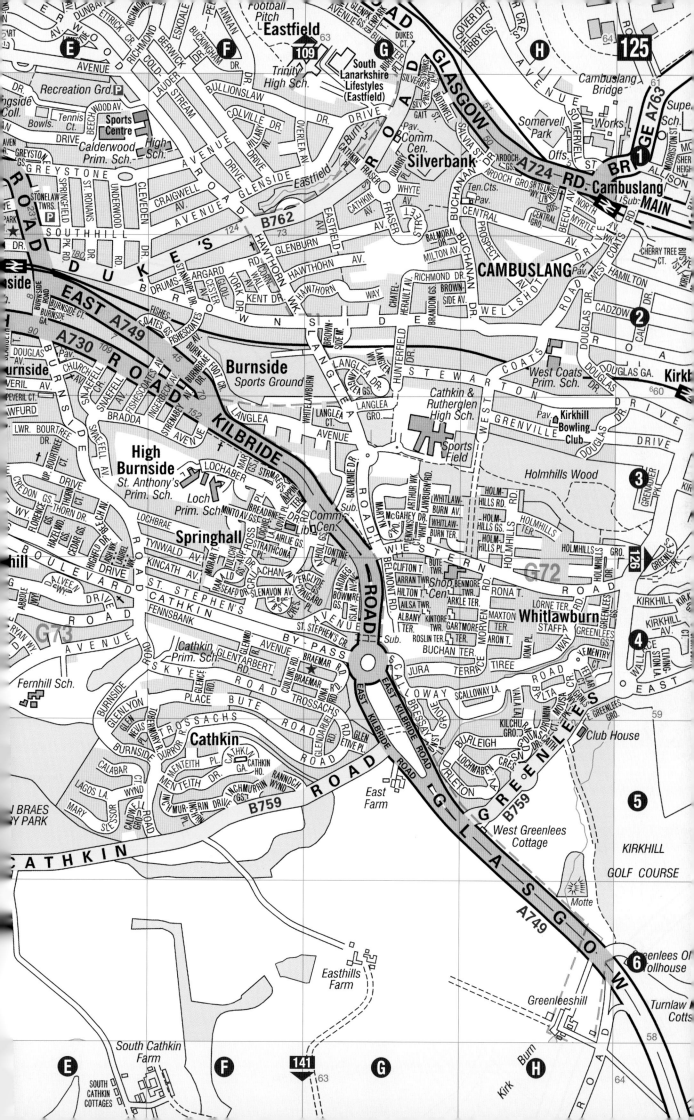

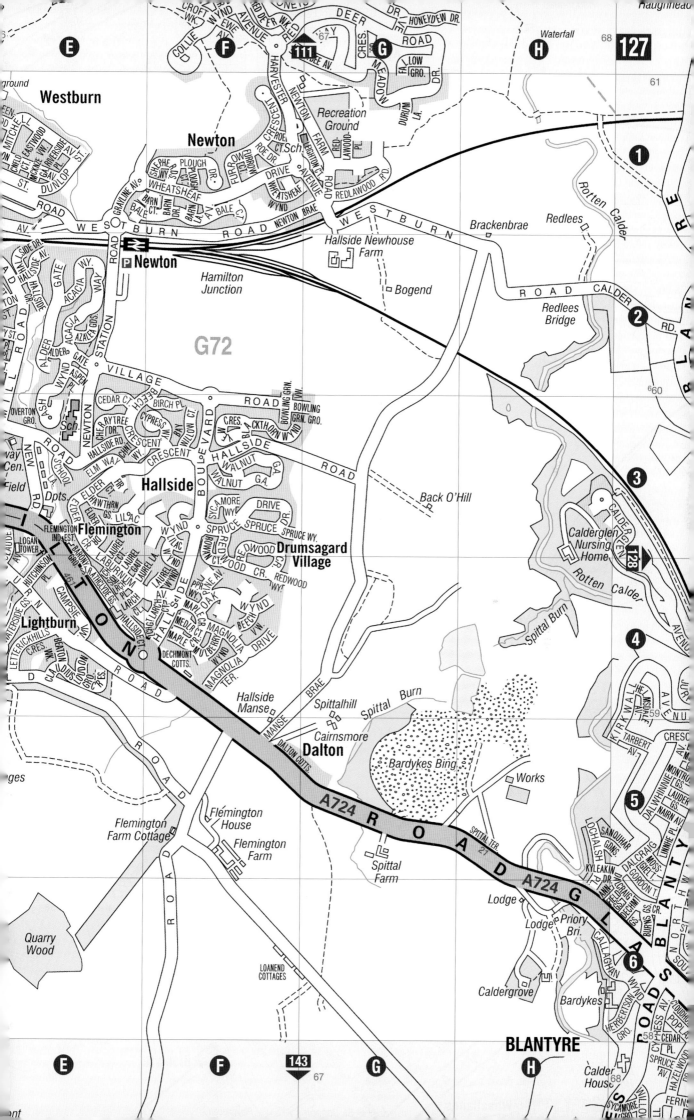

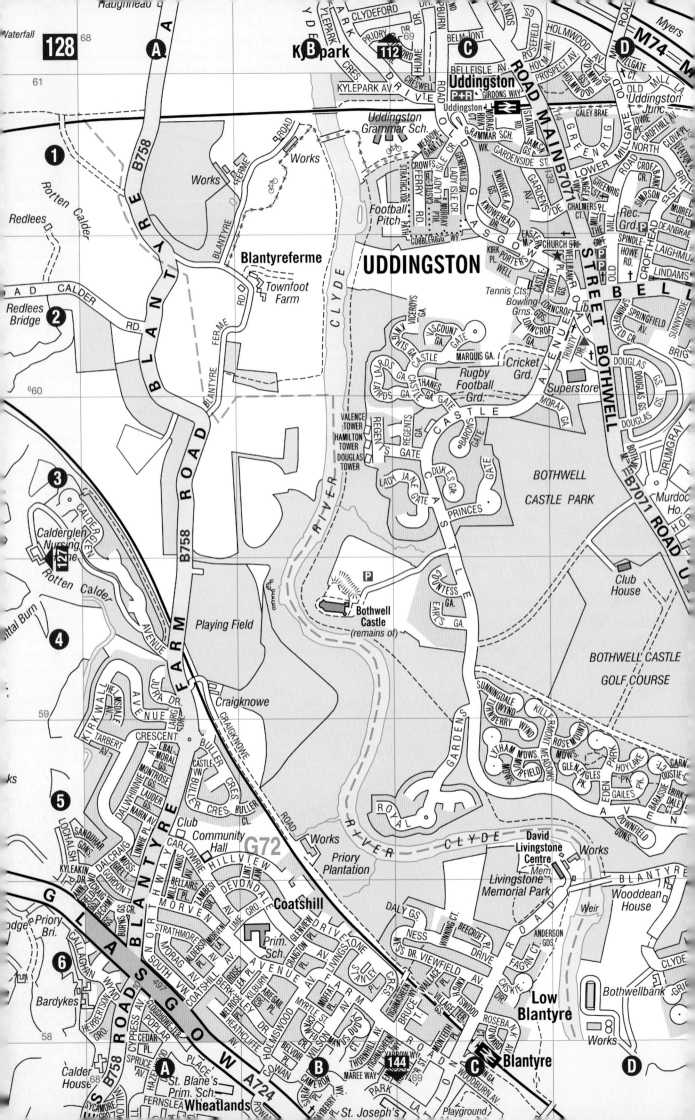

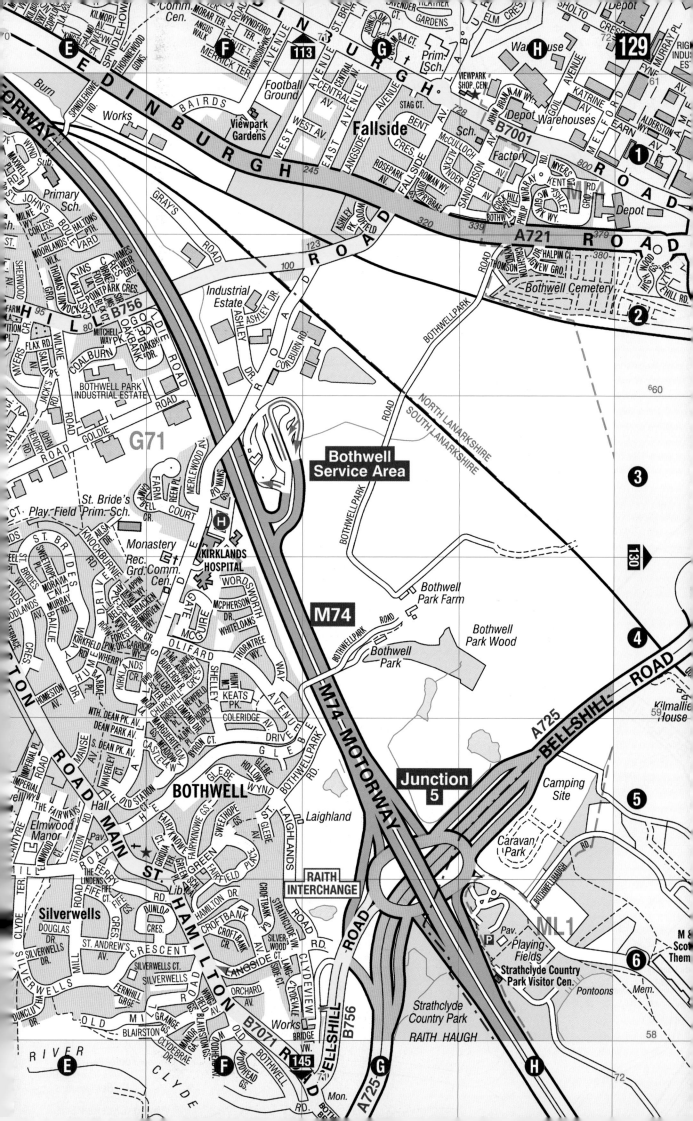

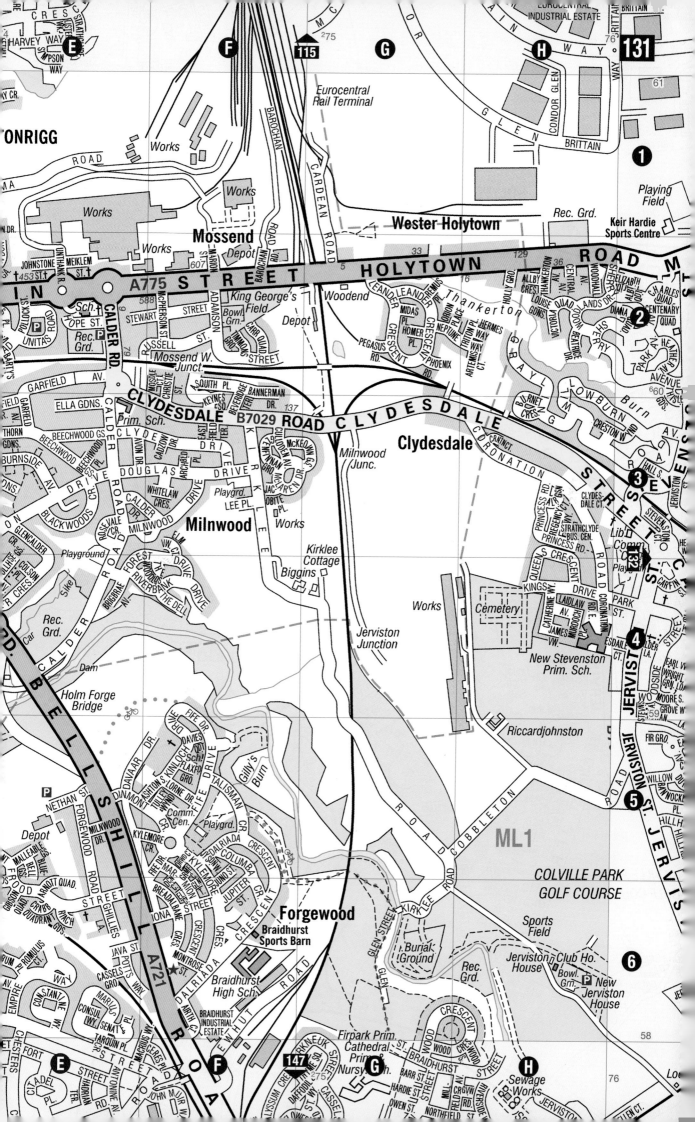

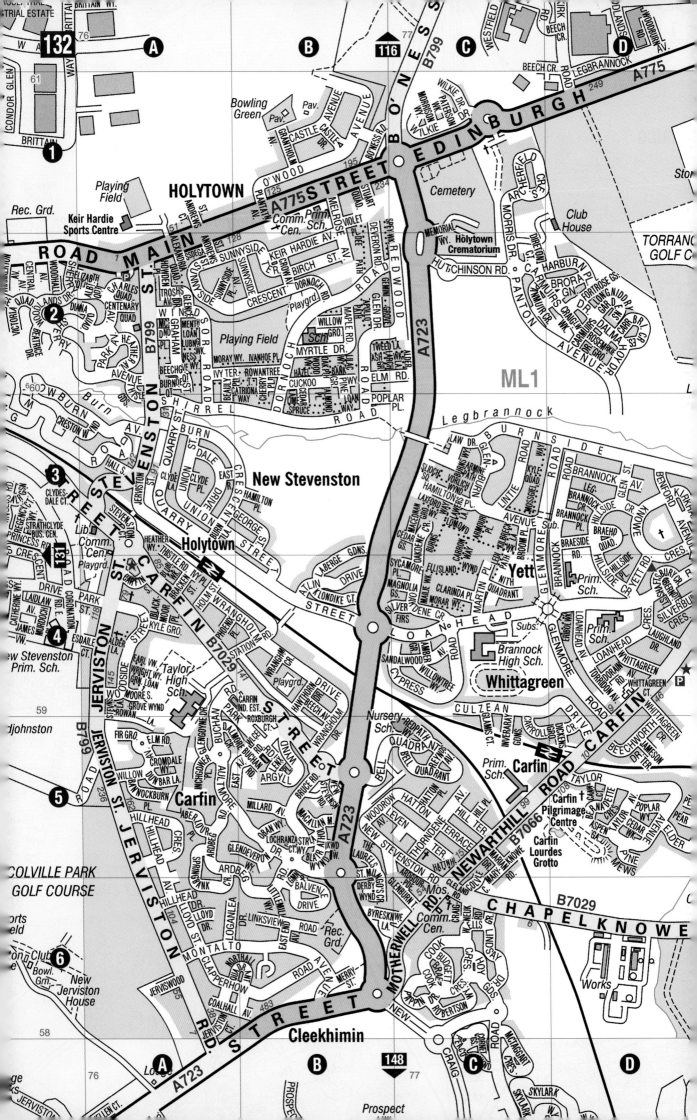

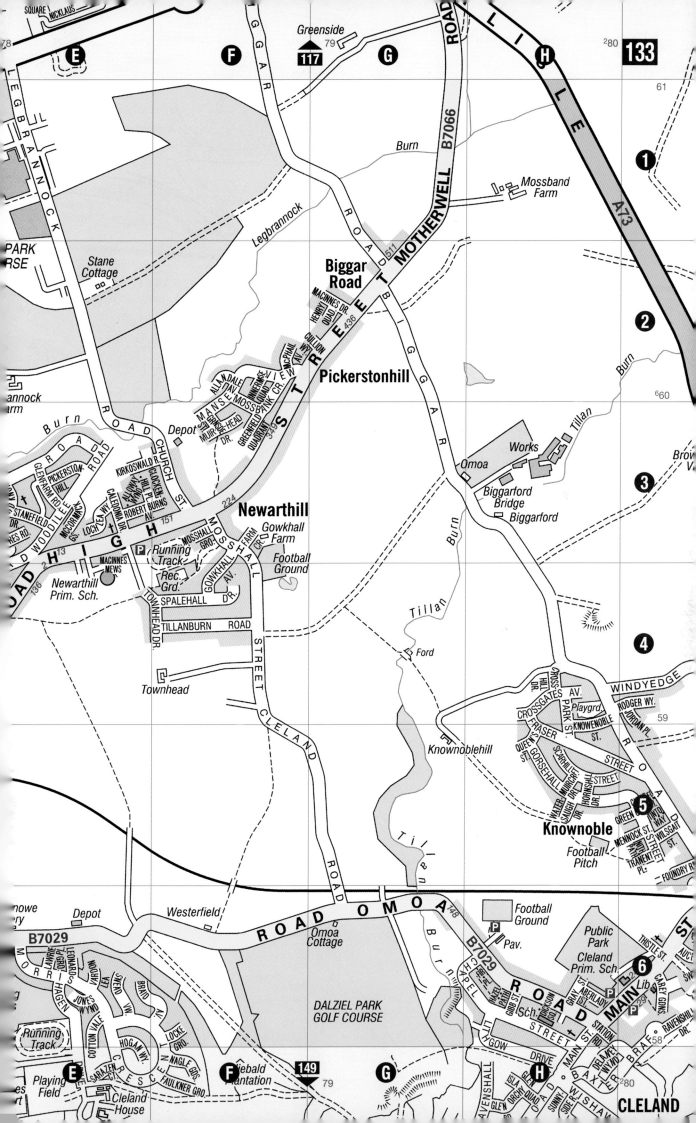

SQUARE NICKLAUS
78

Greenside
117 79

ROAD

LILHLE

280
61

1

B7066 MOTHERWELL

Burn

Mossband
Farm

PARK
RSE

Stane
Cottage

Burn

Legbrannock

Biggar
Road

511

A73

2

annock
arm

Burn

660

Pickerstonhill

MACINNES DR.
HENRY QUAD
VIEW
INNERWISE QUAD 436
ALLAN DALE MCPHAIL AV.
DAV. CULLION WY.
MANSE MOSSBANK CR.
GRASSE-HEAD 349
MUIR-HEAD GREENFIELD QUADRANT
DR. QUADRANT

STREET BIGGAR

Depot

Works

Omoa

Tillan

Brov
V

3

Burn

PARK
RSE

Burn
ROAD ROAD
GLENFARM ROAD
PICKERSTON-
HILL RD
STANEFIELD
HES RD.
WOODILEE
MCCORMACK
GS. LOCH
CALEDONIA DR.
KIRKOSWALD R.
GLOCKEN
HILL PL.
GALLOWAY WYND
ROBERT BURNS AV.
CHURCH ST.
224 151

Newarthill

Gowkhall
Farm

Football
Ground

Biggarford
Bridge
Biggarford

Omoa

Burn

HIGH
13 ROAD
136

MACINNES
MEWS

Newarthill
Prim. Sch.

P
Running
Track
Rec.
Grd.

MOSSHALL GRO.
FARM DR.
GOWKHALL AV.
MOSSHALL
SPALEHALL
TOWNHEAD DR.
TILLANBURN ROAD

Tillan

Ford

WINDYEDGE

4

CROSS
HILL DR.
CROSSGATES AV.
PARK ST.
Playgrd
KNOWENOBLE
FRASER ST.
QUEEN'S SCARNILLET ST.
WATER MINICH DR.
SAUGH HORNSHALL
GORSEHALL DR.
Knownoblehill

RODGER WY.
JORDAN PL.

ROAD

STREET
59

Townhead

STREET CLELAND ROAD

GREEN LINTO WAY
MENNOCK ST. WILSGAIT
TRANENT ST.
PL.
FOUNDRY R

Knownoble 5

Football
Pitch

nowe
ry

Depot

Westerfield

B7029

MORRIS
LEONARD FERGUS
LAWRIE WYND
VARDON JONES
HAGEN WYND
SNEAD
BRAID AV.
LET
HOGAN WY.
LOCKE
GRO.
NAGLE GDS.
COTTON VALE
SARAZEN CRESCE
FAULKNER GRO.

Running
Track

Playing
Field

Cleland
House

Omoa
Cottage

ROAD OMOA 748
ROAD B7029

DALZIEL PARK
GOLF COURSE

iebald
antation
149 79

Football
Ground

P
Pav.

Public
Park
Cleland
Prim. Sch.

THISTLE ST.
ABERLADY
GRAY ST.
CHAPEL
HAZEL DEE ST.
GIBB ST.
DICKSON
Sch.
STREET MAIN ST.
LITHGOW DRIVE
RAVENSHALL GLEN ORCHY SIDE
ISLA QUAD
SUNNY ST.

MAIN ST.
Lib.
STATION RD.
CAREY GDNS.
BRAE 58 280
DEL WY.
WISHAW
AUCY
SWE
SWE

Cleland Prim. Sch.
6

AUCY

E   F   G   H

CLELAND

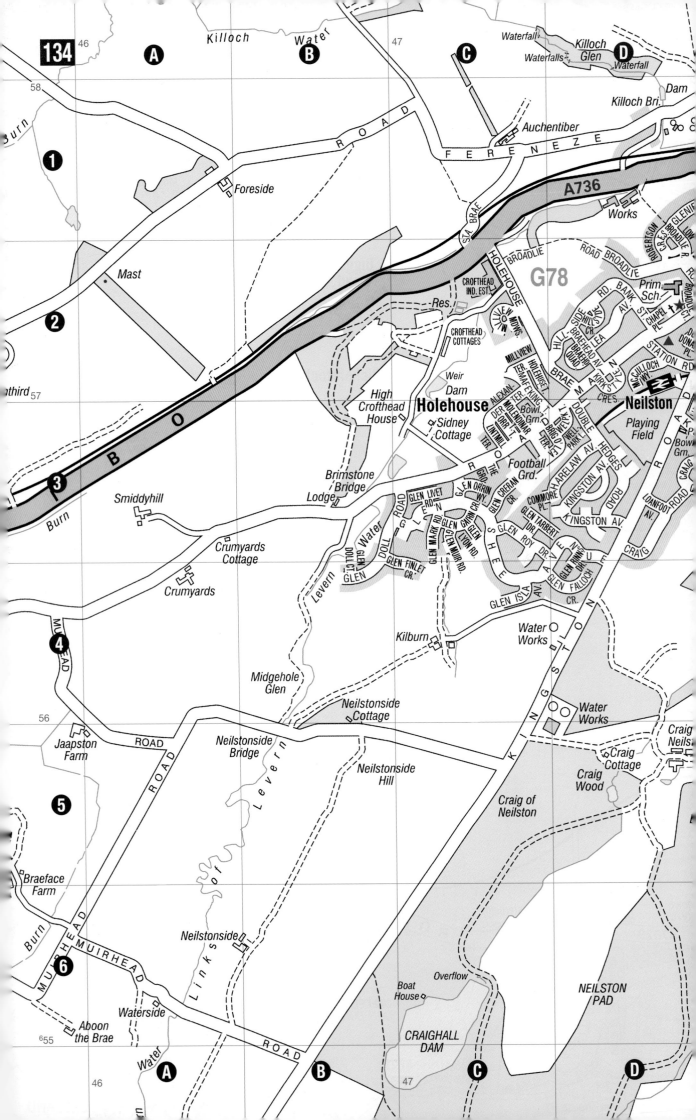

46

58

47

C

Waterfall

Killoch Glen

D

Killoch Water

A

B

Waterfalls

Waterfall

Dam

1

Burn

Foreside

Auchentiber

Killoch Bri.

ROAD

FERENEZE

STA. BRAE

A736

Works

BROADLIE

ROAD BROADLIE

ROBERTSON

CRES

GLENIF

LOW

BROADLIE R

Mast

CROFTHEAD IND. EST.

HOLEHOUSE

G78

Prim. Sch.

BANK ST.

CHAPEL PL.

†

★

STATION RD.

DONA

2

Res.

SIDE

HILL

CR.

HILL

BRAEHEAD AV.

BRAE

QUAD

VIEW MDW.

MILLVIEW TER.

LEA

KIRK ST.

57 thind

CROFTHEAD COTTAGES

Weir

Dam

MCCULLOCH

CRES.

Neilston

BO

Burn

High Crofthead House

Holehouse

Sidney Cottage

ALEXANDER TER.

MOLENDINAR TER.

BRIGO'

UNT MILL

MAFEKING TER.

HOLEHOUSE TER.

ORR.T.

BOWL. GRN.

WELL

PARK L.

WELL PL.

Playing Field

Bowl Grn

3

Smiddyhill

Brimstone Bridge Lodge

GLEN LIVET

GLEN ORRIN WY.

GLEN CRERAN CR.

GLEN TARBERT

DBL

GLEN

Football Grd.

THE GRO.

DOUBLE HEDGES

COMMORE PL.

KINGSTON AV.

ROAD

CRAIG

Crumyards Cottage

GLEN MARK RD.

GLEN CAIRN CR.

GLEN LYON RD.

HARELAW AV.

KINGSTON AV.

LOANFOOT ROAD

ROAD

Levern Water

GLEN DOLL CT.

GLEN MUIR RD.

GLEN ROY DR.

GLEN ISNS DR.

GLEN FALLOCH CR.

Crumyards

DOLL GLEN

GLEN FINLET CR.

GLEN ISLA AV.

MUIRHEAD

4

Kilburn

Water Works

56

Midgehole Glen

Neilstonside Cottage

KINGSTON

Water Works

Craig Neils

ROAD

Neilstonside Bridge

Craig Cottage

Craig Wood

Jaapston Farm

Neilstonside Hill

Craig of Neilston

5

Links of Levern

Braeface Farm

Burn

MUIRHEAD

6

Neilstonside

Overflow

NEILSTON PAD

Waterside

Boat House

Aboon the Brae

ROAD

CRAIGHALL DAM

55

46

A

47

B

C

D

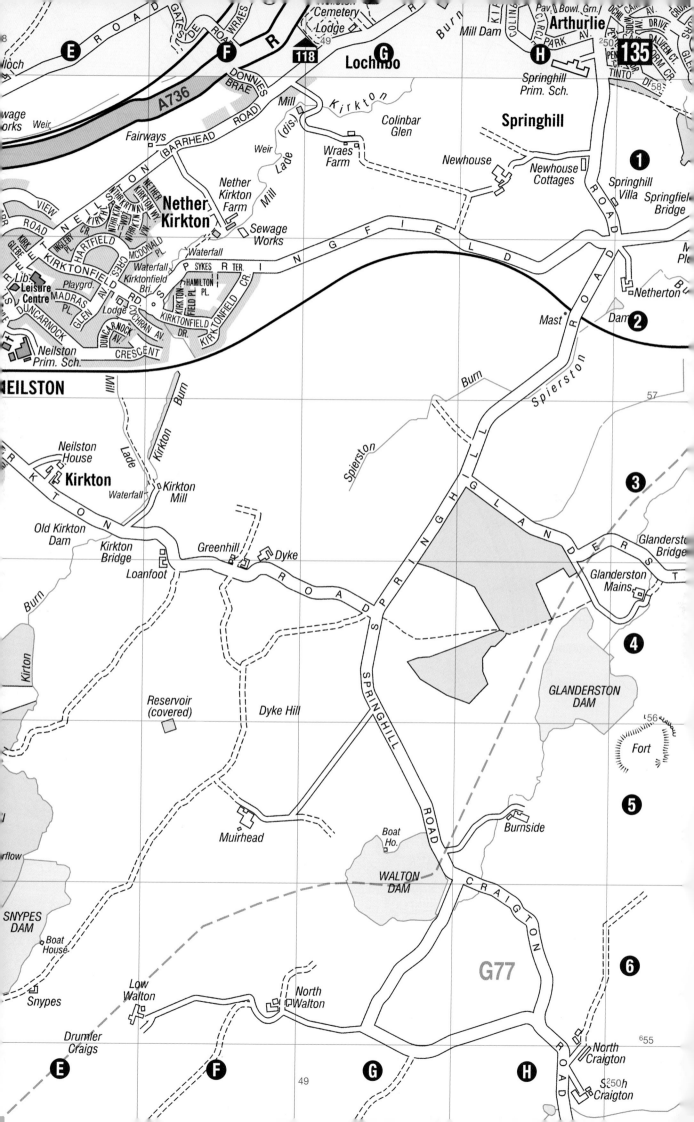

E   **F**   R   118   **G**   Lochlibo   **H**   **Arthurlie**

ROAD   GATESIDE   WRAES   ROAD   DONNIES BRAE   KIRKTON (BARRHEAD) ROAD

A736

Weir   Fairways   Mill (dis.)   Weir   Mill Lade   Kirkton   Colinbar Glen   Mill Dam

Nether Kirkton Farm   Wraes Farm   Newhouse   Springhill Prim. Sch.

sewage Works   Sewage Works   **Springhill**

Nether Kirkton   Waterfall   P SYKES R TER.   Newhouse Cottages   **1**

VIEW ROAD   NETHER KIRKTON   Waterfall   HAMILTON PL.   Springhill Villa   Springfield Bridge

KIRKTONFIELD   Kirktonfield Bri.   KIRKTONFIELD CR.   SPRINGFIELD ROAD

Lib.   Playgrd.   Lodge   KIRKTONFIELD DR.   KIRKTONFIELD   Netherton   **2**

Leisure Centre   MADRAS PL.   GLEN   COCHRAN AV.   Mast   Dam

DUNCARNOCK   Lodge   DUNCARNOCK AV.   CRESCENT   Burn   Spierston   57

Neilston Prim. Sch.

NEILSTON   Mill   Kirkton   Burn   Spierston   **3**

Neilston House   Kirkton   Lade   Burn   SPRINGHILL LANDERSTON   Glanderston Bridge

Kirkton   Waterfall   Kirkton Mill   **4**

Old Kirkton Dam   Kirkton Bridge   Greenhill   Dyke   Glanderston Mains

Loanfoot   ROAD   SPRINGHILL   GLANDERSTON DAM

Kirkton Burn   Reservoir (covered)   Dyke Hill   56   Fort   **5**

Muirhead   Boat Ho.   Burnside

WALTON DAM   **6**

SNYPES DAM   Boat House   CRAIGTON   G77

Snypes   Low Walton   North Walton   ROAD   655

Drumler Craigs   North Craigton

250h   North Craigton

E   **F**   49   **G**   **H**

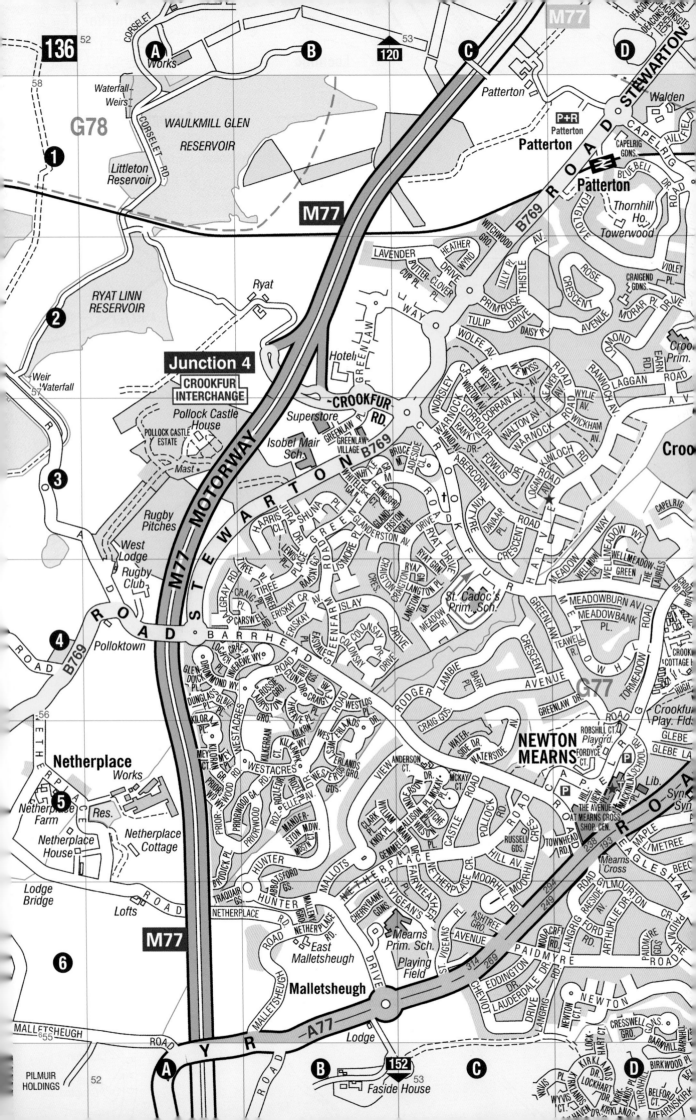

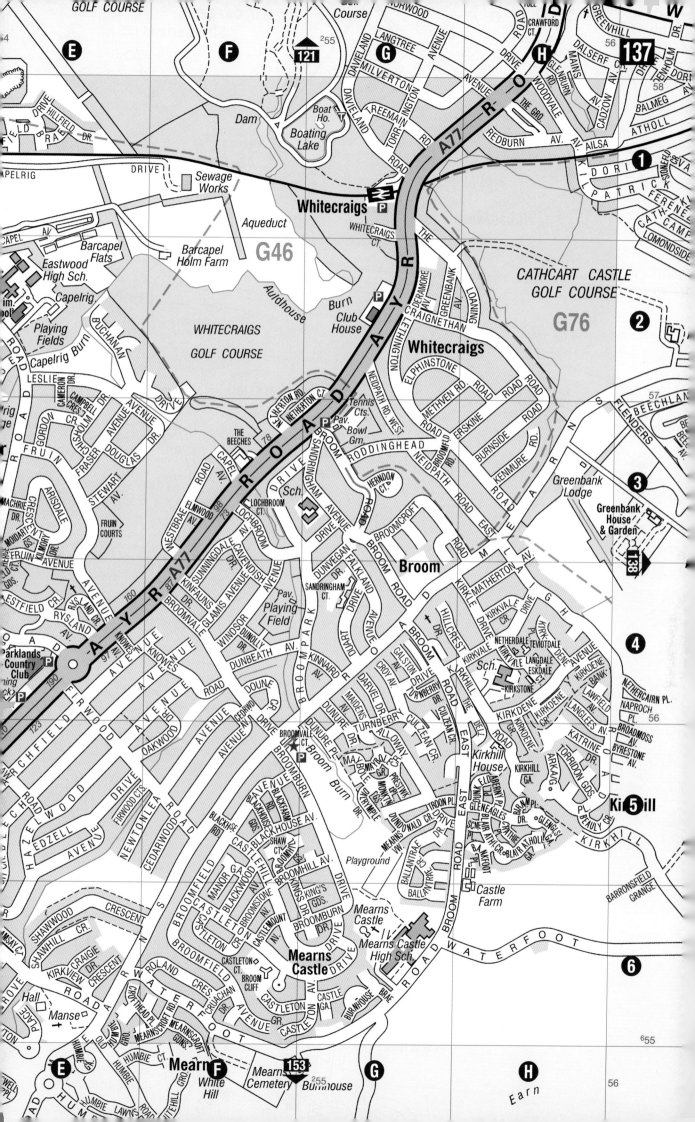

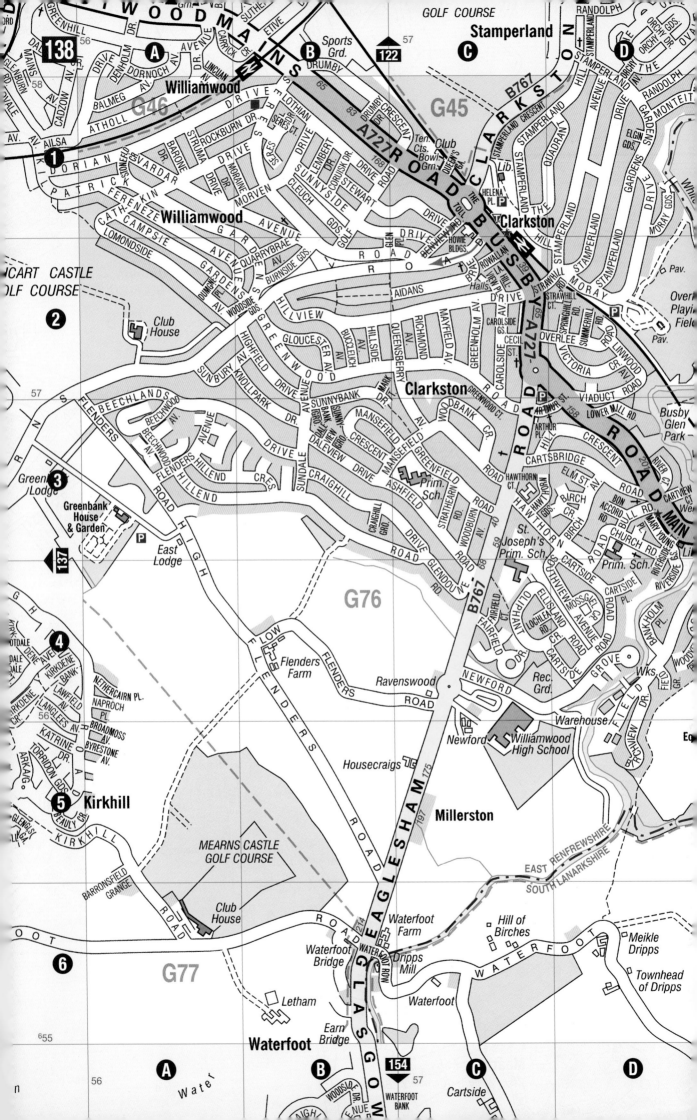

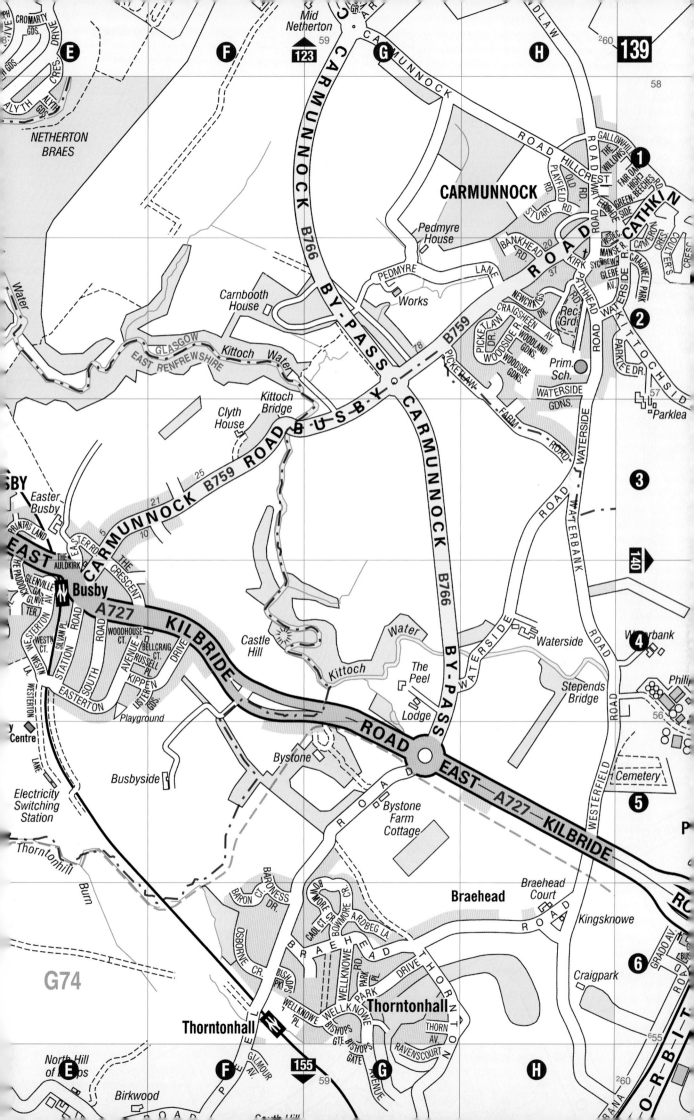

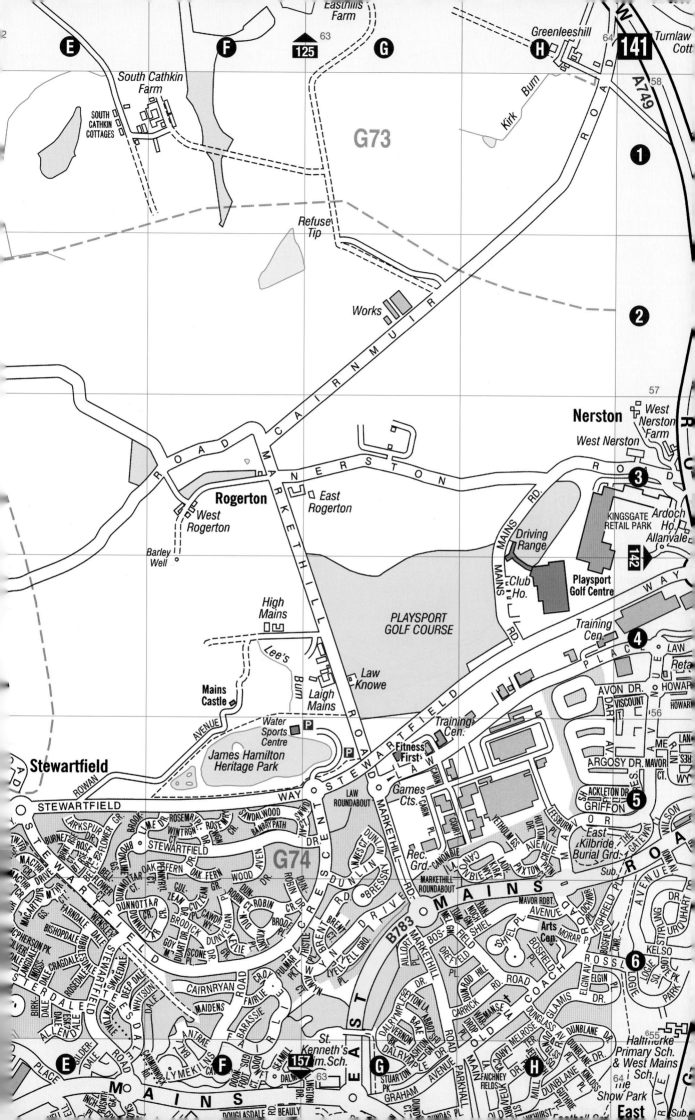

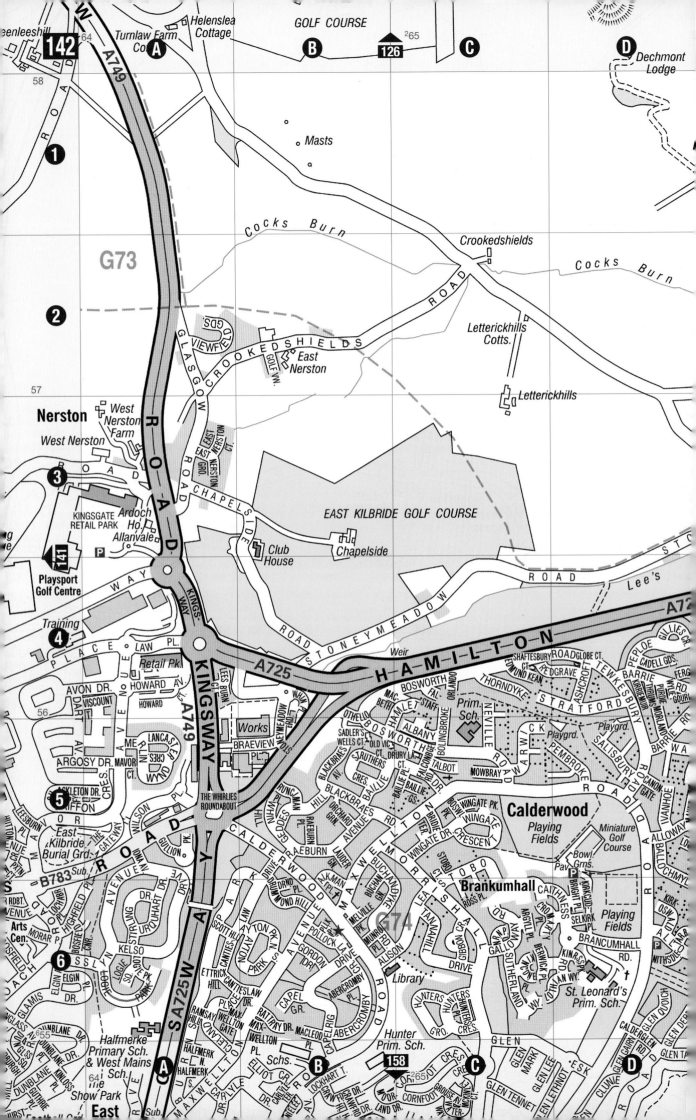

E **F** 127 **G** **H** 143

66

Calderg rove   Bardykes 68

1

Calder House

66

Dechmont Farm Cott.

Spy Wood   Malcolmwood   **Barnhill**

Weir

Iona Path

Playing Field

2

Swinburne Av   Prim. Sch.

Mid Lettrick

Mid Lettrick Farm Cott.

Watson   Stonefield   Sf 57 Gfield

Stonefield   Cres.

Playing Fields

Hunthill La.

Armour   Ct.   Afton   Park Cr.   Kirk Par

3

Crossbow Gdns.

Crossbasket   Spring   Greenhall Estate   **ROAD MAIN**

West Lodge   Dam   East Lodge   Greenhall View   Lady Na   Nancy Cr.   Shott   Shott Ho   Craigmuir Gdns.   Mem   144

Allers   Allers Cotts.   General's L Bridge   Lodge   **HAMILTON ROAD**   Lady Croft Pl.   Nancy Cres.   Archers Croft Pl.   Smithycroft Way   Craigmuir Rd.   Manse V   Priestfield   Forres   Caith

R O A D   **A725**   Douglas

Allers Sewage Purification Works

G72   Hamilton Brae   Hillhouse   **4**   Hill

Craigmuir   Newhouse   Sydes   Stephenson

56

5

Rotten Calder Glen

Calder

South Lanarkshire Crematorium

Red Bur

Park Farm

Craigneith Castle (rems. of)

Blantyre Park Farm

6

Alford

Auchentibber   Clyde Cottage

Auchentibber Farm

Springbank   War Mem.

655

E **F** 159 **G** **H**

Waterfalls   67   Calderside   **ROAD**   68

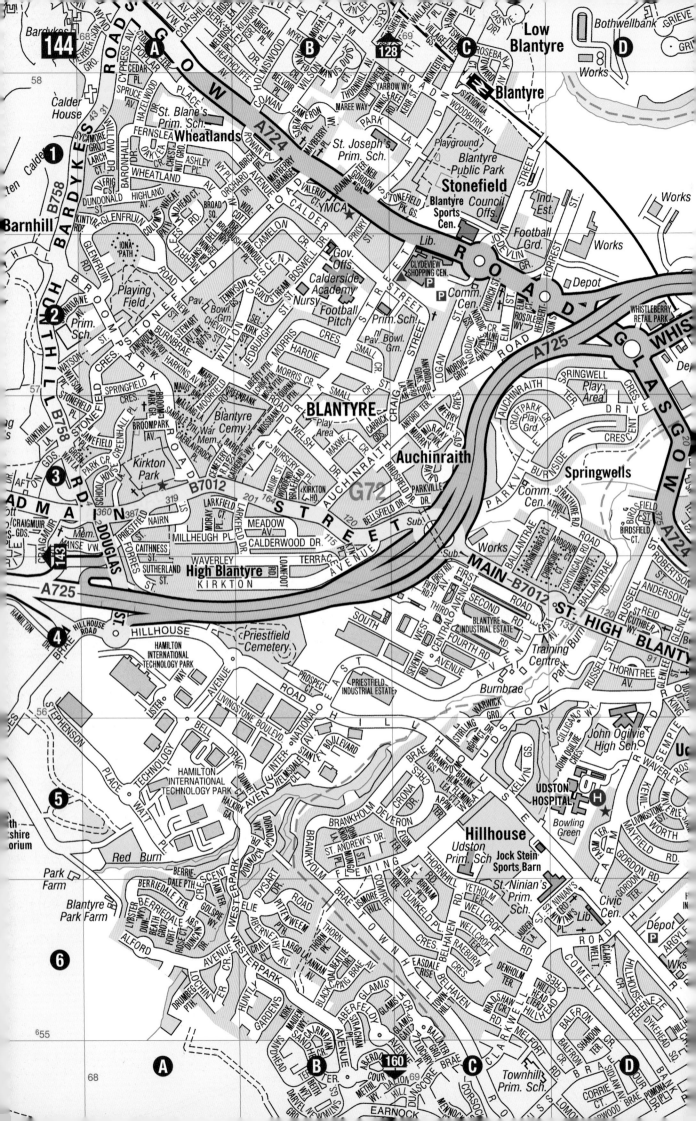

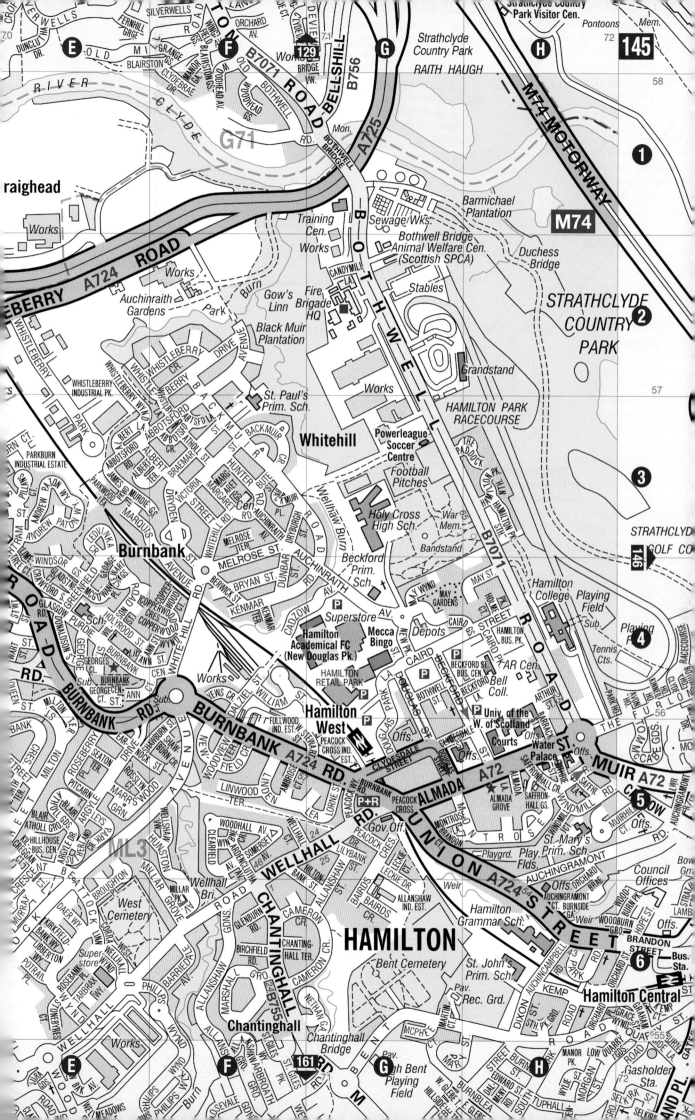

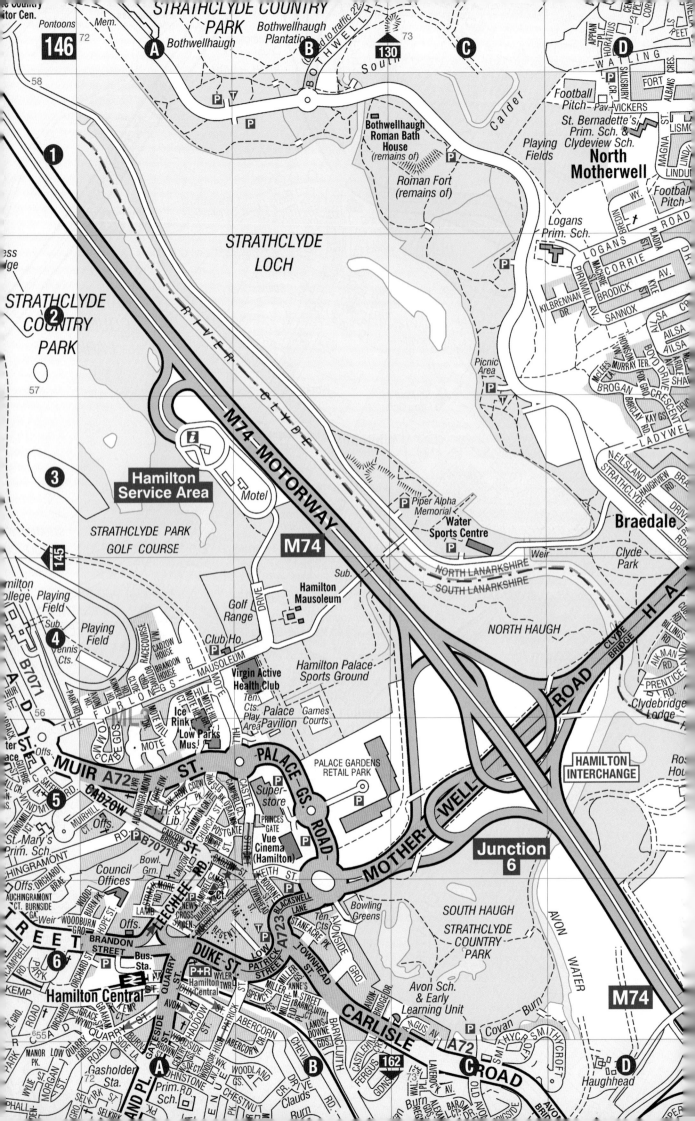

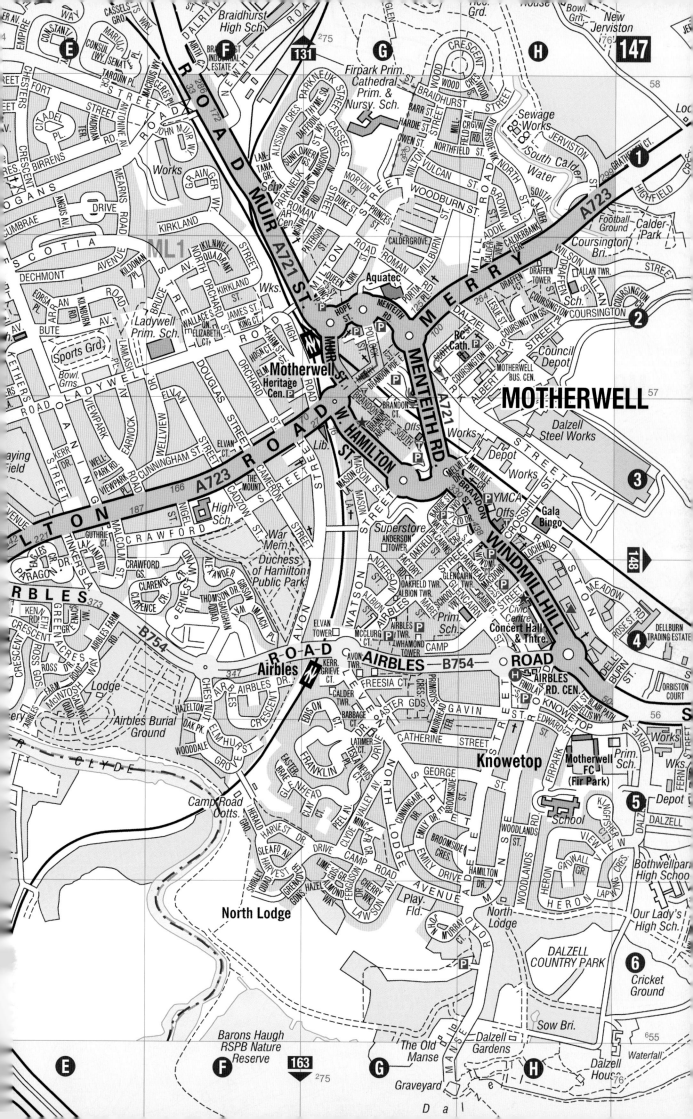

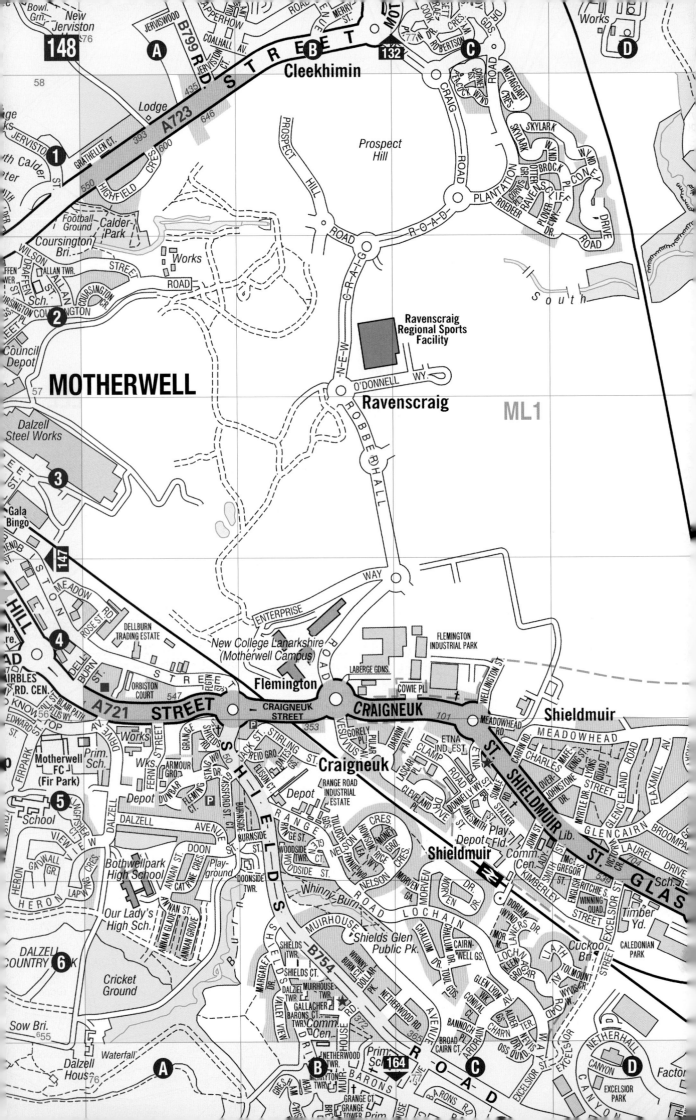

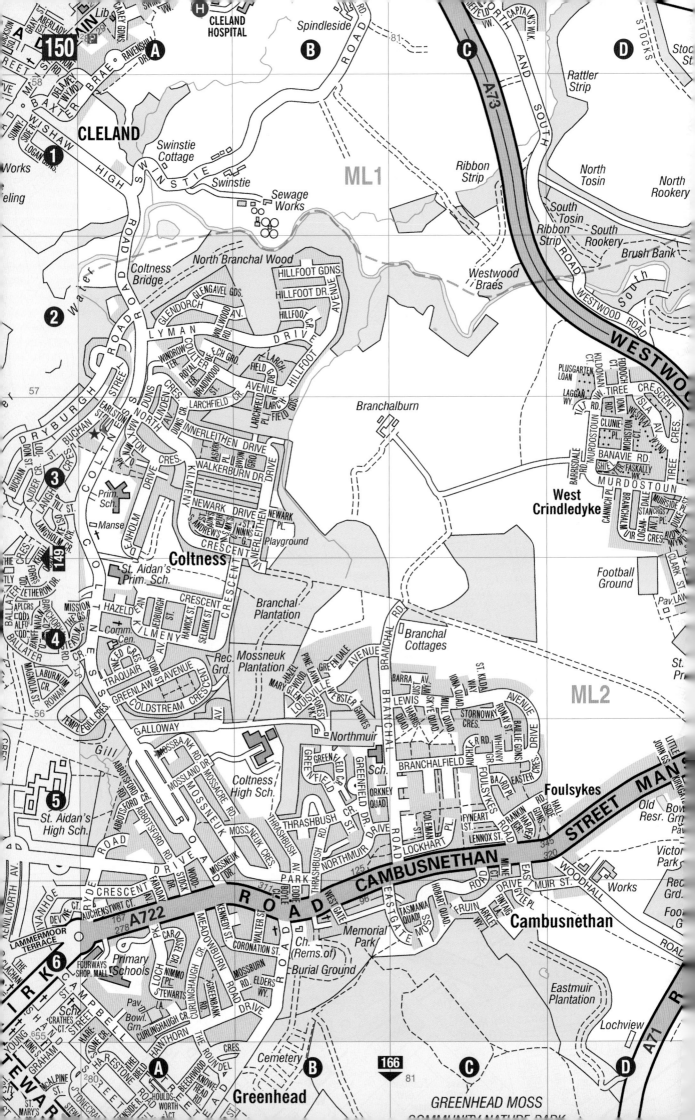

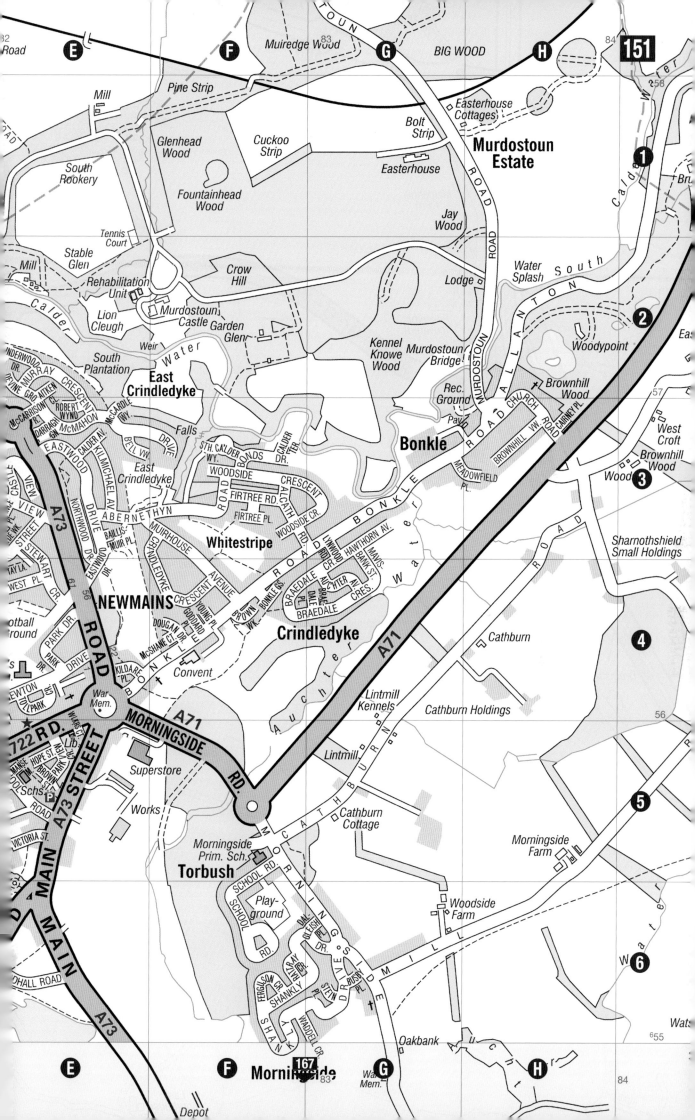

E
F
Muiredge Wood   83
G   BIG WOOD
H   84

Road

Mill

Pine Strip

Glenhead Wood

Cuckoo Strip

Easterhouse Cottages

Bolt Strip

Easterhouse

Murdostoun Estate

58

1

South Rookery

Fountainhead Wood

Jay Wood

Water Splash South

2

Woodypoint

Stable Glen

Mill

Crow Hill

Rehabilitation Unit

Lion Cleugh

Murdostoun Castle

Garden Glen

Weir

Lodge

MURDOSTOUN ROAD

ALLANTON ROAD

Brownhill Wood

57

Calder Water

South Plantation

East Crindledyke

Kennel Knowe Wood

Murdostoun Bridge

Rec. Ground

Pav.

CHURCH ROAD

BROWNHILL VW.

CAIRNEY PL.

West Croft

Brownhill Wood

Wood

3

UNDERWOOD DR.
REVINE GRO.
MURRAY CRESCENT
AITKEN
McCARRISON CT.
R.T.
DARRAGH GN.
ROBERT WYND
McMAHON
CALDER AV.
McCARDLE WY.
BELL VW.
KILMICHAEL AV.
DRIVE
Falls
STH. CALDER WY.
BONDS
CALDER TER.
CRESCENT
WOODSIDE
ALCATH
FIRTREE RD.
WOODSIDE CR.
FIRTREE PL.

East Crindledyke

MEADOWFIELD PL.

Bonkle

Sharnothshield Small Holdings

EASTWOOD

NORTHWOOD DRIVE

ABERNETHYN

BAILLIS

MUIR PL.

MUIRHOUSE

CRINDLEDYKE

EASTWOOD DR.

Whitestripe

WOODSIDE RD.

BONKLE ROAD

LYNWOOD RD.
HAWTHORN AV.
MAVIS
BANK ST.
AUCHTER AV.

Water

ROAD

4

CASTLE VIEW
DERIK VIEW
A73
STEWART CR.
WEST PL.
TAY LA.
61
56
AVENUE
YOUNG PL.
GODDARD
CRESCENT
BROWN WK.
BONKLE RO.
BRAEDALE PL.
DALE PL.
BRAE
BRAEDALE
CRES.

NEWMAINS

Crindledyke

Cathburn

Cathburn Holdings

56

Football Ground

PARK DR.
PARK DRIVE
DOUGAN DR.
McSHANE CT.
KILDARE PL.
Convent

Lintmill Kennels

5

NEWTON TOLL PARK
War Mem.
A71
A722 RD.
MORNINGSIDE

Lintmill

Cathburn Cottage

Morningside Farm

MANSE
HOPE ST.
BROWN ST.
Lib.
Schs.
P
ROAD
A73 STREET
MAIN
Superstore

MORNINGSIDE RD.

Cathburn Holdings

CATHBURN ROAD

MILL

Woodside Farm

VICTORIA ST.

Works

Morningside Prim. Sch.

SCHOOL RD.

6

Torbush

Playground

SCHOOL RD.

DALGLEISH DR.

MORNINGSIDE DRIVE

Water

MAIN

FERGUSON

SHANKLY

HINTLAY DR.

STEIN PL.

BUSSY PL.

WADDELL CR.

Oakbank

655

WOODHALL ROAD

A73

SHANK WK.

Depot

E
F   **Morningside**
167
83
G   War Mem.
H   84

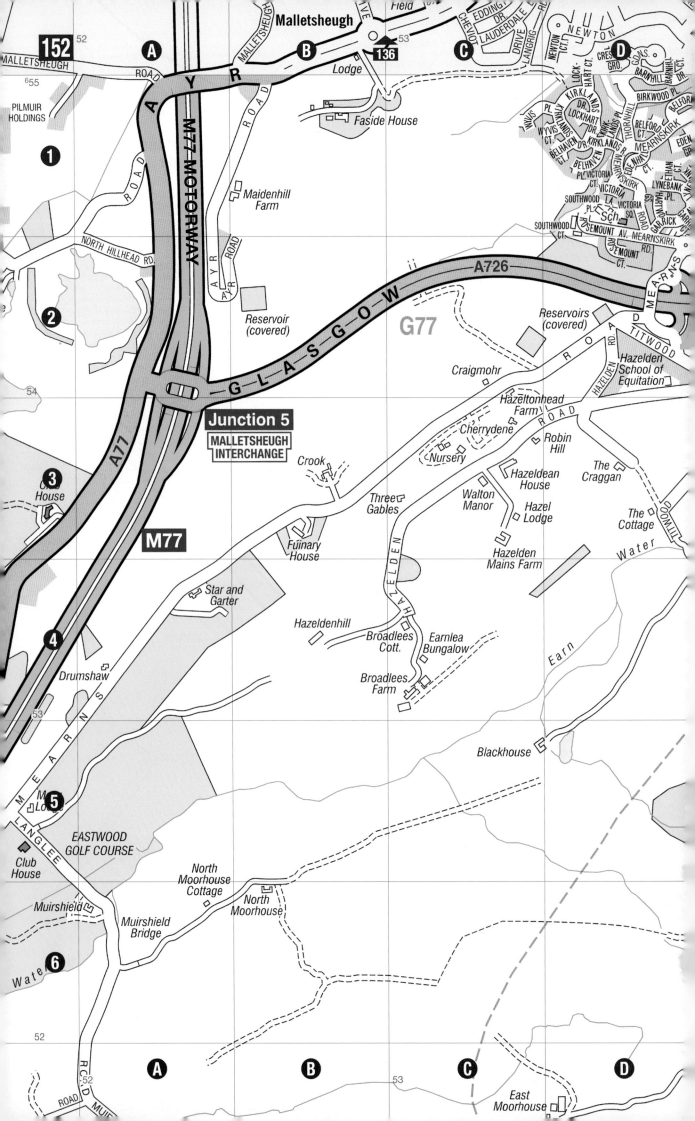

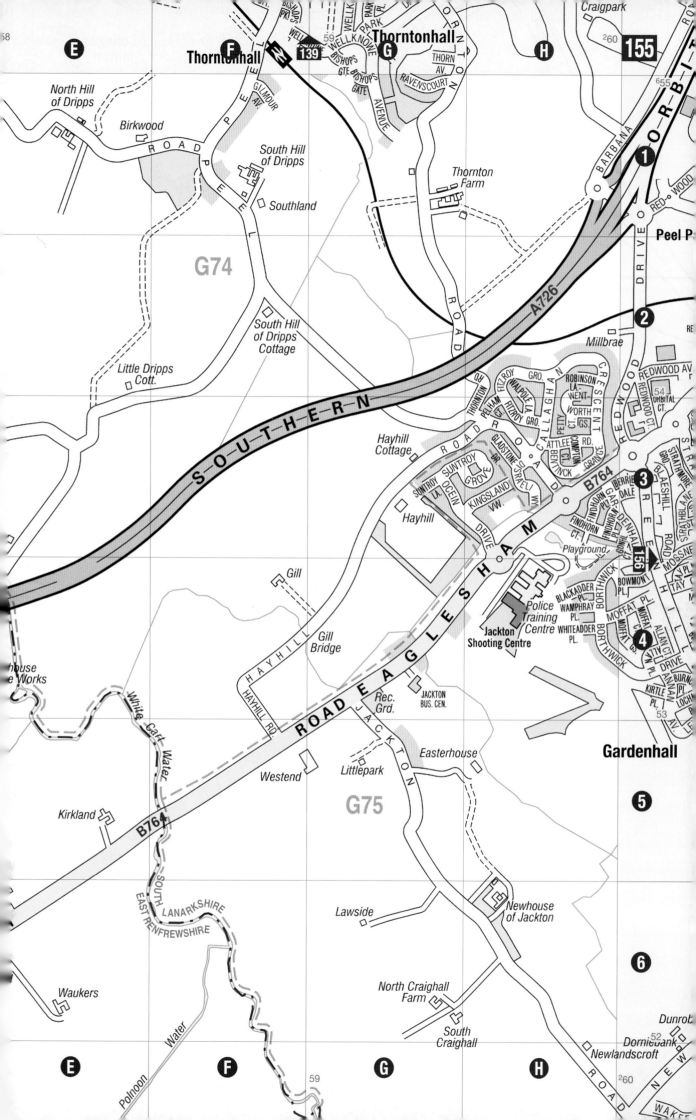

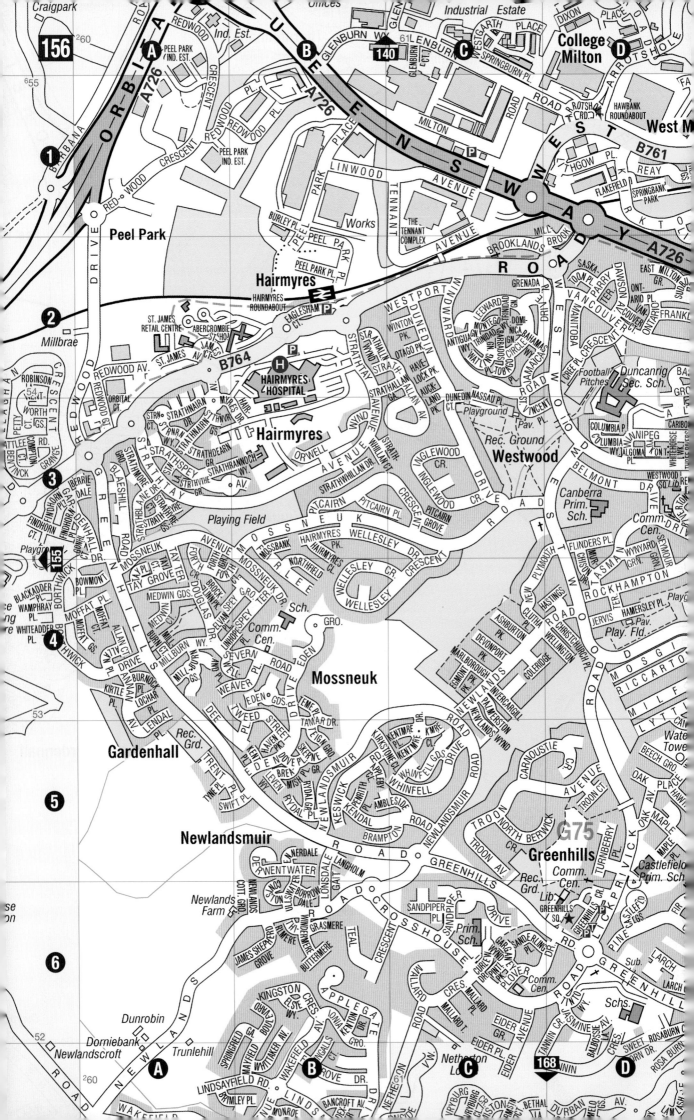

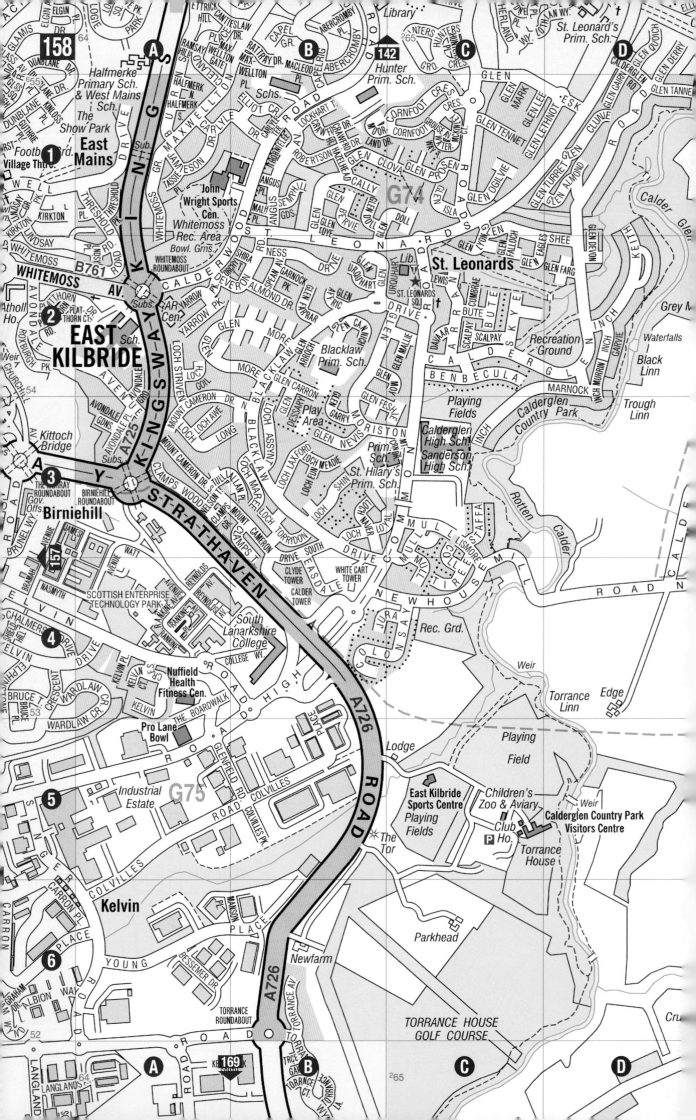

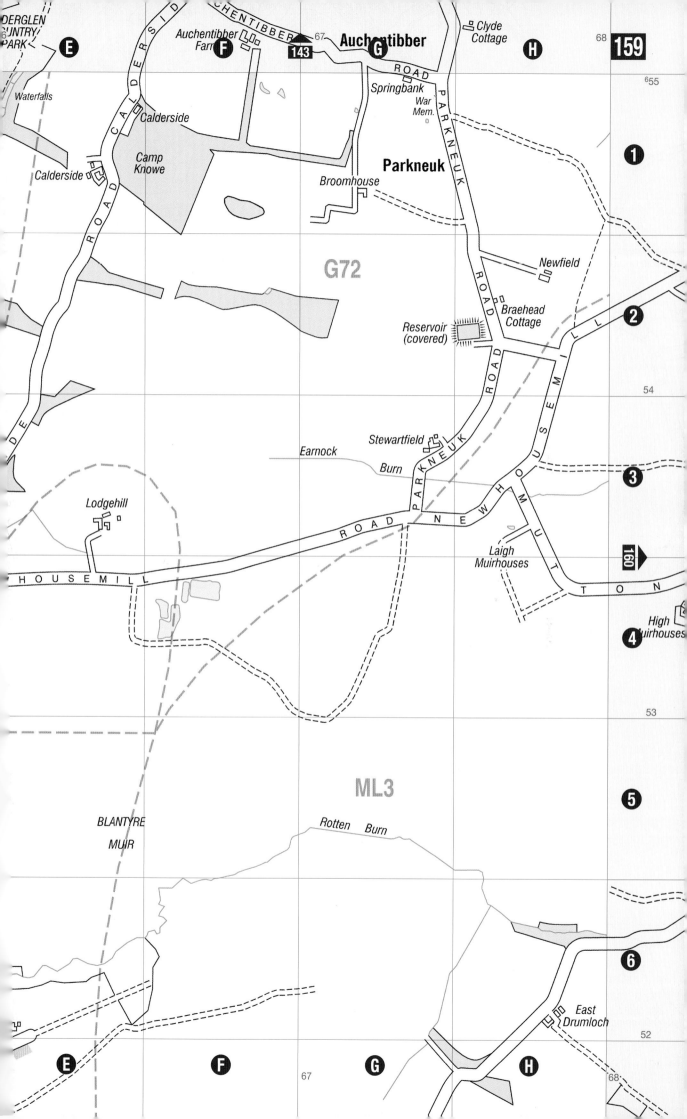

E   **F**   143   **G**   Auchentibber   Clyde Cottage   **H**   68   159

67   655

Auchentibber Farm

DERGLEN
UNTRY
PARK

Waterfalls

CALDERSIDE ROAD

Calderside

Camp Knowe

Calderside

Springbank

War Mem.

Parkneuk

Broomhouse

PARKNEUK ROAD

1

Newfield

G72

Braehead Cottage

Reservoir (covered)

2

54

PARKNEUK ROAD

Stewartfield

Earnock

Burn

NEWHOUSEMILL

3

Lodgehill

ROAD

NEWHOUSETON

Laigh Muirhouses

160

HOUSEMILL

High Muirhouses

4

53

ML3

5

BLANTYRE
MUIR

Rotten   Burn

6

East Drumloch

52

E   **F**   67   **G**   **H**   68

A   B   144   C   D

655

G72

1

Newfield

Dykehead House

Reservoir (covered)

Earnock

Townhill Prim. Sch.

2

54

Muirmains

3

ML3

Kennedies

Weir

159

High Muirhouses

4

Dykend

Electricity Sub Station

Mast

53

Sherriff Faulds

5

Beechfield House

Devonhill

Earnockmuir

Earnockmuir Cottage

6

East Drumloch

52

Cadzow Burn

A   B   C   D   Haspielaw

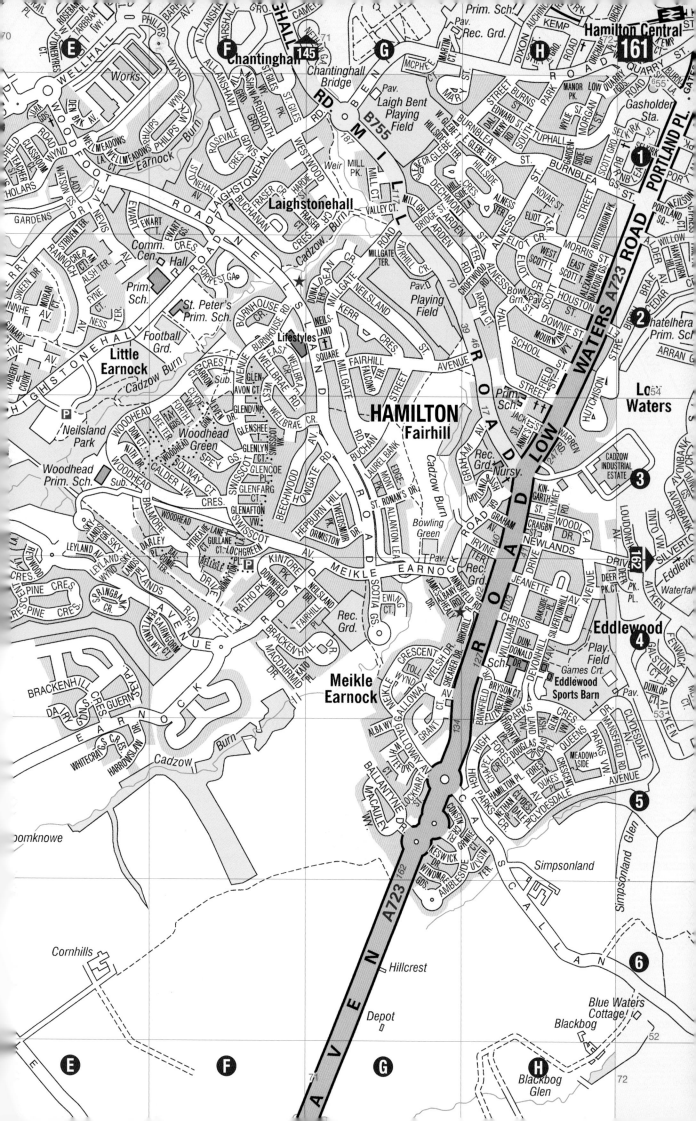

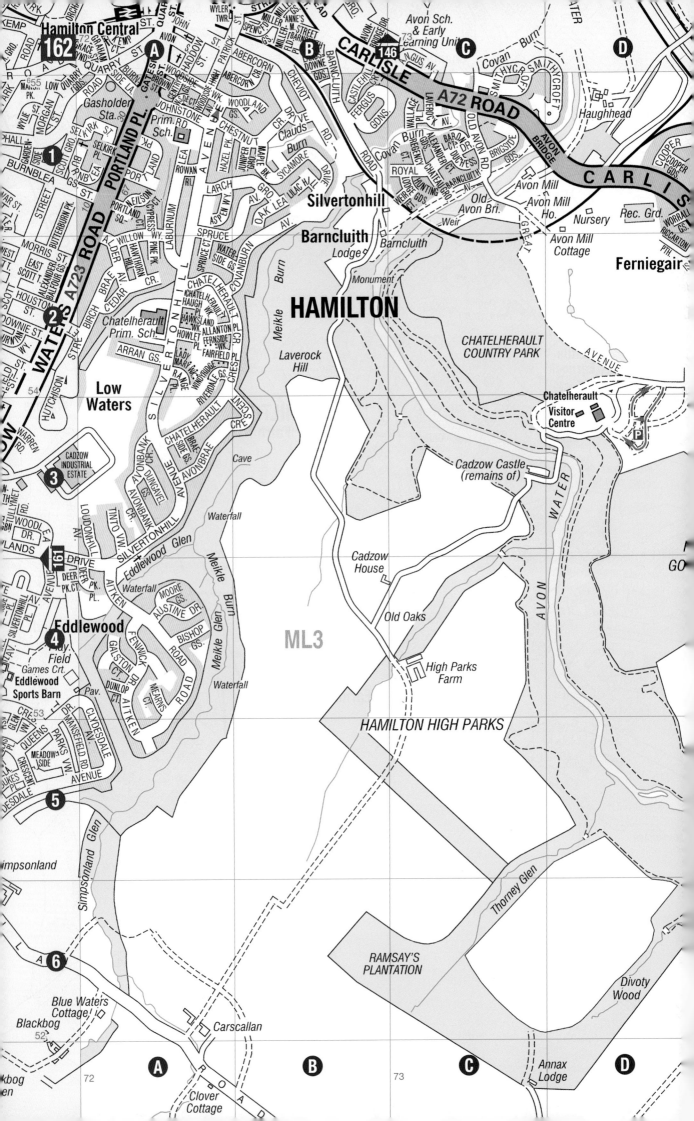

E **F** **G** **H**

147 275

Barons Haugh RSPB Nature Reserve

The Old Manse

MANSE

Dalzell Gardens

Bow Bri. 76

Cricket Ground

Dalzell House

Waterfall 655

Graveyard

D a l z e l

ML1

1

RIVER

NORTH LANARKSHIRE
SOUTH LANARKSHIRE

CLYDE

East
Pla
Pe
We

CRESCENT · TER.
SS
O'DONNELL DR.
GS.
SHEARER AV.
DENBEATH
DCT.
WNOWAY CRES.

A72 162

Chatelherault

Hall +

VALLEYFIELD CR.
METHIL CT.
FAIRHOLM
AV.
PARK DR.
VALLEYFIELD
AV.
ROSS
TER.
LEVEN
RD.
CLYDE
AVENUE
CASTLE HILL CR.
OSPREY
LN.
KINGFISHER AV.
RED
KITE
PL7
G. ROVE
BLACK
GROUSE
GDS.
CAPERCAILLIE
PEREGRINE CRES.

Allanton
Sewage
Works

M74

54

2

CANDYTOFT WND
PRINCRESS
Garden
Centre
HONEYSUCKLE
CT.
DRI
BELVEDE RD.
ALLANTON
TER.

e House

M74

3

TON
OURSE

**BELVIDERE
PLANTATION**

ROAD

CARLISLE

LANARK RD. END **L A N A R K** **A72**

Garden Centre

Low
Merryton

Merryton
Farm Cotts.

164

4

53

ML9

B7078

MERRYTON

ROAD

MERRYTON

ROAD

**Summerlee
Raceway
Larkhall**

5

Dykehead
Cottage

High Merryton

Lodge

FYNE
ETIVE PL.
MORR
CT.
LINNHE
CT.
SHIEL DR.
FYNE CT.
CRESCENT
CRES.

CRESCENT
SDLKW.
WY.
CRES.
PENTLAND
GS.
PENTLAND
LAMMERMUIR
WIND
CAMPSIE
CT.
PENTLAND

LARKHALL

PENTLAND

ROAD

HAMILTON RD.

DAVE BARRIE
AV.
FAIRHOLM
SUMMERLEE

P

Merryton

Glengowan
Prim. Sch.

6

ROAD

MAPLE
CHEST
BROOM
CHESTNUT
TREE
WOOD
BEECH
BIRCH
GROVE
NUT

52

Lodge
Fairholm
Bridge

170 275

AVON

W

BEATON
SUNNY
SIDE
ST.
CLYDE
ST.
MERRYTON
STREET
FAIRHOLM

Glen Vw.
Mem. Pk.

Sewage
Works

Playground

Merryton
Braes

HAMILTON

GLEN
VIEW
LOND
CADZOW
ST.
DOWNE
CLYDES CIR.
NORTH
76
JAS. ST.
BRY

E **F** **G** **H**

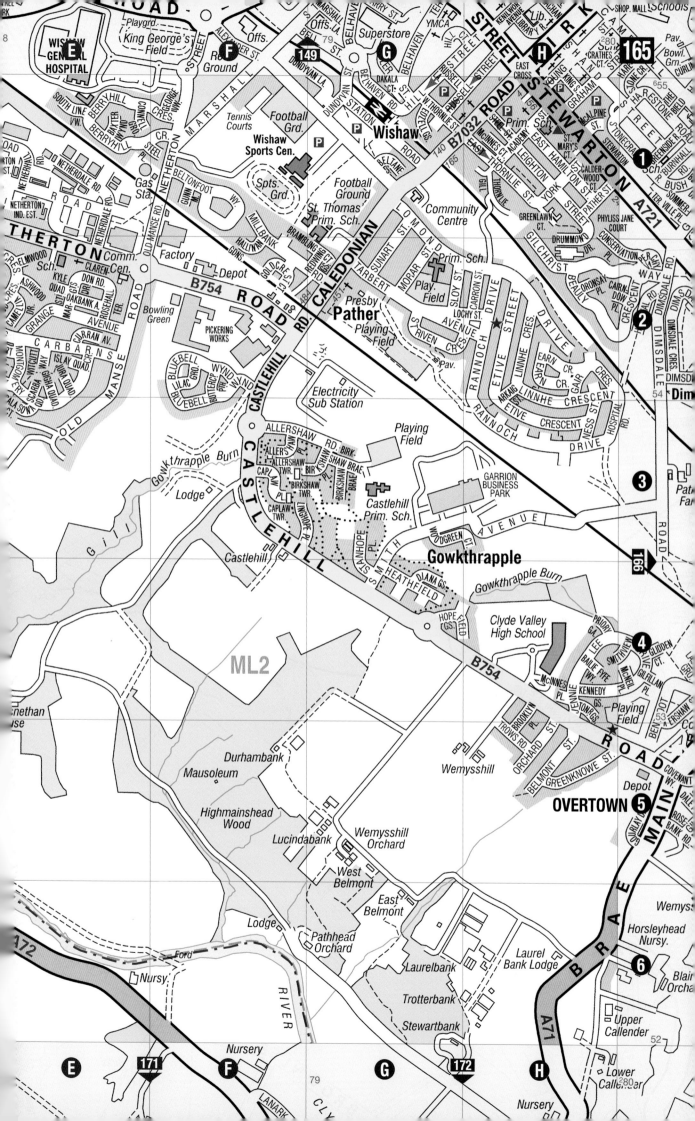

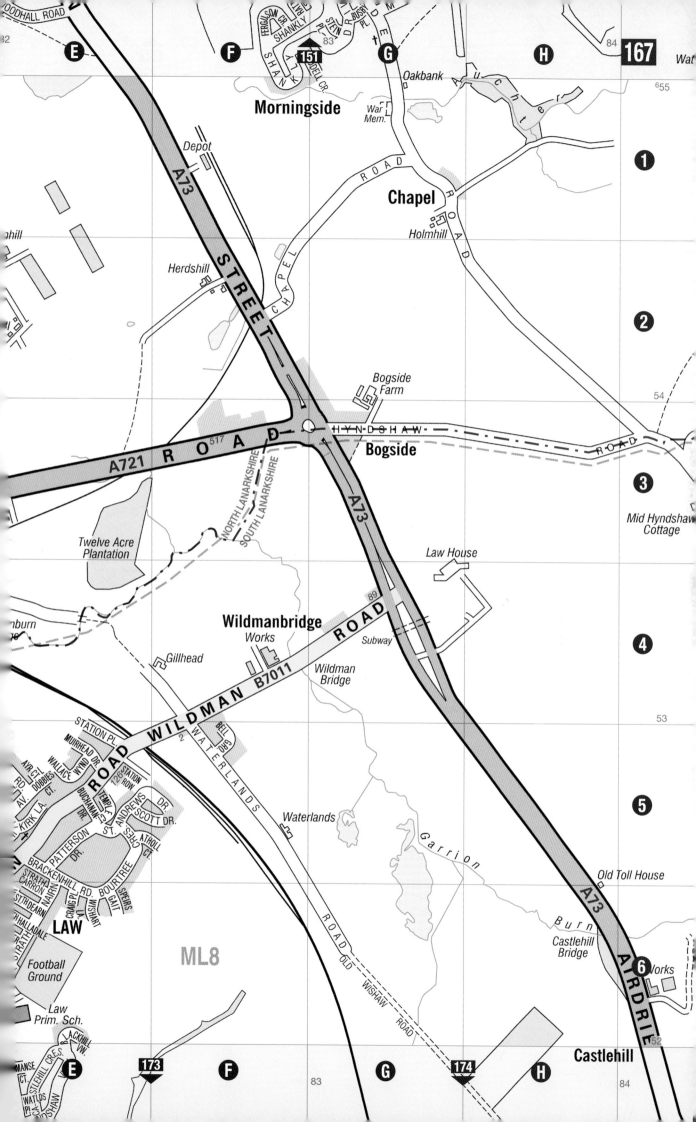

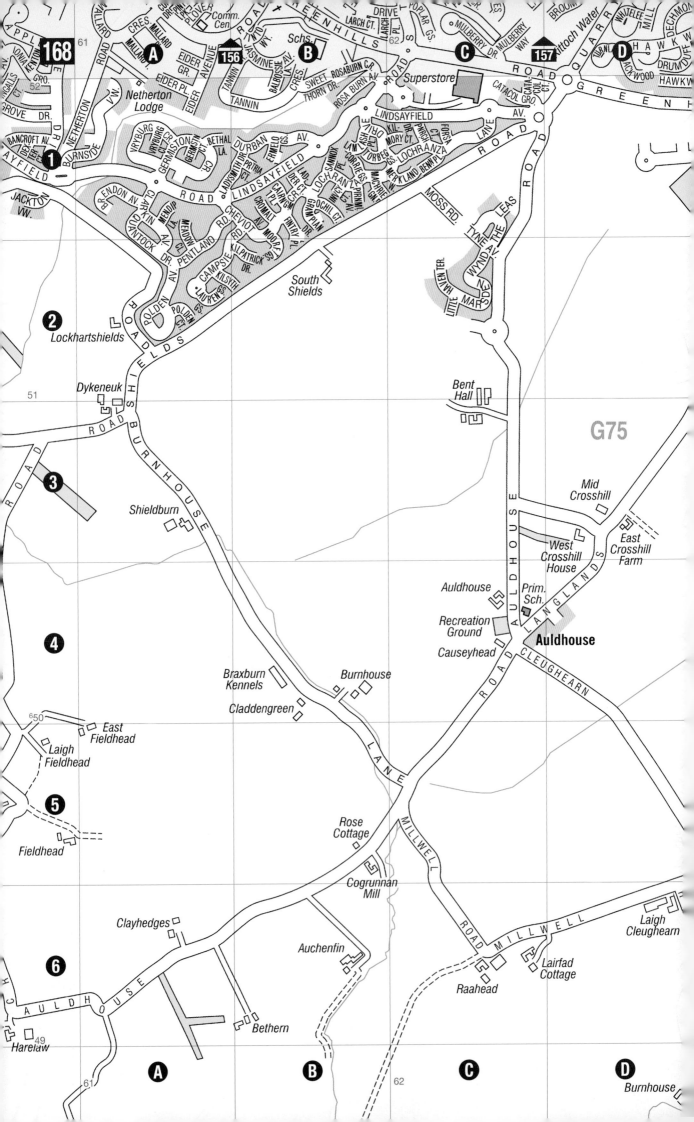

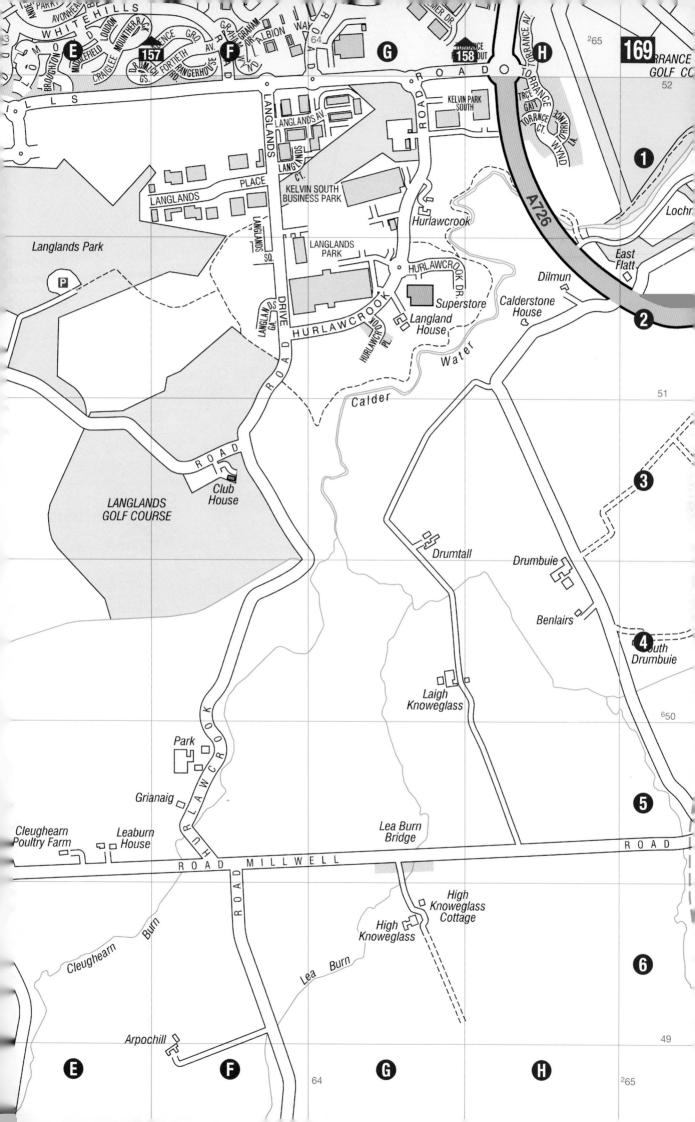

WHITEHILLS

AVONHEAD

E

157

F

G

158

H

265

169

52

TORRANCE GOLF CO

WHITEHILLS

ANDERPARK

MIDDLEFIELD

LODDON

MOUNTHERRICK

CRAIGLEE

DAUMUIR GS.

FORTIETH RD.

RANGERHOUSE

FLORENCE GRO.

AV.

GRAHAM DR.

GRAHAM WAY

ALBION

64

TORRANCE AV.

TORRANCE ROUNDABOUT

TRCE GAIT

TORRNCE CT.

TORRANCE WYND

TORRANCE LA.

1

Langlands Av.

ROAD

KELVIN PARK SOUTH

LANGLANDS

Langlands Ct.

LANGLANDS PLACE

KELVIN SOUTH BUSINESS PARK

Langlands Park

P

LANGLANDS SQ.

LANGLANDS PARK

LANGLANDS GA.

DRIVE

HURLAWCROOK

HURLAWCROOK PL.

ROAD

Hurlawcrook

HURLAWCROOK DR.

Superstore

Langland House

Calder Water

Calder

A726

Lochr

East Flatt

2

Dilmun

Calderstone House

51

Drumtall

Drumbuie

Benlairs

3

South Drumbuie

4

Laigh Knoweglass

650

5

ROAD

Park

HURLAWCROOK

Grianaig

Lea Burn Bridge

ROAD

Cleughearn Poultry Farm

Leaburn House

ROAD MILLWELL

ROAD

High Knoweglass Cottage

High Knoweglass

6

Cleughearn Burn

ROAD

Cleughearn

Lea Burn

Arpochill

49

LANGLANDS GOLF COURSE

Club House

ROAD

E

F

64

G

H

265

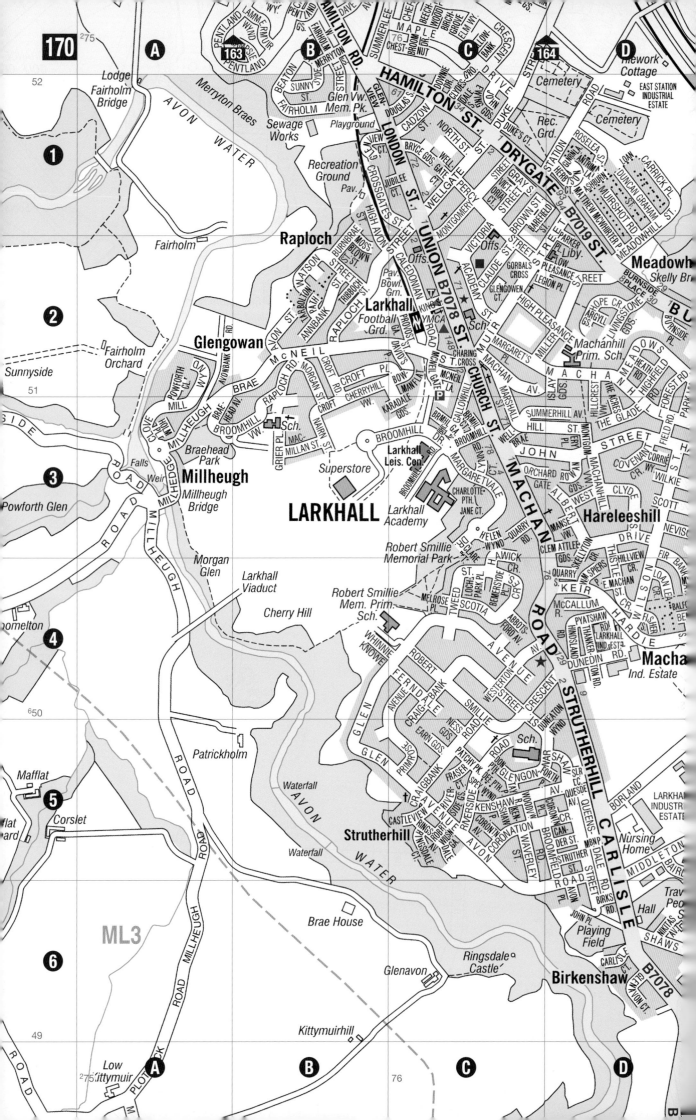

LARKHALL

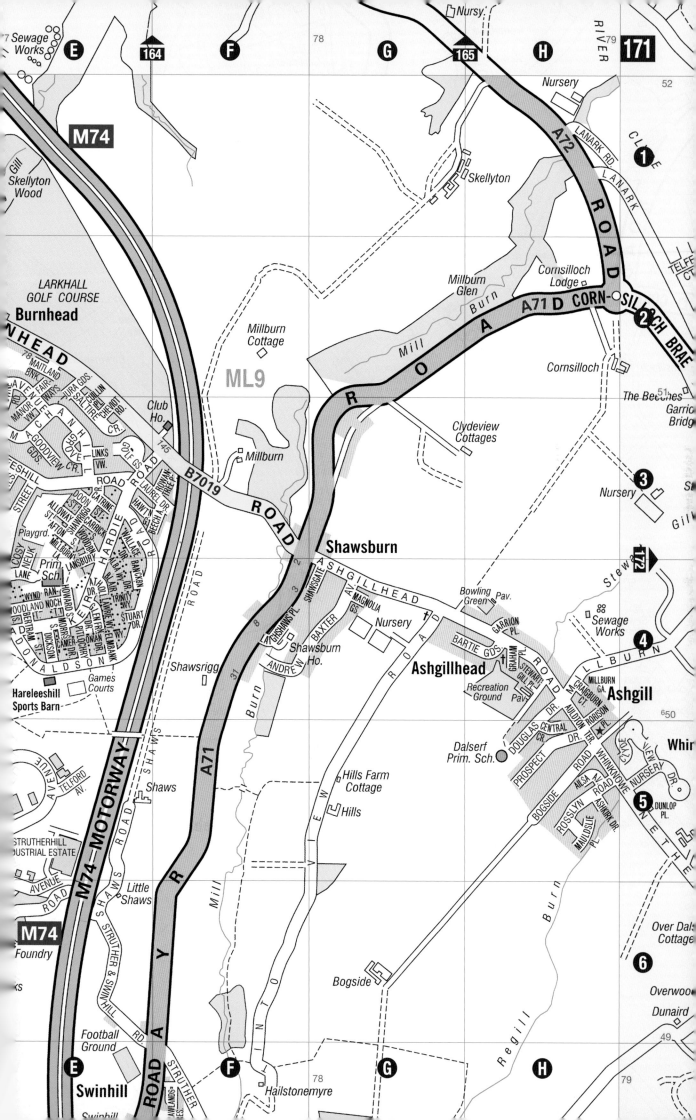

E 164 **F** 78 **G** 165 **H** RIVER 79

Nursy.

Nursery

52

1

Sewage Works

M74

Gill Skellyton Wood

A72

LANARK RD.

LANARK

Skellyton

CLYDE

LARKHALL GOLF COURSE

Burnhead

NHEAD

Millburn Glen

Cornsilloch Lodge

A71 D CORN-SILLOCH BRAE

2

Club Ho.

Millburn Cottage

ML9

Mill Burn

ROAD

Cornsilloch

The Beeches

51

Garrio Bridge

A

MAITLAND FAIR BNK WAYS JURA GDS. SALTIRE CHILLIN CHEVIOT RD. CR.

MANOR WW. AVENUE CH GOODVIEW CR. A LINKS VW. GLF GS. ROAD LAUREL DR. ROWAN TREE

Millburn

Clydeview Cottages

Nursery

3

Gill

B7019

ROAD

ESHILL STREET ALLOWAY ST. AFTON ST. SHAWRIGG WOODBN. CATRINE ST. DOON ST. HARDIE GAVOR HAWT'N BEECH LA. WALLACE RANKIN DR. ALBA WY.

LANSBURY

Shawsrigg

Shawsburn

ASHGILLHEAD

Bowling Green Pav.

172

Stew

Sewage Works

4

COSY NEUK LANE NOCH WYND PRIM. SCH. RAN GLEN FRU. BLAIR DR. LAWRIE WY. ELMBANK STUART DR. TRINITY WY. PITLOCHRY TR.

Playgrd. MILLBURN

2

SHAWSGATE SHAWS PL. ANDREW MAGNOLIA GS. Nursery

BAXTER

D GARRION PL. GRAHAM PL. STEWART GILL PL.

BARTIE GDS.

Ashgill

650

WOODLAND BERTRAM ST. S. DICKSON ST. CAMER. DR. ONIAN DR. DONALDSON

8 3

LATGH SHAWS PL. Shawsburn Ho.

Ashgillhead

Recreation Ground Pav.

Millburn GA.

ROAD

CRAIGBURN DR. AULDTON TER. RORISON PL.

Ashgill

Hareleeshill Sports Barn

Games Courts

31

Burn

Shaws

Dalserf Prim. Sch.

DOUGLAS CENTRAL CR. DR. PROSPECT ROAD

Whir

STRUTHERHILL INDUSTRIAL ESTATE

AVENUE TELFORD AV.

M74—MOTORWAY

A71

SHAWS ROAD

Shaws

Hills Farm Cottage

Hills

BOGSIDE ROAD ROSSLYN PL.

WHINKNOWE AV. AILSA AV. MAULDSLIE PL. ASKIRK DR.

VIEW DR. CLYDE Nursery

ROAD

DUNLOP PL.

5

M74 AVENUE ROAD **M74**

SHAWS RD. STRUTHER & SWINHILL

Little Shaws

Mill

VIEW

Bogside

Burn

Over Dals Cottage

6

Foundry

Football Ground

E 164... Swinhill

STRUTHER ROAD A Y R ROAD

INTO

Hailstonemyre

Regill Burn

Overwoo Dunaird

49

F 78 **G** **H** 79

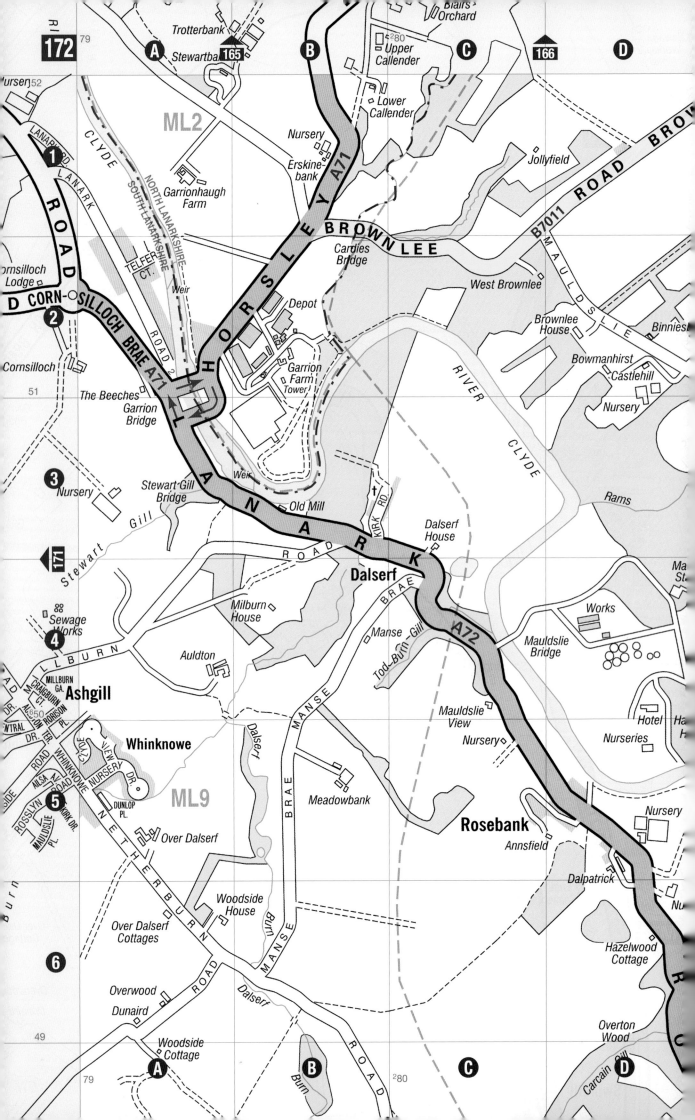

E **166** **F** **167** **G** **H** **173**

83 52

wgill

E 1

BIRKS ROAD

Birks

STRAVENHOUSE ROAD

ANSTRUTHER CT.
ANSTRUTHER CT.
McMILLAN WY.
CARMICHAEL WY.
MICHAEL ST.
BRAEFOOT CT.
BIRK'S CT.
WEIR ST.
BRAEFOOT CT.
WESTEND CT.
SHAW GILL
WEIR PL.
MANSE CT.
TURNER CT.
MURRAY RD.
SWAN WY.
GRIFFITHS
OLD SCHOOL PL.
WATLDS CT.
SILEHILL CRES.
KINGS SHAW VIEW
HYNDSHAW VIEW
BLACKHILL VW.
HILL VW.

Ground

Law Prim.

82

Law Hill

Law of Mauldslie

Park Regis

East Law

QUARRY RD.

LAWHILL ROAD

ROAD

WHITESHAW

ROAD

2

HAMBURG
COTTAGES

51

ROAD

Stravenhouse
Farm

3

Hallcraig

Club House

174

ML8

Mauldslie
Mains

Mauldslie
Cottage

MAULDSLIE

**CARLUKE
GOLF COURSE**

4

East
Lodge

ROAD

Nursery

Mauldslie
House

JOCK'S GILL WOOD

Jock's Gill

Jock's

Whorley Burn

Burn

Burn

5

Jock's Burn

Reas
Gill

Gillbank

RAES ROAD

65 50

Jock's

MILTON

Milton-Lockhart
Farm

Miltonhead
Farm

6

Meadowhead

Milton
Lockhart
Bri.

E

Waterfall

F

Sandilandgate

82 Townhead

G Gill Townhead Burn

Townhead

H

83

49

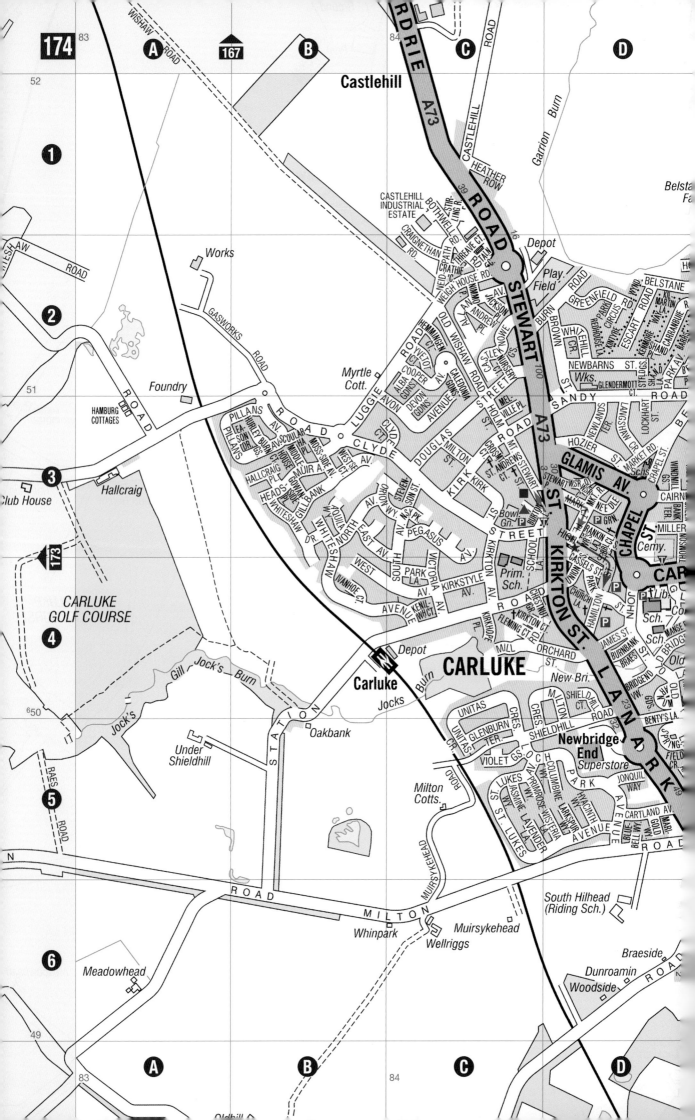

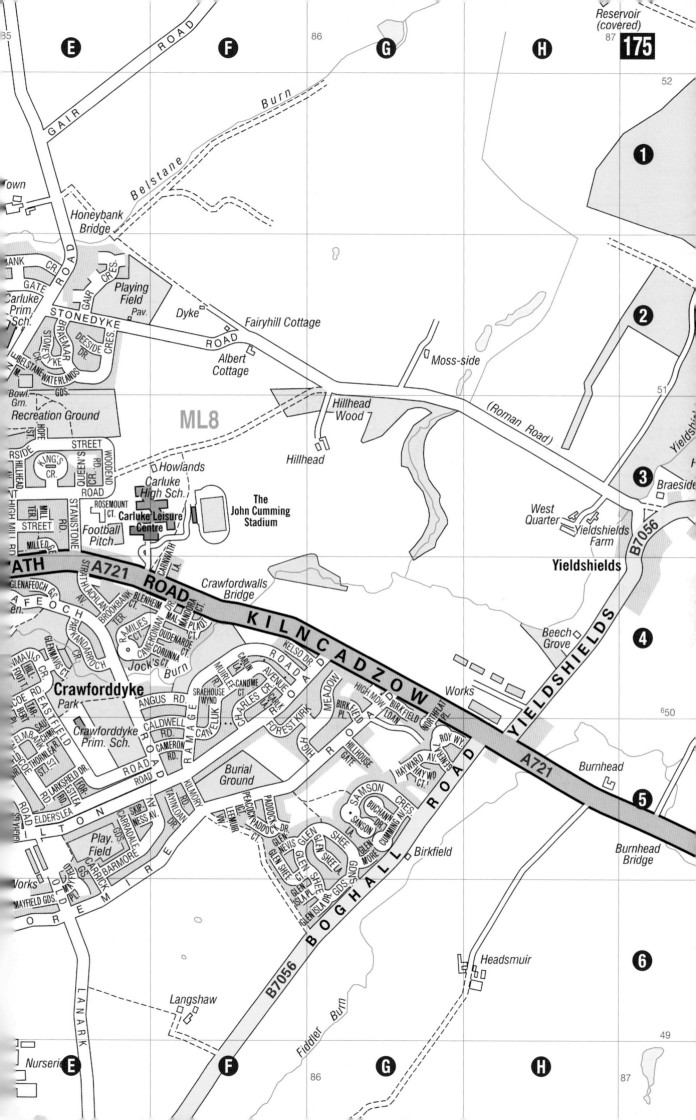

E **F** **G** **H**

35 86 87 52

1

Reservoir
(covered)

Town

GAIR

ROAD

Belstane Burn

Honeybank
Bridge

2

BANK CR.

GATE

Carluke
Prim.
Sch.

BELSTANE

GAIR ROAD

STONEDYKE

STONEDYKE CR.

BRAEMAR

DEESIDE DR.

CRES.

WATERLANDS GDS.

Playing
Field

Pav.

Dyke

Fairyhill Cottage

ROAD

Albert
Cottage

Moss-side

51

Bowl.
Grn.

Recreation Ground

ML8

Hillhead
Wood

(Roman Road)

Yieldshields

3

RSIDE

HILLHEAD

HOPE ST.

KING'S
CR.

STREET

QUEEN'S CR.

WOODEND

N. QUEEN'S RD.

ROAD

STANISTONE RD.

Howlands

Carluke
High Sch.

The
John Cumming
Stadium

West
Quarter

Yieldshields
Farm

Braeside

HIGH MILL RD.

MILL TER.

MILL STREET

MILLED GE

ROSEMOUNT
CT.

Carluke Leisure
Centre

Football
Pitch

CARNWATH LA.

B7056

ATH

A721 **ROAD**

Crawfordwalls
Bridge

KILNCADZOW

Yieldshields

Works

4

GLENAFEOCH GDS.

AFEOCH

en.

STRATHLACHLAN AV.

GLENAFEOCH RD.

GLENMAVIS CR.

BROOKBANK
CT.

BLENHEIM
CT.

PARKANDARROCH CR.

RAMILIES
CT.

CAMERONIAN
CT.

MAL.

MANDORA
CT.

PLAT.

OUDENARDE
CT.

CORUNNA
CT.

Jock's
Burn

KELSO DR.

ROAD A

MUIRIEL
LA.

CANDME
CT.

CARLIN
LA.

CARLIK
CR.

AVENUE

MEADOW

High MDW.

BIRKFIELD

CARLK
LOAN

Birkfield
PL.

NORTHFLAT PL.

Beech
Grove

Burnhead

650

Crawforddyke

MAVIS CR.

HILL FOOT

GLENCOE RD.

ELMBANK ST.

THORNLEA ST.

SAU.

GILBERT ST.

Park

ANGUS RD.

EASTFIELD

RAMAGE ROAD

SRAEHOUSE
WYND

CHARLES ST.

CANELUK

FOREST KIRK

FIRK

HIGH

BIRKFIELD LOAN

ROY WY.

GENERAL RD.

5

Crawforddyke
Prim. Sch.

CALDWELL
RD.

CAMERON
RD.

ROAD

LARKSFIELD DR.

ESK DR.

Burial
Ground

GATE

HILLHOUSE

SAMSON
CRES.

HAYWARD AV.

HAY WD.
CT.

CUMMING AV.

Birkfield

Burnhead
Bridge

ROAD

HIGH

ELDERSLEA

LTON

SKIPNESS AV.

TAYMLOAN

KILMORY DR.

CARRADALE GDS.

BARMORE

PEACOCK CT.

PADDOCK DR.

PADDOCK CT.

LENMUIR VW.

GLEN NEVIS VW.

GLEN SHEE CT.

GLEN SHEE

GLEN SHEE LA.

GLEN MORE GDNS.

BUCHANAN DR.

SANSON LA.

GLEN ISLA DR. GDS.

GLEN ISLA PL.

ROAD

BOGHALL ROAD

6

MAYFIELD GDS.

OLD LANARK ROAD

Play.
Field

CARRICK GDS.

Works

MOOR

Headsmuir

Nurseries

Langshaw

B7056

Fiddler Burn

49

E **F** **G** **H**

35 86 86 87

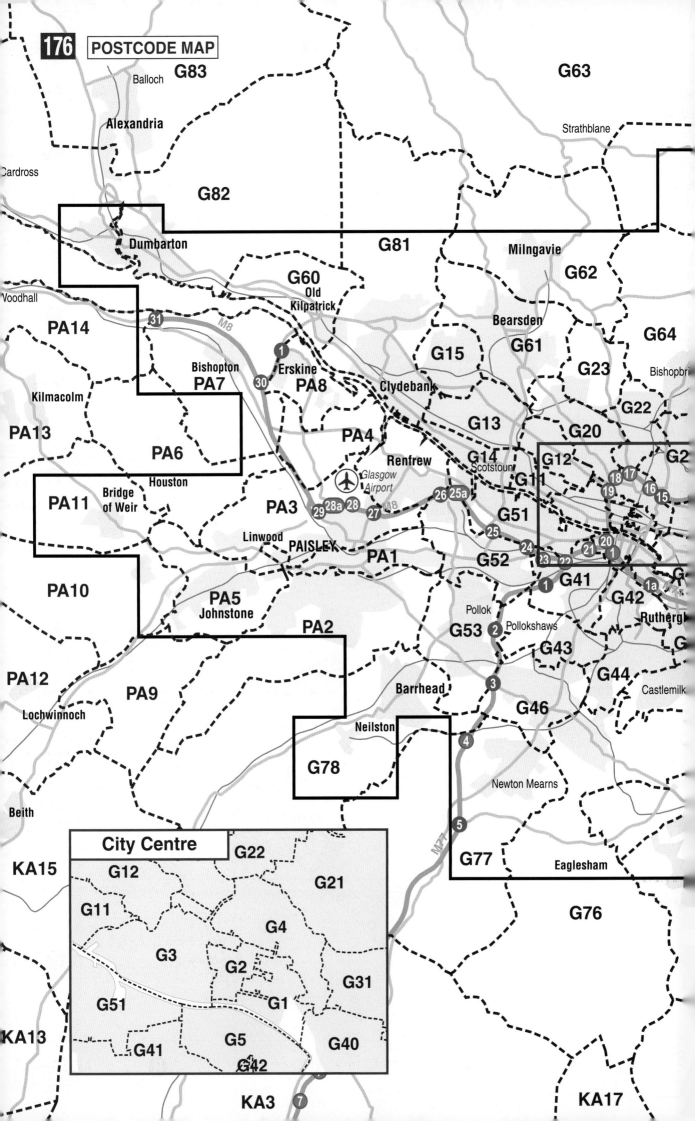

G83
Balloch
Alexandria
Cardross

G82
Dumbarton

G63
Strathblane

G81

Milngavie

G60
Old Kilpatrick

G62

Woodhall

PA14

Bishopton

Erskine

PA7

Kilmacolm

PA13

PA6

Houston

Bridge of Weir

PA11

Linwood

PA3

PAISLEY

PA10

PA5
Johnstone

PA12
Lochwinnoch

PA9

Beith

Bearsden
G61

G23
Bishopbri

G15

G64

Clydebank

G13

G22

PA8

PA4

Renfrew
Glasgow Airport
Scotstoun

G14

G20

G12

G2

G11

18 17
19
16 15

PA1

G51

26 25a

25

24

G52

23 22

21 20
1

G41
1

1a
G

G42
Rutherg

Pollok

G53

Pollokshaws

2

G43

G44
Castlemilk

Barrhead

3

G46

Neilston

4

G78

Newton Mearns

5

G77
Eaglesham

G76

KA15

City Centre

G22

G12

G21

G11

G4

G3

G2

G31

G51

G1

G41

G5

G40

KA13

G42

KA3

7

KA17

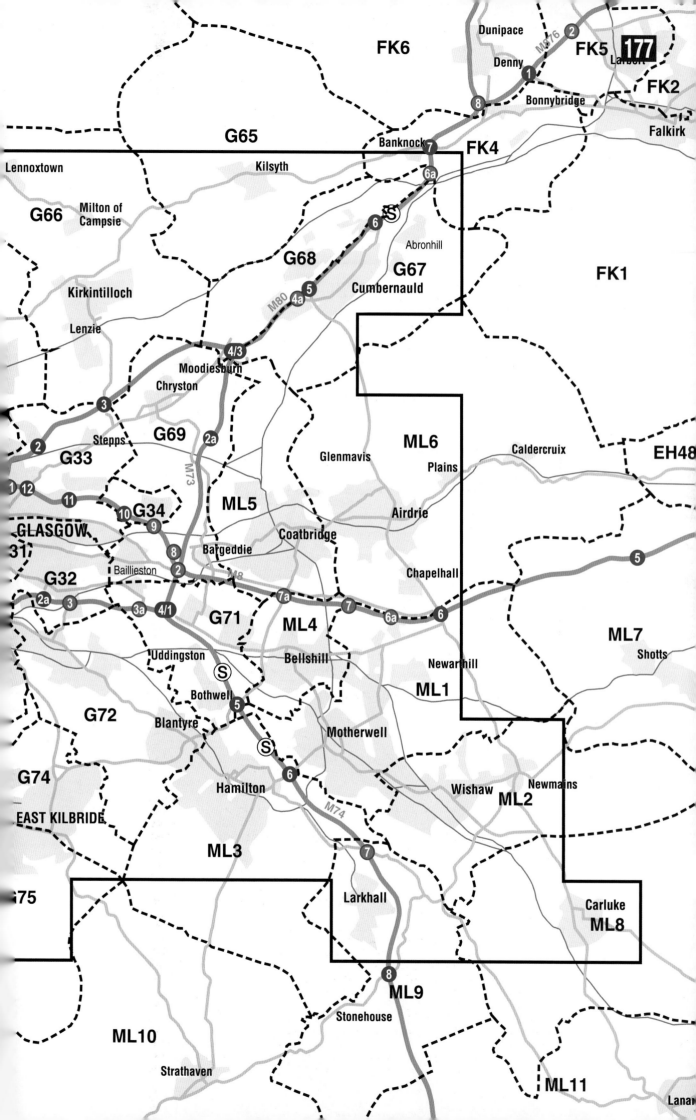

INDEX

Including Streets, Places & Areas, Industrial Estates, Selected Flats & Walkways, Junction Names & Service Areas, Stations and Selected Places of Interest.

HOW TO USE THIS INDEX

1. Each street name is followed by its Postcode District, then by its Locality abbreviation(s) and then by its map reference;
   e.g. **Abbeycraig Rd.** G34: Glas.....2B **92** is in the G34 Postcode District and the Glasgow Locality and is to be found in square 2B on page **92**. The page number is shown in bold type.

2. A strict alphabetical order is followed in which Av., Rd., St., etc. (though abbreviated) are read in full and as part of the street name;
   e.g. **Avon Bri.** appears after **Avonbrae Cres.** but before **Avonbridge Dr.**

3. Streets and a selection of flats and walkways that cannot be shown on the mapping, appear in the index with the thoroughfare to which they are connected shown in brackets; e.g. **Abbey Wlk.** G69: Barg.....6D **92** (*off Abercrombie Cres.*)

4. Addresses that are in more than one part are referred to as not continuous.

5. Places and areas are shown in the index in BLUE TYPE and the map reference is to the actual map square in which the town centre or area is located and not to the place name shown on the map; e.g. AIRDRIE.....4A 96

6. An example of a selected place of interest is **Anatomy Mus. 1B 86**

7. Examples of stations are: Airbles Station (Rail).....4A 96; Bridge Street Station (Subway)..... 6F 87; Kelvinbridge Park & Ride..... 1C 86

8. Junction names and Service Areas are shown in the index in **BOLD CAPITAL TYPE**; e.g. **ARKLESTON INTERCHANGE.....3C 82**

9. Map references for entries that appear on the large scale pages **4–7** are shown first, with small scale map references shown in brackets;
   e.g. **Anderston Quay** G3: GLAS.....6G **5** (5D **86**)

GENERAL ABBREVIATIONS

Arc. : Arcade	**Flds.** : Fields	**Pde.** : Parade
Av. : Avenue	**Gdns.** : Gardens	**Pk.** : Park
Bk. : Back	**Ga.** : Gate	**Pas.** : Passage
Blvd. : Boulevard	**Gt.** : Great	**Pl.** : Place
Bri. : Bridge	**Grn.** : Green	**Quad.** : Quadrant
Bldg. : Building	**Gro.** : Grove	**Res.** : Residential
Bldgs. : Buildings	**Hgts.** : Heights	**Ri.** : Rise
Bus. : Business	**Ho.** : House	**Rd.** : Road
Cvn. : Caravan	**Ho's.** : Houses	**Rdbt.** : Roundabout
Cen. : Centre	**Ind.** : Industrial	**Shop.** : Shopping
Circ. : Circle	**Info.** : Information	**Sth.** : South
Cir. : Circus	**Intl.** : International	**Sq.** : Square
Cl. : Close	**Junc.** : Junction	**Sta.** : Station
Comn. : Common	**La.** : Lane	**St.** : Street
Cnr. : Corner	**Lit.** : Little	**Ter.** : Terrace
Cott. : Cottage	**Lwr.** : Lower	**Twr.** : Tower
Cotts. : Cottages	**Mnr.** : Manor	**Trad.** : Trading
Ct. : Court	**Mans.** : Mansions	**Up.** : Upper
Cres. : Crescent	**Mkt.** : Market	**Va.** : Vale
Cft. : Croft	**Mdw.** : Meadow	**Vw.** : View
Dr. : Drive	**Mdws.** : Meadows	**Vs.** : Villas
E. : East	**M.** : Mews	**Vis.** : Visitors
Ent. : Enterprise	**Mt.** : Mount	**Wlk.** : Walk
Est. : Estate	**Mus.** : Museum	**W.** : West
Fld. : Field	**Nth.** : North	**Yd.** : Yard

LOCALITY ABBREVIATIONS

Airdrie: ML5.....Air	**Bishopbriggs**: G21.....B'rig	**Clydebank**: G81.....Clyd
Airdrie: ML6.....Air	**Bishopbriggs**: G64.....B'rig	**Coatbridge**: G69.....Coat
Allandale: FK4.....Alla	**Bishopton**: PA14.....B'ton	**Coatbridge**: ML5.....Coat
Annathill: ML5.....Anna	**Bishopton**: PA7.....B'ton	**Crossford**: ML8.....Crsfd
Ashgill: ML9.....Ashg	**Blantyre**: G72.....Blan	**Crosslee**: PA6.....C'lee
Auchinloch: G66.....A'loch	**Bothwell**: G71.....Both	**Croy**: G65.....Croy
Baillieston: G69.....Bail	**Bowling**: G60.....Bowl	**Cumbernauld**: G67.....Cumb
Baillieston: G71.....Bail	**Braidwood**: ML8.....Braid	**Cumbernauld**: G68.....Cumb
Baldernock: G62.....Bald	**Bridge of Weir**: PA11.....Bri W	**Dalserf**: ML9.....Dals
Balmore: G62.....Balm	**Brookfield**: PA5.....Brkfld	**Dullatur**: G68.....Dull
Balmore: G64.....Balm	**Busby**: G76.....Busby	**Dumbarton**: G82.....Dumb
Banknock: FK4.....Bank	**Calderbank**: ML6.....C'bnk	**Duntocher**: G81.....Dun
Banton: G65.....Bant	**Cambuslang**: G72.....Camb	**Eaglesham**: G76.....Eag
Bardowie: G62.....Bard	**Campsie Glen**: G66.....Cam G	**Eaglesham**: G77.....Eag
Bargeddie: G69.....Barg	**Carfin**: ML1.....Carf	**East Kilbride**: G74.....E Kil
Bargeddie: G71.....Barg	**Carluke**: ML8.....Carl	**East Kilbride**: G75.....E Kil
Bargeddie: ML5.....Barg	**Carmunnock**: G76.....Crmck	**Elderslie**: PA5.....Eld
Barrhead: G53.....Barr	**Carmyle**: G32.....Carm	**Erskine**: PA8.....Ersk
Barrhead: G78.....Barr	**Castlecary**: G68.....C'cry	**Faifley**: G81.....Faif
Bearsden: G61.....Bear	**Chapelhall**: ML1.....Chap	**Ferniegair**: ML3.....Fern
Bellshill: ML1.....Bell	**Chapelhall**: ML6.....Chap	**Flemington**: G72.....Flem
Bellshill: ML4.....Bell	**Chryston**: G69.....Chry	**Gartcosh**: G33.....G'csh
Bellshill: ML5.....Bell	**Clarkston**: G76.....Clar	**Gartcosh**: G34.....G'csh
Birkenshaw: ML9.....B'haw	**Cleland**: ML1.....Cle	**Gartcosh**: G69.....G'csh

A

Abberlady Way PA7: B'ton..........................6H **41**
Abbey Cl. PA1: Pais 1A **102**
Abbeycraig Rd. G34: Glas..........................2B **92**
Abbeydale Way G73: Ruth..........................4E **125**
Abbey Dr. G14: Glas...................................5E **63**
Abbey Dr. PA5: Eld....................................4A **100**
Abbeyfield Ho. G46: Giff 4H **121**
Abbeyfield Ho. ML5: Coat...........................5A **94**
Abbeygreen St. G34: Glas...........................2C **92**
Abbeyhill St. G32: Glas...............................4G **89**
Abbeylands Rd. G81: Faif............................6E **25**
Abbey Mill Bus. Cen. PA1: Pais...............1B **102**
Abbey Pl. ML6: Air.....................................1C **116**
Abbey Pl. PA1: Pais....................................1B **102**
Abbey Rd. PA5: Eld....................................3H **99**
Abbey Vw. PA1: Pais...................................1B **102**
Abbey Wlk. G69: Barg.................................6D **92**
....(off Abercrombie Cres.)
Abbey Wlk. ML9: Lark 1D **170**
....(off Carrick Pl.)
Abbotsburn Way PA3: Pais.........................3H **81**
Abbotsford G64: B'rig.................................5E **51**
Abbotsford Av. G73: Ruth...........................6D **108**
Abbotsford Av. ML3: Ham 3F **145**
Abbotsford Av. ML9: Lark 4C **170**
Abbotsford Brae G74: E Kil 6G **141**
Abbotsford Ct. G67: Cumb 6H **37**
Abbotsford Cres. ML2: Wis 5A **150**
Abbotsford Cres. ML3: Ham 3F **145**
Abbotsford Cres. PA2: Pais 6B **100**
Abbotsford Dr. G66: Kirkin 5E **33**
Abbotsford Gdns. G77: Newt M...................6B **136**
Abbotsford La. ML3: Ham 3F **145**

Abbotsford La. ML4: Bell............................1B **130**
Abbotsford Pl. G5: Glas 1F **107**
....(not continuous)
Abbotsford Pl. G67: Cumb..........................6H **37**
Abbotsford Pl. ML1: Holy............................2B **132**
....(off Ivy Ter.)
Abbotsford Rd. G61: Bear 1C **46**
Abbotsford Rd. G67: Cumb.........................6H **37**
Abbotsford Rd. G81: Clyd...........................6D **44**
Abbotsford Rd. ML2: Wis 5A **150**
Abbotsford Rd. ML3: Ham 3E **145**
Abbotsford Rd. ML6: Chap 4E **117**
Abbotshall Av. G15: Glas............................4G **45**
Abbotsinch Rd. PA3: Glas A 2A **82**
Abbotsinch Rd. PA4: Renf 6B **60**
Abbots Ter. ML6: Air...................................1C **116**
Abbot St. G41: Glas 4C **106**
Abbot St. PA3: Pais....................................5B **82**
Abbott Cres. G81: Clyd 1F **61**
Abbotts Ct. G68: Dull 4F **15**
Aberconway St. G81: Clyd..........................1E **61**
Abercorn Av. G52: Hill E 3G **83**
Abercorn Cres. ML3: Ham 1B **162**
Abercorn Dr. ML3: Ham 6B **146**
Abercorn Ind. Est. PA3: Pais 5B **82**
Abercorn Pl. G23: Glas...............................6C **48**
Abercorn Rd. G77: Newt M.........................3C **136**
Abercorn St. G81: Faif 6G **25**
Abercorn St. PA3: Pais...............................6A **82**
Abercrombie Cres. G69: Barg 6D **92**
Abercrombie Dr. G61: Bear 5B **26**
Abercrombie Ho. G75: E Kil 2A **156**
Abercrombie Pl. G65: Kils 2F **13**
Abercromby Cres. G74: E Kil 6B **142**
Abercromby Dr. G40: Glas..........................5B **88**

Abercromby Pl. G74: E Kil 6B **142**
Abercromby Sq. G40: Glas 5B **88**
Abercromby St. G40: Glas 6A **88**
....(not continuous)
Aberdalgie Gdns. G34: Glas 3H **91**
Aberdalgie Path G34: Glas 3H **91**
....(off Aberdalgie Rd.)
Aberdalgie Rd. G34: Glas 3H **91**
Aberdeen Rd. ML6: Chap............................1D **116**
Aberdour Ct. G72: Blan...............................1B **160**
Aberdour St. G31: Glas...............................4E **89**
Aberfeldy Av. G72: Blan 6B **144**
Aberfeldy Av. ML6: Plain 6F **75**
Aberfeldy St. G31: Glas 4E **89**
Aberfoyle St. G31: Glas 4E **89**
Aberlady Rd. G51: Glas...............................4E **85**
Aberlady St. ML1: Cle.................................6H **133**
Aberlour Pl. ML1: Carf................................5A **132**
Abernethy Av. G72: Blan 6B **144**
Abernethy Dr. PA3: Lin 6G **79**
Abernethy Rd. ML2: Newm 3E **151**
Abernethy Pk. G74: E Kil 1F **157**
Abernethy Pl. G77: Newt M 5H **137**
Abernethy St. G31: Glas 5E **89**
Aberuthven Dr. G32: Glas...........................2B **110**
Abiegail Pl. G72: Blan 6B **128**
Aboukir St. G51: Glas 3E **85**
Aboyne Dr. PA2: Pais..................................4B **102**
Aboyne St. G51: Glas..................................5F **85**
ABRONHILL 1E **39**
Abronhill Shop. Cen......................................1E **39**
Acacia Dr. G78: Barr 2C **118**
Acacia Dr. PA2: Pais...................................4F **101**
Acacia Pl. PA5: John...................................5G **99**
Acacia Way G72: Camb...............................2E **127**

Acacia Way – Albion St.

Acacia Way G72: Flem ... 2E 127
Academy Ct. ML5: Coat ... 4C 94
Academy Gdns. G61: Bear ... 1F 47
Academy Pk. G51: Glas ... 1A 106
Academy Pk. ML6: Air ... 4A 96
Academy Pl. ML5: Coat ... 4C 94
Academy Rd. G46: Giff ... 5A 122
Academy St. G32: Glas ... 1B 110
Academy St. ML5: Coat ... 4C 94
Academy St. ML6: Air ... 4A 96
Academy St. ML9: Lark ... 2C 170
Academy Ter. ML4: Bell ... 2D 130
Accord Av. PA2: Pais ... 3E 103
Accord Cres. PA2: Pais ... 3E 103
ACCORD HOSPICE ... 3E 103
Accord Pl. PA2: Pais ... 3E 103
Acer Cres. PA2: Pais ... 4F 101
Acer Dr. PA7: B'ton ... 6G 41
Acer Gdns. G71: View ... 5H 113
Acer Gro. ML6: Chap ... 2E 117
Achamore Cres. G15: Glas ... 3G 45
Achamore Dr. G15: Glas ... 3G 45
Achamore Gdns. G15: Glas ... 3G 45
Achamore Rd. G15: Glas ... 3G 45
Achnasheen Rd. ML6: Air ... 5G 97
Achray Dr. PA2: Pais ... 4E 101
Achray Pl. G62: Miln ... 2D 26
Achray Pl. ML5: Coat ... 2G 93
Achray Rd. G67: Cumb ... 6D 36
Acorn Ct. G40: Glas ... 1B 108
Acorn St. G40: Glas ... 1B 108
Acre Dr. G20: Glas ... 6H 47
Acredyke Cres. G21: Glas ... 2E 67
Acredyke Pl. G21: Glas ... 3E 67
Acredyke Rd. G21: Glas ... 2D 66
Acredyke Rd. G73: Ruth ... 5B 108
Acre Rd. G20: Glas ... 6H 47
Acres, The ML9: Lark ... 3D 170
Acre Valley Rd. G64: Torr ... 3D 30
Adam Av. ML6: Air ... 4B 96
Adams Ct. La. G1: Glas ... 6C 6 (5F 87)
Adamslie Cres. G66: Kirkin ... 5A 32
Adamslie Dr. G66: Kirkin ... 5A 32
Adamson St. ML4: Moss ... 2F 131
Adams Pl. G65: Kils ... 3H 13
Adamswell St. G21: Glas ... 6A 66
Adamswell Ter. G69: Mood ... 5E 55
Addie St. ML1: Moth ... 1H 147
Addiewell Pl. ML5: Coat ... 1C 114
Addiewell St. G32: Glas ... 4A 90
Addison Gro. G46: T'bnk ... 3F 121
Addison Pl. G46: T'bnk ... 3F 121
Addison Rd. G12: Glas ... 5B 64
Addison Rd. G46: T'bnk ... 3E 121
Adelaide Ct. G81: Clyd ... 2H 43
Adelaide Rd. G75: E Kil ... 4D 156
Adele St. ML1: Moth ... 5H 147
Adelphi Cen. G5: Glas ... 6H 87
Adelphi St. G5: Glas ... 6G 87
... (not continuous)
Admiral St. G41: Glas ... 6C 86
Admiralty Gdns. G60: Old K ... 2F 43
Admiralty Gro. G60: Old K ... 2F 43
Admiralty Pl. G60: Old K ... 2F 43
Advance Pl. PA11: Bri W ... 3F 77
... (off Main St.)
Advie Pl. G42: Glas ... 5F 107
Affric Av. ML6: Plain ... 6G 75
Affric Dr. PA2: Pais ... 4D 102
Afton Cres. G61: Bear ... 4H 47
Afton Dr. PA4: Renf ... 6G 61
Afton Gdns. G72: Blan ... 3H 143
Afton Gdns. ML5: Coat ... 6F 95
Afton Rd. G67: Cumb ... 2B 38
Afton St. G41: Glas ... 5C 106
Afton St. ML9: Lark ... 3E 171
Afton Vw. G66: Kirkin ... 4F 33
Afton Way PA2: Pais ... 4D 100
Agamemnon St. G81: Clyd ... 5B 44
Agate Ter. ML4: Bell ... 3C 130
... (off Amber Ter.)
Agnew Av. ML5: Coat ... 4E 95
Agnew Av. ML6: Air ... 4F 95
Agnew Gro. ML4: Bell ... 2H 129
Agnew La. G42: Glas ... 4E 107
Aidans Brae G76: Clar ... 2C 138
Aigas Cotts. G13: Glas ... 4F 63
... (off Fern La.)
Aikenhead Rd. G42: Glas ... 2F 107
Aikenhead Rd. G44: Glas ... 1G 123
Aikman Pl. G74: E Kil ... 5B 142
Aikman Rd. ML1: Moth ... 4D 146
Ailean Dr. G32: Glas ... 1E 111
Ailean Gdns. G32: Glas ... 1E 111
Ailish Cres. G33: Glas ... 2A 68
Aillort Pl. G74: E Kil ... 6G 141
Ailort Av. G44: Glas ... 2E 123
Ailort Loan ML2: Newm ... 3D 150
... (off Tiree Cres.)
Ailsa Av. ML1: Moth ... 2D 146
Ailsa Av. ML9: Ashg ... 5H 171
Ailsa Ct. ML3: Ham ... 2B 160
Ailsa Cres. ML1: Moth ... 2D 146
Ailsa Dr. G42: Glas ... 6D 106
Ailsa Dr. G46: Giff ... 1H 137
Ailsa Dr. G66: Kirkin ... 3F 33
Ailsa Dr. G71: Both ... 3E 129
Ailsa Dr. G73: Ruth ... 2B 124
Ailsa Dr. G81: Hard ... 1E 45
Ailsa Dr. PA2: Pais ... 6H 101
Ailsa Pl. ML5: Coat ... 1B 114
Ailsa Rd. G64: B'rig ... 5D 50
Ailsa Rd. ML5: Coat ... 1A 114
Ailsa Rd. PA4: Renf ... 1E 83
Ailsa Twr. G72: Camb ... 4G 125
Ainslie Av. G52: Hill E ... 3A 84
Ainslie Rd. G52: Hill E ... 4A 84
... (not continuous)
Ainslie Rd. G67: Cumb ... 2C 38
Airbles Cres. ML1: Moth ... 4F 147
Airbles Dr. ML1: Moth ... 4F 147
Airbles Farm Rd. ML1: Moth ... 5E 147
Airbles Rd. ML1: Moth ... 4E 147
AIRBLES ROAD CEN. ... 4H 147
Airbles Station (Rail) ... 4G 147
Airbles St. ML1: Moth ... 4G 147
Airbles Twr. ML1: Moth ... 4G 147
Airdale Av. G46: Giff ... 5A 122
AIRDRIE ... 4A 96
Airdrie Bus. Cen. ML6: Air ... 3A 96
Airdrie Golf Course ... 1H 95
Airdriehill Rd. ML6: Air ... 1C 96
Airdriehill St. ML6: Air ... 1C 96
Airdrie Leisure Cen. ... 2C 96
Airdrie Rd. G67: Cumb ... 1D 56
... (Condorrat Ring Rd.)
Airdrie Rd. G67: Cumb ... 6C 36
... (Main Rd.)
Airdrie Rd. G65: Kils ... 2H 13
Airdrie Rd. G67: Mollin ... 3H 55
Airdrie Rd. ML6: Air ... 2F 97
Airdrie Rd. ML6: Plain ... 2F 97
Airdrie Rd. ML8: Carl ... 6H 167
Airdrie Station (Rail) ... 4A 96
Airdrie United ... 5C 96
Aird's La. G1: Glas ... 5G 87
... (off Bridgegate)
Airgold Dr. G15: Glas ... 3H 45
Airgold Pl. G15: Glas ... 3H 45
Airlie Av. G61: Bear ... 6E 27
Airlie Dr. ML4: Bell ... 1C 130
Airlie Gdns. G73: Ruth ... 3F 125
Airlie La. G12: Glas ... 6H 63
Airlie Rd. G69: Bail ... 2G 111
Airlie St. G12: Glas ... 6G 63
Airlour Rd. G43: Glas ... 2C 122
Airth Ct. ML1: Moth ... 6F 131
Airth Dr. G52: Glas ... 2F 105
Airth La. G52: Glas ... 2F 105
Airth Pl. G52: Glas ... 2F 105
... (off Airth La.)
Airthrey Av. G14: Glas ... 6E 63
Airthrey La. G14: Glas ... 5E 63
... (off Airthrey Av.)
Airth Way G68: Cumb ... 5A 36
Airyligg Dr. G76: Eag ... 6C 154
Aitchison Ct. ML6: Air ... 3H 95
Aitchison St. ML6: Air ... 4G 95
Aitkenbar Circ. G82: Dumb ... 2H 19
Aitkenbar Dr. G82: Dumb ... 1H 19
Aitken Cl. ML2: Newm ... 2E 151
Aitkenhead Av. ML5: Coat ... 1F 113
Aitkenhead Rd. G69: Barg ... 2E 113
Aitkenhead Rd. G69: Tann ... 2E 113
Aitkenhead Rd. G71: Barg ... 5E 113
Aitkenhead Rd. G71: Tann ... 5E 113
Aitkenhead Rd. ML6: Chap ... 3D 116
Aitken Rd. ML3: Ham ... 4A 162
Aitken St. G31: Glas ... 4D 88
Aitken St. ML6: Air ... 2A 96
Alasdair Ct. G78: Barr ... 5E 119
Alba Gdns. ML8: Carl ... 2C 174
Alba Ho. G81: Clyd ... 5C 44
Albans Cres. ML1: Moth ... 1D 146
Albany G74: E Kil ... 5C 142
Albany Av. G32: Glas ... 5C 90
Albany Cotts. G13: Glas ... 4F 63
... (off Fern La.)
Albany Dr. G73: Ruth ... 1D 124
Albany Pl. G71: Both ... 5F 129
Albany Quad. G32: Glas ... 5C 90
Albany Rd. ML3: Ham ... 4G 161
Albany St. G40: Glas ... 1C 108
Albany St. ML5: Coat ... 4A 94
Albany Ter. G72: Camb ... 4G 125
Albany Way PA3: Pais ... 3A 82
Albany Wynd ML9: Lark ... 1D 170
... (off Duncan Graham St.)
Alba Way ML3: Ham ... 5G 161
Alba Way ML9: Lark ... 4E 171
Alberta Av. G75: E Kil ... 3D 156
Alberta Av. ML5: Coat ... 3B 94
Alberta Cres. G75: E Kil ... 3E 157
Alberta Pk. G75: E Kil ... 3F 157
Alberta Pl. G75: E Kil ... 3F 157
Albert Av. G42: Glas ... 4D 106
Albert Bri. ... 6G 87
Albert Cres. ML6: Air ... 4B 96
Albert Cross G41: Glas ... 2D 106
Albert Dr. G41: Glas ... 3A 106
Albert Dr. G61: Bear ... 4H 47
Albert Dr. G73: Ruth ... 2D 124
Albert Dr. ML9: Lark ... 3D 170
Albert La. ML3: Ham ... 3E 145
Albert Pl. ML6: Air ... 3B 96
Albert Quad. ML1: Holy ... 2A 132
Albert Rd. G42: Glas ... 4E 107
Albert Rd. G66: Lenz ... 4C 52
Albert Rd. G81: Clyd ... 4B 44
Albert Rd. PA4: Renf ... 6E 61
Albert Rd. PA5: Brkfld ... 6C 78
Albert St. ML1: Moth ... 2H 147
Albert St. ML3: Ham ... 3F 145
Albert St. ML5: Coat ... 4C 94
... (not continuous)
Albert Ter. ML3: Ham ... 3E 145
Albion Ct. ML5: Coat ... 5E 95
... (off Clifton Pl.)
Albion Ga. G1: Glas ... 6F 7 (4H 87)
Albion Ga. PA3: Pais ... 5H 81
Albion Rovers FC ... 5E 95
Albion St. G1: Glas ... 6F 7 (5H 87)
... (not continuous)
Albion St. G69: Bail ... 2F 111
Albion St. ML1: Moth ... 4G 147
Albion St. ML5: Coat ... 4D 94
Albion St. PA3: Pais ... 5A 82

Albion Twr. – Amochrie Rd.

Albion Twr. ML1: Moth 4G **147**
Albion Way G75: E Kil 6H **157**
Albion Works Ind. Est. G13: Glas 2G **61**
Alcaig Rd. G52: Glas 3E **105**
Alcath Rd. ML2: Newm 3F **151**
Alclutha Av. G82: Dumb 4H **19**
Alder Av. G66: Lenz 2B **52**
Alder Av. ML3: Ham 2A **162**
Alder Bank G71: View 4G **113**
Alder Ct. G75: E Kil 6E **157**
Alder Ct. G78: Barr 6E **119**
Alder Cres. G75: E Kil 6E **157**
Alder Gdns. ML1: Moth 6C **148**
Alder Ga. G72: Camb 2E **127**
Alder Ga. G72: Flem 2E **127**
Alder Gro. ML5: Coat 5D **94**
Alder La. ML1: Holy 2C **132**
Alder La. ML1: New S 4A **132**
Alderley Way G68: Cumb 6G **15**
Alderman Pl. G13: Glas 3C **62**
Alderman Rd. G13: Glas 2H **61**
Alder Pl. G43: Glas 2H **121**
Alder Pl. G75: E Kil 6E **157**
Alder Pl. PA5: John 4G **99**
Alder Rd. G43: Glas 2H **121**
Alder Rd. G66: Milt C 6B **10**
Alder Rd. G67: Cumb 3D **38**
Alder Rd. G81: Clyd 2B **44**
Alder Rd. G82: Dumb 3E **19**
Alderside Pl. G71: Both 4F **129**
Alderstocks G75: E Kil 6G **157**
Alderston Pl. ML4: Bell 3A **130**
Alderston Way ML4: Bell 1A **130**
Aldersyde Av. ML2: Wis 5D **148**
Aldersyde Gdns. G71: Udd 6C **112**
Aldersyde Pl. G72: Blan 6A **128**
Aldridge Cres. G68: Cumb 6G **15**
Alexander Av. G65: Twe 1C **34**
Alexander Av. G71: View 1G **129**
Alexander Av. G76: Eag 5D **154**
Alexander Balfour Gdns. ML3: Ham 2H **161**
Alexander Cres. G5: Glas 1G **107**
Alexander Gdns. ML3: Ham 1C **162**
Alexander Gibson Ct. ML1: New S 3H **131**
Alexander Gibson Way ML1: Moth 4F **147**
Alexander Path ML1: Moth 6B **148**
(off Muirhouse Rd.)
Alexander Pl. G66: Kirkin 6H **33**
Alexander St. G81: Clyd 6D **44**
Alexander St. G82: Dumb 3G **19**
Alexander St. ML2: Wis 6F **149**
Alexander St. ML5: Coat 3D **94**
Alexander St. ML6: Air 4G **95**
Alexander Ter. G78: Neil 3C **134**
Alexandra Av. G33: Step 3D **68**
Alexandra Av. G66: Lenz 3C **52**
Alexandra Ct. G31: Glas 3D **88**
Alexandra Dr. PA2: Pais 2F **101**
Alexandra Dr. PA4: Renf 6F **61**
Alexandra Gdns. G66: Lenz 3C **52**
Alexandra Ga. G31: Glas 3C **88**
Alexandra Pde. G31: Glas 3H **7** (3A **88**)
Alexandra Parade Station (Rail) 3D **88**
Alexandra Pk. G66: Lenz 3C **52**
Alexandra Pk. Golf Course **3D 88**
Alexandra Pk. St. G31: Glas 3D **88**
Alexandra Rd. G66: Lenz 3C **52**
Alexandra St. G66: Kirkin 5C **32**
Alexandria Quad. ML1: Holy 2A **132**
Alford Av. G66: Kirkin 5B **32**
Alford Av. G72: Blan 6A **144**
Alford Av. G72: Ham 6A **144**
Alford Pl. PA3: Lin 5E **79**
Alford Quad. ML2: Wis 4H **149**
Alford St. G21: Glas 6H **65**
Alfred La. G12: Glas 6C **64**
(off Cecil St.)
Alfred Ter. G12: Glas 6C **64**
Algie St. G41: Glas 5D **106**
Algoma Pl. G75: E Kil 3D **156**
Alice Av. ML4: Bell 3C **130**
Alice St. PA2: Pais 3A **102**
Alice Ter. G5: Glas 2H **107**
Aline Ct. G78: Barr 3D **118**
Alisa Rd. G81: Clyd 1D **60**
Alison Lea G74: E Kil 6B **142**
Alistair McCoist Complex **5F 157**
Allan Av. ML8: Carl 2C **174**
Allan Av. PA4: Renf 2G **83**
Allan Ct. G75: E Kil 4A **156**
Allan Cres. G82: Dumb 1H **19**
ALLANDALE 1H **17**
Allandale Av. ML1: N'hill 2F **133**
Allandale Cotts. FK4: Alla 1H **17**
Allandale Path G72: Blan 2B **144**
(off Winton Cres.)
Allander Av. G62: Bard 6E **29**
Allander Cres. G69: G'csh 3E **71**
Allander Dr. G64: Torr 5C **30**
Allander Gdns. G64: B'rig 3B **50**
Allander Rd. G61: Bear 4D **46**
Allander Rd. G62: Miln 3G **27**
Allander Sports Complex **6H 27**
Allander St. G22: Glas 5G **65**
Allander Wlk. G67: Cumb 4H **37**
(within The Cumbernauld Shop. Cen.)
Allands Av. PA4: Inch 4G **59**
Allanfauld Rd. G65: Kils 1H **13**
Allanfauld Rd. G67: Cumb 3H **37**
Allan Glen Gdns. G64: B'rig 3C **50**
Allan Gro. ML4: Bell 1D **130**
Allan Pl. G40: Glas 3D **108**
Allan Pl. G75: E Kil 4A **156**
Allan Pl. G82: Dumb 3G **19**
Allanshaw Gdns. ML3: Ham 6F **145**
Allanshaw Gro. ML3: Ham 1F **161**
Allanshaw Ind. Est. ML3: Ham 6G **145**
Allanshaw St. ML3: Ham 6G **145**
Allan St. G40: Glas 3D **108**
Allan St. ML1: Moth 2H **147**
Allan St. ML5: Coat 6H **93**
ALLANTON 2E **163**
Allanton Av. PA1: Pais 1G **103**
Allanton Dr. G52: Glas 6B **84**
Allanton Gro. ML2: Wis 4H **149**
Allanton Lea ML3: Ham 3G **161**
Allanton Pl. ML3: Ham 2A **162**
Allanton Rd. ML2: Newm 2H **151**
Allanton Ter. ML3: Fern 2F **163**
Allan Twr. ML1: Moth 2H **147**
Allbany Cres. ML1: Holy 2H **131**
Allendale G74: E Kil 6E **141**
Allen Glen Pl. G1: Glas 4F **7** (3H **87**)
Allen Way PA4: Renf 2F **83**
Allerdyce Ct. G15: Glas 6G **45**
Allerdyce Dr. G15: Glas 6H **45**
Allerdyce Pl. G15: Glas 6H **45**
Allerdyce Rd. G15: Glas 6G **45**
Allershaw Pl. ML2: Wis 3F **165**
Allershaw Rd. ML2: Wis 3F **165**
Allershaw Twr. ML2: Wis 3F **165**
Allerton Gdns. G69: Bail 1F **111**
Alleysbank Rd. G73: Ruth 4D **108**
Allison Av. PA8: Ersk 5D **42**
Allison Dr. G72: Camb 1A **126**
Allison Pl. G42: Glas 3E **107**
Allison Pl. G77: Newt M 5C **136**
Allison St. G42: Glas 3E **107**
Allnach Pl. G34: Glas 3C **92**
Alloway Av. PA2: Pais 5D **102**
Alloway Ct. G66: Kirkin 3F **33**
Alloway Cres. G73: Ruth 2B **124**
Alloway Cres. PA2: Pais 5D **102**
Alloway Dr. G66: Kirkin 3F **33**
Alloway Dr. G73: Ruth 2B **124**
Alloway Dr. G77: Newt M 5G **137**
Alloway Dr. G81: Clyd 4E **45**
Alloway Dr. PA2: Pais 5D **102**
Alloway Gdns. G66: Kirkin 3G **33**
Alloway Gdns. ML3: Ham 2B **160**
Alloway Gro. G66: Kirkin 3F **33**
Alloway Gro. PA2: Pais 4E **103**
Alloway Quad. G66: Kirkin 4G **33**
Alloway Rd. G43: Glas 1B **122**
Alloway Rd. G74: E Kil 5D **142**
Alloway Rd. ML6: Air 3F **97**
Alloway St. ML9: Lark 3E **171**
Alloway Ter. G66: Kirkin 3F **33**
Alloway Wynd ML1: N'hill 3E **133**
Allwoman Health & Fitness Club **6C 6 (4F 87)**
(Glasgow)
(off Mitchell St.)
Almada Gro. ML3: Ham 5H **145**
Almada La. ML3: Ham 5H **145**
Almada St. ML3: Ham 5G **145**
Alma St. G40: Glas 6C **88**
Almond Av. PA4: Renf 1G **83**
Almond Bank G61: Bear 5C **46**
Almondbank ML6: Plain 6F **75**
Almond Ct. G15: Glas 5B **46**
Almond Cres. PA2: Pais 3D **100**
Almond Dr. FK4: Bank 1E **17**
Almond Dr. G66: Lenz 2B **52**
Almond Dr. G74: E Kil 2B **158**
Almond Dr. PA7: B'ton 5H **41**
Almond Pl. ML1: Holy 3B **132**
Almond Pl. ML5: Coat 2H **93**
Almond Rd. G33: Step 4C **68**
Almond Rd. G61: Bear 5D **46**
Almond Rd. G67: Cumb 6F **17**
Almond St. G33: Glas 2F **89**
Almond Va. G71: Tann 6E **113**
Almond Way ML1: Moth 6G **147**
Almora Dr. G82: Dumb 5H **19**
Alness Cres. G52: Glas 2E **105**
Alness St. ML3: Ham 2H **161**
Alness Ter. ML3: Ham 1H **161**
Alness Way PA7: B'ton 5F **41**
Alnwick Dr. G68: Cumb 6G **15**
Alpha Cen. G81: Clyd 1D **60**
Alpine Gro. G71: Tann 6D **112**
Alpine Path G72: Blan 2C **144**
Alpine Wlk. G72: Blan 2C **144**
Alsatian Av. G81: Clyd 5F **45**
Alsh Ter. ML3: Ham 2E **161**
Alston Av. ML5: Coat 3D **94**
Alston Gdns. G61: Bear 5B **26**
Altnacreag Gdns. G69: Mood 4E **55**
Alton Ct. G66: Kirkin 5E **33**
(off Blackdyke Rd.)
Alton Rd. PA1: Pais 1E **103**
Altpatrick Gdns. PA5: Eld 2H **99**
Altyre St. G32: Glas 2H **109**
Alva Gdns. G52: Glas 3E **105**
Alva Gdns. G61: Bear 6D **26**
Alva Ga. G52: Glas 2E **105**
Alva Pl. G66: Lenz 3E **53**
Alvie Pl. ML6: Air 6D **96**
Alwyn Av. PA6: C'lee 3D **78**
Alwyn Ct. G74: E Kil 6G **141**
Alwyn Dr. G74: E Kil 6F **141**
Alyssum Cres. ML1: Moth 1F **147**
Alyth Cres. G76: Clar 1E **139**
Alyth Gdns. G52: Glas 2E **105**
Alyth Gdns. G76: Clar 1E **139**
Ambassador Way PA4: Renf 2F **83**
Ambercoby Av. PA3: Pais 5A **82**
Amber Gro. ML1: Carf 4C **132**
Amber Ter. ML4: Bell 3C **130**
Ambleside G75: E Kil 5B **156**
Ambleside Ri. ML3: Ham 6G **161**
Ambrose Ct. ML3: Ham 5F **145**
Amethyst Av. ML4: Bell 3C **130**
Amisfield St. G20: Glas 4C **64**
Amochrie Dr. PA2: Pais 5E **101**
Amochrie Glen PA2: Pais 5E **101**
Amochrie Rd. PA2: Pais 4D **100**

A–Z Glasgow 183

Amochrie Way – Ardessie St.

Amochrie Way PA2: Pais 4D **100**
(off Amochrie Rd.)
Amulree Pl. G32: Glas 1A **110**
Amulree St. G32: Glas 6A **90**
Anatomy Mus. 1B **86**
Ancaster Dr. G13: Glas 3F **63**
Ancaster La. G13: Glas 3F **63**
Anchor Av. PA1: Pais 1C **102**
Anchor Bldgs. PA1: Pais 1B **102**
Anchor Cres. PA1: Pais 2C **102**
Anchor Dr. PA1: Pais 1C **102**
Anchor La. G1: Glas 5D **6** (4G **87**)
Anchor Mill PA1: Pais 1B **102**
ANCHOR MILLS 1C **102**
Anchor Wynd PA1: Pais 2C **102**
Ancroft St. G20: Glas 6E **65**
Andersen Ct. G75: E Kil 5G **157**
Anderside G75: E Kil 6G **157**
Anderson Av. G65: Kils 2F **13**
Anderson Ct. G77: Newt M 5C **136**
Anderson Ct. ML2: Wis 6G **149**
Anderson Ct. ML4: Bell 2D **130**
Anderson Cres. G65: Queen 3C **12**
Anderson Dr. G77: Newt M 5C **136**
Anderson Dr. PA4: Renf 5F **61**
Anderson Gdns. G72: Blan 6C **128**
Anderson La. ML6: Air 3A **96**
Anderson Rd. PA7: B'ton 3G **41**
Anderson St. G11: Glas 1H **85**
Anderson St. ML1: Moth 4G **147**
Anderson St. ML3: Ham 4D **144**
Anderson St. ML6: Air 3A **96**
Anderson Twr. ML1: Moth 3G **147**
ANDERSTON 6G **5** (4D **86**)
ANDERSTON CROSS INTERCHANGE 5H **5** (4E **87**)
(M8, Junction 19)
Anderston Quay G3: Glas 6G **5** (5D **86**)
Anderston Station (Rail) 5H **5** (4E **87**)
Andrew Av. G66: Lenz 4D **52**
Andrew Av. PA4: Renf 6G **61**
Andrew Baxter Av. ML9: Shaw 4F **171**
Andrew Dr. G81: Clyd 1E **61**
Andrew Paton Way ML3: Ham 3E **145**
Andrew Pl. ML8: Carl 2C **174**
Andrew Sillars Av. G72: Camb 2B **126**
Andrews St. PA3: Pais 5A **82**
Andrew St. G74: E Kil 2H **157**
Andrew Ure Hall G1: Glas 6G **7** (4H **87**)
(off Parsonage Row)
Anford Gdns. G72: Blan 2C **144**
Anford La. G72: Blan 2C **144**
Anford Pl. G72: Blan 2C **144**
Anford Ter. G72: Blan 3C **144**
Angela Way G71: Udd 1D **128**
Angle Ga. G14: Glas 5D **62**
Angus Av. G52: Glas 2C **104**
Angus Av. G64: B'rig 1E **67**
Angus Av. G74: E Kil 1B **158**
Angus Av. ML1: Moth 1E **147**
Angus Av. ML3: Ham 6C **146**
Angus Av. ML6: Air 6A **96**
Angus Gdns. G71: Tann 5D **112**
Angus Oval G52: Glas 1B **104**
Angus Pl. G52: Glas 1B **104**
Angus Pl. G74: E Kil 1B **158**
Angus Rd. ML8: Carl 4E **175**
Angus St. G21: Glas 5A **66**
Angus St. G81: Clyd 1G **61**
Angus Wlk. G71: View 6F **113**
Anish Pl. G15: Glas 3G **45**
Annan Av. G72: Blan 6B **144**
Annan Av. G75: E Kil 4A **156**
Annan Ct. ML5: Coat 5B **94**
Annan Cres. ML6: Chap 4D **116**
Annandale St. G42: Glas 2F **107**
Annandale Ter. G60: Old K 1G **43**
Annan Dr. G61: Bear 4C **46**
Annan Dr. G73: Ruth 6F **109**
Annan Glade ML1: Moth 6A **148**
Annan Gro. ML1: Moth 6A **148**
Annan Ho. G67: Cumb 4H **37**
(within The Cumbernauld Shop. Cen.)
Annan Pl. PA5: John 5C **98**
Annan St. ML1: Moth 6A **148**
Annan Way G67: Cumb 4H **37**
(within The Cumbernauld Shop. Cen.)
ANNATHILL 5B **56**
Annathill Gdns. ML5: Anna 5B **56**
Annbank Pl. G31: Glas 5B **88**
Annbank St. G31: Glas 5B **88**
Annbank St. ML9: Lark 2B **170**
Ann Ct. ML3: Ham 4E **145**
Anne Av. PA4: Renf 5F **61**
Anne Cres. G66: Lenz 4D **52**
Annerley Ct. ML5: Coat 6A **94**
Annerley Pl. ML5: Coat 6A **94**
Anne's M. ML3: Ham 6B **146**
Annette St. G42: Glas 3E **107**
Annfield Gdns. G72: Blan 6H **127**
Annfield Pl. G31: Glas 4B **88**
Annick Dr. G61: Bear 4C **46**
Annick St. G32: Glas 6B **90**
Annick St. G72: Camb 2D **126**
Anniesdale Av. G33: Step 3D **68**
Annieshill Vw. ML6: Plain 1G **97**
ANNIESLAND 3F **63**
Anniesland Cres. G14: Glas 4A **62**
Anniesland Ind. Est. G13: Glas 1E **63**
Anniesland Rd. G13: Glas 3C **62**
Anniesland Rd. G14: Glas 4A **62**
Anniesland Station (Rail) 3F **63**
Annieston G65: Twe 1D **34**
Anniversary Av. G75: E Kil 4E **157**
Annsfield Rd. ML3: Ham 4G **161**
Ann St. ML3: Ham 4E **145**
Ann St. PA5: John 2G **99**
Ansdell Av. G72: Blan 2A **144**
Anson St. G40: Glas 1B **108**
Anson Way PA4: Renf 2E **83**
Anstruther Ct. ML8: Law 6D **166**
Anstruther St. G32: Glas 6H **89**
Anstruther St. ML8: Law 6D **166**
Antermony Rd. G66: Milt C 5C **10**
Anthony Ct. G81: Clyd 1E **61**
Antigua Way G75: E Kil 2C **156**
Anton Cres. G65: Kils 3A **14**
Antonine G66: Kirkin 3H **33**
Antonine Av. ML1: Moth 1E **147**
Antonine Gdns. G81: Dun 1C **44**
Antonine Ga. FK4: Alla 2G **17**
Antonine Ga. G81: Dun 1B **44**
Antonine Rd. G61: Bear 1B **46**
Antonine Rd. G68: Dull 5E **15**
Antonine Shop. Cen. 4H **37**
Antonine Sports Cen. 1C **44**
Antrim La. ML9: Lark 1D **170**
Anwoth St. G32: Glas 2A **110**
Apartments, The G46: Giff 6H **121**
(off Milverton Rd.)
Apollo Path ML1: Holy 2B **132**
Appian Pl. ML1: Moth 6D **130**
Appin Ct. G66: Kirkin 4H **33**
Appin Cres. G31: Glas 4D **88**
Appin Rd. G31: Glas 4D **88**
Appin Ter. G73: Ruth 3F **125**
Appin Ter. ML3: Ham 5C **144**
Appin Way G71: Both 4E **129**
Appin Way ML5: Coat 1A **114**
Appin Way ML6: Glenm 5H **73**
Appleby Cl. G75: E Kil 5B **156**
Appleby Gro. G69: Barg 5E **93**
Appleby St. G22: Glas 6F **65**
Applecross Dr. PA7: B'ton 5F **41**
Applecross Gdns. G69: Mood 4D **54**
Applecross Quad. ML2: Wis 4H **149**
Applecross Rd. G66: Kirkin 4H **33**
Applecross St. G4: Glas 6F **65**
Appledore Cres. G71: Both 4E **129**
Applegate Dr. G75: E Kil 6B **156**
Apple Way G75: E Kil 5H **157**
Appleyard Ct. ML4: Bell 4B **130**
Apsley La. G11: Glas 1G **85**
Apsley Pl. G5: Glas 6F **87**
Apsley St. G11: Glas 1G **85**
Aqua Av. ML3: Ham 1C **160**
Aqua Ct. ML3: Ham 1C **160**
Aquatec 2G **147**
Aquila Way ML8: Carl 3B **174**
Aquitania Cres. ML9: Lark 6A **164**
Araburn Dr. G75: E Kil 6G **157**
Aranthrue Cres. PA4: Renf 5E **61**
Aranthrue Dr. PA4: Renf 5E **61**
Aray St. G20: Glas 3B **64**
Arbroath Av. G52: Glas 1B **104**
Arbroath Gro. ML3: Ham 1F **161**
Arbuckle Pl. ML6: Plain 6G **75**
Arbuckle Rd. ML6: Plain 6H **75**
Arcadia Pl. G40: Glas 6A **88**
Arcadia St. G40: Glas 6A **88**
(not continuous)
Arcadia St. ML4: Bell 6C **114**
Arcan Cres. G15: Glas 5B **46**
Archerfield Av. G32: Glas 3A **110**
Archerfield Cres. G32: Glas 3A **110**
Archerfield Cres. ML1: N'hse 1C **132**
Archerfield Dr. G32: Glas 3A **110**
Archerfield Gro. G32: Glas 3A **110**
Archerhill Av. G13: Glas 1A **62**
Archerhill Cotts. G13: Glas 1A **62**
Archerhill Cres. G13: Glas 1B **62**
Archerhill Gdns. G13: Glas 1A **62**
Archerhill Rd. G13: Glas 1H **61**
Archerhill Sq. G13: Glas 1H **61**
Archerhill Ter. G13: Glas 1A **62**
(not continuous)
Archerscroft Pl. G72: Blan 3H **143**
Arches, The 6B **6** (4F **87**)
Arches Vw., The G66: Lenz 2F **53**
Archibald Ter. G66: Milt C 5B **10**
Archiebald Pl. ML4: Bell 3F **131**
Arch Way G65: Kils 2H **13**
Ardargie Dr. G32: Carm 5C **110**
Ardargie Gro. G32: Carm 5C **110**
Ardargie Pl. G32: Carm 5C **110**
Ardbeg Av. G64: B'rig 6E **51**
Ardbeg Av. G73: Ruth 4G **125**
Ardbeg Cres. ML6: Air 6A **74**
Ardbeg La. G42: Glas 3E **107**
(off Coplaw St.)
Ardbeg La. G74: T'hall 6G **139**
Ardbeg Rd. ML1: Carf 5A **132**
Ardbeg Rd. ML1: New S 5A **132**
Ardbeg St. G42: Glas 3E **107**
Ardconnel St. G46: T'bnk 3F **121**
ARDEN 3E **121**
Arden Av. G46: T'bnk 5E **121**
Ardenclutha Av. ML3: Ham 5F **145**
Arden Ct. ML3: Ham 2H **161**
Arden Ct. ML6: Air 3F **95**
(off Monkscourt Av.)
Ardencraig Dr. G45: Glas 5B **124**
Ardencraig Gdns. G45: Glas 5C **124**
Ardencraig Pl. G45: Glas 4A **124**
Ardencraig Quad. G45: Glas 5B **124**
Ardencraig Rd. G45: Glas 5A **124**
Ardencraig St. G45: Glas 4C **124**
Ardencraig Ter. G45: Glas 5A **124**
Arden Dr. G46: Giff 5H **121**
Arden Gro. G65: Kils 1G **13**
Ardenlea G71: Tann 6D **112**
Arden Pl. G46: T'bnk 5E **121**
Arden Rd. ML3: Ham 1G **161**
Arden St. ML6: Plain 1G **97**
Arden Ter. ML3: Ham 1G **161**
Ardery St. G11: Glas 1G **85**
Ardessie Pl. G20: Glas 4B **64**
Ardessie St. G23: Glas 6B **48**

Ardfern Rd. – Ascot Ga.

Ardfern Rd. ML6: Air 5F 97
Ardfern St. G32: Glas 2A 110
Ardgay Pl. G32: Glas 1A 110
Ardgay St. G32: Glas 1A 110
Ardgay Way G73: Ruth 4D 124
Ardgoil Dr. G68: Cumb 4B 36
Ardgour Ct. G72: Blan 3D 144
Ardgour Dr. PA3: Lin 6G 79
Ardgour Pde. ML1: Carf 5C 132
Ardgowan Av. PA2: Pais 2B 102
Ardgowan Ct. PA2: Pais 2D 102
Ardgowan Dr. G71: Tann 6D 112
Ardgowan St. PA2: Pais 3B 102
Ardgowan Ter. La. G3: Glas 2C 4 (2B 86)
(off Gray St.)
Ardgryfe Cres. PA6: Hous 1D 78
Ardholm St. G32: Glas 6A 90
Ardhu Pl. G15: Glas 3A 46
Ardlamont Sq. PA3: Lin 6A 80
Ard La. ML2: Newm 3D 150
(off Clunie Pl.)
Ardlaw St. G51: Glas 5F 85
(not continuous)
Ardle Rd. G43: Glas 2C 122
Ard Loan ML1: Holy 2A 132
(off Howden Pl.)
Ardlui Gdns. G62: Miln 2D 26
Ardlui St. G32: Glas 1H 109
Ardmaleish Cres. G45: Glas 5A 124
Ardmaleish Dr. G45: Glas 5H 123
Ardmaleish Rd. G45: Glas 5H 123
Ardmaleish St. G45: Glas 5H 123
Ardmaleish Ter. G45: Glas 5A 124
Ardmay Cres. G44: Glas 6G 107
Ardmillan St. G33: Glas 3H 89
Ardmore Cres. ML6: Air 6A 74
Ardmory Av. G42: Glas 6H 107
Ardmory La. G42: Glas 6A 108
Ardmory Pl. G42: Glas 6A 108
Ardnahoe Av. G42: Glas 5H 107
Ardnahoe Pl. G42: Glas 5H 107
Ardneil Rd. G51: Glas 5F 85
Ardnish St. G51: Glas 4E 85
Ardoch Cres. G82: Dumb 3D 18
Ardoch Gdns. G72: Camb 1H 125
Ardoch Gro. G72: Camb 1H 125
Ardoch Path ML2: Newm 3D 150
(off Tiree Cres.)
Ardochrig G75: E Kil 6H 157
Ardoch Rd. G61: Bear 2H 47
Ardoch St. G22: Glas 5F 65
Ardoch Way G69: Mood 5D 54
(off Arnprior Gdns.)
Ardo Gdns. G51: Glas 6G 85
Ardrain Av. ML1: Moth 1C 164
Ard Rd. PA4: Renf 5D 60
Ardshiel Rd. G51: Glas 4E 85
Ardsloy La. G14: Glas 5A 62
Ardsloy Pl. G14: Glas 5A 62
Ard St. G32: Glas 1A 110
Ardtoe Cres. G33: Step 4E 69
Ardtoe Pl. G33: Step 4E 69
Arduthie Rd. G51: Glas 4E 85
Ardwell Rd. G52: Glas 2E 105
Argosy Dr. G74: E Kil 5H 141
Argosy Way PA4: Renf 2E 83
Argus Av. ML6: Chap 3C 116
Argyle Av. PA3: Glas A 2A 82
Argyle Cres. ML3: Ham 6D 144
Argyle Cres. ML6: Air 1H 115
Argyle Dr. ML3: Ham 5E 145
(not continuous)
Argyle Gdns. G66: Len 4G 9
Argyle St. G2: Glas 6H 5 (4E 87)
Argyle St. G3: Glas 1B 4 (2B 86)
(not continuous)
Argyle St. PA1: Pais 1H 101
Argyle Street Station (Rail) 6D 6 (5G 87)
Argyll Arc. G2: Glas 6C 6 (4G 87)
Argyll Av. G82: Dumb 1C 20
Argyll Av. PA4: Renf 5D 60
Argyll Gdns. ML5: Coat 1A 114
Argyll Gdns. ML9: Lark 2D 170
Argyll Pl. G65: Kils 3A 14
Argyll Pl. G74: E Kil 6C 142
Argyll Pl. G82: Dumb 1C 20
Argyll Pl. ML4: Bell 5B 130
Argyll Rd. G61: Bear 6E 27
Argyll Rd. G81: Clyd 1D 60
Argyll Wynd ML1: New S 5B 132
Arisaig Dr. G52: Glas 2D 104
Arisaig Dr. G61: Bear 4H 47
Arisaig Pl. G52: Glas 2E 105
Arisdale Cres. G77: Newt M 3E 137
Arkaig Av. ML6: Plain 6F 75
Arkaig Pl. G77: Newt M 5H 137
Arkaig St. ML2: Wis 2H 165
Ark La. G31: Glas 4B 88
ARKLESTON 3E 83
Arkleston Ct. PA3: Pais 3D 82
Arkleston Cres. PA3: Pais 4D 82
Arkleston Dr. PA1: Pais 5C 82
ARKLESTON INTERCHANGE 3C 82
Arkleston Rd. PA1: Pais 5D 82
Arkleston Rd. PA3: Pais 4E 83
Arkleston Rd. PA4: Pais 3C 82
Arkleston Rd. PA4: Renf 3C 82
Arkle Ter. G72: Camb 4G 125
Arklet Rd. G51: Glas 5E 85
Arklet Way ML2: Wis 6C 150
Arkwrights Way PA1: Pais 2F 101
Arlington Baths Club 1G 5 (1D 86)
Arlington Pl. G3: Glas 1G 5 (2D 86)
(off Arlington St.)
Arlington St. G3: Glas 1G 5 (2D 86)
Armadale Ct. G31: Glas 3C 88
Armadale Path G31: Glas 3C 88
Armadale Pl. G31: Glas 3C 88
Armadale St. G31: Glas 4C 88
Armadillo 5C 4 (4B 86)
Armine Path ML1: N'hill 3C 132
Armour Av. ML6: Air 4G 95
Armour Ct. G66: Kirkin 4G 33
Armour Ct. G72: Blan 3H 143
Armour Dr. G66: Kirkin 4G 33
Armour Gdns. G66: Kirkin 4G 33
Armour Gro. ML1: Moth 5A 148
Armour Path G31: Glas 5A 88
Armour Pl. G66: Kirkin 4G 33
Armour Pl. ML1: N'hill 3C 132
Armour Pl. PA5: John 2G 99
Armour Sq. PA5: John 2G 99
Armour St. G31: Glas 5A 88
Armour St. PA5: John 2G 99
Armstrong Cres. G71: Tann 5E 113
Armstrong Gro. G75: E Kil 4F 157
Arnbrae Rd. G65: Kils 2F 13
Arngask Rd. G51: Glas 4E 85
Arnhall Pl. G52: Glas 2E 105
Arnhem St. G72: Camb 2D 126
Arnholm Pl. G52: Glas 2E 105
Arnisdale Ct. G34: Glas 3G 91
Arnisdale Ga. G34: Glas 3G 91
Arnisdale Pl. G34: Glas 3G 91
Arnisdale Rd. G34: Glas 3G 91
Arnisdale Vw. G34: Glas 3G 91
Arnisdale Way G73: Ruth 3D 124
Arnish PA8: Ersk 2G 59
Arniston St. G32: Glas 4H 89
Arniston Way PA3: Pais 4C 82
Arnold Av. G64: B'rig 6C 50
Arnol Pl. G33: Glas 4F 91
Arnott Dr. ML5: Coat 1C 114
Arnott Quad. ML1: Moth 6E 131
Arnott Way G72: Camb 1A 126
Arnprior Cres. G45: Glas 4H 123
Arnprior Gdns. G69: Mood 5D 54
Arnprior Quad. G45: Glas 3H 123
Arnprior Rd. G45: Glas 3H 123
Arnprior St. G45: Glas 3H 123
Arnside Av. G46: Giff 4A 122
Arnton Gro. ML6: Chap 5E 117
Arnum Gdns. ML8: Carl 4D 174
Arnum Pl. ML8: Carl 4D 174
Arnwood Dr. G12: Glas 4G 63
Arondale Rd. ML6: Plain 6F 75
Aron Ter. G72: Camb 4H 125
Aros Dr. G52: Glas 2D 104
Aros La. G52: Glas 3D 104
Arran G74: E Kil 2C 158
Arran Av. G82: Dumb 2D 18
Arran Av. ML5: Coat 1F 115
Arran Av. PA3: Glas A 1A 82
(not continuous)
Arran Dr. G46: Giff 5A 122
Arran Dr. G52: Glas 2F 105
Arran Dr. G66: Kirkin 3E 33
Arran Dr. G67: Cumb 5F 37
Arran Dr. ML6: Air 2H 95
Arran Dr. ML6: Glenm 4H 73
Arran Dr. PA2: Pais 6A 102
Arran Dr. PA5: John 4D 98
Arran Gdns. ML3: Ham 2A 162
Arran Gdns. ML8: Carl 5D 174
Arran La. G69: Mood 5E 55
Arran Path ML9: Lark 4E 171
(off Alba Way)
Arran Pl. G81: Clyd 5E 45
Arran Pl. ML5: Coat 1F 115
Arran Pl. PA3: Lin 5G 79
Arran Rd. ML1: Moth 2E 147
Arran Rd. PA4: Renf 1F 83
Arran Ter. G73: Ruth 2B 124
Arran Twr. G72: Camb 4G 125
Arran Vw. G65: Kils 3H 13
Arranview St. ML6: Chap 4E 117
Arran Way G71: Both 5D 128
Arrochar Ct. G23: Glas 1B 64
Arrochar Dr. G23: Glas 6B 48
Arrochar Dr. PA7: B'ton 6G 41
Arrochar Path G23: Glas 6B 48
(off Arrochar Dr.)
Arrochar St. G23: Glas 6B 48
Arrol Pl. G40: Glas 1D 108
Arrol Rd. G40: Glas 1C 108
Arrol St. G52: Hill E 4G 83
Arrol Wynd G72: Camb 1D 126
Arrotshole Ct. G74: E Kil 6D 140
Arrotshole Rd. G74: E Kil 1D 156
Arrowsmith Av. G13: Glas 1D 62
Arthur Av. G78: Barr 6D 118
Arthur Av. ML6: Air 5H 95
Arthur Henderson Av. PA2: Pais 3E 103
ARTHURLIE 6D 118
Arthurlie Av. G78: Barr 5E 119
Arthurlie Dr. G46: Giff 5A 122
Arthurlie Dr. G77: Newt M 6D 136
Arthurlie Gdns. G78: Barr 5E 119
Arthurlie St. G51: Glas 4F 85
Arthurlie St. G78: Barr 5E 119
Arthur Pl. G76: Busby 3C 138
Arthur Rd. PA2: Pais 5A 102
Arthur St. G3: Glas 2B 4 (2B 86)
Arthur St. G76: Busby 3C 138
Arthur St. ML3: Ham 4H 145
Arthur St. PA1: Pais 6G 81
Arthur Wlk. G72: Camb 3G 125
Arundel Dr. G42: Glas 6E 107
Arundel Dr. G64: B'rig 3D 50
Asbury Ct. PA3: Lin 6A 80
(off Melrose Av.)
Ascaig Cres. G52: Glas 3E 105
Ascog Rd. G61: Bear 5F 47
Ascog St. G42: Glas 3E 107
Ascot Av. G12: Glas 3G 63
Ascot Ct. G12: Glas 3G 63
Ascot Ga. G12: Glas 3F 63

Ash Av. G75: E Kil	5E **157**
Ashbank Cres. ML6: Chap	2E **117**
Ashburn Gdns. G62: Miln	4E **27**
Ashburn Loan ML9: Lark	1D **170**
Ashburn Rd. G62: Miln	3E **27**
Ashburton La. G12: Glas	3H **63**
.... (off Winchester Dr.)
Ashburton Pk. G75: E Kil	4C **156**
Ashburton Rd. G12: Glas	3H **63**
Ashby Cres. G13: Glas	6E **47**
Ash Ct. G75: E Kil	5E **157**
Ashcroft G74: E Kil	4D **142**
Ashcroft Av. G66: Len	4G **9**
Ashcroft Dr. G44: Glas	1A **124**
Ashcroft Wlk. G66: Len	4G **9**
Ashdale Dr. G52: Glas	2E **105**
Ashdene St. G22: Glas	2F **65**
Ashen Dr. G66: Milt C	5B **10**
Asher Rd. ML6: Chap	3E **117**
Ashfield G64: B'rig	4C **50**
Ashfield Rd. G62: Miln	4G **27**
Ashfield Rd. G76: Clar	3C **138**
Ashfield Rd. ML8: Law	5D **166**
Ashfield Station (Rail)	4G **65**
Ashfield St. G22: Glas	5G **65**
....(not continuous)
ASHGILL	5H **171**
ASHGILLHEAD	4G **171**
Ashgillhead Rd. ML9: Ashg	4G **171**
Ashgillhead Rd. ML9: Shaw	4G **171**
Ashgill Pl. G22: Glas	3G **65**
Ashgill Rd. G22: Glas	2F **65**
Ash Gro. G64: B'rig	1D **66**
Ash Gro. G66: Lenz	2B **52**
Ash Gro. G71: View	5F **113**
Ash Gro. ML8: Law	5D **166**
Ashgrove G69: Mood	6D **54**
Ashgrove ML5: Coat	1C **114**
Ashgrove ML6: Air	4D **96**
Ashgrove Pl. G40: Glas	3C **108**
Ashgrove Rd. G40: Glas	3C **108**
Ashgrove Rd. ML4: Bell	6D **114**
Ashgrove St. G40: Glas	3C **108**
Ashiestiel Ct. G67: Cumb	6G **37**
Ashiestiel Pl. G67: Cumb	6G **37**
Ashiestiel Rd. G67: Cumb	6G **37**
Ashkirk Dr. G52: Glas	2E **105**
Ashkirk Dr. ML9: Ashg	5H **171**
Ashkirk Pl. ML2: Wis	3A **150**
Ashland Av. ML3: Ham	5H **161**
Ashlar Av. G68: Cumb	6F **15**
Ashlea Dr. G46: Giff	3B **122**
Ashlea Gdns. ML6: Plain	6F **75**
Ashley Dr. G71: Both	2F **129**
Ashley Gro. ML4: Bell	1H **129**
Ashley La. G3: Glas	1G **5** (2D **86**)
.... (off Woodlands Rd.)
Ashley Pk. G71: View	1G **129**
Ashley Pl. G72: Blan	1A **144**
Ashley St. G3: Glas	1G **5** (2D **86**)
Ashmore Cres. G44: Glas	2D **122**
Ashmore Rd. G43: Glas	1D **122**
Ashmore Rd. G44: Glas	2D **122**
Ash Pl. FK4: Bank	1E **17**
Ash Pl. G75: E Kil	5E **157**
Ash Pl. PA5: John	4G **99**
Ash Rd. G67: Cumb	6D **16**
Ash Rd. G69: Bail	2G **111**
Ash Rd. G81: Clyd	2B **44**
Ash Rd. G82: Dumb	3F **19**
Ashton Gdns. G69: G'csh	3E **71**
Ashton Grn. G74: E Kil	1G **157**
Ashton La. G12: Glas	1B **86**
....(Ashton Rd.)
Ashton La. G12: Glas	6B **64**
.... (Gt. George La.)
Ashton La. Nth. G12: Glas	1B **86**
Ashton Rd. G12: Glas	1B **86**
Ashton Rd. G73: Ruth	4C **108**

Ashton St. ML1: Moth	5F **131**
Ashton Vw. G82: Dumb	3B **18**
Ashton Way PA2: Pais	5C **100**
Ashtree Ct. G60: Old K	1F **43**
Ashtree Gro. G77: Newt M	6C **136**
Ashtree Pk. ML2: Wis	6E **149**
Ashtree Rd. G43: Glas	5A **106**
Ashvale Cres. G21: Glas	5A **66**
Ash Wlk. G73: Ruth	4E **125**
Ash Wlk. ML1: Holy	2B **132**
Ashwood ML2: Wis	2E **165**
Ashwood Gdns. G12: Glas	5F **63**
Ashwood Gdns. G13: Glas	5F **63**
Ashworth Ter. ML3: Ham	5E **145**
Ash Wynd G72: Flem	3E **127**
Aspen Dr. G21: Glas	6C **66**
Aspen Ga. ML1: Carf	5D **132**
Aspen Gro. G69: Barg	4F **93**
Aspen Pl. G72: Flem	2E **127**
Aspen Pl. PA5: John	4G **99**
Aspen Way ML3: Ham	1A **162**
Asquith Pl. ML4: Bell	2F **131**
Aster Dr. G45: Glas	4C **124**
Aster Gdns. G53: Glas	4C **120**
Aster Gdns. ML1: Moth	4G **147**
Athelstane Dr. G67: Cumb	6F **37**
Athelstane Rd. G13: Glas	2C **62**
Athena Way G71: Tann	6E **113**
Athole Gdns. G12: Glas	6A **64**
Athole La. G12: Glas	6A **64**
Atholl Av. G52: Hill E	3G **83**
....(not continuous)
Atholl Av. G64: Torr	4D **30**
Atholl Ct. G66: Kirkin	4H **33**
Atholl Ct. G72: Blan	3D **144**
Atholl Ct. ML8: Law	5E **167**
Atholl Cres. PA1: Pais	5G **83**
Atholl Dr. G46: Giff	1A **138**
Atholl Dr. G68: Cumb	5B **36**
Atholl Gdns. G46: T'bnk	5F **121**
Atholl Gdns. G61: Bear	6E **27**
Atholl Gdns. G64: B'rig	4B **50**
Atholl Gdns. G73: Ruth	3G **125**
Atholl La. G69: Mood	5E **55**
Atholl Pl. G46: T'bnk	4F **121**
Atholl Pl. ML5: Coat	2D **114**
Atholl Pl. PA3: Lin	5G **79**
Atholl St. ML3: Ham	3F **145**
Atholl Ter. G46: T'bnk	5F **121**
.... (off Woodlands Pk.)
Atholl Ter. G71: Tann	4D **112**
Atlas Ind. Est. G21: Glas	5B **66**
Atlas Pl. G21: Glas	5B **66**
Atlas Rd. G21: Glas	5A **66**
Atlas Sq. G21: Glas	5B **66**
Atlas St. G81: Clyd	1D **60**
Atlin Dr. ML1: New S	4B **132**
Attercliffe Av. ML2: Wis	1C **164**
Attlee Av. G81: Clyd	6F **45**
Attlee Pl. G81: Clyd	6F **45**
....(off Attlee Av.)
Attlee Rd. G74: T'hall	3H **155**
Attow Rd. G43: Glas	2H **121**
Auburn Dr. G78: Barr	6F **119**
Auchamore Gro. G45: Glas	3A **124**
Auchan Cres. G33: Step	5C **68**
Auchans Rd. PA6: Hous	3F **79**
AUCHENBACK	6F **119**
Auchenbothie Cres. G33: Glas	3G **67**
Auchenbothie Pl. G33: Glas	4F **67**
Auchencrow St. G34: Glas	3B **92**
Auchencruive G62: Miln	5A **28**
Auchendavie Rd. G66: Kirkin	3H **33**
Auchendavie Steading G66: Kirkin	3H **33**
Auchengeich Gdns. G69: Mood	5D **54**
Auchengeich Rd. G69: Mood	3B **54**
Auchengilloch G75: E Kil	6G **157**
Auchenglen Dr. G69: Mood	5D **54**
Auchengreoch Av. PA5: John	5D **98**

Auchengreoch Rd. PA5: John	5D **98**
Auchengreoch Rd. PA9: John	6D **98**
Auchenhowie G62: Miln	5A **28**
Auchenhowie Rd. G62: Bard	5H **27**
Auchenhowie Rd. G62: Miln	5H **27**
Auchenkilns Holdings G68: Cumb	4E **37**
Auchenkilns Pk. G68: Cumb	4E **37**
Auchenkilns Rd. G67: Cumb	1F **57**
Auchenlarie Dr. G73: Ruth	4D **124**
Auchenlodment Rd. PA5: Eld	3G **99**
Auchenlodment Rd. PA5: John	3G **99**
AUCHENREOCH	5H **11**
Auchenreoch Av. G82: Dumb	1H **19**
Auchenstewart Ct. ML2: Wis	6A **150**
AUCHENTIBBER	6G **143**
Auchentibber Rd. G72: Blan	6F **143**
AUCHENTORLIE	2D **102**
Auchentorlie Quad. PA1: Pais	1D **102**
Auchentorlie St. G11: Glas	1F **85**
Auchentoshan Av. G81: Dun	1B **44**
Auchentoshan Est. G81: Clyd	1A **44**
Auchentoshan Ter. G21: Glas	1B **88**
AUCHINAIRN	2C **66**
Auchinairn Gdns. G64: B'rig	1F **67**
Auchinairn Ga. G33: Glas	2F **67**
Auchinairn Rd. G64: B'rig	2B **66**
....(not continuous)
Auchinbee Farm Rd. G68: Cumb	1D **36**
Auchinbee Way G68: Cumb	1D **36**
Auchincampbell Rd. ML3: Ham	6H **145**
AUCHINCLOCH	1C **16**
Auchincloch Dr. FK4: Bank	1F **17**
Auchineden Ct. G61: Bear	6C **26**
Auchingill Path G34: Glas	2B **92**
.... (off Auchingill Pl.)
Auchingill Pl. G34: Glas	2B **92**
Auchingill Rd. G34: Glas	2A **92**
....(not continuous)
Auchingramont Ct. ML3: Ham	6H **145**
Auchingramont Rd. ML3: Ham	5H **145**
Auchinlea Recreation Cen.	2F **91**
Auchinlea Rd. G34: Glas	1F **91**
Auchinlea Way G34: Glas	2F **91**
Auchinleck Av. G33: Glas	3G **67**
Auchinleck Cres. G33: Glas	3G **67**
Auchinleck Dr. G33: Glas	3G **67**
Auchinleck Gdns. G33: Glas	3G **67**
Auchinleck Rd. G33: Glas	2H **67**
Auchinleck Rd. G81: Hard	6D **24**
Auchinleck Ter. G81: Hard	6D **24**
AUCHINLOCH	5D **52**
Auchinloch Rd. G66: Lenz	3D **52**
Auchinloch St. G21: Glas	6B **66**
AUCHINRAITH	3C **144**
Auchinraith Av. ML3: Ham	3F **145**
Auchinraith Rd. G72: Blan	3B **144**
Auchinraith Ter. G72: Blan	3C **144**
AUCHINSTARRY	5H **13**
Auchinstarry Rd. G65: Kils	4A **14**
Auchintibber Ct. G72: Blan	4C **144**
Auchinvole Cres. G65: Kils	3F **13**
Auchmannoch Av. PA1: Pais	6G **83**
Auchnacraig Rd. G81: Faif	6E **25**
Auchnacraig Rd. G81: Hard	6E **25**
Auchter Av. ML2: Newm	4G **151**
Auchter Rd. ML2: Wis	5C **150**
Auckland Pk. G75: E Kil	3C **156**
Auckland Pl. G81: Clyd	3H **43**
Auckland St. G22: Glas	6F **65**
Auckland Wynd G40: Glas	2D **108**
Auld Aisle Vw. G66: Kirkin	6F **33**
Auldbar Rd. G52: Glas	2F **105**
Auldbar Ter. PA2: Pais	3C **102**
Auldburn Pl. G43: Glas	1H **121**
Auldburn Rd. G43: Glas	1H **121**
Auldearn Cl. G21: Glas	2F **67**
Auldearn Rd. G21: Glas	2F **67**
Auldfield Ga. G43: Glas	6H **105**
Auldgirth Rd. G52: Glas	2F **105**

Auldhame St. ML5: Coat..........................3A **94**
AULDHOUSE..4C **168**
Auldhouse Av. G43: Glas.....................1H **121**
Auldhouse Ct. G43: Glas......................1H **121**
Auldhouse Gdns. G43: Glas.................1H **121**
Auldhouse Retail Pk. 6A **106**
Auldhouse Rd. G43: Glas.....................1H **121**
Auldhouse Rd. G75: E Kil.....................6A **168**
Auldhouse Ter. G43: Glas.....................1B **122**
Auldkirk, The G76: Busby.....................4E **139**
Auld Kirk Mus. 4C **32**
Auld Kirk Rd. G72: Camb......................4C **126**
Auldmurroch Dr. G62: Miln....................3D **26**
Auld Rd., The G67: Cumb......................1A **38**
Auld's Brae ML6: Air 3A **96**
Auld St. G81: Clyd 4A **44**
Auldton Ter. ML9: Ashg..........................4H **171**
Auldyards Rd. G69: G'csh......................4E **71**
Aultbea St. G22: Glas..............................1F **65**
Aultmore Dr. ML1: Carf..........................5A **132**
Aultmore Dr. ML1: New S......................5A **132**
Aultmore Gdns. G33: Glas 4F **91**
Aultmore Pk. G33: Glas...........................4F **91**
Aultmore Rd. G33: Glas..........................4F **91**
Aurelia Ct. ML1: Moth.............................2G **147**
....(off Roman Rd.)
Aurora Av. G81: Clyd..............................1D **60**
Aursbridge Cres. G78: Barr....................5F **119**
Aursbridge Dr. G78: Barr.......................5F **119**
Aurs Cres. G78: Barr...............................5F **119**
Aurs Dr. G78: Barr 6F **119**
Aurs Glen G78: Barr................................6E **119**
Aurs Pl. G78: Barr...................................5G **119**
Aurs Rd. G78: Barr 4F **119**
Austen La. G13: Glas...............................4E **63**
Austen Rd. G13: Glas..............................4E **63**
Austine Dr. ML3: Ham 4A **162**
Avenel Rd. G13: Glas..............................6E **47**
Avenue at Mearns Cross Shop. Cen., The
....5D **136**
Avenue End Dr. G33: Glas 1B **90**
Avenue End Ga. G33: Glas 1B **90**
Avenue End Rd. G33: Glas.....................5B **68**
Avenuehead Rd. G69: G'csh..................6D **54**
Avenuehead Rd. G69: Mood...................6D **54**
Avenuepark St. G20: Glas 5C **64**
Avenue St. G40: Glas..............................6C **88**
Avenue St. G73: Ruth..............................4D **108**
Aviemore Gdns. G61: Bear 2H **47**
Aviemore Rd. G52: Glas..........................2E **105**
Avoch St. G34: Glas.................................2H **91**
Avon Av. G61: Bear..................................4H **47**
Avon Av. ML8: Carl 3C **174**
Avonbank Cres. ML3: Ham 3A **162**
Avonbank Rd. G73: Ruth.........................6B **108**
Avonbank Rd. ML9: Lark.........................2A **170**
Avonbrae Cres. ML3: Ham 3A **162**
Avon Bri...1C **162**
Avonbridge Dr. ML3: Ham.......................6B **146**
Avondale Av. G74: E Kil..........................2H **157**
Avondale Dr. PA1: Pais...........................5D **82**
Avondale Gdns. G74: E Kil......................3A **158**
Avondale Gro. G74: E Kil 2A **158**
Avondale Pl. G74: E Kil...........................3A **158**
Avondale St. G33: Glas...........................2A **90**
Avon Dr. G74: E Kil..................................4H **141**
Avon Dr. ML4: Bell...................................3E **131**
Avon Dr. PA3: Lin.....................................5H **79**
Avonhead G75: E Kil................................6G **157**
Avonhead Av. G67: Cumb.......................6E **37**
Avonhead Gdns. G67: Cumb...................6E **37**
Avonhead Pl. G67: Cumb........................6E **37**
Avonhead Rd. G67: Cumb.......................6E **37**
Avon Ho. ML3: Ham 4A **146**
Avon Pl. ML5: Coat..................................2H **93**
Avon Pl. ML9: Lark 6D **170**
Avon Rd. G46: Giff 5H **121**
Avon Rd. G64: B'rig 1C **66**
Avon Rd. ML9: Lark 5C **170**

Avonside Gro. ML3: Ham........................6B **146**
Avonspark Gdns. G21: Glas....................6D **66**
Avonspark Pl. G21: Glas.........................6D **66**
Avonspark St. G21: Glas.........................6C **66**
Avon St. ML1: Moth 4F **147**
Avon St. ML3: Ham 6A **146**
Avon St. ML9: Lark...................................2B **170**
Avon Twr. ML1: Moth................................4G **147**
Avon Wlk. G67: Cumb..............................4H **37**
.................(within The Cumbernauld Shop. Cen.)
Avon Wynd ML2: Newm 3D **150**
Aylmer Rd. G43: Glas..............................1D **122**
Ayr Dr. ML6: Air 6A **96**
Ayr Rd. G46: Giff......................................2G **137**
Ayr Rd. G77: Newt M 1A **152**
Ayr Rd. ML9: Lark....................................6F **171**
Ayr Rd. ML9: Shaw..................................6F **171**
Ayr St. G21: Glas.....................................5B **66**
Ayton Pk. Nth. G74: E Kil........................6B **142**
Ayton Pk. Sth. G74: E Kil........................6B **142**
Aytoun Dr. PA8: Ersk...............................4D **42**
Aytoun Rd. G41: Glas...............................1B **106**
Azalea Gdns. G72: Flem..........................2E **127**

Bardowie Ind. Est. – Bartiebeith Rd.

Bardowie Ind. Est. G22: Glas ... 5G **65**
... *(off Bardowie St.)*
Bardowie Rd. G62: Bard ... 6F **29**
Bardowie St. G22: Glas ... 5F **65**
... (not continuous)
Bardrain Av. PA5: Eld ... 3A **100**
Bardrain Rd. PA2: Pais ... 6G **101**
Bardrill Dr. G64: B'rig ... 6A **50**
Bardykes Rd. G72: Blan ... 1H **143**
Barefield St. ML9: Lark ... 1C **170**
Barfillan Dr. G52: Glas ... 6E **85**
Bargany Ct. G53: Glas ... 4A **104**
Bargany Pl. G53: Glas ... 4A **104**
Bargany Rd. G53: Glas ... 4A **104**
Bargaran Rd. G53: Glas ... 2B **104**
BARGARRAN ... 5D 42
Bargarran Rd. PA8: Ersk ... 5D **42**
Bargarran Sq. PA8: Ersk ... 4D **42**
Bargarron Dr. PA3: Pais ... 4C **82**
BARGEDDIE ... 6D 92
Bargeddie Station (Rail) ... 1E 113
Bargeddie St. G33: Glas ... 1F **89**
Barhill Cotts. G65: Twe ... 1D **34**
... *(off Main St.)*
Bar Hill Fort ... **1F 35**
Barhill La. G65: Twe ... 1D **34**
Bar Hill Pl. G65: Kils ... 3F **13**
Barhill Rd. PA8: Ersk ... 4E **43**
Barhill Way G61: Bear ... 6H **27**
Barholm Cres. PA8: Ersk ... 4E **43**
Barholm Dr. PA8: Ersk ... 4E **43**
Barholm Sq. G33: Glas ... 2D **90**
Barholm St. G33: Glas ... 2D **90**
Baridsland Vw. ML4: Bell ... 1D **130**
Barke Rd. G67: Cumb ... 2A **38**
Barkly Ter. G75: E Kil ... 3E **157**
Barlae Av. G76: Wfoot ... 3C **154**
BARLANARK ... 5E 91
Barlanark Av. G32: Glas ... 4C **90**
Barlanark Cl. G33: Glas ... 5E **91**
Barlanark Cres. G33: Glas ... 4D **90**
Barlanark Dr. G33: Glas ... 4D **90**
Barlanark Pl. G32: Glas ... 5C **90**
Barlanark Pl. G33: Glas ... 4E **91**
Barlanark Rd. G33: Glas ... 4D **90**
Barlandfauld St. G65: Kils ... 3A **14**
Barleybank G66: Kirkin ... 5C **32**
Barleycorn Path ML5: Coat ... 1E **115**
Barlia Dr. G45: Glas ... 4A **124**
Barlia Gdns. G45: Glas ... 4A **124**
Barlia Gro. G45: Glas ... 4A **124**
Barlia Sports Complex ... **4A 124**
Barlia St. G45: Glas ... 4A **124**
Barlia Ter. G45: Glas ... 4A **124**
Barlia Ter. G45: Glas ... 4B **124**
Barlia Way G45: Glas ... 4B **124**
Barloan Ct. G82: Dumb ... 2G **19**
Barloan Cres. G82: Dumb ... 2G **19**
Barloan Pl. G82: Dumb ... 2G **19**
Barloch Av. G62: Miln ... 3G **27**
Barloch Rd. G62: Miln ... 3H **27**
Barloch St. G22: Glas ... 5G **65**
Barlogan Av. G52: Glas ... 6E **85**
Barlogan Quad. G52: Glas ... 6E **85**
Barmore Av. ML8: Carl ... 5E **175**
Barmore Cres. PA7: B'ton ... 5F **41**
Barmore Dr. PA7: B'ton ... 5F **41**
Barmore Wynd PA7: B'ton ... 5G **41**
BARMULLOCH ... 5F 67
Barmulloch Rd. G21: Glas ... 5C **66**
Barnard Gdns. G64: B'rig ... 3C **50**
Barnbeth Rd. G53: Glas ... 3B **104**
BARNCLUITH ... 1C 162
Barncluith Av. ML3: Ham ... 1C **162**
Barncluith Ct. ML3: Ham ... 6B **146**
Barncluith Rd. ML3: Ham ... 6B **146**
Barn Ct. G72: Newt ... 1F **127**
Barn Dr. G72: Newt ... 1F **127**
BARNELLAN ... 4E 29
Barnes Ct. G78: Barr ... 4D **118**
Barness Pl. G33: Glas ... 3A **90**
Barnes St. G78: Barr ... 5D **118**
Barnett Path G72: Blan ... 2B **144**
... *(off Winton Cres.)*
Barnflat Ct. G73: Ruth ... 4D **108**
Barnflat St. G73: Ruth ... 4D **108**
Barn Grn. PA10: Kilba ... 2A **98**
BARNHILL ... 1H 143
Barnhill Ct. G77: Newt M ... 6D **136**
Barnhill Dr. G21: Glas ... 6C **66**
Barnhill Dr. G77: Newt M ... 1D **152**
Barnhill Dr. ML3: Ham ... 1B **160**
Barnhill Rd. G82: Dumb ... 2C **20**
Barnhill Station (Rail) ... 6B 66
Barnkirk Av. G15: Glas ... 4A **46**
Barn La. G72: Newt ... 1F **127**
Barnsford Av. PA4: Inch ... 5F **59**
Barnsford Rd. PA3: Glas A ... 3E **81**
Barnsford Rd. PA4: Inch ... 4E **59**
Barns St. G81: Clyd ... 6E **45**
Barnswood Pl. G71: Both ... 4F **129**
Barnton St. G32: Glas ... 4G **89**
Barnwell Ter. G51: Glas ... 4E **85**
Barochan Cres. PA3: Pais ... 1E **101**
Barochan La. PA5: John ... 6E **79**
Barochan Pl. G53: Glas ... 2B **104**
Barochan Rd. G53: Glas ... 2B **104**
Barochan Rd. ML4: Moss ... 1F **131**
Barochan Rd. PA14: B'ton ... 5B **40**
Barochan Rd. PA5: Brkfld ... 6E **79**
Barochan Rd. PA5: John ... 6E **79**
Barochan Rd. PA6: C'lee ... 2C **78**
Barochan Rd. PA6: Hous ... 2C **78**
Barochan Rd. PA7: B'ton ... 5B **40**
Barochan Way PA3: Pais ... 1E **101**
Baronald Dr. G12: Glas ... 3H **63**
Baronald Ga. G12: Glas ... 3H **63**
Baronald St. G73: Ruth ... 4D **108**
Baron Ct. G74: T'hall ... 6F **139**
Baron Ct. ML3: Ham ... 1C **162**
Barone Dr. G76: Clar ... 1A **138**
Baroness Dr. G74: T'hall ... 5F **139**
Baronhall Dr. G72: Blan ... 1A **144**
Baronhill G67: Cumb ... 6A **16**
Baron Path G69: Barg ... 6D **92**
Baron Rd. PA3: Pais ... 5C **82**
Baronscourt Dr. PA1: Pais ... 1D **100**
Baronscourt Gdns. PA1: Pais ... 1D **100**
Baronscourt Rd. PA1: Pais ... 1D **100**
Barons Ga. G71: Both ... 3C **128**
Baron's Haugh Nature Reserve ... **6F 147**
Barons Rd. ML1: Moth ... 1B **164**
Barons Twr. ML1: Moth ... 6B **148**
Baron St. PA4: Renf ... 1E **83**
Barony Chambers Visitors Cen. ... **4C 32**
... *(off Cowgate)*
Barony Ct. G69: Bail ... 5H **91**
Barony Dr. G66: Lenz ... 1E **53**
Barony Dr. G69: Bail ... 5H **91**
Barony Gdns. G69: Bail ... 6H **91**
Barony Gro. G72: Flem ... 3E **127**
Barony Pl. G68: Cumb ... 4A **36**
Barony Wynd G69: Bail ... 5H **91**
Barra Av. ML2: Wis ... 4C **150**
Barra Av. ML5: Coat ... 1A **114**
Barra Av. PA4: Renf ... 2E **83**
BARRACHNIE ... 1F 111
Barrachnie Av. G69: Bail ... 5G **91**
Barrachnie Ct. G69: Bail ... 5F **91**
Barrachnie Cres. G69: Bail ... 6F **91**
Barrachnie Dr. G69: Bail ... 5G **91**
Barrachnie Gro. G69: Bail ... 5G **91**
Barrachnie Pl. G69: Bail ... 5G **91**
Barrachnie Rd. G69: Bail ... 1F **111**
Barrack St. G4: Glas ... 5A **88**
Barrack St. ML3: Ham ... 5H **145**
Barra Cres. G60: Old K ... 2G **43**
Barra Dr. ML6: Air ... 5E **97**
Barra Gdns. G60: Old K ... 2G **43**
Barrangary Rd. PA7: B'ton ... 6H **41**
Barra Pl. ML5: Coat ... 1A **114**
Barra Rd. G60: Old K ... 2G **43**
Barras, The ... **5A 88**
... *(off Gallowgate)*
Barra St. G20: Glas ... 1A **64**
Barr Av. G78: Neil ... 1E **135**
Barrbridge Rd. G69: Barg ... 1F **113**
Barrbridge Rd. G69: Coat ... 1F **113**
Barrcraig Rd. PA11: Bri W ... 4E **77**
Barr Cres. G81: Hard ... 2D **44**
Barrel Path G53: Glas ... 5D **120**
Barr Farm Rd. G65: Kils ... 4A **14**
Barr Gro. G71: Tann ... 5E **113**
BARRHEAD ... 5E 119
BARRHEAD INTERCHANGE ... 6D **104**
Barrhead Rd. G43: Glas ... 6E **105**
Barrhead Rd. G53: Glas ... 1H **119**
Barrhead Rd. G77: Newt M ... 4A **136**
Barrhead Rd. G78: Barr ... 1F **135**
Barrhead Rd. G78: Neil ... 1F **135**
Barrhead Rd. PA2: Pais ... 2B **102**
Barrhead Sports Cen. ... **4E 119**
Barrhead Station (Rail) ... 4D 118
Barrhill Ct. G66: Kirkin ... 5G **33**
Barrhill Cres. PA10: Kilba ... 3B **98**
Barrhill Rd. G66: Kirkin ... 5G **33**
Barrhill Ter. G65: Twe ... 1E **35**
Barriedale Av. ML3: Ham ... 6F **145**
Barrie Pl. G65: Kils ... 3H **13**
Barrie Quad. G81: Clyd ... 3C **44**
Barrie Rd. G52: Hill E ... 4A **84**
Barrie Rd. G74: E Kil ... 4D **142**
Barrie St. ML1: Moth ... 3G **147**
Barrington Dr. G4: Glas ... 1D **86**
Barrisdale Rd. G20: Glas ... 1B **64**
Barrisdale Rd. ML2: Newm ... 3D **150**
Barrisdale Way G73: Ruth ... 3D **124**
Barrland Ct. G41: Glas ... 2E **107**
Barrland Dr. G46: Giff ... 4A **122**
Barrland St. G41: Glas ... 2E **107**
Barrmill Rd. G43: Glas ... 2G **121**
Barronsfield Grange G77: Newt M ... 6A **138**
BARROW FIELD ... 6D 88
BARROWFIELD ... 1C 114
Barrowfield Dr. G40: Glas ... 6C **88**
Barrowfield Gdns. G40: Glas ... 6D **88**
Barrowfield Ga. G40: Glas ... 1D **108**
Barrowfield Pl. G40: Glas ... 1D **108**
Barrowfield St. G40: Glas ... 6C **88**
Barrowfield St. ML5: Coat ... 1B **114**
Barrpath G65: Kils ... 4B **14**
Barr Pl. G77: Newt M ... 4C **136**
Barr Pl. PA1: Pais ... 1H **101**
Barrs La. ML8: Carl ... 2D **174**
Barr St. G20: Glas ... 6E **65**
Barr St. ML1: Moth ... 1G **147**
Barr Ter. G74: E Kil ... 1G **157**
Barr Way PA1: Pais ... 1A **102**
BARRWOOD ... 3B 14
Barrwood Pl. G71: Tann ... 5E **113**
Barrwood St. G33: Glas ... 1G **89**
Barry Gdns. G72: Blan ... 3A **144**
Barscube Ter. PA2: Pais ... 3C **102**
Barshaw Cl. G52: Glas ... 5G **83**
Barshaw Ct. G52: Glas ... 5H **83**
Barshaw Dr. G52: Glas ... 5H **83**
Barshaw Dr. PA1: Pais ... 5C **82**
Barshaw Ho. PA1: Pais ... 6E **83**
Barshaw Pk. Golf Course ... **6E 83**
Barshaw Pl. PA1: Pais ... 6F **83**
Barshaw Rd. G52: Glas ... 5G **83**
Barskiven Circ. PA1: Pais ... 6D **80**
Barskiven Rd. PA1: Pais ... 1D **100**
Barskiven Rd. PA3: Pais ... 6D **80**
Barterholm Rd. PA2: Pais ... 3A **102**
Bartholomew St. G40: Glas ... 2C **108**
Bartiebeith Rd. G33: Glas ... 4D **90**

Bartie Gdns. – Bellsfield Dr.

Bartie Gdns. ML9: Ashg 4G **171**
Bartonhall Rd. ML2: Wis 2B **166**
Bartonshill Cres. G71: Bail 2B **112**
Bartonshill Dr. G71: Bail 1B **112**
Bartonshill Gdns. G71: Bail 2B **112**
Bartonshill Pl. G71: Bail 1B **112**
Bartonshill Way G71: Bail 2B **112**
Barty's Rd. ML4: Bell 2E **131**
Barwood Dr. PA8: Ersk 4E **43**
Barwood Hill G82: Dumb 1H **19**
Barwood Rd. PA8: Ersk 3E **43**
Basil Gro. G75: E Kil 2D **156**
Bassett Av. G13: Glas 1B **62**
Bassett Cres. G13: Glas 1B **62**
Bathgate St. G31: Glas 5C **88**
Bathgo Av. PA1: Pais 1G **103**
Bath La. G2: Glas 3H **5** (3E **87**)
(not continuous)
Bathlin Cres. G69: Mood 4E **55**
Bath St. G2: Glas 3H **5** (3E **87**)
Batson St. G42: Glas 3F **107**
BATTLEFIELD 6E **107**
Battlefield Av. G42: Glas 6E **107**
Battlefield Cres. G42: Glas 5E **107**
Battlefield Gdns. G42: Glas 5E **107**
Battlefield Rd. G42: Glas 5D **106**
Battle Pl. 5D **106**
Battles Burn Dr. G32: Glas 3A **110**
Battles Burn Ga. G32: Glas 3A **110**
Battles Burn Vw. G32: Glas 3A **110**
Bavelaw St. G33: Glas 1D **90**
Baxter Brae ML1: Cle 1H **149**
Baxter Wynd ML2: Wis 1E **165**
Bayfield Av. G15: Glas 4A **46**
Bayfield Ter. G15: Glas 4A **46**
Bay Willow Ct. G72: Flem 3F **127**
BBC Scotland HQ **6B 4 (4B 86)**
Beacon Pl. G33: Glas 3H **89**
Beaconsfield Rd. G12: Glas 4H **63**
Beard Cres. G69: G'csh 4E **71**
Beardmore Cotts. PA4: Inch 3A **60**
Beardmore Pl. G81: Clyd 4A **44**
Beardmore St. G81: Clyd 4H **43**
Beardmore Way G31: Glas 5D **88**
Beardmore Way G81: Clyd 5H **43**
Bearford Dr. G52: Glas 6B **84**
BEARSDEN 2E **47**
Bearsden Bath House **2F 47**
Bearsden Golf Course **2C 46**
Bearsden Rd. G13: Glas 3F **63**
Bearsden Rd. G61: Bear 2G **63**
Bearsden Shop. Cen. **3G 47**
Bearsden Station (Rail) 3E **47**
Beaton Rd. G41: Glas 3C **106**
Beaton St. ML9: Lark 1B **170**
Beaton Wlk. G72: Flem 4E **127**
Beatrice Dr. ML1: Holy 2H **131**
Beatrice Gdns. PA6: C'lee 3D **78**
BEATSON WEST OF SCOTLAND CANCER CEN. **5G 63**
Beatson Wynd G71: Tann 4E **113**
Beattock St. G31: Glas 6F **89**
Beattock Wynd ML3: Ham 6E **145**
Beatty St. G81: Clyd 4A **44**
Beaufort Av. G43: Glas 1A **122**
Beaufort Dr. G66: Kirkin 5B **32**
Beaufort Gdns. G64: B'rig 6A **50**
Beauly Cres. G77: Newt M 5H **137**
Beauly Cres. ML2: Wis 2H **165**
Beauly Cres. ML6: Air 5E **97**
Beauly Dr. PA2: Pais 4C **100**
Beauly Pl. G20: Glas 3B **64**
Beauly Pl. G64: B'rig 5F **51**
Beauly Pl. G69: Chry 6B **54**
Beauly Pl. G74: E Kil 1F **157**
Beauly Pl. ML1: Holy 2A **132**
Beauly Pl. ML5: Coat 2D **114**
Beauly Rd. G69: Bail 2G **111**
Beaumont Ga. G12: Glas 1A **86**
Beckett Dr. G69: Chry 3H **69**
Beckfield Cres. G33: Glas 2F **67**
Beckfield Dr. G33: Glas 2F **67**
Beckfield Ga. G33: Glas 2F **67**
Beckfield Gro. G33: Glas 2F **67**
Beckfield Pl. G33: Glas 2F **67**
Beckfield Wlk. G33: Glas 2F **67**
Beckford La. ML3: Ham 4H **145**
Beckford St. ML3: Ham 4G **145**
Beckford St. Bus. Cen. ML3: Ham 4G **145**
Bedale Rd. G69: Bail 1F **111**
Bedcow Vw. G66: Kirkin 6F **33**
Bedford Av. G81: Clyd 5F **45**
Bedford La. G5: Glas 6F **87**
Bedford St. G5: Glas 6F **87**
Bedlay Ct. G69: Mood 4E **55**
Bedlay Pl. ML5: Anna 5B **56**
Bedlay Vw. G71: Tann 4F **113**
Bedlay Wlk. G69: Mood 4E **55**
Beech Av. G41: Glas 1H **105**
(not continuous)
Beech Av. G61: Bear 6G **27**
Beech Av. G69: Bail 6G **91**
Beech Av. G72: Camb 1H **125**
Beech Av. G73: Ruth 3E **125**
Beech Av. G77: Newt M 5D **136**
Beech Av. ML1: New S 4B **132**
Beech Av. ML9: Lark 3F **171**
Beech Av. PA11: Bri W 2F **77**
Beech Av. PA2: Pais 4C **102**
Beech Av. PA5: Eld 3A **100**
Beechbank Av. ML6: Air 2H **95**
Beech Cres. G72: Flem 3E **127**
Beech Cres. G77: Newt M 6E **137**
Beech Cres. ML1: N'hse 6D **116**
(not continuous)
Beech Dr. G81: Clyd 2C **44**
Beeches, The G72: Blan 2A **144**
(off Harkins Av.)
Beeches, The G77: Newt M 3F **137**
Beeches, The PA5: Brkfld 5C **78**
Beeches, The PA6: Hous 2D **78**
Beeches Av. G81: Dun 1B **44**
Beeches Rd. G81: Dun 1A **44**
Beeches Ter. G81: Dun 1C **44**
Beechfield Dr. ML8: Carl 5E **175**
Beech Gdns. G69: Bail 6G **91**
Beech Gro. G69: G'csh 4E **71**
Beech Gro. G75: E Kil 5D **156**
Beech Gro. ML2: Wis 2A **150**
Beech Gro. ML8: Law 5D **166**
Beechgrove G69: Mood 5D **54**
Beechgrove Av. G71: View 6G **113**
Beechgrove Quad. ML1: Holy 2A **132**
Beechgrove St. G40: Glas 3D **108**
Beechlands Av. G44: Neth 5C **122**
Beechlands Dr. G76: Clar 3A **138**
Beechmount Rd. G66: Lenz 3C **52**
Beech Pl. G64: B'rig 1D **66**
Beech Rd. G64: B'rig 1D **66**
Beech Rd. G66: Lenz 1C **52**
Beech Rd. ML1: N'hse 6C **116**
Beech Rd. PA5: John 4D **98**
Beech Ter. ML9: Lark 4D **170**
Beechtree Ter. G66: Milt C 6C **10**
Beechwood ML2: Wis 2D **164**
Beechwood ML9: Lark 6A **164**
Beechwood Av. G73: Ruth 1E **125**
Beechwood Av. G76: Clar 3A **138**
Beechwood Av. ML3: Ham 3F **161**
Beechwood Ct. G61: Bear 4F **47**
Beechwood Ct. G67: Cumb 5H **37**
Beechwood Cres. ML2: Wis 1A **166**
Beechwood Dr. G11: Glas 5F **63**
Beechwood Dr. ML5: Coat 6E **95**
Beechwood Dr. PA4: Renf 2D **82**
Beechwood Gdns. G69: Mood 6D **54**
Beechwood Gdns. ML4: Bell 3E **131**
Beechwood Gro. G78: Barr 6E **119**
Beechwood La. G61: Bear 4F **47**
Beechwood Pl. G11: Glas 5F **63**
Beechwood Pl. ML4: Bell 3E **131**
Beechwood Rd. G67: Cumb 4H **37**
Beechworth Dr. ML1: N'hill 5D **132**
Beecraigs Way ML6: Plain 5G **75**
Beecroft Pl. G72: Blan 6C **128**
Beil Dr. G13: Glas 2H **61**
Beith Dr. ML6: Air 1A **116**
Beith Rd. PA10: How 6B **98**
Beith Rd. PA5: How 5D **98**
Beith Rd. PA5: John 5D **98**
Beith St. G11: Glas 2G **85**
Beith Way G72: Blan 1B **160**
Belford Ct. G77: Newt M 1D **152**
Belford Gro. G77: Newt M 1D **152**
Belgowan St. ML4: Bell 6B **114**
Belgrave La. G12: Glas 6C **64**
Belgrave St. ML4: Bell 6B **114**
Belgrave Ter. G12: Glas 6C **64**
Belhaven Ct. G77: Newt M 1D **152**
Belhaven Ho. ML2: Wis 6G **149**
Belhaven Pk. G69: Muirh 2A **70**
Belhaven Pl. G77: Newt M 1D **152**
Belhaven Pl. ML5: Glenb 3A **72**
Belhaven Rd. ML2: Wis 6G **149**
Belhaven Rd. ML3: Ham 6C **144**
Belhaven Ter. G12: Glas 5A **64**
Belhaven Ter. G73: Ruth 1E **125**
Belhaven Ter. ML2: Wis 6G **149**
Belhaven Ter. La. G12: Glas 5A **64**
(off Huntly Rd.)
Belhaven Ter. W. G12: Glas 5A **64**
Belhaven Ter. West La. G12: Glas 5A **64**
BELLAHOUSTON 6F **85**
Bellahouston Dr. G52: Glas 2E **105**
Bellahouston La. G52: Glas 1E **105**
Bellahouston Pk. **1F 105**
Bellairs Pl. G72: Blan 6A **128**
Bellas Pl. ML6: Plain 1G **97**
Bellaville Gro. G69: Chry 1B **70**
Bellcote Pl. G68: Cumb 6F **15**
Bellcraig Ct. G76: Busby 4F **139**
Bell Dr. G72: Blan 5A **144**
Belleisle Av. G71: Udd 6C **112**
Belleisle Ct. G68: Cumb 1G **37**
Belleisle Cres. PA11: Bri W 5E **77**
Belleisle Dr. G68: Cumb 1G **37**
Belleisle Gdns. G68: Cumb 1G **37**
Belleisle Gro. G68: Cumb 1G **37**
Belleisle St. G42: Glas 4F **107**
Bellevue Av. G66: Kirkin 5B **32**
Bellevue Rd. G66: Kirkin 5B **32**
Bellfield Ct. G78: Barr 3D **118**
Bellfield Cres. G78: Barr 3D **118**
Bellfield Dr. ML2: Wis 1A **166**
Bellfield Rd. G66: Kirkin 5B **32**
Bellfield St. G31: Glas 5C **88**
Bellflower Av. G53: Glas 4C **120**
Bellflower Ct. G74: E Kil 6E **141**
Bellflower Gdns. G53: Glas 4C **120**
Bellflower Gro. G74: E Kil 5E **141**
Bellflower Pl. G53: Glas 4C **120**
Bell Grn. E. G75: E Kil 3H **157**
Bell Grn. W. G75: E Kil 3G **157**
Bell Gro. ML8: Law 5F **167**
Bellgrove Station (Rail) 5B **88**
Bellgrove St. G31: Glas 5B **88**
Bellisle Ter. ML3: Ham 4F **161**
Bell Quad. ML1: Carf 5B **132**
Bellrock Cl. G33: Glas 3A **90**
Bellrock Ct. G33: Glas 3B **90**
Bellrock Cres. G33: Glas 3A **90**
Bellrock Path G33: Glas 3B **90**
Bellrock St. G33: Glas 3A **90**
Bellrock Vw. G33: Glas 3A **90**
Bellscroft Av. G73: Ruth 6B **108**
Bellsdyke Rd. ML6: Air 5H **95**
Bellsfield Dr. G72: Blan 3B **144**

Birch Dr. G66: Lenz	2D **52**
Birch Dr. G72: Camb	1B **126**
Birchend Dr. G21: Glas	1D **88**
Birchend Pl. G21: Glas	1D **88**
Birchfield Dr. G14: Glas	5B **62**
Birchfield Rd. ML3: Ham	6F **145**
Birch Gro. G71: View	6F **113**
Birch Gro. G72: Camb	1C **126**
Birchgrove ML9: Lark	6A **164**
Birchgrove PA6: Hous	2D **78**
Birch Knowe G64: B'rig	1D **66**
Birchlea Dr. G46: Giff	3B **122**
Birchmount Ct. ML6: Air	3D **96**
Birch Pl. G72: Blan	1B **144**
Birch Pl. G72: Flem	3F **127**
Birch Pl. PA4: Renf	1D **82**
Birch Quad. ML6: Air	4D **96**
Birch Rd. G67: Cumb	2E **39**
Birch Rd. G81: Clyd	3C **44**
Birch Rd. G82: Dumb	3F **19**
Birch Rd. PA7: B'ton	5G **41**
Birch St. G5: Glas	1H **107**
Birch St. ML1: Holy	2B **132**
Birchtree Rd. PA7: B'ton	6G **41**
Birch Vw. G61: Bear	2G **47**
Birchview Dr. G76: Busby	5D **138**
Birch Way PA4: Renf	1D **82**
Birchwood Av. G32: Glas	1E **111**
Birchwood Courtyards, The ML4: Bell	5A **114**
Birchwood Dr. PA2: Pais	4E **101**
Birchwood Gro. G69: Barg	5E **93**
Birchwood Pl. G32: Glas	1E **111**
Birdsfield Ct. ML3: Ham	3D **144**
Birdsfield Dr. G72: Blan	3C **144**
Birdsfield St. ML3: Ham	3D **144**
BIRDSTON	2C **32**
Birdston Dr. G33: Step	5D **68**
Birdston Rd. G21: Glas	3E **67**
Birdston Rd. G66: Kirkin	5C **10**
Birdston Rd. G66: Milt C	5C **10**
Birgidale Rd. G45: Glas	5H **123**
Birgidale Ter. G45: Glas	5H **123**
Birkbeck Ct. G4: Glas	4G **7** (3H **87**)
Birkdale G74: E Kil	6E **141**
Birkdale Ct. G71: Both	5D **128**
Birkdale Cres. G68: Cumb	5H **15**
Birkdale Wood G68: Cumb	5A **16**
Birkenburn Rd. G67: Cumb	5F **17**
Birken Rd. G66: Lenz	3E **53**
BIRKENSHAW	5D **112**
BIRKENSHAW	6D **170**
Birkenshaw Ind. Est. G71: Tann	4C **112**
Birkenshaw Rd. G69: G'csh	1G **71**
Birkenshaw Rd. ML5: Glenb	1H **71**
Birkenshaw Sports Hall	4D **112**
Birkenshaw St. G31: Glas	4D **88**
Birkenshaw Way PA3: Pais	3A **82**
(off Mosslands Rd.)	
Birkfield Loan ML8: Carl	4G **175**
Birkfield Pl. ML8: Carl	4G **175**
Birkhall Av. G52: Glas	1H **103**
Birkhall Av. PA4: Inch	2H **59**
Birkhall Dr. G61: Bear	5F **47**
Birkhill Av. G64: B'rig	5D **50**
Birkhill Gdns. G64: B'rig	5D **50**
Birkhill Rd. ML3: Ham	4H **161**
Birkmyre Rd. G51: Glas	5F **85**
Birks Ct. ML8: Law	1F **173**
Birkshaw Brae ML2: Wis	3G **165**
Birkshaw Pl. ML2: Wis	3G **165**
Birkshaw Twr. ML2: Wis	3F **165**
Birks Rd. ML8: Carl	1E **173**
Birks Rd. ML9: Lark	6D **170**
Birkwood Ct. ML5: Glenb	3A **72**
Birkwood Pl. G77: Newt M	1D **152**
Birkwood St. G40: Glas	3D **108**
Birmingham Rd. PA4: Renf	2D **82**
Birnam Av. G64: B'rig	5D **50**
Birnam Cres. G61: Bear	2H **47**

Birnam Gdns. G64: B'rig	5D **50**
Birnam Pl. G77: Newt M	5H **137**
Birnam Pl. ML3: Ham	6C **144**
Birnam Rd. G31: Glas	2F **109**
Birness Dr. G43: Glas	5B **106**
Birnie Ct. G21: Glas	5E **67**
BIRNIEHILL	3H **157**
Birniehill Ct. G81: Hard	6C **24**
BIRNIEHILL RDBT.	3A **158**
Birnie Rd. G21: Glas	5E **67**
Birnock Av. PA4: Renf	2G **83**
Birrell Rd. G62: Miln	2F **27**
Birrens Rd. ML1: Moth	1E **147**
Birsay Rd. G22: Glas	2F **65**
BISHOPBRIGGS	6C **50**
Bishopbriggs Golf Course	5B **50**
Bishopbriggs Golf Range	1F **51**
Bishopbriggs Ind. Est. G64: B'rig	2C **66**
Bishopbriggs Station (Rail)	6C **50**
Bishopburn Dr. ML5: Coat	6B **94**
Bishopdale G74: E Kil	6E **141**
Bishop Gdns. G64: B'rig	5A **50**
Bishop Gdns. ML3: Ham	4A **162**
Bishop Loch Ct. G69: G'csh	6B **70**
Bishop Loch Gdns. G69: G'csh	6B **70**
Bishop Loch Local Nature Reserve	1B **92**
Bishopmill Pl. G21: Glas	5E **67**
Bishopmill Rd. G21: Glas	4E **67**
Bishop's Ga. G64: B'rig	6B **50**
Bishops Ga. G74: T'hall	6G **139**
(not continuous)	
Bishopsgate Dr. G21: Glas	2A **66**
Bishopsgate Gdns. G21: Glas	2A **66**
Bishopsgate Pl. G21: Glas	2A **66**
Bishopsgate Rd. G21: Glas	2A **66**
Bishops Pk. G74: T'hall	6F **139**
Bishop St. G3: Glas	5H **5** (4E **87**)
BISHOPTON	3G **41**
Bishopton Station (Rail)	5H **41**
Bisset Ct. PA5: John	4E **99**
(off Tannahill Cres.)	
Bissett Cres. G81: Dun	1A **44**
Blacader Dr. G69: G'csh	1A **92**
Blackadder Pl. G75: E Kil	4H **155**
Blackbog Rd. ML6: Rigg	5H **57**
Blackbraes Av. G74: E Kil	5B **142**
Blackbraes Rd. G74: E Kil	5B **142**
Blackbull Cl. ML8: Carl	3D **174**
Blackburn Cres. G66: Kirkin	5G **33**
Blackburn Cres. G82: Dumb	3C **18**
Blackburn Sq. G78: Barr	6F **119**
Blackburn St. G51: Glas	5B **86**
Blackbyres Ct. G78: Barr	3F **119**
Blackbyres Rd. G78: Barr	1E **119**
(not continuous)	
Blackcraig Av. G15: Glas	4A **46**
Blackcraig Brae G72: Blan	6B **144**
Blackcroft Av. ML6: Gart	6E **97**
Blackcroft Gdns. G32: Glas	1D **110**
Blackcroft Rd. G32: Glas	1D **110**
Blackdyke Rd. G66: Kirkin	5E **33**
Blackfarm Rd. G77: Newt M	5F **137**
Blackfaulds Rd. G73: Ruth	5A **108**
Blackford Cres. PA2: Pais	2C **102**
Blackford Rd. PA2: Pais	3C **102**
Blackfriars Ct. G1: Glas	6F **7** (4H **87**)
(off Blackfriars St.)	
Blackfriars Rd. G1: Glas	6G **7** (4H **87**)
Blackfriars St. G1: Glas	6F **7** (4H **87**)
Black Grouse Gro. ML3: Fern	2F **163**
BLACKHALL	3D **102**
Blackhall Ct. PA2: Pais	2D **102**
Blackhall La. PA1: Pais	2B **102**
Blackhall St. PA1: Pais	2B **102**
BLACKHILL	1F **89**
Blackhill Ct. G23: Glas	6B **48**
Blackhill Cres. G23: Glas	5C **48**
Blackhill Dr. G23: Glas	5C **48**
Blackhill Gdns. G23: Glas	5B **48**

Blackhill Pl. G33: Glas	1F **89**
Blackhill Rd. G23: Glas	5B **48**
Blackhill Vw. ML8: Law	6E **167**
Blackhouse Av. G77: Newt M	5F **137**
Blackhouse Gdns. G77: Newt M	5F **137**
Blackhouse Rd. G77: Newt M	5F **137**
Blackie St. G3: Glas	2B **4** (2B **86**)
Blackland Gro. PA2: Pais	5G **101**
Blacklands Pl. G66: Lenz	3E **53**
Blacklands Rd. G74: E Kil	2F **157**
Blacklaw Dr. G74: E Kil	2B **158**
Blacklaw La. PA3: Pais	6A **82**
Blackmoor Pl. ML1: New S	4A **132**
Blackmoss Dr. ML4: Bell	3B **130**
Blackness St. ML5: Coat	2D **114**
Blacksey Burn Dr. G53: Glas	3H **103**
Blackstone Av. G53: Glas	5C **104**
Blackstone Cres. G53: Glas	4C **104**
Blackstoun Av. PA3: Lin	5H **79**
Blackstoun Oval PA3: Pais	6F **81**
Blackstoun Rd. PA3: Pais	3E **81**
Black St. G4: Glas	2G **7** (2H **87**)
Black St. ML6: Air	2B **96**
Blackswell La. ML3: Ham	6B **146**
Blackthorn Av. G66: Lenz	2A **52**
Blackthorn Gro. G66: Lenz	2B **52**
Blackthorn Rd. G67: Cumb	1D **38**
Blackthorn Rd. G71: View	5G **113**
BLACKTHORN RDBT.	2E **39**
Blackthorn St. G22: Glas	4A **66**
Blackthorn Wynd G72: Flem	3F **127**
BLACKWOOD	4A **36**
Blackwood G75: E Kil	6F **157**
Blackwood Av. G77: Newt M	6F **137**
Blackwood Av. PA3: Lin	6G **79**
Blackwood Rd. G62: Miln	1F **27**
Blackwood Rd. G68: Cumb	4H **35**
BLACKWOOD RDBT.	3A **36**
Blackwoods Cres. G69: Mood	5D **54**
Blackwoods Cres. ML4: Bell	3E **131**
Blackwoods Gdns. ML1: Moth	6E **131**
Blackwood St. G13: Glas	2E **63**
Blackwood St. G78: Barr	5D **118**
Blackwood Ter. PA5: John	5D **98**
BLACKWOOD WEST RDBT.	4H **35**
Bladda La. PA1: Pais	1B **102**
Blades Ct. G69: G'csh	3E **71**
Bladnoch Dr. G15: Glas	5C **46**
Blaeloch Av. G45: Glas	6G **123**
Blaeloch Dr. G45: Glas	6F **123**
Blaeloch Ter. G45: Glas	6F **123**
Blaeshill Rd. G75: E Kil	3A **156**
Blaiklands Cres. ML5: Coat	2C **94**
Blairatholl Av. G11: Glas	6G **63**
Blair Atholl Cres. G77: Newt M	5H **137**
Blair Atholl Dr. ML9: Lark	4E **171**
Blair Atholl Gdns. ML3: Ham	5E **145**
Blairatholl Gdns. G11: Glas	6G **63**
Blair Atholl Ga. G77: Newt M	5H **137**
Blair Atholl Gro. ML3: Ham	5E **145**
Blair Athol Wynd ML1: Carf	5B **132**
Blairbeth Dr. G44: Glas	6F **107**
Blairbeth Golf Course	5C **124**
Blairbeth M. G73: Ruth	2C **124**
Blairbeth Pl. G73: Ruth	2D **124**
(off Blairbeth Rd.)	
Blairbeth Rd. G73: Ruth	2C **124**
Blairbeth Ter. G73: Ruth	2E **125**
Blairbuie Dr. G20: Glas	2A **64**
Blair Ct. G81: Clyd	5D **44**
Blair Cres. G69: Bail	2G **111**
Blairdardie Rd. G13: Glas	6C **46**
Blairdardie Rd. G15: Glas	6B **46**
Blairdenan Av. G69: Mood	4E **55**
Blairdenon Dr. G68: Cumb	2E **37**
Blair Dr. G66: Milt C	6B **10**
Blair Gdns. G64: Torr	4D **30**
Blair Gdns. G77: Newt M	4B **136**
Blairgowrie Rd. G52: Glas	1C **104**

Blairgrove Ct. – Bourtree Cres.

Blairgrove Ct. ML5: Coat 5A **94**
Blairhall Av. G41: Glas 5D **106**
BLAIRHILL 4B **94**
Blairhill Av. G66: Kirkin 1G **53**
Blairhill Pl. ML5: Coat 4A **94**
Blairhill Station (Rail) 3A **94**
Blairhill St. ML5: Coat 4A **94**
Blairholm Dr. ML4: Bell 4D **130**
Blair Ho. G67: Cumb 2A **38**
BLAIRLINN 1H **57**
Blairlinn Ind. Est. G67: Cumb 1H **57**
Blairlinn Rd. G67: Cumb 1H **57**
Blairlogie St. G33: Glas 2B **90**
Blairmore Av. PA1: Pais 6E **83**
Blairpark Av. ML5: Coat 3A **94**
Blair Path ML1: Moth 4H **147**
Blair Rd. ML5: Coat 4A **94**
Blair Rd. PA1: Pais 6G **83**
BLAIRSKAITH 2G **29**
Blairston Av. G71: Both 6E **129**
Blairston Gdns. G71: Both 6F **129**
Blair St. G32: Glas 6H **89**
Blairtum Dr. G73: Ruth 2D **124**
Blairtummock Pl. G33: Glas 3D **90**
Blairtummock Rd. G33: Glas 3C **90**
(not continuous)
Blake Rd. G67: Cumb 3A **38**
Blane Dr. G62: Miln 2H **27**
Blanefield Gdns. G13: Glas 1F **63**
Blane St. ML5: Coat 3C **94**
Blaneview G33: Step 5D **68**
BLANTYRE 2C **144**
Blantyre Ct. PA8: Ersk 4E **43**
Blantyre Cres. G81: Dun 6A **24**
Blantyre Dr. PA7: B'ton 3G **41**
Blantyre Farm Rd. G71: Udd 2A **128**
Blantyre Farm Rd. G72: Blan 6A **128**
BLANTYREFERME 2B **128**
Blantyre Ferme Rd. G71: Udd 2A **128**
Blantyre Gdns. G68: Cumb 4A **36**
Blantyre Ind. Est. G72: Blan 4C **144**
Blantyre Mill Rd. G71: Both 5D **128**
Blantyre Rd. G71: Both 5E **129**
Blantyre Sports Cen. 1C **144**
Blantyre Station (Rail) 1C **144**
Blantyre St. G3: Glas 2B **4** (2B **86**)
Blaven Ct. G69: Bail 1A **112**
Blawarthill St. G14: Glas 4H **61**
Bleachfield G62: Miln 2F **27**
Bleasdale Ct. G81: Clyd 5D **44**
Bleasdale Rd. PA4: Renf 5G **61**
Blenheim Av. G33: Step 3D **68**
Blenheim Av. G75: E Kil 4E **157**
Blenheim Ct. G33: Step 3D **68**
Blenheim Ct. G65: Kils 2H **13**
Blenheim Ct. ML8: Carl 4E **175**
Blenheim Ct. PA1: Pais 6H **81**
BLOCHAIRN INTERCHANGE 3C **88**
Blochairn Pl. G21: Glas 2C **88**
Blochairn Rd. G21: Glas 2C **88**
Bloom Dr. ML5: Coat 1E **115**
Bluebell Dr. G77: Newt M 1D **136**
Bluebell Gdns. G45: Glas 5C **124**
Bluebell Gdns. ML1: Moth 5E **131**
Bluebell Wlk. G67: Cumb 1A **38**
Bluebell Wlk. ML1: New S 4A **132**
Bluebell Way G66: Len 4H **9**
Bluebell Way ML6: Air 1H **95**
Bluebell Way ML8: Carl 5D **174**
Bluebell Wynd ML2: Wis 2F **165**
Blueberry Pl. G68: Cumb 3C **36**
Blueknowes Rd. ML8: Law 6D **166**
Bluevale St. G31: Glas 5C **88**
Blyth Pl. G33: Glas 5D **90**
Blyth Rd. G33: Glas 5E **91**
BLYTHSWOOD 4F **61**
Blythswood Av. PA4: Renf 5F **61**
Blythswood Ct. G2: Glas 5H **5** (4E **87**)
Blythswood Dr. PA3: Pais 5A **82**
Blythswood Ind. Est. PA4: Renf 5D **60**
Blythswood Rd. PA4: Renf 5F **61**
Blythswood Sq. G2: Glas 4A **6** (3E **87**)
Blythswood St. G2: Glas 6A **6** (4E **87**)
Boardwalk, The G75: E Kil 4A **158**
Bobbins Ga. PA1: Pais 2F **101**
Boclair Av. G61: Bear 3F **47**
Boclair Cres. G61: Bear 3G **47**
Boclair Cres. G64: B'rig 5C **50**
Boclair Rd. G61: Bear 3G **47**
Boclair Rd. G62: Miln 1B **48**
Boclair Rd. G64: B'rig 6C **50**
Boclair St. G13: Glas 1E **63**
Bodden Sq. ML1: N'hse 6E **117**
Boden Ind. Est. G40: Glas 1D **108**
Boden Quad. ML1: Moth 5D **130**
Boden St. G40: Glas 1C **108**
Bodmin Gdns. G69: Mood 4D **54**
Bogany Cl. G45: Glas 5A **124**
Bogany Ter. G45: Glas 5A **124**
Bogbain Rd. G34: Glas 3G **91**
Boggknowe G71: Tann 5B **112**
Boghall Dr. PA7: B'ton 6H **41**
Boghall Pl. PA7: B'ton 6H **41**
Boghall Rd. G71: Udd 3G **111**
Boghall St. G33: Glas 2B **90**
BOGHEAD 3A **52**
Boghead Av. G82: Dumb 3H **19**
Boghead Rd. G21: Glas 5C **66**
Boghead Rd. G66: Lenz 3A **52**
Boghead Rd. G82: Dumb 3G **19**
Bogleshole Rd. G72: Camb 6G **109**
Bogmoor Pl. G51: Glas 2C **84**
Bogmoor Rd. G51: Glas 3B **84**
(not continuous)
BOGSIDE 3G **167**
Bogside Rd. G65: Kils 4H **13**
Bogside Rd. ML9: Ashg 5H **171**
Bogside St. G40: Glas 1D **108**
Bogstonhill Rd. PA6: Hous 1B **78**
Bogs Vw. ML4: Bell 4B **130**
Bogton Av. G44: Glas 3D **122**
Bogton Av. La. G44: Glas 3D **122**
Bolerno Av. PA7: B'ton 6H **41**
Bolerno Circ. PA7: B'ton 1A **58**
Bolerno Cres. PA7: B'ton 6H **41**
Bolerno Gdns. PA7: B'ton 6H **41**
Bolerno Pl. PA7: B'ton 6H **41**
Bolerno Wynd PA7: B'ton 6H **41**
Boleyn Rd. G41: Glas 3C **106**
Bolingbroke G74: E Kil 5C **142**
Bolivar Ter. G42: Glas 5G **107**
Bolton Dr. G42: Glas 5F **107**
Bolton Ter. G66: Len 3G **9**
Bon Accord Rd. G76: Busby 3D **138**
Bon Accord Sq. G81: Clyd 1D **60**
Bonar Cres. PA11: Bri W 4G **77**
Bonar La. PA11: Bri W 4G **77**
Bonawe St. G20: Glas 5D **64**
Bond Ct. G43: Glas 6D **104**
Bond Dr. G43: Glas 6D **104**
Bond Pl. G43: Glas 6D **104**
Bonds Dr. ML2: Newm 3F **151**
Bo'ness Rd. ML1: Chap 1B **132**
Bo'ness Rd. ML1: Holy 1B **132**
Bonhill Rd. G82: Dumb 3G **19**
Bonhill St. G22: Glas 6F **65**
BONKLE 3G **151**
Bonkle Gdns. ML2: Newm 4F **151**
Bonkle Rd. ML2: Newm 4E **151**
Bonnaughton Rd. G61: Bear 1B **46**
Bonnyholm Av. G53: Glas 2A **104**
Bonnyrigg Dr. G43: Glas 2G **121**
Bonnyton Dr. G76: Eag 6B **154**
Bonnyton Golf Course 6G **153**
Bonnyton La. ML3: Ham 4F **161**
Bonnyton Moor Rd. G76: Eag 6F **153**
Bontine Av. G82: Dumb 3D **18**
Bonyton Av. G13: Glas 3H **61**
Boon Dr. G15: Glas 5B **46**
Boquhanran Pl. G81: Clyd 4C **44**
(not continuous)
Boquhanran Rd. G81: Clyd 5B **44**
(not continuous)
Borden La. G13: Glas 4E **63**
Borden Rd. G13: Glas 4E **63**
Border Way G66: Kirkin 5E **33**
Boreland Dr. G13: Glas 2A **62**
Boreland Dr. ML3: Ham 1C **160**
Boreland Pl. G13: Glas 3B **62**
Bore Rd. ML6: Air 2B **96**
Borgie Cres. G72: Camb 2A **126**
Borland Cres. G76: Eag 6C **154**
Borland Dr. ML9: Lark 5D **170**
Borland Rd. G61: Bear 4G **47**
Borron St. G4: Glas 6G **65**
Borrowdale G75: E Kil 6B **156**
Borthwick Dr. G75: E Kil 4H **155**
Borthwick Pl. G69: G'csh 5D **70**
Borthwick St. G33: Glas 2B **90**
Bosco Ter. G5: Glas 2H **107**
Bosfield Cnr. G74: E Kil 6H **141**
Bosfield Pl. G74: E Kil 6H **141**
Bosfield Rd. G74: E Kil 6G **141**
Boswell Ct. G42: Glas 6D **106**
Boswell Dr. G72: Blan 2B **144**
Boswell Pk. G74: E Kil 5C **142**
Boswell Sq. G52: Hill E 4H **83**
Bosworth Rd. G74: E Kil 5B **142**
Botanic Cres. G20: Glas 5B **64**
Botanic Cres. La. G20: Glas 5B **64**
Bothlin Ct. G66: Lenz 1F **53**
Bothlin Dr. G33: Step 3D **68**
Bothlyn Av. G66: Kirkin 6E **33**
Bothlyn Cres. G69: G'csh 2D **70**
Bothlyn Rd. G69: Chry 1B **70**
BOTHWELL 5E **129**
Bothwell Bri. G71: Both 1G **145**
Bothwell Castle 4B **128**
Bothwell Castle Golf Course 4D **128**
Bothwellhaugh Quad. ML4: Bell 4B **130**
Bothwellhaugh Rd. G71: Moth 6H **129**
Bothwellhaugh Rd. ML1: Bell 6B **130**
(not continuous)
Bothwellhaugh Rd. ML1: Moth 6B **130**
(not continuous)
Bothwellhaugh Rd. ML4: Bell 5C **130**
Bothwellhaugh Roman Bath House 1B **146**
Bothwell Ho. ML3: Ham 4A **146**
Bothwell La. G12: Glas 1C **86**
(off Glasgow St.)
Bothwell La. G2: Glas 5A **6** (4E **87**)
Bothwell M. G71: Udd 3D **128**
Bothwell Pk. Ind. Est. G71: Udd 2E **129**
Bothwellpark Pl. ML4: Bell 1H **129**
Bothwellpark Rd. G71: Both 5F **129**
(not continuous)
Bothwellpark Rd. G71: View 5F **129**
(not continuous)
Bothwell Pl. ML5: Coat 4B **94**
Bothwell Pl. PA2: Pais 5C **100**
Bothwell Rd. G71: Udd 2D **128**
Bothwell Rd. ML3: Ham 2G **145**
Bothwell Rd. ML8: Carl 1C **174**
BOTHWELL SERVICE AREA 3F **129**
Bothwellshields Rd. ML1: N'hse 4H **117**
Bothwell St. G2: Glas 5A **6** (4E **87**)
Bothwell St. G72: Camb 1G **125**
Bothwell St. ML3: Ham 4G **145**
Bothwick Way PA2: Pais 5C **100**
Boulevard, The G5: Glas 2H **107**
Boundary Rd. G73: Ruth 3A **108**
Bourhill Ct. ML2: Wis 1D **164**
Bourne Ct. PA4: Inch 2H **59**
Bourne Cres. PA4: Inch 2H **59**
Bourne St. ML3: Ham 6B **146**
Bourock Sq. G78: Barr 6F **119**
Bourtree Cres. ML8: Law 6E **167**

A–Z Glasgow 193

Bourtree Rd. ML3: Ham	1C **160**	
Bouverie St. G14: Glas	3G **61**	
Bouverie St. G73: Ruth	6B **108**	
Bowden Dr. G52: Glas	5B **84**	
Bowden Gro. ML2: Wis	3B **150**	
Bowden Pk. G75: E Kil	3E **157**	
Bower St. G12: Glas	6C **64**	
BOWERWALLS	3G **119**	
Bowerwalls Pl. G78: Barr	3G **119**	
Bowes Cres. G69: Bail	1F **111**	
Bowfield Av. G52: Glas	5H **83**	
Bowfield Cres. G52: Glas	5H **83**	
Bowfield Dr. G52: Glas	5H **83**	
Bowfield Path G52: Glas	5H **83**	
Bowfield Pl. G52: Glas	5H **83**	
Bowhill Rd. ML6: Chap	4E **117**	
Bowhousebrae Rd. ML6: Gart	1E **117**	
Bowhouse Dr. G45: Glas	2C **124**	
Bowhouse Gdns. G45: Glas	2C **124**	
Bowhouse Gro. G45: Glas	3C **124**	
Bowhouse Pl. G45: Glas	3C **124**	
Bowhouse Rd. ML6: Gart	6E **97**	
Bowie St. G82: Dumb	4E **19**	
BOWLING	5B **22**	
Bowling Grn. Gro. G72: Flem	3F **127**	
Bowling Grn. La. G14: Glas	6D **62**	
(off Westland Dr.)		
Bowling Grn. Rd. G14: Glas	6D **62**	
Bowling Grn. Rd. G32: Glas	1D **110**	
Bowling Grn. Rd. G44: Glas	2E **123**	
Bowling Grn. Rd. G69: Chry	1B **70**	
Bowling Grn. St. ML4: Bell	2D **130**	
Bowling Grn. Vw. G72: Flem	3F **127**	
Bowling Station (Rail)	5A **22**	
Bowling St. ML5: Coat	4B **94**	
Bowlplex	5H **61**	
(Renfrew)		
Bowmanflat ML9: Lark	2C **170**	
Bowman St. G42: Glas	3E **107**	
Bowmont Gdns. G12: Glas	6A **64**	
Bowmont Hill G64: B'rig	3C **50**	
Bowmont Pl. G72: Camb	2D **126**	
Bowmont Pl. G75: E Kil	4A **156**	
Bowmont Ter. G12: Glas	6A **64**	
Bowmore Cres. G74: T'hall	6G **139**	
Bowmore Gdns. G71: Tann	5C **112**	
Bowmore Gdns. G73: Ruth	4G **125**	
Bowmore Pl. ML6: Rigg	6B **74**	
Bowmore Rd. G52: Glas	6E **85**	
Bowyer Vennel ML4: Bell	1B **130**	
Boyd Dr. ML1: Moth	2D **146**	
Boydstone Path G43: Glas	1E **121**	
Boydstone Pl. G46: T'bnk	2G **121**	
Boydstone Rd. G43: Glas	1E **121**	
Boydstone Rd. G43: T'bnk	1E **121**	
Boydstone Rd. G46: T'bnk	2E **121**	
Boydstone Rd. G53: Glas	1E **121**	
Boyd St. G42: Glas	4F **107**	
Boylestone Rd. G78: Barr	3C **118**	
Boyle St. G81: Clyd	1F **61**	
Boyndie St. G34: Glas	3H **91**	
Brabazon Ct. G66: Kirkin	6F **33**	
Brabloch Cres. PA3: Pais	5B **82**	
Brabloch Pk. PA3: Pais	5B **82**	
Bracadale Dr. G69: Bail	1B **112**	
Bracadale Gdns. G69: Bail	1B **112**	
Bracadale Gro. G69: Bail	1A **112**	
Bracadale Rd. G69: Bail	1A **112**	
Brackenbrae Av. G64: B'rig	5A **50**	
Brackenbrae Rd. G64: B'rig	6B **50**	
Brackendene PA6: Hous	2D **78**	
Brackenhill Cres. ML3: Ham	4E **161**	
Brackenhill Dr. ML3: Ham	4F **161**	
Brackenhill Rd. ML8: Law	5E **167**	
Brackenhirst Gdns. ML6: Glenm	3F **73**	
Brackenhirst Rd. ML6: Glenm	3F **73**	
Brackenhirst Rd. ML6: Rigg	3F **73**	
Brackenhurst St. G82: Dumb	1H **19**	
Bracken Pl. PA11: Bri W	3G **77**	

Brackenrig Cres. G76: Wfoot	2C **154**	
Brackenrig Rd. G46: T'bnk	5E **121**	
Bracken St. G22: Glas	3F **65**	
Bracken St. ML1: New S	4A **132**	
Bracken Ter. G71: Both	4E **129**	
Bracken Way ML9: Lark	4E **171**	
(off Morris St.)		
Brackla Av. G13: Glas	1G **61**	
Brackla Av. G81: Clyd	1G **61**	
Braco Av. ML6: Chap	4D **116**	
Bradan Av. G13: Glas	2G **61**	
Bradan Av. G81: Clyd	2G **61**	
Bradda Av. G73: Ruth	3E **125**	
Bradfield Av. G12: Glas	4A **64**	
Bradgate Ct. G68: Cumb	6H **15**	
Bradley Ct. G33: Step	4F **69**	
Bradshaw Cres. ML3: Ham	6C **144**	
Brady Cres. G69: Mood	4E **55**	
BRAEDALE	3D **146**	
Braedale Av. ML1: Moth	3D **146**	
Braedale Av. ML6: Air	4B **96**	
Braedale Cres. ML2: Newm	4F **151**	
Braedale Pl. ML2: Newm	4G **151**	
Braeface Rd. G67: Cumb	3G **37**	
Braefield Dr. G46: T'bnk	4G **121**	
Braefoot Av. G62: Miln	5G **27**	
Braefoot Ct. ML8: Law	6D **166**	
Braefoot Cres. ML8: Law	1F **173**	
Braefoot Cres. PA2: Pais	6B **102**	
Braefoot La. G71: Udd	2E **129**	
Brae Ga. G33: Glas	2H **67**	
Brae Gro. G33: Glas	3H **67**	
Braehead G72: Blan	3B **144**	
BRAEHEAD	6H **139**	
Braehead Arena	6A **62**	
Braehead Arena Ice Rinks	6A **62**	
Braehead Av. G62: Miln	4F **27**	
Braehead Av. G78: Neil	2D **134**	
Braehead Av. G81: Dun	6C **24**	
Braehead Av. ML5: Coat	2H **113**	
Braehead Av. ML9: Lark	3A **170**	
Braehead Cres. G81: Dun	6C **24**	
Braehead Dr. ML4: Bell	3B **130**	
Braehead Ind. Est. PA4: Renf	6H **61**	
Braehead Loan ML8: Carl	5F **175**	
(off Charles Cres.)		
Braehead Pl. ML4: Bell	3B **130**	
Braehead Quad. G78: Neil	2D **134**	
Braehead Quad. ML1: N'hill	3D **132**	
Braehead Rd. G67: Cumb	2B **38**	
Braehead Rd. G74: T'hall	6G **139**	
Braehead Rd. G81: Dun	6C **24**	
Braehead Shop. Cen.	6A **62**	
Braehead St. G5: Glas	2H **107**	
Braehead St. G66: Kirkin	4C **32**	
Braemar Av. G81: Clyd	3B **44**	
Braemar Ct. G44: Glas	3C **122**	
Braemar Cres. G61: Bear	5F **47**	
Braemar Cres. ML8: Carl	2E **175**	
Braemar Cres. PA2: Pais	4B **102**	
Braemar Dr. PA5: Eld	4H **99**	
Braemar Rd. G73: Ruth	4G **125**	
Braemar Rd. PA4: Inch	2H **59**	
Braemar St. G42: Glas	6D **106**	
Braemar St. ML3: Ham	3F **145**	
Braemar Vw. G81: Clyd	2B **44**	
Braemore Gdns. G22: Glas	5H **65**	
Braemount Av. PA2: Pais	6G **101**	
Braes Av. G81: Clyd	6F **45**	
Braesburn Ct. G67: Cumb	5F **17**	
Braesburn Pl. G67: Cumb	5F **17**	
Braesburn Rd. G67: Cumb	5F **17**	
Braeside Av. G62: Miln	5G **27**	
Braeside Av. G69: Mood	5D **54**	
Braeside Av. G73: Ruth	6E **109**	
Braeside Cres. G69: Barg	6D **92**	
Braeside Cres. G78: Barr	6G **119**	
Braeside Dr. G78: Barr	6F **119**	
Braeside Dr. G82: Dumb	2H **19**	

Braeside Gdns. ML3: Ham	3A **162**	
Braeside La. ML9: Lark	1D **170**	
(off Carrick Pl.)		
Braeside Pl. G72: Camb	3B **126**	
Braeside Rd. ML1: N'hill	3D **132**	
Braeside St. G20: Glas	5D **64**	
Braeside Way ML9: Lark	4D **170**	
(off Beech Ter.)		
Braes o' Yetts G66: Kirkin	5G **33**	
Braes O Yetts Dr. G66: Kirkin	5A **34**	
Braes Shop. Cen., The	4A **124**	
Braeval Way G33: Step	3E **69**	
Braeview Av. PA2: Pais	6F **101**	
Braeview Dr. PA2: Pais	6F **101**	
Braeview Gdns. PA2: Pais	6F **101**	
Braeview Pl. G74: E Kil	5B **142**	
Braeview Rd. PA2: Pais	6F **101**	
Braewell Ct. G33: Glas	3H **67**	
Braewell Dr. G33: Glas	3H **67**	
Braid Av. ML1: Cle	6E **133**	
Braidbar Ct. G46: Giff	4A **122**	
Braidbar Farm Rd. G46: Giff	3B **122**	
(not continuous)		
Braidbar Rd. G46: Giff	4A **122**	
Braidcraft Pl. G53: Glas	5C **104**	
Braidcraft Rd. G53: Glas	4C **104**	
Braidcraft Ter. G53: Glas	4D **104**	
BRAIDFAULD	2G **109**	
Braidfauld Gdns. G32: Glas	2H **109**	
Braidfauld Pl. G32: Glas	3H **109**	
Braidfauld St. G32: Glas	3H **109**	
Braidfield Gro. G81: Hard	2D **44**	
Braidfield Rd. G81: Hard	2D **44**	
Braidholm Cres. G46: Giff	4A **122**	
Braidholm Rd. G46: Giff	4A **122**	
Braidhurst Ind. Est. ML1: Moth	6F **131**	
Braidhurst Sports Barn	6F **131**	
Braidhurst St. ML1: Moth	1G **147**	
Braidley Cres. G75: E Kil	6G **157**	
Braidpark Dr. G46: Giff	4B **122**	
Braids Circ. PA2: Pais	4A **102**	
Braids Ct. PA2: Pais	4H **101**	
Braids Dr. G53: Glas	4H **103**	
Braids Gait PA2: Pais	4H **101**	
Braid Sq. G4: Glas	1E **87**	
Braids Rd. PA2: Pais	4A **102**	
Braid St. G4: Glas	1E **87**	
Braidwood Pl. PA3: Lin	5F **79**	
Braidwood St. ML2: Wis	2A **150**	
Braille Cres. PA4: Renf	2H **83**	
Braille Dr. PA4: Renf	2H **83**	
Bramah Av. G75: E Kil	4H **157**	
Bramble Ct. G66: Len	3E **9**	
Bramble Gdns. ML6: Air	2A **96**	
Bramble Wynd G72: Newt	6F **127**	
Brambling Ct. ML2: Wis	2F **165**	
Brambling Path ML5: Coat	2G **115**	
Brambling Rd. ML5: Air	2F **115**	
Brambling Rd. ML5: Coat	2F **115**	
Bramley Dr. ML4: Bell	5C **114**	
Bramley Pl. G66: Lenz	3E **53**	
Bramley Pl. ML6: Air	5E **97**	
Brampton G75: E Kil	5B **156**	
Branchalfield Dr. ML2: Wis	5C **150**	
Branchalmuir Cres. ML2: Newm	3D **150**	
Branchal Rd. ML2: Wis	4B **150**	
Branchock Av. G72: Camb	3D **126**	
Brancumhall Rd. G74: E Kil	6D **142**	
Brandon Arc. ML1: Moth	3G **147**	
Brandon Ct. ML1: Moth	3G **147**	
Brandon Ct. ML3: Ham	5G **145**	
Brandon Dr. G61: Bear	6E **27**	
Brandon Gdns. G72: Camb	2G **125**	
Brandon Ga. ML4: Bell	2E **131**	
Brandon Ho. ML3: Ham	4A **146**	
Brandon Pde. E. ML1: Moth	2G **147**	
Brandon Pde. Sth. ML1: Moth	3G **147**	
Brandon Pl. ML4: Bell	4A **130**	
Brandon St. G31: Glas	5B **88**	

Brandon St. – BROOM

Brandon St. ML1: Moth 3H 147
Brandon St. ML3: Ham 6A 146
Brandon Way ML5: Coat 1H 113
Brand Pl. G51: Glas 5A 86
Brand St. G51: Glas 5A 86
Brankholm Brae ML3: Ham 5B 144
Brankholm Gdns. ML3: Ham 5C 144
Brankholm Lea ML3: Ham 5C 144
Branklyn Cl. G13: Glas 3D 62
Branklyn Ct. G13: Glas 3D 62
(not continuous)
Branklyn Cres. G13: Glas 3D 62
Branklyn Gro. G13: Glas 3D 62
Branklyn Pl. G13: Glas 3D 62
BRANKUMHALL 6C 142
Brannock Av. ML1: N'hill 3D 132
Brannock Pl. ML1: N'hill 3D 132
Brannock Rd. ML1: N'hill 4D 132
Branscroft PA10: Kilba 1B 98
Brassey St. G20: Glas 3C 64
Breadalbane Cres. ML1: Moth 6F 131
Breadalbane Gdns. G73: Ruth 3F 125
Breadalbane St. G3: Glas 4F 5 (3D 86)
Breadie Dr. G62: Miln 5F 27
Breamish Pl. G75: E Kil 5B 156
Bream Pl. PA6: C'lee 3D 78
Brechanshaw PA8: Inch 2A 60
Brechin Rd. G64: B'rig 6E 51
Brechin St. G3: Glas 3E 5 (3C 86)
Breck Av. PA2: Pais 6B 100
BREDILAND 4E 101
Brediland Rd. PA2: Pais 6C 100
Brediland Rd. PA3: Lin 5G 79
Bredin Way ML1: Moth 1D 146
Bredisholm Cres. G71: View 4G 113
Bredisholm Dr. G69: Bail 1A 112
Bredisholm Rd. G69: Bail 1A 112
Bredisholm Rd. G69: Barg 2C 112
(not continuous)
Bredisholm Ter. G69: Bail 1A 112
Bremners Cotts. G81: Dun 1B 44
Brendan Way ML1: Moth 1B 164
Brendon Av. G75: E Kil 1A 168
Brenfield Av. G44: Glas 3D 122
Brenfield Dr. G44: Glas 3D 122
Brenfield Rd. G44: Glas 3D 122
Brenfield Rd. G44: Neth 3D 122
Brennan Cres. ML6: Air 5A 96
Brent Av. G46: T'bnk 2F 121
Brent Ct. G74: E Kil 6G 141
Brent Cres. PA6: C'lee 3C 78
Brent Dr. G46: T'bnk 2F 121
Brent Gdns. G46: T'bnk 2F 121
Brent Rd. G46: T'bnk 2F 121
Brent Rd. G74: E Kil 6G 141
Brent Way G46: T'bnk 2F 121
Brentwood Av. G53: Glas 3A 120
Brentwood Dr. G53: Glas 3B 120
Brentwood Sq. G53: Glas 3B 120
Brereton St. G42: Glas 4G 107
Bressay G74: E Kil 6G 141
Bressay Cl. G33: Glas 5E 91
Bressay Gro. G33: Glas 5E 91
Bressay Gro. G72: Camb 4G 125
Bressay Pl. G33: Glas 5E 91
Bressay Rd. G33: Glas 5E 91
Bressay Wynd ML2: Newm 3D 150
(off Tiree Cres.)
Breval Ct. G69: Bail 1A 112
Breval Cres. G81: Dun 6C 24
Breval Cres. G81: Hard 6C 24
Brewery St. PA5: John 2F 99
Brewster Av. PA3: Pais 4C 82
Brewster Wynd PA3: Pais 4C 82
Briar Bank G66: Milt C 6B 10
Briarbush Way G72: Blan 1A 144
Briarcroft Dr. G33: Glas 2F 67
Briarcroft Pl. G33: Glas 3G 67
Briarcroft Rd. G33: Glas 3F 67
Briar Dr. G81: Clyd 3D 44
Briar Gdns. G43: Glas 2B 122
Briar Gro. G43: Glas 2B 122
Briarlea Dr. G46: Giff 3A 122
Briar Neuk G64: B'rig 1D 66
Briar Rd. G43: Glas 2B 122
Briar Rd. G66: Kirkin 5F 33
Briar Wlk. G66: Kirkin 5G 33
Briarwell La. G62: Miln 4H 27
Briarwell Rd. G62: Miln 4H 27
Briarwood Ct. G32: Glas 3E 111
Briarwood Gdns. G32: Glas 3E 111
Briarwood Rd. ML2: Wis 5E 149
Brickfield Cres. G41: Glas 1E 107
Brickfield St. G41: Glas 1E 107
Brickfield Vw. G41: Glas 1E 107
Brick La. PA3: Pais 6B 82
Bridge, The 3G 91
Bridgeburn Dr. G69: Mood 5C 54
Bridgeford Av. ML4: Bell 6E 115
Bridgegait G62: Miln 5A 28
Bridgegate G1: Glas 5G 87
Bridgegate Path G1: Glas 5H 87
(off Bridgegate)
Bridge La. PA2: Pais 2F 101
(off The Moorings)
BRIDGEND 4C 54
Bridgend PA7: B'ton 4G 41
Bridgend Cotts. G66: Kirkin 6G 33
Bridgend Ct. G68: C'cry 2F 17
Bridgend Cres. G69: Mood 5C 54
Bridgend Pl. G69: Mood 5C 54
Bridgend Rd. PA5: Eld 2A 100
Bridgend Vw. ML8: Carl 4D 174
BRIDGE OF WEIR 3F 77
Bridge of Weir Rd. PA11: Bri W 4G 77
Bridge of Weir Rd. PA3: Lin 6H 79
Bridge of Weir Rd. PA5: Brkfld 6C 78
Bridge of Weir Rd. PA5: John 6C 78
Bridge of Weir Rd. PA6: Hous 2A 78
Bridge Pl. G62: Miln 4G 27
Bridge St. G5: Glas 5F 87
Bridge St. G72: Camb 1A 126
Bridge St. G81: Clyd 4A 44
Bridge St. G82: Dumb 4E 19
Bridge St. ML2: Wis 6E 149
Bridge St. ML3: Ham 1G 161
Bridge St. PA1: Pais 1B 102
Bridge St. PA3: Lin 5A 80
Bridge Street Park & Ride 6F 87
Bridge Street Station (Subway) 6F 87
BRIDGETON 1B 108
Bridgeton Bus. Cen. G40: Glas 6B 88
Bridgeton Cross G40: Glas 6B 88
Bridgeton Station (Rail) 1B 108
Bridge Vw. G71: Both 6G 129
Bridgewater Ind. Pk. PA8: Ersk 5G 43
Bridgewater Pl. PA8: Ersk 5F 43
Bridgewater Shop. Cen. 5F 43
Bridgeway Ct. G66: Kirkin 6F 33
Bridgeway Pl. G66: Kirkin 6F 33
Bridgeway Rd. G66: Kirkin 6F 33
Bridgeway Ter. G66: Kirkin 6F 33
Bridie Ter. G74: E Kil 5C 142
Brierie Av. PA6: C'lee 2B 78
Brierie Gdns. PA6: C'lee 3B 78
Brierie Hill Gro. PA6: C'lee 3B 78
Brierie Hill Rd. PA6: C'lee 3A 78
Brierie Hills Ct. PA6: C'lee 3B 78
Brierie La. PA6: C'lee 3A 78
Brigbrae Av. ML4: Bell 4E 131
Briggait, The 5G 87
Brigham Pl. G23: Glas 1C 64
Brighton Pl. G51: Glas 5H 85
Brighton St. G51: Glas 5H 85
Brightside Av. G71: Udd 2D 128
Bright St. G21: Glas 2B 88
Brig o' Lea Ter. G78: Neil 3D 134
Brigside Gdns. ML3: Ham 1C 162
Brimley Pl. G75: E Kil 6A 156
Brisbane Ct. G46: Giff 4B 122
Brisbane La. G40: Glas 3D 108
Brisbane Rd. PA7: B'ton 4H 41
Brisbane St. G42: Glas 6E 107
Brisbane St. G81: Clyd 3H 43
Brisbane Ter. G75: E Kil 4E 157
Britannia Way G81: Clyd 5D 44
Britannia Way PA4: Renf 2E 83
Briton St. G51: Glas 4H 85
Brittain Way ML1: Holy 6H 115
Broad Cairn Ct. ML1: Moth 1C 164
Broadcroft G66: Kirkin 5C 32
(not continuous)
Broadcroft Rd. G66: Kirkin 4C 32
Broadford St. G4: Glas 1G 87
Broadholm St. G22: Glas 3F 65
Broadleys Av. G64: B'rig 4B 50
Broadlie Ct. G78: Neil 2D 134
Broadlie Dr. G13: Glas 3A 62
Broadlie Rd. G78: Neil 2C 134
Broadloan PA4: Renf 1E 83
Broadmeadow Ind. Est. G82: Dumb 3F 19
Broadmoss Av. G77: Newt M 5A 138
Broad Sq. G72: Blan 1A 144
Broad St. G40: Glas 6B 88
Broadway, The ML2: Wis 5E 149
Broadwood Bus. Pk. G68: Cumb 5B 36
Broadwood Dr. G44: Glas 1F 123
Broadwood Gymnastics Academy 4B 36
Broadwood Leisure Cen. 4B 36
BROADWOOD RDBT. 5B 36
Broadwood Stadium 4B 36
Brockburn Cres. G53: Glas 5B 104
Brockburn Pl. G53: Glas 3A 104
Brockburn Rd. G53: Glas 3A 104
Brockburn Ter. G53: Glas 5C 104
Brocklinn Pk. G75: E Kil 4A 156
Brock Oval G53: Glas 1C 120
Brock Pl. G53: Glas 6C 104
Brock Pl. ML1: Moth 1D 148
Brock Rd. G53: Glas 1B 120
Brock Ter. G53: Glas 1C 120
Brockville St. G32: Glas 5H 89
Brodick Av. ML1: Moth 2D 146
Brodick Dr. G74: E Kil 6F 141
Brodick Pl. G77: Newt M 5A 136
Brodick Sq. G64: B'rig 1E 67
Brodick St. G21: Glas 2C 88
Brodie Dr. G69: Bail 5A 92
Brodie Gdns. G69: Bail 5A 92
Brodie Gro. G69: Bail 5A 92
Brodie Pk. Av. PA2: Pais 3A 102
Brodie Pk. Cres. PA2: Pais 3H 101
Brodie Pk. Gdns. PA2: Pais 3A 102
Brodie Pl. G74: E Kil 6F 141
Brodie Rd. G21: Glas 2F 67
Brodie Way ML6: Plain 6G 75
Brogan Cres. ML1: Moth 2D 146
Bron Way G67: Cumb 4A 38
Brookbank Ter. ML8: Carl 4E 175
BROOKFIELD 6D 78
Brookfield Av. G33: Glas 2F 67
Brookfield Cnr. G33: Glas 2F 67
Brookfield Dr. G33: Glas 2F 67
Brookfield Gdns. G33: Glas 2F 67
Brookfield Ga. G33: Glas 2F 67
Brookfield Pl. G33: Glas 2G 67
Brookfield Rd. G33: Glas 2F 67
Brooklands G74: E Kil 2C 156
Brooklands Av. G71: Udd 6C 112
Brooklea Dr. G46: Giff 2A 122
Brooklime Dr. G74: E Kil 5E 141
Brooklime Gdns. G74: E Kil 5E 141
Brooklyn Pl. ML2: Over 5H 165
Brookside St. G40: Glas 6C 88
Brook St. G40: Glas 6B 88
Brook St. G81: Clyd 3B 44
BROOM 4G 137

Broom Av. – Buchanan Gdns.

Broom Av. PA8: Ersk ... 2F **59**
Broomburn Dr. G77: Newt M ... 5F **137**
Broom Cliff G77: Newt M ... 6F **137**
Broom Cres. G75: E Kil ... 6F **157**
Broom Cres. G78: Barr ... 2C **118**
Broomcroft Rd. G77: Newt M ... 3G **137**
Broom Dr. G81: Clyd ... 3C **44**
Broom Dr. ML9: Lark ... 6A **164**
Broomdyke Way PA3: Pais ... 4H **81**
... *(off Marchfield Av.)*
Broomfauld Gdns. G82: Dumb ... 3G **19**
... (not continuous)
Broomfield PA6: Hous ... 2D **78**
Broomfield Av. G72: Camb ... 6F **109**
Broomfield Av. G77: Newt M ... 6F **137**
Broomfield Ct. G21: Glas ... 6E **67**
... (not continuous)
Broomfield Cres. G21: Glas ... 6E **67**
Broomfield Dr. G21: Glas ... 6E **67**
Broomfield Ga. G21: Glas ... 6E **67**
Broomfield La. G21: Glas ... 4B **66**
Broomfield Pl. G21: Glas ... 4B **66**
Broomfield Rd. G21: Glas ... 4B **66**
Broomfield Rd. G46: Giff ... 3G **137**
Broomfield Rd. ML9: Lark ... 5D **170**
Broomfield St. ML6: Air ... 4B **96**
Broomfield Ter. G71: Tann ... 4D **112**
Broomfield Wlk. G66: Kirkin ... 5D **32**
Broom Gdns. G66: Lenz ... 1B **52**
BROOMHILL ... **6F 63**
BROOMHILL ... **3D 32**
Broomhill Av. G11: Glas ... 1F **85**
Broomhill Av. G32: Carm ... 5B **110**
Broomhill Av. G77: Newt M ... 5F **137**
Broomhill Av. ML9: Lark ... 3C **170**
Broomhill Ct. G66: Kirkin ... 4D **32**
... *(off Eastside)*
Broomhill Ct. ML9: Lark ... 3C **170**
Broomhill Cres. ML4: Bell ... 4B **130**
Broomhill Cres. PA8: Ersk ... 2F **59**
Broomhill Dr. G11: Glas ... 6F **63**
Broomhill Dr. G73: Ruth ... 2D **124**
Broomhill Dr. G82: Dumb ... 2H **19**
Broomhill Dr. ML9: Lark ... 3B **170**
Broomhill Farm M. G66: Kirkin ... 4E **33**
Broomhill Gdns. G11: Glas ... 6F **63**
Broomhill Gdns. G77: Newt M ... 5F **137**
Broomhill Ga. ML9: Lark ... 3C **170**
Broomhill Ind. Est. G66: Kirkin ... 3E **33**
Broomhill La. G11: Glas ... 6F **63**
Broomhill Path G11: Glas ... 1F **85**
... *(off Balshagray La.)*
Broomhill Pl. G11: Glas ... 1F **85**
Broomhill Rd. ML9: Lark ... 3C **170**
Broomhill Ter. G11: Glas ... 1F **85**
Broomhill Vw. ML9: Lark ... 3A **170**
BROOMHOUSE ... **3H 111**
Broomhouse Cres. G71: Udd ... 3H **111**
Broomhouse Dr. G69: Bail ... 2A **112**
Broomieknowe Dr. G73: Ruth ... 1D **124**
Broomieknowe Gdns. G73: Ruth ... 1C **124**
Broomieknowe Rd. G73: Ruth ... 1D **124**
Broomielaw G1: Glas ... 6A **6** (5E **87**)
Broomknoll St. ML6: Air ... 4A **96**
Broomknowe G68: Cumb ... 2F **37**
Broomknowes Av. G66: Lenz ... 3E **53**
Broomknowes Rd. G21: Glas ... 5C **66**
Broomlands Av. PA8: Ersk ... 1A **60**
Broomlands Ct. PA1: Pais ... 1G **101**
Broomlands Cres. PA8: Ersk ... 1H **59**
Broomlands Gdns. PA8: Ersk ... 1H **59**
Broomlands La. PA1: Pais ... 1F **101**
Broomlands Rd. G67: Cumb ... 5A **38**
Broomlands St. PA1: Pais ... 1F **101**
Broomlands Way PA8: Ersk ... 1A **60**
Broomlea Cres. PA4: Inch ... 2G **59**
Broomlee Rd. G67: Cumb ... 1H **57**
Broomley Dr. G46: Giff ... 6A **122**
Broomley La. G46: Giff ... 6A **122**
Broomloan Ct. G51: Glas ... 6G **85**
Broomloan Cres. G51: Glas ... 3H **85**
Broomloan Pl. G51: Glas ... 5G **85**
Broomloan Rd. G51: Glas ... 5G **85**
Broompark Av. G72: Blan ... 3A **144**
Broompark Cir. G31: Glas ... 4B **88**
Broompark Cres. ML6: Air ... 1A **96**
Broompark Dr. G31: Glas ... 4B **88**
Broompark Dr. G77: Newt M ... 4G **137**
Broompark Dr. PA4: Inch ... 2H **59**
Broompark Gro. G72: Blan ... 3A **144**
Broompark La. G31: Glas ... 4B **88**
Broompark Rd. G72: Blan ... 2A **144**
Broompark Rd. ML2: Wis ... 5D **148**
Broompark St. G31: Glas ... 4B **88**
Broom Path G69: Bail ... 2F **111**
Broom Pl. G43: Glas ... 2B **122**
Broom Pl. ML1: N'hill ... 3C **132**
Broom Pl. ML5: Coat ... 2B **114**
Broom Pl. PA11: Bri W ... 4G **77**
Broom Rd. G43: Glas ... 2B **122**
Broom Rd. G67: Cumb ... 6D **16**
Broom Rd. G77: Newt M ... 3G **137**
Broom Rd. E. G77: Newt M ... 4G **137**
Broomside Cres. ML1: Moth ... 5G **147**
Broomside St. ML1: Moth ... 5G **147**
Broomstone Av. G77: Newt M ... 6F **137**
Broom Ter. PA5: John ... 4F **99**
Broomton Rd. G21: Glas ... 2E **67**
Broomvale Ct. G77: Newt M ... 5F **137**
Broomvale Dr. G77: Newt M ... 4F **137**
Broomward Dr. PA5: John ... 2H **99**
Brora Cres. ML3: Ham ... 3D **160**
Brora Dr. G46: Giff ... 5B **122**
Brora Dr. G61: Bear ... 3H **47**
Brora Dr. PA4: Renf ... 6G **61**
Brora Gdns. G64: B'rig ... 6D **50**
Brora Grn. ML1: N'hse ... 2D **132**
Brora Rd. G64: B'rig ... 6D **50**
Brora St. G33: Glas ... 2F **89**
Broughton G75: E Kil ... 1E **169**
Broughton Dr. G23: Glas ... 1C **64**
Broughton Gdns. G23: Glas ... 6D **48**
Broughton Pl. ML3: Ham ... 6E **145**
Broughton Pl. ML5: Coat ... 2D **114**
Broughton Rd. G23: Glas ... 6C **48**
Brouster Ga. G74: E Kil ... 2G **157**
Brouster Hill G74: E Kil ... 2G **157**
Brouster Pl. G74: E Kil ... 2G **157**
Brown Av. G81: Clyd ... 1F **61**
Brown Av. G82: Dumb ... 1C **20**
Brown Ct. G33: Step ... 4E **69**
Brownhill Rd. G43: Glas ... 3H **121**
Brownhill Vw. ML2: Newm ... 3H **151**
Brownieside Pl. ML6: Plain ... 6G **75**
Brownieside Rd. ML6: Plain ... 1H **97**
Brownlee Rd. ML2: Over ... 1B **172**
Brownlee Rd. ML8: Carl ... 1D **172**
Brownlee Rd. ML8: Law ... 1D **172**
Brownlie St. G42: Glas ... 5F **107**
Brownlow Gdns. PA2: Pais ... 1D **102**
Brownlow Rd. PA2: Pais ... 2D **102**
Brown Pl. G72: Camb ... 1A **126**
Brown Rd. G67: Cumb ... 3H **37**
BROWNSBURN ... **1B 116**
Brownsburn Ind. Est. ML6: Air ... 6B **96**
Brownsburn Rd. ML6: Air ... 1B **116**
Brownsdale Rd. G73: Ruth ... 6B **108**
Brownsfield Av. PA4: Inch ... 5F **59**
Brownsfield Cres. PA4: Inch ... 4F **59**
Brownsfield Rd. PA4: Inch ... 4F **59**
Brownshill Av. ML5: Coat ... 1B **114**
Brownside Av. G72: Camb ... 2G **125**
Brownside Av. G78: Barr ... 2C **118**
Brownside Av. PA2: Pais ... 6G **101**
Brownside Cres. G78: Barr ... 2C **118**
Brownside Dr. G13: Glas ... 3H **61**
Brownside Dr. G78: Barr ... 2C **118**
Brownside Gro. G78: Barr ... 2C **118**
Brownside M. G72: Camb ... 2G **125**
Brownside Rd. G72: Camb ... 2G **125**
Brownside Rd. G73: Ruth ... 2F **125**
Brownsland Ct. G69: G'csh ... 3D **70**
Brown's La. PA1: Pais ... 1A **102**
Brown St. G2: Glas ... 6A **6** (4E **87**)
Brown St. ML1: Moth ... 1H **147**
Brown St. ML2: Newm ... 5E **151**
Brown St. ML3: Ham ... 1A **162**
Brown St. ML5: Coat ... 6C **94**
Brown St. ML8: Carl ... 2D **174**
Brown St. ML9: Lark ... 1C **170**
Brown St. PA1: Pais ... 6G **81**
Brown St. PA4: Renf ... 1D **82**
Brown Wlk. ML2: Newm ... 4F **151**
Bruar Way ML2: Newm ... 3D **150**
... *(off Tiree Cres.)*
Bruce Av. G72: Camb ... 4A **126**
Bruce Av. ML1: Moth ... 2F **147**
Bruce Av. PA3: Pais ... 4C **82**
Bruce Av. PA5: John ... 5E **99**
Bruce Ct. ML6: Air ... 3E **97**
Brucefield Pl. G34: Glas ... 3B **92**
BRUCEHILL ... **3C 18**
Brucehill Rd. G82: Dumb ... 3C **18**
Bruce Ho. G67: Cumb ... 2H **37**
Bruce Loan ML2: Over ... 5A **166**
Bruce Pl. G75: E Kil ... 4H **157**
Bruce Rd. G41: Glas ... 1C **106**
Bruce Rd. ML1: New S ... 5B **132**
Bruce Rd. PA3: Pais ... 5C **82**
Bruce Rd. PA4: Renf ... 2C **82**
Bruce Rd. PA7: B'ton ... 3G **41**
Bruce's Loan ML9: Lark ... 3E **171**
... *(off Wallace Dr.)*
Bruce St. G81: Clyd ... 6D **44**
Bruce St. G82: Dumb ... 5G **19**
Bruce St. ML4: Bell ... 2D **130**
Bruce St. ML5: Coat ... 3D **94**
Bruce St. ML6: Plain ... 1G **97**
Bruce Ter. G72: Blan ... 6C **128**
Bruce Ter. G75: E Kil ... 4H **157**
Brunel Way G75: E Kil ... 3H **157**
Brunstane Rd. G34: Glas ... 2G **91**
Brunswick Cen. ... **4D 66**
Brunswick Gdns. G68: Cumb ... 6H **15**
Brunswick Ho. G81: Clyd ... 1H **43**
Brunswick St. G1: Glas ... 6E **7** (4G **87**)
Brunton St. G44: Glas ... 2D **122**
Brunton Ter. G44: Glas ... 3E **123**
Bruntsfield Av. G53: Glas ... 4B **120**
Bruntsfield Gdns. G53: Glas ... 4B **120**
Bryan St. ML3: Ham ... 4F **145**
Bryce Gdns. ML9: Lark ... 1C **170**
Bryce Pl. G75: E Kil ... 5E **157**
Brydson Pl. PA3: Lin ... 5H **79**
Bryson Ct. ML3: Ham ... 4H **161**
Bryson St. G81: Faif ... 6G **25**
Buccleuch Av. G52: Hill E ... 3G **83**
Buccleuch Av. G76: Clar ... 2B **138**
Buccleuch Ct. G61: Bear ... 6E **27**
Buccleuch Dr. G61: Bear ... 6E **27**
Buccleuch La. G3: Glas ... 2A **6** (2E **87**)
Buccleuch St. G3: Glas ... 2H **5** (2E **87**)
Buchanan Av. PA7: B'ton ... 3H **41**
Buchanan Bus. Pk. G33: Step ... 3F **69**
Buchanan Ct. G33: Step ... 3E **69**
Buchanan Cres. G64: B'rig ... 1E **67**
Buchanan Cres. ML3: Ham ... 1F **161**
Buchanan Dr. G61: Bear ... 3G **47**
Buchanan Dr. G64: B'rig ... 1E **67**
Buchanan Dr. G66: Lenz ... 4D **52**
Buchanan Dr. G72: Camb ... 1G **125**
Buchanan Dr. G73: Ruth ... 1D **124**
Buchanan Dr. G77: Newt M ... 2E **137**
Buchanan Dr. ML8: Carl ... 5G **175**
Buchanan Dr. ML8: Law ... 5E **167**
Buchanan Galleries ... **4D 6 (3G 87)**
Buchanan Gdns. G32: Glas ... 3E **111**

Buchanan Ga. G33: Step	3F **69**
Buchanan Gro. G69: Bail	6H **91**
Buchanan Pl. G64: Torr	4D **30**
Buchanan St. G1: Glas	6C **6** (3G **87**)
Buchanan St. G62: Miln	3H **27**
Buchanan St. G69: Bail	1H **111**
Buchanan St. G82: Dumb	5G **19**
Buchanan St. ML5: Coat	5A **94**
Buchanan St. ML6: Air	4A **96**
Buchanan St. PA5: John	3E **99**
Buchanan Street Station (Subway)	
	4D **6** (3G **87**)
Buchanan Way PA5: John	3E **99**
Buchandyke Rd. G74: E Kil	5B **142**
Buchan Grn. G74: E Kil	6B **142**
Buchan Ho. G67: Cumb	2H **37**
Buchan Rd. ML1: New S	5A **132**
	(not continuous)
Buchan St. ML2: Wis	3H **149**
Buchan St. ML3: Ham	3G **161**
Buchan Ter. G72: Camb	4G **125**
BUCHLEY	2G **49**
Buchlyvie Gdns. G64: B'rig	2B **66**
Buchlyvie Path G34: Glas	4H **91**
Buchlyvie Rd. PA1: Pais	6G **83**
Buchlyvie St. G34: Glas	4H **91**
Buckie PA8: Ersk	4E **43**
Buckie Wlk. ML4: Bell	1C **130**
Buckingham Ct. ML3: Ham	5C **144**
Buckingham Dr. G32: Carm	5B **110**
Buckingham Dr. G73: Ruth	6F **109**
Buckingham St. G12: Glas	6B **64**
Buckingham Ter. G12: Glas	6B **64**
Bucklaw Gdns. G52: Glas	1C **104**
Bucklaw Pl. G52: Glas	1C **104**
Bucklaw Ter. G52: Glas	1C **104**
Buckley St. G22: Glas	3H **65**
Bucksburn Rd. G21: Glas	5E **67**
Buckthorne Pl. G53: Glas	4B **120**
Budgett Brae ML1: Carf	6C **132**
Budhill Av. G32: Glas	6B **90**
Budshaw Av. ML6: Chap	3C **116**
Budshaw Farm Rd. ML6: Chap	4G **117**
Bulldale Ct. G14: Glas	4G **61**
Bulldale Pl. G14: Glas	4G **61**
Bulldale Rd. G14: Glas	4G **61**
Bulldale St. G14: Glas	3G **61**
Buller Cl. G72: Blan	5B **128**
Buller Cres. G72: Blan	5A **128**
Bullionslaw Dr. G73: Ruth	1F **125**
Bulloch Av. G46: Giff	5B **122**
Bull Rd. G76: Busby	3D **138**
Bullwood Av. G53: Glas	5H **103**
Bullwood Ct. G53: Glas	5H **103**
Bullwood Dr. G53: Glas	4H **103**
Bullwood Gdns. G53: Glas	4H **103**
Bullwood Pl. G53: Glas	4H **103**
Bunbury Ter. G75: E Kil	3E **157**
Bunessan St. G52: Glas	6F **85**
Bunhouse Rd. G3: Glas	1A **4** (2A **86**)
Burbank G62: Miln	3G **27**
	(off Sinclair St.)
Burghead Dr. G51: Glas	3E **85**
Burghead Pl. G51: Glas	3E **85**
Burgher St. G31: Glas	6E **89**
Burgh Hall La. G11: Glas	1H **85**
Burgh Hall St. G11: Glas	1H **85**
Burgh La. G12: Glas	6B **64**
	(off Cresswell St.)
Burleigh Gdns. G72: Camb	5H **125**
Burleigh Pl. ML5: Coat	2E **115**
Burleigh Rd. G71: Both	4F **129**
Burleigh St. G51: Glas	3G **85**
Burleigh St. ML5: Coat	2D **114**
Burley Pl. G74: E Kil	1B **156**
Burlington Av. G12: Glas	3H **63**
Burmola St. G22: Glas	5F **65**
Burnacre Gdns. G71: Udd	6C **112**
Burnawn Gdns. G33: Glas	2F **67**

Burnawn Ga. G33: Glas	2F **67**
Burnawn Gro. G33: Glas	2F **67**
Burnawn Pl. G33: Glas	2F **67**
BURNBANK	4E **145**
Burnbank Braes ML8: Carl	4D **174**
Burnbank Cen. ML3: Ham	4E **145**
Burnbank Dr. G78: Barr	6E **119**
Burnbank Gdns. G20: Glas	1D **86**
Burnbank Gdns. ML3: Ham	4E **145**
	(off Burnbank Cen.)
Burnbank La. G20: Glas	1D **86**
Burnbank M. G66: Lenz	3D **52**
Burnbank Pl. G20: Glas	1E **87**
Burnbank Quad. ML6: Air	3H **95**
Burnbank Rd. ML3: Ham	4E **145**
Burnbank St. ML5: Coat	3D **94**
Burnbank St. ML6: Air	3H **95**
Burnbank Ter. G20: Glas	1D **86**
Burnbank Ter. G65: Kils	2H **13**
Burnblea Gdns. ML3: Ham	1A **162**
Burnblea St. ML3: Ham	1H **161**
Burnbrae G81: Dun	1C **44**
Burnbrae Av. G61: Bear	6G **27**
Burnbrae Av. G69: Mood	5D **54**
Burnbrae Dr. G73: Ruth	2F **125**
Burnbrae Dr. PA3: Lin	1A **100**
Burnbrae Gdns. G53: Glas	1D **120**
Burnbrae Gdns. G81: Dun	1C **44**
Burnbrae Pl. G74: E Kil	1E **157**
Burnbrae Rd. G66: A'loch	5E **53**
Burnbrae Rd. G66: Kirkin	6H **33**
Burnbrae Rd. G69: Chry	5G **53**
Burnbrae Rd. G72: Blan	2A **144**
Burnbrae Rd. PA3: Lin	1H **99**
Burnbrae St. G21: Glas	5C **66**
Burnbrae St. G81: Faif	5F **25**
Burnbrae St. ML9: Lark	2B **170**
Burncleuch Av. G72: Camb	3A **126**
Burn Cres. ML1: New S	3A **132**
Burn Cres. ML6: Chap	3D **116**
Burncrooks Av. G61: Bear	6C **26**
Burncrooks Av. G74: E Kil	1E **157**
Burncrooks Ct. G81: Dun	1B **44**
Burndyke Ct. G51: Glas	4H **85**
Burndyke Sq. G51: Glas	4A **86**
Burnet Cres. ML1: New S	3H **131**
Burnet Rose Ct. G74: E Kil	5E **141**
Burnet Rose Gdns. G74: E Kil	5E **141**
Burnet Rose Pl. G74: E Kil	5E **141**
Burnett Ct. G69: Chry	1A **70**
Burnett Rd. G33: Glas	4E **91**
Burnfield Av. G46: Giff	3H **121**
Burnfield Cotts. G46: Giff	3H **121**
Burnfield Dr. G43: Glas	3H **121**
Burnfield Gdns. G46: Giff	3A **122**
Burnfield Rd. G43: Glas	2G **121**
Burnfield Rd. G46: Giff	3A **122**
BURNFOOT	2G **95**
Burnfoot Cres. G73: Ruth	2F **125**
Burnfoot Cres. PA2: Pais	5G **101**
Burnfoot Dr. G52: Glas	6B **84**
Burnfoot Rd. ML6: Air	3G **95**
Burngill Pl. PA11: Bri W	3F **77**
Burngreen G65: Kils	3H **13**
Burngreen Ter. G67: Cumb	6B **16**
Burnhall Pl. ML2: Wis	2B **166**
Burnhall Rd. ML2: Wis	1A **166**
Burnhall St. ML2: Wis	2B **166**
Burnham Rd. G14: Glas	5A **62**
Burnhaven PA8: Ersk	5E **43**
BURNHEAD	2E **171**
Burnhead Rd. G43: Glas	2C **122**
Burnhead Rd. G68: Cumb	3E **37**
Burnhead Rd. ML6: Air	1C **96**
Burnhead Rd. ML9: Lark	2D **170**
Burnhead St. G71: View	5F **113**
Burnhill Quad. G73: Ruth	5B **108**
Burnhill Sports Cen.	5B **108**
Burnhill St. G73: Ruth	5B **108**

Burn Ho. Av. G68: Cumb	3D **36**
Burnhouse Brae G77: Newt M	6G **137**
Burnhouse Cres. ML3: Ham	2F **161**
Burnhouse La. G75: E Kil	3A **168**
Burnhouse Rd. ML3: Ham	2F **161**
Burnhouse St. G20: Glas	3B **64**
Burniebrae ML6: Air	3G **95**
Burniebrae Rd. ML6: Chap	2E **117**
Burn La. ML1: New S	3A **132**
Burnlea Cres. PA6: Hous	1A **78**
Burnlip Rd. ML5: Glenb	5C **72**
Burnlip Rd. ML6: Glenm	5C **72**
Burnmouth Ct. G33: Glas	5F **91**
Burnmouth Pl. G61: Bear	2G **47**
Burnmouth Rd. G33: Glas	5F **91**
Burnock Pl. G75: E Kil	4A **156**
Burnpark Av. G71: Udd	6B **112**
Burn Pl. G72: Camb	6G **109**
Burn Rd. ML8: Carl	2D **174**
Burns Av. PA7: B'ton	4H **41**
Burns Ct. G66: Kirkin	4G **33**
Burn's Cres. ML6: Air	5B **96**
Burns Dr. G66: Kirkin	3G **33**
Burns Dr. PA5: John	5E **99**
Burns Gdns. G72: Blan	6A **128**
Burns Ga. G72: Camb	4A **126**
Burns Gro. G46: T'bnk	5G **121**
Burnshot Wlk. G5: Glas	3A **108**
Burnside G61: Bear	6C **26**
BURNSIDE	2E **125**
Burnside Av. G66: Kirkin	6B **32**
Burnside Av. G78: Barr	3D **118**
Burnside Av. ML4: Bell	3E **131**
Burnside Av. ML6: C'bnk	3B **116**
Burnside Av. PA5: Brkfld	6C **78**
Burnside Ct. G61: Bear	6C **26**
Burnside Ct. G73: Ruth	2E **125**
Burnside Ct. G81: Clyd	3A **44**
Burnside Ct. ML1: Moth	5B **148**
Burnside Ct. ML5: Coat	6B **94**
	(off Kirk St.)
Burnside Cres. G72: Blan	3C **144**
Burnside Cres. G81: Hard	1D **44**
Burnside Gdns. G76: Clar	2B **138**
Burnside Gdns. PA10: Kilba	3B **98**
Burnside Ga. G73: Ruth	2E **125**
Burnside Ga. ML3: Ham	6H **145**
Burnside Gro. PA5: John	3E **99**
Burnside Ind. Est. G65: Kils	3G **13**
Burnside La. ML3: Ham	1A **162**
Burnside Pl. G82: Dumb	5H **19**
Burnside Pl. ML9: Lark	2D **170**
	(not continuous)
Burnside Pl. PA3: Pais	4E **81**
	(not continuous)
Burnside Quad. ML1: Holy	2A **132**
Burnside Rd. G46: Giff	3H **137**
Burnside Rd. G73: Ruth	2E **125**
Burnside Rd. ML1: N'hill	3C **132**
Burnside Rd. ML5: Coat	2E **95**
Burnside Rd. PA5: Eld	4A **100**
Burnside Station (Rail)	2E **125**
Burnside St. G82: Dumb	5H **19**
Burnside St. ML1: Moth	5B **148**
Burnside Ter. G82: Dumb	5H **19**
	(off Glasgow Rd.)
Burnside Ter. PA10: Kilba	3B **98**
Burnside Twr. ML1: Moth	5A **148**
	(off Doon St.)
Burnside Vw. G75: E Kil	1A **168**
Burnside Vw. ML5: Coat	6A **94**
Burnside Wlk. G61: Bear	6C **26**
	(off Burnside)
Burnside Wlk. ML5: Coat	6A **94**
Burns La. ML6: Chap	2D **116**
Burns Loan ML9: Lark	1D **170**
	(off Duncan Graham St.)
Burns Pk. G74: E Kil	1A **158**
Burns Path ML4: Bell	6D **114**

Calderpark Gdns. – Canal St.

Calderpark Gdns. G71: Udd 3H **111**
Calderpark Pl. G71: Udd 3H **111**
Calderpark Rd. G71: Udd 3H **111**
Calderpark Ter. G71: Udd 3H **111**
Calder Pl. G69: Bail 1H **111**
Calder Rd. G71: View 4H **113**
Calder Rd. G72: Blan 2H **127**
Calder Rd. ML4: Bell 2E **131**
Calder Rd. ML4: Moss 2E **131**
Calder Rd. PA3: Pais 6E **81**
Calderside Gro. G74: E Kil 5E **143**
Calderside Rd. G72: Blan 3D **158**
Calderstone Dr. G68: Cumb 5G **15**
Calder St. G42: Glas 3E **107**
Calder St. G72: Blan 1B **144**
Calder St. ML5: Coat 1D **114**
Calder St. ML6: C'bnk 3C **116**
Calder Twr. G74: E Kil 4B **158**
Calder Twr. ML1: Moth 4G **147**
Caldervale St. ML6: Gart 1E **117**
Calder Vw. ML3: Ham 3F **161**
Calderview ML1: Moth 2H **147**
Calderview Av. ML5: Coat 1F **115**
CALDERWOOD 6B **142**
Calderwood Av. G69: Bail 2G **111**
Calderwood Ct. ML2: Wis 1H **165**
Calderwood Dr. G69: Bail 2G **111**
Calderwood Dr. G72: Blan 3B **144**
Calderwood Gdns. G69: Bail 2G **111**
Calderwood Gdns. G74: E Kil 5E **143**
Calderwood Rd. G43: Glas 1B **122**
Calderwood Rd. G73: Ruth 6E **109**
Calderwood Rd. G74: E Kil 5B **142**
Calderwood Sq. G74: E Kil 6B **142**
(off Pollock La.)
Caldwell Av. G13: Glas 3A **62**
Caldwell Av. PA3: Lin 6F **79**
Caldwell Gro. G73: Ruth 5E **125**
Caldwell Gro. ML4: Bell 5C **114**
Caldwell Quad. ML1: Moth 4E **147**
Caldwell Rd. ML8: Carl 5F **175**
Caledonia Av. G5: Glas 2G **107**
Caledonia Av. G73: Ruth 5D **108**
Caledonia Ct. PA3: Pais 5H **81**
Caledonia Dr. G69: Bail 2H **111**
Caledonia Dr. ML1: N'hill 3E **133**
Caledonia Gdns. ML8: Carl 2C **174**
Caledonian Av. ML4: Bell 3B **130**
Caledonian Ct. G4: Glas 2E **7** (2G **87**)
Caledonian Ct. G74: E Kil 3G **157**
Caledonian Cres. G12: Glas 1C **86**
(off Gt. Western Rd.)
Caledonian Ga. ML5: Coat 3C **94**
Caledonian Pk. ML2: Wis 6D **148**
Caledonian Rd. ML2: Wis 2G **165**
Caledonian Rd. ML9: Lark 2C **170**
Caledonia Rd. G5: Glas 1F **107**
Caledonia Rd. G69: Bail 2G **111**
Caledonia St. G5: Glas 2G **107**
Caledonia St. G81: Clyd 4B **44**
Caledonia St. PA3: Pais 6H **81**
Caledonia Ter. G82: Dumb 4C **18**
Caledonia Wlk. ML3: Ham 2A **162**
(off Chatelherault Cres.)
Caledonia Way PA3: Glas A 2H **81**
Caledonia Way E. PA3: Glas A 2A **82**
Caledonia Way W. PA3: Glas A 2H **81**
Caledon La. G12: Glas 1A **86**
Caledon St. G12: Glas 1A **86**
Caley Brae G71: Udd 1D **128**
Calfhill Rd. G53: Glas 2B **104**
Calfmuir Rd. G66: Kirkin 6G **33**
Calfmuir Rd. G66: Lenz 6G **33**
Calgary Pk. G75: E Kil 3F **157**
Calgary Pl. G75: E Kil 3F **157**
Calgary Pl. ML6: Air 5G **95**
Calgary St. G4: Glas 2E **7** (2G **87**)
Calico Way G66: Len 2E **9**
Callaghan Cres. G74: T'hall 3H **155**
Callaghan Wynd G72: Blan 6H **127**
Callander Ct. G68: Cumb 1H **37**
Callander Rd. G68: Cumb 1H **37**
Callander Rd. ML6: Chap 4D **116**
Callander St. G20: Glas 6E **65**
Callieburn Ct. G64: B'rig 1C **66**
Callieburn Rd. G64: B'rig 1C **66**
Callon St. ML6: Air 4A **96**
Cally Av. G15: Glas 4A **46**
Calside PA2: Pais 3H **101**
Calside Av. PA2: Pais 2H **101**
Calside Ct. PA2: Pais 3A **102**
CALTON 5A **88**
Calton Entry G40: Glas 5A **88**
(off Stevenson St.)
Calvary Pk. G65: Kils 2B **14**
Calvay Cres. G33: Glas 4D **90**
Calvay Pl. G33: Glas 4E **91**
Calvay Rd. G33: Glas 4D **90**
Cambourne Rd. G69: Mood 4D **54**
Cambridge Av. G81: Clyd 4D **44**
Cambridge Cres. ML6: Air 2C **96**
Cambridge Rd. PA4: Renf 1E **83**
Cambridge St. G2: Glas 3B **6** (3F **87**)
Cambridge St. G3: Glas 3B **6** (3F **87**)
Camburn St. G32: Glas 6H **89**
Cambusdoon Rd. G33: Glas 1C **90**
Cambuskenneth Gdns. G32: Glas 6D **90**
Cambuskenneth Pl. G33: Glas 1C **90**
CAMBUSLANG 1A **126**
Cambuslang Ct. G32: Glas 5H **109**
Cambuslang Golf Course 6B **110**
Cambuslang Ind. Est. G32: Glas 5A **110**
Cambuslang Ind. Pk. G32: Glas 5A **110**
Cambuslang Investment Pk. G32: Glas 5A **110**
(Clydesmill Pl.)
Cambuslang Rd. G72: Camb 5G **109**
(Dale Av.)
Cambuslang Rd. G32: Glas 5H **109**
Cambuslang Rd. G73: Ruth 4D **108**
CAMBUSLANG ROAD INTERCHANGE 5F **109**
Cambuslang Station (Rail) 1H **125**
Cambuslang Way G32: Glas 5H **109**
Cambusmore Pl. G33: Glas 1C **90**
CAMBUSNETHAN 5C **150**
Cambusnethan St. ML2: Wis 5C **150**
Cambus Pl. G33: Glas 1C **90**
Camden St. G5: Glas 1G **107**
Camden Ter. G5: Glas 1G **107**
Camellia Dr. ML2: Wis 2E **165**
Camelon Cres. G72: Blan 2B **144**
Camelon St. G32: Glas 5H **89**
Cameron Av. PA7: B'ton 3H **41**
Cameron Cotts. G81: Hard 1E **45**
(off Glasgow Rd.)
Cameron Ct. G52: Hill E 4H **83**
Cameron Ct. G73: Ruth 6C **108**
Cameron Ct. G81: Clyd 1E **61**
Cameron Cres. G76: Crmck 2A **140**
Cameron Cres. ML3: Ham 6F **145**
Cameron Dr. G61: Bear 4G **47**
Cameron Dr. G71: Tann 5E **113**
Cameron Dr. G77: Newt M 2E **137**
Cameronian Dr. ML8: Carl 4E **175**
Cameronian Pl. ML4: Bell 4B **130**
Cameronian Way ML9: Lark 4E **171**
Cameron Path ML9: Lark 4E **171**
(off Bannockburn Dr.)
Cameron Rd. ML8: Carl 5F **175**
Cameron Sq. G81: Hard 1E **45**
Cameron St. G52: Hill E 4G **83**
Cameron St. G81: Clyd 1E **61**
Cameron St. ML1: Moth 3F **147**
Cameron St. ML5: Coat 3D **94**
Cameron Way G72: Blan 1B **144**
Camie Ct. G66: Kirkin 5C **32**
CAMLACHIE 6D **88**
Camlachie St. G31: Glas 6D **88**
(not continuous)
Campbell Av. G62: Miln 4G **27**
Campbell Av. G82: Dumb 1C **20**
Campbell Av. PA7: B'ton 3H **41**
Campbell Cl. ML3: Ham 5B **146**
Campbell Cres. G71: Both 3E **129**
Campbell Cres. G77: Newt M 3E **137**
Campbell Dr. G61: Bear 2D **46**
Campbell Dr. G78: Barr 5E **119**
Campbell Dr. G82: Dumb 1C **20**
Campbell Ho. G67: Cumb 4G **37**
Campbell La. ML3: Ham 6A **146**
Campbell Pl. G64: Torr 4D **30**
Campbell Pl. G75: E Kil 4G **157**
Campbell St. G20: Glas 2B **64**
Campbell St. ML2: Wis 6H **149**
Campbell St. ML3: Ham 6A **146**
Campbell St. ML4: Bell 2C **130**
Campbell St. PA4: Renf 5F **61**
Campbell St. PA5: John 3F **99**
Campbell Ter. G82: Dumb 1C **20**
Camphill PA1: Pais 2H **101**
Camphill Av. G41: Glas 6C **106**
Camphill Av. G66: Kirkin 5C **32**
Camphill Ct. PA2: Pais 2H **101**
Camphill Gdns. PA7: B'ton 4A **42**
Camphill Ho. G41: Glas 4D **106**
Campion Rd. ML1: Moth 1G **147**
Camp Rd. G69: Bail 6H **91**
Camp Rd. ML1: Moth 5G **147**
Camps Cres. PA4: Renf 1G **83**
Campsie Av. G78: Barr 6E **119**
Campsie Ct. G66: Kirkin 1C **52**
Campsie Ct. ML5: Coat 2E **115**
Campsie Ct. ML9: Lark 6H **163**
Campsie Cres. ML6: Air 3H **95**
Campsie Dr. G61: Bear 6D **26**
Campsie Dr. G62: Miln 3H **27**
Campsie Dr. PA2: Pais 5H **101**
Campsie Dr. PA3: Glas A 1A **82**
Campsie Dr. PA4: Renf 3C **82**
Campsie Gdns. G76: Clar 1A **138**
Campsie Golf Course 1F **9**
Campsie Pl. G69: Chry 1A **70**
Campsie Rd. G64: Torr 4E **31**
Campsie Rd. G66: Kirkin 4B **32**
Campsie Rd. G66: Len 4H **9**
Campsie Rd. G66: Milt C 4H **9**
Campsie Rd. G75: E Kil 2A **168**
Campsie Rd. ML2: Wis 5E **149**
Campsie St. G21: Glas 4B **66**
Campsie Vw. G33: Step 5D **68**
Campsie Vw. G66: Kirkin 5A **32**
Campsie Vw. G67: Cumb 2B **38**
Campsie Vw. G69: Barg 6D **92**
Campsie Vw. G69: Chry 1A **70**
Campsie Vw. G71: Tann 5E **113**
Campsie Vw. G72: Flem 4E **127**
Campsie Vw. ML3: Ham 1D **160**
Campston Pl. G33: Glas 2B **90**
Camp St. ML1: Moth 4G **147**
Camstradden Dr. E. G61: Bear 3C **46**
Camstradden Dr. W. G61: Bear 3C **46**
Camus Pl. G15: Glas 3H **45**
Canal Av. PA5: John 3G **99**
Canal Bank G13: Glas 1H **61**
Canal Bank G22: Glas 2E **65**
Canal Bank Nth. G22: Glas 2E **65**
(off Canal Bank)
Canal Ct. ML5: Coat 4B **94**
Canal Gdns. PA5: Eld 2B **100**
Canal La. G66: Kirkin 4D **32**
Canal La. PA4: Renf 5F **61**
Canal Rd. PA5: John 3F **99**
Canal St. G4: Glas 1E **7** (2G **87**)
Canal St. G66: Kirkin 4D **32**
Canal St. G81: Clyd 1D **60**
Canal St. PA1: Pais 1H **101**
Canal St. PA4: Renf 5F **61**
Canal St. PA5: Eld 2B **100**

A–Z Glasgow 199

Carnwadric Gro. – Castle Ter.

Carnwadric Gro. G46: T'bnk 3E **121**
Carnwadric Rd. G46: T'bnk 2E **121**
Carnwath Av. G43: Glas 1D **122**
Carnwath La. ML8: Carl 4F **175**
Carnwath Rd. ML8: Carl 4D **174**
Caroline St. G31: Glas 6G **89**
Carolside Av. G76: Clar 2C **138**
Carolside Dr. G15: Glas 4B **46**
Carolside Gdns. G76: Clar 2C **138**
Caronia Way ML9: Lark 6A **164**
Carousel Cres. ML2: Wis 6A **150**
Carradale Cres. G68: Cumb 5B **36**
Carradale Gdns. G64: B'rig 6E **51**
Carradale Gdns. ML8: Carl 5E **175**
Carradale Pl. PA3: Lin 5G **79**
Carradale St. ML5: Coat 4B **94**
(not continuous)
Carranbuie Rd. ML8: Carl 2D **174**
Carrbridge Cres. ML1: N'hse 2D **132**
Carrbridge Dr. G20: Glas 3B **64**
Carresbrook Av. G66: Kirkin 1G **53**
Carresbrooke Pl. G66: Kirkin 1H **53**
CARRIAGEHILL **4A 102**
Carriagehill Av. PA2: Pais 3A **102**
Carriagehill Dr. PA2: Pais 4A **102**
Carrickarden Rd. G61: Bear 4F **47**
Carrick Ct. G66: Kirkin 3G **33**
Carrick Cres. G46: Giff 6A **122**
Carrick Cres. ML2: Wis 5G **149**
Carrick Dr. G32: Glas 1E **111**
Carrick Dr. G73: Ruth 2C **124**
Carrick Dr. ML5: Coat 4H **93**
Carrick Gdns. G72: Blan 3B **144**
Carrick Gdns. ML3: Ham 1C **160**
Carrick Gdns. ML4: Bell 5C **114**
Carrick Gdns. ML8: Carl 5E **175**
Carrick Gro. G32: Glas 1E **111**
Carrick Mans. G32: Glas 2E **111**
(off Carrick Dr.)
Carrick Pl. ML4: Bell 6D **114**
Carrick Pl. ML5: Coat 4H **93**
Carrick Pl. ML5: Glenb 3A **72**
Carrick Pl. ML9: Lark 1D **170**
Carrick Rd. G64: B'rig 6E **51**
Carrick Rd. G67: Cumb 1A **38**
Carrick Rd. G73: Ruth 2B **124**
Carrick Rd. G74: E Kil 6H **141**
Carrick Rd. PA7: B'ton 5A **42**
CARRICKSTONE **6G 15**
Carrickstone Rd. G68: Cumb 6G **15**
CARRICKSTONE RDBT. 6G **15**
Carrickstone Vw. G68: Cumb 6H **15**
Carrick St. G2: Glas 6A **6** (4E **87**)
Carrick St. ML9: Lark 3E **171**
Carrick Ter. G82: Dumb 3B **18**
Carrickvale Ct. G68: Cumb 6H **15**
Carrick Vw. ML5: Glenb 3A **72**
Carrick Way G71: Both 4E **129**
Carriden Pl. G33: Glas 4E **91**
(off Langbar Cres.)
Carrington St. G4: Glas 1G **5** (1D **86**)
Carroglen Gdns. G32: Glas 6D **90**
Carroglen Gro. G32: Glas 6D **90**
Carroll Cres. ML1: Carf 5C **132**
Carron Ct. G72: Camb 2D **126**
Carron Ct. ML3: Ham 2F **161**
Carron Cres. G22: Glas 4H **65**
Carron Cres. G61: Bear 4C **46**
Carron Cres. G64: B'rig 6D **50**
Carron Cres. G66: Lenz 3E **53**
Carron Dr. PA7: B'ton 5A **42**
Carronhall Ct. G71: Udd 3A **112**
Carronhall Dr. G71: Udd 3A **112**
Carronhall Gdns. G71: Udd 3A **112**
Carronhall Gro. G71: Udd 3A **112**
Carron Ho. G67: Cumb 3H **37**
(within The Cumbernauld Shop. Cen.)
Carron Pl. G22: Glas 4A **66**
Carron Pl. G75: E Kil 6H **157**
Carron Pl. ML5: Coat 2H **93**
Carron St. G22: Glas 4A **66**
Carron St. ML2: Wis 2H **165**
Carron Way G67: Cumb 3H **37**
(off St Mungo's Rd.)
Carron Way ML1: N'hill 3C **132**
Carron Way PA3: Pais 4C **82**
Carrour Gdns. G64: B'rig 5B **50**
Carr Quad. ML4: Moss 2F **131**
Carruth Rd. PA11: Bri W 3E **77**
Carsaig Dr. G52: Glas 6E **85**
Carsaig Loan ML5: Glenb 3G **71**
Carscallan Rd. ML3: Ham 5H **161**
Carscallan Rd. ML3: Quart 5H **161**
Carsegreen Av. PA2: Pais 6F **101**
Carsemeadow PA11: Quarr V 1A **76**
Carse Vw. Dr. G61: Bear 1G **47**
Carsphairn Av. PA1: Pais 6D **80**
Carstairs St. G40: Glas 3B **108**
Carswell Gdns. G41: Glas 3C **106**
Carswell Rd. G77: Newt M 4B **136**
Cartbank Gdns. G44: Glas 3E **123**
Cartbank Gro. G44: Glas 3D **122**
Cartbank Rd. G44: Glas 3D **122**
Cartcraigs Rd. G43: Glas 1H **121**
Cartha Cres. PA2: Pais 2C **102**
Cartha St. G41: Glas 6C **106**
Cartland Av. ML8: Carl 5D **174**
Cart La. PA3: Pais 5A **82**
Cartsbridge Rd. G76: Busby 3C **138**
CARTSIDE **4D 98**
Cartside Av. PA4: Inch 5F **59**
Cartside Av. PA5: John 4D **98**
Cartside Dr. G76: Busby 3E **139**
Cartside Pl. G76: Busby 4D **138**
Cartside Quad. G42: Glas 6E **107**
Cartside Rd. G76: Busby 4D **138**
Cartside St. G42: Glas 6D **106**
Cartside Ter. PA10: Kilba 3C **98**
(off Kilbarchan Rd.)
Cart St. G81: Clyd 1D **60**
Cartvale La. PA3: Pais 5A **82**
Cartvale Rd. G42: Glas 6D **106**
Cartview Ct. G76: Busby 3D **138**
Cart Wlk. PA1: Pais 1B **102**
Cartyne Rd. G32: Glas 4B **90**
Caskie Dr. G72: Blan 6C **128**
Cassels Gro. ML1: Moth 6E **131**
Cassels St. ML1: Moth 1G **147**
Cassels St. ML8: Carl 4D **174**
Cassidy Dr. PA5: John 2F **99**
Cassiltoun Gdns. G45: Glas 5H **123**
Cassley Av. PA4: Renf 1H **83**
Castburn Rd. G67: Cumb 5F **17**
Castings Av. ML5: Coat 1E **115**
Castle Av. G71: Both 3C **128**
Castle Av. G71: Udd 3C **128**
Castle Av. ML1: Holy 1B **132**
Castle Av. PA5: Eld 4H **99**
Castlebank Ct. G13: Glas 3E **63**
Castlebank Dr. G11: Glas 2G **85**
Castlebank Gdns. G13: Glas 3E **63**
Castlebank Pl. G11: Glas 2F **85**
Castlebank St. G11: Glas 2F **85**
Castlebank Vs. G13: Glas 3E **63**
Castlebay Dr. G22: Glas 6G **49**
Castlebay Pl. G22: Glas 1G **65**
Castlebay St. G22: Glas 1G **65**
Castlebrae G82: Dumb 2C **18**
Castlebrae Gdns. G44: Glas 1F **123**
CASTLECARY **3E 17**
Castlecary Rd. G68: C'cry 5C **16**
Castlecary Rd. G68: Cumb 5C **16**
Castlecary Way G68: Cumb 4D **16**
Castle Chimmins Av. G72: Camb 3D **126**
Castle Chimmins Gdns. G72: Camb 4D **126**
Castle Chimmins Rd. G72: Camb 4D **126**
Castle Circ. G66: Len 1C **8**
Castle Ct. G66: Kirkin 5D **32**
Castle Ct. G68: C'cry 3F **17**
Castle Ct. G81: Clyd 4A **44**
Castle Cres. PA7: B'ton 5H **41**
Castlecroft Gdns. G71: Udd 2D **128**
Castle Dr. ML1: Holy 1B **132**
Castlefern Cres. G73: Ruth 4C **124**
Castlefern Rd. G73: Ruth 4D **124**
Castlefield Ct. G33: Mille 5B **68**
Castlefield Gdns. G75: E Kil 6D **156**
Castle Gait G53: Glas 5A **104**
Castle Gait PA1: Pais 2H **101**
Castle Gdns. G69: Mood 5D **54**
Castle Gdns. PA2: Pais 2E **101**
Castle Ga. G71: Both 2C **128**
Castle Ga. G77: Newt M 6G **137**
Castleglen Rd. G74: E Kil 5B **140**
Castle Golf Driving Range **5F 99**
Castlegreen Cres. G82: Dumb 5H **19**
Castlegreen Gdns. G82: Dumb 5H **19**
Castlegreen La. G82: Dumb 5G **19**
Castlegreen St. G82: Dumb 5G **19**
Castle Gro. G65: Kils 1G **13**
Castle Gro. G81: Clyd 4A **44**
CASTLEHEAD **2H 101**
CASTLEHILL **2B 18**
CASTLEHILL **1C 174**
Castle Hill Cres. ML3: Fern 2E **163**
Castlehill Cres. FK4: Bank 1E **17**
Castlehill Cres. ML3: Ham 1B **162**
Castlehill Cres. ML6: Chap 4F **117**
Castlehill Cres. ML8: Law 1G **173**
Castlehill Cres. PA4: Renf 5F **61**
Castlehill Dr. G77: Newt M 5F **137**
Castlehill Grn. G74: E Kil 5B **140**
Castlehill Ind. Est. ML8: Carl 1C **174**
Castlehill Quad. G82: Dumb 2C **18**
Castlehill Rd. G61: Bear 1B **46**
Castlehill Rd. G82: Dumb 2C **18**
Castlehill Rd. ML2: Over 2F **165**
Castlehill Rd. ML2: Wis 2F **165**
Castlehill Rd. ML8: Carl 1C **174**
Castlehill Vw. G65: Kils 1G **13**
Castleknowe Gdns. ML8: Carl 2C **174**
Castlelaw Gdns. G32: Glas 5B **90**
Castlelaw St. G32: Glas 5B **90**
Castlemains Cres. G71: Udd 2E **129**
Castle Mains Rd. G62: Miln 3D **26**
CASTLEMILK **4A 124**
Castlemilk Arc. G45: Glas 4A **124**
Castlemilk Cres. G44: Glas 2A **124**
Castlemilk Dr. G45: Glas 4A **124**
Castlemilk Rd. G44: Glas 6A **108**
(not continuous)
Castlemilk Sports Cen. **4A 124**
Castlemilk Swimming Pool **4A 124**
Castlemilk Ter. G45: Glas 5A **124**
Castlemount Av. G77: Newt M 6F **137**
Castle Pl. G71: Udd 1C **128**
Castle Pl. G81: Clyd 4A **44**
(off Castle St.)
Castle Quad. ML6: Air 4D **96**
Castle Rd. G77: Newt M 5C **136**
Castle Rd. G82: Dumb 5G **19**
Castle Rd. ML6: Air 4D **96**
Castle Rd. PA11: Bri W 2F **77**
Castle Rd. PA5: Eld 2A **100**
Castle Sq. G81: Clyd 4A **44**
Castle St. G11: Glas 1A **4** (2A **86**)
Castle St. G4: Glas 2H **7** (3A **88**)
Castle St. G69: Bail 2G **111**
Castle St. G73: Ruth 5C **108**
Castle St. G81: Clyd 4A **44**
Castle St. G82: Dumb 4F **19**
Castle St. ML3: Ham 5B **146**
Castle St. ML6: Chap 3D **116**
Castle St. PA1: Pais 1H **101**
Castle Stuart Pl. G68: Cumb 4B **16**
Castle Ter. G82: Dumb 4F **19**
Castle Ter. PA11: Bri W 4G **77**

Castleton Av. – Chapelton Av.

Castleton Av. G64: B'rig 2A 66
Castleton Av. G77: Newt M 6F 137
Castleton Ct. G77: Newt M 6F 137
Castleton Cres. G77: Newt M 6F 137
Castleton Dr. G77: Newt M 6F 137
Castleton Gro. G77: Newt M 6F 137
Castle Vw. G66: Cam G 1B 8
Castle Vw. G72: Blan 5A 128
Castle Vw. G81: Clyd 4D 44
Castle Vw. ML2: Newm 3E 151
Castleview G68: C'cry 3E 17
Castleview ML9: Lark 5C 170
Castleview Av. PA2: Pais 6E 101
Castleview Dr. PA2: Pais 6E 101
Castleview Pl. PA2: Pais 6E 101
Castleview Ter. FK4: Hag 1G 17
Castle Way G67: Cumb 1C 38
Castle Way G69: Barg 6D 92
Castle Wynd G71: Both 5F 129
Catacol Ct. G75: E Kil 1C 168
Catacol Gro. G75: E Kil 1C 168
Caterpillar La. G71: Tann 5E 113
Cathay St. G22: Glas 1G 65
Cathburn Rd. ML2: Newm 5F 151
CATHCART 1E 123
Cathcart Castle Golf Course 2A 138
Cathcart Ct. G73: Ruth 5B 108
Cathcart Cres. PA2: Pais 2C 102
Cathcart Pl. G73: Ruth 6B 108
Cathcart Rd. G42: Glas 3F 107
Cathcart Rd. G73: Ruth 6A 108
Cathcart Station (Rail) 1E 123
Cathedral Sq. G4: Glas 5H 7 (4A 88)
(not continuous)
Cathedral St. G1: Glas 4D 6 (3G 87)
Cathedral St. G4: Glas 4G 7 (3H 87)
Catherine St. G66: Kirkin 5C 32
Catherine St. ML1: Moth 5G 147
Catherines Wlk. G72: Blan 3B 144
Catherine Way ML1: New S 4H 131
CATHKIN 5F 125
Cathkin Av. G72: Camb 1G 125
Cathkin Av. G73: Ruth 6E 109
Cathkin Braes Country Pk. 5D 124
Cathkin Braes Golf Course 6D 124
Cathkin By-Pass G73: Ruth 4F 125
Cathkin Cres. G68: Cumb 6G 15
Cathkin Dr. G76: Clar 1A 138
Cathkin Gdns. G71: Tann 4C 112
Cathkin Ga. G73: Ruth 5F 125
Cathkin Ho. G73: Ruth 5F 125
Cathkin Pl. G72: Camb 1G 125
Cathkin Recreation Cen. 5F 107
Cathkin Rd. G42: Glas 6D 106
Cathkin Rd. G71: Tann 4C 112
Cathkin Rd. G73: Ruth 5E 125
Cathkin Rd. G76: Crmck 1A 140
Cathkin Rd. G76: Ruth 1B 140
Cathkin Vw. G32: Carm 5B 110
Cathkinview Pl. G42: Glas 6F 107
Cathkinview Rd. G42: Glas 6E 107
Catrine G74: E Kil 1F 157
Catrine Av. G81: Clyd 4F 45
(off Kirkoswald Dr.)
Catrine Ct. G53: Glas 5A 104
Catrine Cres. ML1: Moth 6A 148
Catrine Gdns. G53: Glas 5A 104
Catrine Pl. G53: Glas 5A 104
Catrine Rd. G53: Glas 5A 104
Catrine St. ML9: Lark 3E 171
Catriona Pl. G82: Dumb 3C 20
Catriona Way ML1: Holy 2B 132
Catter Gdns. G62: Miln 2E 27
Cauldstream Pl. G62: Miln 4E 27
Caurnie Vw. G66: Kirkin 6A 34
Causewayside Cres. G32: Glas 2A 110
Causewayside St. G32: Glas 3A 110
Causeyside St. PA1: Pais 1A 102
(Forbes Pl.)
Causeyside St. PA1: Pais 2A 102
(Thompson Brae)
Causeystanes Path G72: Blan 2B 144
(off Winton Cres.)
Cavendish Av. G68: Cumb 6G 15
Cavendish Ct. G5: Glas 1F 107
Cavendish Dr. G77: Newt M 3F 137
Cavendish Pl. G5: Glas 1F 107
Cavendish St. G5: Glas 1F 107
Cavin Dr. G45: Glas 3A 124
Cavin Rd. G45: Glas 3A 124
Cawder Ct. G68: Cumb 6F 15
Cawder Golf Course 1B 50
Cawder Pl. G64: B'rig 4D 50
Cawder Pl. G68: Cumb 6G 15
Cawder Rd. G68: Cumb 6G 15
Cawder Vw. G68: Cumb 6G 15
Cawder Way G68: Cumb 6G 15
Cawdor Cres. ML6: Chap 2E 117
Cawdor Cres. PA7: B'ton 5H 41
Cawdor Way G74: E Kil 6F 141
Cayton Gdns. G69: Bail 1F 111
Cecil St. G12: Glas 6B 64
Cecil St. G76: Clar 2C 138
Cecil St. ML5: Coat 6C 94
Cedar Av. G71: View 5F 113
Cedar Av. G81: Clyd 3H 43
Cedar Av. PA5: John 5F 99
Cedar Ct. G20: Glas 1E 87
Cedar Ct. G72: Flem 3E 127
Cedar Ct. G75: E Kil 6E 157
Cedar Ct. PA10: Kilba 2A 98
Cedar Cres. G78: Barr 6E 119
Cedar Cres. ML3: Ham 2A 162
Cedar Dr. G66: Lenz 2C 52
Cedar Dr. G71: View 5G 113
Cedar Dr. G75: E Kil 6E 157
Cedar Gdns. G73: Ruth 3E 125
Cedar Gdns. ML1: N'hill 3C 132
Cedar Gdns. ML8: Law 5D 166
Cedar La. ML1: Holy 3B 132
Cedar La. ML6: Air 4C 96
Cedar Pl. G72: Blan 6A 128
Cedar Pl. G75: E Kil 6E 157
Cedar Pl. G78: Barr 6F 119
Cedar Rd. FK4: Bank 1E 17
Cedar Rd. G64: B'rig 1D 66
Cedar Rd. G66: Milt C 6C 10
Cedar Rd. G67: Cumb 2D 38
Cedars Gro. G69: Barg 5E 93
Cedar St. G20: Glas 1E 87
Cedar Wlk. G64: B'rig 1D 66
Cedar Wlk. ML1: Carf 5D 132
Cedarwood ML2: Wis 2D 164
Cedarwood Av. G77: Newt M 5F 137
Cedric Pl. G13: Glas 2D 62
Cedric Rd. G13: Glas 2D 62
Celtic FC 6D 88
Celtic FC Training Cen. 2B 8
Celtic FC Visitor Cen. 1D 108
Celtic Pk. 6D 88
Celtic St. G20: Glas 2A 64
Cemetery Rd. G52: Glas 1D 104
Cemetery Rd. G72: Blan 3A 144
Centenary Av. ML6: Air 4F 95
Centenary Ct. G78: Barr 5D 118
(off Cochrane St.)
Centenary Ct. G81: Clyd 6D 44
Centenary Cres. ML4: Bell 1D 130
Centenary Gdns. ML3: Ham 1A 162
Centenary Gdns. ML5: Coat 6B 94
Centenary Quad. ML1: Holy 2A 132
Central Av. G11: Glas 1F 85
Central Av. G32: Glas 2D 110
Central Av. G71: View 1G 129
Central Av. G72: Blan 4C 144
Central Av. G72: Camb 1H 125
Central Av. G81: Clyd 5C 44
Central Av. ML1: Holy 2H 131
Central Cres. ML9: Ashg 5H 171
Central Gro. G32: Glas 1D 110
Central Gro. G72: Camb 1H 125
Central Pk. Vw. PA7: B'ton 6G 41
Central Path G32: Glas 2E 111
Central Rd. PA1: Pais 6A 82
CENTRAL SCOTLAND BRAIN INJURY
REHABILITATION CEN. 2E 151
Central Way G67: Cumb 5G 37
Central Way PA1: Pais 6A 82
Centre, The G78: Barr 5D 118
Centre for Contemporary Arts 3A 6 (3E 87)
(Glasgow)
(off Sauchiehall St.)
Centre Pk. Ct. ML5: Coat 5C 94
Centre Roundabout, The 2H 157
Centre St. G5: Glas 6E 87
Centre St. ML5: Glenb 3G 71
Centre St. ML6: Chap 3D 116
Centre Way G78: Barr 4D 118
Centre W. G74: E Kil 2G 157
Centrum Bus. Pk. ML5: Coat 3D 114
Centurion Pl. ML1: Moth 6D 130
Centurion Way G3: Glas 2A 86
Ceres Gdns. G64: B'rig 6F 51
Ceres Pl. ML1: Moth 1F 147
Cessnock Pl. G72: Camb 2D 126
Cessnock Rd. G33: Mille 4B 68
Cessnock Station (Subway) 5A 86
Cessnock St. G51: Glas 5A 86
Challum Dr. ML1: Moth 6C 148
Chalmers Ct. G40: Glas 5A 88
(off Chalmers St.)
Chalmers Ct. G71: Udd 1D 128
Chalmers Cres. G75: E Kil 4H 157
Chalmers Dr. G75: E Kil 4H 157
Chalmers Ga. G40: Glas 5A 88
(off Claythorn St.)
Chalmers Pl. G40: Glas 5A 88
(off Chalmers St.)
Chalmers St. G40: Glas 5A 88
Chalmers St. G81: Clyd 6D 44
Chamberlain La. G13: Glas 4E 63
Chamberlain Rd. G13: Glas 3E 63
Chancellors Hall G4: Glas 5G 7 (4H 87)
(off Rottenrow East)
Chancellor St. G11: Glas 1H 85
CHANTINGHALL 6F 145
Chantinghall Gdns. ML3: Ham 6F 145
(off St Giles Way)
Chantinghall Rd. ML3: Ham 6F 145
Chantinghall Ter. ML3: Ham 6F 145
CHAPEL 1G 167
Chapel Ct. G73: Ruth 5B 108
Chapel Cres. ML3: Ham 5H 161
Chapelcross Av. ML6: Air 2A 96
CHAPELHALL 3E 117
Chapelhall Ind. Est. ML6: Chap 1D 116
CHAPEL HILL 6D 22
Chapelhill Rd. PA2: Pais 3C 102
Chapelknowe Rd. ML1: Carf 6C 132
Chapelknowe Rd. ML1: Cle 6C 132
Chapel La. ML6: Air 3A 96
Chapel Pl. G78: Neil 2D 134
Chapel Rd. G81: Dun 1C 44
Chapel Rd. ML2: Wis 2F 167
Chapelside Av. ML6: Air 3A 96
Chapelside Rd. G74: Ners 3A 142
Chapel St. G20: Glas 4C 64
Chapel St. G66: Len 3F 9
Chapel St. G73: Ruth 5B 108
Chapel St. ML1: Cle 6H 133
Chapel St. ML3: Ham 6A 146
(off Leechlee Rd.)
Chapel St. ML6: Air 3A 96
Chapel St. ML8: Carl 3D 174
Chapel St. Ind. Est. G20: Glas 3C 64
Chapelton Av. G61: Bear 3F 47
Chapelton Av. G82: Dumb 2G 19

202 A–Z Glasgow

Chapelton Gdns. – Claremont Ter.

Chapelton Gdns. G61: Bear 3F 47
Chapelton Gdns. G82: Dumb 2G 19
Chapelton Rd. G67: Cumb 1E 57
Chapelton St. G22: Glas 3F 65
Chaplet Av. G13: Glas 1C 62
Chapman Av. ML5: Glenb 3G 71
Chapmans Ct. ML2: Wis 5G 149
Chapman St. G42: Glas 3E 107
Chappell St. G78: Barr 4D 118
Charing Cross 2C 170
CHARING CROSS INTERCHANGE 2H 5 (2E 87) (M8, Junction 18)
Charing Cross La. G3: Glas 3G 5 (3D 86) (off Granville St.)
Charing Cross Station (Rail) 3H 5 (3E 87) (Glasgow)
Charles Av. PA4: Renf 5F 61
Charles Cres. G66: Lenz 4D 52
Charles Cres. ML8: Carl 4F 175
Charles Dr. G66: Milt C 5B 10
Charleson Row G65: Croy 2B 36
Charles Path ML6: Chap 4D 116
Charles Quad. ML1: Holy 2A 132
Charles St. G21: Glas 1H 7 (2A 88)
Charles St. G65: Kils 2H 13
Charles St. ML2: Wis 5C 148
CHARLESTON 3A 102
Charleston Sq. PA2: Pais 3A 102
Charlotte Av. G64: Torr 5D 30
Charlotte Path ML9: Lark 3C 170
Charlotte Pl. PA2: Pais 3A 102
Charlotte St. G1: Glas 5H 87
Charlotte St. G82: Dumb 3D 18
Charn Ter. ML1: Moth 6C 148
Charnwood Av. PA5: John 5D 98
Chartwell Rd. PA7: B'ton 4H 41
Chassels St. ML5: Coat 3C 94
Chateau Gro. ML3: Ham 1C 162
Chatelherault 3D 162
Chatelherault Av. G72: Camb 2G 125
Chatelherault Country Pk. 2C 162
Chatelherault Country Pk. Vis. Cen. 3D 162
Chatelherault Cres. ML3: Ham 2A 162
Chatelherault Station (Rail) 2E 163
Chatelherault Wlk. ML3: Ham 2A 162
Chatham G75: E Kil 4E 157
Chatton St. G23: Glas 6B 48
Chatton Wlk. ML5: Coat 3F 115
Cheapside St. G3: Glas 6G 5 (4D 86)
Cheapside St. G76: Eag 6C 154
Chelmsford Dr. G12: Glas 4H 63
Cherry Av. G67: Cumb 6E 17
Cherry Bank G66: Lenz 2B 52
Cherrybank Gdns. G77: Newt M 6B 136
Cherrybank Rd. G43: Glas 1D 122
Cherrybank Wlk. ML6: Air 3F 95
Cherry Cres. G81: Clyd 3C 44
Cherry Gro. G69: Barg 5F 93
Cherryhill Vw. ML9: Lark 2B 170
Cherry La. FK4: Bank 1E 17
Cherry Pl. G64: B'rig 1D 66
Cherry Pl. G66: Milt C 1B 32
Cherry Pl. G71: View 6H 113
Cherry Pl. ML1: Holy 2B 132
Cherry Pl. PA5: John 4G 99
Cherryridge Dr. G69: Barg 5E 93
Cherry Tree Ct. G72: Camb 2A 126
Cherrytree Cres. ML9: Lark 6A 164
Cherrytree Dr. G72: Flem 3E 127
Cherrytree Wynd G75: E Kil 5G 157
Cherry Wlk. ML1: Moth 6G 147
Cherry Wood Cres. G33: Step 5D 68
Cherrywood Rd. PA5: Eld 3A 100
Chesterfield Av. G12: Glas 4G 63
Chesterfield Gdns. G12: Glas 4G 63
Chesters Cres. ML1: Moth 1E 147
Chesters Pl. G73: Ruth 6B 108
Chesters Rd. G61: Bear 3C 46
Chester St. G32: Glas 6A 90
Chestnut Av. G67: Cumb 6E 17
Chestnut Av. PA7: B'ton 2F 41
Chestnut Ct. G66: Milt C 6B 10
Chestnut Ct. G67: Cumb 6E 17
Chestnut Cres. G71: View 6H 113
Chestnut Cres. G75: E Kil 5E 157
Chestnut Cres. ML3: Ham 1A 162
Chestnut Dr. G66: Lenz 1B 52
Chestnut Dr. G81: Clyd 2B 44
Chestnut Gro. G69: G'csh 3G 71
Chestnut Gro. G72: Blan 1A 144
Chestnut Gro. ML1: Moth 4F 147
Chestnut Gro. ML8: Carl 4C 174
Chestnut Gro. ML9: Lark 6A 164
Chestnut La. G62: Miln 4E 27
Chestnut Pl. G67: Cumb 6E 17
Chestnut Pl. PA5: John 5G 99
Chestnut St. G22: Glas 4H 65
Chestnut Wlk. G66: Len 4G 9
Chestnut Way G72: Flem 3E 127
Cheviot Av. G78: Barr 5E 119
Cheviot Cl. G13: Glas 3B 62
Cheviot Ct. ML5: Coat 2E 115
Cheviot Ct. ML6: Air 1B 96
Cheviot Cres. G75: E Kil 1B 168
Cheviot Cres. ML2: Wis 5F 149
Cheviot Dr. G77: Newt M 6C 136
Cheviot Gdns. G61: Bear 6D 26
Cheviot Rd. G43: Glas 2A 122
Cheviot Rd. ML3: Ham 1B 162
Cheviot Rd. ML9: Lark 3E 171
Cheviot Rd. PA2: Pais 4A 102
Cheviot St. G72: Blan 2A 144
Chirmorie Cres. G53: Glas 4A 104
Chirmorie Pl. G53: Glas 4A 104
Chirnside Ct. G72: Blan 4C 144
Chirnside Pl. G52: Glas 5A 84
Chirnside Rd. G52: Glas 5A 84
Chirnsyde Sports Cen. 2H 65
Chisholm Av. PA7: B'ton 4A 42
Chisholm Dr. G77: Newt M 3E 137
Chisholm Pl. ML1: Moth 1B 164
Chisholm St. G1: Glas 5H 87
Chisholm St. ML5: Coat 3D 94
Chrighton Grn. G71: Tann 5E 113
Chriss Av. ML3: Ham 4H 161
Christchurch Dr. G40: Glas 2D 108
Christchurch Pl. G75: E Kil 4D 156
Christian St. G43: Glas 5A 106
Christie La. PA3: Pais 6A 82
Christie Pl. G72: Camb 2A 126
Christie St. ML4: Bell 2F 131
Christie St. PA1: Pais 6B 82
Christopher St. G21: Glas 2C 88
CHRYSTON 1B 70
Chryston Rd. G66: Kirkin 1H 53
Chryston Rd. G69: Chry 1B 70
Chryston Valley Bus. Cen. G69: Chry 1A 70
Chuckie La. PA5: Brkfld 5C 78
Church Av. G33: Step 3D 68
Church Av. G73: Ruth 2E 125
Church Av. ML2: Newm 5D 150
Church Ct. G82: Dumb 4F 19
Church Ct. ML3: Ham 5A 146
Church Cres. ML6: Air 2E 97
Church Dr. G66: Lenz 1C 52
Church Hill PA1: Pais 6A 82
Churchill Av. G74: E Kil 2H 157
Churchill Av. PA5: John 6C 98
Churchill Cres. G71: Both 4F 129
Churchill Dr. G11: Glas 5F 63
Churchill Dr. PA7: B'ton 4H 41
Churchill Pl. PA10: Kilba 2A 98
Churchill Way G64: B'rig 6C 50
Church La. G65: Kils 3H 13 (not continuous)
Church La. ML2: Newm 5D 150
Church La. ML5: Coat 4C 94
Church La. ML8: Carl 4D 174
Church Manse La. PA11: Bri W 3F 77
Church Pl. G60: Old K 1E 43
Church Pl. G73: Ruth 5D 108
Church Rd. G46: Giff 5A 122
Church Rd. G69: Muirh 2A 70
Church Rd. G76: Busby 3D 138
Church Rd. G78: Barr 4E 119
Church Rd. ML2: Newm 2H 151
Church Rd. PA11: Bri W 4G 77
Church Rd. PA11: Quarr V 1A 76
Church St. G11: Glas 1A 4 (1A 86)
Church St. G65: Kils 3H 13
Church St. G69: Bail 1A 112
Church St. G71: Udd 2D 128
Church St. G72: Blan 2C 144
Church St. G81: Clyd 4D 44
Church St. G82: Dumb 4F 19 (not continuous)
Church St. ML1: N'hill 3F 133
Church St. ML3: Ham 5A 146
Church St. ML5: Coat 4C 94
Church St. ML9: Lark 2C 170
Church St. PA10: Kilba 2A 98
Church St. PA5: John 2F 99
Church Vw. G72: Camb 6A 110
Church Vw. ML5: Coat 4C 94
Church Vw. Ct. G66: Len 2F 9
Church Vw. Gdns. ML4: Bell 2C 130
Cineworld Cinema 6C 104 (Glasgow)
Cineworld Cinema 3C 6 (3F 87) (Glasgow, Renfrew St) (off Renfrew St)
Cineworld Cinema 6E 89 (Glasgow, The Forge Shop. Cen.)
Circus Dr. G31: Glas 4B 88
Circus Pl. G31: Glas 4B 88
Circus Pl. La. G31: Glas 3B 88
Citadel Pl. ML1: Moth 1E 147
Citizen La. G2: Glas 5D 6 (4G 87)
Citizens' Theatre 6G 87
Citrus Cres. G71: View 5G 113
Cityford Cres. G73: Ruth 6B 108
Cityford Dr. G73: Ruth 1B 124
City Halls 6F 7 (4H 87) (Glasgow)
City Pk. G31: Glas 3B 88
Civic Sq. ML1: Moth 4H 147 (off Camp St.)
Civic St. G4: Glas 1B 6 (1F 87)
Civic Way G66: Kirkin 6C 32
Clachan, The ML2: Wis 6H 149
Clachan Dr. G51: Glas 3E 85
Clachan Way ML5: Coat 6A 94
CLADDENS 3E 53
Claddens Pl. G22: Glas 3F 65
Claddens Pl. G66: Lenz 3E 53
Claddens Quad. G22: Glas 3G 65
Claddens St. G22: Glas 3F 65
Claddens Wynd G66: Lenz 3E 53
Cladence Gro. G75: E Kil 6H 157
Claire St. ML2: Newm 4D 150
Clairinsh Gdns. PA4: Renf 2E 83
Clairmont Gdns. G3: Glas 2F 5 (2D 86)
Clair Rd. G64: B'rig 6F 51
Clamp Rd. ML2: Wis 5C 148
Clamps Gro. G74: E Kil 3A 158
Clamps Ter. G74: E Kil 3B 158
Clamps Wood G74: E Kil 3A 158
Clanrye Dr. ML5: Coat 1C 114
Clapperhow Rd. ML1: Carf 6A 132
Claremont Av. G66: Kirkin 5B 32
Claremont Dr. G62: Miln 4G 27
Claremont Gdns. G62: Miln 4G 27
Claremont Pl. G3: Glas 2F 5 (2D 86)
Claremont St. G3: Glas 3E 5 (3C 86) (not continuous)
Claremont Ter. G3: Glas 2F 5 (2D 86)

A–Z Glasgow 203

Clyde Pl. – Coltmuir Dr.

Clyde Pl. G72: Camb 3D **126**
Clyde Pl. ML1: New S 3A **132**
Clyde Pl. PA5: John 5C **98**
Clyde Pl. La. G5: Glas 5E **87**
Clyde Pl. Sq. G5: Glas 5F **87**
Clyde Retail Pk. 6E **45**
Clyde Rd. PA3: Pais 4D **82**
CLYDESDALE 3G **131**
Clydesdale Av. ML2: Wis 2D **164**
Clydesdale Av. ML3: Ham 5H **161**
Clydesdale Av. PA3: Pais 2C **82**
Clydesdale Ct. ML1: New S 3H **131**
Clydesdale Cricket Ground **3B 106**
Clydesdale Pl. ML3: Ham 5H **161**
Clydesdale Rd. ML4: Bell 3F **131**
Clydesdale Rd. ML4: New S 3F **131**
Clydesdale St. ML1: New S 3H **131**
Clydesdale St. ML3: Ham 5G **145**
Clydesdale St. ML4: Bell 3G **131**
Clydesdale St. ML9: Lark 1C **170**
Clyde Shop. Cen. **5D 44**
Clydeshore Rd. G82: Dumb 5E **19**
Clydeside Distillery, The G3: Glas **4A 4 (3A 86)**
Clydeside Expressway G11: Glas 1F **85**
Clydeside Expressway G14: Glas 6D **62**
Clydeside Expressway G3: Glas 5D **4** (3B **86**)
Clydeside Ind. Est. G14: Glas 1D **84**
Clydesmill Dr. G32: Glas 6A **110**
Clydesmill Gro. G32: Glas 6A **110**
Clydesmill Pl. G32: Glas 5A **110**
Clydesmill Rd. G32: Glas 5H **109**
Clyde Sq. G67: Cumb 4H **37**
(within The Cumbernauld Shop. Cen.)
Clyde St. G1: Glas 5F **87**
Clyde St. G81: Clyd 1E **61**
Clyde St. ML5: Coat 4E **95**
Clyde St. ML8: Carl 3B **174**
Clyde St. PA4: Renf 4F **61**
Clyde Ter. G71: Both 6E **129**
Clyde Ter. ML1: Moth 1C **164**
Clyde Twr. G74: E Kil 4B **158**
Clyde Twr. ML1: Moth 4G **147**
(off Freesia Ct.)
Clyde Tunnel 2E **85**
Clydevale G71: Both 6F **129**
Clyde Valley Av. ML1: Moth 5G **147**
Clyde Vw. ML3: Ham 2F **161**
Clyde Vw. ML9: Ashg 5A **172**
Clyde Vw. PA2: Pais 3D **102**
Clydeview G71: Both 6G **129**
Clydeview G82: Dumb 5E **19**
Clyde Vw. Ct. G60: Bowl 5A **22**
Clydeview La. G11: Glas 1F **85**
Clydeview Shop. Cen. **2C 144**
Clydeview Ter. G32: Carm 5C **110**
Clyde Wlk. G67: Cumb 4H **37**
(within The Cumbernauld Shop. Cen.)
Clyde Wlk. ML2: Newm 3E **151**
Clyde Walkway G3: Glas 6G **5** (5D **86**)
Clyde Way G67: Cumb 4H **37**
(within The Cumbernauld Shop. Cen.)
Clyde Way PA3: Pais 4D **82**
Clydeway Golf Driving Range **6A 112**
Clydeway Ind. Est. G3: Glas 4E **5** (4C **86**)
(off Finnieston Sq.)
Clyde Workshops G32: Glas 4H **109**
Clynder St. G51: Glas 5H **85**
Clyth Dr. G46: Giff 5B **122**
Coach Cl. G65: Kils 3C **14**
Coach Pl. G65: Kils 4A **14**
Coach Rd. G65: Kils 4B **14**
Coalburn Pk. G71: Udd 2E **129**
Coalburn Rd. G71: Both 2F **129**
Coalhall Av. ML1: Carf 6A **132**
Coalhill St. G31: Glas 6D **88**
Coatbank Bus. Cen. ML5: Coat 5D **94**
Coatbank St. ML5: Coat 6D **94**
Coatbank Way ML5: Coat 5D **94**
COATBRIDGE 4C **94**
Coatbridge Central Station (Rail) **4B 94**
Coatbridge College Leisure Cen. **4D 94**
Coatbridge Golf Course **2G 93**
Coatbridge Indoor Bowling Club **4F 95**
Coatbridge Ind. Est. ML5: Coat 2C **94**
Coatbridge Outdoor Sports Cen. **5A 94**
Coatbridge Rd. G69: Bail 6B **92**
Coatbridge Rd. G69: Barg 5D **92**
Coatbridge Rd. G69: G'csh 5E **71**
Coatbridge Rd. ML5: Coat 2D **94**
Coatbridge Rd. ML5: Glenb 4B **72**
Coatbridge Rd. ML6: Glenm 1E **95**
Coatbridge Sunnyside Station (Rail) **3C 94**
COATDYKE 5F **95**
Coatdyke Station (Rail) **4F 95**
COATHILL HOSPITAL **2C 114**
Coathill St. ML5: Coat 1C **114**
Coats Cres. G69: Bail 6G **91**
Coats Dr. PA2: Pais 2F **101**
COATSHILL 6A **128**
Coatshill Av. G72: Blan 6A **128**
Coats Observatory, The **6H 81**
Coats St. ML5: Coat 5D **94**
Cobbett Rd. ML1: Moth 4D **146**
Cobblerigg Way G71: Udd 2C **128**
Cobbleton Rd. ML1: New S 5H **131**
Cobden Cres. G61: Bear 6H **27**
Cobden Rd. G21: Glas 1B **88**
Cobington Pl. G33: Glas 2B **90**
Cobinshaw St. G32: Glas 5A **90**
Coburg St. G5: Glas 6F **87**
(Kilbarchan St.)
Coburg St. G5: Glas 5F **87**
(Oxford St.)
Cochno Brae G81: Hard 6D **24**
Cochno Gdns. G81: Hard 6D **24**
Cochno Rd. G81: Faif 4B **24**
Cochno Rd. G81: Hard 4B **24**
Cochno Rd. E. G81: Faif 6G **25**
Cochno St. G81: Clyd 1E **61**
Cochran Av. G78: Neil 2E **135**
COCHRANE CASTLE 5E **99**
Cochrane Castle Golf Course **5E 99**
Cochrane Ct. G62: Miln 5A **28**
Cochranemill Rd. PA5: John 4C **98**
Cochrane Sq. PA3: Lin 5H **79**
Cochrane St. G1: Glas 5E **7** (4G **87**)
Cochrane St. G78: Barr 5D **118**
Cochrane St. ML4: Bell 2B **130**
Cochran St. PA1: Pais 1B **102**
Cockburn Pl. ML5: Coat 1B **114**
Cockels Loan PA4: Renf 2D **82**
Cockenzie St. G32: Glas 6A **90**
Cockerhill Rd. G52: Glas 4D **104**
Cockhill Way ML4: Bell 1H **129**
Cockmuir St. G21: Glas 5C **66**
Coddington Cres. ML1: Holy 6H **115**
Cogan Pl. G78: Barr 5D **118**
Cogan Rd. G43: Glas 1A **122**
Cogan St. G43: Glas 6A **106**
Cogan St. G78: Barr 5D **118**
Colbert St. G40: Glas 1B **108**
Colbreggan Ct. G81: Hard 1E **45**
Colbreggan Gdns. G81: Hard 1E **45**
Colbreggan Pl. G81: Hard 1E **45**
Colchester Dr. G12: Glas 3G **63**
Coldingham Av. G14: Glas 3G **61**
Coldstream Cres. ML2: Wis 4A **150**
Coldstream Dr. G73: Ruth 6F **109**
Coldstream Dr. PA2: Pais 4E **101**
Coldstream Gro. ML6: Chap 5E **117**
Coldstream Pl. G21: Glas 6G **65**
Coldstream Rd. G81: Clyd 6D **44**
Coldstream St. G72: Blan 2B **144**
Colebrooke La. G12: Glas 6C **64**
Colebrooke Pl. G12: Glas 6C **64**
Colebrooke St. G12: Glas 6C **64**
Colebrooke Ter. G12: Glas 6C **64**
Colebrook St. G72: Camb 1A **126**
Coleridge G75: E Kil 4C **156**
Coleridge Av. G71: Both 4F **129**
Colfin St. G34: Glas 2A **92**
Colgrain Av. G20: Glas 3E **65**
Colgrain Ter. G20: Glas 3D **64**
Colgrave Cres. G32: Glas 2H **109**
Colinbar Circ. G78: Barr 6D **118**
Colinslee Av. PA2: Pais 4B **102**
Colinslee Cres. PA2: Pais 4B **102**
Colinslee Dr. PA2: Pais 4B **102**
Colinslie Rd. G53: Glas 5D **104**
Colinton Gdns. G69: Chry 6A **54**
Colinton Pl. G32: Glas 4B **90**
Colintraive Av. G33: Glas 6G **67**
Colintraive Cres. G33: Glas 6G **67**
Coll G74: E Kil 3C **158**
Collace Av. PA11: Bri W 4F **77**
Colla Gdns. G64: B'rig 5F **51**
Coll Av. PA4: Renf 2F **83**
Coll Dr. ML5: Coat 1H **113**
College Ga. G61: Bear 1C **46**
COLLEGE MILTON 6D **140**
College St. G1: Glas 6G **7** (4H **87**)
College St. G82: Dumb 3F **19**
College Way G4: Glas 4E **7** (3G **87**)
College Way G75: E Kil 4B **158**
College Way G82: Dumb 4F **19**
College Way Shop. Cen. **4E 19**
Collessie Dr. G33: Glas 1C **90**
Collier St. PA5: John 2F **99**
Colliertree Rd. ML6: Air 3D **96**
Colliery Ga. G32: Glas 3H **109**
Colliery Pl. G65: Twe 2C **34**
Colliery Rd. G32: Glas 3G **109**
Colliery St. G32: Glas 3H **109**
Collie Wynd G72: Newt 6F **111**
Collina Quad. G20: Glas 3B **64**
Collina St. G20: Glas 3A **64**
Collins Gallery **5F 7 (4H 87)**
Collins St. G4: Glas 5H **7** (4A **88**)
Collins St. G81: Faif 1E **45**
Coll Lea ML3: Ham 2D **160**
Coll Pl. G21: Glas 1D **88**
Coll Pl. ML6: Air 6C **96**
Collree Gdns. G34: Glas 4A **92**
Coll St. G21: Glas 1D **88**
Coll St. ML2: Newm 3D **150**
Collylinn Rd. G61: Bear 3E **47**
Colmonell Av. G13: Glas 2H **61**
Colonsay G74: E Kil 4B **158**
Colonsay Av. PA4: Renf 2E **83**
Colonsay Cres. ML5: Coat 1H **113**
Colonsay Dr. G77: Newt M 4B **136**
Colonsay Rd. G52: Glas 6E **85**
Colonsay Rd. PA2: Pais 6H **101**
Colquhoun Av. G52: Hill E 4A **84**
Colquhoun Ct. G41: Glas 1A **106**
Colquhoun Dr. G61: Bear 2D **46**
Colquhoun Pk. G52: Hill E 4B **84**
(off Hepburn Rd.)
Colquhoun Rd. G82: Mil 4E **21**
Colquhoun St. G82: Dumb 3G **19**
Colson Pl. ML4: Bell 4E **131**
COLSTON 2A **66**
Colston Av. G64: B'rig 2B **66**
Colston Dr. G64: B'rig 2B **66**
Colston Gdns. G64: B'rig 2A **66**
Colston Gdns. ML6: Air 4C **96**
Colston Gro. G64: B'rig 2B **66**
Colston Path G64: B'rig 2A **66**
Colston Pl. G64: B'rig 2A **66**
Colston Pl. ML6: Air 4C **96**
Colston Rd. G64: B'rig 2A **66**
Colston Rd. ML6: Air 4C **96**
Colston Row ML6: Air 4C **96**
Colston Ter. ML6: Air 4C **96**
Colt Av. ML5: Coat 2A **94**
Coltmuir Cres. G64: B'rig 1A **66**
Coltmuir Dr. G64: B'rig 1A **66**

Coltmuir Gdns. – Corselet Rd.

Coltmuir Gdns. G64: B'rig 1A 66
Coltmuir St. G22: Glas 3F 65
COLTNESS 3A 150
Coltness Dr. ML4: Bell 3D 130
Coltness La. G33: Glas 4C 90
Coltness Rd. ML2: Wis 3A 150
Coltness St. G33: Glas 3C 90
Coltpark Av. G64: B'rig 1A 66
Coltpark La. G64: B'rig 1B 66
Colt Pl. ML5: Coat 3C 94
Coltsfoot Dr. G53: Glas 4B 120
Coltswood Ct. ML5: Coat 3C 94
Coltswood Rd. ML5: Coat 2C 94
Colt Ter. ML5: Coat 3C 94
Columba G81: Clyd 5F 45
Columba Ct. G71: View 6G 113
Columba Cres. ML1: Moth 5F 131
Columba Ho. G2: Glas 5A 6 (4E 87)
(off Blythswood Ct.)
Columba Path G72: Blan 1A 144
Columba St. G51: Glas 4H 85
Columbia Pl. G75: E Kil 3D 156
Columbia Way G75: E Kil 3D 156
Columbine Way ML8: Carl 5D 174
Colvend Av. G73: Ruth 4C 124
Colvend Dr. G73: Ruth 4D 124
Colvend La. G40: Glas 2B 108
Colvend St. G40: Glas 2B 108
Colville Cl. G72: Camb 1D 126
Colville Ct. ML1: Carf 6C 132
Colville Dr. G73: Ruth 1F 125
Colville Pk. Golf Course 6H 131
Colvilles Pk. G75: E Kil 5B 158
Colvilles Pl. G75: E Kil 5B 158
Colvilles Rd. G75: E Kil 6A 158
Colwood Av. G53: Glas 3A 120
Colwood Gdns. G53: Glas 4A 120
Colwood Path G53: Glas 3A 120
Colwood Pl. G53: Glas 4A 120
Colwood Sq. G53: Glas 4A 120
Colwyn Ct. ML6: Air 2A 96
COLZIUM 2D 14
Colzium-Margaret Lennox Memorial Estate
2B 14
Colzium Vw. G65: Kils 3A 14
Colzium Walled Gdn. 1B 14
Combe Quad. ML4: Bell 4A 130
Comedie Rd. G33: Step 5E 69
Comely Bank ML3: Ham 6D 144
Comelybank La. G82: Dumb 3D 18
Comelybank Rd. G82: Dumb 3D 18
Comelypark Pl. G31: Glas 5C 88
(off Comelypark St.)
Comelypark St. G31: Glas 5B 88
Commerce St. G5: Glas 6F 87
Commercial Ct. G5: Glas 6H 87
Commercial Rd. G5: Glas 6G 87
Commercial Rd. G78: Barr 4E 119
Common Grn. ML3: Ham 5A 146
Commonhead Av. ML6: Air 2H 95
Commonhead La. ML6: Air 2H 95
Commonhead Rd. G34: Glas 3B 92
Commonhead Rd. G69: Barg 3C 92
Commonhead St. ML6: Air 2H 95
Commonside St. ML6: Air 2H 95
Commore Av. G78: Barr 6F 119
Commore Dr. G13: Glas 2A 62
Commore Pl. G78: Neil 3C 134
Community Av. ML4: Bell 5C 130
Community Pl. ML4: Bell 4D 130
Community Rd. ML4: Bell 4B 130
Compton Ct. G74: T'hall 3H 155
Comrie Cres. ML3: Ham 6B 144
Comrie Rd. G33: Step 4C 68
Comrie St. G32: Glas 2B 110
Conacher Dr. G33: Glas 2A 68
Conan Ct. G72: Camb 2D 126
Cona St. G46: T'bnk 3E 121
Condie Cres. ML5: Coat 1E 115
Condor Glen ML1: Holy 6G 115
CONDORRAT 6C 36
CONDORRAT INTERCHANGE 5D 36
Condorrat Ring Rd. G67: Cumb 5D 36
Condorrat Rd. G67: Cumb 4D 56
Condorrat Rd. ML6: Glenm 5F 57
Coney Dr. ML1: Moth 1D 148
Coneypark Cres. FK4: Bank 1C 16
Coneypark Pl. FK4: Bank 1C 16
Congress Rd. G3: Glas 5C 4 (4B 86)
Congress Way G3: Glas 6D 4 (4C 86)
Conifer Pl. G66: Lenz 1B 52
Conisborough Cl. G34: Glas 2G 91
Conisborough Gdns. G34: Glas 2G 91
Conisborough Path G34: Glas 1F 91
Conisborough Pl. G34: Glas 2G 91
Conisborough Rd. G34: Glas 2F 91
Coniston G75: E Kil 6B 156
Coniston Cres. ML3: Ham 5G 161
Coniston Dr. ML4: Bell 4D 130
Conistone Cres. G69: Bail 1F 111
Conival Cl. ML1: Moth 6C 148
Connal St. G40: Glas 2D 108
Connell Cres. G62: Miln 4A 28
Connell Gro. ML2: Wis 1E 165
Connelly Pl. ML1: Moth 2F 147
(off Nth. Orchard St.)
Conniston St. G32: Glas 4G 89
Connollys Land G81: Dun 1C 44
(off Dumbarton Rd.)
Connor Rd. G78: Barr 4D 118
Connor St. ML6: Air 2E 97
Conon Av. G61: Bear 4C 46
Conservation Pl. ML2: Wis 2H 165
Consett La. G33: Glas 3C 90
Consett St. G33: Glas 3C 90
Constantine Way ML1: Moth 6E 131
Constarry Rd. G65: Croy 6A 14
Consul Way ML1: Moth 6E 131
Contin Pl. G20: Glas 4B 64
Convair Way PA4: Renf 2F 83
Conval Way PA3: Pais 3H 81
Convent Rd. G78: Barr 5F 119
Conway Ct. G66: Kirkin 5F 33
Cook Cres. ML1: Carf 6C 132
Cook St. G5: Glas 6E 87
Coo La. G76: Eag 6C 154
Coolgardie Grn. G75: E Kil 4E 157
Coolgardie Pl. G75: E Kil 4E 157
Cooperage Ct. G14: Glas 3F 61
Cooperage Pl. G3: Glas 3A 4 (3A 86)
Co-operative Ter. PA5: John 2G 99
Cooper Av. ML8: Carl 2C 174
Cooper Cres. ML3: Fern 1D 162
Cooper Gdns. ML3: Fern 1D 162
Cooper's Well St. G11: Glas 1A 4 (2A 86)
Copenhagen Av. G75: E Kil 5G 157
Copland Pl. G51: Glas 5H 85
Copland Quad. G51: Glas 5H 85
Copland Rd. G51: Glas 6H 85
Coplaw Ct. G42: Glas 2E 107
Coplaw St. G42: Glas 2E 107
Copperfield La. G71: Tann 6E 113
Copperwood Ct. ML3: Ham 4F 145
Copperwood Cres. ML3: Ham 4F 145
Copperwood Wynd ML3: Ham 4F 145
Copsewood Cres. ML5: Coat 2D 94
Coralmount Gdns. G66: Kirkin 6E 33
Corbeil Pl. G64: B'rig 4D 50
Corbett Ct. G32: Glas 2H 109
Corbette Pl. PA2: Pais 1D 102
Corbett Ga. G32: Glas 2A 110
Corbett Pl. G32: Glas 2A 110
Corbett St. G32: Glas 2H 109
Corbett Wynd G32: Glas 2A 110
Corbie Pl. G62: Miln 3D 26
Corbiston Way G67: Cumb 3B 38
Cordiner La. G44: Glas 6F 107
Cordiner St. G44: Glas 6F 107
CORKERHILL 3D 104
Corkerhill Gdns. G52: Glas 1E 105
Corkerhill Pl. G52: Glas 3D 104
Corkerhill Rd. G52: Glas 2D 104
Corkerhill Station (Rail) 3D 104
Corlaich Av. G42: Glas 6A 108
Corlaich Dr. G42: Glas 6A 108
Corless Ct. G71: Udd 1E 129
Cormack Av. G64: Torr 4E 31
Cormorant Av. PA6: C'lee 3D 78
Cornaig Rd. G53: Glas 5B 104
Cornalee Gdns. G53: Glas 5A 104
Cornalee Pl. G53: Glas 5A 104
(not continuous)
Cornalee Rd. G53: Glas 5B 104
Cornelian Ter. ML4: Bell 3C 130
Cornelia St. ML1: Moth 6D 130
Cornet Gdns. ML1: Carf 1C 148
Cornfield Ct. G72: Camb 1E 127
Cornfoot Cres. G74: E Kil 1C 158
Cornhill Dr. ML5: Coat 3A 94
Cornhill St. G21: Glas 4C 66
Cornish Ct. ML5: Coat 3B 94
Cornmill Ct. G81: Dun 1C 44
Corn Mill Rd. G66: Kirkin 1G 53
Cornock Cres. G81: Clyd 4D 44
Cornock St. G81: Clyd 4D 44
Cornsilloch Brae ML9: Lark 2H 171
Corn St. G4: Glas 1B 6 (1F 87)
Cornwall Av. G73: Ruth 2F 125
Cornwall Ct. G74: E Kil 2H 157
Cornwall St. G41: Glas 6B 86
Cornwall St. G74: E Kil 2F 157
Cornwall St. Sth. G41: Glas 6B 86
Cornwall Way G74: E Kil 2H 157
Coronation Av. ML9: Lark 5C 170
Coronation Ct. ML1: New S 3H 131
Coronation Cres. ML9: Lark 5C 170
Coronation Pl. G69: G'csh 2C 70
Coronation Pl. ML9: Lark 5D 170
Coronation Rd. ML1: New S 3H 131
Coronation Rd. ML4: New S 3H 131
Coronation Rd. E. ML1: New S 4H 131
Coronation Rd. Ind. Est. ML1: New S 3H 131
(off Regency Way)
Coronation St. ML2: Wis 6B 150
Coronation Way G61: Bear 5F 47
Corpach Pl. G34: Glas 2B 92
Corporation Yd. G15: Glas 4H 45
Corra Linn ML3: Ham 6E 145
Corran Av. G77: Newt M 3C 136
Corran St. G33: Glas 3H 89
Correen Gdns. G61: Bear 6B 26
Corrie Brae G65: Kils 2G 13
Corrie Ct. ML3: Ham 1D 160
Corrie Dr. ML1: Moth 2D 146
Corrie Dr. PA1: Pais 1G 103
Corrie Gdns. G75: E Kil 1B 168
Corrie Gro. G44: Neth 3D 122
Corrie Pl. G66: Lenz 3E 53
Corrie Rd. G65: Kils 2G 13
Corrie Vw. G68: Cumb 5B 36
Corrie Vw. Cotts. G65: Twe 1C 34
Corrie Way ML9: Lark 3D 170
Corrour Rd. G43: Glas 6B 106
Corrour Rd. G77: Newt M 3C 136
Corsebar Av. PA2: Pais 3G 101
Corsebar Cres. PA2: Pais 4G 101
Corsebar Dr. PA2: Pais 3G 101
Corsebar La. PA2: Pais 4F 101
Corsebar Rd. PA2: Pais 4F 101
Corsebar Way PA2: Pais 2G 101
CORSEFORD 5C 98
Corseford Av. PA5: John 5C 98
Corsehill Path G34: Glas 3A 92
Corsehill Pl. G34: Glas 3A 92
Corsehill St. G34: Glas 3A 92
Corselet Rd. G53: Glas 5B 120
Corselet Rd. G78: Barr 6A 120

Corse Rd. – Craigie La.

Corse Rd. G52: Glas 5G **83**
Corsewall Av. G32: Glas 2E **111**
Corsewall St. ML5: Coat 4A **94**
Corsford Dr. G53: Glas 1C **120**
Corsock Av. ML3: Ham 1C **160**
Corsock St. G31: Glas 4D **88**
Corson Ct. ML4: Bell 4C **130**
Corston St. G33: Glas 3F **89**
Cortachy Pl. G64: B'rig 6F **51**
Cortmalaw Av. G33: Glas 2G **67**
Cortmalaw Av. G66: Milt C 1C **32**
Cortmalaw Cl. G33: Glas 2G **67**
Cortmalaw Cres. G33: Glas 2G **67**
Cortmalaw Gdns. G33: Glas 2H **67**
Cortmalaw Ga. G33: Glas 2G **67**
Cortmalaw Gro. G33: Glas 2G **67**
Cortmalaw Loan G33: Glas 2G **67**
Cortmalaw Rd. G33: Glas 2G **67**
Coruisk Dr. G76: Clar 1B **138**
Coruisk Way PA2: Pais 5C **100**
Corunna Ct. ML8: Carl 4F **175**
Corunna St. G3: Glas 3D **4** (3C **86**)
Corvus Pl. ML1: Moth 1C **148**
Coshneuk Rd. G33: Mille 4B **68**
Cosy Neuk ML9: Lark 4E **171**
Cottar St. G20: Glas 2C **64**
Cotton Av. PA3: Lin 6H **79**
Cottongrass Ct. G66: Lenz 1F **53**
Cottonmill Ct. ML6: Air 2A **96**
Cottonmill Dr. G66: Milt C 5B **10**
Cotton St. G40: Glas 3C **108**
Cotton St. PA1: Pais 1B **102**
Cotton St. Ent. Pk. G40: Glas 3B **108**
Cotton Va. ML1: Cle 6E **133**
Coulin Gdns. G22: Glas 5H **65**
Coulter Av. ML2: Wis 2A **150**
Coulter Av. ML5: Coat 3A **94**
Coulter's Cres. G76: Crmck 2A **140**
Countess Ga. G71: Both 4C **128**
Countess Way G69: Barg 6E **93**
(off King Pl.)
Counting Ho., The PA1: Pais 2F **101**
(off Turners Av.)
County Av. G72: Camb 6F **109**
County Pl. PA1: Pais 6A **82**
County Sq. PA1: Pais 6A **82**
Couper Pl. G4: Glas 2F **7** (2H **87**)
Couper St. G4: Glas 2F **7** (2H **87**)
Coursington Cres. ML1: Moth 2A **148**
Coursington Gdns. ML1: Moth 2H **147**
Coursington Pl. ML1: Moth 2H **147**
Coursington Rd. ML1: Moth 2H **147**
(not continuous)
Coursington Twr. ML1: Moth 2H **147**
(off Allan St.)
Court Hill G65: Kils 3A **14**
Courthill G61: Bear 1D **46**
Courthill Av. G44: Glas 2F **123**
Courthill Cres. G65: Kils 3A **14**
Coustonholm Rd. G43: Glas 6B **106**
Couther Quad. ML6: Air 1A **96**
Covanburn Av. ML3: Ham 2B **162**
Covenant Cres. ML9: Lark 3D **170**
Covenanters Ct. G65: Kils 2B **14**
Covenanters Way ML2: Over 5A **166**
Covenant Pl. ML2: Wis 1C **164**
Coventry Dr. G31: Glas 3D **88**
Cowal Cres. G66: Kirkin 4H **33**
Cowal Dr. PA3: Lin 6G **79**
Cowal St. G20: Glas 2A **64**
Cowal Vw. G81: Clyd 4D **44**
Cowan Cres. G78: Barr 4F **119**
Cowan La. G12: Glas 1C **86**
(off Glasgow St.)
Cowan Rd. G68: Cumb 3E **37**
Cowan St. G12: Glas 1C **86**
Cowan Wilson Av. G72: Blan 1B **144**
Cowan Wynd G71: Tann 5E **113**
Cowan Wynd ML2: Over 4A **166**
COWCADDENS 2C **6** (2F **87**)
Cowcaddens Rd. G4: Glas 2B **6** (2F **87**)
Cowcaddens Station (Subway) 2B **6** (2F **87**)
Cowden Dr. G64: B'rig 4C **50**
Cowdenhill Cir. G13: Glas 1D **62**
Cowdenhill Pl. G13: Glas 1D **62**
Cowdenhill Rd. G13: Glas 1D **62**
Cowden St. G51: Glas 4D **84**
Cowdray Cres. PA4: Renf 6F **61**
Cowgate G66: Kirkin 4C **32**
Cowglen Golf Course 6F **105**
Cowglen Rd. G53: Glas 6C **104**
Cowie Pl. ML2: Wis 4C **148**
COWLAIRS 5A **66**
Cowlairs Ind. Est. G22: Glas 5H **65**
Cowlairs Rd. G21: Glas 5A **66**
(Millarbank St.)
Coxdale Av. G66: Kirkin 5B **32**
Coxhill St. G21: Glas 6H **65**
Coxton Pl. G33: Glas 2D **90**
Coyle Dr. G69: G'csh 3F **71**
Coylton Cres. ML3: Ham 2C **160**
Coylton Rd. G43: Glas 2C **122**
Crabb Quad. ML1: Moth 6E **131**
Cragdale G74: E Kil 6E **141**
Craggan Dr. G14: Glas 3H **61**
Crags Av. PA2: Pais 4B **102**
Crags Cres. PA2: Pais 3B **102**
Crags Rd. PA2: Pais 4B **102**
Cragwell Pk. G76: Crmck 2A **140**
Craigallian Av. G62: Miln 1F **27**
Craigallian Av. G72: Camb 3D **126**
Craiganour La. G43: Glas 1A **122**
Craigard Pl. G73: Ruth 4F **125**
Craigash Quad. G62: Miln 2E **27**
Craigash Rd. G62: Miln 3E **27**
Craigbank Cres. G76: Eag 5C **154**
Craigbank Dr. G53: Glas 1A **120**
Craigbank Gro. G76: Eag 5C **154**
Craigbank Rd. ML9: Lark 5C **170**
Craigbank St. ML9: Lark 4C **170**
Craigbanzo St. G81: Faif 5F **25**
Craigbarnet Av. G64: Torr 5C **30**
Craigbarnet Cres. G33: Mille 5B **68**
Craigbarnet Rd. G62: Miln 3D **26**
Craigbet Av. PA11: Quarr V 1A **76**
Craigbet Cres. PA11: Quarr V 1A **76**
Craigbet Pl. PA11: Quarr V 1A **76**
Craigbo Av. G23: Glas 6B **48**
Craigbo Ct. G23: Glas 1B **64**
Craigbo Dr. G23: Glas 6B **48**
Craigbog Av. PA5: John 4D **98**
Craigbog Rd. PA5: John 5F **99**
Craigbo Pl. G23: Glas 1B **64**
Craigbo Rd. G23: Glas 1B **64**
Craigbo St. G23: Glas 6B **48**
Craigburn Av. PA6: C'lee 3D **78**
Craigburn Ct. ML9: Ashg 4H **171**
Craigburn Cres. PA6: C'lee 4D **78**
Craigburn Pl. PA6: C'lee 4D **78**
Craigburn St. ML3: Ham 3H **161**
Craig Cres. G66: Kirkin 6H **33**
(off Bk. o'Dykes Rd.)
Craigcrest Pl. G67: Cumb 2A **56**
Craigdhu Av. G62: Miln 4F **27**
Craigdhu Av. ML6: Air 4E **97**
Craigdhu Farm Cotts. G62: Miln 4E **27**
Craigdhu Rd. G61: Bear 5D **26**
Craigdhu Rd. G62: Miln 4E **27**
Craigdonald Pl. PA5: John 2F **99**
Craigellan Rd. G43: Glas 1B **122**
Craigelvan Av. G67: Cumb 1B **56**
Craigelvan Ct. G67: Cumb 1B **56**
Craigelvan Dr. G67: Cumb 1B **56**
Craigelvan Gdns. G67: Cumb 1B **56**
Craigelvan Gro. G67: Cumb 1B **56**
Craigelvan Pl. G67: Cumb 1B **56**
Craigelvan Vw. G67: Cumb 1B **56**
Craigenbay Cres. G66: Lenz 2E **53**
Craigenbay Rd. G66: Lenz 3D **52**
Craigenbay St. G21: Glas 5D **66**
Craigencart Ct. G81: Dun 1B **44**
CRAIGEND 6C **68**
Craigend Cir. G13: Glas 3E **63**
Craigend Cl. G13: Glas 2E **63**
Craigend Ct. G13: Glas 3E **63**
Craigend Cres. G62: Miln 3F **27**
Craigend Dr. ML5: Coat 1G **113**
Craigend Dr. W. G62: Miln 3E **27**
Craigend Gdns. G77: Newt M 2D **136**
Craigend Ho. G82: Dumb 3C **18**
CRAIGENDMUIR 5E **69**
Craigendmuir Cvn. Site G33: Step 5E **69**
Craigendmuir Dr. G33: Glas 1F **89**
Craigendmuir Pl. G33: Glas 1F **89**
Craigendmuir Rd. G33: Step 5E **69**
Craigendmuir St. G33: Glas 1F **89**
Craigendon Oval PA2: Pais 6G **101**
Craigendon Rd. PA2: Pais 6G **101**
Craigend Pl. G13: Glas 3E **63**
Craigend Rd. G67: Cumb 2B **56**
CRAIGENDS 3D **78**
Craigends Av. PA11: Quarr V 1A **76**
Craigends Ct. G65: Kils 3A **14**
Craigends Dr. PA10: Kilba 2A **98**
Craigends Pl. PA11: Quarr V 1A **76**
Craigends Rd. PA6: C'lee 1E **79**
Craigends Rd. PA6: Hous 1E **79**
Craigend St. G13: Glas 3E **63**
Craigend Vw. G67: Cumb 2B **56**
Craigenfeoch Av. PA5: John 4D **98**
Craigens Rd. ML6: Air 6F **97**
Craigens Rd. ML6: Chap 6F **97**
Craigens Rd. ML6: Gart 6F **97**
Craigfaulds Av. PA2: Pais 3F **101**
Craigfell Ct. ML3: Ham 1C **160**
Craigflower Av. G53: Glas 3A **120**
Craigflower Gdns. G53: Glas 3A **120**
Craigflower Rd. G53: Glas 4A **120**
Craig Gdns. G77: Newt M 5C **136**
Craighalbert Rd. G68: Cumb 2E **37**
CRAIGHALBERT RDBT. 1E **37**
Craighalbert Way G68: Cumb 1E **37**
Craighall Quad. G78: Neil 3D **134**
Craighall Rd. G4: Glas 1F **87**
Craighaw St. G81: Faif 5F **25**
CRAIGHEAD 2E **145**
Craighead Av. G33: Glas 6F **67**
Craighead Av. G66: Milt C 5C **10**
Craighead Dr. G62: Miln 3D **26**
Craighead Pl. G33: Glas 6F **67**
Craighead Rd. G66: Milt C 5C **10**
Craighead Rd. PA7: B'ton 5H **41**
Craighead St. G78: Barr 5D **118**
Craighead St. ML6: Air 3E **97**
Craighead Way G78: Barr 5D **118**
Craig Hill G75: E Kil 4E **157**
Craighill Dr. G76: Clar 3B **138**
Craighill Gro. G76: Clar 3B **138**
Craighirst Dr. G81: Dun 6C **24**
Craighirst Dr. G81: Hard 6C **24**
Craighirst Rd. G62: Miln 3D **26**
Craighlaw Av. G76: Wfoot 1B **154**
Craighlaw Dr. G76: Wfoot 1B **154**
Craigholme PA6: Hous 1D **78**
Craighouse St. G33: Glas 2A **90**
Craighton Gdns. G66: Len 3H **9**
Craigiebar Dr. PA2: Pais 5G **101**
Craigieburn Gdns. G20: Glas 1H **63**
Craigieburn Rd. G67: Cumb 4H **37**
Craigie Dr. G77: Newt M 6E **137**
Craigiehall Av. PA8: Ersk 2E **59**
Craigiehall Cres. PA8: Ersk 2E **59**
Craigiehall Pl. G51: Glas 5B **86**
Craigiehall St. G51: Glas 5C **86**
Craigiehall Way PA8: Ersk 2E **59**
Craigie La. ML9: Lark 1D **170**
(off Duncan Graham St.)

A–Z Glasgow 207

Craigielaw Wlk. – Crimond Pl.

Craigielaw Wlk. ML1: N'hse 2D **132**
Craigielea Ct. PA4: Renf 5E **61**
Craigielea Cres. G62: Miln 3E **27**
Craigielea Dr. PA3: Pais 6G **81**
Craigielea Pk. PA4: Renf 6E **61**
Craigielea Rd. G81: Dun 6A **24**
Craigielea Rd. PA4: Renf 6E **61**
Craigielea St. G31: Glas 3C **88**
Craigielinn Av. PA2: Pais 6F **101**
Craigie Pk. G66: Lenz 2E **53**
Craigie Pl. ML5: Coat 6A **94**
Craigie St. G42: Glas 3E **107**
Craigievar Av. G33: Glas 1D **90**
Craigievar Ct. G33: Glas 1E **91**
Craigievar Cres. G33: Glas 1E **91**
Craigievar Pl. G77: Newt M 4B **136**
Craigievar Pl. ML6: Air 5E **97**
Craigievar St. G33: Glas 1E **91**
Craigknowe Rd. G72: Blan 5A **128**
Craiglea Pl. ML6: Air 3C **96**
Craiglea Ter. ML6: Plain 6F **75**
Craiglee G75: E Kil 6G **157**
Craigleith St. G32: Glas 5G **89**
Craiglinn G68: Cumb 3C **36**
CRAIGLINN 4C **36**
Craiglinn Gdns. G45: Glas 5G **123**
Craiglinn Pk. Rd. G68: Cumb 4C **36**
CRAIGLINN RDBT. 4C **36**
Craiglockhart Cres. G33: Glas 1D **90**
Craiglockhart Dr. G33: Glas 1D **90**
Craiglockhart Pl. G33: Glas 1D **90**
Craiglockhart St. G33: Glas 1D **90**
Craigmaddie Gdns. G64: Torr 5C **30**
Craigmaddie Rd. G62: Bald 3D **28**
Craigmaddie Rd. G62: Bard 3D **28**
Craigmaddie Ter. La. G3: Glas 2D **4** (2C **86**)
.... *(off Gray St.)*
CRAIGMARLOCH 1E **37**
Craigmarloch Av. G64: Torr 5D **30**
CRAIGMARLOCH RDBT. 2E **37**
Craigmillar Av. G62: Miln 3H **27**
Craigmillar Pl. G69: G'csh 5C **70**
Craigmillar Rd. G42: Glas 6E **107**
Craigmochan Av. ML6: Air 1H **95**
Craigmont Dr. G20: Glas 3C **64**
Craigmont St. G20: Glas 3C **64**
Craigmore Pl. ML5: Coat 2A **114**
Craigmore Rd. G61: Bear 6B **26**
Craigmore St. G31: Glas 5E **89**
Craigmore Wynd ML9: Lark 1D **170**
.... *(off Duncan Graham St.)*
Craigmount St. G66: Kirkin 6D **32**
Craigmuir Ct. G52: Glas 5H **83**
Craigmuir Cres. G52: Glas 5H **83**
Craigmuir Dr. PA7: B'ton 5G **41**
Craigmuir Gdns. G72: Blan 3H **143**
Craigmuir Pl. G52: Glas 5G **83**
Craigmuir Rd. G52: Glas 5G **83**
Craigmuir Rd. G72: Blan 3H **143**
Craigmuir Rd. PA7: B'ton 5G **41**
Craigmuir Wynd PA7: B'ton 5G **41**
Craigneith Castle 6E **143**
Craigneith Ct. G74: E Kil 5E **143**
Craignethan Dr. G69: G'csh 5E **71**
Craignethan Rd. G46: Giff 2G **137**
Craignethan Rd. ML8: Carl 2C **174**
CRAIGNEUK 4D **96**
CRAIGNEUK 5C **148**
Craigneuk Av. ML6: Air 5C **96**
Craigneuk Rd. ML1: Carf 6C **132**
Craigneuk St. ML1: Moth 4B **148**
Craigneuk St. ML2: Wis 4B **148**
Craignish La. ML6: Air 5G **95**
Craignure Cres. ML6: Air 4E **97**
Craignure Rd. G73: Ruth 4D **124**
Craigpark G31: Glas 4C **88**
Craigpark Dr. G31: Glas 4C **88**
Craigpark St. G81: Faif 6F **25**
Craigpark Ter. G31: Glas 4C **88**
.... *(off Craigpark)*
Craigpark Way G71: Tann 6E **113**
Craig Pl. G77: Newt M 4B **136**
Craig Pl. ML8: Law 6E **167**
Craig Rd. G44: Glas 2E **123**
Craig Rd. G78: Neil 3D **134**
Craig Rd. PA3: Lin 4F **79**
Craigs Av. G81: Faif 1E **45**
Craigs Av. G81: Hard 1E **45**
Craigs Bus. Cen. PA3: Pais 5H **81**
Craigsheen Av. G76: Crmck 2H **139**
Craigside Ct. G68: Cumb 6B **36**
Craigside Pl. G68: Cumb 6B **36**
Craigside Rd. G68: Cumb 6B **36**
Craigson Pl. ML6: Air 5F **97**
Craigstone Vw. G65: Kils 3B **14**
Craigston Pl. PA5: John 3F **99**
Craigston Rd. PA5: John 3E **99**
Craig St. G72: Blan 3C **144**
Craig St. ML5: Coat 1B **114**
Craig St. ML6: Air 4H **95**
Craigswood Cres. G69: Bail 1B **112**
Craigswood Dr. G69: Bail 1B **112**
Craigswood Ga. G69: Bail 1B **112**
Craigswood Pl. G69: Bail 1B **112**
Craigswood Way G69: Bail 1B **112**
CRAIGTON 6D **84**
CRAIGTON 1B **26**
Craigton Av. G62: Miln 3F **27**
Craigton Av. G78: Barr 6G **119**
Craigton Cotts. G62: Miln 1C **26**
Craigton Crematorium 6D **84**
Craigton Cres. G77: Newt M 4B **136**
Craigton Dr. G51: Glas 5F **85**
Craigton Dr. G77: Newt M 4C **136**
Craigton Dr. G78: Barr 6G **119**
Craigton Dr. PA7: B'ton 5F **41**
Craigton Gdns. G62: Miln 2F **27**
Craigton Ind. Est. G52: Glas 6D **84**
CRAIGTON INTERCHANGE 6B **42**
Craigton Pl. G51: Glas 5E **85**
Craigton Pl. G72: Blan 6B **128**
Craigton Rd. G51: Glas 5F **85**
Craigton Rd. G62: Miln 2C **26**
Craigton Rd. G77: Newt M 6H **135**
Craigton St. G81: Faif 5F **25**
Craigvale Cres. ML6: Air 4E **97**
Craigvicar Gdns. G32: Glas 1D **110**
Craigview Av. PA5: John 5D **98**
Craigview Rd. ML1: Moth 1H **147**
Craigview Ter. PA5: John 4D **98**
Craigwell Av. G73: Ruth 1F **125**
Crail Cl. G72: Blan 6B **144**
Crail Cres. PA7: B'ton 6H **41**
Crail Pl. G31: Glas 6F **89**
Crail St. G31: Glas 6F **89**
Craithie Ct. G11: Glas 1G **85**
Crammond Av. ML5: Coat 1G **113**
Cramond Av. PA4: Renf 1G **83**
Cramond Dr. G66: Lenz 1F **53**
Cramond Ter. G32: Glas 6B **90**
Cranborne Rd. G12: Glas 4G **63**
Cranbrooke Dr. G20: Glas 2B **64**
CRANHILL 3B **90**
Crannog Ct. G82: Mil 4E **21**
Crannog Rd. G82: Mil 4E **21**
Cranoch Ga. G69: G'csh 4D **70**
Cranston Av. ML6: Air 2D **96**
CRANSTON HILL 4F **5** (3D **86**)
Cranston St. G3: Glas 5F **5** (4D **86**)
Cranworth La. G12: Glas 6B **64**
.... *(off Gt. George St.)*
Cranworth St. G12: Glas 6B **64**
Crarae Av. G61: Bear 5E **47**
Crarae Pl. G77: Newt M 4A **136**
Crathes Ct. G44: Glas 3C **122**
Crathes Ct. ML2: Wis 6H **149**
Crathie Ct. ML8: Carl 2C **174**
Crathie Dr. G11: Glas 1G **85**
Crathie Dr. ML6: Glenm 5H **73**
Crathie Pl. G77: Newt M 5H **137**
Crathie Quad. ML2: Wis 4H **149**
Crawford Av. G66: Lenz 4D **52**
Crawford Ct. G46: Giff 6H **121**
Crawford Cres. G71: Udd 6C **112**
Crawford Cres. G72: Blan 6B **128**
Crawford Dr. G15: Glas 6H **45**
Crawford Dr. G74: E Kil 1B **158**
Crawford Dr. PA3: Pais 5F **81**
CRAWFORDDYKE 4E **175**
Crawford Gdns. ML1: Moth 4E **147**
Crawford Hill G74: E Kil 1B **158**
Crawford La. G11: Glas 1G **85**
.... *(off Rosevale St.)*
Crawford Path G11: Glas 1G **85**
.... *(off Crawford St.)*
Crawford Rd. G62: Miln 1F **27**
Crawford Rd. PA6: C'lee 2D **78**
Crawford St. G11: Glas 1G **85**
Crawford St. ML1: Moth 3E **147**
Crawford St. ML3: Ham 4E **145**
Crawfurd Gdns. G73: Ruth 3E **125**
Crawfurd Rd. G73: Ruth 3D **124**
Crawhill Dr. G69: Barg 5F **93**
Crawriggs Av. G66: Kirkin 1D **52**
Craw Rd. PA2: Pais 2G **101**
Creamery Rd. ML2: Wis 2B **166**
Crebar Dr. G78: Barr 5E **119**
Crebar St. G46: T'bnk 3E **121**
Credon Dr. ML6: Air 6A **96**
Credon Gdns. G73: Ruth 3E **125**
Cree Av. G64: B'rig 6F **51**
Cree Gdns. G32: Glas 6H **89**
Cree Pl. G75: E Kil 2D **156**
Creggan Ct. ML3: Ham 5E **145**
Creighton Gro. G74: E Kil 2G **157**
Creran Ct. ML3: Ham 2E **161**
Creran Cres. G69: G'csh 4D **70**
Creran Dr. PA4: Renf 5D **60**
Creran Path ML2: Newm 3D **150**
.... *(off Tiree Cres.)*
Crescent, The G62: Miln 5G **27**
Crescent, The G76: Busby 4E **139**
Crescent, The G81: Clyd 4A **44**
Crescent Ct. G81: Clyd 4A **44**
.... *(off The Crescent)*
Crescent Gro. G13: Glas 3B **62**
Crescent Rd. G13: Glas 4B **62**
Crescent Rd. G14: Glas 4B **62**
Cressdale Av. G45: Glas 5H **123**
Cressdale Ct. G45: Glas 5H **123**
Cressdale Dr. G45: Glas 5H **123**
Cressland Dr. G45: Glas 6H **123**
Cressland Pl. G45: Glas 6H **123**
Cresswell Gro. G77: Newt M 6D **136**
Cresswell La. G12: Glas 6B **64**
.... *(off Cresswell St.)*
Cresswell Pl. G77: Newt M 1E **153**
Cresswell St. G12: Glas 6B **64**
Cressy St. G51: Glas 3E **85**
Crest Av. G13: Glas 1B **62**
Crestlea Av. PA2: Pais 5A **102**
Creston Wynd ML1: New S 3H **131**
Creswell Ter. G71: Udd 1C **128**
Crichton Pl. G21: Glas 5A **66**
Crichtons Cairn Dr. G66: Milt C 1C **32**
Crichton St. G21: Glas 5A **66**
Crichton St. ML5: Coat 3C **94**
Crieff Av. G61: Bear 2A **48**
Crieff Av. ML6: Chap 4D **116**
Criffell Gdns. G32: Glas 2D **110**
Criffell Rd. G32: Glas 1D **110**
Criffel Pl. ML1: N'hill 4C **132**
.... *(off Clarinda Pl.)*
Crighton Wynd ML4: Bell 2H **129**
Crimea St. G2: Glas 6H **5** (4E **87**)
Crimond Pl. G65: Kils 2F **13**

Crinan Cres. – Crownhall Pl.

Crinan Cres. ML5: Coat....2H **93**
Crinan Gdns. G64: B'rig....6E **51**
Crinan Pl. ML4: Bell....3D **130**
Crinan Pl. ML5: Coat....2H **93**
Crinan Rd. G64: B'rig....6E **51**
Crinan St. G31: Glas....3D **88**
CRINDLEDYKE....4G 151
Crindledyke Cres. ML2: Newm....3F **151**
Cripps Av. G81: Clyd....6F **45**
Croft ML9: Lark....3B **170**
Croftbank Av. G71: Both....6F **129**
Croftbank Cres. G71: Both....6F **129**
Croftbank Cres. G71: Udd....1D **128**
Croftbank Ga. G71: Both....6F **129**
Croftbank St. G21: Glas....5B **66**
Croftburn Dr. G44: Glas....3H **123**
Croftcot Av. ML4: Bell....4B **130**
Croft Cres. G72: Newt....6F **111**
Croftcroighn Cl. G33: Glas....1E **91**
Croftcroighn Ct. G33: Glas....1E **91**
Croftcroighn Dr. G33: Glas....1E **91**
Croftcroighn Gdns. G33: Glas....1E **91**
Croftcroighn Ga. G33: Glas....1E **91**
Croftcroighn Pl. G33: Glas....1E **91**
Croftcroighn Rd. G33: Glas....2B **90**
Croftend Av. G44: Glas....1A **124**
Croftend La. G44: Glas....2B **124**
CROFTFOOT....2A 124
Croftfoot Cres. G45: Glas....3C **124**
Croftfoot Dr. G45: Glas....3B **124**
Croftfoot Pl. G69: G'csh....3E **71**
Croftfoot Quad. G45: Glas....3A **124**
Croftfoot Rd. G44: Glas....3H **123**
Croftfoot Rd. G45: Glas....3B **124**
Croftfoot Station (Rail)....1A 124
Croftfoot St. G45: Glas....3C **124**
Croftfoot Ter. G45: Glas....3B **124**
Croft Gdns. G72: Camb....2B **126**
Crofthead Cotts. G78: Neil....2C **134**
Crofthead Cres. ML4: Bell....4B **130**
Crofthead Dr. G66: Len....2E **9**
Crofthead Ind. Est. G78: Neil....2C **134**
Crofthead La. G66: Kirkin....4C **32**
....*(off W. High St.)*
Crofthead Pl. G77: Newt M....6E **137**
Crofthead Pl. ML4: Bell....4B **130**
Crofthead St. G71: Udd....2D **128**
Crofthill Av. G71: Udd....1D **128**
Crofthill Rd. G44: Glas....1H **123**
Crofthouse Dr. G44: Glas....3A **124**
Croftmont Av. G44: Glas....3A **124**
Croftmoraig Av. G69: Mood....3E **55**
Crofton Av. G44: Glas....3H **123**
Crofton Av. PA4: Renf....5G **61**
Crofton Dr. PA4: Renf....5G **61**
Crofton Sq. PA4: Renf....5G **61**
Crofton St. PA4: Renf....5G **61**
Crofton Way PA4: Renf....5G **61**
Crofton Wynd ML6: Air....3D **96**
Croftpark G81: Hard....6D **24**
....*(off Cochno Rd.)*
Croftpark Av. G44: Glas....3G **123**
Croftpark Cres. G72: Blan....3C **144**
Croftpark Rd. G81: Hard....6D **24**
Croftpark St. ML4: Bell....1C **130**
Croft Pl. ML9: Lark....2B **170**
Croft Rd. G64: Balm....5A **30**
Croft Rd. G72: Camb....2B **126**
Croft Rd. G75: E Kil....4G **157**
Croft Rd. ML9: Lark....2B **170**
Croftside Av. G44: Glas....3A **124**
Croftspar Av. G32: Glas....5C **90**
Croftspar Ct. G32: Glas....5D **90**
Croftspar Dr. G32: Glas....5C **90**
Croftspar Ga. G32: Glas....5D **90**
Croftspar Gro. G32: Glas....5C **90**
Croftspar Pl. G32: Glas....5C **90**
Croft Wlk. G72: Newt....6F **111**
Croft Way PA4: Renf....2F **83**
Croftwood G64: B'rig....3C **50**
Croftwood Av. G44: Glas....3H **123**
Croftwood Rd. ML3: Ham....2H **161**
Croft Wynd G71: Udd....1E **129**
Crogal Cres. ML6: Chap....3D **116**
Cromalt Av. G75: E Kil....1B **168**
Cromalt Cres. G61: Bear....5C **26**
Cromarty Av. G43: Glas....1D **122**
Cromarty Av. G64: B'rig....5F **51**
Cromarty Cres. G61: Bear....6F **27**
Cromarty Gdns. G76: Clar....6E **123**
Cromarty Pl. G69: Chry....6B **54**
Cromarty Pl. G74: E Kil....6C **142**
Cromarty Rd. ML6: Air....6H **95**
Crombie Gdns. G69: Bail....2F **111**
Cromdale St. G51: Glas....4E **85**
Cromdale St. G51: Glas....5E **85**
Cromdale Way ML1: New S....5A **132**
Cromer Gdns. G20: Glas....4D **64**
Cromer Way PA3: Pais....4H **81**
Cromlet Dr. ML5: Coat....2D **94**
Cromlix Gro. ML6: Plain....6H **75**
Crompton Av. G44: Glas....2F **123**
Cromptons Gro. PA1: Pais....2F **101**
Cromwell La. G20: Glas....1E **87**
Cromwell St. G20: Glas....1E **87**
Crona Dr. ML3: Ham....5C **144**
Cronberry Quad. G52: Glas....2H **103**
Cronberry Ter. G52: Glas....2H **103**
Cronin Pl. ML4: Bell....6D **114**
Cronulla Pl. G65: Kils....3B **14**
Crookedshields Rd. G72: Camb....2B **142**
Crookedshields Rd. G74: Ners....2A **142**
CROOKFUR....3C 136
Crookfur Cott. Homes G77: Newt M....4D **136**
CROOKFUR INTERCHANGE....2B **136**
Crookfur Rd. G77: Newt M....3B **136**
CROOKSTON....1B 104
Crookston Av. G52: Glas....1A **104**
Crookston Castle....**3B 104**
Crookston Ct. G52: Glas....1A **104**
Crookston Dr. G52: Glas....1H **103**
Crookston Dr. PA1: Pais....1H **103**
Crookston Gdns. G52: Glas....1H **103**
Crookston Gro. G52: Glas....1A **104**
Crookstonhill Path G52: Glas....1H **103**
....*(off Ralston Path)*
Crookston Path G52: Glas....1H **103**
....*(off Crookston Quad.)*
Crookston Pl. G52: Glas....1H **103**
Crookston Quad. G52: Glas....1H **103**
Crookston Rd. G52: Glas....2H **103**
Crookston Rd. G53: Glas....6A **104**
Crookston Station (Rail)....1H 103
Crookston Ter. G52: Glas....1A **104**
Crosbie Dr. PA2: Pais....6C **100**
Crosbie La. G20: Glas....1A **64**
....*(off Crosbie St.)*
Crosbie Pl. PA2: Pais....5C **100**
Crosbie St. G20: Glas....1A **64**
Crosbie Woods PA2: Pais....4F **101**
Cross, The....6A **82**
Cross, The PA10: Kilba....2A **98**
Cross Arthurlie St. G78: Barr....5D **118**
Crossbank Av. G42: Glas....4A **108**
Crossbank Dr. G42: Glas....4H **107**
Crossbank Rd. G42: Glas....4H **107**
Crossbank Ter. G42: Glas....4H **107**
CROSSBASKET....3F 143
Crossbow Gdns. G72: Blan....3G **143**
Crossburn Av. G62: Miln....4F **27**
Cross Ct., The G64: B'rig....6B **50**
....*(off Kenmure Av.)*
Crossdykes G66: Kirkin....6G **33**
Crossen La. ML8: Carl....4F **175**
....*(off Ramage Rd.)*
Crossflat Cres. PA1: Pais....6C **82**
Crossford Dr. G23: Glas....6C **48**
Crossgate G66: Kirkin....4D **32**
Cross Gates ML4: Bell....3C **130**
Crossgates PA7: B'ton....3F **41**
Crossgates Av. ML1: Cle....4H **133**
Crossgates St. ML9: Lark....1B **170**
CROSSHILL....4F 107
CROSSHILL....6B 92
Crosshill Av. G42: Glas....4F **107**
Crosshill Av. G66: Kirkin....1D **52**
Crosshill Av. PA7: B'ton....4F **41**
Crosshill Dr. G73: Ruth....1D **124**
Crosshill Dr. ML1: Cle....4H **133**
Crosshill M. PA7: B'ton....5F **41**
Crosshill Rd. G64: B'rig....2E **51**
Crosshill Rd. G64: Lenz....2E **51**
Crosshill Rd. G66: A'loch....4B **52**
Crosshill Rd. G66: Lenz....4B **52**
Crosshill Rd. PA7: B'ton....5F **41**
Crosshill Station (Rail)....4F 107
Crosshill St. G66: Len....2F **9**
Crosshill St. ML1: Moth....3H **147**
Crosshill St. ML5: Coat....1F **113**
Crosshill St. ML6: Air....4H **95**
Crosshill Wynd PA7: B'ton....5F **41**
Crosshouse Rd. G75: E Kil....6B **156**
CROSSLEE....3B 78
Crosslee Cres. PA6: Hous....2C **78**
Crosslee Gdns. PA6: C'lee....2B **78**
Crosslee Pk. PA6: C'lee....2C **78**
Crosslee Rd. PA11: Bri W....5H **77**
Crosslees Dr. G46: T'bnk....4F **121**
Crosslees Pk. G46: T'bnk....4F **121**
Crosslees Rd. G46: T'bnk....5F **121**
Crosslee St. G52: Glas....6D **84**
CROSSLET....1C 20
Crosslet Av. G82: Dumb....1C **20**
Crosslet Ct. G82: Dumb....2C **20**
Crosslet Ho. G82: Dumb....2C **20**
Crosslet Pl. G82: Dumb....4H **19**
Crosslet Rd. G82: Dumb....3G **19**
Crossloan Rd. G51: Glas....4F **85**
Crossloan Ter. G51: Glas....4F **85**
CROSSMILL....3F 119
Crossmill Av. G78: Barr....3F **119**
Crossmill Bus. Pk. G78: Barr....3G **119**
Crossmount Ct. ML8: Carl....3C **174**
CROSSMYLOOF....4B 106
Crossmyloof Gdns. G41: Glas....4B **106**
Crossmyloof Station (Rail)....4B 106
Cross Orchard Way ML4: Bell....2C **130**
Crosspoint Dr. G23: Glas....6C **48**
Cross Rd. PA2: Pais....3F **101**
CROSS STOBS....2C 118
Cross Stone Pl. ML1: Moth....3G **147**
Cross St. G32: Carm....4C **110**
Cross St. PA1: Pais....1G **101**
Crosstobs Rd. G53: Glas....4A **104**
Crossvegate Bus. Pk. G62: Miln....4H **27**
....*(off Fulton Rd.)*
Crossveggate G62: Miln....4H **27**
Crossview Av. G69: Bail....6B **92**
Crossview Pl. G69: Bail....6B **92**
Crossways PA6: Hous....1D **78**
Cross Wynd G74: E Kil....1H **157**
....*(off Hunter St.)*
Crovie Rd. G53: Glas....6A **104**
Crow Av. ML1: Holy....2B **132**
Crowflats Rd. G71: Udd....1C **128**
Crowfoot Vw. G71: View....4G **113**
Crowhall Dr. G33: Glas....5E **91**
Crowhill Cres. ML6: Air....1H **95**
Crowhill Quad. G64: B'rig....1B **66**
Crowhill Rd. G64: B'rig....2B **66**
Crowhill St. G22: Glas....3G **65**
Crow La. G13: Glas....4F **63**
Crowlin Cres. G33: Glas....3B **90**
Crown Av. G81: Clyd....4C **44**
Crown Cir. G12: Glas....6A **64**
Crown Gdns. G12: Glas....6A **64**
Crownhall Pl. G32: Glas....6C **90**

Crownhall Rd. – Dale Dr.

Crownhall Rd. G32: Glas 6C **90**
Crownhill Ct. ML6: Glenm 6G **73**
Crownpoint Rd. G40: Glas 6B **88**
Crown Rd. Nth. G12: Glas 6H **63**
Crown Rd. Sth. G12: Glas 6H **63**
Crown St. G5: Glas 1G **107**
.... *(Alexander Cres.)*
Crown St. G5: Glas 6G **87**
.... *(Ballater St.)*
Crown St. G5: Glas 1F **107**
.... *(Caledonia Rd.)*
Crown St. G69: Bail 2F **111**
Crown St. ML5: Coat 4E **95**
Crown St. ML6: C'bnk 2B **116**
Crown Street Retail Pk. G5: Glas 2F **107**
Crown Ter. G12: Glas 6H **63**
Crow Rd. G11: Glas 5F **63**
Crow Rd. G13: Glas 3F **63**
.... (not continuous)
Crowwood Cres. ML6: C'bnk 3B **116**
Crowwood Dr. ML6: Air 4D **96**
Crow Wood Golf Course 1G **69**
Crow Wood Rd. G69: Chry 2H **69**
Crowwood Rd. ML6: C'bnk 3B **116**
Crow Wood Ter. G69: Chry 2H **69**
CROY 1B **36**
Croy G74: E Kil 6F **141**
Croy Av. G77: Newt M 4G **137**
Croy Bank Ct. G68: Cumb 3B **36**
Croyhill Vw. G68: Cumb 2B **36**
Croy Park & Ride 2B **36**
Croy Pl. G21: Glas 4E **67**
Croy Rd. G21: Glas 4E **67**
Croy Rd. ML5: Coat 1A **114**
Croy Station (Rail) 2B **36**
Cruachan Av. PA2: Pais 5A **102**
Cruachan Av. PA4: Renf 2E **83**
Cruachan Dr. G33: Step 3E **69**
Cruachan Dr. G77: Newt M 6F **137**
Cruachan Dr. G78: Barr 6E **119**
Cruachan Rd. G61: Bear 6B **26**
Cruachan Rd. G73: Ruth 4F **125**
Cruachan St. G46: T'bnk 3F **121**
Cruachan Way G78: Barr 6E **119**
Cruden St. G51: Glas 5F **85**
Crum Av. G46: T'bnk 4G **121**
Crusader Av. G13: Glas 6D **46**
Cubie St. G40: Glas 6B **88**
Cubitt Ct. ML4: Bell 1B **130**
Cuckoo Way ML1: Holy 2B **132**
Cuilhill Dr. G69: Barg 5D **92**
Cuilhill Rd. G69: Barg 3D **92**
Cuillin Pl. ML6: Chap 4F **117**
Cuillin Pl. ML9: Lark 2E **171**
Cuillins, The G69: Mood 3E **55**
Cuillins, The G71: Tann 4C **112**
Cuillins Rd. G73: Ruth 4F **125**
Cuillin Way G78: Barr 5E **119**
Cuilmuir Ter. G65: Croy 1B **36**
Cuilmuir Vw. G65: Croy 6B **14**
Culbin Dr. G13: Glas 1H **61**
Cullen PA8: Ersk 4E **43**
Cullen La. G75: E Kil 4G **157**
Cullen Pl. G71: Tann 5E **113**
Cullen Rd. G75: E Kil 4F **157**
Cullen Rd. ML1: Moth 4E **147**
Cullen St. G32: Glas 1A **110**
Cullion Way ML1: N'hill 2G **133**
Cullochrig Rd. ML6: Glenm 5G **57**
.... (not continuous)
Cullochrig Rd. ML6: Rigg 5G **57**
.... (not continuous)
Culloch Rd. G61: Bear 5C **26**
Culloden Av. ML4: Bell 3F **131**
Culloden St. G31: Glas 3D **88**
Culrain Gdns. G32: Glas 6A **90**
Culrain St. G32: Glas 6A **90**
Culross Hill G74: E Kil 2F **157**
Culross La. G32: Glas 1C **110**
Culross Pl. G74: E Kil 2F **157**
Culross Pl. ML5: Coat 4B **94**
Culross St. G32: Glas 1C **110**
Culross Way G69: Mood 4E **55**
Culter Fell Path ML1: Cle 5H **133**
Cult Rd. G66: Lenz 3E **53**
Cults St. G51: Glas 5F **85**
Culvain Av. G61: Bear 6B **26**
Culzean ML6: Glenm 4H **73**
Culzean Av. ML5: Coat 6A **94**
Culzean Ct. ML5: Coat 6A **94**
.... *(off Torriden St.)*
Culzean Cres. G69: Bail 1G **111**
Culzean Cres. G77: Newt M 4G **137**
Culzean Dr. G32: Glas 1D **110**
Culzean Dr. G74: E Kil 6F **141**
Culzean Dr. ML1: Carf 4C **132**
Culzean Pl. G74: E Kil 6F **141**
Cumberland Pl. G5: Glas 1G **107**
Cumberland Pl. ML5: Coat 6G **93**
Cumberland St. G5: Glas 6F **87**
.... (not continuous)
CUMBERNAULD 4H **37**
Cumbernauld Airport 3B **16**
Cumbernauld Indoor Bowling Club 3A **38**
Cumbernauld Mus. 4H **37**
Cumbernauld Rd. FK4: Bank 1F **17**
Cumbernauld Rd. FK4: Longc 1F **17**
Cumbernauld Rd. G31: Glas 4D **88**
Cumbernauld Rd. G33: Mille 5A **68**
Cumbernauld Rd. G33: Step 5A **68**
Cumbernauld Rd. G67: Mollin 3H **55**
Cumbernauld Rd. G69: Chry 2A **70**
Cumbernauld Rd. G69: Mood 2A **70**
Cumbernauld Rd. G69: Muirh 2A **70**
CUMBERNAULD ROAD INTERCHANGE 1G **89**
Cumbernauld Shop. Cen., The 3H **37**
Cumbernauld Station (Rail) 5A **38**
Cumbernauld Theatre 1B **38**
CUMBERNAULD VILLAGE 6B **16**
Cumbrae G74: E Kil 2C **158**
Cumbrae Ct. G81: Clyd 5D **44**
Cumbrae Cres. ML5: Coat 6G **95**
Cumbrae Cres. Nth. G82: Dumb 2C **18**
Cumbrae Cres. Sth. G82: Dumb 2B **18**
Cumbrae Dr. ML1: Moth 1E **147**
Cumbrae Pl. ML5: Coat 1G **115**
Cumbrae Rd. PA2: Pais 6A **102**
Cumbrae Rd. PA4: Renf 2F **83**
Cumbrae St. G33: Glas 3A **90**
Cumlodden Dr. G20: Glas 2A **64**
Cumming Av. ML8: Carl 5G **175**
Cumming Dr. G42: Glas 5F **107**
Cumnock Dr. G78: Barr 6F **119**
Cumnock Dr. ML3: Ham 2B **160**
Cumnock Dr. ML6: Air 1A **116**
Cumnock Rd. G33: Glas 3G **67**
Cumroch Rd. G66: Len 2E **9**
Cunard Ct. G81: Clyd 1D **60**
Cunard St. G81: Clyd 1D **60**
Cunningair Dr. ML1: Moth 5G **147**
Cunningham Dr. G46: Giff 4C **122**
Cunningham Dr. G81: Dun 1B **44**
Cunninghame Rd. G73: Ruth 4E **109**
Cunninghame Rd. G74: E Kil 2G **157**
Cunninghame Rd. PA10: Kilba 2B **98**
Cunningham Gdns. PA6: C'lee 2D **78**
Cunningham Rd. G52: Hill E 3H **83**
Cunningham St. ML1: Moth 3F **147**
Cuparhead Av. ML5: Coat 1H **113**
Curfew Rd. G13: Glas 6D **46**
Curlers Loan G65: Kils 2B **14**
Curle St. G14: Glas 1D **84**
.... (not continuous)
Curlew Ct. G66: Lenz 1F **53**
Curlew Dr. G75: E Kil 6C **156**
Curlew Pl. PA5: John 6C **98**
Curling Cres. G44: Glas 6G **107**
Curlinghaugh Cres. ML2: Wis 6A **150**
Curlingmire G75: E Kil 5G **157**
Curran Av. ML2: Wis 2E **165**
Currie Ct. PA5: John 4E **99**
.... *(off Tannahill Cres.)*
Currie Pl. G20: Glas 3C **64**
Currie St. G20: Glas 3C **64**
Curtis Av. G44: Glas 5G **107**
Curtis Av. G73: Glas 6A **108**
Curzon St. G20: Glas 3C **64**
Custom Ho. Quay Gdns. 5F **87**
Cut, The G71: Udd 2D **128**
Cuthbertson St. G42: Glas 2E **107**
Cuthbert St. G71: View 6F **113**
Cuthelton Dr. G31: Glas 1G **109**
Cuthelton St. G31: Glas 1F **109**
Cuthelton Ter. G31: Glas 1F **109**
Cutty Sark Pl. G82: Dumb 3C **20**
Cypress Av. G71: View 5F **113**
Cypress Av. G72: Blan 6A **128**
Cypress Ct. G66: Lenz 1B **52**
Cypress Ct. G75: E Kil 6E **157**
Cypress Ct. ML3: Ham 1A **162**
Cypress Cres. G75: E Kil 6E **157**
Cypress Gro. G69: Barg 5F **93**
Cypress Gro. PA11: Quarr V 1B **76**
Cypress La. ML3: Ham 3E **161**
Cypress Pl. G75: E Kil 6E **157**
Cypress Rd. ML1: Carf 4C **132**
Cypress St. G22: Glas 4H **65**
Cypress Way G72: Flem 3F **127**
Cyprian Ct. G66: Lenz 4D **52**
Cyprian Dr. G66: Lenz 4D **52**
Cyprus Av. PA5: Eld 3H **99**
Cyril Cres. PA1: Pais 1C **102**
Cyril Pl. PA1: Pais 1C **102**
Cyril St. PA1: Pais 1C **102**

D

Daer Av. PA4: Renf 2G **83**
Daer Way ML3: Ham 6E **145**
Daffodil Dr. G33: Mille 4A **68**
Daffodil Way G33: Mille 4A **68**
Daffodil Way ML1: Moth 1G **147**
Dairsie Ct. G44: Glas 3D **122**
Dairsie Gdns. G64: B'rig 1F **67**
Dairsie St. G44: Glas 3D **122**
Dairy Gdns. ML3: Ham 4E **161**
Daisy Dr. G72: Newt 5F **111**
Daisy Pl. G77: Newt M 2C **136**
Daisy St. G42: Glas 4F **107**
Dakala Ct. ML2: Wis 1G **165**
Dakota Way PA4: Renf 2F **83**
Dalbeattie Braes ML6: Chap 3E **117**
Dalbeattie Dr. G72: Blan 6B **144**
DALBETH 3G **109**
Dalbeth Pl. G32: Glas 3H **109**
Dalbeth Rd. G32: Glas 3H **109**
Dalby Gro. ML5: Glenb 2B **72**
Dalcharn Path G34: Glas 3G **91**
.... *(off Kildermorie Rd.)*
Dalcharn Pl. G34: Glas 3G **91**
Dalcraig Cres. G72: Blan 5A **128**
Dalcross Pass G11: Glas 1A **86**
.... *(off Dalcross St.)*
Dalcross St. G11: Glas 1A **86**
Dalcross Way ML6: Plain 6G **75**
Dalcruin Gdns. G69: Mood 3E **55**
Daldowie Av. G32: Glas 2D **110**
Daldowie Complex G71: Udd 5G **111**
Daldowie Crematorium 5H **111**
Daldowie Est. G71: Udd 5H **111**
DALDOWIE INTERCHANGE 4H **111**
Daldowie St. ML5: Coat 2A **114**
.... (not continuous)
Dale Av. G72: Camb 5G **109**
Dale Av. G75: E Kil 4E **157**
Dale Ct. ML2: Wis 1C **164**
Dale Dr. ML1: New S 3A **132**

Dale La. G75: E Kil	5F **157**
Dale Path G40: Glas	1B **108**
Dale St. G40: Glas	1B **108**
	(not continuous)
Daleview Av. G12: Glas	3H **63**
Daleview Dr. G76: Clar	3B **138**
Daleview Gro. G76: Clar	3B **138**
Dale Way G73: Ruth	3D **124**
Dalfoil Ct. PA1: Pais	1H **103**
Dalgarroch Av. G81: Clyd	1G **61**
Dalgety Dr. PA7: B'ton	6H **41**
Dalgleish Av. G81: Dun	1A **44**
Dalgleish Dr. G61: Bear	6H **27**
Dalgleish Pl. ML2: Newm	6G **151**
Dalhousie Gdns. G64: B'rig	5B **50**
Dalhousie La. G3: Glas	2A **6** (2E **87**)
Dalhousie Rd. PA10: Kilba	3B **98**
Dalhousie St. G3: Glas	3A **6** (3E **87**)
Dalilea Dr. G34: Glas	2B **92**
Dalilea Gdns. G34: Glas	2B **92**
Dalilea Pl. G34: Glas	2B **92**
Dalintober St. G5: Glas	5E **87**
Dalkeith Av. G41: Glas	1H **105**
Dalkeith Av. G64: B'rig	4D **50**
Dalkeith Rd. G64: B'rig	3D **50**
Dalmacoulter Ct. ML6: Glenm	5G **73**
Dalmacoulter Rd. ML6: Air	6B **74**
Dalmahoy Cres. PA11: Bri W	5D **76**
Dalmahoy Dr. ML1: N'hse	2D **132**
Dalmahoy St. G32: Glas	4G **89**
Dalmally St. G20: Glas	6D **64**
DALMARNOCK	2D **108**
Dalmarnock Bri.	3D **108**
Dalmarnock Ct. G40: Glas	2D **108**
Dalmarnock Dr. G40: Glas	1B **108**
Dalmarnock Rd. G40: Glas	1B **108**
Dalmarnock Rd. G73: Ruth	3D **108**
Dalmarnock Station (Rail)	2C **108**
Dalmary Dr. PA1: Pais	5D **82**
Dalmellington Ct. G74: E Kil	1F **157**
	(off Dalmellington Dr.)
Dalmellington Ct. ML3: Ham	2B **160**
Dalmellington Dr. G53: Glas	5A **104**
Dalmellington Dr. G74: E Kil	1F **157**
Dalmellington Rd. G53: Glas	4A **104**
Dalmeny Av. G46: Giff	4A **122**
Dalmeny Dr. G78: Barr	5C **118**
Dalmeny Ga. G5: Glas	3A **108**
Dalmeny Rd. ML3: Ham	1H **161**
Dalmore Cres. ML1: New S	5A **132**
Dalmore Dr. ML6: Air	5A **96**
DALMUIR	4A **44**
Dalmuir Ct. G81: Clyd	4A **44**
Dalmuir Station (Rail)	4A **44**
Dalnair Pl. G62: Miln	3D **26**
Dalnair St. G3: Glas	2A **4** (2A **86**)
Dalness Cl. G32: Glas	2A **110**
Dalness Cres. G32: Glas	2A **110**
Dalness Pas. G32: Glas	1A **110**
	(off Eckford St.)
Dalness St. G32: Glas	2A **110**
Dalnottar Av. G60: Old K	1F **43**
Dalnottar Dr. G60: Old K	2F **43**
Dalnottar Gdns. G60: Old K	2F **43**
Dalnottar Hill Rd. G60: Old K	1F **43**
Dalnottar Ter. G60: Old K	1F **43**
DALREOCH	2C **18**
Dalreoch Av. G69: Bail	6A **92**
Dalreoch Ct. G82: Dumb	3D **18**
Dalreoch Ho. G82: Dumb	3D **18**
	(off School La.)
Dalreoch Path G69: Bail	6A **92**
Dalreoch Pl. G82: Dumb	3D **18**
Dalreoch Station (Rail)	3E **19**
Dalriada G2: Glas	5H **5** (4E **87**)
	(off Blythswood Ct.)
Dalriada Cres. ML1: Moth	5F **131**
Dalriada Dr. G64: Torr	5E **31**
Dalriada St. G40: Glas	1E **109**

Dalry Gdns. ML3: Ham	1B **160**
Dalrymple Ct. G66: Kirkin	6D **32**
Dalrymple Cres. G73: Ruth	2B **124**
Dalrymple Dr. G74: E Kil	6G **141**
Dalrymple Dr. G77: Newt M	5G **137**
Dalrymple Dr. ML5: Coat	6B **94**
Dalry Pl. ML6: Chap	5E **117**
Dalry Rd. G71: View	6F **113**
Dalry St. G32: Glas	1B **110**
DALSERF	3B **172**
Dalserf Ct. G31: Glas	6D **88**
Dalserf Cres. G46: Giff	6H **121**
Dalserf Gdns. G31: Glas	6D **88**
Dalserf Path ML9: Lark	4E **171**
	(off Alba Way)
Dalserf Pl. G31: Glas	6D **88**
Dalserf St. G31: Glas	6D **88**
Dalsetter Av. G15: Glas	5H **45**
Dalsetter Cres. G15: Glas	5A **46**
Dalsetter Dr. G15: Glas	5H **45**
Dalsetter Pl. G15: Glas	5A **46**
DALSHANNON	1B **56**
Dalshannon Pl. G67: Cumb	6C **36**
Dalshannon Rd. G67: Cumb	6D **36**
Dalshannon Vw. G67: Cumb	6C **36**
Dalshannon Way G67: Cumb	6C **36**
Dalsholm Av. G20: Glas	1H **63**
Dalsholm Ind. Est. G20: Glas	2H **63**
Dalsholm Pl. G20: Glas	1A **64**
Dalsholm Rd. G20: Glas	2H **63**
Dalskeith Av. PA3: Pais	6E **81**
Dalskeith Cres. PA3: Pais	6E **81**
Dalskeith Rd. PA3: Pais	1E **101**
Dalswinton Path G34: Glas	3A **92**
Dalswinton St. G34: Glas	3A **92**
DALTON	5F **127**
Dalton Av. G81: Clyd	6G **45**
Dalton Cotts. G72: Flem	5F **127**
Dalton Ct. G31: Glas	6G **89**
Dalton Hill ML3: Ham	1C **160**
Dalton St. G31: Glas	6G **89**
Dalveen Ct. G78: Barr	6E **119**
Dalveen Dr. G71: Tann	5C **112**
Dalveen Quad. ML5: Coat	6F **95**
Dalveen St. G32: Glas	6H **89**
Dalveen Way G73: Ruth	4E **125**
Dalwhinnie Av. G72: Blan	5A **128**
Dalwhinnie Pl. ML6: Air	6B **74**
Daly Gdns. G72: Blan	6C **128**
Dalzell Av. ML1: Moth	5A **148**
Dalzell Country Pk.	6H **147**
Dalzell Dr. ML1: Moth	5A **148**
Dalziel Ct. ML3: Ham	6E **145**
Dalziel Cres. G72: Camb	1D **126**
Dalziel Dr. G41: Glas	2A **106**
Dalziel Gait G72: Camb	1D **126**
Dalziel Gro. G72: Camb	1D **126**
DALZIEL PK.	6F **133**
Dalziel Pk. Golf Course	1E **149**
Dalziel Path G72: Camb	1D **126**
Dalziel Pl. ML6: Air	5A **96**
Dalziel Quad. G41: Glas	2A **106**
Dalziel Rd. G52: Hill E	3H **83**
Dalziel St. ML1: Moth	2H **147**
Dalziel St. ML3: Ham	4F **145**
Dalziel Twr. ML1: Moth	6B **148**
Dalziel Way G72: Camb	2D **126**
Damshot Cres. G53: Glas	4D **104**
Damshot Rd. G53: Glas	6D **104**
Danby Rd. G69: Bail	1F **111**
Danes Av. G14: Glas	5C **62**
Danes Cres. G14: Glas	4B **62**
Danes Dr. G14: Glas	4B **62**
Danes La. Nth. G14: Glas	5C **62**
Danes La. Sth. G14: Glas	5C **62**
Daniel McLaughlin Pl. G66: Kirkin	4E **33**
Dargarvel Av. G41: Glas	1H **105**
Dargarvel Path G41: Glas	2G **105**
	(off Dumbreck Pl.)

Dargavel Av. PA7: B'ton	4H **41**
Dargavel Rd. PA7: B'ton	6A **42**
Dargavel Rd. PA8: Ersk	6B **42**
Darkwood Ct. PA3: Pais	5F **81**
Darkwood Cres. PA3: Pais	5F **81**
Darkwood Dr. PA3: Pais	5F **81**
Darleith St. G32: Glas	6H **89**
Darley Pl. ML3: Ham	3F **161**
Darley Rd. G68: Cumb	6G **15**
Darluith Pk. PA5: Brkfld	5C **78**
Darluith Rd. PA3: Lin	5E **79**
Darnaway Av. G33: Glas	1D **90**
Darnaway Dr. G33: Glas	1D **90**
Darnaway St. G33: Glas	1D **90**
Darngavel Ct. ML6: Air	3F **95**
	(off Monkscourt Av.)
Darngavil Rd. ML6: Grng	1E **75**
Darnick St. G21: Glas	6C **66**
Darnley Cres. G64: B'rig	4B **50**
Darnley Gdns. G41: Glas	3C **106**
Darnley Ind. Est. G53: Glas	3B **120**
Darnley Mains Rd. G53: Glas	4C **120**
Darnley Path G46: T'bnk	2E **121**
Darnley Pl. G41: Glas	3C **106**
Darnley Rd. G41: Glas	3C **106**
Darnley Rd. G78: Barr	4F **119**
Darnley St. G41: Glas	3D **106**
Darragh Grn. ML2: Newm	3E **151**
Darroch Cres. ML6: Chap	3D **116**
Darroch Dr. PA8: Ersk	4D **42**
Darroch Way G67: Cumb	2A **38**
Dart Av. G74: E Kil	4H **141**
Dartford St. G22: Glas	6F **65**
Darvel Cres. PA1: Pais	1F **103**
Darvel Dr. G77: Newt M	4G **137**
Darvel Gro. G72: Blan	1B **160**
Darwin Av. ML1: Moth	5C **148**
Darwin Pl. G81: Clyd	3H **43**
Darwin Rd. G75: E Kil	3E **157**
Davaar G2: Glas	5A **6** (4E **87**)
	(off Blythswood Ct.)
Davaar G74: E Kil	2C **158**
Davaar Dr. ML1: Moth	5E **131**
Davaar Dr. ML5: Coat	4H **93**
Davaar Dr. PA2: Pais	6A **102**
Davaar Pl. G77: Newt M	3C **136**
Davaar Rd. PA4: Renf	2F **83**
Davaar St. G40: Glas	1D **108**
Davan Loan ML2: Newm	3D **150**
	(off Tiree Cres.)
Dava St. G51: Glas	4G **85**
Dave Barrie Av. ML9: Lark	6H **163**
Daventry Dr. G12: Glas	4G **63**
David Ct. G40: Glas	5C **88**
David Donnelly Pl. G66: Kirkin	4C **32**
David Gray Dr. G66: Kirkin	4G **33**
David Livingstone Cen.	5C **128**
David Lloyd Leisure	1F **63**
	(Glasgow)
David Lloyd Leisure	2D **82**
	(Paisley)
David Pl. G69: Bail	1F **111**
David Pl. PA3: Pais	4D **82**
Davidson Cres. G65: Twe	2D **34**
Davidson Gdns. G14: Glas	5E **63**
Davidson La. G14: Glas	5E **63**
Davidson La. ML8: Carl	4F **175**
	(off Ramage Rd.)
Davidson Pl. G32: Glas	5C **90**
Davidson Quad. G81: Dun	6B **24**
Davidson St. G40: Glas	3C **108**
Davidson St. G81: Clyd	1G **61**
Davidson St. ML5: Coat	1D **114**
Davidson St. ML6: Air	3H **95**
Davidston Pl. G66: Lenz	3F **53**
David St. G40: Glas	6C **88**
David St. ML5: Coat	4E **95**
David Way PA3: Pais	4D **82**
Davieland Rd. G46: Giff	6G **121**

Dodhill Pl. – Drumby Cres.

Dodhill Pl. G13: Glas 3B 62
Dodside Gdns. G32: Glas 1C 110
Dodside Pl. G32: Glas 1C 110
Dodside St. G32: Glas 1C 110
Dolan St. G69: Bail 6H 91
Dollan Aqua Cen. 2G 157
Dollar Pk. ML1: Moth 6B 148
Dollar Ter. G20: Glas 1A 64
(off Crosbie St.)
Dolphington Av. G5: Glas 2A 108
Dolphin Rd. G41: Glas 3B 106
Dominica Grn. G75: E Kil 2C 156
Donald Dewar Leisure Cen. 4A 46
Donaldfield Rd. PA11: Bri W 4D 76
Donald Mackinnon Av. G66: Kirkin 6E 33
Donaldson Av. G65: Kils 4H 13
Donaldson Cres. G66: Kirkin 6C 32
Donaldson Dr. PA4: Renf 6E 61
Donaldson Grn. G71: Tann 5E 113
Donaldson Pl. G66: Kirkin 5D 32
Donaldson Rd. ML9: Lark 4E 171
Donaldson St. G66: Kirkin 6C 32
Donaldson St. ML3: Ham 4E 145
Donaldswood Pk. PA2: Pais 5G 101
Donaldswood Rd. PA2: Pais 5G 101
Donald Ter. ML3: Ham 2G 161
Donald Way G71: Tann 6E 113
Don Av. PA4: Renf 1G 83
Doncaster St. G20: Glas 6E 65
Don Ct. ML3: Ham 3E 161
Don Dr. PA2: Pais 4D 100
Donnelly Way ML2: Wis 5C 148
Donnies Brae G78: Barr 1F 135
Donoghue Ter. PA2: Pais 2D 102
Donohoe Ct. G64: B'rig 6C 50
Don Path ML9: Lark 5C 170
Don Pl. PA5: John 5C 98
Don St. G33: Glas 3F 89
Doon Cres. G61: Bear 4D 46
Doonfoot Ct. G74: E Kil 1F 157
Doonfoot Gdns. G74: E Kil 1F 157
Doonfoot Rd. G43: Glas 1B 122
Doon Pl. G66: Kirkin 3F 33
Doon Rd. G66: Kirkin 4F 33
Doonside G67: Cumb 3B 38
Doonside Twr. ML1: Moth 5B 148
Doon St. G81: Clyd 4F 45
Doon St. ML1: Moth 5A 148
Doon St. ML9: Lark 3E 171
Doon Way G66: Kirkin 4G 33
Dorain Rd. ML1: N'hill 4D 132
Dora St. G40: Glas 2C 108
Dorchester Av. G12: Glas 3G 63
Dorchester Ct. G12: Glas 3G 63
Dorchester Pl. G12: Glas 3G 63
Dorian Dr. G76: Clar 1H 137
Dorian Wynd ML1: Moth 6C 148
Dorlin Rd. G33: Step 4E 69
Dormanside Ct. G53: Glas 2B 104
Dormanside Ga. G53: Glas 2B 104
Dormanside Gro. G53: Glas 2B 104
Dormanside Pl. G53: Glas 4C 104
Dormanside Rd. G53: Glas 2B 104
Dornal Av. G13: Glas 2G 61
Dornford Av. G32: Glas 3D 110
Dornford Rd. G32: Glas 3D 110
Dornie Ct. G46: T'bnk 4E 121
Dornie Dr. G32: Carm 5B 110
Dornie Dr. G46: T'bnk 4E 121
Dornie Path ML2: Newm 3D 150
(off Tiree Cres.)
Dornie Way PA7: B'ton 5F 41
Dornoch Av. G46: Giff 6A 122
Dornoch Ct. ML4: Bell 1C 130
Dornoch Dr. G72: Blan 5B 144
Dornoch Pl. G64: B'rig 5F 51
Dornoch Pl. G69: Chry 6B 54
Dornoch Pl. G74: E Kil 1E 157
Dornoch Rd. G61: Bear 5D 46
Dornoch Rd. ML1: Holy 3B 132
Dornoch St. G40: Glas 6B 88
Dornoch Way G68: Cumb 6A 16
Dornoch Way G72: Blan 5B 144
Dornoch Way ML6: Air 6H 95
Dorset Sq. G3: Glas 3G 5 (3D 86)
(off Dorset St.)
Dorset St. G3: Glas 4F 5 (3D 86)
Dosk Av. G13: Glas 1H 61
Dosk Pl. G13: Glas 1H 61
Double Hedges Rd. G78: Neil 3D 134
Dougalston Av. G62: Miln 4H 27
Dougalston Cres. G62: Miln 4H 27
Dougalston Gdns. Nth. G62: Miln 4H 27
Dougalston Gdns. Sth. G62: Miln 4H 27
Dougalston Rd. G23: Glas 1C 64
Dougan Dr. ML2: Newm 4F 151
Douglas Av. G32: Carm 4B 110
Douglas Av. G46: Giff 6A 122
Douglas Av. G66: Lenz 2D 52
Douglas Av. G73: Ruth 2E 125
Douglas Av. PA5: Eld 3H 99
Douglas Ct. G66: Lenz 2D 52
Douglas Cres. G71: Tann 5F 113
Douglas Cres. G71: View 5F 113
Douglas Cres. ML3: Ham 5H 161
Douglas Cres. ML6: Air 5A 96
Douglas Cres. PA8: Ersk 4D 42
Douglasdale G74: E Kil 1F 157
Douglas Dr. G15: Glas 6H 45
Douglas Dr. G69: Bail 6F 91
Douglas Dr. G71: Both 6E 129
Douglas Dr. G72: Camb 2H 125
Douglas Dr. G75: E Kil 4A 156
Douglas Dr. G77: Newt M 3E 137
Douglas Dr. ML4: Bell 3E 131
Douglas Dr. ML9: Ashg 5H 171
Douglas Gdns. G46: Giff 6A 122
Douglas Gdns. G61: Bear 3F 47
Douglas Gdns. G66: Lenz 2D 52
Douglas Gdns. G71: Udd 2D 128
Douglas Ga. G72: Camb 2H 125
Douglas Ho. G67: Cumb 3H 37
Douglas Ho. G82: Dumb 1H 19
Douglas La. G2: Glas 4A 6 (3E 87)
(off W. George La.)
Douglas Muir Dr. G62: Miln 2C 26
Douglas Muir Gdns. G62: Miln 2C 26
Douglas Muir Pl. G62: Miln 2C 26
Douglas Muir Rd. G62: Miln 3C 26
Douglas Muir Rd. G81: Faif 6F 25
Douglas Pk. Cres. G61: Bear 1G 47
Douglas Pk. Golf Course 2G 47
Douglas Pk. La. ML3: Ham 5G 145
Douglas Pl. G61: Bear 2E 47
Douglas Pl. G66: Lenz 2D 52
Douglas Pl. ML3: Ham 5H 161
Douglas Pl. ML5: Coat 5B 94
Douglas Rd. G82: Dumb 4H 19
Douglas Rd. PA4: Renf 3C 82
Douglas St. G2: Glas 6A 6 (4E 87)
Douglas St. G62: Miln 4G 27
Douglas St. G71: Tann 5F 113
Douglas St. G71: View 5F 113
Douglas St. G72: Blan 3A 144
Douglas St. ML1: Moth 2F 147
Douglas St. ML2: Over 4B 166
Douglas St. ML3: Ham 4G 145
Douglas St. ML6: Air 5A 96
Douglas St. ML8: Carl 3C 174
Douglas St. ML9: Lark 1C 170
Douglas St. PA1: Pais 6G 81
Douglaston Golf Course 2B 28
Douglas Twr. G71: Both 3B 128
Douglas Vw. ML5: Coat 2B 114
Dougray Pl. G78: Barr 5E 119
Dougrie Cl. G45: Glas 4H 123
Dougrie Dr. G45: Glas 4H 123
Dougrie Dr. La. G45: Glas 4H 123
Dougrie Gdns. G45: Glas 5H 123
Dougrie Pl. G45: Glas 4A 124
Dougrie Rd. G45: Glas 5G 123
Dougrie St. G45: Glas 4A 124
Dougrie Ter. G45: Glas 4H 123
Doulton Rd. PA2: Pais 2D 102
Doune Cres. G64: B'rig 3D 50
Doune Cres. G77: Newt M 4F 137
Doune Cres. ML6: Chap 4D 116
Doune Gdns. G20: Glas 6C 64
Doune Gdns. La. G20: Glas 6C 64
Doune Pk. Way ML5: Coat 6B 94
Doune Quad. G20: Glas 6C 64
Doune Ter. ML5: Coat 2H 93
Dovecot G43: Glas 5A 106
Dovecot Dr. ML6: Air 4B 96
Dovecote Rd. ML1: Holy 5H 115
Dovecote Vw. G66: Kirkin 6F 33
DOVECOTHALL 4G 119
Dovecothall St. G78: Barr 4F 119
Dovecotwood G65: Kils 2H 13
DOVECOTWOOD 2H 13
Doveholm G82: Dumb 2G 19
Doveholm Av. G82: Dumb 2H 19
Dove Pl. G75: E Kil 5B 156
Dover St. G3: Glas 4E 5 (3C 86)
Dover St. ML5: Coat 1H 93
Dove St. G53: Glas 2A 120
Dove Wynd ML4: Bell 6A 114
Dowanfield Rd. G67: Cumb 4F 37
DOWANHILL 6A 64
Dowanhill Pk. 1A 86
Dowanhill St. G11: Glas 1A 86
Dowanhill St. G12: Glas 1A 86
Dowan Rd. G62: Bald 6C 28
Dowan Rd. G62: Bard 6C 28
Dowan Rd. G62: Miln 6C 28
Dowanside La. G12: Glas 6B 64
Dowanside Rd. G12: Glas 6A 64
Downcraig Dr. G45: Glas 5H 123
Downcraig Gro. G45: Glas 5G 123
Downcraig Rd. G45: Glas 6G 123
Downcraig Ter. G45: Glas 5H 123
Downfield Dr. ML3: Ham 4F 161
Downfield Gdns. G71: Both 5D 128
Downfield St. G32: Glas 2G 109
Downiebrae Rd. G73: Ruth 3D 108
Downie Cl. G71: Tann 5F 113
Downie Dr. ML9: Lark 1C 170
Downie St. ML3: Ham 2H 161
Downs St. G21: Glas 4B 66
Dow Pl. G69: Barg 5F 93
Dowrie Cres. G53: Glas 4B 104
Draffen Ct. ML1: Moth 2H 147
Draffen St. ML1: Moth 2H 147
Draffen Twr. ML1: Moth 2H 147
Drakemire Av. G45: Glas 3G 123
Drakemire Dr. G44: Glas 3G 123
Drakemire Dr. G45: Glas 5F 123
Drake St. G40: Glas 6A 88
Dreghorn St. G31: Glas 4E 89
Drimnin Rd. G33: Step 4F 69
Drive Rd. G51: Glas 3E 85
Drochil St. G34: Glas 2G 91
Dromore St. G66: Kirkin 6D 32
Drove Hill G68: Cumb 2D 36
Drumaling Ter. G66: Len 3H 9
Drumbathie Rd. ML6: Air 3B 96
Drumbathie Ter. ML6: Air 3C 96
Drumbeg Dr. G53: Glas 1A 120
Drumbeg Path G72: Blan 6A 144
Drumbeg Pl. G53: Glas 1A 120
Drumbeg Pl. G69: Chry 6A 54
Drumbeg Rd. PA7: B'ton 4F 41
Drumbeg Ter. G62: Miln 3D 26
Drumboe Av. G69: G'csh 5D 70
Drumbottie Rd. G21: Glas 4C 66
Drumbowie Vw. G68: Cumb 2E 37
Drumby Cres. G76: Clar 6B 122

Drumby Dr. – Dunalastair Dr.

Drumby Dr. G76: Clar 1B **138**
Drumcarn Dr. G62: Miln 4F **27**
Drumcavel Rd. G69: G'csh 2B **70**
Drumcavel Rd. G69: Muirh 2B **70**
DRUMCHAPEL 4H **45**
Drumchapel Gdns. G15: Glas 5A **46**
Drumchapel Pl. G15: Glas 5B **46**
Drumchapel Rd. G15: Glas 5A **46**
Drumchapel Shop. Cen. 4H **45**
Drumchapel Sports Cen. 5H **45**
Drumchapel Station (Rail) 6A **46**
Drumchapel Swimming Pool 5H **45**
Drumclair Pl. ML6: Air 4D **96**
Drumclog Av. G62: Miln 1G **27**
Drumclog Gdns. G33: Glas 3H **67**
Drumcross Pl. G53: Glas 4C **104**
Drumcross Rd. G53: Glas 4C **104**
Drumcross Rd. PA7: B'ton 4B **42**
Drumduff G75: E Kil 6F **157**
Drumfearn Dr. G22: Glas 3F **65**
Drumfearn Pl. G22: Glas 3F **65**
Drumfearn Rd. G22: Glas 3F **65**
DRUMGELLOCH 3C **96**
Drumgelloch Station (Rail) 3E **97**
Drumgelloch St. ML6: Air 2D **96**
DRUMGLASS 2H **35**
Drumglass Steadings G65: Croy 2H **35**
Drumglass Vw. G65: Croy 1B **36**
Drumgray Av. G71: Udd 3D **128**
DRUMGREW 4F **35**
Drumgrew Quad. G65: Twe 1D **34**
DRUMGREW RDBT. 4F **35**
Drumhead La. G32: Glas 4H **109**
Drumhead Pl. G32: Glas 4H **109**
Drumhead Rd. G32: Glas 4H **109**
Drumhill G66: Kirkin 3H **33**
Drumilaw Cres. G73: Ruth 2C **124**
Drumilaw Rd. G73: Ruth 2C **124**
Drumilaw Way G73: Ruth 2C **124**
Drumin Ct. G72: Camb 5H **125**
Drumlaken Av. G23: Glas 6A **48**
Drumlaken Ct. G23: Glas 6B **48**
Drumlaken Path G23: Glas 6B **48**
(off Drumlaken St.)
Drumlaken Pl. G23: Glas 6B **48**
(off Chatton St.)
Drumlaken St. G23: Glas 6A **48**
Drumlanrig Av. G34: Glas 2A **92**
Drumlanrig Cres. G69: G'csh 5C **70**
Drumlin Dr. G62: Miln 5F **27**
Drumloch Gdns. G75: E Kil 6G **157**
Drumlochy Rd. G33: Glas 2A **90**
Drum Mains Pk. G68: Cumb 6G **35**
Drummond Av. G73: Ruth 5B **108**
Drummond Ct. G22: Glas 2E **65**
Drummond Dr. ML2: Wis 1H **165**
Drummond Dr. PA1: Pais 1F **103**
Drummond Hill G74: E Kil 6B **142**
Drummond Ho. G67: Cumb 2A **38**
Drummond Pl. G74: E Kil 6B **142**
Drummond Way G77: Newt M 4A **136**
Drummore Av. ML5: Coat 2F **115**
Drummore Rd. G15: Glas 2A **46**
Drumnessie Ct. G68: Cumb 5B **36**
Drumnessie Rd. G68: Cumb 5B **36**
Drumnessie Vw. G68: Cumb 5B **36**
Drumore Av. ML6: Chap 4D **116**
Drumover Dr. G31: Glas 1G **109**
DRUMOYNE 5E **85**
Drumoyne Av. G51: Glas 4E **85**
Drumoyne Cir. G51: Glas 5E **85**
Drumoyne Dr. G51: Glas 4E **85**
Drumoyne Pl. G51: Glas 5E **85**
Drumoyne Quad. G51: Glas 5E **85**
Drumoyne Rd. G51: Glas 5E **85**
Drumoyne Sq. G51: Glas 4E **85**
Drumpark St. G46: T'bnk 3F **121**
Drumpark St. ML5: Coat 1F **113**
DRUMPELLIER 4H **93**
Drumpellier Av. G67: Cumb 1E **57**
Drumpellier Av. G69: Bail 2H **111**
Drumpellier Av. ML5: Coat 4G **93**
Drumpellier Country Pk. 3F **93**
Drumpellier Country Pk. Vis. Cen. 2E **93**
Drumpellier Ct. G67: Cumb 6E **37**
Drumpellier Cres. ML5: Coat 5H **93**
Drumpellier Gdns. G67: Cumb 6E **37**
Drumpellier Golf Course 5H **93**
Drumpellier Gro. G67: Cumb 6E **37**
Drumpellier Pl. G67: Cumb 6E **37**
Drumpellier Pl. G69: Bail 1H **111**
Drumpellier Rd. G69: Bail 2G **111**
Drumpellier St. G33: Glas 1F **89**
Drumreoch Dr. G42: Glas 5A **108**
Drumreoch Pl. G42: Glas 5A **108**
DRUMRY 4E **45**
Drumry Pl. G15: Glas 5G **45**
Drumry Rd. G81: Clyd 4D **44**
Drumry Rd. E. G15: Glas 5G **45**
Drumry Station (Rail) 5F **45**
Drumsack Av. G69: Chry 1A **70**
DRUMSAGARD VILLAGE 3F **127**
Drumsargard Rd. G73: Ruth 2F **125**
Drums Av. PA3: Pais 5G **81**
Drums Cres. PA3: Pais 6G **81**
Drumshangie Pl. ML6: Air 1A **96**
Drumshangie St. ML6: Air 1A **96**
Drumshaw Dr. G32: Carm 5C **110**
Drums Rd. G53: Glas 2A **104**
Drumtrocher St. G65: Kils 3H **13**
Drumvale Dr. G69: Mood 5C **54**
Drury La. Ct. G74: E Kil 5C **142**
Drury St. G2: Glas 5C **6** (4F **87**)
Dryad St. G46: T'bnk 2E **121**
Dryburgh Av. G73: Ruth 6D **108**
Dryburgh Av. PA2: Pais 4E **101**
Dryburgh Gdns. G20: Glas 6D **64**
Dryburgh Hill G74: E Kil 2F **157**
Dryburgh La. G74: E Kil 2F **157**
Dryburgh Pl. G66: Kirkin 5F **33**
Dryburgh Pl. ML5: Coat 4B **94**
Dryburgh Rd. G61: Bear 1C **46**
Dryburgh Rd. ML2: Wis 6G **149**
Dryburgh St. ML3: Ham 3F **145**
Dryburgh Wlk. G69: Mood 4E **55**
Dryburgh Way G72: Blan 2B **144**
(off Winton Cres.)
Dryburn Av. G52: Glas 6A **84**
Dryden St. ML3: Ham 3F **145**
Drygate G4: Glas 5H **7** (4A **88**)
Drygate St. ML9: Lark 1C **170**
Drygrange Rd. G33: Glas 1C **90**
Drymen Pl. G66: Lenz 4D **52**
Drymen Rd. G61: Bear 1D **46**
Drymen St. G52: Glas 6E **85**
Drymen Wynd G61: Bear 4F **47**
Drynoch Pl. G22: Glas 2F **65**
Drysdale St. G14: Glas 4H **61**
Duart Dr. G74: E Kil 6F **141**
Duart Dr. G77: Newt M 4G **137**
Duart Dr. PA5: Eld 4H **99**
Duart St. G20: Glas 1A **64**
Duart Way G69: G'csh 5C **70**
Dubs Rd. G78: Barr 4G **119**
Dubton Path G34: Glas 2H **91**
Dubton St. G34: Glas 2H **91**
Duchall Pl. G14: Glas 5B **62**
Duchess Ct. ML3: Ham 1C **162**
Duchess Pl. G73: Ruth 5E **109**
Duchess Rd. G73: Ruth 4E **109**
Duchess Way G69: Barg 6D **92**
(off Park Rd.)
Duchray Dr. PA1: Pais 2G **103**
Duchray La. G33: Glas 2F **89**
Duchray St. G33: Glas 2F **89**
Dudley Dr. G12: Glas 6G **63**
Dudley Dr. ML5: Coat 1G **93**
Dudley La. G12: Glas 6G **63**
Duffus Pl. G32: Carm 5C **110**
Duffus St. G34: Glas 2G **91**
Duffus Ter. G32: Carm 5C **110**
Duich Gdns. G23: Glas 5C **48**
Duisdale Rd. G32: Carm 5C **110**
Duke's Ct. ML9: Lark 1C **170**
Dukes Ct. G72: Camb 6G **109**
Dukes Ga. G71: Both 3C **128**
Dukes Pl. ML3: Ham 5H **161**
Duke's Rd. G72: Camb 1F **125**
Duke's Rd. G73: Ruth 2E **125**
Dukes Rd. G69: Barg 6D **92**
Duke St. G31: Glas 5D **88**
Duke St. G4: Glas 5G **7** (4A **88**)
Duke St. ML1: Moth 1G **147**
Duke St. ML2: Newm 3D **150**
Duke St. ML3: Ham 6A **146**
Duke St. ML9: Lark 1C **170**
Duke St. PA2: Pais 3A **102**
Duke Street Station (Rail) 4D **88**
Duke Wynd G4: Glas 6H **7** (4A **88**)
DULLATUR 5F **15**
Dullatur Golf Course 6E **15**
Dullatur Rd. G68: Dull 5F **15**
DULLATUR RDBT. 6H **15**
Dulnain St. G72: Camb 2D **126**
Dulsie Rd. G21: Glas 3E **67**
DUMBARTON 4E **19**
Dumbarton Castle 6G **19**
Dumbarton Central Station (Rail) 3F **19**
Dumbarton East Station (Rail) 4H **19**
Dumbarton FC 5F **19**
Dumbarton Golf Course 2F **19**
DUMBARTON JOINT HOSPITAL 3C **18**
Dumbarton (Milton) Tourist Info. Cen. 4F **21**
Dumbarton Rd. G11: Glas 1F **85**
(not continuous)
Dumbarton Rd. G14: Glas 3G **61**
Dumbarton Rd. G60: Bowl 5H **21**
Dumbarton Rd. G60: Old K 5H **21**
Dumbarton Rd. G81: Clyd 3G **43**
Dumbarton Rd. G81: Dun 1B **44**
Dumbarton Rd. G81: Hard 1B **44**
Dumbarton Rd. G82: Mil 4E **21**
DUMBRECK 2A **106**
Dumbreck Av. G41: Glas 1G **105**
Dumbreck Ct. G41: Glas 2G **105**
DUMBRECK INTERCHANGE 2G **105**
Dumbreck Path G41: Glas 1G **105**
(off Dumbreck Pl.)
Dumbreck Pl. G41: Glas 2G **105**
Dumbreck Pl. G66: Lenz 3E **53**
Dumbreck Rd. G41: Glas 6G **85**
DUMBRECK ROAD INTERCHANGE 6H **85**
Dumbreck Sq. G41: Glas 1G **105**
Dumbreck Station (Rail) 1A **106**
Dumbreck Ter. G65: Queen 3D **12**
Dumbrock Rd. G62: Miln 3D **26**
DUMBUCK 4E **21**
Dumbuck Cres. G82: Dumb 3C **20**
Dumbuck Gdns. G82: Dumb 5H **19**
Dumbuck Rd. G82: Dumb 3H **19**
(Dumbuie Av.)
(not continuous)
Dumbuck Rd. G82: Dumb 2H **19**
(Stirling Rd.)
Dumbuie Av. G82: Dumb 3H **19**
Dumfries Cres. ML6: Air 6H **95**
Dumgoyne Av. G62: Miln 4F **27**
Dumgoyne Ct. ML6: Air 1B **96**
(off Thrashbush Rd.)
Dumgoyne Dr. G61: Bear 6D **26**
Dumgoyne Gdns. G62: Miln 4F **27**
Dumgoyne Pl. G76: Clar 2A **138**
Dunagoil Gdns. G45: Glas 5A **124**
Dunagoil Pl. G45: Glas 6A **124**
Dunagoil Rd. G45: Glas 5H **123**
Dunagoil St. G45: Glas 5A **124**
Dunalastair Dr. G33: Mille 4B **68**

Dunan Pl. G33: Glas	4E **91**	
Dunard Ct. ML8: Carl	2D **174**	
(off Kenmore Way)		
Dunard Ga. G73: Ruth	6D **108**	
Dunard Rd. G73: Ruth	6D **108**	
Dunard St. G20: Glas	5D **64**	
Dunard Way PA3: Pais	4H **81**	
Dunaskin Ct. G11: Glas	1A **4** (2A **86**)	
Dunaskin St. G11: Glas	1A **4** (2A **86**)	
Dunavon Pl. ML5: Coat	1F **115**	
Dunbar Av. G73: Ruth	6E **109**	
Dunbar Av. ML5: Coat	1H **113**	
Dunbar Av. PA5: John	5E **99**	
Dunbar Dr. ML1: Moth	5A **148**	
Dunbar Hill G74: E Kil	2E **157**	
Dunbar La. ML1: New S	5A **132**	
Dunbar Pl. G74: E Kil	2E **157**	
Dunbar Rd. PA2: Pais	4E **101**	
Dunbar St. ML3: Ham	4F **145**	
Dunbeath Av. G77: Newt M	4F **137**	
Dunbeath Gro. G72: Blan	6A **144**	
Dunbeith Pl. G20: Glas	4B **64**	
DUNBETH	4D **94**	
Dunbeth Av. ML5: Coat	4D **94**	
Dunbeth Ct. ML5: Coat	4D **94**	
Dunbeth Rd. ML5: Coat	3D **94**	
Dunblane Dr. G74: E Kil	6H **141**	
Dunblane Pl. G74: E Kil	1H **157**	
Dunblane Pl. ML5: Coat	1B **114**	
Dunblane St. G4: Glas	1C **6** (2F **87**)	
(not continuous)		
Dunbrach Rd. G68: Cumb	2D **36**	
Dunbritton Rd. G82: Dumb	2C **20**	
Duncan Av. G14: Glas	6C **62**	
Duncan Ct. ML1: Moth	6F **131**	
Duncan Graham St. ML9: Lark	1D **170**	
Duncan La. G14: Glas	6C **62**	
(off Gleneagles La. Nth.)		
Duncan La. Nth. G14: Glas	5C **62**	
(off Norse La. Nth.)		
Duncan La. Sth. G14: Glas	5C **62**	
(off Earlbank La. Sth.)		
Duncan McIntosh Rd. G68: Cumb	4B **16**	
Dun Cann PA8: Ersk	2G **59**	
Duncanrig Cres. G75: E Kil	3E **157**	
Duncansby Dr. G72: Blan	6A **144**	
Duncansby Rd. G33: Glas	5D **90**	
Duncan St. G81: Clyd	4D **44**	
Duncarnock Av. G78: Neil	2E **135**	
Duncarnock Cres. G78: Neil	2E **135**	
Duncarron Ter. G68: Cumb	2B **36**	
Dunchattan Pl. G31: Glas	4B **88**	
Dunchattan St. G31: Glas	4B **88**	
Dunchurch Rd. PA1: Pais	6F **83**	
Dunclutha Dr. G71: Both	6E **129**	
Duncolm Pl. G62: Miln	3D **26**	
Duncombe Av. G81: Hard	6D **24**	
Duncombe St. G20: Glas	2B **64**	
Duncombe Vw. G81: Clyd	4E **45**	
Duncraig Cres. PA5: John	5D **98**	
Duncrub Dr. G64: B'rig	6A **50**	
Duncruin St. G20: Glas	2A **64**	
Duncruin Ter. G20: Glas	2B **64**	
Duncryne Av. G32: Glas	1D **110**	
Duncryne Gdns. G32: Glas	1E **111**	
Duncryne Pl. G64: B'rig	1A **66**	
Dundaff Hill G68: Cumb	3E **37**	
Dundas Av. G64: Torr	5D **30**	
Dundas Cotts. FK4: Alla	1G **17**	
Dundas Ct. G74: E Kil	1G **157**	
Dundas Dr. ML6: Air	5G **95**	
Dundashill G4: Glas	1C **6** (1F **87**)	
Dundas La. G1: Glas	4D **6** (3G **87**)	
Dundas Pl. G74: E Kil	1G **157**	
Dundas St. G1: Glas	4D **6** (3G **87**)	
(not continuous)		
Dundasvale Ct. G4: Glas	1C **6** (2F **87**)	
Dundee Dr. G52: Glas	1B **104**	
Dundee Path G52: Glas	2C **104**	

Dundonald Av. PA5: John	4D **98**	
Dundonald Cres. G77: Newt M	5G **137**	
Dundonald Cres. ML5: Coat	1B **114**	
Dundonald Dr. ML3: Ham	4H **161**	
Dundonald Pl. G78: Neil	2D **134**	
Dundonald Rd. G12: Glas	6A **64**	
Dundonald Rd. PA3: Pais	4C **82**	
Dundonald St. G72: Blan	1A **144**	
Dundrennan Dr. ML6: Chap	3E **117**	
Dundrennan Rd. G42: Glas	6D **106**	
DUNDYVAN	6B **94**	
Dundyvan Gdns. ML5: Coat	6C **94**	
Dundyvan Ga. ML5: Coat	6C **94**	
Dundyvan Ind. Est. ML5: Coat	6B **94**	
Dundyvan La. ML2: Wis	6F **149**	
Dundyvan Rd. ML5: Coat	5B **94**	
Dundyvan St. ML2: Wis	1G **165**	
Dundyvan Way ML5: Coat	6B **94**	
Dunearn Pl. PA2: Pais	2C **102**	
Dunearn St. G4: Glas	1D **86**	
Duneaton Wynd ML9: Lark	5D **170**	
Dunedin Ct. G75: E Kil	3C **156**	
Dunedin Dr. G75: E Kil	2C **156**	
Dunedin Rd. ML9: Lark	4D **170**	
Dunedin Ter. G81: Clyd	1E **61**	
Dunellan Av. G69: Mood	5E **55**	
Dunellan Ct. G69: Mood	5E **55**	
(off Heathfield Av.)		
Dunellan Cres. G69: Mood	5E **55**	
Dunellan Dr. G81: Hard	6D **24**	
Dunellan Gdns. G69: Mood	5E **55**	
Dunellan Gro. G69: Mood	5E **55**	
(off Heathfield Av.)		
Dunellan Pl. G69: Mood	5E **55**	
Dunellan Rd. G62: Miln	3C **26**	
Dunellan St. G52: Glas	6E **85**	
Dunellan Way G69: Mood	5E **55**	
Dungavel Gdns. ML3: Ham	3A **162**	
Dungavel La. ML8: Carl	4F **175**	
(off Kelso Dr.)		
Dungeonhill Rd. G34: Glas	3B **92**	
Dunglass Av. G14: Glas	5C **62**	
Dunglass Av. G74: E Kil	6H **141**	
Dunglass La. G14: Glas	5C **62**	
(off Norse La. Sth.)		
Dunglass La. Nth. G14: Glas	5C **62**	
(off Norse La. Nth.)		
Dunglass Pl. G62: Miln	2E **27**	
Dunglass Pl. G77: Newt M	4A **136**	
Dunglass Rd. PA7: B'ton	5A **42**	
Dunglass Sq. G74: E Kil	1H **157**	
Dungoil Av. G68: Cumb	2D **36**	
Dungoil Rd. G66: Lenz	3E **53**	
Dungoyne St. G20: Glas	1A **64**	
Dunholme Pk. G81: Clyd	4H **43**	
Dunira St. G32: Glas	2H **109**	
Duniston Rd. ML6: Air	1H **117**	
Dunivaig Rd. G33: Glas	4D **90**	
Dunkeld Av. G73: Ruth	6D **108**	
Dunkeld Dr. G61: Bear	3H **47**	
Dunkeld Gdns. G64: B'rig	5D **50**	
Dunkeld La. G69: Mood	5E **55**	
Dunkeld Pl. G77: Newt M	5H **137**	
Dunkeld Pl. ML3: Ham	6C **144**	
Dunkeld Pl. ML5: Coat	1B **114**	
Dunkeld St. G31: Glas	1E **109**	
Dunkenny Pl. G15: Glas	3H **45**	
Dunkenny Rd. G15: Glas	4G **45**	
Dunkenny Sq. G15: Glas	4H **45**	
Dunlin G12: Glas	3G **63**	
Dunlin G74: E Kil	5G **141**	
Dunlin Ct. ML4: Bell	5A **114**	
Dunlin Cres. PA6: C'lee	2C **78**	
Dunlin Way ML5: Coat	3G **115**	
Dunlop Av. G78: Barr	5F **119**	
Dunlop Cl. G33: G'csh	4H **69**	
Dunlop Ct. G33: G'csh	5H **69**	
Dunlop Ct. ML3: Ham	4A **162**	
Dunlop Cres. G33: G'csh	5G **69**	

Dunlop Cres. G33: Step	5G **69**	
Dunlop Cres. G71: Both	6F **129**	
Dunlop Cres. PA4: Renf	5F **61**	
(off Fulbar St.)		
Dunlop Gdns. G33: G'csh	5G **69**	
Dunlop Gdns. ML5: Coat	6E **95**	
Dunlop Ga. G33: G'csh	5H **69**	
Dunlop Gro. G33: Step	4G **69**	
Dunlop Gro. G71: Tann	4E **113**	
Dunlop Pl. G33: Step	4G **69**	
Dunlop Pl. G62: Miln	2F **27**	
Dunlop Pl. ML9: Ashg	5A **172**	
Dunlop St. G1: Glas	5G **87**	
(Howard St.)		
Dunlop St. G1: Glas	6D **6** (5G **87**)	
(Osborne St.)		
Dunlop St. G72: Camb	1E **127**	
Dunlop St. PA3: Lin	5A **80**	
Dunlop St. PA4: Renf	5F **61**	
(off Fulbar St.)		
Dunlop Twr. G75: E Kil	3G **157**	
(off Telford Rd.)		
Dunlop Wynd G33: G'csh	5G **69**	
Dunmore Dr. G62: Miln	5A **28**	
Dunmore St. G81: Clyd	1E **61**	
Dunnachie Dr. ML5: Coat	1F **113**	
Dunnachie Pl. ML5: Coat	1G **113**	
Dunnet Av. ML6: Glenm	4H **73**	
Dunnet Ct. G72: Blan	5B **144**	
Dunnet Dr. PA6: C'lee	2B **78**	
Dunnichen Gdns. G64: B'rig	6F **51**	
Dunnikier Wlk. G68: Cumb	4A **36**	
Dunning Dr. G68: Cumb	6A **16**	
Dunnock Pl. ML5: Coat	2G **115**	
Dunnotar Wlk. ML2: Newm	3D **150**	
(off Tiree Cres.)		
Dunnottar Ct. G74: E Kil	6E **141**	
Dunnottar Cres. G74: E Kil	6E **141**	
Dunnottar St. G33: Glas	1B **90**	
Dunnottar St. G64: B'rig	5F **51**	
Dunn Sq. PA1: Pais	1A **102**	
Dunn St. G40: Glas	2B **108**	
Dunn St. G81: Clyd	4A **44**	
Dunn St. G81: Dun	1B **44**	
Dunn St. PA1: Pais	6C **82**	
Dunnswood Rd. G67: Cumb	5D **16**	
Dunollie Pl. G69: G'csh	5C **70**	
Dunolly Dr. G77: Newt M	4F **137**	
Dunolly St. G21: Glas	2C **88**	
Dunottar Av. ML5: Coat	3D **114**	
Dunottar Pl. ML5: Coat	2D **114**	
Dun Pk. G66: Kirkin	5D **32**	
Dunphail Dr. G34: Glas	3B **92**	
Dunphail Rd. G34: Glas	3B **92**	
Dunragit St. G31: Glas	4E **89**	
Dunree Pl. G69: G'csh	5D **70**	
DUNROBIN	4E **97**	
Dunrobin Av. PA5: Eld	4A **100**	
Dunrobin Ct. G74: E Kil	6F **141**	
Dunrobin Ct. G81: Clyd	5C **44**	
Dunrobin Cres. G74: E Kil	6F **141**	
Dunrobin Dr. G74: E Kil	6F **141**	
Dunrobin Gdns. ML6: Air	5E **97**	
Dunrobin Pl. ML5: Coat	4B **94**	
Dunrobin Rd. ML6: Air	4E **97**	
Dunrobin St. G31: Glas	5D **88**	
Dunrod Hill G74: E Kil	6H **141**	
Dunrod St. G32: Glas	1B **110**	
Dunscaith Dr. G72: Camb	5H **125**	
Dunscore Brae ML3: Ham	1C **160**	
Duns Cres. ML2: Wis	3A **150**	
Dunside Dr. G53: Glas	1A **120**	
Dunskaith Pl. G34: Glas	4B **92**	
Dunskaith St. G34: Glas	4B **92**	
Dunsmore Rd. PA7: B'ton	3G **41**	
Dunsmuir St. G51: Glas	4H **85**	
Duns Path ML5: Coat	2F **115**	
Dunster Gdns. G64: B'rig	3D **50**	
Dunswin Av. G81: Clyd	4A **44**	

E

Eastfield Pl. – Ellangowan Ct.

Eastfield Pl. G82: Dumb 5H **19**
Eastfield Rd. G21: Glas 5A **66**
Eastfield Rd. G68: Cumb 3C **36**
Eastfield Rd. ML8: Carl 4E **175**
Eastfield Ter. ML4: Bell 3F **131**
EAST FULTON 5F **79**
East Ga. ML5: Glenb 2H **71**
Eastgate G69: G'csh 4E **71**
Eastgate ML2: Wis 6B **150**
East George St. ML5: Coat 3D **94**
East Glebe Ter. ML3: Ham 1H **161**
East Greenlees Av. G72: Camb 4C **126**
East Greenlees Cres. G72: Camb 4B **126**
East Greenlees Dr. G72: Camb 4C **126**
East Greenlees Gdns. G72: Camb 4B **126**
East Greenlees Gro. G72: Camb 4H **125**
East Greenlees Rd. G72: Camb 4A **126**
East Hallhill Rd. G69: Bail 5G **91**
Easthall Pl. G33: Glas 4F **91**
East Hamilton St. ML2: Wis 1H **165**
East High St. ML6: Air 3A **96**
EAST KILBRIDE 2H **157**
East Kilbride Arts Cen. 6H **141**
East Kilbride Golf Course 3B **142**
East Kilbride Ice Rink 3H **157**
East Kilbride Rd. G73: Ruth 2E **125**
East Kilbride Rd. G76: Busby 3E **139**
East Kilbride Rd. G76: Crmck 3E **139**
East Kilbride Shop. Cen. 2G **157**
East Kilbride Sports Cen. 5C **158**
East Kilbride Station (Rail) 1G **157**
East Kilbride Village Theatre 1H **157**
East La. PA1: Pais 1C **102**
Eastlea Pl. ML6: Air 5B **96**
East Machan St. ML9: Lark 4D **170**
EAST MAINS 1H **157**
East Mains Rd. G74: E Kil 1G **157**
East Milton Gro. G75: E Kil 2D **156**
Eastmuir St. G32: Glas 6B **90**
Eastmuir St. ML2: Wis 5C **150**
East Nerston Ct. G74: Ners 3A **142**
East Nerston Gro. G74: Ners 3A **142**
Easton Pl. ML5: Coat 6D **94**
East Renfrewshire Golf Course 3A **152**
East Rd. ML1: New S 3A **132**
East Rd. PA10: Kilba 1A **98**
East Scott Ter. ML3: Ham 2H **161**
EAST SHAWHEAD 3E **115**
Eastside G66: Kirkin 4D **32**
Eastside Ind. Est. G66: Kirkin 4D **32**
(off Eastside)
East Springfield Ter. G64: B'rig 1D **66**
East Station Ind. Est. ML9: Lark 1D **170**
East Stewart Gdns. ML5: Coat 4E **95**
East Stewart Pl. ML5: Coat 4E **95**
East Stewart St. ML5: Coat 5E **95**
East Thomson St. G81: Clyd 4D **44**
East Thornlie St. ML2: Wis 1H **165**
Eastvale Pl. G3: Glas 3A **4** (3A **86**)
East Wellbrae Cres. ML3: Ham 2F **161**
East Wellington St. G31: Glas 6F **89**
East Whitby St. G31: Glas 1E **109**
Eastwood Av. G41: Glas 5B **106**
Eastwood Av. G46: Giff 4A **122**
Eastwood Cres. G46: T'bnk 3F **121**
Eastwood Dr. ML2: Newm 3E **151**
Eastwood Golf Course 5A **152**
Eastwoodmains Rd. G46: Giff 6H **121**
Eastwoodmains Rd. G76: Clar 6B **122**
Eastwood Pk. 5H **121**
Eastwood Pk. Leisure 5H **121**
Eastwood Rd. G69: Mood 5D **54**
Eastwood Swimming Pool & Games Hall
2E **137**
Eastwood Toll 6H **121**
Eastwood Vw. G72: Camb 1E **127**
Eastwood Way ML9: Lark 1D **170**
(off Antrim La.)
Easwald Bank PA10: Kilba 3B **98**
Ebroch Dr. G65: Kils 3A **14**
Ebroch Pk. G65: Kils 3A **14**
Eccles St. G22: Glas 4A **66**
Eckford St. G32: Glas 1A **110**
Eck Path ML1: Holy 2A **132**
(off Howden Pl.)
Eday St. G22: Glas 3H **65**
Edderton Pl. G34: Glas 4G **91**
Edderton Way G34: Glas 4G **91**
Eddie Boyle Cl. ML2: Wis 6B **150**
Eddington Dr. G77: Newt M 6C **136**
Eddleston Pl. G72: Camb 2D **126**
EDDLEWOOD 4H **161**
Eddlewood Ct. G33: Glas 4G **91**
Eddlewood Path G33: Glas 4F **91**
Eddlewood Pl. G33: Glas 4F **91**
Eddlewood Rd. G33: Glas 4F **91**
Eddlewood Sports Barn 4H **161**
Eden Ct. ML6: Glenm 4H **73**
Eden Dr. G75: E Kil 5B **156**
Eden Gdns. G75: E Kil 4B **156**
Eden Gro. G75: E Kil 4B **156**
Edenhall Ct. G77: Newt M 1D **152**
Edenhall Gro. G77: Newt M 1D **152**
Eden La. G33: Glas 2F **89**
Eden Pk. G71: Both 5D **128**
Eden Pl. G72: Camb 2D **126**
Eden Pl. PA4: Renf 1G **83**
Edenside G68: Cumb 4B **16**
Eden St. G33: Glas 2F **89**
Edenwood St. G31: Glas 6G **89**
Edgam Dr. G52: Glas 6C **84**
Edgar Circ. PA4: Renf 5G **61**
Edgar Cres. PA4: Renf 5G **61**
Edgar Dr. PA4: Renf 5G **61**
Edgar Pl. PA4: Renf 5G **61**
Edgefauld Av. G21: Glas 6B **66**
Edgefauld Dr. G21: Glas 6B **66**
Edgefauld Pl. G21: Glas 4B **66**
Edgefauld Rd. G21: Glas 5B **66**
Edgehill La. G11: Glas 5G **63**
Edgehill Rd. G11: Glas 5F **63**
Edgehill Rd. G61: Bear 1E **47**
Edgemont Pk. ML3: Ham 3G **161**
Edgemont St. G41: Glas 5C **106**
Edinbeg Av. G42: Glas 5A **108**
Edinbeg Pl. G42: Glas 5A **108**
Edinburgh Dr. G40: Glas 3D **108**
Edinburgh Rd. G33: Glas 4F **89**
Edinburgh Rd. G69: Bail 5F **91**
Edinburgh Rd. ML1: N'hse 1C **132**
Edington Gdns. G69: Mood 4D **54**
Edington St. G4: Glas 1F **87**
Edison Ct. ML1: Moth 4G **147**
Edison St. G52: Hill E 3G **83**
Edmiston Dr. G51: Glas 5F **85**
Edmiston Dr. PA3: Lin 5F **79**
Edmonstone Ct. G81: Clyd 2F **61**
Edmonstone Dr. G65: Kils 4H **13**
Edmonton Ter. G40: Glas 2D **108**
Edmonton Ter. G75: E Kil 3E **157**
Edmund Kean G74: E Kil 4C **142**
Edrom Ct. G32: Glas 6H **89**
Edrom Path G32: Glas 6H **89**
Edrom St. G32: Glas 6H **89**
Edward Av. PA4: Renf 5G **61**
Edward Pl. G33: Step 4D **68**
Edward St. G65: Kils 2H **13**
Edward St. G69: Barg 6D **92**
Edward St. G81: Clyd 2F **61**
Edward St. ML1: Moth 4H **147**
Edward St. ML3: Ham 1H **161**
Edwin St. G51: Glas 6B **86**
Edzell Ct. G14: Glas 1D **84**
Edzell Dr. G77: Newt M 5E **137**
Edzell Dr. PA5: Eld 3B **100**
Edzell Gdns. G64: B'rig 1E **67**
Edzell Gdns. ML2: Wis 1G **165**
Edzell Pl. G14: Glas 6D **62**
Edzell St. G14: Glas 1D **84**
Edzell St. ML5: Coat 1H **113**
Egidia Av. G46: Giff 5A **122**
Egilsay Cres. G22: Glas 1G **65**
Egilsay Pl. G22: Glas 1G **65**
Egilsay St. G22: Glas 1G **65**
Egilsay Ter. G22: Glas 1G **65**
Eglinton Ct. G5: Glas 6F **87**
Eglinton Dr. G46: Giff 5A **122**
Eglinton Dr. G76: Eag 6D **154**
Eglinton St. G5: Glas 1E **107**
Eglinton St. ML5: Coat 3D **94**
Egmont Pk. G75: E Kil 4C **156**
Eider G12: Glas 2G **63**
Eider Av. G75: E Kil 1A **168**
Eider Gro. G75: E Kil 6C **156**
Eider Pl. G75: E Kil 1A **168**
Eighth St. G71: Tann 4C **112**
Eildon Cres. ML6: Chap 4F **117**
Eildon Dr. G78: Barr 6E **119**
Eildon Rd. G66: Kirkin 5F **33**
Eileen Gdns. G64: B'rig 5D **50**
Eilt Wlk. ML2: Newm 3D **150**
(off Tiree Cres.)
Elcho St. G40: Glas 5B **88**
Elderbank G61: Bear 4E **47**
Elder Cres. G72: Flem 3E **127**
Elder Cres. PA7: B'ton 6G **41**
Elder Dr. G72: Flem 3E **127**
Elder Gro. G71: View 5F **113**
Elder Gro. Av. G51: Glas 4D **84**
Elder Gro. Ct. G51: Glas 4D **84**
Elder Gro. Pl. G51: Glas 4D **84**
Elderpark Gdns. G51: Glas 4F **85**
Elderpark Gro. G51: Glas 4F **85**
Elderpark St. G51: Glas 4F **85**
Elderslea Rd. ML8: Carl 5E **175**
ELDERSLIE 4A **100**
Elderslie Ct. G3: Glas 4F **5** (3D **86**)
(off Elderslie St.)
Elderslie Golf Course 2C **100**
Elderslie Leisure Cen. 2B **100**
Elderslie St. G3: Glas 2F **5** (2D **86**)
Elder St. G51: Glas 4F **85**
(not continuous)
Elders Way ML2: Wis 6B **150**
Elder Way ML1: Carf 5D **132**
Eldin Pl. PA11: Bri W 5G **77**
Eldin Pl. PA5: Eld 3H **99**
Eldon Ct. G11: Glas 1H **85**
Eldon Gdns. G64: B'rig 6A **50**
Eldon St. G3: Glas 1C **86**
Elgin Av. G74: E Kil 6H **141**
Elgin Gdns. G76: Clar 1D **138**
Elgin Pl. G65: Kils 2H **13**
Elgin Pl. G74: E Kil 6H **141**
Elgin Pl. ML5: Coat 2D **114**
Elgin Pl. ML6: Air 6G **95**
Elgin Rd. G61: Bear 6F **27**
Elgin Ter. ML3: Ham 5C **144**
Elgin Way ML4: Bell 1C **130**
Elibank St. G33: Glas 2A **90**
Elie Ct. G68: Cumb 6H **15**
Elie Dr. PA7: B'ton 5G **41**
Elie Rd. G72: Blan 6B **144**
Elie St. G11: Glas 1A **86**
Eliot Cres. ML3: Ham 2H **161**
Eliot Ter. ML3: Ham 1H **161**
Elipta, The PA1: Pais 2A **102**
Elison Ct. ML1: Moth 5B **148**
Elizabethan Way PA4: Renf 2E **83**
Elizabeth Av. G66: Milt C 5B **10**
Elizabeth Ct. G74: E Kil 1H **157**
Elizabeth Cres. G46: T'bnk 4G **121**
Elizabeth Quad. ML1: Holy 2A **132**
Elizabeth St. G51: Glas 6A **86**
Elizabeth Wynd ML3: Ham 4H **161**
Ella Gdns. ML4: Bell 3E **131**
Ellangowan Ct. G62: Miln 3G **27**

Ellangowan Rd. G41: Glas	5A **106**
Ellangowan Rd. G62: Miln	3G **27**
Ell Cres. G72: Camb	4C **126**
Ellergreen Rd. G61: Bear	3E **47**
Ellerslie Cres. G14: Glas	3G **61**
Ellerslie Path G14: Glas	3G **61**
Ellerslie Rd. G14: Glas	3G **61**
Ellerslie St. PA5: John	2G **99**
Ellesmere St. G22: Glas	6E **65**
Ellinger Ct. G81: Clyd	3H **43**
Elliot Av. G46: Giff	5A **122**
Elliot Av. PA2: Pais	6C **100**
Elliot Ct. ML1: Moth	6F **131**
Elliot Cres. G74: E Kil	1B **158**
Elliot Dr. G46: Giff	4A **122**
Elliot Ho. G67: Cumb	3B **38**
Elliot Pl. G3: Glas	5E **5** (4C **86**)
Elliot St. G3: Glas	6E **5** (4C **86**)
	(not continuous)
Ellisland G66: Kirkin	3H **33**
Ellisland G74: E Kil	6D **142**
Ellisland Av. G81: Clyd	4E **45**
Ellisland Cres. G73: Ruth	2B **124**
Ellisland Dr. G66: Kirkin	3G **33**
Ellisland Dr. G72: Blan	3H **143**
Ellisland Gdns. ML5: Coat	1E **115**
Ellisland Rd. G43: Glas	1B **122**
Ellisland Rd. G67: Cumb	3B **38**
Ellisland Rd. G76: Busby	4C **138**
Ellisland Wynd ML1: N'hill	4C **132**
Ellismuir Farm Rd. G69: Bail	1B **112**
	(Bredisholm Ter.)
Ellismuir Farm Rd. G69: Bail	2A **112**
	(Mossbeath Cres.)
Ellismuir Pl. G69: Bail	1A **112**
Ellismuir Rd. G69: Bail	1A **112**
Ellismuir St. ML5: Coat	2H **113**
Ellismuir Way G71: Tann	4E **113**
Ellis St. ML5: Coat	4C **94**
Elliston Av. G53: Glas	2C **120**
Elliston Cres. G53: Glas	2C **120**
Elliston Dr. G53: Glas	2C **120**
Ellis Way ML1: Moth	4H **147**
Ellon Dr. PA3: Lin	6G **79**
Ellon Gro. PA3: Pais	4B **82**
Ellon Way PA3: Pais	4B **82**
Ellrig G75: E Kil	6F **157**
Elm Av. G66: Lenz	1C **52**
Elm Av. PA4: Renf	5E **61**
Elm Bank G64: B'rig	6D **50**
Elm Bank G66: Kirkin	4D **32**
Elmbank Av. G71: View	6F **113**
Elmbank Cres. G2: Glas	3H **5** (3E **87**)
Elmbank Cres. ML3: Ham	5E **145**
Elmbank Dr. ML9: Lark	4E **171**
Elmbank Gdns. G2: Glas	3H **5** (3E **87**)
	(off Elmbank Cres.)
Elmbank St. G2: Glas	4H **5** (3E **87**)
Elmbank St. ML4: Bell	2C **130**
Elmbank St. ML8: Carl	5E **175**
Elmbank St. La. G2: Glas	4H **5** (3E **87**)
	(off Elmbank St.)
Elm Ct. G72: Blan	2C **144**
Elm Cres. G71: View	6H **113**
Elm Dr. G67: Cumb	1F **39**
Elm Dr. G72: Camb	2C **126**
Elm Dr. ML6: Chap	2E **117**
Elm Dr. PA5: John	3G **99**
Elmfoot Gro. G5: Glas	3H **107**
Elm Gdns. G61: Bear	1E **47**
Elmhurst ML1: Moth	5F **147**
Elmira Rd. G69: Muirh	2B **70**
Elm La. E. G14: Glas	6D **62**
	(off Elm St.)
Elm La. W. G14: Glas	6D **62**
	(off Lime St.)
Elm Lea PA5: John	3H **99**
Elmore Av. G44: Glas	2F **123**
Elmore La. G44: Glas	2F **123**

Elm Pl. G75: E Kil	5E **157**
Elm Quad. ML6: Air	4D **96**
Elm Rd. G73: Ruth	3D **124**
Elm Rd. G81: Clyd	2C **44**
Elm Rd. G82: Dumb	3F **19**
Elm Rd. ML1: Holy	2B **132**
Elm Rd. ML1: New S	5A **132**
Elm Rd. PA11: Bri W	2G **77**
Elm Rd. PA2: Pais	4C **102**
Elms, The G44: Glas	3E **123**
Elmslie Ct. G69: Bail	1A **112**
Elm St. G14: Glas	6D **62**
Elm St. G66: Len	3G **9**
Elm St. G72: Blan	2C **144**
Elm St. G76: Busby	3D **138**
Elm St. ML1: Moth	2F **147**
Elm St. ML5: Coat	6E **95**
Elmtree Gdns. G45: Glas	3B **124**
Elmvale Row G21: Glas	4A **66**
Elmvale St. G21: Glas	4A **66**
Elm Vw. Ct. ML4: Bell	3F **131**
Elm Wlk. G61: Bear	1E **47**
Elm Way G72: Flem	3E **127**
Elm Way ML9: Lark	6A **164**
Elmwood ML2: Wis	2E **165**
Elmwood Av. G11: Glas	5F **63**
Elmwood Av. G77: Newt M	3F **137**
Elmwood Ct. G71: Both	5E **129**
Elmwood Gdns. G66: Lenz	2A **52**
Elmwood La. G11: Glas	5F **63**
Elphinstone Cres. G75: E Kil	4H **157**
Elphinstone Pl. G51: Glas	6A **4** (4A **86**)
Elphinstone Rd. G46: Giff	2G **137**
Elphin St. G23: Glas	6B **48**
Elrig Rd. G44: Glas	2D **122**
Elsie Way G75: E Kil	6B **156**
Elsinore Path G75: E Kil	6G **157**
Elspeth Gdns. G64: B'rig	5E **51**
Eltham St. G22: Glas	6F **65**
Elvan Ct. ML1: Moth	3F **147**
Elvan Pl. G75: E Kil	4A **156**
Elvan St. G32: Glas	6H **89**
Elvan St. ML1: Moth	2F **147**
Elvan Twr. ML1: Moth	4G **147**
Embo Dr. G13: Glas	3B **62**
Emerald Ter. ML4: Bell	3C **130**
Emerson Rd. G64: B'rig	6C **50**
Emerson Rd. W. G64: B'rig	6C **50**
Emily Dr. ML1: Moth	5G **147**
Emma Jay Rd. ML4: Bell	2D **130**
Empire Cinema	5D **44**
	(Clydebank)
Empire Way ML1: Moth	6E **131**
Endfield Av. G12: Glas	3H **63**
Endrick Bank G64: B'rig	3C **50**
Endrick Ct. ML5: Coat	5B **94**
	(off Turner St.)
Endrick Dr. G61: Bear	4F **47**
Endrick Dr. PA1: Pais	5D **82**
Endrick Gdns. G62: Miln	3E **27**
Endrick Ho. G82: Dumb	1H **19**
Endrick St. G21: Glas	6H **65**
English Row ML6: C'bnk	3C **116**
English St. ML2: Wis	6D **148**
Ennerdale G75: E Kil	5B **156**
Ennisfree Rd. G72: Blan	1B **144**
Ensay St. G22: Glas	2H **65**
Enterkin St. G32: Glas	1H **109**
Enterprise Way ML1: Moth	4B **148**
Eredine Pl. G33: Step	3E **69**
Eriboll Pl. G22: Glas	2F **65**
Eriboll St. G22: Glas	2F **65**
Eribol Wlk. ML1: N'hill	4D **132**
Ericht Rd. G43: Glas	2A **122**
Eriska Av. G14: Glas	4A **62**
Eriskay Av. G77: Newt M	4B **136**
Eriskay Av. ML3: Ham	1D **160**
Eriskay Cres. G77: Newt M	4B **136**
Eriskay Dr. G60: Old K	1G **43**

Eriskay Pl. G60: Old K	1G **43**
Ermelo Gdns. G75: E Kil	1B **168**
Ernest Wynd ML1: Moth	4F **147**
Erradale Pl. G22: Glas	2E **65**
Erradale St. G22: Glas	2E **65**
Errogie St. G34: Glas	3H **91**
Errol Gdns. G5: Glas	1G **107**
ERSKINE	6F **43**
Erskine Av. G41: Glas	1H **105**
Erskine Bridge	3D **42**
Erskine Community Sports Cen.
	5F **43**
Erskine Cres. ML6: Air	6H **95**
Erskinefauld Rd. PA3: Lin	5G **79**
Erskine Ferry Rd. G60: Old K	2F **43**
Erskine Ferry Rd. PA7: B'ton	4G **41**
Erskine Golf Course	2H **41**
Erskine Harbour PA8: Ersk	3E **43**
Erskine Harbour	3E **43**
Erskine Rd. G46: Giff	3H **137**
Erskine Sq. G52: Hill E	4H **83**
Erskine Swimming Pool	5F **43**
Erskine Vw. G60: Old K	1E **43**
Erskine Vw. G81: Clyd	4D **44**
Ervie St. G34: Glas	4A **92**
Escart Rd. ML8: Carl	2D **174**
Esdaile Ct. ML1: New S	4A **132**
Esk Av. PA4: Renf	1G **83**
Eskbank St. G32: Glas	5B **90**
Esk Dale G74: E Kil	6E **141**
Eskdale G77: Newt M	4H **137**
Eskdale Dr. G73: Ruth	6F **109**
Eskdale Rd. G61: Bear	5D **46**
Eskdale St. G42: Glas	4F **107**
Esk Dr. PA2: Pais	4C **100**
Esk St. G14: Glas	4H **61**
Esk Way PA2: Pais	4C **100**
Esmond St. G3: Glas	2A **4** (2A **86**)
Espedair St. PA2: Pais	2A **102**
Espieside Cres. ML5: Coat	3H **93**
Essenside Av. G15: Glas	5B **46**
Essex Dr. G14: Glas	5D **62**
Essex La. G14: Glas	5D **62**
	(not continuous)
Esslemont Av. G14: Glas	4B **62**
Esslemont La. G14: Glas	4C **62**
Estate Quad. G32: Carm	5C **110**
Estate Rd. G32: Carm	5C **110**
Etive Av. G61: Bear	3H **47**
Etive Av. ML3: Ham	2E **161**
Etive Ct. G67: Cumb	1D **56**
Etive Ct. G81: Hard	2E **45**
Etive Ct. ML5: Coat	2D **114**
Etive Cres. G64: B'rig	6D **50**
Etive Cres. G67: Cumb	1D **56**
Etive Cres. ML2: Wis	3H **165**
Etive Dr. G46: Giff	6B **122**
Etive Dr. G67: Cumb	1D **56**
Etive Dr. ML6: Air	6C **96**
Etive Dr. PA7: B'ton	5A **42**
Etive Pl. G67: Cumb	1E **57**
Etive Pl. ML9: Lark	6H **163**
Etive St. G32: Glas	6A **90**
Etive St. ML2: Wis	2H **165**
Etna Ind. Est. ML2: Wis	5C **148**
Etna St. G41: Glas	1E **107**
Etna St. ML2: Wis	5C **148**
Etna Vw. G41: Glas	1E **107**
Etna Way G41: Glas	1E **107**
Eton La. G12: Glas	1C **86**
Etterick Wynd G72: Blan	2A **144**
	(off Cheviot St.)
Ettrick Av. ML4: Bell	6C **114**
Ettrick Av. PA4: Renf	1H **83**
Ettrick Ct. G72: Camb	2D **126**
Ettrick Ct. ML5: Coat	2E **115**
Ettrick Cres. G73: Ruth	6E **109**
Ettrick Dr. G61: Bear	6C **26**
Ettrick Dr. PA7: B'ton	5A **42**

Fernan St. G32: Glas...............6H **89**	Fifth Av. G12: Glas...............4F **63**	Firhill Av. ML6: Air...............5H **95**
Fern Av. G64: B'rig...............1D **66**	Fifth Av. G33: Mille...............4B **68**	Firhill Complex, The...............6E **65**
Fern Av. G66: Lenz...............3C **52**	Fifth Av. ML6: Air...............3C **96**	Firhill Ct. G20: Glas...............5E **65**
Fern Av. PA8: Ersk...............2F **59**	Fifth Av. PA4: Renf...............1E **83**	Firhill Pk...............5E **65**
Fernbank Av. G72: Camb...............3C **126**	Fifth Rd. G72: Blan...............4C **144**	Firhill Rd. G20: Glas...............5D **64**
Fernbank St. G21: Glas...............4A **66**	Fifty Pitches Pl. G51: Glas...............4B **84**	Firhill St. G20: Glas...............5E **65**
Fernbank St. G22: Glas...............4A **66**	Fifty Pitches Rd. G51: Glas...............4B **84**	Firlee G75: E Kil...............3B **156**
Fernbrae Av. G73: Ruth...............4D **124**	Fifty Pitches Way G51: Glas...............4B **84**	Fir Pk...............5H **147**
Fernbrae Way G73: Ruth...............4D **124**	Finart Cres. G69: G'csh...............3E **71**	Firpark Cl. G31: Glas...............3B **88**
Fern Cotts. G13: Glas...............4F **63**	Finart Dr. PA2: Pais...............4D **102**	Firpark Ct. G31: Glas...............3B **88**
Ferncroft Dr. G44: Glas...............2H **123**	Finaven Gdns. G61: Bear...............5B **26**	Firpark Rd. G64: B'rig...............1D **66**
Ferndale ML9: Lark...............4C **170**	Finch Dr. G13: Glas...............1A **62**	Firpark St. G31: Glas...............3B **88**
Ferndale Ct. G23: Glas...............1B **64**	Finch Gro. ML5: Coat...............2G **115**	Firpark St. ML1: Moth...............5H **147**
Ferndale Dr. G23: Glas...............1B **64**	Finch Pl. PA5: John...............6D **98**	Firpark Ter. G31: Glas...............4B **88**
Ferndale Gdns. G23: Glas...............1B **64**	Finch Way ML4: Bell...............5B **114**	Fir Pl. G69: Bail...............2G **111**
Ferndale Pl. G23: Glas...............1B **64**	Findhorn PA8: Ersk...............4E **43**	Fir Pl. G72: Camb...............1C **126**
Fern Dr. G78: Barr...............3D **118**	Findhorn Av. PA2: Pais...............4D **100**	Fir Pl. ML1: Cle...............6H **133**
Ferness Oval G21: Glas...............2E **67**	Findhorn Av. PA4: Renf...............6G **61**	Fir Pl. PA5: John...............4G **99**
Ferness Pl. G21: Glas...............2E **67**	Findhorn Ct. G75: E Kil...............3H **155**	Firs, The G44: Glas...............2F **123**
Ferness Rd. G21: Glas...............3E **67**	Findhorn Pl. G75: E Kil...............3H **155**	First Av. G33: Mille...............4B **68**
Ferness St. G21: Glas...............2E **67**	Findhorn Pl. ML6: Air...............2D **96**	First Av. G44: Neth...............5D **122**
Fern Gro. G64: B'rig...............1D **66**	Findhorn St. G33: Glas...............3F **89**	First Av. G61: Bear...............4G **47**
Fern Gro. G69: G'csh...............3E **71**	Findlay Ct. ML1: Moth...............1F **147**	First Av. G66: A'loch...............6D **52**
Ferngrove Av. G12: Glas...............3H **63**	*...............(off Roman Rd.)*	First Av. G71: Tann...............5C **112**
FERNHILL...............4D **124**	Findlay St. G65: Kils...............3H **13**	First Av. G82: Dumb...............3C **20**
Fernhill Grange G71: Both...............6E **129**	Findlay St. ML1: Moth...............4H **147**	First Av. PA4: Renf...............1E **83**
Fernhill Rd. G73: Ruth...............2C **124**	Findlay Ter. G72: Camb...............1D **126**	First Gdns. G41: Glas...............1G **105**
FERNIEGAIR...............2D **162**	Findochty PA8: Ersk...............4E **43**	First Rd. G72: Blan...............4C **144**
Fernie Gdns. G20: Glas...............2C **64**	Findochty Pl. G33: Glas...............1E **91**	First St. G71: Tann...............5D **112**
Fernington Pl. ML2: Wis...............5H **149**	Findochty St. G33: Glas...............2D **90**	First Ter. G81: Clyd...............4C **44**
Fern La. G13: Glas...............4F **63**	Fingal Av. PA4: Renf...............4G **61**	Firthview Ter. G82: Dumb...............4C **18**
Fern La. G66: Len...............2E **9**	Fingal La. G20: Glas...............2A **64**	Firtree Pl. ML2: Newm...............3F **151**
Fernlea G61: Bear...............4E **47**	Fingal Rd. PA4: Renf...............4G **61**	Firtree Rd. ML2: Newm...............3F **151**
Fernlea Rd. G66: Kirkin...............4E **33**	Fingal St. G20: Glas...............2B **64**	Fir Vw. ML6: C'bnk...............3B **116**
Fernleigh Pl. G69: Mood...............5D **54**	Fingask St. G32: Glas...............1C **110**	Firwood Courts G77: Newt M...............5E **137**
Fernleigh Rd. G43: Glas...............2B **122**	Finglas Av. PA2: Pais...............4D **102**	Firwood Dr. G44: Glas...............1G **123**
Fernside Wlk. ML3: Ham...............2A **162**	Finglen Gdns. G62: Miln...............3E **27**	Firwood Rd. G77: Newt M...............4E **137**
Fernslea Av. G72: Blan...............1A **144**	Finglen Pl. G53: Glas...............3B **120**	Fischer Gdns. PA1: Pais...............1D **100**
Fern St. ML1: Moth...............5A **148**	Fingleton Av. G78: Barr...............6F **119**	Fisher Av. G65: Kils...............3H **13**
Fern Way PA7: B'ton...............6G **41**	Finhaven St. G32: Glas...............2G **109**	Fisher Av. PA1: Pais...............1D **100**
Ferryden Ct. G14: Glas...............1E **85**	Finlarig St. G34: Glas...............4A **92**	Fisher Ct. G31: Glas...............4B **88**
Ferryden St. G11: Glas...............1E **85**	Finlas Pl. G22: Glas...............4H **65**	Fisher Cres. G81: Hard...............1D **44**
Ferryden St. G14: Glas...............1E **85**	Finlas St. G22: Glas...............5H **65**	Fisher Dr. PA1: Pais...............1D **100**
Ferry Rd. G3: Glas...............2A **86**	Finlay Dr. G31: Glas...............4C **88**	Fishers Rd. PA4: Renf...............3E **61**
Ferry Rd. G71: Both...............5E **129**	Finlay Dr. PA3: Lin...............6F **79**	Fisher St. ML9: Lark...............4D **170**
Ferry Rd. G71: Udd...............1C **128**	Finlay Ri. G62: Miln...............5H **27**	Fisher Way PA1: Pais...............1D **100**
Ferry Rd. PA4: Renf...............5F **61**	Finlayson Dr. ML6: Air...............4E **97**	Fishescoates Av. G73: Ruth...............3E **125**
Fersit Ct. G43: Glas...............1A **122**	Finlayson Quad. ML6: Air...............4E **97**	Fishescoates Gdns. G73: Ruth...............2F **125**
...............(off Fersit St.)	Finlaystone St. ML5: Coat...............4A **94**	Fitness First...............5G **141**
Fersit St. G43: Glas...............1A **122**	Finnart Sq. G40: Glas...............2B **108**	*...............(East Kilbride)*
Festival Bus. Cen. G51: Glas...............5A **86**	Finnart St. G40: Glas...............2B **108**	Fitness First...............3F **107**
Festival Ct. G51: Glas...............5B **86**	*...............(not continuous)*	*...............(Glasgow)*
Festival Ga. G51: Glas...............6B **4** (5B **86**)	FINNIESTON...............4E **5** (3C **86**)	Fitzalan Dr. PA3: Pais...............5C **82**
Fetlar Ct. G72: Camb...............4H **125**	Finnieston Crane...............6D **4** (4B **86**)	Fitzalan Rd. PA4: Renf...............2C **82**
Fetlar Dr. G44: Glas...............2G **123**	Finnieston Sq. G3: Glas...............4E **5** (3C **86**)	Fitzpatrick Way PA3: Pais...............5A **82**
Fetlar Rd. PA11: Bri W...............3E **77**	Finnieston St. G3: Glas...............6E **5** (4C **86**)	Fitzroy Gro. G74: T'hall...............2H **155**
Fettercairn Av. G15: Glas...............4G **45**	Finnie Wynd ML1: Moth...............5B **148**	Fitzroy La. G3: Glas...............3D **4** (3C **86**)
Fettercairn Gdns. G64: B'rig...............6E **51**	Finsbay St. G51: Glas...............5D **84**	Fitzroy Pl. G3: Glas...............3E **5** (3C **86**)
Fettercairn Pl. ML6: Air...............6B **74**	Fintaig La. ML2: Wis...............6C **150**	*...............(off Fitzroy La.)*
Fettes St. G33: Glas...............3H **89**	Fintrie Ter. ML3: Ham...............5C **144**	Flakefield G74: E Kil...............1D **156**
Fiddoch Ct. ML2: Newm...............2D **150**	Fintry Av. PA2: Pais...............5A **102**	Flanders St. G81: Hard...............6E **25**
Fidra St. G33: Glas...............3H **89**	Fintry Ct. ML5: Coat...............2E **115**	Flanigan Gro. ML4: Bell...............2C **130**
Fielden Pl. G40: Glas...............6C **88**	Fintry Cres. G64: B'rig...............6E **51**	Flavell Pl. ML6: Air...............5A **96**
Fielden St. G40: Glas...............6C **88**	Fintry Cres. G78: Barr...............6E **119**	Flaxfield Gro. ML1: Moth...............5F **131**
Field Gro. G76: Busby...............4D **138**	Fintry Dr. G44: Glas...............6G **107**	Flaxmill Av. ML2: Wis...............5D **148**
Fieldhead Dr. G43: Glas...............2G **121**	Fintry Gdns. G61: Bear...............5C **26**	Flax Rd. G71: Udd...............2E **129**
Fieldhead Sq. G43: Glas...............2G **121**	Fintry Pl. G75: E Kil...............1B **168**	Fleet Av. PA4: Renf...............2G **83**
Field Rd. G76: Busby...............4D **138**	Fir Bank Av. ML9: Lark...............3D **170**	Fleet St. G32: Glas...............1B **110**
Field Rd. G81: Faif...............5F **25**	Firbank Av. G64: Torr...............5D **30**	Fleming Av. G69: Chry...............1A **70**
Field Rd. ML9: Lark...............3D **170**	Firbank Quad. ML6: Chap...............2E **117**	Fleming Av. G81: Clyd...............1F **61**
Fields La. PA6: Hous...............1B **78**	Firbank Ter. G78: Barr...............6G **119**	Fleming Ct. G81: Clyd...............5D **44**
Field St. ML3: Ham...............2H **161**	Fir Ct. G72: Flem...............3E **127**	Fleming Ct. ML1: Moth...............5A **148**
Fife Av. G52: Glas...............1B **104**	Firdon Cres. G15: Glas...............6A **46**	Fleming Ct. ML3: Ham...............5C **144**
Fife Av. ML6: Air...............6A **96**	Fir Dr. G75: E Kil...............6D **156**	Fleming Ct. ML8: Carl...............4C **174**
Fife Ct. G71: Both...............6E **129**	Firefly La. G74: E Kil...............5H **141**	Fleming Pl. G75: E Kil...............3G **157**
Fife Cres. G71: Both...............6E **129**	Firethorn Dr. G68: Cumb...............1F **57**	Fleming Rd. G67: Cumb...............3H **37**
Fife Dr. ML1: Moth...............5F **131**	Fir Gro. G71: View...............5F **113**	Fleming Rd. ML4: Bell...............1D **130**
Fife Gdns. G71: Both...............6E **129**	Fir Gro. ML1: New S...............5A **132**	Fleming Rd. PA6: Hous...............1A **78**
Fife Way G64: B'rig...............1F **67**	FIRHILL...............5E **65**	Fleming Rd. PA7: B'ton...............4H **41**

Fleming St. G31: Glas 5D **88**
Fleming St. PA3: Pais 4A **82**
FLEMINGTON G72 ....3E **127**
FLEMINGTON ML1 ....5B **148**
Flemington Ind. Est. G72: Flem 3E **127**
Flemington Ind. Pk. ML1: Moth 4C **148**
Flemington Rd. G72: Camb 2E **143**
Flemington St. G21: Glas 6A **66**
Flemington St. ML1: Moth 4A **148**
Flemington Way G69: Chry 1A **70**
Fleming Way ML3: Ham 5B **144**
Fleming Way ML9: Lark 3E **171**
..................(off Wallace Dr.)
Fleming Way PA6: Hous 1A **78**
Flenders Av. G76: Clar 3A **138**
Flenders Rd. G76: Clar 3A **138**
Fleurs Av. G41: Glas 2H **105**
Fleurs Rd. G41: Glas 1H **105**
Flinders Pl. G75: E Kil 3D **156**
Flintlock Way G53: Glas 5D **120**
Flloyd St. ML5: Coat 4B **94**
Floorsburn Cres. PA5: John 3E **99**
Floors Rd. G76: Wfoot 3H **153**
Floors St. PA5: John 3E **99**
Floors St. Ind. Est. PA5: John 3F **99**
Flora Gdns. G64: B'rig 5E **51**
Florence Dr. G46: Giff 5A **122**
Florence Gdns. G73: Ruth 3E **125**
Florence St. G5: Glas 6G **87**
Florida Av. G42: Glas 5F **107**
Florida Cres. G42: Glas 5F **107**
Florida Dr. G42: Glas 5E **107**
Florida Gdns. G69: Bail 6G **91**
Florida Sq. G42: Glas 5F **107**
Florida St. G42: Glas 5F **107**
Florish Rd. PA8: Ersk 1H **59**
Flour Mill Wynd G69: Mood 4E **55**
Flowerdale Pl. G53: Glas 4B **120**
Flowerhill Ind. Est. ML6: Air 3B **96**
Flowerhill St. ML6: Air 3B **96**
FLUCHTER 3E **29**
Fluchter Rd. G62: Balm 4E **29**
Fluchter Rd. G62: Bard 4E **29**
Fluchter Rd. G64: Balm 3F **29**
Flures Av. PA8: Ersk 1A **60**
Flures Cres. PA8: Ersk 1A **60**
Flures Dr. PA8: Ersk 1A **60**
Flures Pl. PA8: Ersk 1A **60**
Flynn Gdns. G33: Step 4G **69**
Fochabers Dr. G52: Glas 5C **84**
Fogo Pl. G20: Glas 3B **64**
Foinaven Dr. G46: T'bnk 2F **121**
Foinaven Gdns. G46: T'bnk 1F **121**
Foinaven Way G46: T'bnk 1G **121**
Footfield Rd. ML4: Bell 3B **130**
Forbes Dr. G40: Glas 6B **88**
Forbes Dr. ML1: Moth 5D **130**
Forbes Hall G4: Glas 5G **7** (4H **87**)
..................(off Rottenrow East)
Forbes Pl. PA1: Pais 1A **102**
Forbes St. G40: Glas 5B **88**
Fordbank Av. PA10: How 6B **98**
Fordbank Dr. PA10: How 6B **98**
Fordbank Pl. PA10: How 6C **98**
Fordbank Wynd PA10: How 6B **98**
Fordneuk St. G40: Glas 6C **88**
Fordoun St. G34: Glas 3B **92**
Ford Rd. G12: Glas 5B **64**
Ford Rd. G77: Newt M 6D **136**
Fordyce Ct. G77: Newt M 5D **136**
Fordyce St. G11: Glas 1H **85**
Foremount Ter. La. G12: Glas 6A **64**
Fore Row ML3: Ham 5A **146**
Forest Av. ML3: Ham 5H **161**
Forestburn Ct. ML6: Air 4F **95**
..................(off Monkscourt Av.)
Forest Dr. G71: Both 4E **129**
Forest Dr. ML4: Bell 4E **131**
Forest Gdns. G66: Lenz 3A **52**

Foresthall Cres. G21: Glas 6C **66**
Foresthall Dr. G21: Glas 6C **66**
Forest Kirk ML8: Carl 5F **175**
Forest La. ML3: Ham 5H **161**
Forestlea Rd. ML8: Carl 5E **175**
Forest Pk. ML2: Wis 4B **150**
Forest Pl. G66: Lenz 3A **52**
Forest Pl. PA2: Pais 3A **102**
Fore St. G14: Glas 6C **62**
Forest Rd. G67: Cumb 5D **16**
Forest Rd. ML9: Lark 3D **170**
Forest Vw. G67: Cumb 2C **38**
Forfar Av. G52: Glas 1B **104**
Forfar Cres. G64: B'rig 1E **67**
Forgan Gdns. G64: B'rig 1F **67**
Forge, The G46: Giff 4B **122**
Forge Cres. PA7: B'ton 6H **41**
Forge Dr. ML5: Coat 4B **94**
Forgehill Cres. ML5: Coat 1E **115**
Forge Pl. G21: Glas 1D **88**
Forge Rd. ML6: Air 5F **97**
Forge Row ML6: C'bnk 2C **116**
Forge Shop. Cen., The 5E **89**
..................(Glasgow)
Forge St. G21: Glas 1D **88**
Forge Way PA7: B'ton 6H **41**
Forgewood ML1: Moth 5F **131**
..................(off Kylemore Cres.)
FORGEWOOD 6F **131**
Forgewood Path ML6: Air 5F **97**
Forgewood Rd. ML1: Moth 5E **131**
Forglen St. G34: Glas 2H **91**
Formakin Estate Country Pk. 5B **40**
Formby Dr. G23: Glas 6B **48**
Forres Av. G46: Giff 4A **122**
Forres Cres. ML4: Bell 1C **130**
Forres Ga. G46: Giff 5B **122**
Forres Quad. ML2: Wis 4H **149**
Forres St. G23: Glas 6C **48**
Forres St. G72: Blan 3A **144**
Forrestburn Rd. ML5: Coat 5C **94**
Forrest Dr. G61: Bear 4B **26**
Forrester Ct. G64: B'rig 1B **66**
Forrestfield Cres. G77: Newt M 4E **137**
Forrestfield Gdns. G77: Newt M 4D **136**
Forrestfield St. G21: Glas 2C **88**
Forrest Ga. G71: Tann 4F **113**
Forrest Ga. ML3: Ham 2F **161**
Forrest St. G40: Glas 6C **88**
Forrest St. G72: Blan 2D **144**
Forrest St. ML6: Air 3C **96**
..................(not continuous)
Forsa Ct. G75: E Kil 1C **168**
Forsyth St. ML6: Air 3B **96**
Forteviot Av. G69: Bail 6A **92**
Forteviot Pl. G69: Bail 6A **92**
Forth Av. PA2: Pais 4D **100**
Forth Ct. G75: E Kil 4A **156**
Forth Cres. G75: E Kil 3A **156**
Forth Gro. G75: E Kil 4A **156**
Forth Pl. ML9: Lark 5D **170**
Forth Pl. PA5: John 5C **98**
Forth Rd. G61: Bear 5D **46**
Forth Rd. G64: Torr 5C **30**
Forth St. G41: Glas 2D **106**
Forth St. G81: Clyd 1E **61**
Forth Ter. ML3: Ham 3F **161**
Forth Wlk. G67: Cumb 4H **37**
..................(within The Cumbernauld Shop. Cen.)
Forth Way G67: Cumb 4H **37**
..................(within The Cumbernauld Shop. Cen.)
Forties Ct. G46: T'bnk 2F **121**
Forties Cres. G46: T'bnk 2G **121**
Forties Gdns. G46: T'bnk 2G **121**
Forties Rd. PA6: C'lee 3C **78**
Forties Way G46: T'bnk 2G **121**
Fortieth Av. G75: E Kil 6H **157**
Fortingall Av. G12: Glas 3A **64**
Fortingall Pl. G12: Glas 3A **64**

Fortingall Rd. G72: Blan 4D **144**
Fortrose Ct. G72: Blan 6A **144**
Fortrose Gdns. ML1: N'hse 2D **132**
Fortrose St. G11: Glas 1H **85**
Fort St. ML1: Moth 1D **146**
Fort Theatre, The 6A **50**
Forum Pl. ML1: Moth 6E **131**
Fossil Gro. G66: Kirkin 4G **33**
Fossil Grove 6D **62**
Fossil House 6D **62**
Foswell Dr. G15: Glas 2H **45**
Foswell Pl. G15: Glas 2H **45**
Fotheringay La. G41: Glas 3B **106**
Fotheringay Rd. G41: Glas 3B **106**
Foulis La. G13: Glas 3F **63**
Foulis St. G13: Glas 3F **63**
FOULSYKES 5C **150**
Foulsykes Rd. ML2: Wis 5C **150**
Foundry, The G41: Glas 2E **107**
Foundry La. G78: Barr 5E **119**
Foundry Rd. ML1: Cle 5H **133**
Foundry St. G21: Glas 5B **66**
Fountain Av. PA4: Inch 5F **59**
Fountain Bus. Cen., The ML5: Coat 5C **94**
..................(off Whittington St.)
Fountain Ct. PA3: Pais 5A **82**
..................(off Love St.)
Fountain Cres. PA4: Inch 4F **59**
Fountain Dr. PA4: Inch 5G **59**
Fountainwell Dr. G21: Glas 1H **87**
Fountainwell Gdns. G21: Glas 1A **88**
Fountainwell Gro. G21: Glas 1A **88**
Fountainwell Path G21: Glas 6H **65**
Fountainwell Rd. G21: Glas 1A **88**
Fourth Av. G33: Mille 4B **68**
Fourth Av. G66: A'loch 6D **52**
Fourth Av. G82: Dumb 2C **20**
Fourth Av. PA4: Renf 1E **83**
Fourth Gdns. G41: Glas 1G **105**
Fourth Rd. G72: Blan 4C **144**
Fourth St. G71: Tann 4D **112**
Fourways Shop. Mall 6A **150**
Four Windings PA6: Hous 1B **78**
Fowlis Dr. G77: Newt M 3C **136**
FOXBAR 4D **100**
Foxbar Cres. PA2: Pais 6C **100**
Foxbar Dr. G13: Glas 3B **62**
Foxbar Dr. PA2: Pais 6C **100**
Foxbar Rd. PA2: Pais 6B **100**
Foxbar Rd. PA5: Eld 6B **100**
Foxes Gro. G66: Lenz 2E **53**
Foxglove Gdns. G66: Lenz 1G **53**
Foxglove Gro. G72: Newt 5F **111**
Foxglove Pl. G53: Glas 4B **120**
Foxglove Rd. G77: Newt M 1D **136**
Fox Gro. ML1: Moth 2D **146**
Foxhills Pl. G23: Glas 6C **48**
Foxknowe Gdns. G81: Faif 6F **25**
FOXLEY 3C **110**
Foxley St. G32: Carm 4C **110**
Fox St. G1: Glas 5F **87**
Foyers Ter. G21: Glas 5C **66**
Foyes Ct. G13: Glas 3B **62**
Foy Gdns. ML4: Bell 5C **114**
Franconia Sq. G81: Clyd 6D **44**
Frankfield Rd. G33: Step 4E **69**
Frankfield St. G33: Glas 1F **89**
Frankfort St. G41: Glas 4C **106**
Franklin Dr. ML1: Moth 5G **147**
Franklin Pl. G75: E Kil 2D **156**
Franklin St. G40: Glas 2B **108**
Fraser Av. G73: Ruth 5E **109**
Fraser Av. G77: Newt M 3E **137**
Fraser Av. G82: Dumb 1C **20**
Fraser Av. PA5: John 3G **99**
Fraser Av. PA7: B'ton 3H **41**
Fraser Ct. ML3: Ham 1G **161**
Fraser Ct. ML9: Lark 5C **170**
Fraser Cres. ML3: Ham 1F **161**

Fraser Gdns. – Garngrew Rd.

Fraser Gdns. G66: Kirkin 5B **32**
Fraser River Twr. G75: E Kil 3F **157**
Fraser St. G72: Camb 1G **125**
Fraser St. ML1: Cle 5H **133**
Frazer St. G40: Glas 6C **88**
Frederick St. ML5: Coat 3A **94**
FREELAND 2F **59**
Freeland Brae G75: E Kil 3H **157**
(off Telford Rd.)
Freeland Ct. G53: Glas 1C **120**
Freeland Cres. G53: Glas 1B **120**
Freeland Dr. G53: Glas 1B **120**
Freeland Dr. PA11: Bri W 2F **77**
Freeland Dr. PA4: Inch 3G **59**
Freeland La. G75: E Kil 3H **157**
(off Telford Rd.)
Freeland Pl. G66: Kirkin 5D **32**
Freeland Rd. PA8: Ersk 2F **59**
Freelands Ct. G60: Old K 2G **43**
Freelands Cres. G60: Old K 2G **43**
Freelands Pl. G60: Old K 3G **43**
Freelands Rd. G60: Old K 2G **43**
Freeneuk La. G72: Camb 1B **126**
Freeneuk Wynd G72: Camb 1B **126**
Freesia Ct. ML1: Moth 4G **147**
Freland Gro. G69: Chry 3H **69**
French St. G40: Glas 2B **108**
French St. G81: Clyd 4A **44**
French St. ML2: Wis 6H **149**
French St. PA4: Renf 1D **82**
Freuchie St. G34: Glas 4H **91**
Frew St. ML6: Air 3A **96**
Friar Av. G64: B'rig 4D **50**
Friarscourt Av. G13: Glas 6D **46**
Friarscourt La. G13: Glas 1D **62**
(off Arrowsmith Av.)
Friarscourt Rd. G69: Chry 6H **53**
Friars Cft. G66: Kirkin 5E **33**
Friarshall Ga. PA2: Pais 3H **101**
Friars Pl. G13: Glas 1D **62**
Friars Way ML6: Air 1C **116**
Friarton Rd. G43: Glas 2D **122**
Friendship Way PA4: Renf 2F **83**
Frood St. ML1: Moth 6E **131**
Fruin Av. G77: Newt M 3E **137**
Fruin Courts G77: Newt M 3E **137**
Fruin Dr. ML2: Wis 6C **150**
Fruin Ho. G82: Dumb 1H **19**
Fruin Pl. G22: Glas 5G **65**
Fruin Ri. ML3: Ham 1C **160**
Fruin Rd. G15: Glas 6H **45**
Fruin St. G22: Glas 5G **65**
Fulbar Av. PA4: Renf 5E **61**
Fulbar Ct. PA4: Renf 5F **61**
Fulbar Cres. PA2: Pais 3D **100**
Fulbar Gdns. PA2: Pais 3D **100**
Fulbar La. PA4: Renf 5F **61**
Fulbar Path G51: Glas 4C **84**
Fulbar Rd. G51: Glas 4C **84**
Fulbar Rd. PA2: Pais 3D **100**
Fulbar St. PA4: Renf 5F **61**
Fullar Ga. ML5: Coat 1E **115**
FULLARTON 3A **110**
Fullarton Av. G32: Glas 3A **110**
Fullarton Dr. G32: Glas 4A **110**
Fullarton La. G32: Glas 3A **110**
Fullarton Pl. ML5: Coat 2H **113**
Fullarton Rd. G32: Glas 5H **109**
Fullarton Rd. G68: Cumb 6G **15**
FULLARTON ROAD INTERCHANGE 4A **110**
Fullarton St. ML5: Coat 2A **114**
Fullers Ga. G81: Faif 6E **25**
Fullerton St. PA3: Pais 4H **81**
Fullwood Ind. Est. ML3: Ham 5F **145**
Fulmar Ct. G64: B'rig 1B **66**
Fulmar Pk. G74: E Kil 6F **141**
Fulmar Pl. PA5: John 6C **98**
Fulton Cres. PA10: Kilba 2A **98**
Fulton Dr. PA6: C'lee 3E **79**
Fulton Gdns. PA6: C'lee 3E **79**
Fulton Rd. G62: Miln 4H **27**
Fulton St. G13: Glas 2D **62**
Fulwood Av. G13: Glas 2H **61**
Fulwood Av. PA3: Lin 5H **79**
Fulwood Pl. G13: Glas 2H **61**
Furlongs, The ML3: Ham 5H **145**
Furrow Ct. G72: Newt 1F **127**
Furrow Cres. G72: Newt 1F **127**
Fyffe Pl. PA5: John 2G **99**
(off Russell St.)
Fyneart St. ML2: Wis 5C **150**
Fyne Av. ML4: Bell 6A **114**
Fyneburn Gdns. ML5: Coat 5C **94**
Fyne Ct. ML3: Ham 2E **161**
Fyne Cres. ML9: Lark 6H **163**
Fyne Way ML1: Holy 2A **132**
(off Howden Pl.)
Fynloch Pl. G81: Dun 6A **24**
Fyvie Av. G43: Glas 2G **121**
Fyvie Cres. ML6: Air 4F **97**

G

Gadie Av. PA4: Renf 1G **83**
Gadie St. G33: Glas 3F **89**
Gadloch Av. G66: A'loch 5D **52**
Gadloch Gdns. G66: Lenz 4D **52**
Gadloch St. G22: Glas 3G **65**
Gadloch Vw. G66: A'loch 5D **52**
Gadsburn Ct. G21: Glas 3E **67**
Gadshill St. G21: Glas 2B **88**
Gadwall Gro. ML1: Moth 5H **147**
Gailes Pk. G71: Both 5D **128**
Gailes Rd. G68: Cumb 6H **15**
Gain & Shankburn Rd. G67: Cumb 6D **56**
Gainburn Ct. G67: Cumb 1B **56**
Gainburn Cres. G67: Cumb 2B **56**
Gainburn Gdns. G67: Cumb 2B **56**
Gainburn Pl. G67: Cumb 1B **56**
Gainburn Vw. G67: Cumb 1C **56**
Gain Rd. G67: Cumb 6D **56**
Gain Rd. ML5: Glenb 6B **56**
Gainside Rd. ML5: Glenb 3G **71**
Gairbraid Av. G20: Glas 3A **64**
Gairbraid Ct. G20: Glas 3A **64**
Gairbraid Pl. G20: Glas 3B **64**
Gairbraid Ter. G69: Barg 6E **93**
Gair Cres. ML2: Wis 2H **165**
Gair Cres. ML8: Carl 2E **175**
Gairloch Gdns. G66: Kirkin 4H **33**
Gair Rd. ML8: Carl 1E **175**
Gala Av. PA4: Renf 1G **83**
Gala Bingo 5E **45**
(Clydebank)
Gala Bingo 5C **94**
(Coatbridge)
Gala Bingo 3A **38**
(Cumbernauld)
Gala Bingo 4G **65**
(Glasgow, Hawthorn St.)
Gala Bingo 3H **147**
(Motherwell)
Gala Cres. ML2: Wis 4G **149**
Galashiels Av. ML6: Chap 4E **117**
Gala St. G33: Glas 1G **89**
Galbraith Cres. ML8: Law 5E **167**
Galbraith Dr. G51: Glas 3D **84**
Galbraith Dr. G62: Miln 5F **27**
Galdenoch St. G33: Glas 1B **90**
Gallacher Av. PA2: Pais 4E **101**
Gallacher Ct. ML1: Moth 6B **148**
Gallacher Ct. PA1: Pais 6G **81**
(off Clavering St. W.)
Gallagher Ct. ML6: Air 5A **96**
Gallan Av. G23: Glas 6C **48**
Gallery Gro. ML5: Coat 5C **94**
Gallery of Modern Art 5D **6** (4G **87**)
(Glasgow)
Galloway Av. ML2: Wis 5A **150**
Galloway Av. ML3: Ham 4G **161**
Galloway Av. PA3: Pais 4H **81**
Galloway Ct. G73: Ruth 4D **124**
Galloway Dr. G73: Ruth 4D **124**
Galloway Rd. G74: E Kil 6C **142**
Galloway Rd. ML6: Air 6H **95**
Galloway St. G21: Glas 3B **66**
Galloway Ter. PA3: Pais 4H **81**
GALLOWFLAT 6E **109**
Gallowflat St. G73: Ruth 5D **108**
Gallowgate G1: Glas 5H **87**
Gallowgate G31: Glas 6D **88**
Gallowgate G4: Glas 5A **88**
Gallowgate G40: Glas 5A **88**
GALLOWGATE 6C **88**
Gallow Grn. Rd. PA1: Pais 1G **101**
Gallowhill ML9: Lark 3C **170**
GALLOWHILL 4D **82**
Gallowhill Av. G66: Lenz 1C **52**
Gallowhill Ct. PA3: Pais 3C **82**
Gallowhill Gro. G66: Kirkin 6C **32**
Gallowhill Rd. G66: Kirkin 1C **52**
Gallowhill Rd. G66: Lenz 1C **52**
Gallowhill Rd. G76: Crmck 1H **139**
Gallowhill Rd. PA3: Pais 5B **82**
Galston Av. G77: Newt M 4G **137**
Galston Ct. ML3: Ham 4A **162**
Galston St. G53: Glas 1H **119**
Galt Pl. G75: E Kil 4F **157**
Gamrie Dr. G53: Glas 6A **104**
Gamrie Gdns. G53: Glas 6A **104**
Gamrie Rd. G53: Glas 5A **104**
Gannochy Dr. G64: B'rig 6E **51**
Gantock Cres. G33: Glas 4B **90**
Gardeners La. G69: Bail 1A **112**
Gardenhall G75: E Kil 3H **155**
GARDENHALL 4A **156**
Gardenhall Ct. G75: E Kil 3A **156**
Garden Ho. G66: Milt C 5B **10**
Gardenia Ga. G76: Crmck 5A **140**
Gardenia Gro. G76: Crmck 5A **140**
Gardenside ML4: Bell 3C **130**
Gardenside Av. G32: Carm 5B **110**
Gardenside Av. G71: Udd 1C **128**
Gardenside Cres. G32: Carm 5B **110**
Gardenside Gro. G32: Carm 5B **110**
Gardenside Pl. G32: Carm 5B **110**
Gardenside Rd. ML3: Ham 1H **161**
Gardenside St. G71: Udd 1C **128**
Garden Sq. Wlk. ML6: Air 3F **95**
Gardner Gro. G71: Tann 5E **113**
Gardner St. G11: Glas 1H **85**
Gardyne St. G34: Glas 2G **91**
Gareloch Av. ML6: Air 1H **95**
Gareloch Av. PA2: Pais 3E **101**
Garfield Av. ML4: Bell 2E **131**
Garfield Dr. ML4: Bell 3E **131**
Garfield Pl. G33: Step 3E **69**
Garfield St. G31: Glas 5C **88**
Garforth Rd. G69: Bail 1F **111**
Garganey Wynd G75: E Kil 6C **156**
Gargrave Av. G69: Bail 1F **111**
Garion Dr. G13: Glas 4B **62**
Garlieston Rd. G33: Glas 5F **91**
Garmouth Ct. G51: Glas 3G **85**
Garmouth Gdns. G51: Glas 3G **85**
Garmouth Pl. G51: Glas 3F **85**
Garmouth St. G51: Glas 3F **85**
Garnet Ct. G4: Glas 1A **6** (2E **87**)
(off Shamrock St.)
GARNETHILL 2A **6** (2E **87**)
Garnethill St. G3: Glas 2A **6** (2E **87**)
Garnet St. G3: Glas 3H **5** (2E **87**)
Garnett Hall G4: Glas 4G **7** (3H **87**)
(off Cathedral St.)
Garngaber Av. G66: Lenz 2D **52**
Garngaber Ct. G66: Lenz 2E **53**
Garngrew Rd. FK4: Hag 1F **17**

222 A–Z Glasgow

Garnhall Farm Rd. – Gibson Av.

Garnhall Farm Rd. G68: Cumb 3E **17**
Garnie Av. PA8: Ersk 6H **43**
Garnie Cres. PA8: Ersk 6H **43**
Garnieland Rd. PA8: Ersk 6H **43**
Garnie La. PA8: Ersk 1H **59**
Garnie Oval PA8: Ersk 6H **43**
Garnie Pl. PA8: Ersk 6H **43**
GARNKIRK 3G **69**
Garnkirk La. G33: Step 4E **69**
Garnock Pk. G74: E Kil 2B **158**
Garnock St. G21: Glas 2B **88**
GARNQUEEN 4H **71**
Garnqueen Cres. ML5: Glenb 4G **71**
Garrell Av. G65: Kils 2H **13**
Garrell Gro. G65: Kils 1H **13**
Garrell Pl. G65: Kils 3G **13**
Garrell Rd. G65: Kils 4G **13**
Garrell Way G65: Kils 3G **13**
Garrell Way G67: Cumb 3G **37**
Garret Pl. G68: Cumb 6F **15**
Garrick Av. G77: Newt M 1D **152**
Garrick Ct. G77: Newt M 1D **152**
Garrioch Cres. G20: Glas 4B **64**
Garrioch Dr. G20: Glas 4B **64**
Garrioch Ga. G20: Glas 4B **64**
Garriochmill Rd. G12: Glas 6C **64**
Garriochmill Rd. G20: Glas 5B **64**
....(not continuous)
Garriochmill Way G20: Glas 6D **64**
.... *(off Henderson St.)*
Garrioch Quad. G20: Glas 4B **64**
Garrioch Rd. G20: Glas 5B **64**
Garrion Bus. Pk. ML2: Wis 3H **165**
Garrion Pl. ML9: Ashg 4H **171**
Garrion St. ML2: Over 5A **166**
GARROWHILL 6G **91**
Garrowhill Dr. G69: Bail 6F **91**
Garrowhill Station (Rail) 6F **91**
Garry Av. G61: Bear 5H **47**
Garry Dr. PA2: Pais 3E **101**
Garry St. G44: Glas 6E **107**
Garscadden Grn. G13: Glas 2H **61**
Garscadden Rd. G15: Glas 5H **45**
Garscadden Rd. Sth. G13: Glas 1A **62**
Garscadden Rd. Sth. G15: Glas 1H **61**
.... *(off Gt. Western Rd.)*
Garscadden Station (Rail) 3A **62**
Garscadden Vw. G81: Clyd 4F **45**
Garscube Rd. G20: Glas 6E **65**
Garscube Rd. G4: Glas 2F **87**
Garscube Sports Complex **6G 47**
.... *(University of Glasgow)*
Garshake Av. G82: Dumb 1C **20**
Garshake Rd. G82: Dumb 3H **19**
Garshake Ter. G82: Dumb 1C **20**
Gartartan Rd. PA1: Pais 6H **83**
Gartcarron Hill G68: Cumb 2E **37**
Gartcloss Rd. ML5: Coat 1G **93**
Gartcolt Pl. ML5: Coat 2B **94**
Gartconnell Dr. G61: Bear 1E **47**
Gartconnell Gdns. G61: Bear 1E **47**
Gartconnell Rd. G61: Bear 1E **47**
Gartconner Av. G66: Kirkin 5H **33**
GARTCOSH 4D **70**
Gartcosh Ind. Pk. G69: G'csh 5E **71**
GARTCOSH INTERCHANGE 4E **71**
Gartcosh Rd. G69: Barg 1E **93**
Gartcosh Rd. G69: Barg 5D **92**
Gartcosh Rd. G69: G'csh 1E **93**
Gartcosh Station (Rail) 5E **71**
Gartcosh Wlk. ML4: Bell 2B **130**
Gartcraig Path G33: Glas 2H **89**
.... *(off Gartcraig Rd.)*
Gartcraig Pl. G33: Glas 2H **89**
Gartcraig Rd. G33: Glas 3H **89**
Gartferry Av. G69: Mood 5D **54**
Gartferry Rd. G68: Mollin 3F **55**
Gartferry Rd. G69: Chry 5B **54**
Gartferry Rd. G69: Mood 5B **54**
Gartferry St. G21: Glas 5C **66**
Gartfield St. ML6: Air 5B **96**
Gartgill Rd. ML5: Coat 1A **94**
GARTHAMLOCK 1E **91**
Garthamlock Recreation Cen. **1D 90**
Garth Dr. G81: Clyd 2D **60**
Garthland Dr. G31: Glas 4C **88**
Garthland La. PA1: Pais 6B **82**
Garth St. G1: Glas 6E **7** (4G **87**)
GARTLEA 5B **96**
Gartlea Av. ML6: Air 4A **96**
Gartlea Gdns. ML6: Air 4B **96**
Gartleahill ML6: Air 5A **96**
Gartlea Rd. ML6: Air 4A **96**
Gartliston Rd. ML5: Coat 6B **72**
Gartliston Ter. G69: Barg 6E **93**
GARTLOCH 6A **70**
Gartloch Ct. G69: G'csh 6A **70**
Gartloch Rd. G33: Glas 1H **89**
....(not continuous)
Gartloch Rd. G34: G'csh 1F **91**
Gartloch Rd. G34: Glas 1F **91**
Gartloch Rd. G69: G'csh 6H **69**
Gartloch Rd. G69: Glas 6H **69**
Gartloch Village G69: G'csh 6A **70**
Gartloch Way G69: G'csh 6A **70**
Gartly St. G44: Glas 3D **122**
Gartmore Gdns. G71: Tann 5C **112**
Gartmore La. G69: Mood 5E **55**
Gartmore Rd. ML6: Air 5G **95**
Gartmore Rd. PA1: Pais 1D **102**
Gartmore Ter. G72: Camb 4G **125**
GARTNAVEL GENERAL HOSPITAL **5G 63**
GARTNAVEL ROYAL HOSPITAL **5G 63**
GARTNESS 6E **97**
Gartness Dr. ML6: Gart 6E **97**
Gartness Rd. ML6: Air 2G **117**
Gartocher Dr. G32: Glas 6C **90**
Gartocher Rd. G32: Glas 6C **90**
Gartocher Ter. G32: Glas 6C **90**
Gartons Rd. G21: Glas 4E **67**
GARTSHERRIE 2B **94**
Gartsherrie Av. ML5: Glenb 4B **72**
Gartsherrie Ind. Est. ML5: Coat 2B **94**
Gartsherrie Rd. ML5: Coat 3A **94**
Gartshore Cres. G65: Twe 3D **34**
Gartshore Est. G66: Kirkin 5C **34**
Gartshore Gdns. G68: Cumb 4A **36**
Garturk St. G42: Glas 3F **107**
Garturk St. ML5: Coat 1D **114**
Gartverrie Gdns. ML5: Coat 2C **94**
Garvald Ct. G40: Glas 2D **108**
Garvald St. G40: Glas 2D **108**
Garve Av. G44: Glas 3E **123**
Garvel Cres. G33: Glas 5E **91**
Garvel Dr. G33: Glas 5E **91**
Garvel Pl. G62: Miln 3D **26**
Garvel Rd. G33: Glas 5E **91**
Garvel Rd. G62: Miln 3D **26**
Garvin Lea ML4: Bell 5C **114**
Garvock Dr. G43: Glas 2H **121**
Garwhitter Dr. G62: Miln 3H **27**
Gary Jacobs Health Club **5C 106**
Gascoyne G75: E Kil 4E **157**
Gaskin Path G33: Step 4E **69**
Gask Pl. G13: Glas 1H **61**
Gas St. PA5: John 2G **99**
Gasworks Rd. ML8: Carl 2A **174**
Gatehead Av. PA7: B'ton 4G **41**
Gatehead Cres. PA7: B'ton 4G **41**
Gatehead Dr. PA7: B'ton 4G **41**
Gatehead Gro. PA7: B'ton 5G **41**
Gatehead Wynd PA7: B'ton 4G **41**
Gatehouse St. G32: Glas 6B **90**
GATESIDE 6B **118**
Gateside Av. G65: Kils 3F **13**
Gateside Av. G72: Camb 2D **126**
Gateside Cres. G78: Barr 6C **118**
Gateside Cres. ML6: Air 3A **96**
Gateside Gdns. G78: Barr 5B **118**
Gateside Pk. G65: Kils 2F **13**
Gateside Pl. PA10: Kilba 2A **98**
Gateside Rd. G78: Barr 6B **118**
Gateside Rd. ML2: Wis 5E **149**
Gateside St. G31: Glas 5D **88**
Gateside St. ML3: Ham 1A **162**
Gateside Way G68: Cumb 5C **36**
Gateway, The G74: E Kil 5A **142**
Gateway Ct. G40: Glas 2C **108**
Gaughan Quad. ML1: Moth 4F **147**
Gauldry Av. G52: Glas 2C **104**
Gauze St. PA1: Pais 6A **82**
Gavell Rd. G65: Kils 4D **12**
Gavell Rd. G65: Queen 4D **12**
Gavinburn Gdns. G60: Old K 6D **22**
Gavinburn Pl. G60: Old K 6E **23**
Gavinburn St. G60: Old K 6E **23**
Gavin's Mill Rd. G62: Miln 4G **27**
Gavins Rd. G81: Hard 2D **44**
Gavin St. ML1: Moth 4G **147**
Gavinton St. G44: Glas 2D **122**
Gayne Dr. ML5: Glenb 3G **71**
Gean Ct. G67: Cumb 1F **39**
Gear Ter. G40: Glas 3D **108**
Geary St. G23: Glas 6B **48**
Geddes Hill G74: E Kil 5B **142**
Geddes Rd. G21: Glas 2E **67**
Geelong Gdns. G66: Len 2F **9**
Geils Av. G82: Dumb 2C **20**
Geils Quad. G82: Dumb 2C **20**
Gelston St. G32: Glas 1B **110**
Gemini Gro. ML1: Holy 2B **132**
Gemmell Pl. G77: Newt M 5B **136**
General Roy Way ML8: Carl 5G **175**
Generals Ga. G71: Udd 1C **128**
Gentle Row G81: Dun 1B **44**
George V Bri. 5F **87**
George Av. G81: Clyd 4E **45**
George Ct. ML3: Ham 4E **145**
George Ct. PA1: Pais 1H **101**
George Cres. G81: Clyd 4E **45**
George La. PA1: Pais 1A **102**
George Mann Ter. G73: Ruth 3C **124**
George Pl. PA1: Pais 1A **102**
George Reith Av. G12: Glas 4F **63**
Georges Cl. ML3: Ham 4E **145**
George Sq. G2: Glas 5D **6** (4G **87**)
George Stewart Gdns. ML3: Ham 4E **145**
George St. PA1: Pais 1G **101**
.... *(Broomlands St.)*
George St. PA1: Pais 1H **101**
.... *(Lady La.)*
George St. G1: Glas 5E **7** (4G **87**)
George St. G69: Bail 1H **111**
George St. G78: Barr 4D **118**
George St. ML1: Moth 5G **147**
George St. ML1: New S 3B **132**
George St. ML3: Ham 4E **145**
George St. ML4: Bell 2B **130**
George St. ML6: Air 4G **95**
George St. ML6: Chap 2D **116**
George St. PA5: John 2F **99**
GEORGETOWN 5B **58**
George Vw. ML2: Wis 1F **165**
George Way ML9: Lark 1D **170**
.... *(off Muirshot Rd.)*
Gerard Pl. ML4: Bell 6D **114**
GERMISTON 1D **88**
Germiston Ct. G75: E Kil 1A **168**
Germiston Cres. G75: E Kil 1A **168**
Gerry Rafferty Dr. PA3: Pais 4H **81**
Gertrude Pl. G78: Barr 5C **118**
Getter Gro. G65: Twe 1D **34**
Ghillies La. ML1: Moth 6E **131**
Gibbon Cres. G74: E Kil 6C **142**
Gibb St. ML1: Cle 6H **133**
Gibb St. ML6: Chap 2D **116**
Gibson Av. G82: Dumb 3H **19**

A–Z Glasgow 223

Gibson Cres. – Glebe Wynd

Gibson Cres. PA5: John 3E **99**
Gibson Hgts. G4: Glas 5H **7** (4A **88**)
(off Drygate)
Gibson Quad. ML1: Moth 6E **131**
Gibson Rd. PA4: Renf 3D **82**
Gibson St. G12: Glas 1B **86**
Gibson St. G40: Glas 5A **88**
Gibson St. G82: Dumb 3G **19**
GIFFNOCK 4A **122**
Giffnock Heritage Cen. 4A **122**
(off Station Rd.)
Giffnock Pk. Av. G46: Giff 3A **122**
Giffnock Station (Rail) 4A **122**
Giffnock Tennis Squash & Hockey Club
6A **122**
Gifford Dr. G52: Glas 6A **84**
Gifford Pl. ML5: Coat 2A **114**
Gifford Wynd PA2: Pais 3D **100**
Gigha Gdns. ML8: Carl 5E **175**
Gigha Quad. ML2: Wis 2E **165**
Gilbertfield Path G33: Glas 1B **90**
Gilbertfield Pl. G33: Glas 1B **90**
Gilbertfield Rd. G72: Camb 4C **126**
Gilbertfield Rd. G72: Flem 4C **126**
Gilbertfield St. G33: Glas 1B **90**
Gilbert St. G3: Glas 3A **4** (3A **86**)
Gilchrist Ct. PA5: John 4E **99**
(off Tannahill Cres.)
Gilchrist St. ML5: Coat 3D **94**
Gilchrist Way ML2: Wis 2H **165**
Gilderdale G74: E Kil 1E **157**
Gilfillan Pl. ML2: Over 4A **166**
Gilfillan Way PA2: Pais 5C **100**
Gilhill St. G20: Glas 2B **64**
Gillbank Av. ML8: Carl 3B **174**
Gillbank La. ML9: Lark 3E **171**
(off Shawrigg Rd.)
Gillburn St. ML2: Over 5A **166**
Gillies Cres. G74: E Kil 4D **142**
Gillies La. G69: Bail 1A **112**
Gilligans Way ML3: Ham 5D **144**
Gill Rd. ML2: Over 4A **166**
(not continuous)
Gilmartin Rd. PA3: Lin 5E **79**
Gilmerton St. G32: Glas 1A **110**
Gilmour Av. G74: T'hall 1F **155**
Gilmour Av. G81: Hard 2D **44**
Gilmour Cres. G73: Ruth 5B **108**
Gilmour Cres. G76: Eag 6C **154**
Gilmour Dr. ML3: Ham 1D **160**
Gilmour Pl. G5: Glas 1G **107**
Gilmour Pl. ML4: Bell 2A **130**
Gilmour Pl. ML5: Coat 3B **94**
Gilmour St. G76: Eag 6C **154**
Gilmour St. G81: Clyd 3E **45**
Gilmour St. PA1: Pais 6A **82**
Gilmourton Cres. G77: Newt M 6D **136**
GILSHOCHILL 2B **64**
Gilshochill Station (Rail) 2C **64**
Gimmerscroft Cres. ML6: Air 5F **97**
Girdons Way G71: Udd 1C **128**
Girthon St. G32: Glas 1C **110**
Girvan Cres. ML6: Chap 4D **116**
Girvan St. G33: Glas 2F **89**
Gisborne Dr. ML6: Air 2C **96**
Glade, The ML9: Lark 3D **170**
Gladney Av. G13: Glas 1G **61**
Gladsmuir Rd. G52: Glas 5A **84**
GLADSTONE 5H **41**
Gladstone Av. G78: Barr 5D **118**
Gladstone Av. PA5: John 6D **98**
Gladstone Ct. ML3: Ham 4E **145**
Gladstone Dr. G74: T'hall 3H **155**
Gladstone St. G4: Glas 1H **5** (1E **87**)
Gladstone St. G81: Clyd 5B **44**
Gladstone St. ML4: Bell 2D **130**
Glaive Rd. G13: Glas 6D **46**
Glamis Av. G77: Newt M 4F **137**
Glamis Av. ML8: Carl 3D **174**
Glamis Av. PA5: Eld 4H **99**
Glamis Ct. ML1: Carf 5C **132**
Glamis Cres. G72: Blan 6B **144**
Glamis Dr. G74: E Kil 6H **141**
Glamis Gait G72: Blan 6C **144**
Glamis Gdns. G64: B'rig 3D **50**
Glamis La. G72: Blan 6B **144**
Glamis Rd. G31: Glas 1F **109**
Glanderston Av. G77: Newt M 3B **136**
Glanderston Av. G78: Barr 5G **119**
Glanderston Ct. G13: Glas 1A **62**
Glanderston Dr. G13: Glas 2A **62**
Glanderston Ga. G77: Newt M 3B **136**
Glanderston Rd. G77: Newt M 3H **135**
Glanderston Rd. G78: Neil 3H **135**
Glanderston Rd. G78: Newt M 3H **135**
GLASGOW 5D **6** (4G **87**)
Glasgow Airlink Ind. Est. PA3: Glas A 3A **82**
GLASGOW AIRPORT 2H **81**
GLASGOW AIRPORT INTERCHANGE 3H **81**
Glasgow & Edinburgh Rd. G69: Bail 6B **92**
Glasgow & Edinburgh Rd. G69: Barg 1D **112**
Glasgow & Edinburgh Rd. ML1: Holy 4H **115**
Glasgow & Edinburgh Rd. ML1: N'hse 4H **115**
Glasgow & Edinburgh Rd. ML1: N'hse 5E **117**
(not continuous)
Glasgow & Edinburgh Rd. ML4: Bell 4G **115**
Glasgow & Edinburgh Rd. ML5: Coat 2F **113**
Glasgow Botanic Gdns. 5B **64**
Glasgow Bri. 5F **87**
Glasgow Bri. Cotts. G66: Kirkin 6G **31**
Glasgow Business Pk. G69: Glas 4H **91**
Glasgow Caledonian University 2E **7** (2G **87**)
Glasgow Central Station (Rail) 6C **6** (4F **87**)
Glasgow City Chambers 5E **7** (4G **87**)
Glasgow City Heliport 2D **84**
Glasgow City Heliport G51: Glas 2E **85**
Glasgow Climbing Cen. 6H **85**
Glasgow Club 1F **105**
(Bellahouston)
Glasgow Club 1E **87**
(North Woodside)
Glasgow Crematorium 1D **64**
GLASGOW DENTAL HOSPITAL 3A **6** (3E **87**)
Glasgow Film Theatre 3B **6** (3F **87**)
Glasgow Fish Mkt. 2D **88**
Glasgow Fort Shop. Pk. 2E **91**
Glasgow Fruit Mkt. G21: Glas 2C **88**
Glasgow Golf Course 5A **48**
GLASGOW GREEN 6H **87**
Glasgow Green Football Cen. 1A **108**
Glasgow Harbour Terraces G11: Glas 2F **85**
Glasgow Hawks RUFC 3E **63**
GLASGOW HOMOEOPATHIC HOSPITAL 5G **63**
Glasgow Museums Resource Cen. 2H **119**
Glasgow Necropolis 3A **88**
GLASGOW NUFFIELD HEALTH HOSPITAL 4H **63**
Glasgow Police Mus. 6F **7** (4H **87**)
Glasgow Rd. G67: Cumb 5E **37**
(Condorrat Ring Rd.)
Glasgow Rd. G72: Camb 6G **109**
(Dukes Ct.)
Glasgow Rd. G72: Camb 6H **125**
(East Kilbride Rd.)
Glasgow Rd. G73: Ruth 5G **125**
(East Kilbride Rd.)
Glasgow Rd. G73: Ruth 3B **108**
(Shawfield Rd.)
Glasgow Rd. G67: Cumb 1B **38**
(Springfield Rd.)
Glasgow Rd. G53: Glas 2G **119**
Glasgow Rd. G62: Miln 5G **27**
Glasgow Rd. G65: Kils 3E **13**
(not continuous)
Glasgow Rd. G66: Kirkin 6H **31**
Glasgow Rd. G69: Bail 1F **111**
Glasgow Rd. G69: Barg 5F **93**
Glasgow Rd. G69: Coat 5F **93**
Glasgow Rd. G71: Tann 4A **112**
Glasgow Rd. G71: Udd 4A **112**
Glasgow Rd. G72: Blan 6H **127**
Glasgow Rd. G74: Ners 2A **142**
Glasgow Rd. G76: Eag 6B **138**
Glasgow Rd. G76: Wfoot 6B **138**
Glasgow Rd. G78: Barr 3F **119**
Glasgow Rd. G81: Clyd 1D **60**
Glasgow Rd. G81: Faif 1D **44**
Glasgow Rd. G81: Hard 1D **44**
Glasgow Rd. G82: Dumb 3E **19**
Glasgow Rd. G82: Mil 3E **19**
Glasgow Rd. ML2: Wis 6D **148**
Glasgow Rd. ML3: Ham 4E **145**
Glasgow Rd. ML5: Barg 5F **93**
Glasgow Rd. ML5: Coat 5F **93**
Glasgow Rd. PA1: Pais 6B **82**
Glasgow Rd. PA4: Renf 6G **61**
Glasgow Rowing Club 6H **87**
Glasgow Royal Concert Hall 3D **6** (3G **87**)
GLASGOW ROYAL INFIRMARY 4H **7** (3A **88**)
Glasgow St Andrew's RC Cathedral 5G **87**
Glasgow St Mary's Episcopal Cathedral 1D **86**
Glasgow St Mungo's Cathedral 4H **7** (3A **88**)
Glasgow School of Art 2B **6** (2F **87**)
(Haldane Bldg.)
Glasgow School of Art 2H **5** (2E **87**)
(JD Kelly & Richmond Bldg.)
Glasgow School of Art 3A **6** (3E **87**)
(Mackintosh Bldg.)
Glasgow School of Art 2A **6** (2E **87**)
(Reid Bldg.)
Glasgow Science Cen. 6A **4** (4A **86**)
Glasgow's Grand Ole Opry 5C **86**
Glasgow Ski Cen. 1G **105**
Glasgow Southern Orbital G77: Eag 2B **152**
Glasgow Southern Orbital G77: Newt M 2B **152**
Glasgow St. G12: Glas 6C **64**
Glasgow Tigers Speedway 4H **65**
Glasgow Tower, The 5A **4** (4A **86**)
Glasgow Visit Scotland Info. Cen. 4D **6** (3G **87**)
Glassel Rd. G34: Glas 2B **92**
Glasserton Pl. G43: Glas 2D **122**
Glasserton Rd. G43: Glas 2D **122**
Glassford St. G1: Glas 6E **7** (4G **87**)
Glassford St. G62: Miln 3H **27**
Glassford St. ML1: Moth 5A **148**
Glassford Twr. ML1: Moth 5A **148**
(off Glassford St.)
Glaudhall Av. G69: G'csh 2C **70**
Glazertbank G66: Len 3E **9**
Glazert Mdw. G66: Len 4G **9**
Glazert Pk. Dr. G66: Len 4G **9**
Glazert Pl. G66: Milt C 6B **10**
Glebe, The G71: Both 5F **129**
Glebe Av. G71: Both 5F **129**
Glebe Av. G76: Crmck 2H **139**
Glebe Av. ML5: Coat 1H **113**
Glebe Ct. G4: Glas 3G **7** (3H **87**)
Glebe Ct. G60: Old K 1E **43**
Glebe Cres. G74: E Kil 2H **157**
Glebe Cres. ML3: Ham 1G **161**
Glebe Cres. ML6: Air 3D **96**
Glebe Gdns. PA6: Hous 1B **78**
Glebe Hollow G71: Both 5F **129**
Glebe La. G77: Newt M 5D **136**
Glebe Pk. G82: Dumb 2H **19**
Glebe Pl. G72: Camb 2B **126**
Glebe Pl. G73: Ruth 5B **108**
Glebe Rd. G77: Newt M 5D **136**
Glebe St. G4: Glas 2G **7** (2H **87**)
(Black St.)
Glebe St. G4: Glas 3H **7** (3A **88**)
(McAslin St.)
(not continuous)
Glebe St. G74: E Kil 1H **157**
Glebe St. ML3: Ham 1G **161**
Glebe St. ML4: Bell 2B **130**
Glebe St. PA4: Renf 6F **61**
Glebe Wynd G71: Both 5F **129**

224 A–Z Glasgow

Gleddoch Cl. G52: Glas................5G **83**
Gleddoch Ct. G52: Glas................5G **83**
Gleddoch Ga. G52: Glas................5H **83**
Gleddoch Rd. G52: Glas................5G **83**
Gleddoch Vw. G82: Dumb................5D **18**
Gledstane Rd. PA7: B'ton................5H **41**
Glenacre Cres. G71: Tann................5C **112**
Glenacre Dr. G45: Glas................4H **123**
Glenacre Dr. ML6: Air................5D **96**
Glenacre Gdns. G45: Glas................3H **123**
Glenacre Gro. G45: Glas................3A **124**
Glenacre Quad. G45: Glas................4H **123**
Glenacre Rd. G67: Cumb................5H **37**
Glenacre St. G45: Glas................4H **123**
Glenacre Ter. G45: Glas................4H **123**
Glenafeoch Gdns. ML8: Carl................4E **175**
Glenafeoch Rd. ML8: Carl................4D **174**
Glen Affric G74: E Kil................2B **158**
Glen Affric Av. G53: Glas................3D **120**
Glen Affric Way ML6: Chap................4D **116**
................(off Glen Avon Dr.)
Glenafton Gro. ML5: Coat................6A **94**
Glenafton Vw. ML3: Ham................3F **161**
Glen Alby Pl. G53: Glas................3C **120**
Glenallan Ter. ML1: Moth................6F **131**
Glenallan Way PA2: Pais................6B **100**
Glen Almond G74: E Kil................1D **158**
Glenalmond Rd. G73: Ruth................4F **125**
Glenalmond St. G32: Glas................1A **110**
Glenalva Ct. G65: Kils................2H **13**
Glenapp Av. PA2: Pais................4D **102**
Glenapp Pl. G69: Mood................4D **54**
Glenapp Rd. PA2: Pais................4D **102**
Glenapp St. G41: Glas................2D **106**
Glenarklet Cres. PA2: Pais................5C **102**
Glenarklet Dr. PA2: Pais................4C **102**
Glen Arroch G74: E Kil................2B **158**
Glenartney PA6: Hous................1A **78**
Glenartney Rd. G69: Chry................6A **54**
Glenashdale Way PA2: Pais................4C **102**
Glen Av. G32: Glas................5B **90**
Glen Av. G69: Mood................5D **54**
Glen Av. G78: Neil................2E **135**
Glen Av. ML9: Lark................5B **170**
Glenavon Ct. ML3: Ham................2F **161**
Glenavon Ct. ML9: B'haw................6D **170**
Glen Avon Dr. ML6: Chap................4D **116**
Glenavon Rd. G20: Glas................2B **64**
Glenbank Av. G66: Lenz................3D **52**
Glenbank Ct. G46: T'bnk................5F **121**
................(off Glenbank Dr.)
Glenbank Dr. G46: T'bnk................5F **121**
Glenbank Rd. G66: Lenz................3D **52**
Glenbarr St. G21: Glas................2B **88**
Glen Bervie G74: E Kil................1B **158**
Glenbervie Cres. G68: Cumb................1H **37**
Glenbervie Pl. G23: Glas................6B **48**
Glenbervie Pl. G77: Newt M................4A **136**
GLENBOIG................3A **72**
Glenboig Cotts. ML5: Glenb................3H **71**
Glenboig Farm Rd. ML5: Glenb................3A **72**
Glenboig New Rd. ML5: Glenb................3B **72**
Glenboig Rd. G69: G'csh................1F **71**
Glenboig Rd. G69: Glenb................1F **71**
Glenboig Rd. ML5: Glenb................3G **71**
Glen Brae PA11: Bri W................3E **77**
Glenbrittle Dr. PA2: Pais................4C **102**
Glenbrittle Way PA2: Pais................4C **102**
Glenbuck Av. G33: Glas................3H **67**
Glenbuck Dr. G33: Glas................3H **67**
GLENBURN................5H **101**
Glenburn Av. G69: Bail................6A **92**
Glenburn Av. G69: Mood................5D **54**
Glenburn Av. G72: Camb................2F **125**
Glenburn Av. ML1: N'hill................3C **132**
Glenburn Cl. ML6: Grng................1C **74**
Glenburn Ct. G66: Kirkin................5D **32**
................(off Willowbank Gdns.)
Glenburn Ct. G74: E Kil................6C **140**

Glenburn Cres. G66: Milt C................6C **10**
Glenburn Cres. G71: View................5G **113**
Glenburn Cres. PA2: Pais................5H **101**
Glenburn Gdns. G64: B'rig................5B **50**
Glenburn Gdns. ML5: Glenb................3G **71**
Glenburnie Pl. G34: Glas................4F **91**
Glenburn La. G20: Glas................2C **64**
Glenburn Rd. G46: Giff................6H **121**
Glenburn Rd. G61: Bear................2D **46**
Glenburn Rd. G74: E Kil................6C **140**
Glenburn Rd. ML3: Ham................6F **145**
Glenburn Rd. PA2: Pais................5F **101**
Glenburn St. G20: Glas................2C **64**
Glenburn Ter. ML1: Carf................6C **132**
Glenburn Ter. ML8: Carl................5C **174**
Glenburn Wlk. G69: Bail................6A **92**
Glenburn Way G74: E Kil................6B **140**
Glenburn Wynd ML9: Lark................1D **170**
................(off Muirshot Rd.)
Glencairn Av. ML2: Wis................5D **148**
Glencairn Ct. PA3: Pais................3D **82**
................(off Montgomery Rd.)
Glencairn Dr. G41: Glas................3B **106**
Glencairn Dr. G69: Mood................5C **54**
Glencairn Dr. G73: Ruth................5B **108**
Glencairn Dr. ML5: Coat................6A **94**
Glencairn Gdns. G41: Glas................3C **106**
Glencairn Gdns. G72: Camb................2D **126**
Glencairn La. G41: Glas................3C **106**
Glencairn Path G32: Glas................5C **90**
................(off Hallhill Rd.)
Glencairn Rd. G67: Cumb................3C **38**
Glencairn Rd. G82: Dumb................4C **18**
Glencairn Rd. PA3: Pais................4C **82**
Glencairn St. G66: Kirkin................6D **32**
Glencairn St. ML1: Moth................4G **147**
Glencairn Twr. ML1: Moth................4G **147**
Glencalder Cres. ML4: Bell................4D **130**
Glen Cally G74: E Kil................1B **158**
Glencally Av. PA2: Pais................4D **102**
Glencalvie Rd. G82: Dumb................1F **19**
Glen Cannich G74: E Kil................2B **158**
Glen Carron G74: E Kil................2B **158**
Glencart Gro. PA10: Kilba................4C **98**
Glencleland Rd. ML2: Wis................5D **148**
Glenclora Dr. PA2: Pais................4C **102**
Glen Clova G74: E Kil................1B **158**
Glen Clova Dr. G68: Cumb................1E **37**
Glencloy St. G20: Glas................2A **64**
Glen Clunie G74: E Kil................1D **158**
Glen Clunie Dr. G53: Glas................3C **120**
Glen Clunie Pl. G53: Glas................3C **120**
Glencoats Dr. PA3: Pais................6E **81**
Glencoe Dr. ML1: Holy................2A **132**
Glencoe Pl. G13: Glas................2F **63**
Glencoe Pl. ML3: Ham................3F **161**
Glencoe Rd. G73: Ruth................4F **125**
Glencoe Rd. ML8: Carl................5E **175**
Glencoe St. G13: Glas................2F **63**
Glen Cona Dr. G53: Glas................2C **120**
Glenconner Way G66: Kirkin................4G **33**
Glencorse Rd. PA2: Pais................3G **101**
Glencorse St. G32: Glas................4G **89**
Glen Ct. ML1: Moth................5B **148**
Glen Ct. ML5: Coat................6H **93**
Glencraig St. ML6: Air................4G **95**
Glen Creran Cres. G78: Neil................3C **134**
Glen Cres. G13: Glas................2G **61**
Glencroft Av. G71: Tann................5C **112**
Glencroft Rd. G44: Glas................1H **123**
Glencryan Rd. G67: Cumb................5A **38**
Glendale Av. ML6: Air................5D **96**
Glendale Cres. G64: B'rig................1E **67**
Glendale Dr. G64: B'rig................1E **67**
Glendale Gro. ML5: Coat................2A **114**
Glendale Pl. G31: Glas................5D **88**
Glendale Pl. G64: B'rig................2E **67**
Glendale St. G31: Glas................5D **88**
Glendaruel Av. G61: Bear................3H **47**

Glendaruel Rd. G73: Ruth................5G **125**
Glendarvel Gdns. G22: Glas................5H **65**
Glendee Gdns. PA4: Renf................1F **83**
Glendee Rd. PA4: Renf................1F **83**
Glen Dene Way G53: Glas................3C **120**
Glendentan Rd. PA11: Bri W................4E **77**
Glendermott Ct. ML8: Carl................2D **174**
Glen Derry G74: E Kil................6D **142**
Glen Dessary G74: E Kil................3B **158**
Glen Dessary La. G82: Dumb................1F **19**
Glendeveron Way ML1: Carf................5A **132**
Glen Devon G74: E Kil................2D **158**
Glendevon Cotts. G81: Clyd................4B **44**
Glen Devon Gro. G68: Cumb................6E **15**
Glendevon Pl. G81: Clyd................4B **44**
Glendevon Pl. ML3: Ham................3F **161**
Glendevon Sq. G33: Glas................1B **90**
Glen Dewar Pl. G53: Glas................3C **120**
Glendinning Pl. G76: Eag................6B **154**
Glendinning Rd. G13: Glas................6E **47**
Glen Dochart Dr. G68: Cumb................6E **15**
Glendoick Pl. G77: Newt M................4A **136**
Glen Doll G74: E Kil................1B **158**
Glen Doll Rd. G78: Neil................4B **134**
Glendorch Av. ML2: Wis................2A **150**
Glendore St. G14: Glas................1E **85**
Glen Douglas Dr. G68: Cumb................1E **37**
Glendoune Rd. G76: Clar................4C **138**
Glendower Way PA2: Pais................5C **100**
Glen Dr. ML1: Holy................2B **132**
Glenduffhill Rd. G69: Bail................6F **91**
Glen Dye G74: E Kil................1B **158**
Glen Eagles G74: E Kil................2C **158**
Gleneagles Av. G68: Cumb................6A **16**
Gleneagles Ct. G64: B'rig................4C **50**
................(off Hilton Rd.)
Gleneagles Dr. G64: B'rig................4C **50**
Gleneagles Dr. G77: Newt M................5H **137**
Gleneagles Gdns. G64: B'rig................4B **50**
Gleneagles Ga. G77: Newt M................5H **137**
Gleneagles La. Nth. G14: Glas................5C **62**
Gleneagles La. Sth. G14: Glas................6C **62**
Gleneagles Pk. G71: Both................5D **128**
Glenelg Cres. G66: Kirkin................4G **33**
Glenelg Path ML5: Glenb................3G **71**
Glenelg Quad. G34: Glas................2B **92**
Glenelm Pl. ML4: Bell................1C **130**
Glen Esk G74: E Kil................1C **158**
Glen Esk Cres. G53: Glas................3C **120**
Glen Esk Dr. G53: Glas................3C **120**
Glen Esk Pl. G53: Glas................3C **120**
Glen Etive Pl. G73: Ruth................5G **125**
Glen Falloch G74: E Kil................2C **158**
Glen Falloch Cres. G78: Neil................4D **134**
Glen Falloch Way G68: Cumb................6E **15**
Glen Farg G74: E Kil................2D **158**
Glenfarg Ct. ML3: Ham................3F **161**
Glenfarg Cres. G61: Bear................3H **47**
Glenfarg Rd. G73: Ruth................3D **124**
Glenfarg St. G20: Glas................1E **87**
Glenfarm Rd. ML1: N'hill................3E **133**
Glen Farrar G74: E Kil................2B **158**
Glen Feshie G74: E Kil................3B **158**
Glenfield Av. PA2: Pais................1A **118**
Glenfield Cres. PA2: Pais................1A **118**
Glenfield Gdns. PA2: Pais................1A **118**
Glenfield Grange PA2: Pais................1A **118**
Glenfield Gro. PA2: Pais................1A **118**
Glenfield Rd. G75: E Kil................5A **158**
Glenfield Rd. PA2: Pais................6G **101**
Glen Finlet Cres. G78: Neil................4C **134**
Glenfinnan Dr. G20: Glas................3B **64**
Glenfinnan Dr. G61: Bear................4H **47**
Glenfinnan Dr. G82: Dumb................2G **19**
Glenfinnan Gro. ML4: Bell................3F **131**
Glenfinnan Pl. G20: Glas................3B **64**
................(off Glenfinnan Rd.)
Glenfinnan Rd. G20: Glas................3B **64**
Glen Fruin Ct. G82: Dumb................2G **19**

Glenfruin Cres. PA2: Pais	4D **102**	
Glen Fruin Dr. ML9: Lark	4E **171**	
Glen Fruin Pl. ML6: Chap	4D **116**	
.... (off Glen Rannoch Dr.)		
Glenfruin Rd. G72: Blan	1A **144**	
Glen Fyne Rd. G68: Cumb	1D **36**	
Glen Gairn G74: E Kil	1D **158**	
Glen Gairn Cres. G78: Neil	3C **134**	
Glen Gdns. PA5: Eld	2A **100**	
Glengariff Way PA5: Eld	4A **100**	
Glen Garrell Pl. G65: Kils	2F **13**	
Glengarriff Rd. ML4: Bell	5D **114**	
Glen Garry G74: E Kil	3B **158**	
Glen Garry Cl. G82: Dumb	1F **19**	
Glengarry Dr. G52: Glas	6C **84**	
Glengavel Cres. G33: Glas	3H **67**	
Glengavel Gdns. ML2: Wis	2A **150**	
Glen Gavin Way PA2: Pais	4D **102**	
Glengonnar St. ML9: Lark	5C **170**	
GLENGOWAN	2A **170**	
Glengowan Rd. PA11: Bri W	3E **77**	
Glengowen Ct. ML9: Lark	2C **170**	
Glengoyne Dr. ML1: New S	5A **132**	
Glen Gro. G65: Kils	1H **13**	
Glen Gro. G75: E Kil	4F **157**	
Glengyle Dr. G66: Len	2E **9**	
Glengyre Pl. G34: Glas	3A **92**	
Glengyre St. G34: Glas	2A **92**	
Glenhead Cres. G22: Glas	3G **65**	
Glenhead Cres. G81: Dun	6C **24**	
Glenhead Cres. G81: Hard	6C **24**	
Glenhead Dr. ML1: Moth	5F **147**	
Glenhead Rd. G66: Lenz	3D **52**	
Glenhead Rd. G81: Clyd	2B **44**	
Glenhead St. G22: Glas	3G **65**	
Glenheath Dr. ML5: Glenb	4G **71**	
Glenholme Av. PA2: Pais	4F **101**	
Glenhouse Cres. PA5: Eld	4A **100**	
Glenhove Rd. G67: Cumb	3A **38**	
Gleniffer Av. G13: Glas	3A **62**	
Gleniffer Ct. PA2: Pais	6F **101**	
Gleniffer Cres. PA5: Eld	4A **100**	
Gleniffer Dr. G78: Barr	2C **118**	
Gleniffer Rd. PA4: Renf	3D **82**	
Gleniffer Vw. G78: Neil	1D **134**	
Gleniffer Vw. G81: Clyd	4F **45**	
Glen Isla G74: E Kil	1C **158**	
Glen Isla Av. G78: Neil	4C **134**	
Glenisla Av. G69: Mood	3E **55**	
Glen Isla Dr. ML8: Carl	6G **175**	
Glen Isla Pl. ML8: Carl	6F **175**	
Glen Isla Quad. ML1: Cle	1H **149**	
Glenisla St. G31: Glas	2F **109**	
Glenkirk Dr. G15: Glas	5B **46**	
Glen Kyle Dr. G53: Glas	3C **120**	
Glen La. PA3: Pais	6A **82**	
Glen Lednock Dr. G68: Cumb	1D **36**	
Glen Lee G74: E Kil	1C **158**	
Glenlee St. ML3: Ham	4D **144**	
Glen Lethnot G74: E Kil	1C **158**	
Glen Livet Pl. G53: Glas	3C **120**	
Glen Livet Rd. G78: Neil	3C **134**	
Glen Lochay Gdns. G68: Cumb	1D **36**	
Glenlora Dr. G53: Glas	6A **104**	
Glenlora Ter. G53: Glas	6B **104**	
Glen Loy Pl. G53: Glas	3C **120**	
Glenluce Dr. G32: Glas	2D **110**	
Glenluce Gdns. G69: Mood	4E **55**	
Glenluce Ter. G74: E Kil	1E **157**	
Glenluggie Rd. G66: Kirkin	6G **33**	
Glenlui Av. G73: Ruth	2D **124**	
Glen Luss Gdns. G68: Cumb	1D **36**	
Glen Luss Pl. G53: Glas	3C **120**	
Glen Luss Pl. ML5: Coat	6F **95**	
Glen Lyon G74: E Kil	2C **158**	
Glen Lyon Ct. G68: Cumb	1D **36**	
Glenlyon Ct. ML3: Ham	3F **161**	
Glenlyon Pl. G73: Ruth	4E **125**	
Glen Lyon Rd. G78: Neil	3C **134**	
Glen Lyon Wlk. ML1: Moth	6C **148**	
Glen Mallie G74: E Kil	2C **158**	
Glenmalloch Pl. PA5: Eld	2A **100**	
Glenmanor Av. G69: Mood	5C **54**	
Glenmanor Rd. G69: Mood	5C **54**	
Glenmare Av. G66: Kirkin	6G **33**	
Glen Mark G74: E Kil	1C **158**	
Glen Mark Rd. G78: Neil	3C **134**	
GLENMAVIS	5G **73**	
Glenmavis Ct. ML8: Carl	4E **175**	
Glenmavis Cres. ML8: Carl	4E **175**	
Glenmavis Rd. ML6: Air	6G **73**	
Glenmavis Rd. ML6: Glenm	6G **73**	
Glenmavis St. G4: Glas	1C **6** (2F **87**)	
Glenmill Av. G53: Glas	6C **120**	
Glenmill Cres. G53: Glas	6C **120**	
Glenmill Dr. G53: Glas	5C **120**	
Glenmill Rd. G53: Glas	5C **120**	
Glenmill Way G53: Glas	5C **120**	
Glen More G74: E Kil	2A **158**	
Glen More ML8: Carl	5G **175**	
Glenmore Av. G42: Glas	5A **108**	
Glenmore Av. ML4: Bell	4D **130**	
Glenmore Pl. G42: Glas	5A **108**	
Glenmore Rd. ML1: N'hill	4C **132**	
Glen Moriston G74: E Kil	2C **158**	
Glen Moriston Rd. G53: Glas	4C **120**	
Glen Moriston Rd. G68: Cumb	1D **36**	
Glenmoss Av. PA8: Ersk	6D **42**	
Glen Moy G74: E Kil	2B **158**	
Glenmuir Av. G53: Glas	2C **120**	
Glenmuir Ct. G53: Glas	2D **120**	
Glenmuir Cres. G53: Glas	2C **120**	
Glenmuir Dr. G53: Glas	2B **120**	
Glen Muir Rd. G78: Neil	3C **134**	
Glen Nevis G74: E Kil	3B **158**	
Glen Nevis ML8: Carl	5F **175**	
Glen Nevis Pl. G73: Ruth	5E **125**	
Glen Noble ML1: Cle	1G **149**	
Glen Ochil Rd. ML6: Chap	4D **116**	
Glen Ogilvie G74: E Kil	1C **158**	
Glen Ogle St. G32: Glas	1D **110**	
Glenoran La. ML9: Lark	1D **170**	
Glenorchard Rd. G64: Balm	3H **29**	
Glen Orchy Ct. G68: Cumb	6D **14**	
Glen Orchy Dr. G53: Glas	3C **120**	
Glen Orchy Dr. G68: Cumb	1D **36**	
Glen Orchy Gro. G53: Glas	3D **120**	
Glen Orchy Pl. G53: Glas	4D **120**	
Glen Orchy Pl. G68: Cumb	1D **36**	
Glen Orchy Pl. ML6: Chap	4D **116**	
.... (off Glen Rannoch Dr.)		
Glen Orchy Rd. ML1: Cle	1H **149**	
Glen Orchy Way G53: Glas	4C **120**	
Glen Orrin Way G78: Neil	3C **134**	
Glenpark ML6: Air	5E **97**	
Glenpark Av. G46: T'bnk	5F **121**	
Glenpark Gdns. G72: Camb	6G **109**	
Glenpark Ind. Est. G31: Glas	5D **88**	
Glenpark Rd. G31: Glas	5D **88**	
Glenpark St. G31: Glas	5D **88**	
Glenpark St. ML2: Wis	5G **149**	
Glenpark Ter. G72: Camb	6G **109**	
Glenpath G82: Dumb	2C **20**	
Glenpatrick Rd. PA5: Eld	5A **100**	
Glen Pl. G76: Clar	2C **138**	
Glen Prosen G74: E Kil	1C **158**	
Glen Quoich G74: E Kil	6D **142**	
Glenraith Path G33: Glas	6B **68**	
Glenraith Rd. G33: Glas	6B **68**	
Glenraith Sq. G33: Glas	6B **68**	
Glenraith Wlk. G33: Glas	6C **68**	
Glen Rannoch Dr. ML6: Chap	4D **116**	
Glenrigg Ct. ML6: Air	6H **95**	
Glen Rinnes Dr. G78: Neil	4D **134**	
Glen Rd. G32: Glas	4B **90**	
Glen Rd. G60: Old K	1F **43**	
Glen Rd. G66: Cam G	1C **8**	
Glen Rd. G66: Len	1C **8**	
Glen Rd. G68: Dull	4F **15**	
Glen Rd. G74: E Kil	5B **140**	
Glen Rd. ML1: N'hse	6D **116**	
Glen Rd. ML2: Wis	5G **149**	
Glen Rd. ML6: Air	5E **97**	
Glen Rd. PA7: B'ton	3G **41**	
Glen Rosa Gdns. G68: Cumb	1D **36**	
Glen Roy Dr. G78: Neil	3C **134**	
Glen Sannox Dr. G68: Cumb	1D **36**	
Glen Sannox Gro. G68: Cumb	1E **37**	
Glen Sannox Loan G68: Cumb	1D **36**	
Glen Sannox Vw. G68: Cumb	1D **36**	
Glen Sannox Way G68: Cumb	1E **37**	
Glen Sannox Wynd G68: Cumb	1E **37**	
Glen Sax Dr. PA4: Renf	2G **83**	
Glen Shee G74: E Kil	1C **158**	
Glen Shee Av. G78: Neil	3C **134**	
Glen Shee Ct. ML8: Carl	5F **175**	
Glenshee Ct. G31: Glas	1F **109**	
Glen Shee Cres. ML6: Chap	4D **116**	
Glen Shee Gdns. ML8: Carl	5F **175**	
Glenshee Gdns. G31: Glas	1G **109**	
Glen Shee La. ML8: Carl	5G **175**	
Glenshee St. G31: Glas	1F **109**	
Glenshee Ter. ML3: Ham	3F **161**	
Glenshiel Av. PA2: Pais	4C **102**	
Glenshira Av. PA2: Pais	4C **102**	
Glen Shira Dr. G82: Dumb	1F **19**	
Glen Shirva Rd. G65: Twe	1C **34**	
Glenside Av. G53: Glas	3B **104**	
Glenside Cotts. PA11: Bri W	3F **77**	
.... (off Mill of Gryffe Rd.)		
Glenside Dr. G73: Ruth	1F **125**	
Glenside Rd. G82: Dumb	1H **19**	
Glenspean Pl. ML5: Coat	6F **95**	
Glenspean St. G43: Glas	1A **122**	
Glen St. G72: Camb	3D **126**	
Glen St. G78: Barr	4E **119**	
Glen St. ML1: Moth	6G **131**	
Glen St. ML1: N'hill	3D **132**	
Glen St. PA3: Pais	5H **81**	
Glentanar Ct. PA1: Pais	1C **102**	
Glentanar Dr. G69: Mood	5E **55**	
Glentanar Pl. G22: Glas	2F **65**	
Glentanar Rd. G22: Glas	2F **65**	
Glen Tanner G74: E Kil	1D **158**	
Glen Tarbert Dr. G78: Neil	3C **134**	
Glentarbert Rd. G73: Ruth	4F **125**	
Glen Tennet G74: E Kil	1C **158**	
Glentore Quad. ML6: Air	1A **96**	
Glen Twr. ML1: Moth	5B **148**	
.... (off Glen Ct.)		
Glentrool Gdns. G22: Glas	5G **65**	
Glentrool Gdns. G69: Mood	4E **55**	
Glen Turret G74: E Kil	1C **158**	
Glenturret St. G32: Glas	1A **110**	
Glentyan Av. PA10: Kilba	1A **98**	
Glentyan Dr. G53: Glas	6A **104**	
Glentyan Pl. G53: Glas	6A **104**	
Glen Urquhart G74: E Kil	2B **158**	
Glen Vw. G67: Cumb	2C **38**	
Glen Vw. ML3: Ham	5H **161**	
Glenview G66: Kirkin	5D **32**	
Glenview ML6: Air	5D **96**	
Glenview ML9: Lark	1B **170**	
Glenview Av. FK4: Bank	1E **17**	
Glenview Ct. ML9: Lark	1B **170**	
Glenview Cres. G69: Mood	4D **55**	
Glenview Pl. G72: Blan	6B **128**	
Glenview St. ML6: Glenm	5G **73**	
Glenvilla Circ. PA2: Pais	6H **101**	
Glenvilla Cres. PA2: Pais	1A **118**	
Glenvilla Pl. PA2: Pais	6H **101**	
Glenvilla Rd. PA2: Pais	6H **101**	
Glenvilla Wynd PA2: Pais	6H **101**	
Glenville Av. G46: Giff	4H **121**	
Glenville Ga. G76: Busby	4E **139**	
Glenville Ter. G76: Busby	4E **139**	
Glenward Av. G66: Len	3G **9**	

Glenwell St. – Gray St.

Glenwell St. ML6: Glenm 6G **73**
Glenwood Av. ML6: Air 1C **116**
Glenwood Bus. Cen. G45: Glas 4A **124**
Glenwood Ct. G66: Lenz 2A **52**
Glenwood Dr. G46: T'bnk 5F **121**
Glenwood Gdns. G66: Lenz 2A **52**
Glenwood Path G45: Glas 4A **124**
Glenwood Pl. G45: Glas 4A **124**
Glenwood Pl. G66: Lenz 2A **52**
Glenwood Rd. G66: Lenz 2A **52**
Glidden Ct. ML2: Over 4A **166**
Globe Ct. G74: E Kil 4D **142**
Glorat Av. G66: Len 3G **9**
Gloucester Av. G73: Ruth 2F **125**
Gloucester Av. G76: Clar 2B **138**
Glynhill Leisure Club **2D 82**
Goals Soccer Cen. **4D 106**
(Glasgow South, Pollokshaws Rd.)
Goals Soccer Cen. **4F 45**
(Glasgow West, Gt. Western Rd.)
GOCKSTON **3H 81**
Gockston Rd. PA3: Pais 4H **81**
Goddard Pl. ML2: Newm 4F **151**
Gogar Pl. G33: Glas 3G **89**
Gogar St. G33: Glas 3G **89**
Goil Av. ML4: Bell 1H **129**
Goil Way ML1: Holy 2A **132**
(off Glencoe Dr.)
Golberry La. G14: Glas 4B **62**
(off Esslemont Av.)
Goldberry Av. G14: Glas 4B **62**
Gold Coast La. G40: Glas 2D **108**
Goldcrest Ct. ML2: Wis 2F **165**
Goldenacre Pl. ML6: Plain 6F **75**
Goldenhill Ct. G81: Hard 1D **44**
GOLDEN JUBILEE NATIONAL HOSPITAL **5A 44**
Goldenlee Vw. PA6: C'lee 3A **78**
Goldie Rd. G71: Udd 3E **129**
Golf Av. ML4: Bell 4C **130**
Golf Course Rd. G64: Balm 5A **30**
Golf Course Rd. PA11: Bri W 3D **76**
Golf Ct. G44: Neth 5C **122**
Golf Dr. G15: Glas 6H **45**
Golf Dr. PA1: Pais 1E **103**
Golf Gdns. ML9: Lark 3E **171**
GOLFHILL **1H 95**
Golfhill Dr. G31: Glas 3C **88**
Golfhill Quad. ML6: Air 1A **96**
Golfhill Rd. ML2: Wis 5D **148**
Golf Pl. ML4: Bell 4D **130**
Golf Rd. G73: Ruth 3D **124**
Golf Rd. G76: Clar 2B **138**
Golf Rd. PA7: B'ton 2H **41**
Golf Vw. G61: Bear 2B **46**
Golf Vw. G74: Ners 2B **142**
Golf Vw. G81: Clyd 3B **44**
Golfview Dr. ML5: Coat 4G **93**
Golfview Pl. ML5: Coat 5G **93**
Golspie Av. ML6: Air 1G **115**
Golspie St. G51: Glas 3G **85**
Golspie Way G72: Blan 6A **144**
Goodview Gdns. ML9: Lark 3E **171**
Goosedubbs G1: Glas 5G **87**
Gooseholm Cres. G82: Dumb 2G **19**
Gooseholm Rd. G82: Dumb 2G **19**
Gopher Av. G71: View 5F **113**
GORBALS **1G 107**
Gorbals Cross **6G 87**
Gorbals Cross **2C 170**
Gorbals Leisure Cen. **6G 87**
Gorbals St. G5: Glas 6F **87**
Gordon Av. G44: Neth 5C **122**
Gordon Av. G52: Hill E 4G **83**
Gordon Av. G69: Bail 6F **91**
Gordon Av. PA7: B'ton 3G **41**
Gordon Ct. ML6: Air 3E **97**
Gordon Cres. G77: Newt M 3E **137**
Gordon Dr. G44: Neth 5D **122**
Gordon Dr. G74: E Kil 6B **142**
Gordon La. G1: Glas 5C **6** (4F **87**)
Gordon McMaster Gdns. PA5: John 2G **99**
Gordon Pl. ML4: Bell 4B **130**
Gordon Rd. G44: Neth 5C **122**
Gordon Rd. ML3: Ham 5D **144**
Gordon Sq. PA5: John 3F **99**
Gordon St. G1: Glas 5C **6** (4F **87**)
Gordon St. PA1: Pais 1A **102**
Gordon Ter. G72: Blan 5A **128**
Gordon Ter. ML3: Ham 6D **144**
Gorebridge St. G32: Glas 4G **89**
Gorely Pl. ML1: Moth 5B **148**
Goremire Rd. ML8: Carl 6E **175**
Gorget Av. G13: Glas 6C **46**
Gorget Pl. G13: Glas 6C **46**
Gorget Quad. G13: Glas 6B **46**
Gorse Cres. PA11: Bri W 4G **77**
Gorse Dr. G78: Barr 3D **118**
Gorsehall St. ML1: Cle 5H **133**
Gorse Pl. G71: View 5F **113**
Gorsewood G64: B'rig 6A **50**
Gorstan Path G23: Glas 1B **64**
Gorstan Pl. G20: Glas 4A **64**
Gorstan St. G23: Glas 1B **64**
Gosford La. G14: Glas 5A **62**
Gotter Bank PA11: Quarr V 1A **76**
Goudie St. PA3: Pais 4H **81**
Gough La. G33: Glas 3F **89**
(off Gough St.)
Gough St. G33: Glas 3F **89**
Gourlay G74: E Kil 4D **142**
Gourlay Dr. ML2: Over 5A **166**
Gourlay St. G21: Glas 6H **65**
(not continuous)
Gourock St. G5: Glas 1E **107**
Gour Pl. G69: G'csh 4C **70**
GOVAN **3G 85**
Govan Cross Shop. Cen. **3G 85**
GOVANHILL **3F 107**
Govanhill St. G42: Glas 3F **107**
(not continuous)
Govanhill Swimming Pool **3E 107**
Govan Rd. G51: Glas 2D **84**
Govan Station (Subway) **3G 85**
Gowanbank Gdns. PA5: John 3E **99**
Gowanbrae G66: Lenz 1C **52**
Gowanlea Av. G15: Glas 6A **46**
Gowanlea Dr. G46: Giff 3B **122**
Gowanlea Ter. G71: View 6F **113**
Gowan Pl. ML6: Chap 2D **116**
Gowanside Pl. ML8: Carl 3B **174**
Gower St. G41: Glas 1A **106**
Gower St. G51: Glas 1A **106**
Gower Ter. G41: Glas 6A **86**
Gowkhall Av. ML1: N'hill 4F **133**
GOWKTHRAPPLE **3G 165**
Goyle Av. G15: Glas 4C **46**
Grace Av. G69: Barg 6D **92**
Grace St. G3: Glas 5F **5** (4D **86**)
Grace Wynd ML3: Ham 6A **146**
Grado Av. G74: E Kil 6A **140**
Graeme Ct. ML1: Moth 5F **131**
Graffham Av. G46: Giff 4B **122**
Grafton Pl. G1: Glas 3E **7** (3G **87**)
Graham Av. G72: Camb 2D **126**
Graham Av. G74: E Kil 1G **157**
Graham Av. G81: Clyd 4D **44**
Graham Av. ML3: Ham 3H **161**
(not continuous)
Graham Dr. G62: Miln 3E **27**
Graham Dr. G75: E Kil 6H **157**
Graham Ho. G67: Cumb 3G **37**
Graham Pl. G65: Kils 1G **13**
Graham Pl. ML9: Ashg 4H **171**
Graham Rd. G82: Dumb 3D **18**
Grahamsdyke Pl. G66: Kirkin 4E **33**
Grahamsdyke Rd. G66: Kirkin 4E **33**
Grahamshill Av. ML6: Air 3D **96**
Grahamshill St. ML6: Air 3C **96**
Graham Sq. G31: Glas 5B **88**
Grahamston Ct. PA2: Pais 5E **103**
Grahamston Cres. PA2: Pais 5E **103**
Grahamston Pk. G78: Barr 2D **118**
Grahamston Pl. PA2: Pais 5E **103**
Grahamston Rd. G78: Barr 2D **118**
Grahamston Rd. PA2: Pais 1E **119**
Graham St. G78: Barr 4D **118**
Graham St. ML1: Holy 2A **132**
Graham St. ML2: Wis 1H **165**
Graham St. ML3: Ham 6A **146**
Graham St. ML6: Air 4A **96**
Graham St. PA5: John 3E **99**
Graham Ter. G64: B'rig 2D **66**
Graham Wynd G75: E Kil 6H **157**
Graignestock Pl. G40: Glas 6A **88**
Grainger Rd. G64: B'rig 6F **51**
Grainger Way ML1: Moth 1F **147**
Grammar School Sq. ML3: Ham 5A **146**
Grammar School Wlk. G71: Udd 1C **128**
Grampian Av. PA2: Pais 5H **101**
Grampian Ct. G61: Bear 5C **26**
Grampian Cres. G32: Glas 1B **110**
Grampian Cres. ML6: Chap 4F **117**
Grampian Dr. G75: E Kil 1B **168**
Grampian Pl. G32: Glas 1B **110**
Grampian Rd. ML2: Wis 5F **149**
Grampian St. G32: Glas 1B **110**
Grampian Way G61: Bear 6B **26**
Grampian Way G68: Cumb 3C **36**
Grampian Way G78: Barr 6E **119**
Granby La. G12: Glas 6B **64**
Grand Ole Opry **5C 86**
Grandtully Dr. G12: Glas 3A **64**
Grange, The G42: Glas 5E **107**
Grange Av. G62: Miln 3H **27**
Grange Av. ML2: Wis 2E **165**
Grange Ct. G42: Glas 5E **107**
Grange Ct. ML1: Moth 1B **164**
Grange Gdns. G71: Both 6F **129**
Grangeneuk Gdns. G68: Cumb 4D **36**
Grange Rd. G42: Glas 5E **107**
Grange Rd. G61: Bear 2F **47**
Grange St. ML1: Moth 5A **148**
Grange Twr. ML1: Moth 1B **164**
Grannoch Pl. ML5: Coat 3F **115**
Gran St. G81: Clyd 1G **61**
Grant Ct. ML3: Ham 5G **161**
Grant Ct. ML6: Air 3E **97**
Grant Gro. ML4: Bell 3C **130**
Grantholm Av. ML1: Holy 1B **132**
Grantlea Gro. G32: Glas 1D **110**
Grantlea Ter. G32: Glas 1D **110**
Grantley Gdns. G41: Glas 5B **106**
Grantley St. G41: Glas 5B **106**
Grantoften Path G75: E Kil 5F **157**
Granton Ter. G5: Glas 3A **108**
Grantown Av. ML6: Air 5E **97**
Grantown Gdns. ML6: Glenm 4H **73**
Grant Pl. G61: Bear 6H **27**
Grant Rd. G66: Kirkin 1G **53**
Grants Av. PA2: Pais 4G **101**
Grants Cres. PA2: Pais 5H **101**
Grants Pl. PA2: Pais 5G **101**
Grant St. G3: Glas 1G **5** (2D **86**)
Grants Way PA2: Pais 4G **101**
Granville St. G3: Glas 3G **5** (3D **86**)
Granville St. G81: Clyd 4D **44**
Grasmere G75: E Kil 6B **156**
Grasmere Ct. ML3: Ham 5H **161**
Grathellen Ct. ML1: Moth 1A **148**
Gray Dr. G61: Bear 4F **47**
Grayline Av. G72: Newt 1E **127**
Grayling Rd. ML1: New S 2H **131**
Grayshill Rd. G68: Cumb 6H **35**
Gray's Rd. G71: Udd 1F **129**
Grayston Mnr. G69: Chry 6C **54**
Gray St. G3: Glas 2C **4** (2B **86**)
Gray St. G66: Kirkin 6H **33**

A–Z Glasgow 227

Gray St. – Groves, The

Gray St. ML1: Cle 6H 133
Gray St. ML9: Lark 1C 170
Great Av. ML3: Fern 2C 162
Great Dovehill G1: Glas 5H 87
Great George La. G12: Glas 6B 64
Great George St. G12: Glas 6B 64
Great Hamilton St. PA2: Pais 3A 102
Great Kelvin La. G12: Glas 1C 86
(off Glasgow St.)
Great Western Retail Pk. 5G 45
Great Western Rd. G12: Glas 4G 63
Great Western Rd. G13: Glas 6B 46
Great Western Rd. G15: Glas 6H 45
Great Western Rd. G4: Glas 1D 86
Great Western Rd. G60: Bowl 5H 21
Great Western Rd. G60: Old K 5H 21
Great Western Rd. G81: Clyd 1H 43
Great Western Rd. G81: Dun 1H 43
Great Western Rd. G81: Hard 1H 43
Great Western Ter. G12: Glas 5A 64
Great Western Ter. La. G12: Glas 5A 64
Grebe Dr. G68: Cumb 5B 36
Green, The G40: Glas 1A 108
Green, The G65: Twe 1D 34
Greenacres ML1: Moth 4E 147
Greenacres Ct. G53: Glas 3C 120
Greenacres Dr. G53: Glas 3C 120
Greenacres Vw. ML1: Moth 4E 147
Greenacres Way G53: Glas 3C 120
Greenan Av. G42: Glas 6A 108
Greenbank G72: Blan 2A 144
Greenbank Av. G46: Giff 2G 137
Greenbank Dr. PA2: Pais 6H 101
Greenbank House & Gdn. 3H 137
Green Bank Rd. G68: Cumb 3E 37
Greenbank Rd. ML2: Wis 6A 150
Greenbank St. G73: Ruth 5C 108
Greenbank Ter. ML8: Carl 3D 174
Green Cl. G40: Glas 6A 88
Green Dale ML2: Wis 4B 150
Greendyke St. G1: Glas 5H 87
GREENEND 1F 115
Greenend Av. PA5: John 4D 98
Greenend Pl. G32: Glas 4C 90
Greenend Vw. ML4: Bell 3B 130
Greenfarm Rd. G77: Newt M 4B 136
Greenfarm Rd. PA3: Lin 5H 79
GREENFAULDS 6G 37
Greenfaulds Cres. G67: Cumb 5A 38
Greenfaulds Rd. G67: Cumb 6G 37
Greenfaulds Station (Rail) 6H 37
GREENFIELD 5B 90
Greenfield Av. G32: Glas 4B 90
Greenfield Cres. ML2: Wis 5B 150
Greenfield Dr. ML2: Wis 5B 150
Greenfield Pl. G32: Glas 5B 90
Greenfield Quad. ML1: N'hill 3F 133
Greenfield Rd. G32: Glas 4C 90
Greenfield Rd. G76: Clar 3C 138
Greenfield Rd. ML3: Ham 4E 145
Greenfield Rd. ML8: Carl 2D 174
Greenfields Rd. G67: Cumb 5A 38
Greenfield St. G51: Glas 4F 85
Greenfield St. ML2: Wis 5B 150
Greenfinch Av. G68: Cumb 5B 36
GREENFOOT 2C 72
Greengairs Av. G51: Glas 3D 84
Greengairs Rd. ML6: Grng 2B 74
Green Gdns. ML1: Cle 5H 133
Greenhall Pl. G72: Blan 3A 144
GREENHEAD 1A 166
Greenhead Av. G82: Dumb 4H 19
Greenhead Gdns. G82: Dumb 4H 19
(not continuous)
Greenhead Moss Community Nature Pk. 1C 166
Greenhead Rd. G61: Bear 3F 47
Greenhead Rd. G66: Len 3G 9
Greenhead Rd. G82: Dumb 4H 19
Greenhead Rd. ML2: Wis 1A 166
Greenhead Rd. PA4: Inch 2G 59
Greenhead St. G40: Glas 6A 88
Greenhill G64: B'rig 1E 67
GREENHILL 2D 94
Greenhill Av. G46: Giff 6H 121
Greenhill Av. G69: G'csh 2C 70
Greenhill Bus. Pk. PA3: Pais 5G 81
Greenhill Ct. G73: Ruth 5C 108
Greenhill Cres. PA3: Lin 5H 79
Greenhill Cres. PA5: Eld 3B 100
Greenhill Dr. PA3: Lin 6A 80
Greenhill Ind. Est. ML5: Coat 2D 94
Greenhill Rd. G73: Ruth 5C 108
Greenhill Rd. PA3: Pais 5G 81
GREENHILLS 6D 156
Greenhills Cres. G75: E Kil 6D 156
Greenhills Rd. G75: E Kil 3A 156
Greenhills Sports Cen. 5E 157
Greenhills Sq. G75: E Kil 6D 156
Greenhill St. G73: Ruth 6C 108
Greenhills Way G75: E Kil 5F 157
Greenholm Av. G71: Udd 6C 112
Greenholm Av. G76: Clar 2C 138
Greenholme Ct. G44: Glas 1F 123
Greenholme St. G44: Glas 1F 123
Greenknowe Ct. G43: Glas 1H 121
Greenknowe Dr. ML8: Law 5D 166
Greenknowe Rd. G43: Glas 1H 121
Greenknowe St. ML2: Over 5H 165
Greenlaw Av. ML2: Wis 4A 150
Greenlaw Av. PA1: Pais 6C 82
Greenlaw Ct. G14: Glas 3F 61
Greenlaw Cres. PA1: Pais 5C 82
Greenlaw Dr. G77: Newt M 4C 136
Greenlaw Dr. PA1: Pais 6C 82
Greenlaw Gdns. PA1: Pais 5C 82
Greenlaw Ho. PA1: Pais 6C 82
Greenlaw Ind. Est. PA3: Pais 5B 82
Greenlawn Ct. ML2: Wis 1H 165
Greenlaw Path ML6: Chap 4E 117
Greenlaw Pl. G77: Newt M 3B 136
Greenlaw Rd. G14: Glas 3F 61
Greenlaw Rd. G77: Newt M 4C 136
Greenlaw Village 3B 136
Greenlaw Way G77: Newt M 2B 136
Greenlea Rd. G69: Chry 1H 69
Greenlea St. G13: Glas 3E 63
GREENLEES 4B 126
Greenlees Gdns. G72: Camb 4H 125
Greenlees Gro. ML5: Coat 6F 95
Greenlees Pk. G72: Camb 4A 126
Greenlees Rd. G72: Camb 5H 125
Greenlees Way G72: Camb 4H 125
Green Loan ML1: New S 4A 132
Greenloan Av. G51: Glas 3D 84
Greenloan Vw. ML9: Lark 4D 170
(off Fisher St.)
Greenlodge Ter. G40: Glas 1B 108
Greenmoss Pl. ML4: Bell 2D 130
Greenmount Rd. G22: Glas 2E 65
Greenoakhill Av. G71: Udd 3H 111
Greenoakhill Ct. G71: Udd 3H 111
Greenoakhill Cres. G71: Udd 3G 111
Greenoakhill Ga. G71: Udd 2H 111
Greenoakhill Pl. G71: Udd 3G 111
Greenoakhill Rd. G71: Udd 2G 111
Greenock Av. G44: Glas 2F 123
Greenock Rd. PA3: Pais 3G 81
(not continuous)
Greenock Rd. PA4: Inch 3F 59
Greenock Rd. PA7: B'ton 1B 40
Green Pl. G71: Both 5F 129
Green Pl. ML6: C'bnk 3B 116
Greenrig G71: Udd 1D 128
Greenrigg Rd. G67: Cumb 4A 38
Greenrig St. G33: Glas 6F 67
Greenrig St. G71: Udd 1D 128
Green Rd. G73: Ruth 5C 108
Green Rd. PA2: Pais 2D 100
GREENS, THE 6C 32
Greens Av. G66: Kirkin 6C 32
Greens Cres. G66: Kirkin 6C 32
Greenshields Rd. G69: Bail 6H 91
Greenside G76: Crmck 1A 140
Greenside Cres. G33: Glas 6G 67
Greenside Pl. G61: Bear 5C 26
Greenside Rd. G81: Hard 6D 24
Greenside Rd. ML1: Chap 6C 116
Greenside Rd. ML1: N'hse 6C 116
Greenside Rd. ML2: Wis 1A 166
Greenside St. G33: Glas 6G 67
Greenside St. ML1: N'hill 3F 133
Greenside St. ML5: Coat 2D 94
Greens Rd. G67: Cumb 1H 57
Green St. G40: Glas 6A 88
Green St. G71: Both 5F 129
Green St. G81: Clyd 4C 44
Greentree Dr. G69: Bail 2F 111
Greenview St. G43: Glas 5A 106
Greenway La. G72: Blan 3H 143
Greenways Av. PA2: Pais 3E 101
Greenways Ct. PA2: Pais 3E 101
Greenwood Av. G69: Mood 5D 54
Greenwood Av. G72: Camb 1E 127
Greenwood Ct. G76: Clar 2C 138
Greenwood Cres. ML5: Coat 6E 95
Greenwood Dr. G61: Bear 3G 47
Greenwood Dr. PA5: John 5D 98
Greenwood Quad. G81: Clyd 6F 45
Greenwood Rd. G76: Clar 2B 138
Green Wynd G40: Glas 6A 88
GREENYARDS INTERCHANGE 4C 38
Greer Quad. G81: Clyd 3D 44
Grenada Pl. G75: E Kil 2C 156
Grenadier Gdns. ML1: Moth 6F 147
Grenadier Pk. G72: Camb 3A 126
Grenville Dr. G72: Camb 3H 125
Gresham Vw. ML1: Moth 1B 164
Greta Meek La. G66: Milt C 5C 10
Greyfriars Rd. G71: Udd 5A 112
Greyfriars St. G32: Glas 4H 89
Greystone Av. G73: Ruth 1E 125
Greystone Gdns. G73: Ruth 1E 125
Greywood St. G13: Glas 2E 63
Grier Path G31: Glas 6F 89
Grier Pl. ML9: Lark 3B 170
Grierson La. G33: Glas 3F 89
(off Dee St.)
Grierson St. G33: Glas 3F 89
Grieve Cft. G71: Both 6D 128
Grieve Rd. G67: Cumb 2A 38
Griffen Av. PA1: Pais 6B 80
Griffin Pl. ML4: Bell 5C 114
Griffiths Way ML8: Law 1F 173
Griffon Cres. G74: E Kil 5H 141
Griqua Ter. G71: Both 5F 129
Grogarry Rd. G15: Glas 3A 46
Grosvenor Cinema 6B 64
(Glasgow)
Grosvenor Cres. G12: Glas 6B 64
Grosvenor Cres. La. G12: Glas 6B 64
Grosvenor La. G12: Glas 6B 64
Grosvenor Ter. G12: Glas 6B 64
Grouse Av. G74: E Kil 1C 158
Grove, The G46: Giff 1H 137
Grove, The G78: Neil 3C 134
Grove, The PA10: Kilba 1A 98
Grove, The PA11: Bri W 5G 77
Grove, The PA7: B'ton 4G 41
Groveburn Av. G46: T'bnk 3G 121
Grove Cres. ML9: Lark 3E 171
Grove Pk. G66: Lenz 3D 52
Grovepark Ct. G20: Glas 1E 87
Grovepark Gdns. G20: Glas 1E 87
Grovepark Pl. G20: Glas 6E 65
Grovepark St. G20: Glas 6E 65
Groves, The G64: B'rig 1E 67

228 A–Z Glasgow

Grove Way – Hapland Av.

Grove Way ML4: Bell 3B **130**
Grove Wood G71: View 4H **113**
Grovewood Bus. Cen. ML4: Bell 5A **114**
Grove Wynd ML1: New S 4A **132**
Grudie St. G34: Glas 3G **91**
Gryfebank Av. PA6: C'lee 2E **79**
Gryfebank Cl. PA6: C'lee 2E **79**
Gryfebank Cres. PA6: C'lee 2E **79**
Gryfebank Way PA6: C'lee 2E **79**
Gryfewood Cres. PA6: C'lee 2E **79**
Gryfewood Way PA6: C'lee 2E **79**
Gryffe Av. PA11: Bri W 2E **77**
Gryffe Av. PA4: Renf 4D **60**
Gryffe Castle PA11: Bri W 2E **77**
Gryffe Cres. PA2: Pais 4D **100**
Gryffe Gro. PA11: Bri W 3F **77**
Gryffe Pl. PA11: Bri W 3F **77**
Gryffe Rd. PA11: Bri W 4F **77**
Gryffe St. G44: Glas 6E **107**
GSO Bus. Pk. G74: E Kil 6A **140**
Guernsey Pl. ML3: Ham 4E **161**
Guildford Dr. G33: Glas 2C **90**
Guildford St. G33: Glas 2C **90**
Gullane Ct. ML3: Ham 3F **161**
Gullane Cres. G68: Cumb 5H **15**
Gullane Dr. ML5: Coat 3A **114**
Gullane St. G11: Glas 2H **85**
Gullion Pk. G74: E Kil 5A **142**
Gunn M. ML2: Wis 1F **165**
Gunn Quad. ML4: Bell 4A **130**
Gushetfaulds Pl. G5: Glas 2F **107**
Gushet Ho. ML6: Air 4G **95**
(off Aitchison St.)
Guthrie Ct. ML1: Moth 3E **147**
Guthrie Dr. G71: Tann 4E **113**
Guthrie Pl. G64: Torr 5E **31**
Guthrie Pl. G74: E Kil 1H **157**
Guthrie St. G20: Glas 3B **64**
Guthrie St. ML3: Ham 5H **145**
Gyle Pl. ML2: Wis 6C **150**

H

Haberlea Av. G53: Glas 4C **120**
Haberlea Gdns. G53: Glas 5C **120**
Haddington Way ML5: Coat 2A **114**
(not continuous)
Haddow Gro. G71: Tann 5E **113**
Haddow St. ML3: Ham 6A **146**
Hadrian Ter. ML1: Moth 1E **147**
Hagart Rd. PA6: Hous 1B **78**
Hagen Dr. ML1: Cle 6E **133**
Hagg Cres. PA5: John 2E **99**
Hagg Pl. PA5: John 2E **99**
Hagg Rd. PA5: John 3E **99**
Haggs Castle Golf Course **2G 105**
Haggs Ga. G41: Glas 5A **106**
Haggs La. G41: Glas 3A **106**
Haggs Rd. G41: Glas 4A **106**
Haggswood Av. G41: Glas 3A **106**
HAGHILL 4E 89
Haghill Rd. G31: Glas 5E **89**
Hagmill Cres. ML5: Coat 3E **115**
Hagmill Rd. ML5: Coat 3C **114**
Haig Dr. G69: Bail 1F **111**
Haig St. G21: Glas 5C **66**
Hailes Av. G32: Glas 6D **90**
Haining, The PA4: Renf 1F **83**
Haining Rd. PA4: Renf 6F **61**
Haining Wynd G69: Chry 3H **69**
HAIRMYRES 3B 156
Hairmyres Dr. G75: E Kil 3B **156**
HAIRMYRES HOSPITAL **2B 156**
Hairmyres Pk. G75: E Kil 3B **156**
HAIRMYRES RDBT. 2B **156**
Hairmyres Station (Rail) 2B 156
Hairmyres St. G42: Glas 3G **107**
Hairst St. PA4: Renf 5F **61**
Halbeath Av. G15: Glas 4H **45**
Halbert St. G41: Glas 4C **106**
Haldane La. G14: Glas 6D **62**
(off Victoria Pk. St.)
Haldane Pl. G75: E Kil 4H **157**
Haldane St. G14: Glas 6D **62**
Haldon Gro. ML5: Glenb 2B **72**
Halfmerk Nth. G74: E Kil 1A **158**
Halfmerk Sth. G74: E Kil 1A **158**
HALFWAY 3D 126
Halgreen Av. G15: Glas 4G **45**
Halidon Av. G67: Cumb 6H **37**
Halifax Way PA4: Renf 2E **83**
(off Tiree Av.)
Halkirk Ga. G72: Blan 5A **144**
Hallbrae St. G33: Glas 1G **89**
Hallcraig Pl. ML8: Carl 3B **174**
Hallcraig St. ML6: Air 3A **96**
Halley Ct. G13: Glas 2G **61**
Halley Dr. G13: Glas 2G **61**
Halley Pl. G13: Glas 2G **61**
Halley Sq. G13: Glas 2H **61**
Halley St. G13: Glas 2G **61**
Hallforest St. G33: Glas 1B **90**
Hallhill Circ. PA5: John 6C **98**
Hallhill Cres. G33: Glas 5E **91**
Hallhill Cres. PA5: John 6C **98**
Hallhill Dr. PA5: John 6C **98**
Hallhill Rd. G32: Glas 6B **90**
Hallhill Rd. G33: Glas 5D **90**
Hallhill Rd. G69: Bail 5G **91**
Hallhill Rd. PA5: John 6C **98**
Hallhill Wynd PA5: John 6C **98**
Halliburton Rd. G34: Glas 3F **91**
Halliburton Ter. G34: Glas 4G **91**
Hallidale Cres. PA4: Renf 1H **83**
Hallinan Gdns. ML2: Wis 2F **165**
Hall Pl. G33: Step 4F **69**
Hallrule Dr. G52: Glas 6C **84**
HALLSIDE 3F 127
Hallside Av. G72: Camb 2E **127**
Hallside Blvd. G72: Flem 4F **127**
Hallside Ct. G72: Flem 4E **127**
Hallside Cres. G72: Camb 2E **127**
Hallside Dr. G72: Camb 2E **127**
Hallside Gdns. ML2: Wis 5C **150**
Hallside Pl. G5: Glas 1G **107**
Hallside Rd. G72: Flem 3E **127**
(Newton Sta. Rd.)
Hallside Rd. G72: Flem 3F **127**
(Walnut Ga.)
Halls Land Pl. G81: Hard 6D **24**
Hall St. G81: Clyd 6C **44**
Hall St. ML1: New S 3A **132**
Hall St. ML3: Ham 2H **161**
Hallydown Dr. G13: Glas 4C **62**
Halpin Cl. ML4: Bell 2H **129**
Halton Gdns. G69: Bail 1F **111**
Haltons Path G71: Udd 1E **129**
Hamburg Cotts. ML8: Carl 3A **174**
Hamersley Pl. G75: E Kil 4D **156**
Hamilcomb Rd. ML4: Bell 4C **130**
Hamill Dr. G65: Kils 3B **14**
HAMILTON 6A 146
Hamilton Academical FC **4G 145**
Hamilton Av. G41: Glas 2H **105**
Hamilton Bus. Pk. ML3: Ham 4H **145**
Hamilton Central Park & Ride 6A 146
Hamilton Central Station (Rail) 6A 146
Hamilton Ct. PA2: Pais 3A **102**
Hamilton Cres. G61: Bear 6E **27**
Hamilton Cres. G72: Camb 3C **126**
Hamilton Cres. ML5: Coat 6C **94**
Hamilton Cres. PA4: Renf 4F **61**
Hamilton Cres. PA7: B'ton 4F **41**
Hamilton Dr. G12: Glas 6C **64**
Hamilton Dr. G46: Giff 5B **122**
Hamilton Dr. G71: Both 6F **129**
Hamilton Dr. G72: Blan 4H **143**
Hamilton Dr. G72: Camb 2A **126**
Hamilton Dr. ML1: Moth 5H **147**
Hamilton Dr. ML6: Air 2B **96**
Hamilton Dr. PA8: Ersk 4D **42**
Hamilton Dr. La. G12: Glas 6C **64**
HAMILTON FARM 5G 109
Hamilton Gdns. G12: Glas 6C **64**
Hamilton Golf Course **3E 163**
HAMILTONHILL 5F 65
Hamiltonhill Cres. G22: Glas 5F **65**
Hamiltonhill Gdns. G22: Glas 5F **65**
Hamiltonhill Rd. G22: Glas 6F **65**
HAMILTON INTERCHANGE 5C **146**
Hamilton Intl. Technology Pk. G72: Blan 4A **144**
(not continuous)
Hamilton Mausoleum **4B 146**
Hamilton Pk. Av. G12: Glas 6C **64**
Hamilton Pk. Nth. ML3: Ham 3H **145**
Hamilton Pk. Racecourse **3G 145**
Hamilton Pk. Sth. ML3: Ham 3H **145**
Hamilton Pl. G40: Glas 1E **109**
Hamilton Pl. G75: E Kil 4G **157**
Hamilton Pl. G78: Neil 2F **135**
Hamilton Pl. ML1: N'hill 3C **132**
Hamilton Pl. ML1: New S 3B **132**
Hamilton Pl. ML3: Ham 5H **161**
Hamilton Retail Pk. **4G 145**
Hamilton Rd. G32: Glas 2B **110**
Hamilton Rd. G71: Both 6F **129**
Hamilton Rd. G71: Udd 3F **111**
Hamilton Rd. G72: Blan 4F **143**
Hamilton Rd. G72: Camb 1A **126**
Hamilton Rd. G72: Flem 1A **126**
Hamilton Rd. G73: Ruth 5D **108**
Hamilton Rd. G74: E Kil 4C **142**
Hamilton Rd. ML1: Moth 4D **146**
Hamilton Rd. ML4: Bell 4B **130**
Hamilton Rd. ML9: Lark 6H **163**
HAMILTON SERVICE AREA 3A **146**
Hamilton Service Area Tourist Info. Cen. **3A 146**
Hamilton St. G42: Glas 4G **107**
Hamilton St. G81: Clyd 2F **61**
Hamilton St. G82: Dumb 3G **19**
Hamilton St. ML8: Carl 4D **174**
Hamilton St. ML9: Lark 1C **170**
Hamilton St. PA3: Pais 6B **82**
Hamilton Ter. G81: Clyd 2F **61**
Hamilton Twr. G71: Both 3B **128**
Hamilton Vw. G71: Tann 6E **113**
Hamilton Water Palace **5H 145**
Hamilton West Park & Ride 5G 145
Hamilton West Station (Rail) 5G 145
Hamlet G74: E Kil 4C **142**
Hampden Dr. G42: Glas 6F **107**
Hampden La. G42: Glas 5F **107**
Hampden Pk. **6F 107**
Hampden Ter. G42: Glas 5F **107**
Hampden Way PA4: Renf 2F **83**
Handel Pl. G5: Glas 1G **107**
Handley Pl. G69: Muirh 3A **70**
HANGINGSHAW 5G 107
Hangingshaw Pl. G42: Glas 5G **107**
Hannah Gdns. G64: B'rig 6F **51**
Hannay St. PA1: Pais 6G **81**
(off Well St.)
Hanover Cl. G42: Glas 5E **107**
Hanover Ct. G1: Glas 4E **7** (3G **87**)
Hanover Ct. G11: Glas 1G **85**
Hanover Ct. PA1: Pais 6C **82**
Hanover Ct. PA5: John 2F **99**
Hanover Gdns. G64: B'rig 6C **50**
Hanover Gdns. PA1: Pais 1G **101**
(off Wilson St.)
Hanover Pl. G11: Glas 1G **85**
Hanover St. G1: Glas 5D **6** (4G **87**)
Hanson Pk. G31: Glas 3B **88**
Hanson St. G31: Glas 4B **88**
Hapland Av. G53: Glas 3C **104**

Hapland Rd. G53: Glas	3C **104**	
Harbour La. PA3: Pais	6A **82**	
Harbour Pl. G11: Glas	2G **85**	
Harbour Rd. PA3: Pais	4A **82**	
Harburn Pl. G23: Glas	6C **48**	
Harburn Pl. ML1: N'hse	2D **132**	
Harbury Pl. G14: Glas	3H **61**	
Harcourt Dr. G31: Glas	3D **88**	
HARDGATE	1D **44**	
Hardgate Dr. G51: Glas	3C **84**	
Hardgate Gdns. G51: Glas	3C **84**	
Hardgate Path G51: Glas	3C **84**	
Hardgate Pl. G51: Glas	3C **84**	
Hardgate Rd. G51: Glas	3C **84**	
Hardie Av. G73: Ruth	5E **109**	
Hardie St. G72: Blan	2B **144**	
Hardie St. ML1: Moth	1G **147**	
Hardie St. ML3: Ham	1F **161**	
Hardmuir Gdns. G66: Kirkin	4E **33**	
Hardmuir Rd. G66: Kirkin	4E **33**	
Hardridge Av. G52: Glas	3E **105**	
Hardridge Pl. G52: Glas	3E **105**	
Hardridge Rd. G52: Glas	3D **104**	
Harefield Dr. G14: Glas	4B **62**	
Harelaw Av. G44: Glas	3C **122**	
Harelaw Av. G78: Barr	6F **119**	
Harelaw Av. G78: Neil	3D **134**	
Harelaw Cres. PA2: Pais	6G **101**	
HARELEESHILL	3D **170**	
Hareleeshill Rd. ML9: Lark	3D **170**	
Hareleeshill Sports Barn	4E **171**	
HARESTANES	3H **33**	
Harestanes Gdns. G66: Kirkin	4G **33**	
Harestone Cres. ML2: Wis	6A **150**	
Harestone Rd. ML2: Wis	1A **166**	
Harfield Dr. G33: Glas	5E **91**	
Harfield Gdns. G33: Glas	5E **91**	
Harhill St. G51: Glas	4F **85**	
Harkins Av. G72: Blan	2A **144**	
Harkness Av. G66: Milt C	6B **10**	
Harland Cotts. G14: Glas	6C **62**	
Harland St. G14: Glas	6C **62**	
Harlaw Gdns. G64: B'rig	5F **51**	
Harlequin Ct. ML3: Ham	4D **160**	
Harley St. G51: Glas	5A **86**	
Harmetray St. G22: Glas	3H **65**	
Harmony Pl. G51: Glas	4G **85**	
Harmony Row G51: Glas	4G **85**	
	(not continuous)	
Harmony Sq. G51: Glas	4G **85**	
Harmsworth St. G11: Glas	1E **85**	
Harnett Wynd G64: B'rig	1F **67**	
Harper Cres. ML2: Wis	5C **150**	
Harport St. G46: T'bnk	2E **121**	
Harriet Pl. G43: Glas	1H **121**	
Harriet St. G73: Ruth	6C **108**	
Harrington Rd. G74: E Kil	2G **157**	
Harris Cl. G77: Newt M	3B **136**	
Harris Cres. G60: Old K	2F **43**	
Harris Dr. G60: Old K	2F **43**	
Harris Gdns. G60: Old K	2G **43**	
Harrison Dr. G51: Glas	5H **85**	
Harris Pl. ML6: Air	6C **96**	
Harris Quad. ML2: Wis	4C **150**	
Harris Rd. G23: Glas	6C **48**	
Harris Rd. G60: Old K	2F **43**	
Harrow Ct. G15: Glas	4H **45**	
Harrow Pl. G15: Glas	4H **45**	
Harrowslaw Dr. ML3: Ham	5E **161**	
Hartfield Ct. G82: Dumb	3G **19**	
Hartfield Cres. G78: Neil	2E **135**	
Hartfield Gdns. G82: Dumb	3G **19**	
Hartfield Ter. PA2: Pais	3B **102**	
Hartlaw Cres. G52: Glas	5A **84**	
Hartree Av. G13: Glas	1G **61**	
Hartstone Pl. G53: Glas	6B **104**	
Hartstone Rd. G53: Glas	6B **104**	
Hartstone Ter. G53: Glas	6B **104**	
Hart St. G31: Glas	6G **89**	

Hart St. G81: Faif	6F **25**	
Hart St. PA3: Lin	6H **79**	
Hartwood Gdns. G77: Newt M	1D **152**	
Harvest Dr. ML1: Moth	5F **147**	
Harvester Av. G72: Newt	6F **111**	
Harvey St. G4: Glas	1G **87**	
Harvey Way ML4: Bell	6E **115**	
Harvie Av. G77: Newt M	4C **136**	
Harvie St. G51: Glas	5B **86**	
Harwood Gdns. G69: Mood	4E **55**	
Harwood St. G32: Glas	4G **89**	
Hastie St. G3: Glas	2B **4** (2B **86**)	
Hastings G75: E Kil	4D **156**	
Hatfield Dr. G12: Glas	4F **63**	
Hathaway Dr. G46: Giff	5H **121**	
Hathaway La. G20: Glas	4C **64**	
Hathaway St. G20: Glas	4C **64**	
Hathersage Av. G69: Bail	6H **91**	
Hathersage Dr. G69: Bail	6H **91**	
Hathersage Gdns. G69: Bail	6H **91**	
Hatton Gdns. G52: Glas	1A **104**	
Hatton Hill ML1: Carf	5C **132**	
Hatton Path G52: Glas	1A **104**	
	(off Hatton Gdns.)	
Hatton Pl. ML1: Carf	5C **132**	
HATTONRIGG	1D **130**	
Hattonrigg Rd. ML4: Bell	6C **114**	
Hatton Ter. ML1: Carf	5C **132**	
Haughburn Pl. G53: Glas	6B **104**	
Haughburn Rd. G53: Glas	6B **104**	
Haughburn Ter. G53: Glas	6C **104**	
Haughhead G66: Cam G	1B **8**	
HAUGHHEAD	1C **8**	
Haughhead Bri.	5A **112**	
Haugh Pl. ML3: Ham	2A **162**	
Haugh Rd. G3: Glas	3B **4** (3B **86**)	
Haugh Rd. G65: Kils	3G **13**	
Haughton Av. G65: Kils	3A **14**	
Haughview Rd. ML1: Moth	3D **146**	
Haughview Ter. G5: Glas	2H **107**	
Havannah St. G4: Glas	6H **7** (4A **88**)	
Havelock La. G11: Glas	1A **86**	
Havelock Pk. G75: E Kil	2C **156**	
Havelock St. G11: Glas	1A **86**	
Haven Pk. G75: E Kil	5B **156**	
Havoc Rd. G82: Dumb	4B **18**	
Hawbank Rd. G74: E Kil	6C **140**	
Hawick Av. PA2: Pais	4F **101**	
Hawick Ct. G13: Glas	2F **61**	
Hawick Cres. ML9: Lark	3C **170**	
Hawick Dr. ML5: Coat	2F **115**	
Hawick St. G13: Glas	3G **61**	
Hawick St. ML2: Wis	4A **150**	
HAWKBANK RDBT.	1D **156**	
HAWKHEAD	3E **103**	
Hawkhead Av. PA2: Pais	3D **102**	
Hawkhead Rd. PA1: Pais	1D **102**	
Hawkhead Rd. PA2: Pais	1D **102**	
Hawkhead Station (Rail)	1D **102**	
Hawksland Wlk. ML3: Ham	2A **162**	
Hawkwood G75: E Kil	6F **157**	
Hawkwood Rd. ML6: Glenm	5H **73**	
Hawthorn Av. G61: Bear	6G **27**	
Hawthorn Av. G64: B'rig	1D **66**	
Hawthorn Av. G66: Lenz	2C **52**	
Hawthorn Av. G72: Camb	2F **125**	
Hawthorn Av. G82: Dumb	2B **18**	
Hawthorn Av. ML2: Newm	3G **151**	
Hawthorn Av. PA5: John	4G **99**	
Hawthorn Av. PA8: Ersk	1A **60**	
Hawthorn Ct. G22: Glas	4G **65**	
Hawthorn Ct. G76: Busby	3C **138**	
Hawthorn Cres. PA8: Ersk	1A **60**	
Hawthornden Gdns. G23: Glas	5C **48**	
Hawthorn Dr. FK4: Bank	1E **17**	
Hawthorn Dr. G78: Barr	6F **119**	
Hawthorn Dr. ML1: New S	4B **132**	
Hawthorn Dr. ML2: Wis	1A **166**	
Hawthorn Dr. ML5: Coat	6F **95**	

Hawthorn Dr. ML6: Air	4D **96**	
Hawthorn Gdns. G72: Flem	3E **127**	
Hawthorn Gdns. G76: Busby	3C **138**	
Hawthorn Gdns. ML4: Bell	3E **131**	
Hawthorn Gdns. ML9: Lark	3E **171**	
Hawthorn Gro. ML8: Law	5D **166**	
Hawthorn Hill ML3: Ham	2A **162**	
Hawthornhill Rd. G82: Dumb	2B **18**	
Hawthorn Pl. G64: Torr	4E **31**	
Hawthorn Quad. G22: Glas	4G **65**	
Hawthorn Rd. G67: Cumb	1F **39**	
Hawthorn Rd. G76: Busby	3C **138**	
Hawthorn Rd. PA8: Ersk	1A **60**	
Hawthorn St. G22: Glas	4G **65**	
Hawthorn St. G64: Torr	4E **31**	
Hawthorn St. G81: Clyd	3C **44**	
Hawthorn Ter. G71: View	6F **113**	
Hawthorn Ter. G75: E Kil	5D **156**	
Hawthorn Wlk. G72: Camb	2F **125**	
Hawthorn Way G66: Milt C	6C **10**	
Hawthorn Way G72: Camb	2G **125**	
Hawthorn Way G82: Dumb	3B **18**	
Hawthorn Way PA8: Ersk	1A **60**	
Hay Av. PA7: B'ton	4A **42**	
Hayburn Ct. G11: Glas	1G **85**	
	(off Hayburn St.)	
Hayburn Cres. G11: Glas	6G **63**	
Hayburn Ga. G11: Glas	1H **85**	
Hayburn La. G11: Glas	6G **63**	
Hayburn La. G12: Glas	6G **63**	
Hayburn Pl. G11: Glas	1H **85**	
	(off Hayburn St.)	
Hayburn St. G11: Glas	2H **85**	
Hay Cres. G72: Newt	6G **111**	
Hayfield Ct. G5: Glas	1H **107**	
Hayfield St. G5: Glas	1H **107**	
Hayhill Rd. G74: T'hall	4F **155**	
Hayle Gdns. G69: Mood	4D **54**	
Haylynn St. G14: Glas	1E **85**	
Haymarket St. G32: Glas	4G **89**	
Haystack Pl. G66: Lenz	3D **52**	
HAYSTON	5A **32**	
Hayston Ct. G66: Kirkin	5B **32**	
Hayston Cres. G22: Glas	4F **65**	
Hayston Golf Course	4A **32**	
Hayston Rd. G66: Kirkin	5A **32**	
Hayston Rd. G68: Cumb	1G **37**	
Hayston St. G22: Glas	4F **65**	
Hayward Av. ML8: Carl	5G **175**	
Hayward Ct. ML8: Carl	5G **175**	
Haywood St. G22: Glas	3F **65**	
Hazel Av. G44: Glas	3D **122**	
Hazel Av. G61: Bear	6G **27**	
Hazel Av. G66: Lenz	1D **52**	
Hazel Av. G82: Dumb	2B **18**	
Hazel Av. PA5: John	4G **99**	
Hazel Bank G66: Milt C	1B **32**	
Hazel Bank ML6: Plain	6F **75**	
	(off Arondale Rd.)	
Hazelbank ML1: Holy	2B **132**	
Hazelbank Wlk. ML6: Air	3F **95**	
Hazeldean Cres. ML2: Wis	4A **150**	
Hazel Dene G64: B'rig	6D **50**	
Hazeldene La. ML9: Lark	4E **171**	
	(off Dickson St.)	
Hazelden Gdns. G44: Glas	3C **122**	
Hazelden Pk. G44: Glas	3C **122**	
Hazelden Rd. G77: Newt M	4C **152**	
Hazelfield Gro. ML6: Chap	4E **117**	
Hazel Gdns. ML1: Moth	6G **147**	
Hazel Gro. G66: Lenz	1D **52**	
Hazel Gro. ML8: Law	5D **166**	
Hazelhead G74: E Kil	1B **158**	
Hazellea Dr. G46: Giff	3C **122**	
Hazel Pk. ML3: Ham	1A **162**	
Hazel Path ML1: Cle	6H **133**	
Hazel Rd. FK4: Bank	1E **17**	
Hazel Rd. G67: Cumb	2D **38**	
Hazel Ter. G71: View	6F **113**	

Hazelton ML1: Moth	4F **147**
Hazel Wood ML2: Wis	4B **150**
Hazelwood Av. G77: Newt M	5E **137**
Hazelwood Av. PA11: Bri W	4F **77**
Hazelwood Av. PA2: Pais	6C **100**
Hazelwood Dr. G72: Blan	1A **144**
Hazelwood Gdns. G73: Ruth	3E **125**
Hazelwood Gro. G69: Barg	5E **93**
Hazelwood La. PA11: Bri W	4F **77**
Hazelwood Rd. G41: Glas	1A **106**
Hazelwood Rd. PA11: Bri W	4F **77**
Hazlitt Gdns. G20: Glas	3E **65**
Hazlitt Pl. G20: Glas	3E **65**
Hazlitt St. G20: Glas	3F **65**
Headhouse Ct. G75: E Kil	3F **157**
Headhouse Grn. G75: E Kil	3G **157**
Headline Bldg., The G1: Glas	5F **7** (4H **87**)
(off Albion St.)	
Headsmuir Av. ML8: Carl	3B **174**
Heath Av. G64: B'rig	1D **66**
Heath Av. G66: Lenz	3C **52**
Heathcliffe Av. G72: Blan	6A **128**
Heathcot Av. G15: Glas	5G **45**
Heathcot Pl. G15: Glas	5F **45**
Heather Av. G61: Bear	5D **26**
Heather Av. G78: Barr	2C **118**
Heather Av. G81: Hard	6C **24**
Heather Av. ML1: Holy	2A **132**
Heatherbank Av. G69: G'csh	6A **70**
Heatherbank Dr. G69: G'csh	6A **70**
Heatherbank Gro. G69: G'csh	6A **70**
Heatherbank Rd. G69: G'csh	6A **70**
Heatherbank Wlk. ML6: Air	3F **95**
HEATHERBELL	6A **72**
Heatherbell Rd. ML5: Coat	2B **94**
Heatherbell Rd. ML5: Coat	2C **94**
Heatherbrae G64: B'rig	6A **50**
Heather Dr. G66: Lenz	3A **52**
Heather Gdns. G66: Lenz	3A **52**
Heather Gdns. G71: View	6G **113**
Heather Gro. G75: E Kil	4G **157**
(off The Murray Rd.)	
Heatherhall ML1: Cle	1H **149**
Heather Pl. G66: Lenz	2A **52**
Heather Pl. PA5: John	3G **99**
Heather Row ML8: Carl	1C **174**
Heather Vw. G66: Len	2G **9**
Heather Way ML1: New S	3A **132**
Heather Wynd G77: Newt M	2C **136**
Heatheryford Gdns. ML6: Plain	6G **75**
Heathery Knowe G75: E Kil	4G **157**
Heatheryknowe Rd. G69: Barg	4C **92**
(not continuous)	
Heathery Lea Av. ML5: Coat	2F **115**
Heathery Rd. ML2: Wis	6F **149**
Heathfield ML2: Wis	4G **165**
Heathfield Av. G69: Mood	5D **54**
Heathfield Dr. G62: Miln	2H **27**
Heathfield St. G33: Glas	3C **90**
Heath Rd. ML9: Lark	2D **170**
Heathside Rd. G46: Giff	4B **122**
Heathwood Dr. G46: T'bnk	4G **121**
Hecla Av. G15: Glas	4H **45**
Hecla Pl. G15: Glas	4H **45**
Hecla Sq. G15: Glas	5H **45**
Hector Rd. G41: Glas	5B **106**
Helena Pl. G76: Clar	1C **138**
Helena Ter. G81: Dun	1C **44**
Helensburgh Dr. G13: Glas	3D **62**
Helenslea G60: Bowl	6C **22**
Helenslea G72: Camb	3D **126**
Helenslea Pl. ML4: Bell	3B **130**
Helenslee Ct. G82: Dumb	4D **18**
Helenslee Cres. G82: Dumb	4D **18**
Helenslee Pl. G82: Dumb	5D **18**
Helenslee Rd. G82: Dumb	5D **18**
Helen St. G51: Glas	4G **85**
Helen St. G52: Glas	6F **85**
HELEN STREET INTERCHANGE	6F **85**

Helenvale Ct. G31: Glas	6F **89**
Helenvale St. G31: Glas	1E **109**
Helen Wynd ML9: Lark	3C **170**
Helmsdale Av. G72: Blan	4A **128**
Helmsdale Cl. G72: Blan	5B **144**
Helmsdale Ct. G72: Camb	2D **126**
Helmsdale Dr. PA2: Pais	3D **100**
Helve Pl. ML5: Coat	6E **95**
Hemlock St. G13: Glas	2F **63**
Hemmingen Ct. ML8: Carl	2C **174**
Henderland Dr. G61: Bear	5E **47**
Henderland Rd. G61: Bear	5E **47**
Henderson Av. G72: Camb	1D **126**
Henderson Ct. ML1: Moth	2F **147**
Henderson St. G20: Glas	6D **64**
Henderson St. G81: Clyd	1G **61**
Henderson St. ML5: Coat	5B **94**
Henderson St. ML6: Air	3B **96**
Henderson St. PA1: Pais	6H **81**
Henrietta St. G14: Glas	6C **62**
Henry Bell Grn. G75: E Kil	3H **157**
(off Muirhouse La.)	
Henry Quad. ML1: N'hill	2G **133**
Henry St. G78: Barr	4D **118**
Henry Wood Hall	3E **5** (3C **86**)
Hepburn Hill ML3: Ham	3F **161**
Hepburn Rd. G52: Hill E	4B **84**
Herald Av. G13: Glas	6D **46**
Herald Gro. ML1: Moth	5F **147**
Herald Way PA4: Renf	2E **83**
Herbertson Gro. G72: Blan	6A **128**
Herbertson St. G5: Glas	6F **87**
Herbertson St. G72: Blan	2C **144**
Herbert St. G20: Glas	6D **64**
Herbison Ct. ML9: Lark	1D **170**
Hercules Way PA4: Renf	2F **83**
Heriot Av. PA2: Pais	5C **100**
Heriot Cres. G64: B'rig	4C **50**
Heriot Rd. G66: Lenz	4C **52**
Heriot Way PA2: Pais	5D **100**
(off Heriot Av.)	
Heritage Ct. G77: Newt M	4E **137**
Heritage Vw. ML5: Coat	3B **94**
Heritage Way ML5: Coat	4B **94**
Herma St. G23: Glas	1C **64**
Hermes Way ML4: Moss	2H **131**
Hermiston Av. G32: Glas	5C **90**
Hermiston Gdns. G69: Chry	6A **54**
Hermiston Pl. G32: Glas	5C **90**
Hermiston Pl. ML1: Holy	2A **132**
(off Windsor Rd.)	
Hermiston Rd. G32: Glas	4B **90**
Hermitage Av. G13: Glas	2C **62**
Hermitage Cres. ML5: Coat	2D **114**
Herndon Ct. G77: Newt M	3G **137**
Heron Ct. G81: Hard	2D **44**
Heron Pl. PA5: John	6D **98**
Heron St. G40: Glas	1B **108**
Heron Vw. ML1: Moth	6H **147**
Heron Way PA4: Renf	2E **83**
Herries Rd. G41: Glas	4A **106**
Herriet St. G41: Glas	2D **106**
Herriot St. ML5: Coat	3A **94**
Herschell St. G13: Glas	3F **63**
Hertford Av. G12: Glas	3H **63**
Hewett Cres. PA6: C'lee	2C **78**
Hexham Gdns. G41: Glas	4B **106**
Heys St. G78: Barr	5E **119**
Hickman St. G42: Glas	4F **107**
Hickman Ter. G42: Glas	3G **107**
Hickory Cres. G71: View	4G **113**
Hickory St. G22: Glas	4A **66**
Hidden Gdns., The	2E **107**
High Avon St. ML9: Lark	1B **170**
HIGH BALMALLOCH	2G **13**
High Barholm PA10: Kilba	2A **98**
High Barrwood Rd. G65: Kils	3A **14**
High Beeches G76: Crmck	1A **140**
HIGH BLANTYRE	3A **144**

High Blantyre Rd. ML3: Ham	4D **144**
Highburgh Dr. G73: Ruth	2D **124**
Highburgh Rd. G12: Glas	6A **64**
HIGH BURNSIDE	3E **125**
High Burnside Av. ML5: Coat	6A **94**
High Calside PA2: Pais	2H **101**
High Cleughearn Rd. G75: E Kil	6D **168**
High Coats ML5: Coat	4D **94**
High Comn. Rd. G74: E Kil	4B **158**
High Comn. Rd. G75: E Kil	4B **158**
High Court	5G **87**
(Glasgow)	
Highcraig Av. PA5: John	4D **98**
High Craigends G65: Kils	3H **13**
High Craighall Rd. G4: Glas	1F **87**
Highcroft Av. G44: Glas	2H **123**
Highcross Av. ML5: Coat	1H **113**
HIGH CROSSHILL	1E **125**
Higherness Way ML5: Coat	2H **113**
Highfield Av. G66: Kirkin	4E **33**
Highfield Av. PA2: Pais	6H **101**
Highfield Ct. G66: Kirkin	4F **33**
Highfield Cres. G66: Kirkin	4E **33**
Highfield Cres. ML1: Moth	1A **148**
Highfield Cres. PA2: Pais	6H **101**
Highfield Dr. G12: Glas	3H **63**
Highfield Dr. G73: Ruth	4E **125**
Highfield Dr. G76: Clar	2B **138**
Highfield Gro. G66: Kirkin	4E **33**
Highfield Pl. G12: Glas	3H **63**
Highfield Pl. G74: E Kil	6H **141**
Highfield Rd. G66: Kirkin	4E **33**
Highfield Rd. ML9: Lark	2D **170**
High Flenders Rd. G76: Clar	3A **138**
HIGH GALLOWHILL	2B **52**
Highgrove Ct. PA4: Renf	6G **61**
Highgrove Rd. PA4: Renf	6G **61**
High Kirk Vw. PA5: John	3F **99**
HIGH KNIGHTSWOOD	1D **62**
Highland Av. G72: Blan	1A **144**
Highland La. G51: Glas	3A **86**
Highland Pk. G65: Kils	2G **13**
HIGHLAND PK.	1G **13**
Highland Pl. G65: Kils	1G **13**
Highland Rd. G62: Miln	3G **27**
High Mains Av. G82: Dumb	2C **20**
High Mair PA4: Renf	1E **83**
High Mdw. ML8: Carl	5G **175**
(not continuous)	
High Mill Rd. ML8: Carl	3E **175**
High Parksail PA8: Ersk	1G **59**
High Parks Cres. ML3: Ham	5H **161**
High Patrick St. ML3: Ham	1A **162**
High Pleasance ML9: Lark	2C **170**
High Rd. ML1: Moth	2F **147**
High Rd. PA2: Pais	2G **101**
High Row Cotts. G64: B'rig	2D **50**
Highstonehall Rd. ML3: Ham	4C **160**
High St. G1: Glas	6F **7** (4H **87**)
High St. G4: Glas	5G **7** (4H **87**)
High St. G66: Kirkin	4C **32**
High St. G73: Ruth	5C **108**
High St. G78: Neil	2D **134**
High St. G82: Dumb	4E **19**
High St. ML1: N'hill	3E **133**
High St. ML6: Air	3H **95**
High St. ML8: Carl	3D **174**
High St. PA1: Pais	1H **101**
High St. PA4: Renf	5F **61**
High St. PA5: John	2E **99**
High Street Station (Rail)	6G **7** (4H **87**)
High Whitehills Rd. G75: E Kil	6F **157**
High Wood Gdns. ML4: Bell	2A **130**
Hilary Dr. G69: Bail	6F **91**
Hilda Cres. G33: Glas	5G **67**
Hillary Av. G73: Ruth	1F **125**
Hill Av. G77: Newt M	5C **136**
Hillbrae St. G51: Glas	5D **84**
Hill Ct. ML2: Wis	6G **149**

Hill Cres. G76: Busby		3C **138**
Hillcrest G69: Chry		1B **70**
Hillcrest G76: Crmck		1H **139**
Hillcrest Av. G32: Carm		5B **110**
Hillcrest Av. G44: Glas		3C **122**
Hillcrest Av. G67: Cumb		5G **37**
Hillcrest Av. G81: Dun		6C **24**
Hillcrest Av. ML2: Wis		6E **149**
Hillcrest Av. ML5: Coat		5E **95**
Hillcrest Ct. G67: Cumb		4H **37**
Hillcrest Dr. G77: Newt M		4G **137**
Hillcrest Rd. G32: Carm		4C **110**
Hillcrest Rd. G61: Bear		3F **47**
Hillcrest Rd. G65: Queen		3C **12**
Hillcrest Rd. G71: Tann		6E **113**
Hillcrest St. G62: Miln		3G **27**
Hillcrest Ter. G71: Both		4F **129**
Hillcrest Vw. ML9: Lark		3D **170**
Hillcroft Ter. G64: B'rig		1B **66**
Hillend Cotts. G66: Lenz		1C **52**
Hillend Cres. G76: Clar		3A **138**
Hillend Cres. G81: Dun		1B **44**
Hillend Rd. G22: Glas		2E **65**
Hillend Rd. G73: Ruth		2D **124**
Hillend Rd. G76: Clar		3A **138**
Hillfield Brae G77: Newt M		1E **137**
Hillfield Dr. G77: Newt M		1D **136**
Hillfoot PA6: C'lee		3D **78**
Hillfoot Av. G61: Bear		2F **47**
Hillfoot Av. G73: Ruth		6C **108**
Hillfoot Av. G82: Dumb		1C **20**
Hillfoot Av. ML2: Wis		2B **150**
Hillfoot Ct. G61: Bear		2F **47**
Hillfoot Cres. ML2: Wis		2B **150**
Hillfoot Dr. G61: Bear		2F **47**
Hillfoot Dr. ML2: Wis		2B **150**
Hillfoot Dr. ML5: Coat		5H **93**
Hillfoot Gdns. G71: Tann		5C **112**
Hillfoot Gdns. ML2: Wis		2B **150**
Hillfoot Rd. ML6: Air		5A **96**
Hillfoot Station (Rail)		2G **47**
Hillfoot St. G31: Glas		4C **88**
Hillfoot Ter. ML8: Carl		4E **175**
Hill Gro. G69: Barg		5E **93**
HILLHEAD		6B **64**
HILLHEAD		4D **32**
Hillhead Av. FK4: Bank		1E **17**
Hillhead Av. G69: Mood		5D **54**
Hillhead Av. G73: Ruth		3D **124**
Hillhead Av. ML1: Carf		5A **132**
Hillhead Av. ML8: Carl		3E **175**
Hillhead Cres. ML1: Carf		5A **132**
Hillhead Cres. ML3: Ham		6C **144**
Hillhead Cres. PA3: Lin		1C **100**
Hillhead Dr. ML1: Carf		6A **132**
Hillhead Dr. ML6: Air		5A **96**
Hillhead Dr. PA3: Lin		1C **100**
Hillhead Pl. G73: Ruth		3D **124**
Hillhead Pl. PA3: Lin		1C **100**
Hillhead Rd. G21: Glas		2F **67**
Hillhead Rd. G66: Kirkin		4D **32**
Hillhead Station (Subway)		6B **64**
Hillhead St. G12: Glas		1B **86**
Hillhead St. G62: Miln		3G **27**
Hillhead Ter. ML3: Ham		6C **144**
HILLHOUSE		6D **144**
Hillhouse Bus. Cen. ML3: Ham		5E **145**
Hillhouse Cres. ML3: Ham		6D **144**
Hillhouse Ga. ML8: Carl		5G **175**
Hillhouse Pk. Ind. Est. ML3: Ham		6D **144**
Hillhouse Rd. G72: Blan		4A **144**
Hillhouse Rd. ML3: Ham		5C **144**
Hillhouse St. G21: Glas		5C **66**
Hillhouse Ter. ML3: Ham		6D **144**
HILLINGTON		6A **84**
Hillington East Station (Rail)		5B **84**
Hillington Gdns. G52: Glas		1C **104**
Hillington Ind. Est. G52: Hill E		4A **84**
		(not continuous)

HILLINGTON INDUSTRIAL ESTATE		3H **83**
HILLINGTON INTERCHANGE		2H **83**
Hillington Pk. G52: Hill E		3H **83**
Hillington Pk. Cir. G52: Glas		6C **84**
Hillington Quad. G52: Glas		6A **84**
Hillington Rd. G52: Hill E		2H **83**
		(not continuous)
Hillington Rd. Sth. G52: Glas		5A **84**
Hillington Ter. G52: Glas		6A **84**
Hillington West Station (Rail)		4H **83**
Hillkirk Pl. G21: Glas		5B **66**
Hillkirk St. G21: Glas		5B **66**
Hillkirk St. La. G21: Glas		5B **66**
		(off Hillkirk St.)
Hillman Cres. PA3: Pais		1C **100**
Hillman Rd. PA3: Pais		1C **100**
Hillneuk Av. G61: Bear		2F **47**
Hillneuk Dr. G61: Bear		2G **47**
Hillpark Av. PA2: Pais		4H **101**
Hillpark Dr. G43: Glas		1A **122**
Hill Pl. ML1: Carf		5C **132**
Hill Pl. ML4: Bell		4B **130**
Hillrigg ML6: Grng		1D **74**
Hillrigg Av. ML6: Air		3C **96**
Hill Rd. G65: Kils		1H **13**
Hill Rd. G67: Cumb		3G **37**
Hillsborough La. G12: Glas		6C **64**
Hillsborough Rd. G69: Bail		6F **91**
Hillside G65: Croy		6B **14**
HILLSIDE		5B **118**
Hillside PA6: C'lee		3E **79**
Hillside Av. G61: Bear		2F **47**
Hillside Av. G76: Clar		2B **138**
Hillside Cotts. ML5: Glenb		3A **72**
Hillside Ct. G46: T'bnk		4F **121**
Hillside Cres. G78: Neil		2D **134**
Hillside Cres. ML1: N'hill		3D **132**
Hillside Cres. ML3: Ham		1H **161**
Hillside Cres. ML5: Coat		1B **114**
Hillside Dr. G61: Bear		2G **47**
Hillside Dr. G64: B'rig		5C **50**
Hillside Dr. G78: Barr		4C **118**
Hillside Gdns. La. G11: Glas		6H **63**
		(off Nth. Gardner St.)
Hillside Gro. G78: Barr		5C **118**
Hillside La. ML3: Ham		1G **161**
Hillside Pk. G81: Hard		1D **44**
Hillside Pl. ML1: N'hill		4D **132**
Hillside Quad. G43: Glas		2H **121**
Hillside Rd. G43: Glas		2H **121**
Hillside Rd. G78: Barr		5B **118**
Hillside Rd. G78: Neil		2D **134**
Hillside Rd. PA2: Pais		3C **102**
Hillside Ter. G60: Old K		2G **43**
Hillside Ter. G66: Milt C		6B **10**
Hillside Ter. ML3: Ham		1G **161**
Hill St. G3: Glas		2H **5** (2E **87**)
Hill St. G82: Dumb		4D **18**
Hill St. ML2: Wis		1G **165**
Hill St. ML3: Ham		6D **144**
Hill St. ML6: Chap		3D **116**
Hill St. ML9: Lark		3C **170**
Hillsview G69: Chry		1H **69**
Hillswick Cres. G22: Glas		1F **65**
Hill Ter. ML1: Carf		5C **132**
Hilltop Av. ML4: Bell		6C **114**
Hilltop Rd. G69: Mood		5D **54**
Hilltree Ct. G46: Giff		3A **122**
Hill Vw. G66: Kirkin		6F **33**
Hill Vw. G75: E Kil		3G **157**
Hillview G82: Mil		4F **21**
Hillview Av. G65: Kils		4H **13**
Hillview Av. G66: Len		3G **9**
Hillview Cotts. G65: Twe		1D **34**
Hillview Ct. G81: Clyd		4B **44**
Hillview Cres. G71: Tann		5C **112**
Hillview Cres. ML4: Bell		5C **114**
Hillview Cres. ML9: Lark		3D **170**
Hillview Dr. G72: Blan		5A **128**

Hillview Dr. G76: Clar		2B **138**
Hillview Gdns. G64: B'rig		1F **67**
Hillview Gdns. G81: Clyd		4B **44**
Hillview Pl. G76: Clar		2C **138**
Hillview Pl. G77: Newt M		5D **136**
Hillview Rd. PA11: Bri W		4G **77**
Hillview Rd. PA5: Eld		3H **99**
Hillview St. G32: Glas		6H **89**
Hillview Ter. G60: Old K		1F **43**
Hiltonbank St. ML3: Ham		5F **145**
Hilton Ct. G64: B'rig		4C **50**
Hilton Ct. ML3: Ham		1A **162**
		(off Silvertonhill Av.)
Hilton Gdns. G13: Glas		1F **63**
Hilton Gdns. La. G13: Glas		2F **63**
Hilton Pk. G64: B'rig		3B **50**
Hilton Rd. G62: Miln		3E **27**
Hilton Rd. G64: B'rig		4B **50**
Hilton Ter. G13: Glas		2E **63**
Hilton Ter. G64: B'rig		3B **50**
Hilton Ter. G72: Camb		4G **125**
Hilton Vw. ML4: Bell		5C **114**
Hindsland Rd. ML9: Lark		4D **170**
Hinshaw St. G20: Glas		6E **65**
Hinshelwood Dr. G51: Glas		5G **85**
Hinshelwood Pl. G51: Glas		6H **85**
Hirsel Pl. G71: Both		5F **129**
HMP Barlinnie		2H **89**
HMP Low Moss		2F **51**
Hobart Cres. G81: Clyd		2H **43**
Hobart Quad. ML2: Wis		6C **150**
Hobart Rd. G75: E Kil		4E **157**
Hobart St. G22: Glas		5F **65**
Hobden St. G21: Glas		6C **66**
Hoddam Av. G45: Glas		4B **124**
Hoddam Ter. G45: Glas		4C **124**
Hoey Dr. ML2: Over		4A **166**
Hogan Ct. G81: Dun		1B **44**
Hogan Way ML1: Cle		6E **133**
Hogarth Av. G32: Glas		4F **89**
Hogarth Cres. G32: Glas		4F **89**
Hogarth Dr. G32: Glas		4F **89**
Hogarth Gdns. G32: Glas		4F **89**
HOGGANFIELD		1B **90**
Hogganfield Ct. G33: Glas		1F **89**
Hogganfield Pk. Local Nature Reserve		6A **68**
Hogganfield St. G33: Glas		1F **89**
Hogg Av. PA5: John		4E **99**
Hogg Rd. ML6: Chap		1D **116**
Hogg St. ML6: Air		4A **96**
Holeburn La. G43: Glas		1A **122**
Holeburn Rd. G43: Glas		1A **122**
HOLEHILLS		2B **96**
Holehills Dr. ML6: Air		1B **96**
Holehills Pl. ML6: Air		1B **96**
HOLEHOUSE		2C **134**
Holehouse Brae G78: Neil		2C **134**
Holehouse Dr. G13: Glas		3A **62**
Holehouse Rd. G76: Eag		6C **154**
Holehouse Ter. G78: Neil		2C **134**
Hollandbush Gro. ML3: Ham		3H **161**
Hollandhurst Rd. ML5: Coat		2B **94**
Holland St. G2: Glas		4H **5** (3E **87**)
Hollinwell Rd. G23: Glas		1B **64**
Hollowfield Cres. G69: G'csh		2D **70**
Hollowglen Rd. G32: Glas		5B **90**
Hollows, The G46: Giff		6H **121**
		(off Ayr Rd.)
Hollows Av. PA2: Pais		6D **100**
Hollows Cres. PA2: Pais		6D **100**
Holly Av. G66: Milt C		6B **10**
Hollybank Pl. G72: Camb		3B **126**
Hollybank St. G21: Glas		2C **88**
Hollybrook Pl. G42: Glas		3F **107**
		(off Hollybrook St.)
Hollybrook St. G42: Glas		3F **107**
Hollybush Av. PA2: Pais		6F **101**
Hollybush Rd. G52: Glas		6H **83**
Holly Dr. G21: Glas		6C **66**

Holly Dr. – Humbie Rd.

Holly Dr. G82: Dumb 2B **18**
Holly Gro. FK4: Bank 1F **17**
Holly Gro. ML4: Moss 2H **131**
Hollyhill Gro. G69: Barg 5E **93**
Hollymount G61: Bear 5F **47**
Holly Pl. PA5: John 5G **99**
Holly St. G81: Clyd 3C **44**
Holly St. ML6: Air 4C **96**
Hollytree Gdns. G66: Len 3E **9**
Hollywood Bowl **1F 113**
(Glasgow)
Hollywood Bowl **5D 86**
(Glasgow, Springfield Quay)
Holm Av. G71: Udd 6C **112**
Holm Av. PA2: Pais 3B **102**
Holmbank Av. G41: Glas 6B **106**
Holmbrae Av. G71: Tann 5D **112**
Holmbrae Rd. G71: Tann 6D **112**
Holmbyre Ct. G45: Glas 6F **123**
Holmbyre Ga. G45: Glas 5G **123**
Holmbyre Rd. G45: Glas 6F **123**
Holmbyre Ter. G45: Glas 5G **123**
Holmes Av. PA4: Renf 2E **83**
Holmes Quad. ML4: Bell 4C **130**
Holmfauldhead Dr. G51: Glas 3E **85**
Holmfauldhead Pl. G51: Glas 3E **85**
Holmfauld Rd. G51: Glas 3E **85**
Holmfield G66: Kirkin 6E **33**
Holm Gdns. ML4: Bell 3E **131**
Holmhead Cres. G44: Glas 1E **123**
Holmhead Pl. G44: Glas 1E **123**
Holmhead Rd. G44: Glas 2E **123**
Holmhill Av. G72: Camb 3A **126**
Holmhills Dr. G72: Camb 4H **125**
Holmhills Gdns. G72: Camb 3H **125**
Holmhills Gro. G72: Camb 3H **125**
Holmhills Pl. G72: Camb 3H **125**
Holmhills Rd. G72: Camb 3H **125**
Holmhills Ter. G72: Camb 3H **125**
Holm La. G74: E Kil 2G **157**
Holmlea Ct. G42: Glas 6F **107**
Holmlea Rd. G44: Glas 6E **107**
Holmpark PA7: B'ton 4H **41**
HOLMPARK **4H 41**
Holm Pl. ML9: Lark 3A **170**
Holm Pl. PA3: Lin 4H **79**
Holms Cres. PA8: Ersk 5D **42**
Holms Pl. G69: G'csh 2C **70**
Holm St. G2: Glas 6A **6** (4E **87**)
Holm St. ML1: New S 4A **132**
Holm St. ML8: Carl 3C **174**
Holmswood Av. G72: Blan 1B **144**
Holmwood Av. G71: Udd 6D **112**
Holmwood Gdns. G71: Udd 6D **112**
Holmwood House **3F 123**
Holyknowe Cres. G66: Len 3G **9**
Holyknowe Rd. G66: Len 4G **9**
Holyrood Cres. G20: Glas 1D **86**
Holyrood Quad. G20: Glas 1D **86**
(off Napiershall St.)
Holyrood Sports Cen. **4G 107**
Holyrood St. ML3: Ham 4E **145**
HOLYTOWN **2A 132**
Holytown Crematorium 2C **132**
Holytown Rd. ML1: Holy 2H **131**
Holytown Rd. ML4: Moss 2G **131**
Holytown Station (Rail) **4A 132**
Holywell St. G31: Glas 6D **88**
Homeblair Ho. G46: Giff 2A **122**
Home Farm Ct. ML5: Coat 4H **93**
Home Farm Steading PA7: B'ton 2A **42**
Homer Pl. ML4: Moss 2G **131**
Homeston Av. G71: Both 4E **129**
Honeybank Cres. ML8: Carl 2D **174**
Honeybee Av. G72: Newt 6G **111**
Honeybog Rd. G52: Glas 5G **83**
Honeydew Dr. G72: Newt 6G **111**
Honeysuckle Ct. ML3: Fern 3E **163**
Honeysuckle Cres. G72: Newt 6G **111**
Honeysuckle Dr. G68: Cumb 1F **57**
Honeysuckle Dr. G72: Newt 6F **111**
Honeywell Av. G33: Step 5G **69**
Honeywell Ct. G33: Step 5F **69**
Honeywell Cres. ML6: Chap 4E **117**
Honeywell Dr. G33: Step 5F **69**
Honeywell Gro. G33: Step 5G **69**
Honeywell Pl. G33: Step 5G **69**
Hood St. G81: Clyd 5E **45**
Hooper Pl. ML4: Bell 1D **130**
Hoover Dr. G72: Camb 6G **109**
Hope Av. PA11: Quarr V 1A **76**
Hope Cres. ML9: Lark 2D **170**
Hopefield Av. G12: Glas 4A **64**
Hopefield Gdns. ML2: Wis 4G **165**
Hopehill Gdns. G20: Glas 6E **65**
Hopehill Rd. G20: Glas 6E **65**
Hopeman PA8: Ersk 4E **43**
Hopeman Av. G46: T'bnk 3E **121**
Hopeman Dr. G46: T'bnk 3E **121**
Hopeman Path G46: T'bnk 2E **121**
Hopeman Rd. G46: T'bnk 3E **121**
Hopeman St. G46: T'bnk 3E **121**
Hopepark Dr. G68: Cumb 3A **36**
Hope St. G2: Glas 6B **6** (4F **87**)
Hope St. ML1: Moth 2G **147**
Hope St. ML2: Newm 5E **151**
Hope St. ML3: Ham 6A **146**
Hope St. ML4: Moss 2E **131**
Hope St. ML8: Carl 3E **175**
Hopetoun Pl. G23: Glas 6C **48**
Hopetoun Ter. G21: Glas 6C **66**
Hopkins Brae G66: Kirkin 4D **32**
Horatius St. ML1: Moth 6D **130**
Hornal Rd. G71: Udd 3D **128**
Hornbeam Dr. G81: Clyd 3C **44**
Hornbeam Rd. G67: Cumb 6E **17**
Hornbeam Rd. G71: View 5F **113**
Horndean Ct. G64: B'rig 3C **50**
Horne St. G22: Glas 4A **66**
Hornock Cotts. ML5: Coat 3B **94**
Hornock Rd. ML5: Coat 2B **94**
Hornshill Dr. ML1: Cle 5H **133**
Hornshill Farm Rd. G33: Step 3E **69**
HORNSHILL INTERCHANGE 1E **69**
Hornshill St. G21: Glas 5C **66**
Horsbrugh Av. G65: Kils 2H **13**
Horselethill Rd. G12: Glas 5A **64**
Horseshoe La. G61: Bear 3F **47**
Horseshoe Rd. G61: Bear 2E **47**
Horsewood Rd. PA11: Bri W 4E **77**
Horslet St. ML5: Coat 1G **113**
Horsley Brae ML2: Over 2A **172**
Hospital Rd. ML2: Wis 3H **165**
(not continuous)
Hospital St. G5: Glas 1F **107**
Hospital St. ML5: Coat 1C **114**
Hotspur St. G20: Glas 4C **64**
Houldsworth Ct. ML2: Wis 1A **166**
Houldsworth La. G3: Glas 4E **5** (3C **86**)
(off Elliot St.)
Houldsworth St. G3: Glas 4E **5** (3C **86**)
House for an Art Lover **1G 105**
Househillmuir Cres. G53: Glas 1C **120**
Househillmuir La. G53: Glas 6C **104**
(off Househillmuir Rd.)
Househillmuir Pl. G53: Glas 6C **104**
Househillmuir Rd. G53: Glas 2A **120**
HOUSEHILLWOOD **6B 104**
Househillwood Cres. G53: Glas 6B **104**
Househillwood Rd. G53: Glas 1A **120**
Housel Av. G13: Glas 2B **62**
HOUSTON **1A 78**
Houston Ct. PA4: Renf 5F **61**
(off Fulbar St.)
Houstonfield Quad. PA6: Hous 1A **78**
Houstonfield Rd. PA6: Hous 1A **78**
Houston Pl. G5: Glas 5D **86**
Houston Pl. PA5: Eld 3A **100**
Houston Rd. PA11: Bri W 3F **77**
Houston Rd. PA3: Lin 6B **58**
Houston Rd. PA4: Inch 5D **58**
Houston Rd. PA6: C'lee 1B **78**
(not continuous)
Houston Rd. PA6: Hous 1B **78**
(not continuous)
Houston Rd. PA7: B'ton 5C **40**
Houston St. G5: Glas 6D **86**
Houston St. ML2: Wis 1B **166**
Houston St. ML3: Ham 2H **161**
Houston St. PA4: Renf 5F **61**
Houston Ter. G74: E Kil 1F **157**
Houstoun Ct. PA5: John 2F **99**
(off William St.)
Houstoun Sq. PA5: John 2F **99**
Howard Av. G74: E Kil 4A **142**
Howard Ct. G74: E Kil 4A **142**
Howard St. G1: Glas 6C **6** (5F **87**)
Howard St. ML9: Lark 4E **171**
Howard St. PA1: Pais 6C **82**
Howatshaws Rd. G82: Dumb 1H **19**
Howat St. G51: Glas 3G **85**
Howcraigs Ct. G81: Clyd 2F **61**
(off Clydeholm Ter.)
Howden Av. ML1: N'hse 5D **116**
Howden Dr. PA3: Lin 6G **79**
Howden Pl. ML1: Holy 2A **132**
Howe Gdns. G71: Tann 6E **113**
Howe Rd. G65: Kils 4H **13**
Howes St. ML5: Coat 1D **114**
Howe St. PA1: Pais 1D **100**
Howford Rd. G52: Glas 1B **104**
Howgate Av. G15: Glas 4H **45**
Howgate Rd. ML3: Ham 3F **161**
Howie Bldgs. G76: Clar 2C **138**
Howieshill Av. G72: Camb 2B **126**
Howieshill Rd. G72: Camb 3B **126**
Howie St. ML9: Lark 4D **170**
Howletnest Rd. ML6: Air 5C **96**
Howlet Pl. ML3: Ham 2A **162**
Howson Lea ML1: Moth 5B **148**
Howson Vw. ML1: Moth 2D **146**
Howth Dr. G13: Glas 1F **63**
Howth Ter. G13: Glas 1F **63**
Howwood Rd. PA10: How 6B **98**
HOWWOOD ROAD **4E 99**
Hoy Gdns. ML1: Carf 6C **132**
Hoylake Pk. G71: Both 5D **128**
Hoylake Pl. G23: Glas 6C **48**
Hozier Cres. G71: Tann 5D **112**
Hozier Loan ML9: Lark 1D **170**
(off Muirshot Rd.)
Hozier Pl. G71: Both 4F **129**
Hozier St. ML5: Coat 6C **94**
Hozier St. ML8: Carl 3D **174**
Hudson Ter. G75: E Kil 3D **156**
Hudson Way G75: E Kil 3E **157**
Hughenden Ct. G12: Glas 5H **63**
(off Hughenden Rd.)
Hughenden Dr. G12: Glas 5H **63**
Hughenden Gdns. G12: Glas 5G **63**
Hughenden La. G12: Glas 5H **63**
Hughenden Rd. G12: Glas 5H **63**
Hughenden Ter. G12: Glas 5H **63**
Hugh Fraser Ct. G77: Newt M 4D **136**
Hugh Murray Gro. G72: Camb 2C **126**
Hugo St. G20: Glas 4D **64**
Humbie Ct. G77: Newt M 1E **153**
Humbie Ga. G77: Newt M 1E **153**
Humbie Gro. G77: Newt M 6E **137**
Humbie Lawns G77: Newt M 1E **153**
Humbie Rd. G76: Eag 2F **153**
(not continuous)
Humbie Rd. G76: Wfoot 2F **153**
(not continuous)
Humbie Rd. G77: Eag 1E **153**
Humbie Rd. G77: Newt M 1E **153**
Humbie Rd. G77: Wfoot 1E **153**

A–Z Glasgow 233

I

J

John Ewing Gdns. – Kelvin Dr.

John Ewing Gdns. ML9: Lark ... 1C **170**
John Hannah Av. PA2: Pais ... 3E **103**
John Hendry Rd. G71: Udd ... 3E **129**
John Jarvie Sq. G65: Kils ... 2H **13**
John Knox La. ML3: Ham ... 5B **144**
John Knox St. G4: Glas ... 5H **7** (4A **88**)
John Knox St. G81: Clyd ... 1E **61**
John Lang St. PA5: John ... 2G **99**
John McEwan Way G64: Torr ... 4D **30**
John Marshall Dr. G64: B'rig ... 1A **66**
John Muir Way ML1: Moth ... 1F **147**
John Mulgrew Normandy Golf Cen. ... **5D 60**
John Murray Ct. ML1: Moth ... 6G **147**
John Neilson Av. PA1: Pais ... 1E **101**
John Ogilvie Cres. ML3: Ham ... 5D **144**
John Pl. ML9: Lark ... 6D **170**
Johnsburn Dr. G53: Glas ... 1B **120**
Johnsburn Rd. G53: Glas ... 1B **120**
Johnshaven PA8: Ersk ... 5E **43**
Johnshaven St. G43: Glas ... 6A **106**
John Smith Ct. ML3: Ham ... 3H **161**
... *(off Hollandbush Gro.)*
John Smith Ct. ML6: Air ... 3H **95**
John Smith Gdns. ML5: Coat ... 6F **95**
John Smith Ga. G78: Barr ... 3E **119**
John Smith Swimming Pool ... **4H 95**
Johnson Dr. G72: Camb ... 2A **126**
Johnston Av. G65: Kils ... 4H **13**
Johnston Av. G81: Clyd ... 1F **61**
JOHNSTONE ... **2G 99**
Johnstone Av. G52: Hill E ... 3B **84**
Johnstone Castle ... **4G 99**
... *(off Tower Pl.)*
JOHNSTONE CASTLE ... **4G 99**
Johnstone Community Sports Hub ... **5D 98**
Johnstone Cres. G71: View ... 6G **113**
Johnstone Dr. G73: Ruth ... 6C **108**
Johnstone La. ML8: Carl ... 4F **175**
... *(off Ramage Rd.)*
Johnstone Rd. ML3: Ham ... 1A **162**
Johnstone Rd. PA11: Bri W ... 4H **77**
Johnstone Station (Rail) ... **3G 99**
Johnstone St. ML4: Moss ... 2E **131**
Johnstone Swimming Pool ... **2F 99**
Johnstone Ter. G65: Twe ... 2D **34**
Johnston Rd. G69: G'csh ... 3E **71**
Johnston St. ML6: Air ... 3B **96**
Johnston St. PA1: Pais ... 1A **102**
John St. G1: Glas ... 5E **7** (4G **87**)
John St. G66: Kirkin ... 4D **32**
John St. G72: Blan ... 2C **144**
John St. G78: Barr ... 4D **118**
John St. ML2: Wis ... 5C **148**
John St. ML3: Ham ... 6A **146**
John St. ML4: Bell ... 2C **130**
John St. ML8: Carl ... 4D **174**
John St. ML9: Lark ... 3C **170**
John Wilson Dr. G65: Kils ... 2F **13**
John Wright Sports Cen. ... **1A 158**
Jones Wynd ML1: Cle ... 6E **133**
Jonquil Way ML8: Carl ... 5D **174**
Jonquin La. ML6: Air ... 5A **96**
Joppa St. G33: Glas ... 4G **89**
JORDANHILL ... **4E 63**
Jordanhill Cres. G13: Glas ... 4D **62**
Jordanhill Dr. G13: Glas ... 4C **62**
Jordanhill La. G13: Glas ... 4E **63**
Jordanhill Station (Rail) ... **5F 63**
Jordan Pl. ML1: Cle ... 4H **133**
Jordan St. G14: Glas ... 1D **84**
Jordanvale Av. G14: Glas ... 1D **84**
Jowitt Av. G81: Clyd ... 6F **45**
Jubilee Bank G66: Lenz ... 4C **52**
Jubilee Ct. G52: Hill E ... 4H **83**
Jubilee Ct. ML9: Lark ... 1C **170**
Jubilee Gdns. G61: Bear ... 3F **47**
Jubilee Ter. PA5: John ... 3D **98**
Jubilee Way ML4: Bell ... 1D **130**
Julian Av. G12: Glas ... 5A **64**
Julian Ct. G12: Glas ... 5A **64**
... *(off Julian Av.)*
Julian La. G12: Glas ... 5A **64**
Junction 29 PA1: Lin ... 1B **100**
Juniper Av. G75: E Kil ... 5F **157**
Juniper Av. PA11: Quarr V ... 2A **76**
Juniper Ct. G66: Lenz ... 2B **52**
Juniper Dr. G66: Milt C ... 1B **32**
Juniper Dr. ML3: Ham ... 4D **160**
Juniper Gro. ML3: Ham ... 1B **162**
Juniper Pl. G32: Glas ... 1E **111**
Juniper Pl. G71: View ... 5H **113**
Juniper Pl. PA5: John ... 5G **99**
Juniper Rd. G71: View ... 6H **113**
Juniper Ter. G32: Glas ... 1E **111**
Juniper Wynd ML1: Holy ... 2B **132**
... *(off Dornoch Rd.)*
Juno St. ML1: Moth ... 6F **131**
Jupiter St. ML1: Moth ... 6F **131**
Jura G74: E Kil ... 4B **158**
Jura Av. PA4: Renf ... 2F **83**
Jura Ct. G52: Glas ... 6E **85**
Jura Dr. G60: Old K ... 2G **43**
Jura Dr. G66: Kirkin ... 5G **33**
Jura Dr. G72: Blan ... 4A **128**
Jura Dr. G77: Newt M ... 3B **136**
Jura Gdns. G60: Old K ... 2G **43**
Jura Gdns. ML3: Ham ... 1E **161**
Jura Gdns. ML8: Carl ... 5E **175**
Jura Gdns. ML9: Lark ... 2E **171**
Jura Pl. G60: Old K ... 2G **43**
Jura Quad. ML2: Wis ... 2E **165**
Jura Rd. G60: Old K ... 2G **43**
Jura Rd. PA2: Pais ... 6H **101**
Jura St. G52: Glas ... 6F **85**
Jura Ter. G72: Camb ... 4G **125**
Jura Wynd ML5: Glenb ... 3G **71**
Justice of the Peace Court ... **5E 95**
... *(Coatbridge)*
Justice of the Peace Court ... **4A 38**
... *(Cumbernauld)*
Justice of the Peace Court ... **4F 19**
... *(Dumbarton)*
Justice of the Peace Court ... **5H 87**
... *(Glasgow)*
Justice of the Peace Court ... **6A 146**
... *(Hamilton)*
Justice of the Peace Court ... **6A 82**
... *(Paisley)*

K

Kaim Dr. G53: Glas ... 1C **120**
Kames Cl. G69: G'csh ... 4D **70**
Karadale Gdns. ML9: Lark ... 3C **170**
Karol Path G4: Glas ... 1E **87**
Katewell Av. G15: Glas ... 3G **45**
Katewell Pl. G15: Glas ... 3G **45**
Katherine St. ML6: Air ... 3E **97**
Katrine Av. G64: B'rig ... 6D **50**
Katrine Av. ML4: Bell ... 1H **129**
Katrine Ct. G20: Glas ... 1E **87**
... *(off Cedar St.)*
Katrine Cres. ML6: Air ... 2H **95**
Katrine Dr. G77: Newt M ... 5H **137**
Katrine Dr. PA2: Pais ... 3D **100**
Katrine Pl. G72: Camb ... 1A **126**
Katrine Pl. ML5: Coat ... 1H **93**
Katrine Way G71: Both ... 4E **129**
Katrine Wynd ML1: Holy ... 2A **132**
... *(off Glencoe Dr.)*
Katriona Path ML9: Lark ... 4E **171**
... *(off Stuart Dr.)*
Kay Gdns. ML1: Moth ... 3D **146**
Kaystone Rd. G15: Glas ... 6A **46**
Kay St. G21: Glas ... 5B **66**
Keal Av. G15: Glas ... 1A **62**
Keal Cres. G15: Glas ... 1A **62**
Keal Dr. G15: Glas ... 1A **62**
Keal Pl. G15: Glas ... 1A **62**
Keane Path ML1: Moth ... 6B **148**
... *(off Shields Dr.)*
Kearn Av. G15: Glas ... 6B **46**
Kearn Gdns. G15: Glas ... 6A **46**
Kearn Pl. G15: Glas ... 6B **46**
Keats Pk. G71: Both ... 4F **129**
Kebbuckston Pl. PA1: Pais ... 6D **80**
Keen Gro. ML1: Moth ... 6C **148**
Keil Cres. G82: Dumb ... 4D **18**
Keil Gdns. G82: Dumb ... 4D **18**
Keir Cres. ML2: Wis ... 5H **149**
Keir Dr. G64: B'rig ... 5B **50**
Keir Hardie Av. ML1: Holy ... 2B **132**
Keir Hardie Ct. G64: B'rig ... 6C **50**
Keir Hardie Dr. G65: Kils ... 4H **13**
Keir Hardie Dr. ML4: Bell ... 3B **130**
Keir Hardie Pl. ML4: Bell ... 3B **130**
Keir Hardie Rd. ML9: Lark ... 4D **170**
Keir Hardie Sports Cen. ... **1A 132**
Keir St. G41: Glas ... 2D **106**
Keir's Wlk. G72: Camb ... 1A **126**
Keith Av. G46: Giff ... 4B **122**
Keith Ct. G11: Glas ... 2A **86**
Keith Quad. ML2: Wis ... 3H **149**
Keith St. G11: Glas ... 1A **86**
Keith St. ML3: Ham ... 5B **146**
Keith St. ML4: Bell ... 1C **130**
Kelbourne Cres. ML4: Bell ... 2B **130**
Kelbourne St. G20: Glas ... 5C **64**
Kelburne Ct. PA1: Pais ... 6C **82**
Kelburne Dr. PA1: Pais ... 6D **82**
Kelburne Gdns. G69: Bail ... 2G **111**
Kelburne Gdns. PA1: Pais ... 6C **82**
Kelburne Oval PA1: Pais ... 6C **82**
Kelburn Gro. ML6: Air ... 5G **95**
Kelburn St. G78: Barr ... 6C **118**
Kelhead Av. G52: Glas ... 6H **83**
... (not continuous)
Kelhead Dr. G52: Glas ... 6H **83**
Kelhead Path G52: Glas ... 6H **83**
Kelhead Pl. G52: Glas ... 6H **83**
Kellas St. G51: Glas ... 4G **85**
Kellie Gro. G74: E Kil ... 6F **141**
Kells Pl. G15: Glas ... 3G **45**
Kelly's La. ML8: Carl ... 4F **175**
... *(off Kelso Dr.)*
Kelso Av. G73: Ruth ... 6D **108**
Kelso Av. PA11: Bri W ... 4F **77**
Kelso Av. PA2: Pais ... 4E **101**
Kelso Cres. ML2: Wis ... 3H **149**
Kelso Dr. G74: E Kil ... 6A **142**
Kelso Dr. ML8: Carl ... 4F **175**
Kelso Gdns. G69: Mood ... 4D **54**
Kelso Pl. G14: Glas ... 3G **61**
Kelso Quad. ML5: Coat ... 3B **94**
Kelso St. G13: Glas ... 2H **61**
Kelso St. G14: Glas ... 3G **61**
Kelton St. G32: Glas ... 1B **110**
KELVIN ... **6A 158**
Kelvin Av. G52: Hill E ... 2H **83**
Kelvinbridge Park & Ride ... **1C 86**
KELVINBRIDGE RDBT. ... 5D **30**
Kelvinbridge Station (Subway) ... **1C 86**
Kelvin Ct. G12: Glas ... 4G **63**
Kelvin Ct. G66: Kirkin ... 4C **32**
Kelvin Ct. G75: E Kil ... 4A **158**
Kelvin Cres. G61: Bear ... 5F **47**
Kelvin Cres. G75: E Kil ... 4A **158**
KELVINDALE ... **4H 63**
Kelvindale G64: Torr ... 4E **31**
Kelvindale Bldgs. G12: Glas ... 4A **64**
Kelvindale Ct. G12: Glas ... 3A **64**
Kelvindale Gdns. G20: Glas ... 3A **64**
Kelvindale Pl. G20: Glas ... 3B **64**
Kelvindale Rd. G12: Glas ... 4H **63**
Kelvindale Rd. G20: Glas ... 4A **64**
Kelvindale Station (Rail) ... **2H 63**
Kelvin Dr. G20: Glas ... 5B **64**

236 A–Z Glasgow

Kelvin Dr. – Kilbeg Ter.

Kelvin Dr. G64: B'rig 5C **50**
Kelvin Dr. G66: Kirkin 5A **32**
Kelvin Dr. G69: Mood 5C **54**
Kelvin Dr. G75: E Kil 4H **157**
Kelvin Dr. G78: Barr 6F **119**
Kelvin Dr. ML6: Air 2B **96**
Kelvin Gdns. G65: Kils 4H **13**
Kelvin Gdns. ML3: Ham 5C **144**
KELVINGROVE 1C 4 (2B 86)
Kelvingrove Art Gallery & Mus. 1C **4** (2B **86**)
Kelvingrove Lawn Bowls Cen. 2C **4** (2B **86**)
Kelvingrove Pk. 1D **4** (2C **86**)
Kelvingrove St. G3: Glas 3D **4** (3C **86**)
Kelvin Hall 1A **4** (2B **86**)
Kelvinhall Station (Subway) 1A 86
KELVINHAUGH 3B 4 (3B 86)
Kelvinhaugh Ga. G3: Glas 3B **4** (3B **86**)
Kelvinhaugh Pl. G3: Glas 3C **4** (3B **86**)
Kelvinhaugh St. G3: Glas 3A **4** (3A **86**)
KELVINHEAD 1H 15
Kelvinhead Rd. G65: Bant 1G **15**
Kelvin Pk. Sth. G75: E Kil 1G **169**
Kelvin Pl. G75: E Kil 4A **158**
Kelvin Rd. G62: Miln 2E **27**
Kelvin Rd. G67: Cumb 5A **38**
Kelvin Rd. G71: Tann 6C **112**
Kelvin Rd. G75: E Kil 4H **157**
Kelvin Rd. ML4: Bell 6D **114**
Kelvin Rd. Nth. G67: Cumb 5A **38**
KELVINSIDE 4G 63
Kelvinside Av. G20: Glas 5C **64**
Kelvinside Dr. G20: Glas 5D **64**
Kelvinside Gdns. G20: Glas 5C **64**
Kelvinside Gdns. E. G20: Glas 6D **64**
Kelvinside Gdns. La. G20: Glas 5C **64**
Kelvinside Gro. G20: Glas 5C **64**
Kelvinside Ter. Sth. G20: Glas 6C **64**
Kelvinside Ter. W. G20: Glas 6C **64**
Kelvin Sth. Bus. Pk. G75: E Kil 1F **169**
Kelvin St. ML5: Coat 6E **95**
Kelvin Ter. G65: Twe 3D **34**
Kelvinvale G66: Kirkin 4D **32**
Kelvin Vw. G64: Torr 5E **31**
Kelvin Vw. G65: Twe 3D **34**
Kelvinview Av. FK4: Bank 1E **17**
Kelvin Way G12: Glas 1C **4** (2B **86**)
Kelvin Way G3: Glas 2C **4** (2B **86**)
Kelvin Way G65: Kils 2G **13**
Kelvin Way G66: Kirkin 5A **32**
Kelvin Way G71: Both 4E **129**
Kemp Av. PA3: Pais 2C **82**
Kemp Ct. ML3: Ham 6A **146**
Kempsthorn Cres. G53: Glas 4B **104**
Kempsthorn Path G53: Glas 4B **104**
(off Kempsthorn Rd.)
Kempsthorn Pl. G53: Glas 4B **104**
Kempsthorn Rd. G53: Glas 4A **104**
Kemp St. G21: Glas 5A **66**
Kemp St. ML3: Ham 6H **145**
Kenbank Cres. PA11: Bri W 3F **77**
Kenbank Rd. PA11: Bri W 3F **77**
Kendal Av. G12: Glas 3G **63**
Kendal Av. G46: Giff 4A **122**
Kendal Dr. G12: Glas 3G **63**
Kendal Rd. G75: E Kil 5B **156**
Kendoon Av. G15: Glas 4G **45**
Kenilburn Av. ML6: Air 1B **96**
Kenilburn Cres. ML6: Air 1B **96**
Kenilworth G74: E Kil 5D **142**
Kenilworth Av. G41: Glas 5B **106**
Kenilworth Av. ML2: Wis 6H **149**
Kenilworth Av. PA2: Pais 5D **100**
Kenilworth Ct. G67: Cumb 5G **37**
Kenilworth Ct. ML1: Holy 2B **132**
(off Catriona Way)
Kenilworth Ct. ML8: Carl 4C **174**
Kenilworth Cres. G61: Bear 1C **46**
Kenilworth Cres. ML3: Ham 5D **144**
Kenilworth Cres. ML4: Bell 1C **130**
Kenilworth Dr. ML6: Air 3C **96**
Kenilworth Rd. G66: Kirkin 5E **33**
Kenilworth Way PA2: Pais 4D **100**
Kenley Rd. PA4: Renf 5G **61**
Kenmar Gdns. G71: Tann 5C **112**
Kenmar Rd. ML3: Ham 4F **145**
Kenmar Ter. ML3: Ham 4F **145**
Kenmore Gdns. G61: Bear 2H **47**
Kenmore Rd. G67: Cumb 3B **38**
Kenmore St. G32: Glas 6A **90**
Kenmore Way ML5: Coat 2E **115**
Kenmore Way ML8: Carl 2D **174**
Kenmuiraid Pl. ML4: Bell 4B **130**
Kenmuir Av. G32: Glas 2E **111**
Kenmuirhill Gdns. G32: Glas 3D **110**
Kenmuirhill Ga. G32: Glas 3D **110**
Kenmuirhill Rd. G32: Glas 3D **110**
Kenmuir Rd. G32: Carm 5C **110**
(not continuous)
Kenmuir Rd. G32: Glas 5C **110**
(not continuous)
Kenmuir Rd. G71: Udd 3E **111**
Kenmuir St. ML5: Coat 1F **113**
Kenmure Av. G64: B'rig 6A **50**
Kenmure Cres. G64: B'rig 6B **50**
Kenmure Dr. G64: B'rig 6B **50**
Kenmure Gdns. G64: B'rig 6A **50**
Kenmure La. G64: B'rig 6B **50**
Kenmure Rd. G46: Giff 3H **137**
Kenmure St. G41: Glas 2D **106**
Kenmure Way G73: Ruth 4D **124**
Kennedar Dr. G51: Glas 3E **85**
Kennedy Av. G65: Twe 2E **35**
Kennedy Ct. G46: Giff 3A **122**
Kennedy Dr. ML6: Air 4G **95**
Kennedy Gdns. ML2: Over 4H **165**
Kennedy Path G4: Glas 3F **7** (3H **87**)
Kennedy St. G4: Glas 3E **7** (3G **87**)
Kennedy St. ML2: Wis 6A **150**
Kennelburn Rd. ML6: Chap 4D **116**
Kenneth Rd. ML1: Moth 4E **147**
Kennihill ML6: Air 1A **96**
Kennihill Quad. ML6: Air 2A **96**
KENNISHEAD 2E 121
Kennishead Av. G46: T'bnk 2E **121**
Kennishead Path G46: T'bnk 2E **121**
(off Kennisholme Av.)
Kennishead Pl. G46: T'bnk 3E **121**
Kennishead Rd. G46: T'bnk 3F **121**
(Lochiel Rd.)
Kennishead Rd. G46: T'bnk 2D **120**
(Millview Pl.)
Kennishead Rd. G43: Glas 2E **121**
Kennishead Rd. G53: Glas 3B **120**
Kennishead Station (Rail) 2E 121
Kennisholm Av. G46: T'bnk 2E **121**
Kennisholm Path G46: T'bnk 2E **121**
(off Kennisholme Av.)
Kennisholm Pl. G46: T'bnk 2E **121**
Kennoway Cres. ML3: Fern 2E **163**
Kennoway Dr. G11: Glas 1F **85**
Kennoway La. G11: Glas 1F **85**
(off Auchentorlie St.)
Kennyhill Sq. G31: Glas 3D **88**
(not continuous)
Kenshaw Av. ML9: Lark 5C **170**
Kenshaw Pl. ML9: Lark 5C **170**
Kensington Ct. G12: Glas 5A **64**
(off Kensington Rd.)
Kensington Dr. G46: Giff 6B **122**
Kensington Ga. G12: Glas 5A **64**
Kensington Ga. La. G12: Glas 5A **64**
Kensington Rd. G12: Glas 5A **64**
Kentallen Rd. G33: Glas 5E **91**
Kent Dr. G73: Ruth 2F **125**
Kentigern Ter. G64: B'rig 1D **66**
Kentmere Cl. G75: E Kil 5C **156**
Kentmere Dr. G75: E Kil 5C **156**
Kentmere Pl. G75: E Kil 5C **156**
Kenton Dr. G75: E Kil 6B **156**
Kent Pl. G75: E Kil 5B **156**
Kent Rd. G3: Glas 3E **5** (3C **86**)
Kent Rd. ML4: Bell 1H **129**
Kent St. G40: Glas 5A **88**
Keppel Dr. G44: Glas 6A **108**
Keppochhill Dr. G21: Glas 6H **65**
Keppochhill Pl. G21: Glas 1H **87**
Keppochhill Rd. G21: Glas 6G **65**
Keppochhill Rd. G22: Glas 6G **65**
Keppochhill Way G21: Glas 1H **87**
Keppoch St. G21: Glas 6H **65**
Kerfield La. G15: Glas 3G **45**
(off Achamore Rd.)
Kerfield Pl. G15: Glas 3G **45**
Kerr Cres. ML3: Ham 2G **161**
Kerr Dr. G40: Glas 6B **88**
Kerr Dr. ML1: Moth 3E **147**
Kerrera Pl. G33: Glas 5D **90**
Kerrera Rd. G33: Glas 5D **90**
Kerr Gdns. G71: Tann 5E **113**
Kerr Grieve Ct. ML1: Moth 4G **147**
Ker Rd. G62: Miln 2E **27**
Kerr Pl. G40: Glas 6B **88**
Kerr St. G40: Glas 6B **88**
Kerr St. G66: Kirkin 5C **32**
Kerr St. G72: Blan 1C **144**
Kerr St. G78: Barr 5C **118**
Kerr St. PA3: Pais 6H **81**
Kerrycroy Av. G42: Glas 6H **107**
Kerrycroy Pl. G42: Glas 5H **107**
Kerrycroy St. G42: Glas 5H **107**
Kerrydale St. G40: Glas 1D **108**
Kerrylamont Av. G42: Glas 6A **108**
Kerry Pl. G15: Glas 4G **45**
Kershaw St. ML2: Over 4A **166**
Kersland Dr. G62: Miln 3H **27**
Kersland La. G12: Glas 6B **64**
(off Kersland St.)
Kersland La. G62: Miln 3H **27**
Kersland St. G12: Glas 6B **64**
Kesh Pl. G68: Cumb 5B **36**
Kessington Dr. G61: Bear 3G **47**
Kessington Rd. G61: Bear 4G **47**
Kessington Sq. G61: Bear 4H **47**
Kessock Dr. G22: Glas 6F **65**
Kessock Pl. G22: Glas 6F **65**
Kestrel Ct. G81: Hard 2C **44**
Kestrel Ct. ML5: Coat 2G **115**
Kestrel Pl. G68: Cumb 5A **36**
Kestrel Pl. PA5: John 6D **98**
Kestrel Rd. G13: Glas 3C **62**
Kestrel Vw. ML4: Bell 4A **114**
Keswick Dr. ML3: Ham 5G **161**
Keswick Rd. G75: E Kil 5B **156**
Kethers La. ML1: Moth 2E **147**
Kethers St. ML1: Moth 2E **147**
Kew Gdns. G71: Tann 6F **113**
Kew La. G12: Glas 6B **64**
Kew Ter. G12: Glas 6B **64**
Keynes Sq. ML4: Bell 3F **131**
Keystone Av. G62: Miln 5G **27**
Keystone Quad. G62: Miln 5F **27**
Keystone Rd. G62: Miln 5G **27**
Kibble Palace 6B 64
Kibbleston Rd. PA10: Kilba 2A **98**
Kidston Pl. G5: Glas 1G **107**
Kidston Ter. G5: Glas 1G **107**
Kierhill Rd. G68: Cumb 3E **37**
Kilallan Av. PA11: Bri W 2F **77**
KILBARCHAN 2A 98
Kilbarchan Rd. PA10: John 3C **98**
(not continuous)
Kilbarchan Rd. PA10: Kilba 3C **98**
(not continuous)
Kilbarchan Rd. PA11: Bri W 4G **77**
Kilbarchan Rd. PA5: John 4D **98**
Kilbarchan St. G5: Glas 6F **87**
Kilbeg Ter. G46: T'bnk 4D **120**

Kilberry St. G21: Glas	2C **88**	
Kilbirnie Pl. G5: Glas	1E **107**	
Kilbirnie St. G5: Glas	1E **107**	
KILBOWIE	4D **44**	
Kilbowie Ct. G81: Clyd	4D **44**	
Kilbowie Pl. ML6: Air	5D **96**	
Kilbowie Retail Pk.	5E **45**	
Kilbowie Rd. G67: Cumb	4A **38**	
Kilbowie Rd. G81: Clyd	2D **44**	
Kilbowie Rd. G81: Hard	2D **44**	
Kilbreck Gdns. G61: Bear	5C **26**	
Kilbreck La. ML1: N'hill	3C **132**	
Kilbrennan Dr. ML1: Moth	2D **146**	
Kilbrennan Rd. PA3: Lin	5H **79**	
Kilbride Ter. G5: Glas	2H **107**	
Kilbride Vw. G71: Tann	6E **113**	
KILBRYDE HOSPICE	3E **157**	
Kilburn Gro. G72: Blan	6B **128**	
Kilburn Pl. G13: Glas	3B **62**	
Kilchattan Dr. G44: Glas	6G **107**	
Kilchoan Rd. G33: Glas	1C **90**	
Kilchurn Gro. G72: Camb	5H **125**	
Kilcloy Av. G15: Glas	3A **46**	
Kildale Way G73: Ruth	5B **108**	
Kildare Pl. ML2: Newm	4E **151**	
Kildary Av. G44: Glas	2E **123**	
Kildary Rd. G44: Glas	2E **123**	
Kildermorie Pl. G34: Glas	3G **91**	
Kildermorie Rd. G34: Glas	3F **91**	
Kildonan Ct. ML2: Newm	2D **150**	
Kildonan Dr. G11: Glas	1G **85**	
Kildonan Pl. ML1: Moth	2E **147**	
Kildonan St. ML5: Coat	4D **94**	
Kildrostan St. G41: Glas	3D **106**	
KILDRUM	2B **38**	
Kildrummy Dr. G69: G'csh	5D **70**	
Kildrummy Pl. G74: E Kil	6F **141**	
Kildrum Rd. G67: Cumb	2B **38**	
KILDRUM SOUTH RDBT.	4B **38**	
Kilearn Rd. PA3: Pais	4D **82**	
Kilearn Sq. PA3: Pais	4D **82**	
Kilearn Way PA3: Pais	4D **82**	
(not continuous)		
Kilfinan Ct. G69: G'csh	4D **70**	
Kilfinan St. G22: Glas	2F **65**	
Kilgarth Dr. G71: Bail	2B **112**	
Kilgarth Rd. G71: Bail	2B **112**	
Kilgarth St. ML5: Coat	1F **113**	
Kilgraston Rd. PA11: Bri W	5E **77**	
Kilkerran Ct. G77: Newt M	5B **136**	
Kilkerran Dr. G33: Glas	3H **67**	
Kilkerran Pk. G77: Newt M	5B **136**	
Kilkerran Way G77: Newt M	5B **136**	
Killearn Cres. ML6: Plain	6G **75**	
Killearn Dr. PA1: Pais	1H **103**	
Killearn St. G22: Glas	5F **65**	
(not continuous)		
Killermont Av. G61: Bear	5G **47**	
Killermont Ct. G61: Bear	4H **47**	
Killermont Mdws. G71: Both	4C **128**	
Killermont Rd. G61: Bear	4F **47**	
Killermont St. G2: Glas	3D **6** (3G **87**)	
Killermont Vw. G20: Glas	5G **47**	
Killiegrew Rd. G41: Glas	3B **106**	
Killin Ct. ML5: Coat	2D **114**	
Killin Dr. G32: Glas	6B **90**	
Killin Dr. PA3: Lin	6F **79**	
Killin St. G32: Glas	2B **110**	
Killoch Av. PA3: Pais	6E **81**	
Killoch Dr. G13: Glas	2A **62**	
Killoch Dr. G78: Barr	6F **119**	
Killoch La. PA3: Pais	6E **81**	
Killoch Rd. PA3: Pais	6E **81**	
Killoch Way PA3: Pais	6E **81**	
Kilmailing Rd. G44: Glas	2F **123**	
Kilmair Pl. G20: Glas	4B **64**	
Kilmaluag Ter. G46: T'bnk	4D **120**	
Kilmannan Gdns. G62: Miln	2D **26**	
Kilmany Dr. G32: Glas	6H **89**	

Kilmany Gdns. G32: Glas	6H **89**	
Kilmardinny Art Cen.	1G **47**	
Kilmardinny Av. G61: Bear	2F **47**	
Kilmardinny Cres. G61: Bear	1F **47**	
Kilmardinny Dr. G61: Bear	1F **47**	
Kilmardinny Ga. G61: Bear	2F **47**	
Kilmardinny Gro. G61: Bear	1F **47**	
Kilmari Gdns. G15: Glas	3G **45**	
Kilmarnock Rd. G41: Glas	5B **106**	
Kilmarnock Rd. G43: Glas	2B **122**	
Kilmartin La. ML8: Carl	2D **174**	
Kilmartin Pl. G46: T'bnk	3E **121**	
Kilmartin Pl. G71: Tann	4E **113**	
Kilmartin Pl. ML6: Air	5D **96**	
Kilmaurs Dr. G46: Giff	4C **122**	
Kilmaurs St. G51: Glas	5F **85**	
Kilmeny Cres. ML2: Wis	4A **150**	
Kilmichael Av. ML2: Newm	3E **151**	
Kilmore Cres. G15: Glas	3G **45**	
Kilmore Gro. ML5: Coat	1B **114**	
Kilmorie Dr. G73: Ruth	6A **108**	
Kilmory Av. G71: Tann	6E **113**	
Kilmory Ct. G75: E Kil	1C **168**	
Kilmory Dr. G77: Newt M	3E **137**	
Kilmory Gdns. ML8: Carl	2D **174**	
Kilmory Rd. ML8: Carl	5F **175**	
Kilmuir Cl. G46: T'bnk	4E **121**	
Kilmuir Cres. G46: T'bnk	3D **120**	
Kilmuir Dr. G46: T'bnk	4E **121**	
Kilmuir Rd. G46: T'bnk	3E **121**	
Kilmuir Rd. G71: Tann	4D **112**	
Kilmun St. G20: Glas	2A **64**	
Kilnburn Rd. ML1: Moth	2E **147**	
Kilncadzow Rd. ML8: Carl	4F **175**	
Kilncroft La. PA2: Pais	4A **102**	
Kilnside La. PA1: Pais	6B **82**	
Kilnside Rd. PA1: Pais	6B **82**	
Kilnwell Quad. ML1: Moth	2F **147**	
Kiloran Gro. G77: Newt M	5A **136**	
Kiloran Pl. G77: Newt M	4A **136**	
Kiloran St. G46: T'bnk	3F **121**	
Kilpatrick Av. PA2: Pais	3F **101**	
Kilpatrick Av. PA8: Ersk	4F **43**	
Kilpatrick Ct. G33: Step	4F **69**	
Kilpatrick Ct. G60: Old K	1E **43**	
Kilpatrick Cres. PA2: Pais	4H **101**	
Kilpatrick Dr. G33: Step	4E **69**	
Kilpatrick Dr. G61: Bear	5C **26**	
Kilpatrick Dr. G75: E Kil	2B **168**	
Kilpatrick Dr. PA4: Renf	3D **82**	
Kilpatrick Dr. PA8: Ersk	4F **43**	
Kilpatrick Gdns. G76: Clar	1H **137**	
Kilpatrick Station (Rail)	1F **43**	
Kilpatrick Vw. G82: Dumb	3H **19**	
Kilpatrick Way G71: Tann	5E **113**	
KILSYTH	2H **13**	
Kilsyth Gdns. G75: E Kil	2A **168**	
Kilsyth Heritage Mus.	3A **14**	
Kilsyth Lennox Golf Course	1A **14**	
Kilsyth Rd. FK4: Bank	1B **16**	
Kilsyth Rd. FK4: Hag	1B **16**	
Kilsyth Rd. FK4: Longc	1B **16**	
Kilsyth Rd. G65: Queen	4C **12**	
Kilsyth Rd. G66: Kirkin	4D **32**	
Kilsyth Swimming Pool	2G **13**	
Kiltarie Cres. ML6: Air	4F **97**	
Kiltearn Rd. G33: Glas	4F **91**	
Kiltongue Cotts. ML6: Air	3F **95**	
(off Monkscourt Av.)		
Kilvaxter Dr. G46: T'bnk	3E **121**	
Kilwinning Cres. ML3: Ham	2C **160**	
Kilwinning Cres. ML6: Air	2E **97**	
Kilwynet Way PA3: Pais	4C **82**	
Kimberley Gdns. G75: E Kil	3E **157**	
Kimberley St. G81: Clyd	2H **43**	
Kimberley St. ML2: Wis	5C **148**	
Kinalty Rd. G44: Glas	2E **123**	
Kinarvie Cres. G53: Glas	6H **103**	
Kinarvie Gdns. G53: Glas	6H **103**	

Kinarvie Pl. G53: Glas	6H **103**	
Kinarvie Rd. G53: Glas	6H **103**	
Kinarvie Ter. G53: Glas	6H **103**	
Kinbuck Pas. G22: Glas	5G **65**	
Kinbuck St. G22: Glas	5G **65**	
Kincaid Dr. G66: Len	2E **9**	
Kincaid Fld. G66: Milt C	6C **10**	
Kincaid Gdns. G72: Camb	1A **126**	
Kincaid Way G66: Milt C	6B **10**	
Kincardine Dr. G64: B'rig	1D **66**	
Kincardine Pl. G64: B'rig	2E **67**	
Kincardine Pl. G74: E Kil	6C **142**	
Kincardine Sq. G33: Glas	1D **90**	
Kincath Av. G73: Ruth	4F **125**	
Kinclaven Av. G15: Glas	4A **46**	
Kinclaven Gdns. G15: Glas	4B **46**	
Kinclaven Pl. G15: Glas	4B **46**	
Kincraig St. G51: Glas	5D **84**	
Kinellan Rd. G61: Bear	6F **47**	
Kinellar Dr. G14: Glas	3A **62**	
Kinfauns Dr. G15: Glas	3H **45**	
Kinfauns Dr. G77: Newt M	4F **137**	
Kingarth St. G42: Glas	3E **107**	
Kingarth St. ML3: Ham	3H **161**	
King Ct. ML1: Moth	2F **147**	
King Edward La. G13: Glas	4E **63**	
King Edward Rd. G13: Glas	4F **63**	
Kingfisher Av. ML3: Fern	2F **163**	
Kingfisher Ct. ML1: Moth	5H **147**	
Kingfisher Cres. G68: Cumb	5A **36**	
Kingfisher Dr. G13: Glas	2H **61**	
Kingfisher Gdns. G13: Glas	2A **62**	
Kingfisher Rd. G66: Lenz	1F **53**	
King George Ct. PA4: Renf	2G **83**	
King George Gdns. PA4: Renf	1G **83**	
King George Pk. Av. PA4: Renf	2G **83**	
King George Pl. PA4: Renf	2G **83**	
King George Way PA4: Renf	2G **83**	
Kinghorn Dr. G44: Glas	6G **107**	
Kinghorn La. G44: Glas	6G **107**	
Kinglas Dr. G82: Dumb	2G **19**	
Kinglas Ho. G82: Dumb	1H **19**	
Kinglass Rd. G61: Bear	5C **46**	
King Pl. G69: Barg	6E **93**	
Kingsacre Rd. G44: Glas	6G **107**	
Kingsacre Rd. G73: Ruth	1A **124**	
Kings Av. G72: Camb	2B **126**	
Kingsbarns Dr. G44: Glas	6F **107**	
Kingsbarns Gdns. G68: Cumb	4A **16**	
Kingsborough Gdns. G12: Glas	5H **63**	
(not continuous)		
Kingsborough Ga. G12: Glas	6H **63**	
Kingsborough La. G12: Glas	6H **63**	
Kingsborough La. E. G12: Glas	6H **63**	
Kingsbrae Av. G44: Glas	6G **107**	
King's Bri.	1H **107**	
Kingsbridge Cres. G44: Glas	1H **123**	
Kingsbridge Dr. G44: Glas	1H **123**	
Kingsbridge Dr. G73: Ruth	1A **124**	
Kingsbridge Pk. Gdns. G44: Glas	1H **123**	
Kingsburgh Dr. PA1: Pais	6D **82**	
Kingsburn Dr. G73: Ruth	1C **124**	
Kingsburn Gro. G73: Ruth	1B **124**	
Kingscliffe Av. G44: Glas	1G **123**	
Kings Ct. G1: Glas	5G **87**	
(off King St.)		
Kingscourt Av. G44: Glas	6H **107**	
King's Cres. ML8: Carl	3E **175**	
Kings Cres. G72: Camb	2B **126**	
Kings Cres. PA5: Eld	2A **100**	
Kingsdale Av. G44: Glas	6G **107**	
King's Dr. G40: Glas	1A **108**	
King's Dr. G68: Cumb	5H **15**	
Kings Dr. G77: Newt M	6F **137**	
Kings Dr. ML1: New S	4H **131**	
Kingsdyke Av. G44: Glas	6G **107**	
Kingsferry Ct. PA4: Renf	5G **61**	
Kingsford Av. G44: Glas	3C **122**	
Kingsford Ct. G77: Newt M	3B **136**	

King's Gdns. – Kirkness St.

King's Gdns. G77: Newt M 6G 137
Kingsgate Retail Pk. 3A 142
Kingsheath Av. G73: Ruth 1A 124
Kingshill Av. G68: Cumb 4A 36
Kingshill Dr. G44: Glas 1G 123
Kingshill Vw. ML8: Law 1G 173
Kingshouse Av. G44: Glas 6G 107
Kingshurst Av. G44: Glas 6G 107
Kings Inch Dr. G51: Glas 1A 84
Kings Inch Pl. PA4: Renf 1H 83
King's Inch Rd. G51: Renf 6H 61
King's Inch Rd. PA4: Renf 4G 61
King's Inch Way PA4: Renf 5G 61
Kingsknowe Dr. G73: Ruth 1A 124
Kingsland Cres. G52: Glas 5B 84
Kingsland Dr. G52: Glas 5B 84
Kingsland La. G52: Glas 5C 84
Kingsland Vw. G75: T'hall 3H 155
Kingslea Rd. PA6: Hous 1B 78
Kingsley Av. G42: Glas 4F 107
Kingsley Ct. G71: Tann 6E 113
Kingslynn Dr. G44: Glas 1H 123
Kingslynn La. G44: Glas 1H 123
Kingsmuir Dr. G68: Cumb 3B 36
Kingsmuir Dr. G73: Ruth 1A 124
KING'S PK. 1A 124
King's Pk. G64: Torr 4E 31
King's Pk. Av. G44: Glas 1F 123
Kings Pk. Av. G73: Ruth 1A 124
King's Pk. Golf Course 2H 123
King's Pk. La. G44: Glas 1F 123
King's Pk. Rd. G44: Glas 6F 107
King's Park Station (Rail) 1G 123
King's Pl. G22: Glas 3F 65
King's Rd. PA5: Eld 3H 99
King's Rd. PA5: John 3H 99
King's Theatre 3H 5 (3E 87)
(Glasgow)
(off Bath St.)
KINGSTON G5 6E 87
KINGSTON PA7 4A 42
Kingston Av. G71: Tann 5E 113
Kingston Av. G78: Neil 3D 134
Kingston Av. ML6: Air 3C 96
Kingston Bri. 5D 86
Kingston Bri. Trad. Est. G5: Glas 5D 86
Kingston Cres. G75: E Kil 6B 156
Kingston Flats G65: Kils 2H 13
Kingston Gro. PA7: B'ton 4H 41
Kingston Ind. Est. G5: Glas 6D 86
KINGSTON INTERCHANGE 6E 87
Kingston Pl. G40: Glas 3E 109
Kingston Pl. G81: Clyd 3H 43
Kingston Rd. G65: Kils 2H 13
Kingston Rd. G78: Neil 5C 134
Kingston Rd. PA7: B'ton 5H 41
Kingston St. G5: Glas 5E 87
King St. G1: Glas 5G 87
King St. G65: Kils 3H 13
King St. G73: Ruth 5C 108
King St. G81: Clyd 1F 61
King St. ML2: Newm 4D 150
King St. ML2: Wis 1H 165
King St. ML3: Ham 4D 144
King St. ML5: Coat 5A 94
King St. ML9: Lark 2C 170
King St. PA1: Pais 6G 81
King St. La. G65: Kils 3H 13
King St. La. G73: Ruth 5C 108
King's Vw. G68: Cumb 5H 15
Kings Vw. G73: Ruth 6B 108
King's Way G82: Dumb 2C 18
Kingsway G14: Glas 4A 62
Kingsway G65: Kils 2H 13
Kingsway G66: Kirkin 3H 33
Kingsway G74: E Kil 4A 142
Kingsway Ct. G14: Glas 4A 62
Kingswood Dr. G44: Glas 1G 123
Kingswood Rd. PA7: B'ton 3F 41
Kingussie Dr. G44: Glas 1G 123
Kiniver Dr. G15: Glas 6A 46
Kinkell Gdns. G66: Kirkin 4H 33
Kinloch Av. G72: Camb 3B 126
Kinloch Av. PA3: Lin 6G 79
Kinloch Dr. ML1: Moth 5F 131
Kinloch Rd. G77: Newt M 3C 136
Kinloch Rd. PA4: Renf 3D 82
Kinloch St. G40: Glas 1E 109
Kinloss Pl. G74: E Kil 1H 157
Kinmount Av. G44: Glas 6F 107
Kinmount La. G44: Glas 6G 107
Kinnaird Av. G77: Newt M 4G 137
Kinnaird Cres. G61: Bear 3G 47
Kinnaird Dr. PA3: Lin 5H 79
Kinnaird Pl. G64: B'rig 2D 66
Kinnear Rd. G40: Glas 2C 108
Kinneil Ho. ML3: Ham 4A 146
Kinneil Pl. ML3: Ham 1D 160
Kinnell Av. G52: Glas 2C 104
Kinnell Cres. G52: Glas 2C 104
Kinnell Path G52: Glas 2C 104
Kinnell Pl. G52: Glas 2D 104
Kinnell Sq. G52: Glas 2C 104
KINNING PK. 6B 86
Kinning Park Station (Subway) 6B 86
Kinning St. G5: Glas 6E 87
Kinnoul Gdns. G61: Bear 6D 26
Kinnoul La. G12: Glas 6A 64
Kinnoull Pl. G72: Blan 2B 144
Kinpurnie Rd. PA1: Pais 6F 83
Kinross Av. G52: Glas 1B 104
Kinross Pk. G74: E Kil 6D 142
Kinsail Dr. G52: Glas 5H 83
Kinstone Av. G14: Glas 4A 62
Kintail Gdns. G66: Kirkin 4H 33
Kintessack Pl. G64: B'rig 5F 51
Kintillo Dr. G13: Glas 3B 62
Kintore Pk. ML3: Ham 4F 161
Kintore Rd. G43: Glas 1D 122
Kintore Twr. G72: Camb 4G 125
Kintra St. G51: Glas 5H 85
Kintyre Av. PA3: Lin 6G 79
Kintyre Cres. G77: Newt M 3C 136
Kintyre Cres. ML5: Coat 1A 114
Kintyre Cres. ML6: Plain 6F 75
Kintyre Dr. ML5: Coat 1A 114
Kintyre Gdns. G66: Kirkin 4H 33
Kintyre Rd. G72: Blan 1A 144
Kintyre St. G21: Glas 2C 88
Kintyre Wynd ML8: Carl 2D 174
Kipland Wlk. ML5: Coat 6F 95
Kippen Dr. G76: Busby 4E 139
Kippen St. G22: Glas 3H 65
Kippen St. ML6: Air 5F 95
Kippford Pl. ML6: Chap 4F 117
Kippford St. G32: Glas 1C 110
Kippford Ter. G73: Ruth 4D 124
Kipps Av. ML6: Air 3G 95
Kippsbyre Ct. ML6: Air 4F 95
(off Monkscourt Av.)
Kirby Gdns. G72: Camb 6H 109
Kirkaig Av. PA4: Renf 1H 83
Kirkandrews Pl. ML6: Chap 4F 117
Kirkbean Av. G73: Ruth 3C 124
Kirkburn Av. G72: Camb 3A 126
Kirkcaldy Rd. G41: Glas 3B 106
Kirkconnel Av. G13: Glas 3H 61
Kirkconnel Av. G68: Cumb 4A 36
Kirkconnel Dr. G73: Ruth 2B 124
Kirk Cres. G60: Old K 6E 23
Kirkcudbright Pl. G74: E Kil 6D 142
Kirkdale Dr. G52: Glas 1E 105
Kirkdene Av. G77: Newt M 4H 137
Kirkdene Bank G77: Newt M 4H 137
Kirkdene Cres. G77: Newt M 4H 137
Kirkdene Gro. G77: Newt M 5H 137
Kirkdene Pl. G77: Newt M 4H 137
Kirkfieldbank Way ML3: Ham 6E 145
Kirkfield Gdns. PA4: Renf 6D 60
Kirkfield Rd. G71: Both 4E 129
Kirkford Rd. G69: Mood 5C 54
Kirkgate ML2: Newm 5D 150
Kirk Glebe G78: Neil 2E 135
Kirkhall Rd. ML1: N'hill 3D 132
KIRKHILL G72 2B 126
KIRKHILL G77 5H 137
Kirkhill Av. G72: Camb 4A 126
Kirkhill Bowling Club 3H 125
Kirkhill Cres. G78: Neil 1E 135
Kirkhill Dr. G20: Glas 4B 64
Kirkhill Gdns. G72: Camb 4A 126
Kirkhill Ga. G77: Newt M 5H 137
Kirkhill Golf Course 5H 125
Kirkhill Gro. G72: Camb 4A 126
Kirkhill Pl. G20: Glas 4B 64
Kirkhill Pl. ML2: Wis 1C 164
Kirkhill Rd. G69: G'csh 4D 70
Kirkhill Rd. G71: Tann 5C 112
Kirkhill Rd. G77: Newt M 4H 137
(not continuous)
Kirkhill Rd. ML2: Wis 2B 164
Kirkhill Station (Rail) 2A 126
Kirkhill St. ML2: Wis 2D 164
Kirkhill Ter. G72: Camb 4A 126
Kirkhope Dr. G15: Glas 6B 46
Kirkhope Pl. ML8: Carl 4C 174
Kirkinner Pl. PA11: Bri W 3F 77
(off Main Rd.)
Kirkinner Rd. G32: Glas 2D 110
KIRKINTILLOCH 4C 32
Kirkintilloch Golf Course 3B 32
Kirkintilloch Ind. Est. G66: Kirkin 3C 32
Kirkintilloch Leisure Cen. 6D 32
Kirkintilloch Rd. G66: Kirkin 2H 31
(Campsie Rd.)
Kirkintilloch Rd. G66: Kirkin 1G 51
(Glasgow Rd.)
Kirkintilloch Rd. G64: B'rig 2B 66
Kirkintilloch Rd. G66: Lenz 2C 52
Kirkland Gro. PA5: John 2F 99
KIRKLANDNEUK 5D 60
Kirklandneuk Cres. PA4: Renf 5C 60
Kirklandneuk Rd. PA4: Renf 5C 60
Kirklands PA4: Renf 6D 60
Kirklands Cres. G65: Kils 4H 13
Kirklands Cres. G71: Both 4E 129
Kirklands Dr. G77: Newt M 1D 152
KIRKLANDS HOSPITAL 3F 129
Kirklands Pl. G77: Newt M 1D 152
Kirklands Rd. G77: Newt M 1D 152
Kirkland St. G20: Glas 6D 64
Kirkland St. ML1: Moth 1F 147
Kirk La. G43: Glas 6A 106
Kirk La. G61: Bear 2E 47
Kirk La. ML8: Law 5E 167
Kirklea Gdns. PA3: Pais 6E 81
Kirkle Dr. G77: Newt M 4H 137
Kirklee Cir. G12: Glas 5A 64
Kirklee Gdns. G12: Glas 4B 64
Kirklee Gdns. La. G12: Glas 4B 64
Kirklee Ga. G12: Glas 4B 64
Kirklee Pl. G12: Glas 5B 64
Kirklee Quad. G12: Glas 5B 64
Kirklee Quad. La. G12: Glas 5B 64
Kirklee Rd. G12: Glas 5A 64
Kirklee Rd. ML1: New S 6G 131
Kirklee Rd. ML4: Bell 3F 131
Kirklee Ter. G12: Glas 5A 64
Kirklee Ter. La. G12: Glas 5B 64
Kirklee Ter. Rd. G12: Glas 5A 64
Kirkliston St. G32: Glas 5H 89
Kirkmaiden Way G72: Blan 6B 144
Kirk M. G72: Camb 2A 126
Kirkmichael Av. G11: Glas 6G 63
Kirkmichael Gdns. G11: Glas 6G 63
Kirkmuir Dr. G73: Ruth 4D 124
Kirkness St. ML6: Air 3A 96

A–Z Glasgow 239

Lady in Leisure Health & Fitness Cen. – Langside Gdns.

Lady in Leisure Health & Fitness Cen. .... **5C 6 (4F 87)**
.... *(Glasgow)*
.... *(off Mitchell St.)*
Lady Isle Cres. G71: Udd 1C **128**
Lady Jane Ga. G71: Both 3B **128**
Ladykirk Cres. G52: Glas 5B **84**
Ladykirk Cres. PA2: Pais 2B **102**
Ladykirk Dr. G52: Glas 5B **84**
Ladykirk Way G74: E Kil 5H **141**
Lady La. PA1: Pais 1H **101**
Ladyloan Av. G15: Glas 3G **45**
Ladyloan Ct. G15: Glas 3H **45**
Ladyloan Gdns. G15: Glas 3H **45**
Ladyloan Gro. G15: Glas 3H **45**
Ladyloan Pl. G15: Glas 3G **45**
Lady Mary Wlk. ML3: Ham 2A **162**
Ladymuir Circ. PA8: Ersk 6D **42**
Ladymuir Cres. G53: Glas 3C **104**
Lady Nancy Cres. G72: Blan 3G **143**
Ladysmith Av. PA10: Kilba 3B **98**
Ladysmith Dr. G75: E Kil 1A **168**
Ladysmith St. ML2: Wis 5C **148**
Lady Watson Gdns. ML3: Ham 1E **161**
Ladywell Bus. Cen. G4: Glas 6H **7** (4A **88**)
Ladywell Rd. ML1: Moth 3D **146**
Ladywell St. G4: Glas 5H **7** (4A **88**)
Lady Wilson St. ML6: Air 5B **96**
Ladywood G62: Miln 3H **27**
LA Fitness **6G 27**
.... *(Milngavie)*
Lagan Rd. ML8: Carl 4D **174**
Laggan Quad. ML6: Air 2G **95**
Laggan Rd. G43: Glas 2C **122**
Laggan Rd. G64: B'rig 6D **50**
Laggan Rd. G77: Newt M 2D **136**
Laggan Rd. ML6: Air 2H **95**
Laggan Ter. PA4: Renf 5D **60**
Laggan Way ML2: Newm 2D **150**
Lagholm Dr. PA3: Lin 6A **80**
Lagoon Leisure Cen. **1B 102**
Lagos La. G73: Ruth 5E **125**
Laidlaw Av. ML1: New S 4H **131**
Laidlaw Gdns. G71: Tann 4D **112**
Laidlaw St. G5: Glas 6E **87**
.... (not continuous)
Laidon Rd. ML6: Air 2H **95**
Laidon Wlk. ML2: Newm 3D **150**
.... *(off Murdostoun Vw.)*
Laighcartside St. PA5: John 2G **99**
Laigh Kirk La. PA1: Pais 1A **102**
.... *(off Causeyside St.)*
Laighlands Rd. G71: Both 5F **129**
Laighmuir St. G71: Udd 2D **128**
LAIGH PK. **5A 82**
Laighpark Av. PA7: B'ton 4H **41**
Laighpark Vw. PA3: Pais 4A **82**
Laigh Rd. G77: Newt M 4H **137**
Laighshaws Pl. ML9: Shaw 4F **171**
LAIGHSTONEHALL **1F 161**
Laighstonehall Rd. ML3: Ham 1F **161**
Laightoun Ct. G67: Cumb 1C **56**
Laightoun Dr. G67: Cumb 1C **56**
Laightoun Gdns. G67: Cumb 1C **56**
Lainshaw Dr. G45: Glas 5E **123**
Laird Gro. G71: Tann 5E **113**
Laird Pl. G40: Glas 1B **108**
Lairds Ga. G71: Both 2B **128**
Lairds Hill G67: Cumb 3G **37**
Laird's Hill Ct. G65: Kils 3E **13**
Laird's Hill Pl. G65: Kils 3E **13**
Lairdsland Rd. G66: Kirkin 5D **32**
Laird St. ML5: Coat 4D **94**
Lairg Dr. G72: Blan 5A **128**
Lairg Vw. PA7: B'ton 5F **41**
Lairhills Rd. G75: E Kil 4G **157**
Lakeview Gro. G33: Glas 6H **67**
Lamberton Dr. G52: Glas 5B **84**
LAMBHILL **2E 65**
Lambhill Quad. G41: Glas 6C **86**
Lambhill St. G41: Glas 6B **86**
Lambie Cres. G77: Newt M 4C **136**
Lamb St. G22: Glas 3F **65**
Lamb St. ML3: Ham 6A **146**
Lamerton Rd. G67: Cumb 3C **38**
Lamington Rd. G52: Glas 1B **104**
Lamlash Cres. G33: Glas 3B **90**
Lamlash Pl. G33: Glas 3B **90**
Lamlash Pl. G75: E Kil 1B **168**
Lamlash Pl. ML1: Moth 2E **147**
Lamlash Sq. G33: Glas 3C **90**
Lammermoor G74: E Kil 5E **143**
Lammermoor Av. G52: Glas 1C **104**
Lammermoor Cres. G66: Kirkin 5F **33**
Lammermoor Dr. G67: Cumb 6G **37**
Lammermoor Gdns. G66: Kirkin 5F **33**
Lammermoor Rd. G66: Kirkin 5F **33**
Lammermoor Ter. ML2: Wis 6H **149**
Lammermuir Ct. PA2: Pais 5A **102**
Lammermuir Dr. PA2: Pais 5H **101**
Lammermuir Gdns. G61: Bear 6C **26**
Lammermuir Pl. ML1: Holy 3B **132**
.... *(off Cherry Pl.)*
Lammermuir Way ML6: Chap 3F **117**
Lammermuir Wynd ML9: Lark 6H **163**
Lammer Wynd ML9: Lark 4E **171**
.... *(off Cameronian Way)*
Lamont Av. PA7: B'ton 4A **42**
Lamont Rd. G21: Glas 3D **66**
Lanark Av. ML6: Air 1H **115**
Lanark Rd. ML8: Braid 4D **174**
Lanark Rd. ML8: Carl 4D **174**
Lanark Rd. ML8: Crsfd 4C **172**
Lanark Rd. ML8: Roseb 4C **172**
Lanark Rd. ML9: Dals 4H **163**
.... (not continuous)
Lanark Rd. ML9: Lark 4H **163**
.... (not continuous)
Lanark Rd. End ML9: Lark 4G **163**
Lanarkshire Ice Rink **4A 146**
Lanark St. G1: Glas 5H **87**
Lancaster Av. ML6: Chap 4D **116**
Lancaster Cres. G12: Glas 5A **64**
Lancaster Cres. G74: E Kil 5A **142**
Lancaster Cres. La. G12: Glas 5A **64**
Lancaster Rd. G64: B'rig 3D **50**
Lancaster Ter. G12: Glas 5A **64**
Lancaster Ter. La. G12: Glas 5A **64**
Lancaster Way PA4: Renf 2E **83**
Lancefield Quay G3: Glas 6D **4** (4C **86**)
Lancefield St. G3: Glas 6F **5** (4D **86**)
Landemer Ct. G73: Ruth 1C **124**
Landemer Dr. G73: Ruth 1B **124**
Landemer Gait G73: Ruth 1C **124**
Landressy Pl. G40: Glas 1B **108**
Landressy St. G40: Glas 6B **88**
Landsdowne Gdns. ML3: Ham 6B **146**
Landsdowne Rd. ML9: Lark 3E **171**
Lane, The G68: Dull 5F **15**
Lanfine Rd. PA1: Pais 1D **102**
Langa Gro. G20: Glas 2C **64**
.... *(off Lochburn Cres.)*
Langa St. G20: Glas 2C **64**
Lang Av. PA4: Renf 1E **83**
Lang Av. PA7: B'ton 4A **42**
Langbank St. G5: Glas 6F **87**
Langbar Cres. G33: Glas 4E **91**
Langbar Gdns. G33: Glas 4F **91**
Langbar Path G33: Glas 4D **90**
.... *(off Langbar Cres.)*
Langcraigs G82: Dumb 2G **19**
Langcraigs Ct. PA2: Pais 5G **101**
Langcraigs Dr. PA2: Pais 6G **101**
Langcraigs Ter. PA2: Pais 6G **101**
Langcroft Av. G72: Camb 3C **126**
Langcroft Dr. G72: Camb 3C **126**
Langcroft Pk. G72: Camb 3C **126**
Langcroft Pl. G51: Glas 4C **84**
Langcroft Rd. G51: Glas 4C **84**
Langcroft Ter. G51: Glas 4D **84**
Langdale G74: E Kil 6E **141**
Langdale G77: Newt M 4H **137**
Langdale Av. G33: Glas 6G **67**
Langdale Rd. G69: Mood 5D **54**
Langdales Av. G68: Cumb 3F **37**
Langdale St. G33: Glas 6G **67**
Langfaulds Cres. G81: Faif 6F **25**
Langford Dr. G53: Glas 4A **120**
Langford Pl. G53: Glas 4B **120**
Langhaul Av. G53: Glas 4H **103**
Langhaul Ct. G53: Glas 4H **103**
Langhaul Pl. G53: Glas 4H **103**
Langhaul Rd. G53: Glas 4H **103**
Langhill Dr. G68: Cumb 2F **37**
Langholm G75: E Kil 5B **156**
Langholm Ct. G69: Mood 5D **54**
Langholm Cres. ML2: Wis 3H **149**
Langholm Path G72: Blan 2A **144**
Langlade Rd. PA5: Eld 4A **100**
Langlands Av. G51: Glas 4D **84**
Langlands Av. G75: E Kil 1F **169**
Langlands Ct. G51: Glas 3F **85**
Langlands Ct. G75: E Kil 1F **169**
Langlands Dr. G51: Glas 3C **84**
Langlands Dr. G75: E Kil 1F **169**
Langlands Ga. G75: E Kil 2F **169**
Langlands Golf Course **3F 169**
Langlands Pk. G75: E Kil 2G **169**
Langlands Path G51: Glas 4E **85**
.... *(off Langlands Rd.)*
Langlands Pl. G67: Cumb 5H **37**
Langlands Pl. G75: E Kil 1F **169**
Langlands Rd. G51: Glas 4D **84**
Langlands Rd. G75: E Kil 4C **168**
LANGLANDS-SEAFAR INTERCHANGE 5G **37**
Langlands Sq. G75: E Kil 1F **169**
Langlands Ter. G82: Dumb 1H **19**
Langlea Av. G72: Camb 3F **125**
Langlea Ct. G72: Camb 3G **125**
Langlea Dr. G72: Camb 2G **125**
Langlea Gdns. G72: Camb 2G **125**
Langlea Gro. G72: Camb 3G **125**
Langlea Rd. G73: Ruth 2G **125**
.... *(Langlea Dr.)*
Langlea Rd. G72: Camb 3G **125**
Langlea Way G72: Camb 2G **125**
Langlee Rd. G77: Newt M 5A **152**
Langlees Av. G77: Newt M 4H **137**
Langley Av. G13: Glas 1B **62**
LANGLOAN **6A 94**
Langloan Cres. ML5: Coat 6A **94**
Langloan Pl. ML5: Coat 5A **94**
Langloan St. ML5: Coat 6A **94**
Langlook Cres. G53: Glas 5H **103**
Langlook Pl. G53: Glas 5H **103**
Langlook Rd. G53: Glas 5H **103**
LANGMUIR **4H 33**
Langmuir Av. G66: Kirkin 4E **33**
Langmuirhead Rd. G66: A'loch 1H **67**
Langmuir Rd. G66: Kirkin 4G **33**
Langmuir Rd. G69: Barg 6E **93**
Langmuir Way G69: Barg 6E **93**
Langness Rd. G33: Glas 3B **90**
Langoreth Av. ML3: Ham 1D **160**
Lang Pl. PA5: John 2F **99**
Langrig Rd. G21: Glas 4C **66**
Langrig Rd. G77: Newt M 6C **136**
Langroods Circ. PA3: Pais 4A **82**
Langshaw Cres. ML8: Carl 3D **174**
Langshot St. G51: Glas 6B **86**
LANGSIDE **5D 106**
Langside Av. G41: Glas 4C **106**
Langside Av. G71: View 1G **129**
Langside Ct. G71: Both 6F **129**
Langside Dr. G43: Glas 3C **122**
Langside Dr. PA10: Kilba 3A **98**
Langside Gdns. G42: Glas 6E **107**

A–Z Glasgow 241

Langside La. G42: Glas	4E **107**
Langside Pk. PA10: Kilba	3A **98**
Langside Pl. G41: Glas	5D **106**
Langside Rd. G42: Glas	5D **106**
(not continuous)
Langside Rd. G71: Both	6F **129**
Langside Station (Rail)	1C **122**
Langside St. G81: Faif	1G **45**
Langstile Pl. G52: Glas	6H **83**
Langstile Rd. G52: Glas	6H **83**
Lang St. PA1: Pais	1C **102**
Langton Cres. G53: Glas	4C **104**
Langton Cres. G78: Barr	6F **119**
Langton Gdns. G69: Bail	1F **111**
Langton Ga. G77: Newt M	4C **136**
Langton Pl. G77: Newt M	4C **136**
Langton Rd. G53: Glas	4C **104**
Langtree Av. G46: Giff	6G **121**
LANRIGG	6A **54**
Lanrig Pl. G69: Chry	1A **70**
Lanrig Rd. G69: Chry	6A **54**
Lansbury Gdns. PA3: Pais	4H **81**
Lansbury Ter. ML9: Lark	4E **171**
Lansdowne Cres. G20: Glas	1D **86**
Lansdowne Cres. La. G20: Glas	1D **86**
(off Gt. Western Rd.)
Lansdowne Dr. G68: Cumb	6H **15**
Lantana Gro. ML1: Moth	1F **147**
Lanton Dr. G52: Glas	6B **84**
Lanton Path ML6: Chap	4E **117**
Lanton Rd. G43: Glas	2C **122**
Lappin St. G81: Clyd	1F **61**
Lapsley Av. PA2: Pais	4A **102**
Lapwing Av. G66: Lenz	1F **53**
Lapwing Cres. ML1: Moth	6H **147**
Lapwing Cres. PA4: Renf	4G **61**
Lapwing Dr. PA4: Renf	4G **61**
Lapwing Rd. PA4: Renf	4G **61**
Larbert St. G4: Glas	2C **6** (2F **87**)
Larch Av. G64: B'rig	1D **66**
Larch Av. G66: Lenz	1C **52**
Larch Cl. G72: Flem	4E **127**
Larch Ct. G67: Cumb	1D **38**
Larch Ct. G72: Blan	1A **144**
Larch Ct. G72: Flem	4F **127**
Larch Ct. G75: E Kil	6D **156**
Larch Cres. G66: Lenz	1C **52**
Larch Dr. FK4: Bank	1E **17**
Larch Dr. G75: E Kil	6D **156**
Larches, The G69: Mood	3E **55**
Larchfield Av. G14: Glas	5B **62**
Larchfield Av. G77: Newt M	5E **137**
Larchfield Ct. G77: Newt M	5D **136**
Larchfield Cres. ML2: Wis	3A **150**
Larchfield Dr. G73: Ruth	3D **124**
Larchfield Gdns. ML2: Wis	3B **150**
Larchfield Gro. ML2: Wis	2B **150**
Larchfield Pl. G14: Glas	5B **62**
Larchfield Pl. ML2: Wis	3B **150**
Larchfield Rd. G61: Bear	6F **47**
Larchfield Rd. G69: Mood	5D **54**
Larch Gait G72: Flem	4F **127**
Larch Gro. G66: Milt C	6B **10**
Larch Gro. G67: Cumb	1D **38**
Larch Gro. ML1: Holy	2B **132**
Larch Gro. ML3: Ham	1A **162**
Larchgrove Av. G32: Glas	5C **90**
Larchgrove Pl. G32: Glas	4C **90**
Larchgrove Rd. G32: Glas	4C **90**
Larch Pl. G67: Cumb	1D **38**
Larch Pl. G71: View	5H **113**
Larch Pl. G72: Flem	4E **127**
Larch Pl. G75: E Kil	6D **156**
Larch Pl. PA5: John	5F **99**
Larch Rd. G41: Glas	1H **105**
Larch Rd. G67: Cumb	1D **38**
Larch Sq. G72: Flem	4E **127**
Larchwood Ter. G78: Barr	6F **119**
Largie Rd. G43: Glas	2D **122**

Largo La. G72: Blan	6B **144**
Largo Pl. G51: Glas	4E **85**
Larkfield Cl. G42: Glas	2F **107**
Larkfield Ct. G72: Blan	3A **144**
Larkfield Dr. G72: Blan	3B **144**
Larkfield Ga. G42: Glas	2F **107**
Larkfield Rd. G66: Lenz	1E **53**
Larkfield St. G42: Glas	2F **107**
LARKHALL	2C **170**
Larkhall Golf Course	3F **171**
Larkhall Ind. Est. ML9: Lark	5D **170**
(Borland Dr.)
Larkhall Ind. Est. ML9: Lark	4D **170**
(Pyatshaw Rd.)
LARKHALL INTERCHANGE	5A **164**
Larkhall Leisure Cen.	3C **170**
Larkhall Station (Rail)	2C **170**
Larkin Gdns. PA3: Pais	4H **81**
Larkin Way ML4: Bell	6B **114**
Larksfield Dr. ML8: Carl	5E **175**
Larkspur Dr. G74: E Kil	5E **141**
Larkspur Pl. G68: Cumb	1E **57**
Larkspur Way ML8: Carl	5D **174**
Lark Way ML4: Bell	5B **114**
Larocca La. G74: E Kil	1H **157**
Lascar Pl. ML1: Moth	5C **148**
Lashley Gro. ML2: Over	4A **166**
Lasswade St. G14: Glas	3G **61**
Latherton Dr. G20: Glas	4B **64**
Latimer Ct. ML1: Moth	5G **147**
Latimer Gdns. G52: Glas	1A **104**
Latimer Path G52: Glas	1A **104**
(off Hatton Gdns.)
Latta St. G82: Dumb	3G **19**
Lauchlin Pl. G66: Kirkin	6H **33**
Lauchope Rd. ML1: N'hse	6D **116**
Lauchope St. ML6: Chap	3E **117**
Lauder Cres. ML2: Wis	3H **149**
Lauderdale Dr. G77: Newt M	6C **136**
Lauderdale Gdns. G12: Glas	6H **63**
(not continuous)
Lauderdale La. G12: Glas	6H **63**
Lauderdale Pl. G65: Kils	2B **14**
Lauder Dr. G73: Ruth	1F **125**
Lauder Dr. PA3: Lin	6H **79**
Lauder Gdns. G72: Blan	5A **128**
Lauder Gdns. ML5: Coat	2F **115**
Lauder Grn. G74: E Kil	5B **142**
Lauder La. ML3: Ham	6C **144**
Lauder St. G5: Glas	1E **107**
Laughland Dr. ML1: N'hill	4D **132**
Lauranne Pl. ML4: Bell	2A **130**
Laundry La. G33: Step	4C **68**
Lauranne Pl. ML4: Bell	2A **130**
Laurel Av. G66: Lenz	1D **52**
Laurel Av. G81: Clyd	3H **43**
Laurel Bank ML3: Ham	3G **161**
Laurelbank ML5: Coat	3C **94**
Laurelbank Rd. G32: Carm	5C **110**
Laurelbank Rd. G69: Chry	2H **69**
Laurel Ct. G72: Flem	3E **127**
Laurel Ct. G75: E Kil	6F **157**
Laurel Dr. G75: E Kil	6E **157**
Laurel Dr. ML2: Wis	5D **148**
Laurel Dr. ML9: Lark	3E **171**
Laurel Gait G72: Flem	4E **127**
Laurel Gdns. G71: Tann	5D **112**
Laurel Gdns. ML6: Chap	3E **117**
Laurel La. G72: Flem	4E **127**
Laurel La. ML9: Lark	4E **171**
(off Donaldson Rd.)
Laurel Pk. Cl. G13: Glas	4C **62**
Laurel Pk. Gdns. G13: Glas	3C **62**
Laurel Pk. Sports Club	3D **62**
Laurel Pl. G11: Glas	1G **85**
Laurel Pl. G75: E Kil	6F **157**
Laurels, The G77: Newt M	4D **136**
Laurels, The ML1: Carf	5B **132**
Laurel Sq. FK4: Bank	1E **17**
Laurel St. G11: Glas	1G **85**

Laurel Wlk. G73: Ruth	4E **125**
Laurel Way G78: Barr	4D **118**
Laurel Way PA11: Quarr V	2B **76**
Laurel Wynd G72: Flem	4F **127**
Laurence Ct. G15: Glas	4G **45**
Laurence Dr. G15: Glas	4G **45**
Laurence Dr. G61: Bear	1D **46**
Laurence Gdns. G15: Glas	4G **45**
Laurenstone Ter. G74: E Kil	6B **142**
(off Capelrig Dr.)
Lauren Vw. ML6: Air	4H **95**
Lauren Way PA2: Pais	4D **100**
Laurie Ct. G71: Tann	6E **113**
LAURIESTON	6F **87**
Laurieston Cres. ML6: Chap	4D **116**
Lauriestone Pl. ML5: Coat	2F **115**
Laurieston Rd. G5: Glas	1F **107**
Laurieston Way G73: Ruth	3C **124**
Lauriston Gro. G77: Newt M	4B **136**
Lavelle Dr. ML5: Coat	4E **95**
Lavender Ct. G71: View	6G **113**
Lavender Cres. G33: Mille	4A **68**
Lavender Dr. G75: E Kil	6F **157**
Lavender Dr. G77: Newt M	2B **136**
Lavender La. ML8: Carl	5C **174**
Lavender St. G33: Mille	4A **68**
Laverock Av. ML3: Ham	1C **162**
Laverockhall St. G21: Glas	6B **66**
Laverock Rd. ML6: Air	6B **74**
Laverock Ter. G69: Mood	6D **54**
LAW	6D **166**
Law Dr. ML1: N'hill	3C **132**
Lawers Dr. G61: Bear	1C **46**
Lawers Dr. ML1: Moth	6C **148**
Lawers La. ML1: N'hill	3C **132**
Lawers Rd. G43: Glas	2H **121**
Lawers Rd. PA4: Renf	2E **83**
Lawfield Av. G77: Newt M	4H **137**
LAW HILL	1G **173**
Lawhill Av. G45: Glas	3H **123**
Lawhill Rd. ML8: Carl	6D **166**
Lawhill Rd. ML8: Law	6D **166**
Lawhope Mill Rd. ML6: Chap	2F **117**
Lawmarnock Cres. PA11: Bri W	4E **77**
Lawmarnock Rd. PA11: Bri W	5E **77**
Lawmoor Rd. G5: Glas	2G **107**
Lawmoor St. G5: Glas	2G **107**
Lawmuir Cres. G81: Faif	6G **25**
Lawmuir Pl. ML4: Bell	5C **130**
Lawmuir Rd. ML4: Bell	4C **130**
Lawmuir Rd. ML8: Law	6D **166**
Lawn Pk. G62: Miln	4A **28**
(not continuous)
LAWN PK.	4A **28**
Lawn St. PA1: Pais	6B **82**
LAW OF MAULDSLIE	1F **173**
Law Pl. G74: E Kil	5G **141**
Lawrence Av. G46: Giff	6A **122**
Lawrence St. G11: Glas	1A **86**
Lawrie Pl. ML1: Cle	6E **133**
Lawrie St. G11: Glas	1H **85**
Lawrie St. ML2: Newm	4D **150**
Lawrie Way ML9: Lark	4E **171**
LAW RDBT.	5G **141**
Lawson Av. ML1: Moth	6G **147**
Law St. G40: Glas	6D **88**
Law Vw. ML2: Over	5A **166**
Laxford Av. G44: Glas	3E **123**
Laxford Pl. ML5: Coat	6F **95**
Laxford Rd. PA8: Ersk	6C **42**
Laxford Way ML1: N'hill	3C **132**
Laxton Dr. G66: Lenz	3E **53**
Layland Rd. ML1: Moth	3E **147**
Laymoor Av. PA4: Renf	6H **61**
Laymoor Pl. PA4: Renf	6G **61**
Laymoor Sq. PA4: Renf	6G **61**
Laymoor Wlk. PA4: Renf	6H **61**
Lea Av. G78: Neil	2D **134**
Leabank Av. PA2: Pais	5A **102**

Leadburn Rd. G21: Glas.............5E 67
Leadburn St. G32: Glas.............4G 89
Leader St. G33: Glas.............2F 89
Leaend Rd. ML6: Air.............2G 95
Leander Cres. ML4: Moss.............2G 131
Leander Cres. PA4: Renf.............1G 83
Learigg Rd. ML6: Plain.............6H 75
Learmont Pl. G62: Miln.............3F 27
Leas, The G75: E Kil.............1C 168
Leathem Pl. ML2: Wis.............2C 164
Leathen Pl. PA8: Ersk.............6C 42
Leckethill Av. G68: Cumb.............6B 36
Leckethill Ct. G68: Cumb.............6B 36
Leckethill Pl. G68: Cumb.............6A 36
Leckethill Vw. G68: Cumb.............6B 36
Leckie Ct. ML3: Ham.............5G 145
Leckie Dr. ML3: Ham.............5G 145
Leckie St. G43: Glas.............5A 106
Leck Wynd G33: Glas.............2H 67
Ledaig Pl. G31: Glas.............4E 89
Ledaig St. G31: Glas.............4E 89
Ledard Rd. G42: Glas.............5D 106
Ledcameroch Cres. G61: Bear.............3D 46
Ledcameroch Pk. G61: Bear.............3D 46
Ledcameroch Rd. G61: Bear.............3D 46
Ledgate G66: Kirkin.............4D 32
Ledgowan Pl. G20: Glas.............1B 64
Ledi Dr. G61: Bear.............6B 26
Ledi Path ML1: N'hill.............4C 132
Ledi Rd. G43: Glas.............2A 122
Ledmore Dr. G15: Glas.............3H 45
Lednock Rd. G33: Step.............4C 68
Lednock Rd. G52: Glas.............6A 84
Ledvinka Cres. ML3: Ham.............3E 145
Lee Av. G33: Glas.............2G 89
Leebank Dr. G44: Neth.............6D 122
Leeburn Av. PA6: Hous.............2C 78
Leeburn Gdns. PA6: Hous.............2C 78
Leechlee Rd. ML3: Ham.............6A 146
Leechman Gdns. G64: B'rig.............6F 51
Lee Cres. G64: B'rig.............1C 66
Leefield Dr. G44: Neth.............5D 122
Leehill Rd. G21: Glas.............2A 66
Leemuir Vw. ML8: Carl.............5F 175
Lee Pl. ML4: Bell.............3F 131
Lees Burn Ct. G74: E Kil.............4A 142
Leesburn Pl. G74: E Kil.............5H 141
Lee's Ct. ML5: Coat.............6C 94
Leeside Rd. G21: Glas.............2A 66
Leesland G71: Tann.............5E 113
Leeward Circ. G75: E Kil.............2C 156
Leewood Dr. G44: Neth.............5E 123
Le Froy Gdns. G75: E Kil.............3E 157
Le Froy La. G75: E Kil.............3E 157
Lefroy St. ML5: Coat.............4A 94
Legbrannock Av. ML1: N'hse.............6D 116
Legbrannock Cres. ML1: N'hill.............3D 132
Legbrannock Rd. ML1: N'hill.............1E 133
Legbrannock Rd. ML1: N'hse.............1E 133
Leggate Way ML4: Bell.............5C 114
Leggatston Av. G53: Glas.............6C 120
Leggatston Dr. G53: Glas.............5C 120
Leggatston Pl. G53: Glas.............5C 120
Leggatston Rd. G53: Glas.............4C 120
Leggatston Rd. G53: Glas.............5C 120
Legion Pl. ML9: Lark.............2C 170
Leglen Wood Cres. G21: Glas.............3F 67
Leglen Wood Dr. G21: Glas.............3F 67
Leglen Wood Gdns. G21: Glas.............3F 67
Leglen Wood Pl. G21: Glas.............3G 67
Leglen Wood Rd. G21: Glas.............3F 67
Leicester Av. G12: Glas.............4H 63
Leighton Ct. G72: Newt.............1G 127
Leighton St. G20: Glas.............3C 64
Leighton St. ML2: Wis.............1H 165
Leishman Pl. ML6: Air.............2D 96
Leisuredrome, The.............3A 50
.............(Bishopbriggs Sports Centre)
Leitchland Rd. PA2: Pais.............5B 100

Leitchland Rd. PA5: Eld.............5B 100
Leithland Av. G53: Glas.............4B 104
Leithland Rd. G53: Glas.............4B 104
Leith St. G33: Glas.............3F 89
Leman Dr. PA6: C'lee.............3D 78
Leman Gro. PA6: C'lee.............3D 78
Lembert Dr. G76: Clar.............1B 138
Lemondgate Dr. G82: Dumb.............1G 19
Lendale La. G64: B'rig.............3C 50
Lendalfoot Gdns. ML3: Ham.............1B 160
Lendal Pl. G75: E Kil.............5A 156
Lendel Pl. G51: Glas.............5B 86
Lenihall Dr. G45: Glas.............5A 124
Lenihall Ter. G45: Glas.............5A 124
Lennox Av. G14: Glas.............6C 62
Lennox Av. G62: Miln.............4G 27
Lennox Av. ML5: Coat.............4A 94
Lennox Av. PA7: B'ton.............4H 41
Lennox Ct. G65: Kils.............3H 13
Lennox Ct. G66: Kirkin.............5E 33
.............(off Newdyke Rd.)
Lennox Cres. G64: B'rig.............1B 66
Lennox Dr. G61: Bear.............1F 47
Lennox Dr. G77: Newt M.............1E 153
Lennox Dr. G81: Faif.............6E 25
Lennox Gdns. G14: Glas.............5D 62
Lennox Ga. G33: Step.............5D 68
Lennox Ho. G67: Cumb.............3H 37
Lennox La. E. G14: Glas.............6D 62
Lennox La. W. G14: Glas.............6C 62
.............(Gleneagles La. Nth.)
.............(off Gleneagles La. Nth.)
Lennox La. W. G14: Glas.............5D 62
.............(Norse La. Nth.)
.............(off Norse La. Nth.)
Lennoxmill La. G66: Len.............3E 9
Lennox Pl. G66: Len.............3F 9
Lennox Pl. G81: Clyd.............4A 44
Lennox Pl. ML1: New S.............5B 132
Lennox Rd. G66: Len.............2E 9
Lennox Rd. G67: Cumb.............3H 37
Lennox Rd. G82: Dumb.............4H 19
Lennox Rd. G82: Mil.............4E 21
Lennox Sq. G66: Len.............3F 9
.............(off Winston Cres.)
Lennox St. G20: Glas.............2A 64
Lennox St. G82: Dumb.............4G 19
Lennox St. ML2: Wis.............5C 150
Lennox Ter. PA3: Pais.............3C 82
LENNOXTOWN.............3F 9
Lennox Vw. G81: Clyd.............4D 44
Lentran St. G34: Glas.............4A 92
Leny St. G20: Glas.............5D 64
LENZIE.............3C 52
Lenzie Ga. G21: Glas.............4B 66
Lenzie Golf Course.............4D 52
LENZIEMILL.............5A 38
Lenziemill Rd. G67: Cumb.............1G 57
Lenzie Pl. G21: Glas.............3B 66
Lenzie Rd. G33: Step.............2D 68
Lenzie Rd. G66: Kirkin.............6D 32
Lenzie Station (Rail).............3C 52
Lenzie St. G21: Glas.............4B 66
Lenzie Ter. G21: Glas.............3A 66
Lenzie Way G21: Glas.............3A 66
Leonard Gro. ML1: Cle.............6E 133
Lesley Quad. ML4: Bell.............5B 130
Leslie Av. G77: Newt M.............2E 137
Leslie Av. PA7: B'ton.............4H 41
Leslie Rd. G41: Glas.............3C 106
Leslie St. G41: Glas.............2D 106
Leslie St. ML1: Moth.............2H 147
Lesmuir Dr. G14: Glas.............4H 61
Lesmuir Pl. G14: Glas.............4H 61
Letham Ct. G43: Glas.............2C 122
Letham Dr. G43: Glas.............2C 122
Letham Dr. G64: B'rig.............1E 67
Letham Grange G68: Cumb.............1H 37
Lethamhill Cres. G33: Glas.............2H 89

Lethamhill Golf Course.............6H 67
Lethamhill Pl. G33: Glas.............2G 89
Lethamhill Rd. G33: Glas.............2G 89
Letham Oval G64: B'rig.............1F 67
Lethbridge Pl. G75: E Kil.............3E 157
Letherby Dr. G42: Glas.............6F 107
Letherby Dr. G44: Glas.............6F 107
Letheron Dr. ML2: Wis.............4H 149
Lethington Av. G41: Glas.............5C 106
Lethington Pl. G41: Glas.............5D 106
Lethington Rd. G46: Giff.............2G 137
Letterfearn Dr. G23: Glas.............6C 48
Letterickhills Cres. G72: Flem.............4E 127
Lettoch St. G51: Glas.............4G 85
Leven Av. G64: B'rig.............6D 50
Leven Ct. G78: Barr.............2D 118
Leven Ct. G82: Dumb.............3E 19
Leven Dr. G61: Bear.............3F 47
Leven Dr. ML3: Ham.............3F 161
Levenford Ho. (County Library HQ).............4E 19
Levenford Ter. G82: Dumb.............4E 19
Levengrove Ct. G82: Dumb.............4E 19
Levengrove Ter. G82: Dumb.............4E 19
Leven Path ML1: Holy.............2A 132
.............(off Graham St.)
Leven Pl. PA8: Ersk.............6C 42
Leven Quad. ML6: Air.............1H 95
Leven Rd. ML3: Fern.............2E 163
Leven Rd. ML5: Coat.............2G 93
Leven Sq. PA4: Renf.............5D 60
Leven St. G41: Glas.............2D 106
Leven St. G82: Dumb.............4G 19
Leven St. ML1: Moth.............4G 147
Leven Ter. ML1: Carf.............5C 132
Leven Valley Ent. Cen. G82: Dumb.............3D 18
Leven Vw. G81: Clyd.............4D 44
Leven Way G67: Cumb.............4H 37
.............(within The Cumbernauld Shop. Cen.)
Leven Way G75: E Kil.............5B 156
Leven Way PA2: Pais.............4C 100
Levern Bri. Ct. G53: Glas.............6H 103
Levern Bri. Gro. G53: Glas.............6H 103
Levern Bri. Pl. G53: Glas.............1H 119
Levern Bri. Rd. G53: Glas.............1H 119
Levern Bri. Way G53: Glas.............1H 119
Levern Cres. G78: Barr.............5D 118
Leverndale Ct. G53: Glas.............4H 103
LEVERNDALE HOSPITAL.............3H 103
Leverndale Rd. G53: Glas.............4H 103
Levern Gdns. G78: Barr.............4D 118
Leverngrove Ct. G53: Glas.............1H 119
Levernside Av. G53: Glas.............5C 104
Levernside Av. G78: Barr.............5C 118
Levernside Cres. G53: Glas.............4B 104
Levernside Rd. G53: Glas.............4B 104
Lewis G74: E Kil.............2C 158
Lewis Av. ML2: Wis.............4A 150
Lewis Av. PA4: Renf.............2F 83
Lewis Cres. G60: Old K.............2G 43
Lewis Cres. PA10: Kilba.............3C 98
Lewis Dr. G60: Old K.............2F 43
Lewis Gdns. G60: Old K.............2G 43
Lewis Gdns. G61: Bear.............1B 46
Lewis Gro. G60: Old K.............2G 43
Lewis Pl. G60: Old K.............2G 43
Lewis Pl. G77: Newt M.............3B 136
Lewis Pl. ML6: Air.............5D 96
Lewiston Dr. G23: Glas.............6B 48
.............(off Lewiston Rd.)
Lewiston Pl. G23: Glas.............6B 48
.............(off Lewiston Rd.)
Lewiston Rd. G23: Glas.............6B 48
Lexwell Av. PA5: Eld.............2B 100
Leyden Ct. G20: Glas.............4C 64
Leyden Gdns. G20: Glas.............4D 64
Leyden St. G20: Glas.............4C 64
Leyland Av. ML3: Ham.............3E 161
Leyland Wynd ML3: Ham.............4E 161
Leys, The G64: B'rig.............6C 50

Leys Pk. ML3: Ham	5E **145**	
Liath Av. ML1: Moth	6C **148**	
Libberton Way ML3: Ham	6E **145**	
Liberton St. G33: Glas	3F **89**	
Liberty Av. G69: Barg	6E **93**	
Liberty Path G72: Blan	2B **144**	
Liberty Rd. ML4: Bell	3C **130**	
Libo Av. G53: Glas	4D **104**	
Libo Pl. PA8: Ersk	5C **42**	
Library & Community Cen.	2B **100**	
Library Gdns. G72: Camb	1H **125**	
Library La. G46: T'bnk	4F **121**	
Library Rd. ML2: Wis	6H **149**	
Lickprivick Rd. G75: E Kil	6D **156**	
Liddell Gro. G75: E Kil	4F **157**	
Liddell Rd. G67: Cumb	4A **38**	
Liddells Ct. G64: B'rig	2C **66**	
Liddell St. G32: Carm	4C **110**	
Liddel Rd. G67: Cumb	4G **37**	
Liddesdale Av. PA2: Pais	6B **100**	
Liddesdale Pl. G22: Glas	2A **66**	
Liddesdale Rd. G22: Glas	2F **65**	
Liddesdale Sq. G22: Glas	2H **65**	
Liddesdale Ter. G22: Glas	2A **66**	
Liddlesdale Pas. G22: Glas	2G **65**	
Liddoch Way G73: Ruth	5B **108**	
Liff Gdns. G64: B'rig	1F **67**	
Liff Pl. G34: Glas	2A **92**	
LIGHTBURN	**4A 90**	
LIGHTBURN	**4E 127**	
LIGHTBURN HOSPITAL	**4B 90**	
Lightburn Pl. G32: Glas	4B **90**	
Lightburn Rd. G31: Glas	5E **89**	
Lightburn Rd. G72: Camb	3D **126**	
Lightburn Rd. G72: Flem	3D **126**	
Lighthouse, The	6C 6 (4F **87**)	
(off Mitchell St.)		
Lilac Av. G67: Cumb	6E **17**	
Lilac Av. G81: Clyd	2H **43**	
Lilac Ct. G67: Cumb	6E **17**	
Lilac Cres. G71: View	5F **113**	
Lilac Gdns. G64: B'rig	1D **66**	
Lilac Gro. ML2: Wis	2F **165**	
Lilac Hill G67: Cumb	6F **17**	
Lilac Hill ML3: Ham	1B **162**	
Lilac Pl. G67: Cumb	6F **17**	
Lilac Pl. PA5: John	4H **99**	
Lilac Way ML1: Holy	2B **132**	
Lilac Wynd G72: Flem	3E **127**	
Lillie Art Gallery	3H **27**	
Lillieleaf Dr. ML6: Chap	4E **117**	
Lillyburn Pl. G15: Glas	3G **45**	
Lilly Pl. G77: Newt M	2C **136**	
Lilybank Av. G69: Muirh	2A **70**	
Lilybank Av. G72: Camb	3B **126**	
Lilybank Av. ML6: Air	1B **96**	
Lilybank Gdns. G12: Glas	1B **86**	
Lilybank Gdns. La. G12: Glas	1B **86**	
Lilybank La. G12: Glas	1B **86**	
Lilybank St. ML3: Ham	5G **145**	
Lilybank Ter. G12: Glas	1B **86**	
Lilybank Ter. La. G12: Glas	1B **86**	
(off Gt. George St.)		
Lilybank Wynd PA5: John	2F **99**	
Lily Gdns. G66: Kirkin	5E **33**	
Lily St. G40: Glas	2D **108**	
Limecraigs Av. PA2: Pais	6G **101**	
Limecraigs Cres. PA2: Pais	6G **101**	
Limecraigs Rd. PA2: Pais	6F **101**	
Lime Cres. G67: Cumb	2E **39**	
Lime Cres. ML6: Air	4C **96**	
Lime Gro. G66: Lenz	2D **52**	
Lime Gro. G72: Blan	6A **128**	
Lime Gro. ML1: Moth	5G **147**	
Limegrove St. ML4: Bell	6C **114**	
Limekilns Dr. G66: Kirkin	5A **34**	
Limekilns Rd. G67: Cumb	1H **57**	
Limekilns St. G81: Faif	6F **25**	
Lime La. G14: Glas	6D **62**	

Lime Loan ML1: Holy	3B **132**	
Lime Rd. G82: Dumb	3F **19**	
Limes, The G44: Glas	3F **123**	
Limeside Av. G73: Ruth	6D **108**	
Limeside Gdns. G73: Ruth	6E **109**	
Lime St. G14: Glas	6D **62**	
Limetree Av. G71: View	5F **113**	
Limetree Ct. ML3: Ham	4E **145**	
Limetree Cres. G77: Newt M	5D **136**	
Limetree Dr. G81: Clyd	3C **44**	
Limetree La. PA7: B'ton	5G **41**	
Limetree Quad. G71: View	5G **113**	
Limetree Wlk. G66: Milt C	1B **32**	
Limeview Av. PA2: Pais	6F **101**	
Limeview Cres. PA2: Pais	6F **101**	
Limeview Rd. PA2: Pais	6F **101**	
Limeview Way PA2: Pais	6F **101**	
Limewood Pl. G69: Barg	5E **93**	
Linacre Dr. G32: Glas	6C **90**	
Linacre Gdns. G32: Glas	6D **90**	
LINBURN	**6D 42**	
Linburn Pl. G52: Glas	5A **84**	
Linburn Rd. G52: Glas	4G **83**	
Linburn Rd. PA8: Ersk	6C **42**	
LINCLIVE INTERCHANGE	6B **80**	
Linclive Spur PA3: Lin	6B **80**	
Linclive Spur PA3: Pais	6B **80**	
Linclive Ter. PA3: Lin	6B **80**	
Lincluden Path G41: Glas	1D **106**	
Lincoln Av. G13: Glas	2C **62**	
Lincoln Av. G71: Tann	4D **112**	
Lincoln Ct. ML5: Coat	3C **94**	
Lincoln Path ML6: Air	2C **96**	
Lincuan Av. G46: Giff	6A **122**	
Lindams G71: Udd	2D **128**	
Lindcres Av. G73: Ruth	6D **108**	
Lindean Dr. ML6: Chap	5E **117**	
Linden Av. ML2: Wis	3A **150**	
Linden Ct. G81: Hard	1C **44**	
Linden Dr. FK4: Bank	1E **17**	
Linden Dr. G81: Hard	1C **44**	
Linden Lea G66: Milt C	6B **10**	
Linden Lea ML3: Ham	5F **145**	
Linden Pl. G13: Glas	2F **63**	
Lindens, The G71: Both	5E **129**	
Linden St. G13: Glas	2F **63**	
Linden Way G13: Glas	2F **63**	
Lindores Dr. G33: Step	5C **68**	
Lindores Dr. G74: E Kil	2E **157**	
Lindores Pl. G74: E Kil	2E **157**	
Lindores St. G42: Glas	5F **107**	
Lind Pl. ML6: Air	3D **96**	
Lindrick Dr. G23: Glas	6C **48**	
Lindsaybeg Ct. G69: Chry	1A **70**	
Lindsaybeg Rd. G66: Lenz	3D **52**	
Lindsaybeg Rd. G69: Chry	5H **53**	
Lindsay Dr. G12: Glas	3H **63**	
Lindsay Dr. ML1: Carf	6C **132**	
Lindsayfield Av. G75: E Kil	1B **168**	
Lindsayfield Rd. G75: E Kil	6A **156**	
Lindsayfield Rd. G75: E Kil	6B **156**	
Lindsay Gro. G74: E Kil	1H **157**	
Lindsay Pl. G12: Glas	3H **63**	
Lindsay Pl. G66: Lenz	4D **52**	
Lindsay Pl. G74: E Kil	2A **158**	
Lindsay Pl. PA5: John	2G **99**	
(off Thorn Brae)		
Lindsay Rd. G74: E Kil	2H **157**	
Lindsay Ter. G66: Len	3G **9**	
Lindseyhill G72: Blan	1H **143**	
Lindum Cres. ML1: Moth	1D **146**	
Lindum St. ML1: Moth	1D **146**	
Linfern Rd. G12: Glas	6A **64**	
Linghope Pl. ML2: Wis	3F **165**	
Lingley Av. ML6: Air	5A **96**	
Linhope Pl. G75: E Kil	4A **156**	
Links, The G68: Cumb	5B **16**	
Links Rd. G32: Glas	2D **110**	
Links Rd. G44: Glas	3G **123**	

Links Vw. ML9: Lark	3E **171**	
Linksview Rd. ML1: Carf	6B **132**	
Linkwood Av. G15: Glas	4H **45**	
Linkwood Cres. G15: Glas	4A **46**	
Linkwood Dr. G15: Glas	4H **45**	
Linkwood Gdns. G15: Glas	4B **46**	
Linkwood Gro. G15: Glas	4B **46**	
Linkwood Pl. G15: Glas	4H **45**	
Linkwood Rd. ML6: Air	6B **74**	
Linlithgow Gdns. G32: Glas	6D **90**	
Linlithgow Pl. G69: G'csh	5C **70**	
Linn Crematorium	5E **123**	
Linn Cres. PA2: Pais	6G **101**	
Linndale Dr. G45: Glas	6G **123**	
Linndale Gdns. G45: Glas	6G **123**	
Linndale Gro. G45: Glas	6G **123**	
Linndale Oval G45: Glas	5G **123**	
Linndale Rd. G45: Glas	6G **123**	
Linndale Way G45: Glas	5G **123**	
Linn Dr. G44: Neth	4D **122**	
Linnet Av. PA5: John	6C **98**	
Linnet Dr. G66: Lenz	1F **53**	
Linnet Pl. G13: Glas	2H **61**	
Linnet Rd. ML4: Bell	3D **130**	
Linnet Way ML4: Bell	5B **114**	
Linn Gdns. G68: Cumb	3B **36**	
Linn Ga. G68: Cumb	3C **36**	
Linn Glen G66: Len	3H **9**	
Linnhead Dr. G53: Glas	1B **120**	
Linnhead Pl. G14: Glas	5B **62**	
Linnhe Av. G44: Glas	3E **123**	
Linnhe Av. G64: B'rig	6D **50**	
Linnhe Av. ML3: Ham	2E **161**	
Linnhe Ct. ML9: Lark	6H **163**	
Linnhe Cres. ML2: Wis	2H **165**	
Linnhe Dr. G78: Barr	2D **118**	
Linnhe Pl. G72: Blan	5A **128**	
Linnhe Pl. PA8: Ersk	6C **42**	
Linnpark Av. G44: Neth	5D **122**	
Linnpark Ct. G44: Glas	4D **122**	
Linn Pk. Gdns. PA5: John	3G **99**	
Linn Pk. Golf Course	4F **123**	
Linnpark Ind. Est. G45: Glas	4G **123**	
Linnvale Way G68: Dull	5E **15**	
Linn Valley Vw. G45: Glas	4H **123**	
Linnview Av. G44: Glas	4F **123**	
Linnview Ct. G44: Glas	3F **123**	
Linnview Dr. G44: Glas	3F **123**	
Linnwell Cres. PA2: Pais	6H **101**	
Linnwood Ct. G44: Glas	2E **123**	
Linside Av. PA1: Pais	1C **102**	
Lint Butts G72: Blan	2A **144**	
Lintfield Loan G71: Udd	2E **129**	
(off Flax Rd.)		
Linthaugh Rd. G53: Glas	3A **104**	
Linthaugh Ter. G53: Glas	4D **104**	
LINTHOUSE	**3E 85**	
Linthouse Bldgs. G51: Glas	3E **85**	
Linthouse Dr. G51: Glas	2E **85**	
Linthouse Rd. G51: Glas	2E **85**	
Lintie Rd. ML1: N'hill	3C **132**	
Lintlaw G72: Blan	5B **128**	
Lintlaw Dr. G52: Glas	5B **84**	
Lint Mill Rd. G66: Kirkin	1G **53**	
Lintmill Ter. G78: Neil	3C **134**	
Lint Mill Way G68: Cumb	3C **36**	
Linton Pl. ML5: Coat	2A **114**	
Linton St. G33: Glas	3G **89**	
Lintwhite Ct. PA11: Bri W	4G **77**	
(off Lintwhite Cres.)		
Lintwhite Cres. PA11: Bri W	3G **77**	
LINVALE	**6G 45**	
LINWOOD	**6A 80**	
Linwood Av. G74: E Kil	1B **156**	
Linwood Av. G76: Busby	2D **138**	
Linwood Community Sports Hub	4G **79**	
Linwood Ind. Est. PA3: Lin	1H **99**	
Linwood Rd. PA1: Lin	6B **80**	
Linwood Rd. PA1: Pais	6B **80**	

Linwood Rd. – Loch Meadie

Linwood Rd. PA3: Lin 6B **80**
Linwood Ter. ML3: Ham 5F **145**
Lion Bank G66: Kirkin 4D **32**
Lion M. G66: Kirkin 1G **53**
Lipton Gdns. G5: Glas 2H **107**
Lismore G74: E Kil 3C **158**
Lismore Av. ML1: Moth 1D **146**
Lismore Av. PA4: Renf 2F **83**
Lismore Dr. ML5: Coat 1H **113**
Lismore Dr. PA2: Pais 6H **101**
Lismore Dr. PA3: Lin 6F **79**
Lismore Gdns. PA10: Kilba 3C **98**
Lismore Hill ML3: Ham 6B **144**
Lismore Pl. G69: Mood 4E **55**
Lismore Pl. G77: Newt M 4B **136**
Lismore Pl. ML6: Air 6C **96**
Lismore Rd. G12: Glas 4H **63**
Lister Gdns. G76: Busby 4E **139**
Lister Hgts. G4: Glas 5H **7** (4A **88**)
.... *(off Drygate)*
Lister Pl. G52: Hill E 4A **84**
Lister Rd. G52: Hill E 4H **83**
.... (not continuous)
Lister St. G4: Glas 2G **7** (2H **87**)
Lister Twr. G75: E Kil 3H **157**
.... *(off Sinclair Pl.)*
Lister Wlk. ML4: Bell 6E **115**
Lister Way G72: Blan 4A **144**
Lithgow Av. G66: Kirkin 6E **33**
Lithgow Cres. PA2: Pais 3C **102**
Lithgow Dr. ML1: Cle 6H **133**
Lithgow Pl. G74: E Kil 1D **156**
Little Corseford PA5: John 6C **98**
.... *(off Corseford Av.)*
Little Dovehill G1: Glas 5H **87**
Little Drum Rd. G68: Cumb 5F **35**
LITTLE EARNOCK 2E **161**
Little Haven Ter. G75: E Kil 2C **168**
Littlehill Golf Course **2C 66**
Littlehill St. G21: Glas 5C **66**
Littleholm Pl. G81: Clyd 3A **44**
Little John Gdns. ML2: Newm 5D **150**
Littlemill Av. G68: Cumb 4A **36**
Littlemill Ct. G60: Bowl 5H **21**
Littlemill Cres. G53: Glas 5A **104**
Littlemill Dr. G53: Glas 5A **104**
Littlemill Gdns. G53: Glas 5A **104**
Littlemill La. G60: Bowl 5A **22**
Littlemill Pl. G60: Bowl 5A **22**
Littlemill Way ML1: Carf 6B **132**
Littleston Gdns. PA8: Ersk 6D **42**
Little St. G3: Glas 5F **5** (4D **86**)
Littleton Dr. G23: Glas 6B **48**
Littleton St. G23: Glas 6B **48**
Lively Pl. G72: Blan 2A **144**
.... *(off Harkins Av.)*
Livery Wlk. PA11: Bri W 3F **77**
.... *(off Main St.)*
Livingston Dr. ML6: Plain 1G **97**
Livingstone Av. G52: Hill E 3A **84**
Livingstone Blvd. G72: Blan 4A **144**
Livingstone Cres. G72: Blan 6B **128**
Livingstone Cres. G75: E Kil 4F **157**
Livingstone Dr. G75: E Kil 3F **157**
Livingstone Gdns. ML9: Lark 2D **170**
Livingstone La. G71: Both 4E **129**
Livingstone Pk. G65: Kils 1F **13**
Livingstone Pl. ML6: Air 4B **96**
Livingstone St. G81: Clyd 6E **45**
Livingstone St. ML3: Ham 5D **144**
Livingston La. G72: Camb 4A **126**
LivingWell Health Club .... **4H 5 (3E 87)**
.... *(Glasgow)*
.... *(off St Vincent St.)*
LivingWell Health Club **5B 114**
.... *(Strathclyde)*
Lloyd Av. G32: Glas 3A **110**
Lloyd Ct. G73: Ruth 4D **108**
Lloyd Dr. ML1: Carf 6A **132**
Lloyds St. ML5: Coat 6C **94**
Lloyd St. G31: Glas 3C **88**
Lloyd St. G73: Ruth 4D **108**
Lloyd St. ML1: Carf 6A **132**
Lloyd St. Ind. Est. G73: Ruth 4D **108**
Loan, The G62: Miln 1C **26**
Loanbank Pl. G51: Glas 4G **85**
Loanbank Quad. G51: Glas 4F **85**
Loancroft Av. G69: Bail 2A **112**
Loancroft Gdns. G71: Udd 2D **128**
Loancroft Ga. G71: Udd 2C **128**
Loancroft Ho. G69: Bail 2H **111**
Loancroft Pl. G69: Bail 2H **111**
Loanend Cotts. G72: Flem 6F **127**
Loanfoot Av. G13: Glas 2A **62**
Loanfoot Av. G78: Neil 3D **134**
Loanfoot Rd. G72: Blan 4B **144**
LOANHEAD 1E **83**
Loanhead Av. ML1: N'hill 4D **132**
Loanhead Av. PA3: Lin 5G **79**
Loanhead Av. PA4: Renf 6F **61**
Loanhead Cres. ML1: N'hill 4D **132**
Loanhead La. PA3: Lin 5G **79**
Loanhead Rd. ML1: N'hill 4C **132**
Loanhead Rd. PA3: Lin 5G **79**
Loanhead St. G32: Glas 4H **89**
Loanhead St. ML5: Coat 2A **114**
Loaning ML9: Lark 3E **171**
.... *(off Doon St.)*
Loaning, The G46: Giff 1G **137**
Loaning, The G61: Bear 2E **47**
Loaning, The G66: Kirkin 6C **32**
Loaning, The ML1: Moth 2E **147**
Loaninghead Dr. G82: Dumb 1H **19**
Loan Lea Cres. ML9: Lark 4D **170**
Lobnitz Av. PA4: Renf 6F **61**
Lochaber Dr. G73: Ruth 3F **125**
Lochaber Path G72: Blan 2B **144**
Lochaber Pl. G74: E Kil 6H **141**
Lochaber Rd. G61: Bear 5G **47**
Lochaber Wlk. G66: Milt C 4C **10**
Loch Achray Gdns. G32: Glas 1C **110**
Loch Achray St. G32: Glas 1C **110**
Lochain Way ML1: Moth 6C **148**
Lochaline Av. PA2: Pais 3E **101**
Lochaline Dr. G44: Glas 3E **123**
Lochalsh Cres. G66: Milt C 5C **10**
Lochalsh Dr. PA2: Pais 3E **101**
Lochalsh Pl. G72: Blan 5H **127**
Lochalsh Pl. ML6: Air 6C **96**
Lochan Rd. G65: Kils 2A **14**
Lochar Cres. G53: Glas 3D **104**
Lochard Dr. PA2: Pais 4E **101**
Lochar Pl. G75: E Kil 4A **156**
Loch Assynt G74: E Kil 3B **158**
Loch Awe G74: E Kil 3A **158**
Loch Awe Pl. ML5: Coat 5B **94**
Lochay St. G32: Glas 1C **110**
Lochbrae Dr. G73: Ruth 3E **125**
Lochbridge Rd. G34: Glas 4G **91**
Lochbroom Ct. G77: Newt M 3F **137**
Lochbroom Dr. G77: Newt M 3F **137**
Lochbroom Dr. PA2: Pais 3E **101**
Loch Brora Cres. ML5: Coat 5A **94**
Lochbuie La. ML6: Glenm 5G **73**
Lochburn Cres. G20: Glas 2C **64**
Lochburn Gdns. G20: Glas 2D **64**
Lochburn Ga. G20: Glas 2C **64**
Lochburn Gro. G20: Glas 2C **64**
.... *(off Lochburn Cres.)*
Lochburn Pas. G20: Glas 2C **64**
Lochburn Rd. G20: Glas 3B **64**
Lochdochart Gdns. G34: Glas 2B **92**
Lochdochart Path G34: Glas 4B **92**
.... *(off Lentran St.)*
Lochdochart Rd. G34: Glas 3A **92**
Lochearn Cres. ML6: Air 1H **95**
Lochearn Cres. PA2: Pais 3E **101**
Lochearnhead Rd. G33: Step 4B **68**
Lochend Av. G69: G'csh 2C **70**
Lochend Cres. G61: Bear 4D **46**
Lochend Dr. G61: Bear 4D **46**
Lochend Path G34: Glas 2H **91**
Lochend Rd. G69: G'csh 2D **70**
.... *(Drumcavel Rd.)*
.... (not continuous)
Lochend Rd. G69: G'csh 2B **92**
.... *(Dubton St.)*
Lochend Rd. G34: Glas 2H **91**
Lochend Rd. G61: Bear 4E **47**
Lochend St. ML1: Moth 3H **147**
Locher Av. PA6: C'lee 2E **79**
Locherburn Av. PA6: C'lee 3D **78**
Locherburn Gro. PA6: C'lee 3D **78**
Locherburn Pl. PA6: C'lee 3D **78**
Locher Cres. PA6: C'lee 3E **79**
Locher Gait PA6: C'lee 3E **79**
Locher Gdns. PA6: C'lee 3E **79**
Locher Pl. ML5: Coat 2F **115**
Locher Rd. PA11: Bri W 6H **77**
Locher Wlk. ML5: Coat 2E **115**
Locher Way PA6: C'lee 3E **79**
Lochfauld Rd. G23: Glas 5E **49**
LOCHFIELD 4B **102**
Lochfield Cres. PA2: Pais 4B **102**
Lochfield Dr. PA2: Pais 4C **102**
Lochfield Gdns. G34: Glas 2B **92**
Lochfield Rd. PA2: Pais 4A **102**
Lochgarry Way ML5: Coat 1H **113**
Lochgilp St. G20: Glas 2A **64**
Loch Goil G74: E Kil 2A **158**
Lochgoin Av. G15: Glas 3G **45**
Lochgoin Gdns. G15: Glas 3G **45**
Lochgreen Pl. ML3: Ham 3F **161**
Lochgreen Pl. ML5: Coat 1G **93**
Lochgreen St. G33: Glas 6F **67**
Loch Gro. G69: G'csh 1A **92**
Lochhead Av. PA3: Lin 6H **79**
Lochiel Ct. ML6: Air 4F **95**
.... *(off Monkscourt Av.)*
Lochiel Dr. G66: Milt C 5C **10**
Lochiel La. G73: Ruth 3F **125**
Lochiel Rd. G46: T'bnk 3F **121**
Lochinch Pl. G77: Newt M 4A **136**
Lochinch Rd. G41: Glas 3G **105**
Lochinvar Rd. G67: Cumb 6F **37**
Lochinver Cres. G72: Blan 6A **144**
Lochinver Cres. PA2: Pais 3E **101**
Lochinver Dr. G44: Glas 3E **123**
Lochinver Gro. G72: Camb 2B **126**
Loch Laidon Ct. G32: Glas 1C **110**
Loch Laidon St. G32: Glas 1D **110**
Loch Laxford G74: E Kil 3B **158**
Loch Lea G66: Kirkin 3F **33**
Lochlea G74: E Kil 5D **142**
Lochlea Av. G81: Clyd 4E **45**
Lochlea Loan ML9: Lark 3E **171**
.... *(off Catrine St.)*
Lochlea Rd. G73: Ruth 2B **124**
.... *(Ailsa Dr.)*
Lochlea Rd. G43: Glas 1B **122**
Lochlea Rd. G67: Cumb 2B **38**
Lochlea Rd. G76: Busby 4C **138**
Lochlea Way ML1: N'hill 3E **133**
Lochleven La. G42: Glas 6E **107**
Lochleven Rd. G42: Glas 6E **107**
LOCHLIBO 6C **118**
Lochlibo Av. G13: Glas 3H **61**
Lochlibo Cres. G78: Barr 6C **118**
Lochlibo Ter. G78: Barr 6C **118**
Loch Long G74: E Kil 3A **158**
Loch Loyal G74: E Kil 3B **158**
Lochmaben Cres. G72: Camb 5H **125**
Lochmaben Rd. G52: Glas 1H **103**
Lochmaben Rd. G69: G'csh 5D **70**
Lochmaddy Av. G44: Glas 3E **123**
Loch Maree G74: E Kil 3B **158**
Loch Meadie G74: E Kil 3B **158**

A–Z Glasgow 245

Lochnagar Dr. G61: Bear	6B **26**	
Lochnagar Rd. ML1: Moth	6C **148**	
Lochnagar Way ML9: Lark	4E **171**	
.... (off Bannockburn Dr.)		
Loch Naver G74: E Kil	3B **158**	
Lochore Av. PA3: Pais	4B **82**	
Loch Pk. ML2: Wis	6A **150**	
Loch Pk. Av. ML8: Carl	5C **174**	
Lochpark Pl. ML9: Lark	4C **170**	
Loch Pl. PA11: Bri W	3F **77**	
Lochranza Ct. ML1: Carf	5B **132**	
Lochranza Cres. ML6: Air	5G **95**	
Lochranza Dr. G75: E Kil	1B **168**	
Lochranza La. G75: E Kil	1C **168**	
Lochrin St. ML5: Coat	6D **94**	
Loch Rd. G33: Step	4D **68**	
Loch Rd. G62: Miln	2H **27**	
Loch Rd. G66: Kirkin	6D **32**	
Loch Rd. ML6: Chap	3D **116**	
Loch Rd. PA11: Bri W	3F **77**	
Loch Shin G74: E Kil	3B **158**	
Lochside G61: Bear	4F **47**	
Lochside G69: G'csh	3D **70**	
Lochside Av. PA7: B'ton	6G **41**	
Lochside Cres. ML6: Air	6A **74**	
Lochside St. G41: Glas	4C **106**	
Lochsloy Ct. G22: Glas	5H **65**	
Loch St. ML6: C'bnk	3B **116**	
Loch Striven G74: E Kil	2A **158**	
Loch Torridon G74: E Kil	3B **158**	
Loch Vw. ML6: C'bnk	3B **116**	
Lochview Cres. G33: Glas	6H **67**	
Lochview Dr. G33: Glas	6H **67**	
Lochview Gdns. G33: Glas	6H **67**	
Lochview Ga. G33: Glas	6H **67**	
Lochview Pl. G33: Glas	6H **67**	
Lochview Quad. ML4: Bell	4B **130**	
Lochview Rd. G61: Bear	4E **47**	
Lochview Rd. ML5: Coat	2G **93**	
Lochview Ter. G69: G'csh	4D **70**	
Loch Voil St. G32: Glas	1D **110**	
Loch Way G69: G'csh	6A **70**	
LOCHWOOD	1C **92**	
Lochwood Loan G69: Mood	4E **55**	
Lochwood St. G33: Glas	1G **89**	
Lochy Av. PA4: Renf	2H **83**	
Lochy Gdns. G64: B'rig	6D **50**	
Lochy Pl. PA8: Ersk	6C **42**	
Lochy St. ML2: Wis	2G **165**	
Locke Gro. ML1: Cle	6F **133**	
Lockerbie Av. G43: Glas	1D **122**	
Locket Yett Vw. ML4: Bell	2A **130**	
Lockhart Av. G72: Camb	1D **126**	
Lockhart Ct. G77: Newt M	1D **152**	
Lockhart Dr. G72: Camb	1D **126**	
Lockhart Dr. G77: Newt M	1D **152**	
Lockhart Pl. ML2: Wis	5C **150**	
Lockhart St. G21: Glas	1D **88**	
Lockhart St. ML3: Ham	5G **161**	
Lockhart St. ML8: Carl	3D **174**	
Lockhart Ter. G74: E Kil	1B **158**	
Locksley Av. G13: Glas	1C **62**	
Locksley Av. G67: Cumb	1G **57**	
Locksley Ct. G67: Cumb	1G **57**	
Locksley Cres. G67: Cumb	1G **57**	
Locksley Pl. G67: Cumb	1G **57**	
Locksley Rd. G67: Cumb	1G **57**	
Locksley Rd. PA2: Pais	4D **100**	
Locksley Way PA2: Pais	4D **100**	
Locks St. ML5: Coat	5F **95**	
Lodge Twr. ML1: Moth	5A **148**	
.... (off Glassford St.)		
Logan Av. G77: Newt M	3C **136**	
Logandale Av. ML2: Newm	3D **150**	
Logan Dr. G68: Cumb	2F **37**	
Logan Gdns. G5: Glas	2H **107**	
Logan Gdns. ML1: Cle	1H **149**	
Loganlea Dr. ML1: Carf	6A **132**	
Logans Rd. ML1: Moth	2D **146**	

Logan St. G72: Blan	2C **144**	
Loganswell Dr. G46: T'bnk	5E **121**	
Loganswell Gdns. G46: T'bnk	5E **121**	
Loganswell Pl. G46: T'bnk	5E **121**	
Loganswell Rd. G46: T'bnk	5E **121**	
Logan Twr. G72: Camb	3E **127**	
Logie Pk. G74: E Kil	6A **142**	
Logie Sq. G74: E Kil	6A **142**	
Lomax St. G33: Glas	3F **89**	
Lomond G75: E Kil	6G **157**	
Lomond Av. PA4: Renf	2D **82**	
Lomond Ct. G67: Cumb	6E **37**	
Lomond Ct. G78: Barr	5E **119**	
Lomond Ct. G82: Dumb	3E **19**	
Lomond Ct. ML5: Coat	4F **95**	
Lomond Cres. G67: Cumb	6E **37**	
Lomond Cres. PA11: Bri W	3E **77**	
Lomond Cres. PA2: Pais	5H **101**	
Lomond Dr. G64: B'rig	4B **50**	
Lomond Dr. G67: Cumb	6D **36**	
Lomond Dr. G71: Both	4F **129**	
Lomond Dr. G77: Newt M	2D **136**	
Lomond Dr. G78: Barr	3D **118**	
Lomond Dr. G82: Dumb	1H **19**	
Lomond Dr. ML2: Wis	1G **165**	
Lomond Dr. ML6: Air	1G **95**	
Lomond Gdns. PA5: Eld	3A **100**	
Lomond Gro. G67: Cumb	6E **37**	
Lomond Pl. G33: Step	5D **68**	
.... (not continuous)		
Lomond Pl. G67: Cumb	6D **36**	
Lomond Pl. ML5: Coat	2A **94**	
Lomond Pl. PA8: Ersk	6C **42**	
Lomond Rd. G61: Bear	5E **47**	
Lomond Rd. G66: Lenz	2D **52**	
Lomond Rd. G71: Tann	4D **112**	
Lomond Rd. ML5: Coat	1G **93**	
Lomondside Av. G76: Clar	1A **138**	
Lomond St. G22: Glas	4F **65**	
Lomond Vw. G67: Cumb	6E **37**	
Lomond Vw. G72: Camb	6A **126**	
Lomond Vw. G81: Clyd	4C **44**	
Lomond Vw. ML3: Ham	1D **160**	
Lomond Wlk. ML1: N'hill	3C **132**	
Lomond Wlk. ML9: Lark	1D **170**	
.... (off Muirshot Rd.)		
Lomond Way ML1: Holy	2A **132**	
.... (off Graham St.)		
London Av. G40: Glas	2D **108**	
London Dr. G32: Glas	3E **111**	
London La. G1: Glas	5H **87**	
.... (off St Andrew's St.)		
London Rd. G1: Glas	5H **87**	
London Rd. G31: Glas	1E **109**	
London Rd. G32: Glas	4A **110**	
London Rd. G40: Glas	5A **88**	
London Rd. Trade Pk. G32: Glas	4B **110**	
London St. ML9: Lark	1C **170**	
London St. PA4: Renf	4F **61**	
London Way G1: Glas	5H **87**	
Lonend PA1: Pais	1B **102**	
Longay Pl. G22: Glas	1G **65**	
Longay St. G22: Glas	1G **65**	
Long Calderwood Cotts. G74: E Kil	5C **142**	
.... (off Maxwellton Rd.)		
Long Crags Vw. G82: Dumb	1H **19**	
Longcroft Dr. PA4: Renf	5E **61**	
Longden St. G81: Clyd	1F **61**	
Longford St. G33: Glas	3F **89**	
Longlee G69: Bail	1H **111**	
Longmeadow PA5: John	4D **98**	
Longmorn Pl. ML1: Carf	6B **132**	
Longniddry Gdns. ML1: N'hse	2D **132**	
Long Row G66: Kirkin	6H **33**	
Long Row G69: Bail	5A **92**	
Longstone Pl. G33: Glas	3B **90**	
Longstone Rd. G33: Glas	3B **90**	
Longwill Ter. G67: Cumb	1B **38**	
Lonmay Dr. G33: Glas	3D **90**	

Lonmay Pl. G33: Glas	3D **90**	
Lonmay Rd. G33: Glas	3D **90**	
Lonsdale Av. G46: Giff	4A **122**	
Lonsdale Gait G75: E Kil	6B **156**	
Loom Wlk. PA10: Kilba	2A **98**	
.... (not continuous)		
Lora Dr. G52: Glas	1E **105**	
Lord Way G69: Barg	6D **92**	
Loretto Pl. G33: Glas	3H **89**	
Loretto St. G33: Glas	3H **89**	
Lorimer Cres. G75: E Kil	4F **157**	
Lorn Av. G69: Chry	1B **70**	
Lorne Ct. G20: Glas	1E **87**	
.... (off Cedar Ct.)		
Lorne Cres. G64: B'rig	5F **51**	
Lorne Dr. ML1: Moth	5F **131**	
Lorne Dr. PA3: Lin	6G **79**	
Lorne Pl. ML5: Coat	6F **95**	
Lorne Rd. G52: Hill E	3H **83**	
Lorne St. G51: Glas	5B **86**	
Lorne St. ML3: Ham	5G **145**	
Lorne Ter. G72: Camb	4H **125**	
Lorn Pl. G66: Kirkin	4A **34**	
Lorraine Gdns. G12: Glas	5A **64**	
Lorraine Gardens La. G12: Glas	5A **64**	
.... (off Westbourne Gardens La.)		
Lorraine Rd. G12: Glas	5A **64**	
Loskin Dr. G22: Glas	2F **65**	
Lossie Cres. PA4: Renf	1H **83**	
Lossie St. G33: Glas	2F **89**	
Lothian Cres. PA2: Pais	4H **101**	
Lothian Dr. G76: Clar	1B **138**	
Lothian Gdns. G20: Glas	6C **64**	
Lothian St. G52: Hill E	3G **83**	
Lothian Way G74: E Kil	6C **142**	
Loubcroy Pl. G33: Glas	2A **68**	
Louden Hill Dr. G33: Glas	3G **67**	
Louden Hill Gdns. G33: Glas	3G **67**	
Louden Hill Pl. G33: Glas	3G **67**	
Louden Hill Rd. G33: Glas	3G **67**	
Louden Hill Way G33: Glas	3G **67**	
Louden St. ML6: Air	4A **96**	
Loudon G75: E Kil	6G **157**	
Loudon Gdns. PA5: John	2G **99**	
Loudon Gro. G72: Flem	4E **127**	
Loudonhill Av. ML3: Ham	3A **162**	
Loudon Rd. G33: Mille	5B **68**	
Loudon St. ML2: Wis	3H **149**	
Loudon Ter. G12: Glas	6B **64**	
.... (off Observatory Rd.)		
Loudon Ter. G61: Bear	6D **26**	
.... (off Grampian Way)		
Louis Braille Cres. G75: E Kil	5F **157**	
Louis Braille Lea G75: E Kil	5F **157**	
Louise Gdns. ML1: Holy	2H **131**	
Louisville Av. ML2: Wis	4B **150**	
LOUNSDALE	3E **101**	
Lounsdale Av. PA2: Pais	2F **101**	
Lounsdale Cres. PA2: Pais	3E **101**	
Lounsdale Dr. PA2: Pais	3F **101**	
Lounsdale Gro. PA2: Pais	2F **101**	
Lounsdale Ho. PA2: Pais	4D **100**	
Lounsdale Pl. G14: Glas	5B **62**	
Lounsdale Rd. PA2: Pais	3F **101**	
Lounsdale Way PA2: Pais	2F **101**	
Lourdes Av. G52: Glas	1D **104**	
Lourdes Ct. G52: Glas	1D **104**	
Lovat Av. G61: Bear	6E **27**	
Lovat Dr. G66: Kirkin	5B **32**	
Lovat Path ML9: Lark	3E **171**	
.... (off Shawrigg Rd.)		
Lovat Pl. G52: Hill E	4G **83**	
Lovat Pl. G73: Ruth	3F **125**	
Love Av. PA11: Quarr V	1A **76**	
Love Dr. ML4: Bell	1D **130**	
Love St. PA3: Pais	5A **82**	
Low Barholm PA10: Kilba	3B **98**	
LOW BLANTYRE	6C **128**	
Low Borland Way G76: Wfoot	3C **154**	

McGregor Path – Mallaig Path

McGregor Path ML5: Glenb 3G **71**
McGregor Rd. G67: Cumb 4G **37**
McGregor St. G51: Glas 5F **85**
McGregor St. G81: Clyd 1F **61**
McGregor St. ML2: Wis 5D **148**
McGrigor Rd. G62: Miln 2F **27**
Mcguire Ga. G71: Both 4F **129**
McGurk Way ML4: Bell 1H **129**
MACHAN **4C 170**
Machan Av. ML9: Lark 2C **170**
Machanhill ML9: Lark 2D **170**
Machanhill Vw. ML9: Lark 3D **170**
Machan Rd. ML9: Lark 3C **170**
Machrie Cres. PA3: Lin 5H **79**
Machrie Dr. G45: Glas 3B **124**
Machrie Dr. G77: Newt M 3E **137**
Machrie Grn. G75: E Kil 1B **168**
Machrie Rd. G45: Glas 3A **124**
Machrie St. G45: Glas 4A **124**
Machrie St. ML1: Moth 2D **146**
McInnes Ct. ML2: Wis 1H **165**
Macinnes Dr. ML1: N'hill 2G **133**
Macinnes M. ML1: N'hill 3E **133**
McInnes Pl. ML2: Over 4H **165**
Macintosh Ct. G72: Camb 4A **126**
McIntosh Ct. G31: Glas 4B **88**
Macintosh Pl. G75: E Kil 4E **157**
McIntosh Quad. ML4: Bell 5B **130**
McIntosh St. G31: Glas 4B **88**
McIntosh Way G67: Cumb 4H **37**
McIntosh Way ML1: Moth 4E **147**
McIntyre Pl. PA2: Pais 3A **102**
McIntyre St. G3: Glas 5G **5** (4D **86**)
McIntyre Ter. G72: Camb 1A **126**
McIver Av. PA2: Pais 3E **103**
McIver St. G72: Camb 1D **126**
Macivor Cres. G74: E Kil 5C **140**
McKay Ct. G77: Newt M 5C **136**
McKay Cres. PA5: John 3G **99**
McKay Gro. ML4: Bell 2B **130**
McKay Pl. G74: E Kil 5C **140**
McKay Pl. G77: Newt M 5C **136**
McKean St. PA3: Pais 5G **81**
McKechnie St. G51: Glas 3G **85**
Mackeith St. G40: Glas 1B **108**
McKenna Dr. ML6: Air 4G **95**
McKenzie Av. G81: Clyd 3D **44**
Mackenzie Dr. PA10: Kilba 4B **98**
Mackenzie Gdns. G74: E Kil 5C **140**
McKenzie Ga. G72: Camb 1E **127**
McKenzie St. PA3: Pais 6G **81**
Mackenzie Ter. ML4: Bell 6C **114**
McKeown Gdns. ML4: Bell 3F **131**
McKerrell St. PA1: Pais 6C **82**
Mackie's Mill Rd. PA5: Eld 5B **100**
Mackinlay Pl. G77: Newt M 5D **136**
McKinley Ct. G74: E Kil 1C **158**
Mackinnon Mills **2C 114**
Mackintosh House, The **1B 86**
Mack St. ML6: Air 3A **96**
McLaren Ct. G46: Giff 6H **121**
McLaren Cres. G20: Glas 2C **64**
McLaren Dr. ML4: Bell 3F **131**
McLaren Gdns. G20: Glas 2C **64**
McLaren Gro. G74: E Kil 5C **140**
Maclaren Pl. G44: Neth 5D **122**
McLaurin Cres. PA5: John 4D **98**
Maclay Av. PA10: Kilba 3A **98**
McLean Av. PA4: Renf 2E **83**
Maclean Ct. G74: E Kil 5D **140**
McLean Dr. ML4: Bell 5B **130**
Maclean Gro. G74: E Kil 5D **140**
Maclean Pl. G74: E Kil 5D **140**
McLean Pl. G67: Cumb 6C **36**
.... *(off Airdrie Rd.)*
McLean Pl. PA3: Pais 4H **81**
Maclean Sq. G51: Glas 5B **86**
Maclean St. G51: Glas 5B **86**
Maclean St. G81: Clyd 1G **61**
McLees La. ML1: Moth 2D **146**
Maclehose Rd. G67: Cumb 2C **38**
McLelland Dr. ML6: Plain 1H **97**
Maclellan Rd. G78: Neil 3E **135**
Maclellan St. G41: Glas 6B **86**
McLennan St. G42: Glas 5F **107**
Macleod Cres. ML6: Air 3D **96**
Macleod Pl. G74: E Kil 6B **142**
McLeod Rd. G82: Dumb 1C **20**
Macleod St. G4: Glas 5H **7** (4A **88**)
Macleod Way G72: Camb 2C **126**
McMahon Dr. ML2: Newm 3E **151**
McMahon Gro. ML4: Bell 1D **130**
McMaster Sports Cen. **4E 99**
Macmillan Gdns. G71: Tann 5E **113**
McMillan Gdns. ML6: Air 5A **96**
McMillan Rd. ML2: Wis 1D **164**
Macmillan St. ML9: Lark 3B **170**
McMillan Way ML8: Law 6D **166**
McNab Cres. G33: Step 4G **69**
McNair St. G32: Glas 6A **90**
McNeil Av. G81: Clyd 6G **45**
McNeil Dr. ML1: Holy 6G **115**
McNeil Gdns. G5: Glas 1H **107**
McNeil Ga. ML9: Lark 2C **170**
McNeil La. ML9: Lark 2C **170**
Macneill Dr. G74: E Kil 5D **140**
Macneill Gdns. G74: E Kil 5C **140**
McNeil Pl. ML2: Over 4A **166**
McNeil St. G5: Glas 1H **107**
McNeil St. ML9: Lark 2B **170**
Macneish Way G74: E Kil 5D **140**
Macnicol Ct. G74: E Kil 5C **140**
Macnicol Pk. G74: E Kil 5C **140**
Macnicol Pl. G74: E Kil 5C **140**
McPhail Av. ML1: N'hill 2F **133**
McPhail St. G40: Glas 1A **108**
McPhater St. G4: Glas 2C **6** (2F **87**)
McPhee Ct. ML3: Ham 6G **145**
McPherson Cres. ML6: Chap 4E **117**
McPherson Dr. G71: Both 4F **129**
Macpherson Pk. G74: E Kil 6E **141**
McPherson St. G1: Glas 6F **7** (5H **87**)
McPherson St. ML4: Moss 2F **131**
Macphie Rd. G82: Dumb 1C **20**
Macquisten Bri. 6B **106**
Macrae Ct. PA5: John 4E **99**
.... *(off Tannahill Cres.)*
Macrae Gdns. G74: E Kil 6E **141**
Macrimmon Pl. G75: E Kil 3G **157**
Macrius Way ML1: Moth 1F **147**
McShane Ct. ML2: Newm 4F **151**
McShannon Gro. ML4: Bell 4C **130**
McSparran Rd. G65: Croy 1B **36**
McTaggart Cres. ML1: Carf 1C **148**
Mactaggart Rd. G67: Cumb 5G **37**
McVey Pl. G33: Step 4G **69**
Madison Av. G44: Glas 2F **123**
Madison La. G44: Glas 2F **123**
Madison Path G72: Blan 2B **144**
Madras Pl. G40: Glas 2B **108**
Madras Pl. G78: Neil 2E **135**
Madras St. G40: Glas 2B **108**
Mafeking St. G51: Glas 5H **85**
Mafeking St. ML2: Wis 5D **148**
Mafeking Ter. G78: Neil 2C **134**
Magdalen Way PA2: Pais 6B **100**
Maggie Lawson Ct. G71: Udd 3E **129**
MAGGIE'S CEN. **5G 63**
Magna St. ML1: Moth 1D **146**
Magnolia Dr. G72: Flem 4F **127**
Magnolia Gdns. ML1: N'hill 4C **132**
Magnolia Gdns. ML9: Shaw 4G **171**
Magnolia Pl. G71: View 5G **113**
Magnolia St. ML2: Wis 4H **149**
Magnolia Ter. G72: Flem 4F **127**
Magnus Cres. G44: Glas 3F **123**
Magnus Rd. PA6: C'lee 3C **78**
Mahon Ct. G69: Mood 6D **54**
Maida St. G43: Glas 6H **105**
Maidens G74: E Kil 6F **141**
Maidens Av. G77: Newt M 4G **137**
Maidland Rd. G53: Glas 5C **104**
Mailerbeg Gdns. G69: Mood 4D **54**
Mailie Wlk. ML1: N'hill 4C **132**
Mailing Av. G64: B'rig 5D **50**
Mainhead Ter. G67: Cumb 6B **16**
Mainhill Av. G69: Bail 6B **92**
Mainhill Dr. G69: Bail 6A **92**
Mainhill Pl. G69: Bail 5B **92**
Mainhill Rd. G69: Barg 6C **92**
Main Rd. G67: Cumb 3A **56**
Main Rd. G67: Mollin 3A **56**
Main Rd. PA1: Pais 2D **100**
Main Rd. PA2: Pais 1H **101**
Main Rd. PA5: Eld 3H **99**
Mains Av. G46: Giff 6H **121**
Mains Castle **4F 141**
Mainscroft PA8: Ersk 6G **43**
Mains Dr. PA8: Ersk 6G **43**
Mains Hill PA8: Ersk 6F **43**
Mainshill Av. PA8: Ersk 6F **43**
Mainshill Gdns. PA8: Ersk 6F **43**
Mains Pl. ML4: Bell 4C **130**
Mains River PA8: Ersk 6G **43**
Mains Rd. G74: E Kil 3H **141**
Mains Rd. G74: E Kil 6H **141**
Mains Rd. G74: Ners 3H **141**
Main St. G40: Glas 2B **108**
Main St. G46: T'bnk 4F **121**
Main St. G62: Miln 4G **27**
.... (not continuous)
Main St. G64: Torr 5D **30**
Main St. G65: Kils 2H **13**
Main St. G65: Twe 1D **34**
Main St. G66: Len 3F **9**
Main St. G67: Cumb 6B **16**
Main St. G69: Bail 1H **111**
Main St. G69: Chry 1A **70**
Main St. G71: Both 5E **129**
Main St. G71: Udd 1D **128**
Main St. G72: Blan 3H **143**
.... (not continuous)
Main St. G72: Camb 1A **126**
Main St. G73: Ruth 5C **108**
Main St. G74: E Kil 1H **157**
Main St. G76: Busby 3D **138**
Main St. G78: Barr 5D **118**
Main St. G78: Neil 2D **134**
Main St. ML1: Cle 1H **149**
Main St. ML1: Holy 2A **132**
Main St. ML2: Newm 5E **151**
Main St. ML2: Over 5A **166**
Main St. ML2: Wis 5E **151**
Main St. ML2: Wis 5F **149**
Main St. ML4: Bell 2B **130**
Main St. ML4: Moss 2B **130**
Main St. ML5: Coat 4C **94**
.... (not continuous)
Main St. ML5: Glenb 3H **71**
Main St. ML6: C'bnk 2C **116**
Main St. ML6: Chap 2E **117**
Main St. ML6: Plain 1G **97**
Main St. PA11: Bri W 3F **77**
Main St. PA6: Hous 1A **78**
Mains Wood PA8: Ersk 6H **43**
Mair St. G51: Glas 5C **86**
Maitland Bank ML9: Lark 2E **171**
Maitland Dr. G64: Torr 4D **30**
Maitland Pl. PA4: Renf 1D **82**
Maitland St. G4: Glas 1C **6** (2F **87**)
.... (not continuous)
Malcolm Gdns. G74: E Kil 1E **157**
Malcolm St. ML1: Moth 3E **147**
Mal Fleming's Brae G65: Kils 4B **14**
Malin Pl. G33: Glas 3H **89**
Mallaig Path G51: Glas 4D **84**
.... *(off Langlands Rd.)*

Mallaig Pl. G51: Glas	4D 84
Mallaig Rd. G51: Glas	4D 84
Mallard Cres. G75: E Kil	6C 156
Mallard La. G71: Both	4E 129
Mallard Pl. G75: E Kil	6C 156
Mallard Rd. G81: Hard	2D 44
Mallard Ter. G75: E Kil	6C 156
Mallard Way ML4: Bell	4B 114
Malleable Gdns. ML1: Moth	5E 131
Malleny Gro. G77: Newt M	6B 136
MALLETSHEUGH	6B 136
MALLETSHEUGH INTERCHANGE	3A 152
Malloch Cres. PA5: Eld	3H 99
Malloch Pl. G74: E Kil	1B 158
Malloch St. G20: Glas	4C 64
Mallots Vw. G77: Newt M	5B 136
Malov Ct. G75: E Kil	6G 157
Malplaquet Ct. ML8: Carl	4F 175
Malta Ter. G5: Glas	1F 107
Maltbarns St. G20: Glas	6E 65
Malvaig La. G72: Blan	3A 144
Malvern Ct. G31: Glas	5C 88
Malvern Way PA3: Pais	3H 81
Mambeg Dr. G51: Glas	3E 85
Mamore Pl. G43: Glas	1A 122
Mamore St. G43: Glas	1A 122
Manchester Dr. G12: Glas	3G 63
Manchester Pl. G40: Glas	1E 109
Manderston Ct. G77: Newt M	5B 136
Manderston Mdw. G77: Newt M	5B 136
Mandora Ct. ML8: Carl	4F 175
Mandrel Dr. ML5: Coat	1E 115
Manitoba Cres. G75: E Kil	2D 156
Mannering G74: E Kil	5D 142
Mannering Ct. G41: Glas	5A 106
Mannering Rd. G41: Glas	5A 106
Mannering Rd. PA2: Pais	6C 100
Mannering Way PA2: Pais	5C 100
Mannoch Pl. ML5: Coat	2F 115
Mannofield G61: Bear	3D 46
Manor Dr. ML5: Coat	4H 93
Manor Dr. ML6: Air	3G 95
Manor Ga. G71: Both	6F 129
Manor Ga. G77: Newt M	6F 137
Manor Pk. ML3: Ham	1H 161
Manor Pk. Av. PA2: Pais	4F 101
Manor Pk. Gro. PA2: Pais	4F 101
Manor Rd. G14: Glas	5E 63
Manor Rd. G15: Glas	6H 45
Manor Rd. G69: G'csh	4D 70
Manor Rd. PA2: Pais	4D 100
Manor Vw. ML6: C'bnk	3B 116
Manor Vw. ML9: Lark	3E 171
Manor Way G73: Ruth	3E 125
Manresa Pl. G4: Glas	1F 87
Manscroft Pl. G32: Glas	6G 89
Manse Av. G61: Bear	2F 47
Manse Av. G71: Both	5E 129
Manse Av. ML5: Coat	1H 113
Manse Brae G44: Glas	1F 123
Manse Brae G72: Flem	5F 127
Manse Brae ML9: Ashg	6B 172
Manse Brae ML9: Dals	6B 172
Manse Bri. ML8: Carl	4D 174
Manse Ct. G65: Kils	4H 13
Manse Ct. G78: Barr	4F 119
Manse Ct. ML8: Law	1G 173
Manse Cres. PA6: Hous	1B 78
Mansefield Av. G72: Camb	3A 126
Mansefield Cres. G60: Old K	1E 43
Mansefield Cres. G76: Clar	3B 138
Mansefield Rd. G76: Clar	3C 138
Mansefield Rd. ML3: Ham	5H 161
Manse Gdns. G32: Glas	1D 110
Manse La. G74: E Kil	6H 141
Mansel St. G21: Glas	4B 66
Manse M. ML2: Newm	5E 151
Manse Pl. ML6: Air	4A 96
	(not continuous)

Manse Rd. G32: Glas	1D 110
Manse Rd. G60: Bowl	5B 22
Manse Rd. G61: Bear	2E 47
Manse Rd. G65: Kils	4H 13
Manse Rd. G69: Barg	5C 92
Manse Rd. G76: Crmck	2H 139
Manse Rd. G78: Neil	2D 134
Manse Rd. ML1: Moth	1G 163
Manse Rd. ML2: Newm	5D 150
Manse Rd. Gdns. G61: Bear	2F 47
Manse St. ML5: Coat	5B 94
Manse St. PA4: Renf	5F 61
Manse Vw. G72: Blan	3H 143
Manse Vw. ML1: N'hill	3F 133
Manse Vw. ML9: Lark	3D 170
Manseview Ter. G76: Eag	6C 154
MANSEWOOD	1H 121
Mansewood Dr. G82: Dumb	2H 19
Mansewood Rd. G43: Glas	1H 121
Mansfield Dr. G71: Udd	1D 128
Mansfield Rd. G52: Hill E	4H 83
Mansfield Rd. ML4: Bell	3B 130
Mansfield St. G11: Glas	1A 86
Mansion Ct. G72: Camb	1A 126
Mansionhouse Av. G32: Carm	5C 110
Mansionhouse Dr. G32: Glas	5C 90
Mansionhouse Gdns. G41: Glas	6C 106
Mansionhouse Gro. G32: Glas	2E 111
Mansionhouse Rd. G32: Glas	1E 111
Mansionhouse Rd. G41: Glas	6C 106
Mansionhouse Rd. PA1: Pais	6C 82
Mansion St. G22: Glas	4G 65
Mansion St. G72: Camb	1A 126
Manson Pl. G75: E Kil	6B 158
Manswrae Steading PA11: Bri W	5G 77
Manus Duddy Ct. G72: Blan	6B 128
Maple Av. G66: Milt C	6B 10
Maple Av. G77: Newt M	5D 136
Maple Av. G82: Dumb	2B 18
Maple Bank ML3: Ham	1B 162
Maple Ct. G67: Cumb	6F 17
Maple Cres. G72: Flem	4F 127
Maple Dr. G66: Lenz	2A 52
Maple Dr. G78: Barr	6F 119
Maple Dr. G81: Clyd	2B 44
Maple Dr. ML9: Lark	6A 164
Maple Dr. PA5: John	5F 99
Maple Gro. G69: Barg	5E 93
Maple Gro. G75: E Kil	6D 156
Maple Pl. FK4: Bank	1E 17
Maple Pl. G71: View	5H 113
Maple Pl. G75: E Kil	5D 156
Maple Pl. PA5: John	5G 99
Maple Quad. ML6: Air	5D 96
Maple Rd. G41: Glas	1H 105
Maple Rd. G67: Cumb	6F 17
Maple Rd. ML1: Holy	2B 132
Maple Ter. G75: E Kil	5D 156
Maple Wlk. G66: Milt C	6B 10
Maple Way G72: Blan	2A 144
Maplewood ML2: Wis	2D 164
Mar Av. PA7: B'ton	4H 41
Marchbank Gdns. PA1: Pais	1F 103
Marchburn Dr. PA3: Glas A	3H 81
Marchfield G62: Miln	3A 28
Marchfield G64: B'rig	4A 50
Marchfield Av. PA3: Pais	3H 81
Marchfield Dr. PA3: Pais	4A 82
Marchfield Pl. PA3: Pais	4A 82
Marchglen Pl. G51: Glas	4D 84
Marchmont Gdns. G64: B'rig	4B 50
Marchmont Ter. G12: Glas	6A 64
	(off Observatory Rd.)
March St. G41: Glas	3D 106
Mardale G74: E Kil	6E 141
Mar Dr. G61: Bear	6F 27
Maree Dr. G52: Glas	1E 105
Maree Dr. G67: Cumb	6D 36
Maree Gdns. G64: B'rig	6D 50

Maree Rd. PA2: Pais	3E 101
Maree Wlk. ML2: Newm	3D 150
	(off Banavie Rd.)
Maree Way G72: Blan	1B 144
Marfield Pl. G32: Glas	5H 89
Marfield St. G32: Glas	4G 89
Mar Gdns. G73: Ruth	3F 125
Margaret Av. FK4: Hag	1G 17
Margaret Ct. G66: Len	3F 9
Margaret Dr. ML1: Moth	6B 148
Margaret Gdns. ML3: Ham	3F 145
Margaret Macdonald Ho. G3: Glas	2A 6 (2E 87)
	(off Buccleuch St.)
Margaret Pl. ML4: Bell	2A 130
Margaret Rd. ML3: Ham	3F 145
Margaret's Pl. ML9: Lark	2C 170
Margaret St. G5: Glas	6F 87
Margaret St. ML5: Coat	1C 114
Margaretta Bldgs. G44: Glas	1E 123
Margaretvale Dr. ML9: Lark	3C 170
Marguerite Av. G66: Lenz	1C 52
Marguerite Dr. G66: Lenz	1C 52
Marguerite Gdns. G66: Lenz	1C 52
Marguerite Gdns. G71: Both	5F 129
Marguerite Gro. G66: Lenz	1C 52
Marguerite Pl. G66: Milt C	5B 10
Mar Hall Av. PA7: B'ton	2B 42
Mar Hall Dr. PA7: B'ton	2B 42
Mar Hall Golf Course	1C 42
Marian Dr. ML1: Carf	5C 132
Maric La. ML6: Plain	1G 97
MARIE CURIE HOSPICE	2B 66
	(Glasgow)
Marigold Av. ML1: Moth	1G 147
Marigold Way ML8: Carl	5D 174
Marina Ct. ML4: Bell	4B 130
Marina Way G66: Kirkin	6C 32
Marine Cres. G51: Glas	5C 86
Marine Gdns. G51: Glas	5C 86
Mariner Ct. G81: Clyd	5C 44
Marion St. ML4: Moss	2F 131
Mariscat Rd. G41: Glas	3C 106
Maritime Ct. PA4: Inch	5F 59
Marius Cres. ML1: Moth	6E 131
Marjory Dr. PA3: Pais	4C 82
Marjory Rd. PA4: Renf	2C 82
Markdow Av. G53: Glas	4A 104
Market Cl. G65: Kils	3H 13
Market Ct. G65: Kils	3H 13
	(off Market St.)
Markethill Rd. G74: E Kil	3F 141
	(not continuous)
Markethill Rd. G74: Roger	3F 141
	(not continuous)
MARKETHILL RDBT.	6G 141
Market Pl. G65: Kils	3H 13
Market Pl. G71: View	6G 113
Market Pl. ML8: Carl	3D 174
Market Rd. G66: Kirkin	6G 33
Market Rd. G71: View	6G 113
Market Rd. ML8: Carl	3D 174
Market Sq. G65: Kils	3H 13
Market St. G31: Glas	5B 88
Market St. G65: Kils	3H 13
Market St. G71: View	6G 113
Market St. ML6: Air	4A 96
Marlach Pl. G53: Glas	5A 104
Marlborough Av. G11: Glas	6F 63
Marlborough La. Nth. G11: Glas	6F 63
Marlborough La. Sth. G11: Glas	6F 63
Marlborough Pk. G75: E Kil	4C 156
Marldon La. G11: Glas	6F 63
Marley Way G66: Milt C	5B 10
Marlfield Gdns. ML4: Bell	6C 114
Marlin Cres. G51: Glas	6A 62
Marlin Dr. G51: Glas	6A 62
Marlin Rd. G51: Glas	1A 84
Marlin Way G51: Glas	1A 84
Marlow St. G41: Glas	1C 106

Marlow Ter. – Meadside Av.

Marlow Ter. G41: Glas 1C **106**
Marmion Cres. ML1: Moth 5F **131**
Marmion Dr. G66: Kirkin 5F **33**
Marmion Pl. G67: Cumb 6G **37**
Marmion Rd. G67: Cumb 6G **37**
Marmion Rd. PA2: Pais 5C **100**
Marne St. G31: Glas 4D **88**
Marnoch Dr. ML5: Glenb 2H **71**
Marnoch Way G69: Mood 5D **54**
(off Arnprior Gdns.)
MARNOCK 3G **71**
Marnock Ter. PA2: Pais 2C **102**
Maroney Dr. G33: Step 4G **69**
Marquis Av. ML3: Ham 3E **145**
Marquis Ga. G71: Both 2C **128**
Marrswood Grn. ML3: Ham 5E **145**
Marsden Wynd G75: E Kil 2C **168**
Marshall Gro. ML3: Ham 6F **145**
Marshall La. ML2: Wis 6G **149**
Marshall's La. PA1: Pais 1A **102**
Marshall St. ML2: Wis 1F **165**
Marshall St. ML9: Lark 2C **170**
Martha Pl. ML9: Lark 3D **170**
Martha St. G1: Glas 4E **7** (3G **87**)
Martin Ct. ML3: Ham 6G **145**
Martin Cres. G69: Bail 6A **92**
Martin Pl. ML1: N'hill 4C **132**
Martinside G75: E Kil 6G **157**
Martin St. G40: Glas 2B **108**
Martin St. ML5: Coat 4F **95**
Martlet Dr. PA5: John 6C **98**
Mart St. G1: Glas 5G **87**
(not continuous)
Martyn Gro. G72: Camb 3G **125**
Martyn St. ML6: Air 4G **95**
Martyrs Pl. G64: B'rig 1C **66**
Martyrs School **3H 7 (3A 88)**
(off Glebe St.)
Marwick St. G31: Glas 4D **88**
Mary Dr. ML4: Bell 4A **130**
Mary Fisher Cres. G82: Dumb 3C **20**
Mary Glen ML2: Wis 4B **150**
MARYHILL 1A **64**
Maryhill Leisure Cen. **3B 64**
Maryhill Rd. G20: Glas 3B **64**
Maryhill Rd. G61: Bear 5F **47**
Maryhill Shop. Cen. **4C 64**
Maryhill Station (Rail) **1A 64**
Maryknowe Rd. ML1: Carf 5C **132**
Maryland Dr. G52: Glas 6E **85**
Maryland Gdns. G52: Glas 6E **85**
Maryland Rd. G82: Dumb 1H **19**
Mary Rae Rd. ML4: Bell 4A **130**
Mary Slessor Wynd G73: Ruth 5E **125**
Mary Sq. G69: Barg 6D **92**
Maryston Dr. G33: Glas 1F **89**
Maryston Rd. G33: Glas 1F **89**
Maryston St. G33: Glas 1F **89**
Mary St. ML3: Ham 1G **161**
Mary St. PA2: Pais 3A **102**
Mary St. PA5: John 2G **99**
Maryville Av. G46: Giff 5A **122**
Maryville Gdns. G46: Giff 5A **122**
MARYVILLE INTERCHANGE 5A **112**
Maryville La. G71: Tann 5B **112**
Maryville Vw. G71: Tann 4B **112**
Marywell Path G68: Cumb 3B **36**
Marywood Sq. G41: Glas 3D **106**
Mary Young Pl. G76: Busby 3D **138**
Masonfield Av. G68: Cumb 3F **37**
Mason La. ML1: Moth 3G **147**
(not continuous)
Mason St. ML1: Moth 3G **147**
Mason St. ML9: Lark 4E **171**
Masterton Pl. G21: Glas 6G **65**
Masterton Way G71: Tann 4F **113**
Matherton Av. G77: Newt M 4H **137**
Mathieson Cres. G33: Step 4F **69**
Mathieson Rd. G73: Ruth 4E **109**
Mathieson St. PA1: Pais 6D **82**
Mathieson Ter. G5: Glas 1H **107**
Matilda Rd. G41: Glas 1C **106**
Matthew McWhirter Pl. ML9: Lark 1D **170**
Mauchline G74: E Kil 6D **142**
Mauchline Av. G66: Kirkin 3G **33**
Mauchline Ct. G66: Kirkin 3G **33**
Mauchline Ct. ML3: Ham 1B **160**
Mauchline Dr. ML5: Coat 1F **115**
Mauchline St. G5: Glas 6E **87**
Mauchline Wynd G73: Ruth 1B **124**
Maukinfauld Ct. G32: Glas 2F **109**
Maukinfauld Gdns. G31: Glas 1G **109**
Maukinfauld Rd. G32: Glas 2G **109**
Mauldslie Dr. ML8: Law 5D **166**
Mauldslie Pl. ML9: Ashg 5H **171**
Mauldslie Rd. ML8: Carl 2D **172**
Mauldslie St. ML4: Bell 3C **130**
Mauldslie St. ML5: Coat 6C **94**
Maule Dr. G11: Glas 1G **85**
Mausoleum Dr. ML3: Ham 4A **146**
Mavis Bank G64: B'rig 1B **66**
Mavis Bank G72: Blan 2A **144**
Mavisbank Gdns. G51: Glas 6D **4** (5C **86**)
Mavisbank Gdns. ML4: Bell 1C **130**
Mavisbank St. ML2: Newm 3G **151**
Mavisbank St. ML6: Air 3G **95**
Mavisbank Ter. PA1: Pais 2B **102**
Mavisbank Ter. PA5: John 3F **99**
Mavis Valley Rd. G64: B'rig 3A **50**
Mavor Av. G74: E Kil 5H **141**
Mavor Ct. G74: E Kil 5A **142**
MAVOR RDBT. 6H **141**
Maxton Av. G78: Barr 4C **118**
Maxton Cres. ML2: Wis 3A **150**
Maxton Gro. G78: Barr 5C **118**
Maxton Ter. G72: Camb 4H **125**
Maxwell Av. G41: Glas 1C **106**
Maxwell Av. G61: Bear 4E **47**
Maxwell Av. G69: Bail 1G **111**
Maxwell Ct. G41: Glas 1C **106**
Maxwell Ct. ML5: Coat 4D **94**
Maxwell Cres. G72: Blan 3B **144**
Maxwell Dr. G41: Glas 1A **106**
Maxwell Dr. G69: Bail 6F **91**
Maxwell Dr. G74: E Kil 1H **157**
Maxwell Dr. PA8: Ersk 4D **42**
Maxwell Gdns. G41: Glas 1B **106**
Maxwell Gro. G41: Glas 1B **106**
Maxwell La. G41: Glas 1C **106**
Maxwell Oval G41: Glas 1D **106**
Maxwell Park Station (Rail) **3B 106**
Maxwell Path ML9: Lark 3E **171**
(off Wallace Dr.)
Maxwell Pl. G41: Glas 2E **107**
Maxwell Pl. G65: Kils 2H **13**
Maxwell Pl. G71: Udd 1E **129**
Maxwell Pl. ML5: Coat 6B **94**
Maxwell Pl. PA11: Bri W 3F **77**
Maxwell Rd. G41: Glas 1D **106**
Maxwell Rd. PA7: B'ton 4H **41**
Maxwell St. G1: Glas 5F **87**
(Fox St.)
Maxwell St. G1: Glas 6D **6** (4G **87**)
(Osborne St.)
Maxwell St. G69: Bail 1H **111**
Maxwell St. G81: Clyd 3B **44**
Maxwell St. PA3: Pais 6A **82**
Maxwell Ter. G41: Glas 1C **106**
Maxwellton Av. G74: E Kil 1A **158**
Maxwellton Ct. PA1: Pais 1G **101**
Maxwellton Ga. G74: E Kil 6A **142**
Maxwellton Pl. G74: E Kil 6B **142**
Maxwellton Rd. G74: E Kil 6B **142**
Maxwellton Rd. PA1: Pais 1F **101**
Maxwellton St. PA1: Pais 1G **101**
Maxwelton Rd. G33: Glas 1F **89**
Maybank La. G42: Glas 4E **107**
Maybank St. G42: Glas 4E **107**
Mayberry Cres. G32: Glas 6D **90**
Mayberry Gdns. G32: Glas 6D **90**
Mayberry Grange G72: Blan 1B **144**
Mayberry Gro. G32: Glas 6D **90**
Mayberry Pl. G72: Blan 1B **144**
Maybole Cres. G77: Newt M 5G **137**
Maybole Dr. ML6: Air 1A **116**
Maybole Gdns. ML3: Ham 1B **160**
Maybole Gro. G77: Newt M 5G **137**
Maybole Pl. ML5: Coat 2F **115**
Maybole St. G53: Glas 1H **119**
Mayburn Pl. ML5: Coat 5C **94**
Mayfield Av. G76: Clar 2C **138**
Mayfield Blvd. G75: E Kil 6B **156**
Mayfield Gdns. ML8: Carl 6E **175**
Mayfield Pl. ML5: Coat 2C **114**
Mayfield Pl. ML8: Carl 6E **175**
Mayfield Rd. ML3: Ham 5D **144**
Mayfield St. G20: Glas 4D **64**
May Gdns. ML2: Wis 5G **149**
May Gdns. ML3: Ham 4G **145**
May Rd. PA2: Pais 6A **102**
May St. ML3: Ham 4H **145**
May Ter. G42: Glas 5F **107**
May Ter. G46: Giff 4A **122**
May Wynd ML3: Ham 4G **145**
M&D's Scotland Theme Pk. **6A 130**
Meadow Av. G72: Blan 3B **144**
Meadowbank La. G71: Udd 1C **128**
Meadowbank Pl. G77: Newt M 4D **136**
Meadowbank St. G82: Dumb 3E **19**
(not continuous)
Meadowburn G64: B'rig 3C **50**
Meadowburn Av. G66: Lenz 2E **53**
Meadowburn Av. G77: Newt M 4D **136**
Meadowburn Rd. ML2: Wis 6A **150**
Meadow Cen., The **3F 19**
Meadow Cl. G75: E Kil 1A **168**
Meadow Ct. G82: Dumb 2F **19**
Meadow Ct. ML8: Carl 4G **175**
(off High Mdw.)
Meadow Dr. G72: Newt 6G **111**
Meadowfield Pl. ML2: Newm 3G **151**
Meadowhead Av. G69: Mood 5D **54**
Meadowhead Rd. ML2: Wis 5C **148**
(not continuous)
Meadowhead Rd. ML6: Plain 6F **75**
Meadowhill G77: Newt M 4D **136**
MEADOWHILL 2D **170**
Meadowhill St. ML9: Lark 2D **170**
Meadow La. G71: Both 5F **129**
Meadow La. PA4: Renf 4F **61**
Meadowpark St. G31: Glas 4D **88**
(not continuous)
Meadow Path ML6: Chap 4D **116**
Meadow Ri. G77: Newt M 4C **136**
Meadow Rd. G11: Glas 1G **85**
Meadow Rd. G82: Dumb 3G **19**
Meadow Rd. ML1: Moth 4H **147**
Meadows, The PA6: Hous 2D **78**
Meadows Av. ML9: Lark 2D **170**
Meadows Av. PA8: Ersk 6G **43**
Meadows Dr. PA8: Ersk 6G **43**
Meadowside ML3: Ham 5H **161**
Meadowside Av. PA5: Eld 3B **100**
Meadowside Gdns. ML6: Air 4D **96**
Meadowside Ind. Est. PA4: Renf 3F **61**
Meadowside Pl. ML6: Air 4D **96**
Meadowside Quay Sq. G11: Glas 2G **85**
Meadowside Quay Wlk. G11: Glas 2G **85**
Meadowside Rd. G65: Queen 3C **12**
Meadowside St. PA4: Renf 4F **61**
Meadow St. ML5: Coat 1D **114**
Meadow Vw. G67: Cumb 1C **38**
Meadow Vw. ML6: Plain 6G **75**
Meadow Wlk. ML5: Coat 5D **94**
Meadow Way G77: Newt M 4D **136**
Meadowwell St. G32: Glas 6B **90**
Meadside Av. PA10: Kilba 1A **98**

Meadside Rd. – Middleton St.

Meadside Rd. PA10: Kilba 1A **98**
Mealkirk St. G81: Faif 6E **25**
MEARNS 6E 137
MEARNS CASTLE 6G 137
Mearns Castle Golf Course 6A **138**
Mearns Ct. ML3: Ham 4A **162**
Mearnscroft Gdns. G77: Newt M 6F **137**
Mearnscroft Rd. G77: Newt M 6F **137**
Mearns Cross Bowling Green 5D **136**
Mearnskirk Rd. G77: Newt M 1D **152**
Mearns Rd. G76: Clar 3H **137**
Mearns Rd. G77: Newt M 5A **152**
Mearns Rd. ML1: Moth 1E **147**
Mearns Way G64: B'rig 5F **51**
Mecca Bingo 5D **86** *(Glasgow)* *(off The Quay)*
Mecca Bingo 4G **145** *(Hamilton)*
Mecca Bingo G15: Glas 6H **45**
Medlar Ct. G72: Flem 4F **127**
Medlar Rd. G67: Cumb 3D **38**
Medrox Gdns. G67: Cumb 2B **56**
Medwin Ct. G75: E Kil 4A **156**
Medwin Gdns. G75: E Kil 4A **156**
Medwin St. G72: Camb 2D **126**
Medwyn St. G14: Glas 6D **62** (not continuous)
Meek Pl. G72: Camb 2B **126**
Meetinghouse La. PA1: Pais 6A **82**
Megabowl 6E **45** *(Clydebank)*
Megan Ga. G40: Glas 1B **108**
Megan St. G40: Glas 1B **108**
Meigle Rd. ML6: Air 1H **115**
Meikle Av. PA4: Renf 1E **83**
Meikle Bin Brae G66: Len 3G **9**
Meikle Cres. ML3: Ham 4G **161**
Meikle Cres. ML6: Grng 1D **74**
Meikle Drumgray Rd. ML6: Grng 1D **74**
MEIKLE EARNOCK 4G 161
Meikle Earnock Rd. ML3: Ham 5D **160**
Meiklehill Av. G66: Kirkin 4E **33**
Meiklehill Rd. G66: Kirkin 4E **33**
Meiklem St. ML4: Moss 2E **131**
Meiklerig Ct. G53: Glas 3C **104**
Meiklerig Cres. G53: Glas 3C **104**
MEIKLERIGGS 3F 101
Meikleriggs Ct. PA2: Pais 3F **101**
Meikleriggs Dr. PA2: Pais 4E **101**
Meikle Rd. G53: Glas 5C **104**
Meiklewood Rd. G51: Glas 5D **84**
Melbourne Av. G75: E Kil 4E **157**
Melbourne Av. G81: Clyd 2H **43**
Melbourne Ct. G46: Giff 4B **122**
Melbourne Grn. G75: E Kil 3E **157**
Melbourne Pl. G40: Glas 1E **109**
Melbourne St. G31: Glas 5B **88**
Meldon Pl. G51: Glas 4D **84**
Meldrum Gdns. G41: Glas 3B **106**
Meldrum Mains ML6: Glenm 5G **73**
Meldrum St. G81: Clyd 1F **61**
Melford Av. G46: Giff 5B **122**
Melford Av. G66: Kirkin 5B **32**
Melford Rd. ML4: Bell 1H **129**
Melford Way PA3: Pais 3D **82**
Melfort Av. G41: Glas 1H **105**
Melfort Av. G81: Clyd 4D **44**
Melfort Ct. G81: Clyd 5E **45**
Melfort Gdns. G81: Clyd 5E **45**
Melfort Gdns. PA10: Kilba 4C **98**
Melfort Path ML2: Newm 2D **150** *(off Murdostoun Vw.)*
Melfort Quad. ML1: N'hill 4D **132** *(off Glenmore Rd.)*
Melfort Rd. ML3: Ham 6C **144**
Mellerstain Dr. G14: Glas 3G **61**
Mellerstain Gro. G14: Glas 3H **61**
Melness Gro. PA7: B'ton 5F **41**
Melness Pl. G51: Glas 4D **84**
Melrose Av. G69: Barg 6D **92**
Melrose Av. G73: Ruth 6D **108**
Melrose Av. ML1: Holy 1B **132**
Melrose Av. ML6: Chap 3D **116**
Melrose Av. PA2: Pais 4E **101**
Melrose Av. PA3: Lin 6H **79**
Melrose Ct. G73: Ruth 6D **108**
Melrose Cres. ML2: Wis 4G **149**
Melrose Gdns. G20: Glas 6D **64**
Melrose Gdns. G65: Twe 1C **34**
Melrose Gdns. G71: Tann 4D **112**
Melrose Pl. G72: Blan 6A **128**
Melrose Pl. ML5: Coat 4B **94**
Melrose Pl. ML9: Lark 4C **170**
Melrose Rd. G67: Cumb 6G **37**
Melrose St. G4: Glas 1H **5** (1E **87**) *(off Queen's Cres.)*
Melrose St. ML3: Ham 4F **145**
Melrose Ter. G74: E Kil 6H **141**
Melrose Ter. ML3: Ham 3F **145**
Melvaig Pl. G20: Glas 4B **64**
Melvick Pl. G51: Glas 4D **84**
Melville Cres. ML1: Moth 3H **147**
Melville Dr. ML1: Moth 3G **147**
Melville Gdns. G64: B'rig 5C **50**
Melville Pk. G74: E Kil 6B **142**
Melville Pl. ML8: Carl 3C **174**
Melville St. G41: Glas 2D **106**
Memel St. G21: Glas 4A **66**
Memorial Way ML1: N'hse 1C **132**
Memus Av. G52: Glas 1C **104**
Mendip La. G75: E Kil 1A **168**
Mennock Ct. ML3: Ham 1C **160**
Mennock Dr. G64: B'rig 3C **50**
Mennock St. ML1: Cle 5H **133**
Menock Rd. G44: Glas 1F **123**
Menteith Av. G64: B'rig 6D **50**
Menteith Ct. ML1: Moth 3H **147** *(off Melville Cres.)*
Menteith Dr. G73: Ruth 5F **125**
Menteith Gdns. G61: Bear 5C **26**
Menteith Loan ML1: Holy 2A **132**
Menteith Pl. G73: Ruth 5F **125**
Menteith Rd. ML1: Moth 2G **147**
Menzies Dr. G21: Glas 4C **66**
Menzies Dr. G66: Lenz 2E **53**
Menzies Pl. G21: Glas 4C **66**
Menzies Rd. G21: Glas 3D **66**
Merchant La. G1: Glas 5G **87**
Merchants Cl. PA10: Kilba 2A **98**
Merchiston Av. PA3: Lin 6F **79**
Merchiston Dr. PA5: Brkfld 6D **78**
Merchiston Oval PA5: John 6E **79**
Merchiston St. G32: Glas 4G **89**
Mere Ct. G68: Dull 5F **15**
Merkins Av. G82: Dumb 1H **19**
MERKLAND 4G 33
Merkland Ct. G11: Glas 1H **85**
Merkland Ct. G66: Kirkin 4F **33**
Merkland Dr. G66: Kirkin 4G **33**
Merkland Pl. G66: Kirkin 4F **33**
Merkland Rd. ML5: Coat 1G **93**
Merkland St. G11: Glas 1H **85**
Merkland Way G75: E Kil 1C **168**
Merksworth Way PA3: Pais 4A **82** *(off Mosslands Rd.)*
Merlewood Av. G71: Both 3F **129**
Merlin Av. ML4: Bell 6C **114**
Merlinford Av. PA4: Renf 6G **61**
Merlinford Cres. PA4: Renf 6G **61**
Merlinford Dr. PA4: Renf 6G **61**
Merlinford Way PA4: Renf 6G **61**
Merlin Way PA3: Pais 4D **82**
Merlin Wynd G74: E Kil 5A **142**
Merrick Ct. ML6: Air 1B **96**
Merrick Gdns. G51: Glas 6H **85**
Merrick Gdns. G61: Bear 6C **26**
Merrick Path G51: Glas 6H **85** *(off Ibroxholm Oval)*
Merrick Ter. G71: View 6F **113**
Merrick Way G73: Ruth 4D **124**
Merryburn Av. G46: Giff 2B **122**
Merry Ct. G72: Blan 3C **144**
Merrycrest Av. G46: Giff 3A **122**
Merrycroft Av. G46: Giff 3B **122**
Merryland Pl. G51: Glas 4A **86**
Merryland St. G51: Glas 4H **85** (not continuous)
MERRYLEE 3B 122
Merrylee Cres. G46: Giff 2A **122**
Merrylee Pk. Av. G46: Giff 3A **122**
Merrylee Pk. La. G46: Giff 3A **122**
Merrylee Pk. M. G46: Giff 2A **122**
Merrylee Rd. G43: Glas 2B **122**
Merrylee Rd. G44: Glas 2D **122**
Merrylees Rd. G72: Blan 2A **144**
Merryston Ct. ML5: Coat 5A **94**
Merrystone St. ML5: Coat 4B **94**
Merrystown Dr. ML5: Coat 2C **94**
Merry St. ML1: Carf 6B **132**
Merry St. ML1: Moth 2G **147**
Merryton Av. G15: Glas 4B **46**
Merryton Av. G46: Giff 3A **122**
Merryton Gdns. G15: Glas 4B **46**
Merryton Rd. ML1: Moth 1B **164**
Merryton Rd. ML9: Lark 5H **163** (not continuous)
Merryton Station (Rail) 6H **163**
Merryton St. ML9: Lark 6H **163**
Merryton Twr. ML1: Moth 1B **164**
Merryvale Av. G46: Giff 2B **122**
Merryvale Pl. G46: Giff 2B **122**
Merton Dr. G52: Glas 6A **84**
Meryon Gdns. G32: Glas 3D **110**
Meryon Rd. G32: Glas 2D **110**
Methil Ct. ML3: Fern 2E **163**
Methil St. G14: Glas 6C **62**
Methil Way G72: Blan 1B **160**
Methlan Pk. G82: Dumb 5E **19**
Methlan Pk. Gdns. G82: Dumb 5D **18**
Methlick Av. ML6: Air 1G **115**
Methuen Rd. PA3: Pais 2B **82**
Methven Av. G61: Bear 2H **47**
Methven Pl. G74: E Kil 1E **157**
Methven Rd. G46: Giff 3G **137**
Methven St. G31: Glas 2F **109**
Methven St. G81: Clyd 3B **44**
Methven Ter. ML5: Coat 2D **94**
Metropole La. G1: Glas 5G **87**
Mews La. PA3: Pais 4B **82**
Mey Ct. G77: Newt M 5A **136**
Mey Pl. G77: Newt M 5A **136**
Michael McParland Dr. G64: Torr 5D **30**
Michael Ter. ML6: Chap 4D **116**
Micklehouse Oval G69: Bail 5H **91**
Micklehouse Pl. G69: Bail 5H **91**
Micklehouse Rd. G69: Bail 5H **91**
Micklehouse Wynd G69: Bail 5H **91**
Midas Pl. ML4: Moss 2G **131**
Mid Barrwood Rd. G65: Kils 4A **14**
Mid Carbarns ML2: Wis 2D **164**
Midcroft G64: B'rig 4A **50**
Midcroft Av. G44: Glas 2H **123**
Middlefield G75: E Kil 6G **157**
Middlehouse Ct. ML8: Carl 3B **174**
Middlemuir Av. G66: Lenz 2D **52**
Middlemuir Rd. G66: Lenz 1D **52**
Middlerigg Rd. G68: Cumb 3F **37**
Middlesex Gdns. G41: Glas 5C **86**
Middlesex St. G41: Glas 6C **86**
Middleton Av. ML9: Lark 5D **170**
Middleton Dr. G62: Miln 3H **27**
Middleton Pl. G68: Cumb 3B **36**
Middleton Rd. PA3: Lin 5A **80**
Middleton Rd. PA3: Pais 4F **81**
Middleton St. G51: Glas 5A **86**

A–Z Glasgow 251

Milton Rd. – Moorland Dr.

Milton Rd. ML8: Carl 5H **173**
Milton St. G4: Glas 2C **6** (2F **87**)
Milton St. ML1: Moth 2G **147**
Milton St. ML3: Ham 5E **145**
Milton St. ML6: Air 3A **96**
Milton St. ML8: Carl 3C **174**
Milton Ter. ML3: Ham 4E **145**
Milverton Av. G61: Bear 1C **46**
Milverton Rd. G46: Giff 6G **121**
Mimosa Rd. PA11: Bri W 3F **77**
Mimosas, The PA11: Bri W 3F **77**
.... *(off Mimosa Rd.)*
Minard Rd. G41: Glas 4C **106**
Minard Way G71: Tann 6E **113**
Mincher Cres. ML1: Moth 5G **147**
Minch Way ML6: Air 6C **96**
Minella Gdns. ML4: Bell 5C **114**
Miners Way G65: Twe 2D **34**
Miners' Welfare & Social Club **6A 14**
Minerva Ct. G3: Glas 4E **5** (3C **86**)
.... *(off Elliot St.)*
Minerva St. G3: Glas 5D **4** (3C **86**)
Minerva Way G3: Glas 4C **4** (3B **86**)
Mingarry La. G20: Glas 5C **64**
Mingarry St. G20: Glas 5C **64**
Mingulay Cres. G22: Glas 1H **65**
Mingulay Pl. G22: Glas 1A **66**
Mingulay St. G22: Glas 1H **65**
Minister's Pk. G74: E Kil 5B **140**
Minmoir Rd. G53: Glas 6H **103**
Minster Wlk. G69: Barg 6D **92**
Minstrel Rd. G13: Glas 6D **46**
Mintlaw Way G69: Chry 6A **54**
Minto Av. G73: Ruth 3F **125**
Minto Cres. G52: Glas 6F **85**
Minton Av. PA2: Pais 2D **102**
Minto Pk. ML2: Wis 3A **150**
Minto St. G52: Glas 6F **85**
Mireton St. G22: Glas 4F **65**
Mirin Dr. PA3: Pais 4A **82**
Mirin Wynd PA3: Pais 4H **81**
Mirren Ct. PA3: Pais 4B **82**
Mirren Dr. G81: Dun 6B **24**
Mirrlees Dr. G12: Glas 5A **64**
Mirrlees La. G12: Glas 5A **64**
Mission Gdns. ML2: Wis 4H **149**
Mission Pl. ML1: Moth 1F **147**
Mitchell Arc. G73: Ruth 5D **108**
Mitchell Av. G72: Camb 1E **127**
Mitchell Av. PA4: Renf 1D **82**
Mitchell Ct. G74: E Kil 1E **157**
Mitchell Dr. G62: Miln 4A **28**
Mitchell Dr. G73: Ruth 1D **124**
Mitchell Gdns. G66: Kirkin 5F **33**
Mitchell Gro. G74: E Kil 1E **157**
Mitchell La. G1: Glas 5C **6** (4F **87**)
Mitchell Library, The .... **3G 5 (3D 86)**
Mitchell Rd. G67: Cumb 3A **38**
Mitchell St. G1: Glas 6C **6** (4F **87**)
Mitchell St. ML5: Coat 1F **113**
Mitchell St. ML6: Air 3H **95**
Mitchell Way G71: Udd 2E **129**
Mitchison Rd. G67: Cumb 2A **38**
Mitre Ct. G11: Glas 5F **63**
Mitre Ga. G11: Glas 6F **63**
Mitre La. G14: Glas 5E **63**
Mitre La. W. G14: Glas 5D **62**
Mitre Rd. G11: Glas 5F **63**
Mitre Rd. G14: Glas 5D **62**
Moat Av. G13: Glas 2C **62**
Mochrum Rd. G43: Glas 1C **122**
Moffat Ct. G75: E Kil 4A **156**
Moffat Gdns. G75: E Kil 4A **156**
Moffathill ML6: Gart 6E **97**
MOFFAT MILLS **5F 97**
Moffat Pl. G72: Blan 6B **128**
Moffat Pl. G75: E Kil 4A **156**
Moffat Pl. ML5: Coat 1F **115**
Moffat Pl. ML6: Air 3F **97**
Moffat Rd. ML6: Air 4F **97**
Moffat St. G5: Glas 1H **107**
Moffat Vw. ML6: Plain 1G **97**
Mogarth Av. PA2: Pais 5D **100**
Moidart Av. PA4: Renf 5D **60**
Moidart Ct. G78: Barr 3D **118**
Moidart Cres. G52: Glas 6F **85**
Moidart Gdns. G66: Kirkin 4H **33**
Moidart Gdns. G77: Newt M 3E **137**
Moidart Pl. G52: Glas 6F **85**
Moidart Rd. G52: Glas 6E **85**
Moir St. G1: Glas 5H **87**
Molendinar Cl. G33: Glas 1G **89**
Molendinar Gdns. G33: Glas 1F **89**
Molendinar St. G1: Glas 5H **87**
Molendinar Ter. G78: Neil 3C **134**
MOLLINSBURN **3H 55**
MOLLINSBURN JUNC. 4G **55**
Mollinsburn Rd. G67: Cumb 3A **56**
Mollinsburn Rd. ML5: Anna 6B **56**
Mollinsburn Rd. ML5: Glenb 6B **56**
Mollinsburn Rd. ML6: Glenm 3D **72**
Mollinsburn St. G21: Glas 6A **66**
Mollins Ct. G68: Cumb 2H **55**
Mollins Rd. G68: Cumb 1G **55**
Monach Rd. G33: Glas 3C **90**
Monar Dr. G22: Glas 6F **65**
Monar Pl. G22: Glas 6F **65**
Monar St. G22: Glas 6F **65**
Monart Pl. G20: Glas 5D **64**
Monar Way ML2: Newm 3D **150**
.... *(off Murdostoun Vw.)*
Moncrieff Av. G66: Lenz 2C **52**
Moncrieffe Rd. ML6: Chap 1D **116**
Moncrieff Gdns. G66: Lenz 2D **52**
Moncrieff St. PA3: Pais 6A **82**
Moncur St. G40: Glas 5A **88**
Moness Dr. G52: Glas 1E **105**
Money Gro. ML1: Moth 5B **148**
Monieburgh Cres. G65: Kils 2A **14**
Monieburgh Rd. G65: Kils 2A **14**
Monifieth Av. G52: Glas 2D **104**
Monikie Gdns. G64: B'rig 6F **51**
Monkcastle Dr. G72: Camb 1A **126**
Monkdyke Ho. PA4: Renf 6F **61**
Monkland Av. G66: Kirkin 6D **32**
Monkland Av. G66: Lenz 6D **32**
MONKLANDS HOSPITAL **4F 95**
Monklands Ind. Est. ML5: Coat 3B **114**
Monkland St. ML6: Air 4B **96**
Monkland Ter. ML5: Glenb 3H **71**
Monkland Vw. G71: Tann 4E **113**
Monkland Vw. ML6: C'bnk 3B **116**
Monkland Vw. Cres. G69: Barg 1D **112**
Monksbridge Av. G13: Glas 6C **46**
Monkscourt Av. ML6: Air 3G **95**
Monkscroft Av. G11: Glas 1G **85**
Monkscroft Ct. G11: Glas 1G **85**
Monkscroft Gdns. G11: Glas 6G **63**
Monks Rd. ML6: Air 1C **116**
Monkton Brae G69: Chry 6A **54**
Monkton Cres. ML5: Coat 1A **114**
Monkton Dr. G15: Glas 5B **46**
Monkton Gdns. G77: Newt M 5G **137**
Monmouth Av. G12: Glas 3G **63**
Monreith Av. G61: Bear 5D **46**
Monreith Rd. G43: Glas 1B **122**
Monreith Rd. E. G44: Glas 2E **123**
Monroe Dr. G71: Tann 4D **112**
Monroe Pl. G71: Tann 4D **112**
Montague La. G12: Glas 5H **63**
Montague St. G4: Glas 1D **86**
Montalto Av. ML1: Carf 6A **132**
Montclair Pl. PA3: Lin 5H **79**
Montclare Pl. ML9: Lark 6A **164**
Montego Grn. G75: E Kil 2C **156**
Monteith Dr. G76: Clar 1D **138**
Monteith Gdns. G76: Clar 1D **138**
Monteith Path G69: Chry 3H **69**
Monteith Pl. G40: Glas 6A **88**
Monteith Pl. G72: Blan 1C **144**
Monteith Row G40: Glas 5H **87**
Montford Av. G44: Glas 6H **107**
Montford Av. G73: Ruth 6A **108**
Montfort Ga. G78: Barr 4G **119**
Montfort Pk. G78: Barr 4G **119**
Montgarrie St. G51: Glas 5D **84**
Montgomery Av. ML5: Coat 4B **94**
Montgomery Av. PA3: Pais 4D **82**
Montgomery Ct. G76: Eag 6C **154**
Montgomery Ct. PA3: Pais 4D **82**
Montgomery Cres. ML2: Wis 2E **165**
Montgomery Dr. G46: Giff 6A **122**
Montgomery Dr. PA10: Kilba 1A **98**
Montgomery Pl. G74: E Kil 1H **157**
Montgomery Pl. ML9: Lark 3D **170**
Montgomery Rd. PA3: Pais 3C **82**
Montgomery Sq. G76: Eag 6C **154**
Montgomery St. G40: Glas 1C **108**
Montgomery St. G72: Camb 2D **126**
Montgomery St. G74: E Kil 1H **157**
Montgomery St. ML9: Lark 1C **170**
Montgomery Ter. G66: Milt C 6B **10**
Montgomery Wynd G74: E Kil 1H **157**
.... *(off Montgomery St.)*
Montraive St. G73: Ruth 4E **109**
Montrave Path G52: Glas 1D **104**
Montrave St. G52: Glas 1D **104**
Montreal Ho. G81: Clyd 1H **43**
Montreal Pk. G75: E Kil 2E **157**
Montrose Av. G32: Carm 4B **110**
Montrose Av. G52: Hill E 3G **83**
Montrose Ct. ML1: Carf 5B **132**
.... *(off Bruce Rd.)*
Montrose Cres. ML3: Ham 5H **145**
Montrose Dr. G61: Bear 6E **27**
Montrose Gdns. G62: Miln 2H **27**
Montrose Gdns. G65: Kils 2G **13**
Montrose Gdns. G72: Blan 5A **128**
Montrose La. ML3: Ham 5G **145**
Montrose Pl. PA3: Lin 5G **79**
Montrose Rd. PA2: Pais 5D **100**
Montrose St. G1: Glas 5F **7** (4H **87**)
Montrose St. G81: Clyd 5D **44**
Montrose St. ML1: Moth 6F **131**
Montrose Ter. G64: B'rig 2E **67**
Montrose Ter. PA11: Bri W 4F **77**
Montrose Way PA2: Pais 5D **100**
Monument Dr. G33: Glas 4G **67**
Monymusk Gdns. G64: B'rig 5F **51**
Monymusk Pl. G15: Glas 2G **45**
MOODIESBURN **5D 54**
Moodiesburn St. G33: Glas 1F **89**
Moorburn Av. G46: Giff 4H **121**
Moorburn Pl. PA3: Lin 5E **79**
Moorcroft Dr. ML6: Air 4E **97**
Moorcroft Rd. G77: Newt M 6C **136**
Moore Dr. G61: Bear 4F **47**
Moore Gdns. ML3: Ham 4A **162**
Moore St. G40: Glas 5B **88**
Moore St. ML1: New S 4A **132**
Moorfield Cres. ML6: Air 4F **97**
Moorfield Rd. G72: Blan 3A **144**
Moorfoot G64: B'rig 5E **51**
Moorfoot Av. G46: T'bnk 4G **121**
Moorfoot Av. PA2: Pais 4H **101**
Moorfoot Dr. ML2: Wis 6F **149**
Moorfoot Gdns. G75: E Kil 2B **168**
Moorfoot Path PA2: Pais 5H **101**
Moorfoot St. G32: Glas 5G **89**
Moorfoot Way G61: Bear 5C **26**
Moorhill Cres. G77: Newt M 6C **136**
Moorhill Rd. G77: Newt M 5C **136**
Moorhouse Av. G13: Glas 3H **61**
Moorhouse Av. PA2: Pais 3F **101**
Moorhouse St. G78: Barr 5E **119**
Moorings, The PA2: Pais 2F **101**
Moorland Dr. G74: E Kil 1B **158**

Moorland Dr. – Mossvale Wlk.

Moorland Dr. ML6: Air 4F **97**
Moorlands Wlk. G71: Udd 2E **129**
MOORPARK 1D 82
Moorpark Av. G52: Glas 5H **83**
Moorpark Av. G69: Muirh 2A **70**
Moorpark Av. ML6: Air 4E **97**
Moorpark Ct. PA4: Renf 1D **82**
Moorpark Dr. G52: Glas 5A **84**
Moorpark Pl. G52: Glas 5H **83**
Moorpark Sq. PA4: Renf 1D **82**
Moor Rd. G62: Miln 3H **27**
Moorside St. ML8: Carl 3E **175**
Morag Av. G72: Blan 6A **128**
Morag Riva Ct. G71: Udd 1C **128**
Moraine Av. G15: Glas 6A **46**
Moraine Cir. G15: Glas 6A **46**
Moraine Dr. G15: Glas 6A **46**
Moraine Dr. G76: Clar 1B **138**
Moraine Pl. G15: Glas 6B **46**
Morar Av. G81: Clyd 3D **44**
Morar Ct. G67: Cumb 5D **36**
Morar Ct. G81: Clyd 3D **44**
Morar Ct. ML3: Ham 2E **161**
Morar Ct. ML9: Lark 6H **163**
Morar Cres. G64: B'rig 5B **50**
Morar Cres. G81: Clyd 3D **44**
Morar Cres. ML5: Coat 2H **93**
Morar Cres. ML6: Air 1G **95**
Morar Cres. PA7: B'ton 5A **42**
Morar Dr. G61: Bear 4H **47**
Morar Dr. G67: Cumb 6D **36**
Morar Dr. G73: Ruth 4D **124**
Morar Dr. G81: Clyd 3D **44**
Morar Dr. PA2: Pais 3D **100**
Morar Dr. PA3: Lin 6G **79**
Morar Pl. G74: E Kil 6H **141**
Morar Pl. G77: Newt M 2D **136**
Morar Pl. G81: Clyd 3D **44**
Morar Pl. PA4: Renf 5D **60**
Morar Rd. G52: Glas 6E **85**
Morar Rd. G81: Clyd 3D **44**
Morar St. ML2: Wis 2G **165**
Morar Ter. G71: View 6F **113**
Morar Ter. G73: Ruth 4F **125**
Morar Way ML1: N'hill 4C **132**
Moravia Av. G71: Both 4E **129**
Moray Av. ML6: Air 6A **96**
Moray Ct. G73: Ruth 5C **108**
Moray Dr. G64: Torr 4D **30**
Moray Dr. G76: Clar 2D **138**
Moray Gdns. G68: Cumb 6H **15**
Moray Gdns. G71: Tann 5D **112**
Moray Gdns. G76: Clar 1D **138**
Moray Ga. G71: Both 3C **128**
Moray Pl. G41: Glas 3C **106**
Moray Pl. G64: B'rig 6E **51**
Moray Pl. G66: Kirkin 4G **33**
Moray Pl. G69: Chry 1B **70**
Moray Pl. G72: Blan 3A **144**
Moray Pl. PA3: Lin 5G **79**
Moray Quad. ML4: Bell 2C **130**
Moray Way ML1: Holy 2A **132**
Mordaunt St. G40: Glas 2C **108**
Moredun Cres. G32: Glas 4C **90**
Moredun Dr. PA2: Pais 4F **101**
Moredun Rd. PA2: Pais 4F **101**
Moredun St. G32: Glas 4C **90**
Morefield Rd. G51: Glas 4D **84**
Morgan M. G42: Glas 2F **107**
Morgan St. ML3: Ham 1H **161**
Morgan St. ML9: Lark 2B **170**
Morgan Wynd G61: Bear 6D **26**
Morina Gdns. G53: Glas 4C **120**
Morion Rd. G13: Glas 1D **62**
Morison Ho. G67: Cumb 3A **38**
Moriston Ct. ML2: Newm 3D **150**
Morland G74: E Kil 5D **142**
Morley St. G42: Glas 6E **107**
Mor M. ML1: Moth 6C **148**
Morna La. G14: Glas 1E **85**
(off Victoria Pk. Dr. Sth.)
MORNINGSIDE 6G 151
Morningside Rd. ML2: Newm 5F **151**
Morningside St. G33: Glas 3F **89**
Morrin Path G21: Glas 6A **66**
Morrin St. G21: Glas 5A **66**
Morris Cres. G72: Blan 2B **144**
Morris Cres. ML1: Cle 6E **133**
Morris Dr. ML1: N'hse 1C **132**
Morrishall Rd. G74: E Kil 5C **142**
Morrison Dr. G66: Len 4G **9**
Morrison Gdns. G64: Torr 5E **31**
Morrison Pl. PA11: Bri W 3F **77**
(off Main St.)
Morrison Quad. G81: Clyd 6G **45**
Morrisons Ct. G1: Glas 6C **6** (4F **87**)
(off Buchanan St.)
Morrison St. G5: Glas 5E **87**
Morrison St. G81: Dun 1B **44**
Morrison Way G61: Bear 6H **27**
Morrison Way ML1: N'hse 1C **132**
Morris Pl. G40: Glas 6A **88**
Morris St. ML3: Ham 2H **161**
Morris St. ML9: Lark 4E **171**
Morriston Cres. PA4: Renf 2H **83**
Morriston Pk. Dr. G72: Camb 1A **126**
Morriston St. G72: Camb 1A **126**
Morton Av. PA2: Pais 3E **103**
Morton Dr. PA2: Pais 3E **103**
Morton Gdns. G41: Glas 4A **106**
Morton Pl. PA2: Pais 3E **103**
Morton St. ML1: Moth 1G **147**
Morton Ter. PA11: Bri W 3E **77**
(off Horsewood Rd.)
Morven Av. G64: B'rig 6E **51**
Morven Av. G72: Blan 6A **128**
Morven Av. PA2: Pais 5H **101**
Morven Ct. G61: Bear 1E **47**
(not continuous)
Morven Dr. G76: Clar 1B **138**
Morven Dr. ML1: Moth 6C **148**
Morven Dr. PA3: Lin 6G **79**
Morven Gait PA8: Ersk 1A **60**
Morven Gdns. G71: Tann 5D **112**
Morven Ga. ML1: Moth 6C **148**
Morven La. G72: Blan 6A **128**
Morven Rd. G61: Bear 1E **47**
Morven Rd. G72: Camb 4H **125**
Morven St. G52: Glas 6E **85**
Morven St. ML5: Coat 3C **94**
Morven Way G66: Kirkin 5H **33**
Morven Way G71: Both 4F **129**
Mosesfield St. G21: Glas 4B **66**
Mosgiel G75: E Kil 4D **156**
Mosque Av. G5: Glas 6G **87**
Mossacre Rd. ML2: Wis 5A **150**
Moss Av. PA3: Lin 5H **79**
Mossbank G72: Blan 3B **144**
Mossbank G75: E Kil 3B **156**
Mossbank Av. G33: Glas 5H **67**
Mossbank Cres. ML1: N'hill 3F **133**
Mossbank Dr. G33: Glas 5H **67**
Mossbank Rd. ML2: Wis 5A **150**
Mossbeath Ct. G69: Bail 2A **112**
Mossbeath Cres. G69: Bail 2A **112**
Mossbeath Gdns. G69: Bail 2H **111**
Mossbeath Gro. G69: Bail 2A **112**
Mossbell Rd. ML4: Bell 1A **130**
Mossblown St. ML9: Lark 2B **170**
Mossburn Rd. ML2: Wis 6B **150**
Mossburn St. ML2: Wis 2B **166**
Mosscastle Rd. G33: Glas 1C **90**
Mossdale G74: E Kil 6E **141**
Mossdale Ct. ML4: Bell 2F **131**
Mossdale Gdns. ML3: Ham 1C **160**
Moss Dr. G78: Barr 2C **118**
Moss Dr. PA8: Ersk 2F **59**
Mossedge Ind. Est. PA3: Lin 5A **80**
MOSSEND 2E 131
Mossend La. G33: Glas 3D **90**
Mossend St. G33: Glas 3D **90**
Mossgiel Av. G73: Ruth 2C **124**
Mossgiel Cres. G76: Busby 4D **138**
Mossgiel Dr. G81: Clyd 4E **45**
Mossgiel Gdns. G66: Kirkin 4F **33**
Mossgiel Gdns. G71: Tann 5C **112**
Mossgiel La. ML9: Lark 4E **171**
(off Keir Hardie La.)
Mossgiel Pl. G73: Ruth 2C **124**
Mossgiel Rd. G43: Glas 1B **122**
(Doonfoot Rd.)
Mossgiel Rd. G43: Glas 6B **106**
(Riverton Ct.)
Mossgiel Rd. G67: Cumb 2B **38**
Mossgiel Ter. G72: Blan 5A **128**
Mossgiel Way ML1: N'hill 3C **132**
Mosshall Dr. PA7: B'ton 4G **41**
Mosshall Gro. ML1: N'hill 3F **133**
Mosshall Rd. ML1: N'hse 6D **116**
Mosshall St. ML1: N'hill 3F **133**
Mosshead Rd. G61: Bear 6F **27**
Moss Hgts. Av. G52: Glas 6D **84**
Mosshill Rd. ML4: Bell 5D **114**
Moss Knowe G67: Cumb 3C **38**
Mossland Dr. G52: Hill E 2H **83**
Mossland Dr. ML2: Wis 5A **150**
Mossland Rd. G52: Hill E 3F **83**
Mossland Rd. PA4: Renf 2H **83**
Mosslands Rd. PA3: Pais 3H **81**
Mosslingal G75: E Kil 6G **157**
Mossmulloch G75: E Kil 6G **157**
MOSSNEUK 4B 156
Mossneuk Av. G75: E Kil 3A **156**
Mossneuk Cres. ML2: Wis 5B **150**
Mossneuk Dr. G75: E Kil 4B **156**
Mossneuk Dr. ML2: Wis 5A **150**
Mossneuk Dr. PA2: Pais 5G **101**
Mossneuk Pk. ML2: Wis 5A **150**
Mossneuk Rd. G75: E Kil 3B **156**
Mossneuk St. ML5: Coat 2B **114**
MOSSPARK 2E 105
Mosspark Av. G52: Glas 2F **105**
Mosspark Av. G62: Miln 2G **27**
Mosspark Blvd. G52: Glas 1E **105**
Mosspark Dr. G52: Glas 1C **104**
Mosspark La. G52: Glas 2E **105**
Mosspark Oval G52: Glas 2E **105**
Mosspark Rd. G62: Miln 2G **27**
Mosspark Rd. ML5: Coat 3H **93**
Mosspark Sq. G52: Glas 2E **105**
Mosspark Station (Rail) 2C 104
Moss Path G69: Bail 2F **111**
Moss Rd. G51: Glas 3D **84**
Moss Rd. G66: Kirkin 6H **33**
Moss Rd. G66: Lenz 1B **52**
Moss Rd. G67: Cumb 2E **39**
Moss Rd. G69: Muirh 2A **70**
Moss Rd. G75: E Kil 1C **168**
Moss Rd. ML2: Wis 6C **150**
Moss Rd. ML6: Air 5A **96**
Moss Rd. PA11: Bri W 3G **77**
Moss Rd. PA3: Lin 5A **80**
Moss Rd. PA6: Hous 6A **58**
Moss Side Av. ML6: Air 3G **95**
Moss-Side Av. ML8: Carl 3B **174**
Moss-Side Rd. G41: Glas 4B **106**
Moss St. PA1: Pais 6A **82**
Moss St. PA3: Pais 6A **82**
Mossvale Cres. G33: Glas 1C **90**
Mossvale La. PA3: Pais 5H **81**
Mossvale Path G33: Glas 6C **68**
Mossvale Rd. G33: Glas 6B **68**
Mossvale Sq. G33: Glas 1B **90**
Mossvale Sq. PA3: Pais 5H **81**
Mossvale St. PA3: Pais 4H **81**
Mossvale Ter. G69: Mood 4E **55**
Mossvale Wlk. G33: Glas 1C **90**

Mossvale Way – Murray Gro.

Mossvale Way G33: Glas ... 1C **90**
Mossview Cres. ML6: Air ... 5A **96**
Mossview La. G52: Glas ... 6C **84**
Mossview Quad. G52: Glas ... 6D **84**
Mossview Rd. G33: Step ... 4E **69**
Mosswater Wynd G68: Cumb ... 3B **36**
Mosswell Rd. G62: Miln ... 2H **27**
Mossywood Ct. G68: Cumb ... 6B **36**
Mossywood Ct. ML6: Air ... 3D **96**
Mossywood Pl. G68: Cumb ... 6B **36**
Mossywood Rd. G68: Cumb ... 6B **36**
Mote Hill ML3: Ham ... 5A **146**
Mote Hill Ct. ML3: Ham ... 4A **146**
Mote Hill Gro. ML3: Ham ... 4A **146**
Motehill Rd. PA3: Pais ... 5C **82**
MOTHERWELL ... 2G 147
Motherwell Bus. Cen. ML1: Moth ... 2H **147**
Motherwell Concert Hall & Theatre ... **4H 147**
Motherwell FC ... **5H 147**
Motherwell Food Pk. ... 1B **130**
Motherwell Our Lady of Good Aid RC Cathedral ... **2G 147**
Motherwell Rd. ML1: Carf ... 6C **132**
Motherwell Rd. ML1: N'hse ... 2G **133**
Motherwell Rd. ML3: Ham ... 5C **146**
Motherwell Rd. ML4: Bell ... 2C **130**
Motherwell Station (Rail) ... 2G 147
Motherwell St. ML6: Air ... 2C **96**
Moulin Cir. G52: Glas ... 1A **104**
Moulin Pl. G52: Glas ... 1A **104**
Moulin Rd. G52: Glas ... 1A **104**
Moulin Ter. G52: Glas ... 1A **104**
Mount, The ML1: Moth ... 3F **147**
Mountainblue St. G31: Glas ... 6D **88**
Mount Annan Ct. G64: B'rig ... 4D **50**
Mount Annan Dr. G44: Glas ... 6F **107**
MOUNTBLOW ... 2G 43
Mountblow Ho. G81: Clyd ... 2H **43**
Mountblow Rd. G81: Clyd ... 1H **43**
Mountblow Rd. G81: Dun ... 1H **43**
Mount Cameron Dr. G74: E Kil ... 3C **158**
Mount Cameron Dr. Nth. G74: E Kil ... 3A **158**
Mount Cameron Dr. Sth. G74: E Kil ... 3A **158**
MOUNT ELLEN ... 2C 70
Mount Ellen Golf Course ... **2D 70**
MOUNT FLORIDA ... 5F 107
Mount Florida Station (Rail) ... 5E 107
Mountgarrie Path G51: Glas ... 4D **84**
Mountgarrie Rd. G51: Glas ... 4D **84**
Mount Harriet Av. G33: Step ... 3E **69**
Mount Harriet Dr. G33: Step ... 3D **68**
Mountherrick G75: E Kil ... 6G **157**
Mount Lockhart G71: Udd ... 3H **111**
Mount Lockhart Gdns. G71: Udd ... 3H **111**
Mount Lockhart Pl. G71: Udd ... 3H **111**
Mount Pleasant Cres. G66: Milt C ... 5B **10**
Mount Pleasant Dr. G60: Old K ... 6F **23**
Mount Pleasant Ho. G60: Old K ... 1E **43**
Mount Pleasant Pl. G60: Old K ... 1F **43**
... *(off Station Rd.)*
Mount Stewart St. ML8: Carl ... 3C **174**
Mount St. G20: Glas ... 6D **64**
Mount Stuart St. G41: Glas ... 5C **106**
MOUNT VERNON ... 3D 110
Mount Vernon Av. G32: Glas ... 3E **111**
Mount Vernon Av. ML5: Coat ... 4A **94**
Mount Vernon Station (Rail) ... 3F 111
Mournian Way ML3: Ham ... 2H **161**
Mousa Pk. G72: Camb ... 4H **125**
Mowbray G74: E Kil ... 5C **142**
Mowbray Av. G69: G'csh ... 4D **70**
Moyne Rd. G53: Glas ... 3A **104**
Moy Path ML2: Newm ... 3D **150**
... *(off Murdostoun Vw.)*
Moy St. G11: Glas ... 1A **4** (1A **86**)
... *(off Church St.)*
Muckcroft Rd. G66: Kirkin ... 3H **53**
Muckcroft Rd. G66: Lenz ... 3H **53**
Muckcroft Rd. G69: Chry ... 3H **53**
Muckcroft Rd. G69: Lenz ... 3H **53**
Muckcroft Rd. G69: Mood ... 3H **53**
Mugdock Rd. G62: Miln ... 3G **27**
Mugdock Rd. Sth. G62: Miln ... 3G **27**
Muirbank Av. G73: Ruth ... 6B **108**
Muirbank Gdns. G73: Ruth ... 6B **108**
Muirbrae Rd. G73: Ruth ... 3D **124**
Muirbrae Way G73: Ruth ... 3D **124**
Muirburn Av. G44: Glas ... 3C **122**
Muir Cl. G64: B'rig ... 6F **51**
Muir Ct. G44: Neth ... 5C **122**
... (not continuous)
Muircroft Dr. ML1: Cle ... 5H **133**
Muirdrum Av. G52: Glas ... 2D **104**
Muirdyke Rd. ML5: Coat ... 3H **93**
Muirdyke Rd. ML5: Glenb ... 5B **72**
Muirdyke Rd. ML6: Glenm ... 4D **72**
Muirdykes Av. G52: Glas ... 6A **84**
Muirdykes Rd. G52: Glas ... 6A **84**
Muiredge Ct. G71: Udd ... 1D **128**
Muiredge Ter. G69: Bail ... 1H **111**
MUIREND ... 3D 122
Muirend Av. G44: Glas ... 3D **122**
Muirend Rd. G44: Glas ... 3C **122**
Muirend Station (Rail) ... 3D 122
Muirfield Ct. G44: Glas ... 3D **122**
Muirfield Cres. G23: Glas ... 6C **48**
Muirfield Mdws. G71: Both ... 5C **128**
Muirfield Rd. G68: Cumb ... 6A **16**
MUIRHEAD G69: Bail ... 1H 111
MUIRHEAD G69: Chry ... 2A 70
MUIRHEAD-BRAEHEAD INTERCHANGE ... 3A **38**
Muirhead Cotts. G66: Kirkin ... 6H **33**
Muirhead Ct. G69: Bail ... 1A **112**
Muirhead Dr. ML1: N'hill ... 3F **133**
Muirhead Dr. ML8: Law ... 5E **167**
Muirhead Dr. PA3: Lin ... 6G **79**
Muirhead Gdns. G69: Bail ... 1A **112**
Muirhead Ga. G71: Tann ... 5F **113**
Muirhead Gro. G69: Bail ... 1A **112**
Muirhead Rd. G69: Bail ... 2H **111**
Muirhead Rd. G78: Neil ... 4A **134**
MUIRHEAD RDBT. ... 2B **38**
Muirhead St. G66: Kirkin ... 6C **32**
Muirhead Ter. ML1: Moth ... 5G **147**
Muirhead Way G64: B'rig ... 6F **51**
Muirhill Av. G44: Glas ... 3C **122**
Muirhill Ct. ML3: Ham ... 5A **146**
Muirhill Cres. G13: Glas ... 2A **62**
MUIRHOUSE ... 1B 164
Muirhouse Av. ML1: Moth ... 6B **148**
Muirhouse Av. ML2: Newm ... 3F **151**
Muirhouse Dr. ML1: Moth ... 1C **164**
Muirhouse La. G75: E Kil ... 3H **157**
Muirhouse Pk. G61: Bear ... 5D **26**
Muirhouse Rd. ML1: Moth ... 1B **164**
Muirhouse St. G41: Glas ... 2E **107**
Muirhouse Twr. ML1: Moth ... 6B **148**
Muirhouse Works G41: Glas ... 2E **107**
Muirkirk Dr. G13: Glas ... 2F **63**
Muirkirk Dr. ML3: Ham ... 1B **160**
Muirlee Rd. ML8: Carl ... 4F **175**
Muirlees Cres. G62: Miln ... 3E **27**
Muirmadkin Rd. ML4: Bell ... 2D **130**
Muirpark Av. PA4: Renf ... 1E **83**
Muirpark Dr. G64: B'rig ... 1C **66**
Muirpark St. G11: Glas ... 1H **85**
Muirpark Ter. G64: B'rig ... 1B **66**
Muir Rd. G82: Dumb ... 1H **19**
Muirshiel Av. G53: Glas ... 1C **120**
Muirshiel Ct. G53: Glas ... 2C **120**
Muirshiel Cres. G53: Glas ... 1C **120**
Muirshot Rd. ML9: Lark ... 1D **170**
Muirside Av. G32: Glas ... 2E **111**
Muirside Av. G66: Kirkin ... 5G **33**
Muirside Pl. ML2: Newm ... 3D **150**
Muirside Rd. G69: Bail ... 1H **111**
Muirside St. G69: Bail ... 1H **111**
Muirskeith Cres. G43: Glas ... 1D **122**
Muirskeith Pl. G43: Glas ... 1D **122**
Muirskeith Rd. G43: Glas ... 1D **122**
Muir St. G64: B'rig ... 6C **50**
Muir St. G72: Blan ... 3B **144**
Muir St. ML1: Moth ... 1F **147**
Muir St. ML3: Ham ... 5H **145**
Muir St. ML5: Coat ... 4A **94**
Muir St. ML8: Law ... 5D **166**
Muir St. ML9: Lark ... 2C **170**
Muir St. PA4: Renf ... 5F **61**
Muirsykehead Rd. ML8: Carl ... 6C **174**
Muir Ter. PA3: Pais ... 4C **82**
Muirton Dr. G64: B'rig ... 4B **50**
Muiryfauld Dr. G31: Glas ... 1G **109**
Muiryhall St. ML5: Coat ... 4C **94**
Muiryhall St. E. ML5: Coat ... 4D **94**
Mulben Cres. G53: Glas ... 6H **103**
Mulben Pl. G53: Glas ... 6H **103**
Mulben Ter. G53: Glas ... 6H **103**
Mulberry Cres. ML6: Chap ... 2E **117**
Mulberry Cres. PA4: Renf ... 4G **61**
Mulberry Dr. G75: E Kil ... 6E **157**
Mulberry Rd. G43: Glas ... 2B **122**
Mulberry Rd. G71: View ... 4G **113**
Mulberry Rd. PA4: Renf ... 4G **61**
Mulberry Sq. PA4: Renf ... 4G **61**
Mulberry Way G75: E Kil ... 6E **157**
Mulberry Wynd G72: Flem ... 4F **127**
Mull G74: E Kil ... 3C **158**
Mull ML6: Air ... 6D **96**
Mullardoch St. G23: Glas ... 6B **48**
Mull Av. PA2: Pais ... 6A **102**
Mull Av. PA4: Renf ... 2E **83**
Mull Ct. ML3: Ham ... 2D **160**
Mullen Ct. G33: Step ... 4F **69**
Mull Quad. ML2: Wis ... 4C **150**
Mull St. G21: Glas ... 1D **88**
Mulvey Cres. ML6: Air ... 4G **95**
Mungo Pk. G75: E Kil ... 3F **157**
Mungo Pl. G71: Tann ... 4E **113**
Munlochy Rd. G51: Glas ... 4D **84**
Munro Ct. G81: Dun ... 1B **44**
Munro Dr. G66: Milt C ... 6B **10**
Munro La. G13: Glas ... 4E **63**
Munro La. E. G13: Glas ... 4E **63**
Munro Pl. G13: Glas ... 2E **63**
Munro Pl. G74: E Kil ... 6B **142**
Munro Rd. G13: Glas ... 4E **63**
Murano Cres. G20: Glas ... 5D **64**
Murano Pl. G20: Glas ... 5D **64**
Murano St. G20: Glas ... 4D **64**
Murchison G12: Glas ... 3G **63**
Murchison Dr. G75: E Kil ... 4D **156**
Murchison Rd. PA6: C'lee ... 2C **78**
Murdoch Av. G72: Camb ... 4B **126**
Murdoch Ct. PA5: John ... 4E **99**
... *(off Tannahill Cres.)*
Murdoch Dr. G62: Miln ... 5B **28**
Murdoch Dr. G81: Clyd ... 5C **44**
Murdoch Pl. ML1: New S ... 4H **131**
Murdoch Rd. G75: E Kil ... 3G **157**
Murdoch Sq. ML4: Bell ... 6E **115**
MURDOSTOUN ESTATE ... 1H 151
Murdostoun Gdns. ML2: Wis ... 4H **149**
Murdostoun Vw. ML2: Newm ... 3D **150**
Muriel La. G78: Barr ... 4E **119**
Muriel St. G78: Barr ... 4E **119**
MURRAY, THE ... 4G 157
Murray Av. G65: Kils ... 4H **13**
Murray Bus. Area PA3: Pais ... 5H **81**
Murray Ct. ML3: Ham ... 6E **145**
Murray Cres. G72: Blan ... 3C **144**
Murray Cres. ML2: Newm ... 2E **151**
Murrayfield G64: B'rig ... 4C **50**
Murrayfield Dr. G61: Bear ... 6E **47**
Murrayfield St. G32: Glas ... 4G **89**
Murray Gdns. G66: Milt C ... 5C **10**
Murray Gro. G61: Bear ... 5B **26**

Murray Hall – Netherhouse Rd.

Murray Hall G4: Glas 4G **7** (3H **87**)
....(off Collins St.)
Murrayhill G75: E Kil 3F **157**
Murray Path G71: Udd 1C **128**
Murray Pl. G78: Barr 3F **119**
Murray Pl. G82: Dumb 1C **20**
Murray Pl. ML4: Bell 6A **114**
Murray Rd. G71: Both 4E **129**
Murray Rd. ML8: Law 1F **173**
Murray Rd., The G75: E Kil 3E **157**
Murray Roundabout, The 3H **157**
Murray Sq., The G75: E Kil 4G **157**
Murray St. PA3: Pais 5G **81**
Murray St. PA4: Renf 6E **61**
Murray Ter. ML1: Moth 2D **146**
Murray Wlk. G72: Blan 3C **144**
Murrin Av. G64: B'rig 6F **51**
Murroch Av. G82: Dumb 1H **19**
Murroes Rd. G51: Glas 4D **84**
Museum Bus. Pk. G53: Glas 2H **119**
Museum of 602 (City of Glasgow) Squadron **4H 83**
Museum of Piping ....**2C 6 (2F 87)**
....(off McPhater St.)
Musgrove Pl. G75: E Kil 3E **157**
Musket Gro. G53: Glas 5C **120**
Muslin St. G40: Glas 1B **108**
Muttonhole Rd. ML3: Ham 3H **159**
Mybster Pl. G51: Glas 4D **84**
Myers Ct. G71: Udd 3D **128**
Myers Ct. ML4: Bell 1H **129**
Myers Cres. G71: Udd 2E **129**
Myreside Cres. G32: Glas 5F **89**
Myreside Dr. G32: Glas 5F **89**
Myreside Ga. G32: Glas 5G **89**
Myreside Pl. G32: Glas 5F **89**
Myreside St. G32: Glas 5F **89**
....(not continuous)
Myreside Way G32: Glas 5F **89**
Myres Rd. G53: Glas 5D **104**
Myrie Gdns. G64: B'rig 5D **50**
Myroch Pl. G34: Glas 2A **92**
Myrtle Av. G66: Lenz 2C **52**
Myrtle Dr. ML1: Holy 2B **132**
Myrtle Dr. ML2: Wis 5D **148**
Myrtle Hill La. G42: Glas 5G **107**
Myrtle La. ML9: Lark 4D **170**
Myrtle Pk. G42: Glas 4F **107**
Myrtle Pl. G42: Glas 5G **107**
Myrtle Rd. G71: View 5F **113**
Myrtle Rd. G81: Clyd 3H **43**
Myrtle Sq. G64: B'rig 1C **66**
Myrtle St. G72: Blan 6B **128**
Myrtle Vw. Rd. G42: Glas 5G **107**
Myrtle Wlk. G72: Camb 1H **125**
Myvot Av. G67: Cumb 1D **56**
Myvot Rd. G67: Cumb 3A **56**
....(Mollinsburn Rd.)
Myvot Rd. G67: Cumb 1D **56**
....(Myvot Av.)

N

Naburn Ga. G5: Glas 1G **107**
Nagle Gdns. ML1: Cle 1F **149**
Nairn Av. G72: Blan 5A **128**
Nairn Av. ML4: Bell 1C **130**
Nairn Cres. ML6: Air 6A **96**
Nairn Dr. PA7: B'ton 5F **41**
Nairn Pl. G74: E Kil 6C **142**
Nairn Pl. G81: Clyd 4B **44**
Nairn Pl. PA5: John 5C **98**
Nairn Quad. ML2: Wis 4H **149**
Nairnside Rd. G21: Glas 2E **67**
Nairn St. G3: Glas 2B **4** (2B **86**)
Nairn St. G72: Blan 3A **144**
Nairn St. G81: Clyd 4B **44**
Nairn St. ML9: Lark 3B **170**
Nairn Way G68: Cumb 6A **16**
Naismith St. G32: Carm 5C **110**
Naismith Wlk. ML4: Bell 6E **115**
Nansen St. G20: Glas 6E **65**
Napier Ct. G60: Old K 2G **43**
Napier Ct. G68: Cumb 3D **16**
Napier Cres. G82: Dumb 4C **18**
Napier Dr. G51: Glas 3H **85**
Napier Gdns. PA3: Lin 5A **80**
Napier Hill G75: E Kil 3G **157**
Napier La. G75: E Kil 3G **157**
Napier Pk. G68: Cumb 4C **16**
Napier Pl. G51: Glas 3H **85**
Napier Pl. G60: Old K 2G **43**
Napier Pl. G68: Cumb 3C **16**
Napier Rd. G51: Glas 3H **85**
Napier Rd. G52: Hill E 2H **83**
Napier Rd. G68: Cumb 4C **16**
Napiershall La. G20: Glas 1D **86**
....(off Napiershall St.)
Napiershall Pl. G20: Glas 1D **86**
Napiershall St. G20: Glas 1D **86**
Napier Sq. ML4: Bell 6D **114**
Napier St. G51: Glas 3H **85**
Napier St. G81: Clyd 2E **61**
Napier St. PA3: Lin 5A **80**
Napier St. PA5: John 2E **99**
Napier Ter. G51: Glas 3H **85**
Napier Way G68: Cumb 4C **16**
Naproch Pl. G77: Newt M 4A **138**
Naseby Av. G11: Glas 6F **63**
Naseby Av. Open Space **6F 63**
....(off Naseby Avenue)
Naseby La. G11: Glas 6F **63**
Nasmyth Av. G61: Bear 5B **26**
Nasmyth Av. G75: E Kil 4H **157**
Nasmyth Pl. G52: Hill E 4A **84**
Nasmyth Rd. G52: Hill E 4A **84**
Nasmyth Rd. Nth. G52: Hill E 4A **84**
....(not continuous)
Nasmyth Rd. Sth. G52: Hill E 4A **84**
Nassau Pl. G75: E Kil 2C **156**
National Bank La. G1: Glas 5C **6** (4F **87**)
National Ct. G43: Glas 6E **105**
National Cres. G43: Glas 6E **105**
National Dr. G43: Glas 6D **104**
National Ga. G43: Glas 6D **104**
National Hockey Cen. **1A 108**
National Indoor Sports Arena **1D 108**
National Mus. of Rural Life Scotland **5B 140**
Navar Pl. PA2: Pais 3C **102**
Naver St. G33: Glas 2G **89**
Naylor La. ML6: Air 3B **96**
Naysmyth Bank G75: E Kil 4H **157**
Needle Grn. ML8: Carl 3D **174**
Neidpath G69: Bail 1G **111**
Neidpath Av. ML5: Coat 2D **114**
Neidpath E. G74: E Kil 1F **157**
Neidpath Pl. ML5: Coat 2C **114**
Neidpath Rd. ML8: Carl 2C **174**
Neidpath Rd. E. G46: Giff 3G **137**
Neidpath Rd. W. G46: Giff 2G **137**
Neidpath W. G74: E Kil 1F **157**
Neil Gordon Ga. G72: Blan 1B **144**
Neilsland Dr. ML1: Moth 3D **146**
Neilsland Dr. ML3: Ham 4G **161**
Neilsland Oval G53: Glas 5D **104**
Neilsland Rd. ML3: Ham 2F **161**
Neilsland Sq. G53: Glas 4D **104**
Neilsland Sq. ML3: Ham 2G **161**
Neilsland St. ML3: Ham 2G **161**
Neilson Ct. ML3: Ham 1A **162**
Neilson St. ML4: Bell 2C **130**
NEILSTON 2D **134**
Neilston Av. G53: Glas 2C **120**
Neilston Ct. G53: Glas 2C **120**
Neilston Leisure Cen. **2E 135**
Neilston Pl. G65: Kils 2F **13**
Neilston Rd. G78: Barr 1E **135**
Neilston Rd. G78: Neil 1E **135**
Neilston Rd. PA2: Pais 2A **102**
Neilston Station (Rail) **2D 134**
Neilston Wlk. G65: Kils 2H **13**
....(Garrell Av.)
Neilston Wlk. G65: Kils 2F **13**
....(Gateside Pk.)
Neilston Wlk. G65: Kils 3E **13**
....(Glasgow Rd.)
Neilston Wlk. G65: Kils 2G **13**
....(Kelvin Way)
Neil St. PA4: Renf 4F **61**
Neilvaig Cres. G73: Ruth 3D **124**
Neilvaig Dr. G73: Ruth 4D **124**
Neistpoint Dr. G33: Glas 3A **90**
Nelson Av. ML5: Coat 1A **114**
Nelson Cres. ML1: Moth 5B **148**
Nelson Mandela Pl. G2: Glas 4D **6** (3G **87**)
Nelson Pl. G69: Bail 1H **111**
Nelson St. G5: Glas 5E **87**
Nelson St. G69: Bail 1H **111**
Nelson Ter. G74: E Kil 3A **158**
Neptune St. G51: Glas 4H **85**
Neptune Way ML4: Moss 2G **131**
NERSTON 3A **142**
Nerston Rd. G74: Ners 3G **141**
Nerston Rd. G74: Roger 3G **141**
Ness Av. PA5: John 5C **98**
Ness Dr. G72: Blan 6C **128**
Ness Dr. G74: E Kil 2B **158**
Ness Gdns. G64: B'rig 6D **50**
Ness Gdns. ML9: Lark 5C **170**
Ness Rd. PA4: Renf 5D **60**
Ness St. G33: Glas 2G **89**
Ness St. ML2: Wis 3H **165**
Ness Ter. ML3: Ham 2E **161**
Ness Way ML1: Holy 2A **132**
Nethan Av. ML2: Wis 1C **164**
Nethan Ga. ML3: Ham 6G **145**
Nethan Pl. ML3: Ham 5H **161**
Nethan St. G51: Glas 3G **85**
Nethan St. ML1: Moth 5E **131**
Nether Auldhouse Rd. G43: Glas 6H **105**
Netherbank Rd. ML2: Wis 1D **164**
Netherbog Av. G82: Dumb 3H **19**
Netherbog Rd. G82: Dumb 3H **19**
Netherburn Av. G44: Neth 5D **122**
Netherburn Av. PA6: C'lee 3E **79**
Netherburn Gdns. PA6: C'lee 3E **79**
Netherburn Rd. ML9: Ashg 5A **172**
Netherby Dr. G41: Glas 1B **106**
Nethercairn Pl. G77: Newt M 4A **138**
Nethercairn Rd. G43: Glas 3A **122**
Nethercliffe Av. G44: Neth 5D **122**
Nethercommon Ind. Est. PA3: Pais 3A **82**
....(not continuous)
Nethercraigs Ct. PA2: Pais 6F **101**
Nethercraigs Dr. PA2: Pais 5G **101**
Nethercraigs Rd. PA2: Pais 6F **101**
Nethercroy Rd. G65: Croy 6A **14**
Netherdale G77: Newt M 4H **137**
Netherdale Cres. ML2: Wis 1C **164**
Netherdale Dr. PA1: Pais 1H **103**
Netherdale Rd. ML2: Wis 1E **165**
Nethergreen Cres. PA4: Renf 6D **60**
Nethergreen Rd. PA4: Renf 6D **60**
Nethergreen Wynd PA4: Renf 6D **60**
Netherhall Rd. ML2: Wis 1D **164**
Netherhill Av. G44: Neth 6D **122**
Netherhill Cotts. PA3: Pais 4C **82**
....(off Priory Av.)
Netherhill Cres. PA3: Pais 5C **82**
Netherhill Rd. G69: Mood 6D **54**
Netherhill Rd. PA3: Pais 5B **82**
Netherhill Way PA3: Pais 4D **82**
Netherhouse Av. G66: Lenz 3E **53**
Netherhouse Av. ML5: Coat 2B **114**
Netherhouse Pl. G34: Glas 3C **92**
Netherhouse Rd. G34: Glas 4B **92**
Netherhouse Rd. G69: Barg 4B **92**

256 A–Z Glasgow

NEW VICTORIA HOSPITAL – Nursery Pl.

NEW VICTORIA HOSPITAL 5E **107**
(Glasgow)
New Vw. Cres. ML4: Bell 4C **130**
New Vw. Dr. ML4: Bell 4C **130**
New Vw. Pl. ML4: Bell 4C **130**
New Way G73: Ruth 5D **108**
New Wynd G1: Glas 5G **87**
Niamh Ct. PA4: Inch 2G **59**
Nicholas St. G1: Glas 5G **7** (4H **87**)
Nicholson St. G5: Glas 6F **87**
Nicholson St. G5: Glas 6F **87**
Nicklaus Way ML1: N'hse 6E **117**
Nicolson Ct. G33: Step 4D **68**
Nicol St. ML6: Air 2C **96**
Niddrie Rd. G42: Glas 3D **106**
Niddrie Sq. G42: Glas 3D **106**
Niddry St. PA3: Pais 6B **82**
Nigel Gdns. G41: Glas 4B **106**
Nigel St. ML1: Moth 3F **147**
Nigg Pl. G34: Glas 3G **91**
Nightingale Pl. PA5: John 6D **98**
Nikitas Av. ML9: B'haw 6D **170**
Nimmo Dr. G51: Glas 4E **85**
Nimmo Pl. ML2: Wis 6A **150**
Nimmo Pl. ML8: Carl 2C **174**
Ninian Av. PA6: C'lee 3C **78**
Ninian Cres. G66: Kirkin 6F **33**
Ninian Rd. ML6: Air 6B **96**
Ninian's Ri. G66: Kirkin 6F **33**
Nisbet St. G31: Glas 6F **89**
Nisbett Pl. ML6: Chap 2E **117**
Nisbett St. ML6: Chap 3E **117**
Nissen Pl. G53: Glas 4H **103**
Nith Dr. ML3: Ham 3E **161**
Nith Dr. PA4: Renf 1G **83**
Nith La. ML2: Newm 3D **150**
(off King St.)
Nith Path ML1: Cle 5H **133**
Nith Pl. PA5: John 5C **98**
Nith Quad. ML1: N'hill 4C **132**
Nithsdale G74: E Kil 6D **142**
Nithsdale Cres. G61: Bear 1C **46**
Nithsdale Dr. G41: Glas 3D **106**
Nithsdale Pl. G41: Glas 2D **106**
Nithsdale Rd. G41: Glas 1H **105**
(Dargarvel Av.)
Nithsdale Rd. G41: Glas 3D **106**
(Nithsdale St.)
Nithsdale St. G41: Glas 3D **106**
Nith St. G33: Glas 2F **89**
Nith Way PA4: Renf 1G **83**
NITSHILL 2A **120**
NITSHILL INTERCHANGE 5D **120**
Nitshill Rd. G46: T'bnk 4E **121**
Nitshill Rd. G53: Glas 1H **119**
Nitshill Rd. G53: T'bnk 1H **119**
Nitshill Station (Rail) 2A **120**
Niven St. G20: Glas 3A **64**
Noble Dr. G33: Glas 2H **67**
Noble Gro. G33: Glas 2A **68**
Noble Rd. ML4: Bell 2C **130**
Nobles Pl. ML4: Bell 3B **130**
Nobles Vw. ML4: Bell 3B **130**
Noldrum Av. G32: Carm 5C **110**
Noldrum Gdns. G32: Carm 5C **110**
Norbreck Dr. G46: Giff 3A **122**
Norby Rd. G11: Glas 6F **63**
Nordic Cres. G72: Blan 2C **144**
Nordic Gdns. G72: Blan 2C **144**
Nordic Gro. G72: Blan 2C **144**
Noremac Way ML4: Bell 6B **114**
Norfield Dr. G44: Glas 6F **107**
Norfolk Ct. G5: Glas 6F **87**
Norfolk Cres. G64: B'rig 4A **50**
Norfolk St. G5: Glas 6F **87**
Norham St. G41: Glas 4C **106**
Normal Av. G13: Glas 4D **62**
Norman MacLeod Cres. G61: Bear 1E **47**
Norman St. G40: Glas 2B **108**
Norse La. Nth. G14: Glas 5C **62**
Norse La. Sth. G14: Glas 5C **62**
Norse Pl. G14: Glas 5C **62**
Norse Rd. G14: Glas 5C **62**
North Alderston Belt 5B **114**
(within Strathclyde Business Park)
Northall Quad. ML1: Carf 6A **132**
Northampton Dr. G12: Glas 3H **63**
Northampton La. G12: Glas 3H **63**
(off Northampton Dr.)
North Av. G72: Camb 1H **125**
North Av. G81: Clyd 4C **44**
North Av. ML8: Carl 3B **174**
North Bank PA3: Pais 5A **82**
North Bank PA6: Hous 1B **78**
Northbank Av. G66: Kirkin 5C **32**
Northbank Av. G72: Camb 1D **126**
North Bank Pl. G81: Clyd 1E **61**
Northbank Rd. G66: Kirkin 5C **32**
Northbank St. G72: Camb 1D **126**
North Bank St. G81: Clyd 1E **61**
NORTH BARR 4E **43**
North Barr Av. PA8: Ersk 4E **43**
NORTH BARRWOOD 3A **14**
North Berwick Av. G68: Cumb 6H **15**
North Berwick Cres. G75: E Kil 5C **156**
North Berwick Gdns. G68: Cumb 6H **15**
North Biggar Rd. ML6: Air 3B **96**
North Birbiston Rd. G66: Len 3F **9**
Northbrae Dr. PA7: B'ton 5F **41**
Northbrae Pl. G13: Glas 3B **62**
Northbrae Vw. PA7: B'ton 5F **41**
North Bri. St. ML6: Air 3H **95**
North British Rd. G71: Udd 1D **128**
Northburn Av. ML6: Air 2B **96**
Northburn Pl. ML6: Air 1B **96**
Northburn Rd. ML5: Coat 2E **95**
Northburn St. ML6: Plain 1H **97**
North Bute St. ML5: Coat 1D **114**
North Caldeen Rd. ML5: Coat 6E **95**
North Calder Dr. ML6: Air 5D **96**
North Calder Gro. G71: Udd 3H **111**
North Calder Pl. G71: Udd 3G **111**
North Calder Rd. G71: View 4G **113**
North Campbell Av. G62: Miln 4F **27**
North Canal Bank St. G4: Glas 1D **6** (1G **87**)
North Carbrain Rd. G67: Cumb 5G **37**
NORTH CARDONALD 4B **84**
North Claremont La. G62: Miln 3G **27**
North Claremont St. G3: Glas 2E **5** (2C **86**)
North Corsebar Rd. PA2: Pais 3G **101**
North Ct. G1: Glas 5D **6** (4G **87**)
North Ct. La. G1: Glas 5D **6** (4G **87**)
Northcroft Rd. G69: Mood 5C **54**
North Cft. St. PA3: Pais 6B **82**
North Dean Pk. Av. G71: Both 4E **129**
North Douglas St. G81: Clyd 1E **61**
North Dr. G1: Glas 6C **6** (4F **87**)
North Dr. PA3: Lin 5H **79**
North Dryburgh Rd. ML2: Wis 4G **149**
North Dumgoyne Av. G62: Miln 2F **27**
North Elgin Pl. G81: Clyd 2E **61**
North Elgin St. G81: Clyd 2E **61**
North Erskine Pk. G61: Bear 2D **46**
NORTHFIELD 2F **13**
Northfield G75: E Kil 4B **156**
Northfield Rd. G65: Kils 2F **13**
Northfield St. ML1: Moth 1G **147**
Northflat Pl. ML8: Carl 5G **175**
North Frederick Path G1: Glas 4E **7** (3G **87**)
North Frederick St. G1: Glas 5E **7** (4G **87**)
North Gardner St. G11: Glas 1H **85**
Northgate Quad. G21: Glas 2E **67**
Northgate Rd. G21: Glas 2E **67**
North Gower St. G51: Glas 6A **86**
North Grange Rd. G61: Bear 1E **47**
North Hanover St. G1: Glas 5E **7** (3G **87**)
North Hillhead Rd. G77: Newt M 2A **152**
Northinch Ct. G14: Glas 1D **84**
Northinch St. G14: Glas 1D **84**
North Iverton Pk. Rd. PA5: John 2G **99**
NORTH KELVIN 5C **64**
North Kilmeny Cres. ML2: Wis 3A **150**
North Lanarkshire Heritage Cen. 2F **147**
Northland Av. G14: Glas 4C **62**
Northland Dr. G14: Glas 4C **62**
Northland Gdns. G14: Glas 4C **62**
Northland La. G14: Glas 5C **62**
North La. PA3: Lin 5A **80**
North LODGE 5F **147**
North Lodge Av. ML1: Moth 5G **147**
North Lodge Ga. G33: Glas 4D **90**
North Lodge Rd. PA4: Renf 5E **61**
North Lodge Wynd G33: Glas 4D **90**
North Moraine La. G15: Glas 5C **46**
NORTH MOTHERWELL 2E **147**
Northmuir Dr. ML2: Wis 5B **150**
Northmuir Rd. G15: Glas 3B **46**
North Orchard St. ML1: Moth 2F **147**
North Pk. Av. G46: T'bnk 3F **121**
North Pk. Av. G78: Barr 4D **118**
Northpark St. G20: Glas 5D **64**
North Pk. Vs. G46: T'bnk 4F **121**
North Portland St. G1: Glas 5F **7** (4H **87**)
North Porton Rd. PA7: B'ton 3A **42**
North Rd. G68: Cumb 5C **36**
North Rd. ML4: Bell 3C **114**
North Rd. ML5: Coat 3C **114**
North Rd. PA5: John 3E **99**
North Sq. ML5: Coat 3A **94**
North St. G3: Glas 2G **5** (2D **86**)
North St. ML1: Moth 1H **147**
North St. ML9: Lark 1C **170**
North St. PA3: Pais 5A **82**
North St. PA6: Hous 1A **78**
Northumberland St. G20: Glas 5C **64**
North Vw. G61: Bear 5D **46**
North Vw. Rd. PA11: Bri W 5H **77**
North Wallace St. G4: Glas 2F **7** (2H **87**)
Northway G72: Blan 6A **128**
Northwood Cl. G43: Glas 1D **120**
Northwood Dr. ML2: Newm 3E **151**
Northwood Ga. G43: Glas 1D **120**
North Woodside Rd. G20: Glas 6D **64**
(not continuous)
Northwood Ter. G43: Glas 1D **120**
Northwood Wynd G43: Glas 1D **120**
Norval St. G11: Glas 1G **85**
Norwich Dr. G12: Glas 4H **63**
Norwood Av. G66: Kirkin 5B **32**
Norwood Dr. G46: Giff 6G **121**
Norwood Pk. G61: Bear 4F **47**
Norwood Ter. G71: Tann 6E **113**
Nottingham Av. G12: Glas 3H **63**
Nottingham La. G12: Glas 3H **63**
(off Northampton Dr.)
Novar Dr. G12: Glas 5G **63**
Novar Gdns. G64: B'rig 5A **50**
Novar St. ML3: Ham 1H **161**
Nova Technology Pk. G33: Glas 4G **67**
Nuffield Health 4A **158**
(East Kilbride)
Nuffield Health 3C **122**
(Giffnock)
Nuffield Health 6E **5** (4C **86**)
(Glasgow, Central)
Nuffield Health 4D **4** (3C **86**)
(Glasgow, West End)
Nuneaton St. G40: Glas 2C **108**
Nuneaton St. Ind. Est. G40: Glas 2C **108**
Nurseries Rd. G69: Bail 5F **91**
Nursery Av. PA7: B'ton 3C **42**
Nursery Av. PA7: B'ton 3C **42**
Nursery Ct. ML8: Carl 2C **174**
Nursery Dr. ML9: Ashg 5A **172**
Nursery La. G41: Glas 3D **106**
Nursery Pk. ML8: Carl 3C **174**
Nursery Pl. G72: Blan 3B **144**

258 A–Z Glasgow

Nursery St. – Oran Ga.

Nursery St. G41: Glas 2E **107**
Nutberry Ct. G42: Glas 4F **107**

O

Oak Av. G61: Bear 6F **27**
Oak Av. G75: E Kil 5D **156**
Oakbank Av. ML2: Wis 2E **165**
Oakbank Cres. G71: Udd 2E **129**
Oakbank Dr. G71: Udd 2E **129**
Oakbank Dr. G78: Barr 6F **119**
Oakbank Ind. Est. G20: Glas 6F **65**
Oakbank St. ML6: Air 4D **96**
Oakburn Av. G62: Miln 4F **27**
Oakburn Cres. G62: Miln 3F **27**
Oak Cres. G69: Bail 1G **111**
Oakdene Av. G71: Tann 6F **113**
Oakdene Av. ML4: Bell 6C **114**
Oakdene Cres. ML1: N'hill 3C **132**
Oak Dr. G66: Lenz 2B **52**
Oak Dr. G72: Camb 3C **126**
Oak Fern Dr. G74: E Kil 5F **141**
Oak Fern Gro. G74: E Kil 5F **141**
Oakfield Av. G12: Glas 1C **86**
Oakfield Dr. ML1: Moth 3G **147**
Oakfield La. G12: Glas 1C **86**
.... *(off Gibson St.)*
Oakfield Rd. ML1: Moth 3G **147**
Oakfield Twr. ML1: Moth 4G **147**
Oak Gdns. G66: Lenz 1B **52**
Oak Gro. ML6: Chap 2E **117**
Oakhill Av. G69: Bail 2F **111**
Oak Lea ML3: Ham 1B **162**
Oaklea Cres. G72: Blan 1A **144**
Oakley Dr. G44: Neth 4D **122**
Oakley Ter. G31: Glas 4B **88**
Oak Pk. G64: B'rig 6D **50**
Oak Pk. ML1: Moth 5F **147**
Oak Path ML1: Holy 2B **132**
Oak Pl. G71: View 6G **113**
Oak Pl. G75: E Kil 5D **156**
Oak Pl. ML5: Coat 6E **95**
Oakridge Cres. PA3: Pais 6F **81**
Oakridge Rd. G69: Barg 5E **93**
Oak Rd. G67: Cumb 1E **39**
Oak Rd. G81: Clyd 2B **44**
Oak Rd. PA2: Pais 4C **102**
Oaks, The G44: Glas 3F **123**
Oaks, The PA5: John 3E **99**
Oakshaw Brae PA1: Pais 6H **81**
Oakshawhead PA1: Pais 6H **81**
Oakshaw St. E. PA1: Pais 6H **81**
Oakshaw St. W. PA1: Pais 6H **81**
Oakside Pl. ML3: Ham 4H **161**
Oak St. G2: Glas 5H **5** (4E **87**)
Oaktree Gdns. G45: Glas 3B **124**
Oaktree Gdns. G82: Dumb 3C **20**
Oaktree Gro. G45: Glas 3B **124**
Oakwood Av. PA2: Pais 4F **101**
Oakwood Ct. G33: Step 5D **68**
Oakwood Cres. G34: Glas 2B **92**
Oakwood Dr. G34: Glas 2B **92**
Oakwood Dr. G77: Newt M 5F **137**
Oakwood Dr. ML5: Coat 6H **93**
Oak Wynd G72: Flem 4F **127**
Oates Gdns. ML1: Moth 5B **148**
Oatfield St. G21: Glas 5D **66**
OATLANDS **2H 107**
Oatlands Ga. G5: Glas 2H **107**
Oatlands Sq. G5: Glas 2H **107**
Oban Ct. G20: Glas 5C **64**
Oban Dr. G20: Glas 5C **64**
Oban La. G20: Glas 5C **64**
Oban Pass G20: Glas 5C **64**
Oban Pl. ML6: Air 5D **96**
Oban Way ML1: Carf 5B **132**
Observatory La. G12: Glas 6B **64**
Observatory Rd. G12: Glas 6A **64**
Occupation Gdns. G71: Tann 5F **113**
Ocean Fld. G81: Clyd 1B **44**
Ocein Dr. G75: T'hall 3G **155**
Ochel Path ML6: Chap 4F **117**
Ochil Ct. G75: E Kil 1B **168**
Ochil Dr. G78: Barr 6D **118**
Ochil Dr. PA2: Pais 5H **101**
Ochill Vw. Home G67: Cumb 2A **38**
.... *(off Hume Rd.)*
Ochil Pl. G32: Glas 1A **110**
Ochil Rd. G61: Bear 6B **26**
Ochil Rd. G64: B'rig 6E **51**
Ochil Rd. PA4: Renf 2D **82**
Ochil St. G32: Glas 1A **110**
Ochil St. ML2: Wis 5F **149**
Ochiltree Av. G13: Glas 2F **63**
Ochiltree Cres. ML5: Coat 6A **94**
Ochiltree Dr. ML3: Ham 2C **160**
Ochil Vw. G71: Tann 5E **113**
Odense Ct. G75: E Kil 5G **157**
Odeon Cinema **3H 157**
.... *(East Kilbride)*
Odeon Cinema **5D 86**
.... *(Glasgow)*
Odeon Cinema **5H 61**
.... *(Renfrew)*
O'Donnell Dr. ML3: Fern 1E **163**
O'Donnell Gdns. ML3: Fern 1E **163**
O'Donnell Way ML1: Moth 2B **148**
Ogilvie Athletic Ground **5A 68**
Ogilvie Pl. G31: Glas 1F **109**
Ogilvie St. G31: Glas 1F **109**
Oki Way G68: Cumb 4C **16**
Old Aisle Rd. G66: Kirkin 6F **33**
Old Anniesland **3E 63**
Old Avon Rd. ML3: Ham 1C **162**
OLD BALORNOCK **4D 66**
Oldbar Cres. G53: Glas 5G **103**
Oldbar Ga. G53: Glas 5H **103**
Oldbar Rd. G53: Glas 5H **103**
Old Bars Dr. G69: Mood 4E **55**
Oldbar Sq. G53: Glas 5G **103**
Old Bore Rd. ML6: Air 3E **97**
Old Bothwell Rd. G71: Both 6F **129**
Old Bridgend ML8: Carl 4D **174**
Old Bridge of Weir Rd. PA6: Hous 1A **78**
Old Castle Gdns. G44: Glas 1F **123**
Old Castle Rd. G44: Glas 1E **123**
Old Church Gdns. G69: Barg 6E **93**
Old Coach Rd. G74: E Kil 6H **141**
Old Cross 3A **96**
Old Dalmarnock Rd. G40: Glas 1B **108**
Old Dalnottar Rd. G60: Old K 2F **43**
Old Dullatur Rd. G68: Dull 5F **15**
Old Dumbarton Rd. G3: Glas 1A **4** (2A **86**)
.... (not continuous)
Old Duntiblae Rd. G66: Kirkin 6G **33**
Old Edinburgh Rd. G71: Tann 4B **112**
Old Edinburgh Rd. G71: View 4B **112**
Old Edinburgh Rd. ML4: Bell 1H **129**
Old Farm Rd. G61: Bear 1F **63**
Old Farm Rd. PA2: Pais 4F **103**
Old Ferry Rd. PA8: Ersk 3D **42**
Old Fruitmarket .... **6F 7 (4H 87)**
.... *(Glasgow)*
.... *(within City Hall)*
Old Gartloch Rd. G69: G'csh 5D **70**
Old Glasgow Rd. G71: Udd 1C **128**
.... *(Grammar School Wlk.)*
Old Glasgow Rd. G71: Udd 6B **112**
.... *(Kylepark Dr.)*
Old Glasgow Rd. G67: Cumb 1H **37**
Old Govan Rd. PA4: Renf 6H **61**
Old Greenock Rd. PA4: Inch 6D **42**
.... *(Drumcross Rd.)*
Old Greenock Rd. PA4: Inch 2G **59**
.... *(Newshot Dr.)*
.... (not continuous)
Old Greenock Rd. PA7: B'ton 2A **40**
Old Greenock Rd. PA8: Ersk 6C **42**
OLDHALL **6G 83**
Oldhall Rd. PA1: Pais 6E **83**
Old Howwood Rd. PA9: How 6C **98**
Old Humbie Rd. G77: Newt M 6E **137**
OLD INNS INTERCHANGE 5B **16**
OLD INNS RDBT. 5B **16**
OLD KILPATRICK **1E 43**
Old Lanark Rd. ML8: Carl 4D **174**
.... (not continuous)
Old Lindsaybeg Rd. G69: Chry 6A **54**
Old Manse Gdns. ML5: Coat 4C **94**
Old Manse Rd. G32: Glas 1D **110**
Old Manse Rd. ML2: Wis 3E **165**
Old Mill Ct. G81: Dun 2C **44**
Old Mill Ga. G73: Ruth 1C **124**
.... *(off Rodger Pl.)*
Old Mill La. G71: Udd 1D **128**
Old Mill Park Ind. Est. G66: Kirkin 4C **32**
Old Mill Rd. G71: Both 6E **129**
Old Mill Rd. G71: Udd 2D **128**
.... (not continuous)
Old Mill Rd. G72: Camb 2D **126**
Old Mill Rd. G74: E Kil 1H **157**
Old Mill Rd. G81: Dun 1C **44**
Old Mill Rd. G81: Hard 1C **44**
Old Mill Rd. PA2: Pais 2F **101**
Old Mill Vw. G65: Croy 1B **36**
OLD MONKLAND **1A 114**
Old Monkland Rd. ML5: Coat 2H **113**
Old Playfield Rd. G76: Crmck 1H **139**
Old Polmadie Rd. G5: Glas 3H **107**
Old Quarry Rd. G68: Cumb 2H **55**
Old Ranfurly Golf Course **4F 77**
Old Rd. PA5: Eld 2H **99**
Old Rutherglen Rd. G5: Glas 6G **87**
Old School, The PA11: Bri W 3F **77**
Old School Ct. ML5: Coat 1C **114**
Old Schoolhouse La. PA6: Hous 1B **78**
Old School Pl. ML8: Law 1G **173**
Old School Sq. PA10: Kilba 2A **98**
Old Shettleston Rd. G32: Glas 6H **89**
Old Sneddon St. PA3: Pais 6A **82**
Old Stable Row ML5: Coat 4D **94**
Old Sta. Ct. G71: Both 5E **129**
Old St. G81: Dun 1B **44**
Old Tower Rd. G68: Cumb 3B **36**
Old Union St. ML6: Air 4B **96**
Old Vic Ct. G74: E Kil 5B **142**
Old Wishaw Rd. ML8: Carl 2C **174**
Old Wishaw Rd. ML8: Law 6G **167**
Old Wood Rd. G69: Bail 2G **111**
Old Wynd G1: Glas 5G **87**
Olifard Av. G71: Both 4F **129**
Oliphant Ct. PA2: Pais 5D **100**
Oliphant Cres. G76: Busby 4C **138**
Oliphant Cres. PA2: Pais 5C **100**
Oliphant Oval PA2: Pais 5C **100**
Olive Bank G71: View 4G **113**
Olive Ct. ML1: Holy 2B **132**
.... *(off Elm Rd.)*
Olive St. G33: Glas 5F **67**
Ollach PA8: Ersk 2G **59**
Olympia Arc. G74: E Kil 2H **157**
Olympia Ct. G74: E Kil 2H **157**
.... *(within East Kilbride Shop. Cen.)*
Olympia Mall **3H 157**
Olympia St. G40: Glas 6B **88**
Olympia Way G74: E Kil 2H **157**
Omoa Rd. ML1: Cle 6G **133**
O'Neill Av. G64: B'rig 1D **66**
Onslow G75: E Kil 4E **157**
Onslow Dr. G31: Glas 4C **88**
Onslow Rd. G81: Clyd 5E **45**
Onslow Sq. G31: Glas 4C **88**
Ontario Pk. G75: E Kil 2D **156**
Ontario Pl. G75: E Kil 2D **156**
Onyx St. ML4: Bell 3C **130**
Oran Gdns. G20: Glas 4C **64**
Oran Ga. G20: Glas 4C **64**

A–Z Glasgow 259

Oran Pl. G20: Glas	5C **64**	
Oran St. G20: Glas	4C **64**	
ORBISTON	3B **130**	
Orbiston Ct. ML1: Moth	4A **148**	
Orbiston Dr. G81: Faif	6F **25**	
Orbiston Dr. ML4: Bell	4D **130**	
Orbiston Gdns. G32: Glas	6A **90**	
Orbiston Pl. G81: Faif	6F **25**	
Orbiston Rd. ML4: Bell	5D **130**	
(Community Av.)		
Orbiston Rd. ML4: Bell	3B **130**	
(Strachan St.)		
Orbiston Sq. ML4: Bell	4B **130**	
Orbiston St. ML1: Moth	3H **147**	
Orbital Ct. G74: E Kil	3A **156**	
Orcades Dr. G44: Glas	3F **123**	
Orchard Av. G71: Both	6F **129**	
Orchard Brae G66: Lenz	3E **53**	
Orchard Brae ML3: Ham	5H **145**	
Orchard Ct. G32: Carm	5B **110**	
Orchard Ct. G46: T'bnk	4G **121**	
Orchard Ct. PA4: Renf	5F **61**	
(off Orchard St.)		
Orchard Dr. G46: Giff	4H **121**	
(not continuous)		
Orchard Dr. G72: Blan	1A **144**	
Orchard Dr. G73: Ruth	5B **108**	
Orchard Fld. G66: Lenz	3E **53**	
Orchard Ga. ML9: Lark	3C **170**	
Orchard Grn. G74: E Kil	5B **142**	
Orchard Gro. G46: Giff	3H **121**	
Orchard Gro. ML5: Coat	5D **94**	
Orchard Pk. G46: Giff	4A **122**	
ORCHARD PK.	4H **121**	
ORCHARD PK.	4D **52**	
Orchard Pk. Av. G46: T'bnk	3G **121**	
Orchard Pl. G66: Kirkin	6G **33**	
Orchard Pl. ML3: Ham	6H **145**	
Orchard Pl. ML4: Bell	4B **130**	
Orchard St. G69: Bail	2F **111**	
Orchard St. ML1: Moth	2F **147**	
Orchard St. ML2: Over	5H **165**	
Orchard St. ML3: Ham	6H **145**	
Orchard St. ML8: Carl	4D **174**	
Orchard St. PA1: Pais	1A **102**	
Orchard St. PA4: Renf	5F **61**	
Orchardton Rd. G68: Cumb	1G **55**	
(Mollins Rd.)		
Orchardton Rd. G68: Cumb	2H **55**	
(Old Quarry Rd.)		
Orchardton Woods Ind. Pk. G68: Cumb	5G **35**	
Orchid Dr. G33: Mille	3A **68**	
Orchid Gro. G33: Mille	3A **68**	
Orchid Pl. G66: Len	3E **9**	
Orchid Pl. G71: View	5H **113**	
Orchill Dr. ML6: Plain	6G **75**	
Orchy Av. G76: Clar	6D **122**	
Orchy Ct. G81: Hard	2E **45**	
Orchy Cres. G61: Bear	5D **46**	
Orchy Cres. ML6: Air	6C **96**	
Orchy Cres. PA2: Pais	4D **100**	
Orchy Dr. G76: Clar	6D **122**	
Orchy Gdns. G76: Clar	6D **122**	
Orchy St. G44: Glas	1E **123**	
Orchy Ter. G74: E Kil	2B **158**	
Orefield Pl. G74: E Kil	6G **141**	
Oregon Pl. G5: Glas	1G **107**	
Oregon St. G5: Glas	1H **107**	
Orion Pl. ML4: Moss	2G **131**	
Orion Way G72: Camb	1A **126**	
Orion Way ML8: Carl	3B **174**	
Orissa Dr. G82: Dumb	5H **19**	
Orkney Pl. G51: Glas	4H **85**	
Orkney Quad. ML2: Wis	5B **150**	
Orkney St. G51: Glas	4H **85**	
Orlando G74: E Kil	4C **142**	
Orleans Av. G14: Glas	6E **63**	
Orleans La. G14: Glas	6E **63**	
Orlington Ct. ML5: Coat	3B **94**	

Ormiston Av. G14: Glas	5C **62**	
Ormiston Dr. ML3: Ham	3G **161**	
Ormiston La. G14: Glas	5C **62**	
(off Norse La. Sth.)		
Ormiston La. Nth. G14: Glas	5C **62**	
(off Norse La. Nth.)		
Ormonde Av. G44: Neth	4D **122**	
Ormonde Ct. G44: Neth	4C **122**	
Ormonde Cres. G44: Neth	4D **122**	
Ormonde Dr. G44: Neth	4D **122**	
Ornsay St. G22: Glas	2H **65**	
Oronsay Ct. G60: Old K	1G **43**	
Oronsay Cres. G60: Old K	1G **43**	
Oronsay Cres. G61: Bear	4H **47**	
Oronsay Gdns. G60: Old K	1G **43**	
Oronsay Ga. ML9: Lark	6A **164**	
Oronsay Pl. G60: Old K	1G **43**	
Oronsay Pl. ML2: Wis	2H **165**	
Oronsay Rd. ML6: Air	6D **96**	
Oronsay Sq. G60: Old K	1G **43**	
Orr Sq. PA1: Pais	6A **82**	
Orr St. G40: Glas	6B **88**	
(not continuous)		
Orr St. PA1: Pais	6A **82**	
Orr St. PA2: Pais	2A **102**	
Orr Ter. G78: Neil	3C **134**	
Orton Pl. G51: Glas	5G **85**	
Orwell Wynd G75: E Kil	3B **156**	
Osborne Cres. G74: T'hall	6F **139**	
Osborne St. G1: Glas	6D **6** (5G **87**)	
Osborne St. G81: Clyd	4C **44**	
Oskaig PA8: Ersk	2G **59**	
Osprey Cres. ML2: Wis	5H **149**	
Osprey Cres. PA3: Pais	3H **81**	
Osprey Dr. G71: Tann	6E **113**	
Osprey Ho. PA3: Pais	3A **82**	
Osprey La. ML3: Fern	2E **163**	
Osprey Rd. PA3: Pais	3H **81**	
Osprey Vw. PA3: Pais	3H **81**	
Ossian Av. PA1: Pais	6H **83**	
Ossian Rd. G43: Glas	1C **122**	
Ossian Way G81: Clyd	2D **60**	
Oss Quad. ML1: Moth	1C **164**	
Oswald St. G1: Glas	6B **6** (5F **87**)	
Oswald Wlk. G62: Miln	5A **28**	
Otago La. G12: Glas	1C **86**	
Otago La. Nth. G12: Glas	1C **86**	
(off Glasgow St.)		
Otago Pk. G75: E Kil	2C **156**	
Otago Pl. G82: Dumb	3C **20**	
Otago St. G12: Glas	1C **86**	
Othello G74: E Kil	5B **142**	
Ottawa Cres. G81: Clyd	3H **43**	
Otterburn Dr. G46: Giff	6A **122**	
Otter Gro. ML1: Moth	1C **148**	
Otterswick Pl. G33: Glas	1C **90**	
Oudenarde Ct. ML8: Carl	4F **175**	
Oval, The G76: Clar	6D **122**	
Oval, The ML5: Glenb	3G **71**	
Oval Path G52: Glas	2E **105**	
Overbrae Gdns. G15: Glas	2H **45**	
Overbrae Pl. G15: Glas	2H **45**	
Overburn Av. G82: Dumb	3F **19**	
Overburn Cres. G82: Dumb	2F **19**	
Overburn Ter. G82: Dumb	2F **19**	
Overcroy Rd. G65: Croy	1B **36**	
Overdale Av. G42: Glas	5D **106**	
Overdale Gdns. G42: Glas	5D **106**	
Overdale Pl. ML2: Over	5A **166**	
Overdale St. G42: Glas	5D **106**	
Overjohnstone Dr. ML2: Wis	5D **148**	
Overlea Av. G73: Ruth	1F **125**	
Overlee Rd. G76: Busby	2D **138**	
Overnewton Pl. G3: Glas	3C **4** (3B **86**)	
Overnewton Sq. G3: Glas	2B **4** (2B **86**)	
Overnewton St. G3: Glas	2B **4** (2B **86**)	
Overton Cres. PA5: John	2H **99**	
Overton Gro. G72: Camb	3E **127**	
Overton Rd. G72: Camb	3D **126**	

Overton Rd. G72: Flem	3D **126**	
Overton Rd. PA5: John	3G **99**	
Overton St. G72: Camb	3D **126**	
Overtoun G82: Dumb	1C **20**	
Overtoun Av. G82: Dumb	4H **19**	
Overtoun Ct. G81: Clyd	4A **44**	
Overtoun Dr. G73: Ruth	6C **108**	
Overtoun Dr. G81: Clyd	3B **44**	
Overtoun Rd. G81: Clyd	3B **44**	
OVERTOWN	5A **166**	
Overtown Av. G53: Glas	1A **120**	
Overtown Pl. G31: Glas	6C **88**	
Overtown Rd. ML2: Newm	4B **166**	
Overtown Rd. ML2: Wis	4B **166**	
Overtown St. G31: Glas	6C **88**	
Overwood Dr. G44: Glas	1G **123**	
Overwood Dr. G82: Dumb	3H **19**	
Overwood Gro. G82: Dumb	3H **19**	
Owen Av. G75: E Kil	4E **157**	
Owendale Av. ML4: Bell	6D **114**	
Owen Pk. G75: E Kil	4E **157**	
Owen St. ML1: Moth	1G **147**	
O'Wood Av. ML1: Holy	1B **132**	
Oxford Dr. PA3: Lin	5H **79**	
Oxford La. G5: Glas	6F **87**	
Oxford La. PA4: Renf	6E **61**	
Oxford Rd. PA4: Renf	6E **61**	
Oxford St. G5: Glas	5F **87**	
Oxford St. G66: Kirkin	5C **32**	
Oxford St. ML5: Coat	5B **94**	
OXGANG	6F **33**	
Oxgang Holdings G66: Kirkin	6F **33**	
Oxgang Pl. G66: Kirkin	6E **33**	
Oxhill Pl. G82: Dumb	4D **18**	
Oxhill Rd. G82: Dumb	3D **18**	
Oxton Dr. G52: Glas	6B **84**	
Oykel Cres. G33: Glas	2H **67**	
Oykel Dr. G33: Glas	2H **67**	
Oykel Ga. G33: Glas	1H **67**	
Oykel Wlk. G33: Glas	1H **67**	

P

PACIFIC DR.	6C **4** (4B **86**)	
Pacific Quay G51: Glas	5A **86**	
Paddock, The G76: Busby	4E **139**	
Paddock, The ML3: Ham	3H **145**	
Paddock Ct. ML8: Carl	5F **175**	
Paddock Dr. ML8: Carl	5F **175**	
Paddock St. ML5: Coat	1F **115**	
Paidmyre Cres. G77: Newt M	6D **136**	
Paidmyre Gdns. G77: Newt M	6D **136**	
Paidmyre Rd. G77: Newt M	6C **136**	
PAISLEY	6A **82**	
Paisley Abbey	1B **102**	
Paisley Arts Cen.	1A **102**	
Paisley Canal Station (Rail)	2A **102**	
Paisley Cen., The	1A **102**	
Paisley Gilmour Street Station (Rail)		
	6A **82**	
Paisley Leisure Pk.	6C **80**	
Paisley Mus.	6H **81**	
Paisley Retail Pk. PA3: Pais	5B **82**	
Paisley Rd. G5: Glas	5D **86**	
Paisley Rd. G78: Barr	2D **118**	
Paisley Rd. PA4: Renf	3C **82**	
Paisley Rd. W. G51: Glas	6G **85**	
Paisley Rd. W. G52: Glas	1A **104**	
Paisley St James Station (Rail)	5G **81**	
Paisley St Mirin's RC Cathedral	6B **82**	
Paisley Tourist Info. Cen.	1A **102**	
Palacecraig St. ML5: Coat	2C **114**	
Palace Gdns. Retail Pk.	5B **146**	
Palace Grounds Rd. ML3: Ham	5B **146**	
Palace of Art	6F **85**	
Palacerigg Country Pk.	6E **39**	
Palacerigg Country Pk. Vis. Cen.	6F **39**	
Palacerigg Family Golf Cen.	6B **38**	
Palacerigg Golf Course	6F **39**	

Parsonage Sq. – Pillans Av.

Parsonage Sq. G4: Glas 6G 7 (4H 87)
(not continuous)
Parson St. G4: Glas 3H 7 (3A 88)
PARTICK 1H 85
Partick Bri. St. G11: Glas 1A 4 (2A 86)
PARTICKHILL 1H 85
Partickhill Av. G11: Glas 6H 63
Partickhill Ct. G11: Glas 6H 63
Partickhill Rd. G11: Glas 6H 63
Partick Station (Rail & Subway) 1H 85
Partick St. ML5: Coat 6E 95
Partick Thistle FC 5E 65
Partridge Pl. G66: Lenz 1F 53
Patchy Pk. ML9: Lark 5C 170
Paterson Pl. G61: Bear 5C 26
Paterson's Laun G64: Balm 6A 30
Paterson St. G3: Glas 4G 5 (3D 86)
Paterson St. G5: Glas 6E 87
(not continuous)
Paterson St. ML1: Moth 2G 147
Paterson Ter. G75: E Kil 4F 157
Paterson Wlk. ML1: N'hse 1C 132
PATHER 2G 165
Pather St. ML2: Wis 1H 165
Pathhead Gdns. G33: Glas 3H 67
Pathhead Rd. G76: Crmck 2H 139
Patna Ct. ML3: Ham 2C 160
Patna St. G40: Glas 2D 108
Paton Ct. ML2: Wis 2D 164
Paton St. G31: Glas 4D 88
Patrickbank Cres. PA5: Eld 4A 100
Patrickbank Gdns. PA5: Eld 4A 100
Patrickbank Vw. PA5: Eld 4A 100
Patrickbank Wynd PA5: Eld 4A 100
Patrick St. PA2: Pais 2B 102
Patrick Thomas Ct. G1: Glas 6F 7 (4H 87)
(off Candleriggs)
Patterson Dr. ML8: Law 5E 167
PATTERTON 1D 136
Patterton Dr. G78: Barr 6F 119
Patterton Park & Ride 1D 136
Patterton Range Dr. G53: Glas 5C 120
Patterton Range Ga. G53: Glas 5D 120
Patterton Range St. G53: Glas 5C 120
Patterton Range Way G53: Glas 5D 120
Patterton Station (Rail) 1D 136
Pattison St. G81: Clyd 4A 44
Pavilion Theatre 3C 6 (3F 87)
(Glasgow)
(off Renfield St.)
Pavilion Way ML5: Coat 2C 94
Paxton Ct. G74: E Kil 5H 141
Paxton Cres. G74: E Kil 5H 141
Payne St. G4: Glas 1D 6 (1G 87)
Peace Av. PA11: Quarr V 1B 76
Peach Ct. ML1: Carf 5D 132
Peacock Av. PA2: Pais 3D 100
Peacock Ct. ML8: Carl 5F 175
Peacock Cross 5G 145
Peacock Cross Ind. Est. ML3: Ham 5G 145
Peacock Dr. ML3: Ham 5G 145
Peacock Dr. PA2: Pais 3D 100
Peacock Loan ML8: Carl 2D 174
(off Carranbuie Rd.)
Peacock Way ML3: Ham 5G 145
Peacock Wynd ML1: Carf 1C 148
Pearce La. G51: Glas 3G 85
Pearce St. G51: Glas 3G 85
Pear Gro. ML1: Carf 5D 132
Pearl St. ML4: Bell 4D 130
Pearson Dr. PA4: Renf 1F 83
Pearson Pl. PA3: Lin 6H 79
Pear Tree Dr. G33: Step 4C 68
Peathill Av. G69: Chry 6H 53
Peathill St. G21: Glas 6G 65
Peat Pl. G53: Glas 2A 120
Peat Rd. G53: Glas 2A 120
Peat Rd. PA11: Bri W 4G 77
Pedmyre La. G76: Crmck 2G 139
Peebles Dr. G73: Ruth 6F 109
Peebles Path ML5: Coat 2F 115
Peel Av. ML1: Moth 5G 147
Peel Brae G66: Kirkin 4C 32
Peel Ct. G72: Camb 1A 126
Peel Glen Gdns. G15: Glas 2A 46
Peel Glen Rd. G15: Glas 1A 46
Peel La. G11: Glas 1H 85
PEEL PK. 1A 156
Peel Pk. Ind. Est. G74: E Kil 6A 140
(not continuous)
Peel Pk. Pl. G74: E Kil 1B 156
Peel Pl. G71: Both 4E 129
Peel Pl. ML5: Coat 6H 93
Peel Rd. G74: T'hall 1F 155
Peel St. G11: Glas 1H 85
Peel Vw. G81: Clyd 4F 45
Pegasus Av. ML8: Carl 3C 174
Pegasus Av. PA1: Pais 6B 80
Pegasus Rd. ML4: Moss 2G 131
Peinchorran PA8: Ersk 2G 59
Peiter Pl. G72: Blan 2A 144
(off Harkins Av.)
Pelham Ct. G74: T'hall 3H 155
Pembroke G74: E Kil 5D 142
Pembroke St. G3: Glas 4F 5 (3D 86)
Pembury Cres. ML3: Ham 4D 160
Pencaitland Dr. G32: Glas 2A 110
Pencaitland Gro. G32: Glas 3A 110
Pencaitland Pl. G23: Glas 6C 48
Pendale Ri. G45: Glas 4H 123
Pend Cl. PA5: John 4F 99
Pendeen Cres. G33: Glas 6E 91
Pendeen Pl. G33: Glas 5F 91
Pendeen Rd. G33: Glas 6E 91
Pendicle Cres. G61: Bear 4D 46
Pendicle Rd. G61: Bear 4D 46
Pendle Ct. G69: G'csh 3D 70
Penfold Cres. G75: E Kil 3F 157
Penicuik Dr. G32: Glas 5F 89
Penicuik Ga. G32: Glas 5F 89
Penicuik La. G32: Glas 5F 89
Penicuik Pl. G32: Glas 5F 89
Penicuik St. G32: Glas 5F 89
Penicuik Way G32: Glas 5F 89
PENILEE 5G 83
Penilee Rd. G52: Glas 3F 83
Penilee Rd. G52: Hill E 3F 83
Penilee Rd. PA1: Pais 6G 83
Penilee Ter. G52: Glas 4G 83
Peninver Dr. G51: Glas 3E 85
Penkill Av. ML6: Air 5H 95
Penman Av. G73: Ruth 5B 108
Pennan PA8: Ersk 5E 43
Pennan Pl. G14: Glas 4A 62
Penneld Rd. G52: Glas 6H 83
Penniecroft Av. G82: Dumb 2H 19
Pennine Gro. ML6: Chap 4F 117
Penny Cres. G43: Glas 6D 104
Pennycress Dr. ML3: Fern 2E 163
Penny Ga. G43: Glas 6D 104
Penny Pl. G43: Glas 6D 104
Pennyroyal Ct. G74: E Kil 5F 141
Penrioch Dr. G75: E Kil 1C 168
Penrith Av. G46: Giff 4A 122
Penrith Dr. G12: Glas 3G 63
Penrith Pl. G75: E Kil 5B 156
Penryn Gdns. G32: Glas 2D 110
Penston Rd. G33: Glas 3D 90
Pentagon Cen., The G3: Glas 6H 5 (4E 87)
Pentland Av. PA3: Lin 6G 79
Pentland Ct. G78: Barr 6D 118
Pentland Ct. ML5: Coat 2E 115
Pentland Ct. ML6: Air 1B 96
Pentland Cres. ML9: Lark 6G 163
Pentland Cres. PA2: Pais 5H 101
Pentland Dr. G64: B'rig 5F 51
Pentland Dr. G78: Barr 6D 118
Pentland Dr. PA4: Renf 3D 82
Pentland Gdns. ML9: Lark 6H 163
Pentland Pl. G61: Bear 6B 26
Pentland Rd. G43: Glas 2A 122
Pentland Rd. G69: Chry 1B 70
Pentland Rd. G75: E Kil 2A 168
Pentland Rd. ML2: Wis 5E 149
Pentland Way ML3: Ham 4E 161
Penzance Way G69: Mood 4C 54
Peockland Gdns. PA5: John 2G 99
Peockland Pl. PA5: John 2G 99
People's Palace & Winter Gdns. 6H 87
Peploe Dr. G74: E Kil 4D 142
Perchy Vw. ML2: Wis 2A 166
Percy Dr. G46: Giff 6A 122
Percy Rd. PA4: Renf 3C 82
Percy St. G51: Glas 6B 86
Percy St. ML9: Lark 1C 170
Peregrine Gdns. ML3: Fern 2F 163
Perimeter Rd. PA3: Lin 6H 79
Perran Gdns. G69: Mood 5C 54
Perray Av. G82: Dumb 2B 18
Perrays Ct. G82: Dumb 2A 18
Perrays Cres. G82: Dumb 2A 18
Perrays Dr. G82: Dumb 3A 18
Perrays Gro. G82: Dumb 2A 18
Perrays Way G82: Dumb 2A 18
Perth Av. ML6: Air 1A 116
Perth Cres. G81: Clyd 2H 43
Perth La. G40: Glas 1D 108
Perth St. G3: Glas 5G 5 (4D 86)
Peter Coats Bldg. PA2: Pais 2A 102
Peter D Stirling Rd. G66: Kirkin 4D 32
PETERSBURN 5E 97
Petersburn Pl. ML6: Air 5D 96
Petersburn Rd. ML6: Air 6C 96
Peters Ga. G61: Bear 6D 26
PETERSHILL 6C 66
Petershill Dr. G21: Glas 5D 66
Petershill Rd. G21: Glas 6B 66
Peterson Dr. G13: Glas 1G 61
Peterson Gdns. G13: Glas 1G 61
Petition Pl. G71: Udd 2E 129
Pettigrew St. G32: Glas 6A 90
Petty Ct. G74: T'hall 3H 155
Peveril Av. G41: Glas 4B 106
Peveril Av. G73: Ruth 2E 125
Peveril Ct. G73: Ruth 3E 125
Pharonhill St. G31: Glas 6G 89
Philip Ct. ML4: Bell 3C 130
Philip Murray Rd. ML4: Bell 1H 129
PHILIPSHILL 5A 140
Philipshill Ga. G74: E Kil 5A 140
Philipshill Gro. G76: Crmck 5A 140
Philipshill Rd. G76: Crmck 5A 140
Philips Wlk. ML3: Ham 1F 161
Philips Wynd ML3: Ham 6F 145
Phoenix Bus. Pk. PA1: Pais 6C 80
Phoenix Ct. G74: E Kil 4D 142
(off Redgrave)
Phoenix Cres. ML4: Bell 5A 114
Phoenix Pl. ML1: New S 4A 132
Phoenix Pl. PA5: Eld 2B 100
Phoenix Retail Pk. 1D 100
(Paisley)
Phoenix Rd. G4: Glas 1H 5 (1E 87)
Phoenix Rd. ML4: Moss 2G 131
Phyliss Jane Ct. ML2: Wis 1H 165
Piazza Shop. Cen. 6A 82
Piccadilly St. G3: Glas 6G 5 (4D 86)
Pickering Works ML2: Wis 2F 165
Pickerstonhill ML1: N'hill 3E 133
PICKERSTONHILL 2F 133
Picketlaw Dr. G76: Crmck 2H 139
Picketlaw Farm Rd. G76: Crmck 2G 139
Picton Gro. ML6: Air 1C 96
Piershill St. G32: Glas 4H 89
Pikeman Rd. G13: Glas 3C 62
Pillans Av. ML8: Carl 3B 174

262 A–Z Glasgow

Raymond Pl. – River Cart Wlk.

Raymond Pl. G75: E Kil ... 2E **157**
Rayne Pl. G15: Glas ... 3B **46**
Ream Av. ML6: Air ... 5F **97**
Reay Av. G74: E Kil ... 1D **156**
Reay Gdns. G74: E Kil ... 1D **156**
Redan St. G40: Glas ... 6B **88**
Redbrae Pl. G66: Kirkin ... 4E **33**
Redbrae Rd. G66: Kirkin ... 4D **32**
Red Bri. Ct. ML5: Coat ... 3C **94**
Redburn Av. G46: Giff ... 1H **137**
Redburn Ct. G67: Cumb ... 5F **17**
Redburn Pl. G67: Cumb ... 6F **17**
Redburn Rd. G67: Cumb ... 5F **17**
Redcastle Sq. G33: Glas ... 2E **91**
Redcliffe Dr. G75: E Kil ... 3D **156**
Red Deer Rd. G72: Newt ... 6F **111**
Red Deer Rd. G75: E Kil ... 3E **157**
Red Deer Village Res. Pk. G33: Step ... 5D **68**
Red Deer Wlk. G72: Newt ... 6F **111**
Rederech Cres. ML3: Ham ... 1D **160**
Redford St. G33: Glas ... 3F **89**
Redgate Pl. G14: Glas ... 5B **62**
Redgrave G74: E Kil ... 4C **142**
Redhill Rd. G68: Cumb ... 2F **37**
Redhills Vw. G66: Len ... 4G **9**
Redholme Path ML9: Lark ... 4D **170**
... *(off Fisher St.)*
Redhouse La. ML8: Carl ... 2D **174**
Redhurst Cres. PA2: Pais ... 6G **101**
Redhurst La. PA2: Pais ... 6G **101**
Redhurst Way PA2: Pais ... 6F **101**
Red Kite Pl. ML3: Fern ... 2F **163**
Redlands La. G12: Glas ... 5A **64**
Redlands Rd. G12: Glas ... 5A **64**
Redlands Ter. G12: Glas ... 5A **64**
Redlands Ter. La. G12: Glas ... 5A **64**
Redlawood Pl. G72: Newt ... 1G **127**
Redlawood Rd. G72: Newt ... 1G **127**
Redmoss Rd. G66: Milt C ... 6B **10**
Redmoss Rd. G81: Dun ... 1B **44**
Redmoss St. G22: Glas ... 4F **65**
Rednock St. G22: Glas ... 5G **65**
Redpath Dr. G52: Glas ... 5B **84**
Redpath Dr. G72: Camb ... 1D **126**
Redpath Way ML1: Carf ... 5C **132**
Red Rd. G21: Glas ... 5D **66**
Red Rd. Ct. G21: Glas ... 6D **66**
Redshank Av. PA4: Renf ... 5G **61**
Redshank Way PA4: Renf ... 4G **61**
Redwing Cres. ML5: Coat ... 3G **115**
Redwing Gdns. ML2: Wis ... 2G **165**
Redwood Av. G74: E Kil ... 2A **156**
Redwood Cl. G33: Step ... 5D **68**
Redwood Cl. ML3: Ham ... 4D **160**
Redwood Ct. G74: E Kil ... 2A **156**
Redwood Cres. G71: View ... 5G **113**
Redwood Cres. G72: Flem ... 3F **127**
Redwood Cres. G74: E Kil ... 6A **140**
Redwood Cres. ML3: Ham ... 4D **160**
Redwood Cres. PA7: B'ton ... 4A **42**
Redwood Dr. G21: Glas ... 6C **66**
Redwood Dr. G74: T'hall ... 3A **156**
Redwood Gro. ML5: Coat ... 5D **94**
Redwood La. ML3: Ham ... 4E **161**
Redwood Pl. G66: Lenz ... 2B **52**
Redwood Pl. G71: View ... 5G **113**
Redwood Pl. G74: E Kil ... 1A **156**
Redwood Rd. G67: Cumb ... 3D **38**
Redwood Rd. ML1: Holy ... 2C **132**
Redwood Way G72: Flem ... 4F **127**
Reelick Av. G13: Glas ... 1G **61**
Reelick Quad. G13: Glas ... 1G **61**
Reema Rd. ML4: Bell ... 1D **130**
Reema Rd. ML4: Moss ... 1D **130**
Reen Pl. G71: Both ... 3F **129**
Regency Ct. ML3: Ham ... 1C **162**
Regency Way ML1: New S ... 3H **131**
Regent Cen., The ... **5C 32**
Regent Dr. G73: Ruth ... 5C **108**
Regent Moray St. G3: Glas ... 2B **4** (2B **86**)
Regent Pk. Sq. G41: Glas ... 3D **106**
Regent Pl. G81: Clyd ... 3A **44**
Regent Pl. ML6: Air ... 2D **96**
Regents Ga. G71: Both ... 3B **128**
Regent Sq. G66: Lenz ... 3C **52**
Regent St. G66: Kirkin ... 5C **32**
Regent St. G81: Clyd ... 3A **44**
Regent St. PA1: Pais ... 6D **82**
Regent Way ML3: Ham ... 6A **146**
Register Av. ML4: Bell ... 4C **130**
Register Rd. G65: Kils ... 3A **14**
Regwood St. G41: Glas ... 5B **106**
Reid Av. G61: Bear ... 1G **47**
Reid Av. PA3: Lin ... 6H **79**
Reid Ct. G73: Ruth ... 5D **108**
Reid Gro. ML1: Moth ... 5B **148**
Reidhouse St. G21: Glas ... 5B **66**
Reid Pl. G40: Glas ... 1B **108**
Reid St. G40: Glas ... 2B **108**
Reid St. G73: Ruth ... 5D **108**
Reid St. ML3: Ham ... 4D **144**
Reid St. ML5: Coat ... 3C **94**
Reid St. ML6: Air ... 2B **96**
Reidvale St. G31: Glas ... 5B **88**
... (not continuous)
Reilly Rd. PA6: Hous ... 6B **40**
Reith Dr. G75: E Kil ... 4F **157**
Remus Pl. ML4: Moss ... 2G **131**
Renfield La. G2: Glas ... 5C **6** (4F **87**)
Renfield St. G2: Glas ... 5C **6** (4F **87**)
Renfield St. PA4: Renf ... 5F **61**
RENFREW ... **5F 61**
Renfrew Community Mus. ... **5F 61**
Renfrew Ct. G2: Glas ... 3D **6** (3G **87**)
Renfrew Cross ... **5F 61**
Renfrew Football Club PA4: Renf ... **5D 60**
Renfrew Golf Course ... **4D 60**
Renfrew La. G2: Glas ... 3C **6** (3F **87**)
Renfrew Leisure Cen. ... **1E 83**
Renfrew Pl. ML5: Coat ... 1G **113**
Renfrew Rd. G51: Glas ... 1A **84**
Renfrew Rd. PA3: Pais ... 5B **82**
Renfrew St. G2: Glas ... 3B **6** (3F **87**)
Renfrew St. G3: Glas ... 2H **5** (2E **87**)
Renfrew St. ML5: Coat ... 1G **113**
Rennie Pl. G74: E Kil ... 6C **140**
Rennie Rd. G65: Kils ... 2F **13**
Renshaw Dr. G52: Glas ... 5B **84**
Renshaw Pl. ML1: Holy ... 5H **115**
Renshaw Rd. PA5: Eld ... 4A **100**
Renshaw Rd. PA7: B'ton ... 4H **41**
Renton Rd. G82: Dumb ... 1D **18**
Renton Rd. G82: Rent ... 1D **18**
Renton St. G4: Glas ... 1D **6** (2G **87**)
Resipol Rd. G33: Step ... 4E **69**
Reston Dr. G52: Glas ... 5B **84**
Reuther Av. G73: Ruth ... 6D **108**
Revoch Dr. G13: Glas ... 2A **62**
Reynolds Av. G75: E Kil ... 4A **158**
Reynolds Av. ML1: Carf ... 5C **132**
Reynolds Dr. G33: Step ... 4F **69**
Reynolds Path ML2: Wis ... 2B **166**
Rhannan Rd. G44: Glas ... 2E **123**
Rhannan Ter. G44: Glas ... 2E **123**
Rhindhouse Pl. G69: Bail ... 6B **92**
Rhindhouse Rd. G69: Bail ... 6B **92**
Rhindmuir Av. G69: Bail ... 6A **92**
Rhindmuir Ct. G69: Bail ... 5A **92**
Rhindmuir Cres. G69: Bail ... 5B **92**
Rhindmuir Dr. G69: Bail ... 5A **92**
Rhindmuir Gdns. G69: Bail ... 5A **92**
Rhindmuir Ga. G69: Bail ... 5B **92**
Rhindmuir Gro. G69: Bail ... 5B **92**
Rhindmuir Path G69: Bail ... 5B **92**
Rhindmuir Pl. G69: Bail ... 5A **92**
Rhindmuir Rd. G69: Bail ... 5A **92**
Rhindmuir Vw. G69: Bail ... 5B **92**
Rhindmuir Wynd G69: Bail ... 5B **92**
Rhinds Cl. G69: Bail ... 1B **112**
Rhinds Cres. G69: Bail ... 6B **92**
Rhinds Ga. G69: Bail ... 1B **112**
Rhinds Pl. G69: Bail ... 6B **92**
Rhinds St. ML5: Coat ... 1F **113**
Rhinsdale Cres. G69: Bail ... 6A **92**
Rhumhor Gdns. PA10: Kilba ... 3C **98**
Rhu Quad. ML2: Over ... 5A **166**
Rhymer St. G21: Glas ... 2A **88**
Rhymie Rd. G32: Glas ... 2D **110**
Rhynie Dr. G51: Glas ... 6H **85**
Riach Gdns. ML1: Moth ... 6E **131**
Ribblesdale G74: E Kil ... 6E **141**
Riccarton G75: E Kil ... 4D **156**
Riccarton Path ML3: Fern ... 2D **162**
Riccarton St. G42: Glas ... 3G **107**
Riccartsbar Av. PA2: Pais ... 2G **101**
Rice Way ML1: Moth ... 5B **148**
Richmond Av. G76: Clar ... 2C **138**
Richmond Ct. G73: Ruth ... 5E **109**
Richmond Dr. G64: B'rig ... 3D **50**
Richmond Dr. G72: Camb ... 2G **125**
Richmond Dr. G73: Ruth ... 6E **109**
Richmond Dr. PA3: Lin ... 4G **79**
Richmond Gdns. G69: Chry ... 1H **69**
Richmond Gro. G73: Ruth ... 6E **109**
Richmond Pk. Gdns. G5: Glas ... 2A **108**
Richmond Pk. Ter. G5: Glas ... 2H **107**
Richmond Pl. G73: Ruth ... 5E **109**
Richmond Rd. G73: Ruth ... 6F **109**
Richmond St. G1: Glas ... 5F **7** (4H **87**)
Richmond St. G81: Clyd ... 6E **45**
Riddell St. G81: Clyd ... 4D **44**
Riddell St. ML5: Coat ... 4E **95**
Riddon Av. G13: Glas ... 1G **61**
Riddon Av. G81: Clyd ... 1G **61**
Riddon Pl. G13: Glas ... 1G **61**
RIDDRIE ... **2F 89**
Riddrie Cres. G33: Glas ... 3G **89**
Riddrie Knowes G33: Glas ... 3G **89**
RIDDRIE KNOWES ... **3G 89**
Riddrievale Ct. G33: Glas ... 2G **89**
Riddrievale St. G33: Glas ... 2G **89**
Rigby Av. G32: Glas ... 5G **89**
Rigby Cres. G32: Glas ... 5G **89**
Rigby Dr. G32: Glas ... 5G **89**
Rigby Gdns. G32: Glas ... 5G **89**
Rigby St. G32: Glas ... 4F **89**
RIGGEND ... **1B 74**
Rigghead Av. G67: Cumb ... 6B **16**
Rigg Pl. G33: Glas ... 4E **91**
Riggs, The G62: Miln ... 2G **27**
Riggside Rd. G33: Glas ... 1C **90**
Righead Ga. G74: E Kil ... 2G **157**
... *(within East Kilbride Shop. Cen.)*
Righead Ind. Est. ML4: Bell ... 6A **114**
RIGHEAD RDBT. ... 2F **157**
Riglands Ga. PA4: Renf ... 5E **61**
Riglands Way PA4: Renf ... 6E **61**
Riglaw Pl. G13: Glas ... 2A **62**
Rigmuir Rd. G51: Glas ... 4C **84**
Rimsdale St. G40: Glas ... 6C **88**
Ringford St. G21: Glas ... 6B **66**
Ringsdale Av. ML9: Lark ... 5C **170**
Ringsdale Ct. ML9: Lark ... 5C **170**
Ripon Dr. G12: Glas ... 3G **63**
Risk St. G81: Clyd ... 3B **44**
Risk St. G82: Dumb ... 4E **19**
Ristol Rd. G13: Glas ... 4B **62**
Ritchie Cres. PA5: Eld ... 2A **100**
Ritchie Pk. PA5: John ... 2H **99**
Ritchie Pl. G77: Newt M ... 5C **136**
Ritchie St. G5: Glas ... 1E **107**
Ritchie St. ML2: Wis ... 6D **148**
Ritz Pl. G5: Glas ... 2H **107**
Riverbank Dr. ML4: Bell ... 4E **131**
Riverbank St. G43: Glas ... 6A **106**
River Cart Wlk. PA1: Pais ... 1A **102**
... *(off Marshall's La.)*

River Ct. – Rosemount Gdns.

River Ct. G76: Busby 3D **138**
Riverdale Gdns. ML3: Ham 2A **162**
River Dr. PA4: Inch 4H **59**
Riverford Ct. G43: Glas 6A **106**
Riverford Gdns. G43: Glas 6A **106**
Riverford Rd. G43: Glas 6A **106**
Riverford Rd. G73: Ruth 4E **109**
River Rd. G32: Carm 6B **110**
Riversdale La. G14: Glas 4A **62**
Riverside G62: Miln 3G **27**
Riverside PA6: Hous 2D **78**
Riverside Ct. G44: Glas 4D **122**
Riverside Ct. G76: Wfoot 2C **154**
Riverside Gdns. G76: Busby 4D **138**
Riverside Gdns. ML9: Lark 5C **170**
Riverside La. G82: Dumb 4E **19**
Riverside Mus. **3H 85**
(Museum of Transport & Travel)
Riverside Pk. G44: Neth 5E **123**
Riverside Pl. G72: Camb 1E **127**
Riverside Rd. G43: Glas 6C **106**
Riverside Rd. G76: Wfoot 2C **154**
Riverside Rd. ML9: Lark 5C **170**
Riverside Ter. G76: Busby 4D **138**
Riverside Wlk. ML1: Moth 1H **147**
Riverton Ct. G43: Glas 6B **106**
Riverton Dr. G75: E Kil 3D **156**
Riverview Dr. G5: Glas 5E **87**
Riverview Gdns. G5: Glas 5E **87**
Riverview Pl. G5: Glas 5E **87**
RNIB Springfield Cen. G64: B'rig 6D **50**
Roaden Av. PA2: Pais 6D **100**
Roaden Rd. PA2: Pais 6D **100**
Roadside G67: Cumb 6A **16**
Roadside Pl. ML6: Grng 1D **74**
Robberhall Rd. ML1: Moth 3B **148**
Robb Ter. G66: Kirkin 1G **53**
Robert Burns Av. G81: Clyd 4E **45**
Robert Burns Av. ML1: N'hill 3E **133**
Robert Burns Dr. G61: Bear 1F **47**
Robert Burns Quad. ML4: Bell 2B **130**
Robert Dr. G51: Glas 4G **85**
Robert Gilson Gdns. ML5: Coat 6D **94**
Roberton St. ML6: Chap 2E **117**
Robert Smillie Cres. ML9: Lark 4C **170**
Robertson Av. G41: Glas 3A **106**
Robertson Av. PA4: Renf 6D **60**
Robertson Cl. PA4: Renf 6E **61**
Robertson Cres. G78: Neil 2D **134**
Robertson Dr. G74: E Kil 1B **158**
Robertson Dr. ML4: Bell 3C **130**
Robertson Dr. PA4: Renf 6D **60**
Robertson La. G2: Glas 6B **6** (4F **87**)
Robertsons Gait PA2: Pais 2A **102**
Robertson Sports Cen. **6B 102**
Robertson St. G2: Glas 6B **6** (5F **87**)
Robertson St. G78: Barr 5D **118**
Robertson St. ML3: Ham 4D **144**
Robertson St. ML6: Air 4G **95**
Robertson Ter. G69: Bail 6A **92**
Robertson Way ML1: Carf 6C **132**
Roberts Quad. ML4: Bell 4D **130**
Roberts St. G81: Clyd 4A **44**
Roberts St. ML2: Wis 6G **149**
Robert St. G51: Glas 4G **85**
Robert Templeton Dr. G72: Camb 2B **126**
Robert Wilson Ga. ML9: Lark 5C **170**
Robert Wynd ML2: Newm 3E **151**
Robin Pl. G68: Cumb 5B **36**
Robin Pl. ML2: Wis 6H **149**
Robinson La. G74: T'hall 2H **155**
Robin Way G32: Carm 5C **110**
ROBROYSTON **3G 67**
Robroyston Av. G33: Glas 6G **67**
Robroyston Ga. G33: Glas 4G **67**
ROBROYSTON INTERCHANGE 4H **67**
Robroyston Oval G33: Glas 4G **67**
Robroyston Park & Ride **4A 68**
Robroyston Rd. G33: Glas 2G **67**
Robroyston Rd. G64: B'rig 6H **51**
Robroyston Rd. G66: A'loch 5A **52**
Robroyston Station (Rail)
4A 68
Robroyston Way G33: Glas 4G **67**
Robshill Ct. G77: Newt M 5D **136**
Robslee Cres. G46: Giff 4G **121**
Robslee Dr. G46: Giff 4H **121**
Robslee Rd. G46: Giff 5G **121**
Robslee Rd. G46: T'bnk 5G **121**
Robson Gro. G42: Glas 2F **107**
Rocep Dr. PA4: Renf 1H **83**
Rocep Way PA4: Renf 1H **83**
Rochdale Pl. G66: Kirkin 5C **32**
Rochsoles Cres. ML6: Air 1A **96**
Rochsoles Dr. ML6: Air 1H **95**
Rochsolloch Farm Cotts. ML6: Air 4G **95**
Rochsolloch Rd. ML6: Air 5F **95**
Rockall Dr. G44: Glas 3F **123**
Rockbank Cres. ML5: Glenb 3A **72**
Rockbank Pl. G40: Glas 6C **88**
Rockbank Pl. G81: Hard 1E **45**
Rockbank St. G40: Glas 6C **88**
Rockburn Cres. ML4: Bell 6C **114**
Rockburn Dr. G76: Clar 1A **138**
Rockcliffe Path ML6: Chap 4E **117**
Rockcliffe St. G40: Glas 2B **108**
Rock Dr. PA10: Kilba 3B **98**
Rockfield Pl. G21: Glas 4E **67**
Rockfield Rd. G21: Glas 4E **67**
Rockhampton Av. G75: E Kil 4D **156**
Rockmount Av. G46: T'bnk 3G **121**
Rockmount Av. G78: Barr 6F **119**
Rockshill Pl. ML6: C'bnk 3B **116**
Rockwell Av. PA2: Pais 5G **101**
Roddans La. G76: Eag 6D **154**
Roddinghead Rd. G46: Giff 3G **137**
Rodger Av. G77: Newt M 4C **136**
Rodger Dr. G73: Ruth 1C **124**
Rodger Pl. G73: Ruth 1C **124**
Rodger Way ML1: Cle 4H **133**
Rodil Av. G44: Glas 3G **123**
Rodney St. G4: Glas 1F **87**
Roebank Dr. G78: Barr 6E **119**
Roebank St. G31: Glas 3D **88**
(not continuous)
Roe Ct. G72: Newt 1F **127**
Roedeer Dr. ML1: Moth 1C **148**
Roe Dr. G72: Newt 1F **127**
Roffey Pk. Rd. PA1: Pais 6F **83**
Rogart St. G40: Glas 6B **88**
(not continuous)
Rogerfield Rd. G69: Barg 4A **92**
ROGERTON **3F 141**
Rokeby La. G12: Glas 6C **64**
(off Southpark Av.)
Roland Cres. G77: Newt M 6F **137**
Roman Av. G15: Glas 6A **46**
Roman Av. G61: Bear 2F **47**
Roman Ct. G61: Bear 2F **47**
Roman Ct. G81: Hard 1C **44**
Roman Cres. G60: Old K 6D **22**
Roman Dr. G61: Bear 2F **47**
Roman Dr. ML4: Bell 3D **130**
Roman Gdns. G61: Bear 2F **47**
Roman Hill Rd. G81: Hard 6D **24**
Roman Pl. ML4: Bell 4A **130**
Roman Rd. G61: Bear 2E **47**
Roman Rd. G66: Kirkin 5B **32**
Roman Rd. G81: Hard 1C **44**
Roman Rd. ML1: Moth 1F **147**
(not continuous)
Roman Way G71: View 1G **129**
Romney Av. G44: Glas 2G **123**
Romulus Ct. ML1: Moth 6E **131**
Ronaldsay Dr. G64: B'rig 5F **51**
Ronaldsay Pass G22: Glas 2H **65**
Ronaldsay Pl. G67: Cumb 5F **37**
Ronaldsay St. G22: Glas 2G **65**
Ronald St. ML5: Coat 3C **94**
Rona St. G21: Glas 1D **88**
Rona Ter. G72: Camb 4H **125**
Ronay St. G22: Glas 2H **65**
Ronay St. ML2: Wis 4C **150**
Rooksdell Av. PA2: Pais 4G **101**
Rooney Way ML4: Bell 2C **130**
Ropework La. G1: Glas 5G **87**
Rorison Pl. ML9: Ashg 4H **171**
Rosa Burn Av. G75: E Kil 1B **168**
Rosaburn Cres. G75: E Kil 6D **156**
ROSEBANK G66 **5G 33**
ROSEBANK ML8 **5C 172**
Rosebank Av. G66: Kirkin 4E **33**
Rosebank Av. G72: Blan 6C **128**
Rosebank Dr. G71: View 6G **113**
Rosebank Dr. G72: Camb 3C **126**
Rosebank Gdns. G71: Udd 3H **111**
Rosebank Gdns. PA5: John 3F **99**
Rosebank La. G71: Both 4F **129**
Rosebank Pl. G68: Dull 5E **15**
Rosebank Pl. G71: Udd 3H **111**
Rosebank Pl. ML3: Ham 6E **145**
Rosebank Rd. ML2: Over 5A **166**
Rosebank Rd. ML4: Bell 5D **114**
Rosebank St. ML6: Air 3E **97**
Rosebank Ter. G69: Barg 1D **112**
Rosebank Twr. G72: Camb 1A **126**
(off Allison Dr.)
Roseberry La. ML6: Chap 2E **117**
Roseberry Pl. G81: Clyd 6D **44**
Roseberry Pl. ML3: Ham 5E **145**
Roseberry Rd. ML6: Chap 1D **116**
Rosebery Ter. G5: Glas 3H **107**
Roseburn Ct. G67: Cumb 6F **17**
Roseburn Pl. ML5: Coat 6C **94**
Rose Cres. G77: Newt M 2D **136**
Rose Cres. ML3: Ham 5D **144**
Rose Dale G64: B'rig 1D **66**
Rosedale G74: E Kil 6E **141**
Rosedale Av. PA2: Pais 6B **100**
Rosedale Dr. G69: Bail 1G **111**
Rosedale Gdns. G20: Glas 1A **64**
Rose Dene Dr. G61: Bear 6H **27**
Rosedene Ter. ML4: Bell 1C **130**
Rosefield Gdns. G71: Udd 6C **112**
Rose Gdns. ML5: Coat 2B **114**
Rosegreen Cres. ML4: Bell 5C **114**
ROSEHALL **2D 114**
Rosehall Av. ML5: Coat 1D **114**
Rosehall Cl. G69: Bail 2B **112**
Rosehall Cres. G69: Bail 2B **112**
Rosehall Dr. G69: Bail 2B **112**
Rosehall Gdns. G69: Bail 2B **112**
Rosehall Ga. G69: Bail 2B **112**
Rosehall Ind. Est. ML5: Coat 2C **114**
Rosehall Rd. ML4: Bell 1B **130**
Rosehall Ter. ML2: Wis 2E **165**
Rosehall Way G69: Bail 2B **112**
Rosehill Cres. G53: Glas 1A **120**
Rosehill Dr. G53: Glas 1A **120**
Rosehill Dr. G67: Cumb 1C **56**
Rosehill Pl. G67: Cumb 1C **56**
Rosehill Rd. G64: Torr 5D **30**
Rose Knowe Rd. G42: Glas 5H **107**
Roselea Dr. G62: Miln 2H **27**
Roselea Gdns. G13: Glas 2F **63**
Roselea Pl. G72: Blan 6A **128**
Roselea Rd. G71: Tann 5C **112**
Roselea St. ML9: Lark 1D **170**
Rosemarkie Gro. ML1: N'hse 2D **132**
Rosemary Cres. G74: E Kil 5F **141**
Rosemary Pl. G74: E Kil 5F **141**
Rosemount G68: Cumb 6H **15**
Rosemount Av. G77: Newt M 1D **152**
Rose Mt. Ct. ML6: Air 3C **96**
Rosemount Ct. G77: Newt M 2D **152**
Rosemount Ct. ML8: Carl 3E **175**
Rosemount Gdns. ML6: Air 4A **96**

Rosemount La. – Rutherford Av.

Rosemount La. ML9: Lark 4E **171**
(off Dickson St.)
Rosemount La. PA11: Bri W 5D **76**
Rosemount Mdws. G71: Both 5D **128**
Rosemount St. G21: Glas 2B **88**
Rosendale Way G72: Blan 2C **144**
Roseneath Ga. G74: E Kil 1E **157**
Roseness Pl. G33: Glas 3A **90**
Rosepark Av. G71: View 1G **129**
Rosepark Cotts. ML5: Coat 2B **114**
Rose St. G3: Glas 3B **6** (3F **87**)
Rose St. G66: Kirkin 5D **32**
Rose St. G67: Cumb 6D **36**
Rose St. ML1: Moth 4A **148**
Rosevale Cres. ML3: Ham 1F **161**
Rosevale Cres. ML4: Bell 3E **131**
Rosevale Rd. G61: Bear 3E **47**
Rosevale St. G11: Glas 1G **85**
Rosewood ML2: Wis 2E **165**
Rosewood Av. ML4: Bell 6D **114**
Rosewood Av. PA2: Pais 4F **101**
Rosewood Gdns. G71: View 5H **113**
Rosewood Path ML4: Bell 2A **130**
Rosewood Pl. G69: Barg 5E **93**
Rosewood St. G13: Glas 2E **63**
Roslea Dr. G31: Glas 4C **88**
Roslin Pl. ML6: Chap 3E **117**
Roslin Twr. G72: Camb 4G **125**
Roslyn Dr. G69: Barg 6D **92**
Rosneath St. G51: Glas 3G **85**
Ross Av. G66: Kirkin 5F **33**
Ross Av. PA4: Renf 2C **82**
Ross Cott. Dr. ML3: Fern 1E **163**
Ross Cres. ML1: Moth 4E **147**
Ross Dr. G71: View 4G **113**
Ross Dr. ML1: Moth 4E **147**
Ross Dr. ML6: Air 1G **115**
Rossendale Ct. G43: Glas 5A **106**
Rossendale Rd. G41: Glas 5B **106**
Rossendale Rd. G43: Glas 5A **106**
Ross Gdns. ML1: Moth 4E **147**
ROSSHALL 2A **104**
Rosshall Av. PA1: Pais 1E **103**
ROSS HALL BMI HOSPITAL 2A **104**
Rosshall Pl. PA4: Renf 6F **61**
Rosshill Av. G52: Glas 6H **83**
Rosshill Rd. G52: Glas 6H **83**
Rossie Cres. G64: B'rig 1E **67**
Rossie Gro. G77: Newt M 4B **136**
ROSSLAND 5A **42**
Rossland Cres. PA7: B'ton 4G **41**
Rossland Gdns. PA7: B'ton 4G **41**
Rossland Pl. PA7: B'ton 5H **41**
Rossland Vw. PA7: B'ton 4G **41**
Rosslea Dr. G46: Giff 5A **122**
Rosslyn Av. G73: Ruth 6D **108**
Rosslyn Av. G74: E Kil 6H **141**
Rosslyn Ct. ML3: Ham 5E **145**
Rosslyn Rd. G61: Bear 1B **46**
Rosslyn Rd. ML9: Ashg 5H **171**
Rosslyn Ter. G12: Glas 5A **64**
Ross Pl. G73: Ruth 3F **125**
Ross Pl. G74: E Kil 6C **142**
Ross St. G40: Glas 5H **87**
Ross St. ML5: Coat 4C **94**
Ross St. PA1: Pais 2C **102**
Ross Ter. ML3: Fern 2E **163**
Rostan Rd. G43: Glas 2A **122**
Rosyth Rd. G5: Glas 3A **108**
Rotary Way G66: Kirkin 5A **34**
Rotherwick Dr. PA1: Pais 1G **103**
Rotherwood Av. G13: Glas 6C **46**
Rotherwood Av. PA2: Pais 5D **100**
Rotherwood La. G13: Glas 5C **46**
Rotherwood Pl. G13: Glas 1D **62**
Rotherwood Way PA2: Pais 5D **100**
Rothesay Cres. ML5: Coat 1D **114**
Rothesay Cres. PA4: Renf 1F **83**
Rothesay Pl. ML5: Coat 1D **114**
Rothesay Pl. PA4: Renf 1F **83**
Rothesay St. G74: E Kil 2F **157**
Rothes Dr. G23: Glas 6A **48**
Rothes Pl. G23: Glas 6A **48**
Rottenrow G1: Glas 4F **7** (3H **87**)
Rottenrow G4: Glas 5H **7** (4A **88**)
Rottenrow E. G4: Glas 5G **7** (4H **87**)
Roughcraig St. ML6: Air 1A **96**
Roughrigg Rd. ML6: Air 5G **97**
Roukenburn St. G46: T'bnk 3E **121**
Rouken Glen Pk. 6F **121**
Rouken Glen Rd. G46: Giff 5F **121**
Rouken Glen Rd. G46: T'bnk 5F **121**
Roundel, The ML2: Wis 6A **150**
Roundhill Dr. PA5: Eld 2C **100**
Roundhouse Circ. PA4: Renf 6H **61**
Roundhouse Cres. PA4: Renf 1H **83**
Roundhouse Pl. PA4: Renf 6H **61**
Roundknowe Rd. G71: Udd 4A **112**
Round Riding Rd. G82: Dumb 3G **19**
Rowallan Gdns. G11: Glas 6G **63**
Rowallan La. G11: Glas 6F **63**
Rowallan La. G76: Clar 2C **138**
Rowallan Rd. G46: T'bnk 5F **121**
Rowallan Ter. G33: Mille 5B **68**
Rowallen La. E. G11: Glas 6G **63**
Rowan Av. G66: Milt C 6B **10**
Rowan Av. G74: E Kil 5E **141**
Rowan Av. PA4: Renf 5E **61**
Rowanbank Pl. ML6: Air 3E **95**
Rowanberry Ct. G66: Len 1C **8**
Rowan Bus. Pk. G51: Glas 5F **85**
Rowan Ct. G72: Flem 3F **127**
Rowan Ct. ML2: Wis 1D **164**
Rowan Ct. PA2: Pais 3A **102**
Rowan Cres. G66: Lenz 2C **52**
Rowan Cres. ML6: Chap 2E **117**
Rowandale Av. G69: Bail 1G **111**
Rowand Av. G46: Giff 4A **122**
Rowanden Av. ML4: Bell 1C **130**
Rowan Dr. FK4: Bank 1E **17**
Rowan Dr. G61: Bear 6F **27**
Rowan Dr. G81: Clyd 3B **44**
Rowan Dr. G82: Dumb 3A **18**
Rowan Gdns. G41: Glas 1H **105**
Rowan Gdns. ML9: Lark 3D **170**
Rowan La. ML1: New S 4A **132**
Rowanlea ML6: Plain 6F **75**
(off Craiglea Ter.)
Rowanlea PA5: John 3E **99**
Rowanlea Av. PA2: Pais 6B **100**
Rowanlea Dr. G46: Giff 3B **122**
Rowanpark Dr. G78: Barr 2C **118**
Rowan Pl. G72: Blan 1B **144**
Rowan Pl. ML5: Coat 1A **114**
Rowan Ri. ML3: Ham 1A **162**
Rowan Rd. G41: Glas 1H **105**
Rowan Rd. G67: Cumb 2D **38**
Rowan Rd. PA3: Lin 4F **79**
Rowans, The G64: B'rig 5B **50**
Rowans Gdns. G71: Both 3F **129**
Rowans Ga. PA2: Pais 3B **102**
Rowan St. ML2: Wis 4H **149**
Rowan St. PA2: Pais 3A **102**
Rowantree Av. G71: View 6G **113**
Rowantree Av. G73: Ruth 2D **124**
Rowantree Av. ML1: N'hse 6C **116**
Rowantree Gdns. G73: Ruth 2D **124**
Rowantree Pl. G66: Len 4G **9**
Rowantree Pl. ML9: Lark 3F **171**
Rowantree Pl. PA5: John 4F **99**
(off Rowantree Rd.)
Rowantree Rd. PA5: John 4F **99**
Rowantree Ter. G66: Len 4G **9**
Rowantree Ter. ML1: Holy 2B **132**
Rowanwood Cres. ML5: Coat 6H **93**
Rowan Wynd PA2: Pais 3A **102**
Row Av. G51: Glas 2B **84**
Rowchester St. G40: Glas 6C **88**
Rowena Av. G13: Glas 6D **46**
Roxburgh Ct. ML1: New S 5B **132**
Roxburgh Dr. G61: Bear 6E **27**
Roxburgh Dr. ML5: Coat 1F **115**
Roxburgh La. G12: Glas 6B **64**
Roxburgh Pk. G74: E Kil 2H **157**
Roxburgh Pl. G72: Blan 2B **144**
(off Winton Cres.)
Roxburgh Rd. PA2: Pais 6B **100**
Roxburgh St. G12: Glas 6B **64**
ROYAL ALEXANDRA HOSPITAL 3H **101**
Royal Bank Pl. G1: Glas 5D **6** (4G **87**)
(off Buchanan St.)
Royal Conservatoire of Scotland 3C **6** (3F **87**)
Royal Cres. G3: Glas 3D **4** (3C **86**)
Royal Dr. ML3: Ham 1C **162**
Royal Exchange Ct. G1: Glas 5D **6** (4G **87**)
(off Queen St.)
Royal Exchange Sq. G1: Glas 5D **6** (4G **87**)
Royal Gdns. G71: Both 5B **128**
Royal Highland Fusiliers Mus. 2H **5** (2E **87**)
Royal Inch Cres. PA4: Renf 4F **61**
Royal Ter. G3: Glas 2D **4** (2C **86**)
Royal Ter. ML2: Wis 2A **150**
Royal Ter. La. G3: Glas 2D **4** (2C **86**)
Royellen Av. ML3: Ham 1D **160**
ROYSTON 2B **88**
Roystonhill G21: Glas 2B **88**
Roystonhill Pl. G21: Glas 2B **88**
Royston Rd. G21: Glas 2H **7** (2A **88**)
Royston Rd. G33: Glas 6G **67**
Royston Sq. G21: Glas 2A **88**
Roy St. G21: Glas 6H **65**
Rozelle Av. G15: Glas 4B **46**
Rozelle Av. G77: Newt M 5B **136**
Rozelle Dr. G77: Newt M 5B **136**
Rozelle Pl. G77: Newt M 5B **136**
Rubislaw Dr. G61: Bear 4E **47**
Ruby St. G40: Glas 1C **108**
Ruby Ter. ML4: Bell 3C **130**
RUCHAZIE 2B **90**
Ruchazie Pl. G33: Glas 3H **89**
Ruchazie Rd. G32: Glas 5H **89**
Ruchazie Rd. G33: Glas 3H **89**
RUCHILL 4D **64**
Ruchill Golf Course 3D **64**
Ruchill Pl. G20: Glas 4D **64**
Ruchill St. G20: Glas 4C **64**
Ruel St. G44: Glas 6E **107**
Rufflees Av. G78: Barr 3F **119**
Rugby Av. G13: Glas 1B **62**
Rullion Pl. G33: Glas 3H **89**
Rumford St. G40: Glas 2B **108**
Runciman Pl. G74: E Kil 5B **142**
Rundell Dr. G66: Milt C 6C **10**
Rupert St. G4: Glas 1D **86**
Rushyhill St. G21: Glas 5C **66**
Ruskin La. G12: Glas 6C **64**
Ruskin Pl. G12: Glas 6C **64**
Ruskin Pl. G65: Kils 3H **13**
Ruskin Sq. G64: B'rig 6C **50**
Ruskin Ter. G12: Glas 6C **64**
Ruskin Ter. G73: Ruth 4D **108**
Russell Colt St. ML5: Coat 3C **94**
Russell Dr. G61: Bear 1E **47**
Russell Gdns. G71: Tann 5E **113**
Russell Gdns. G77: Newt M 5C **136**
Russell La. ML2: Wis 6G **149**
Russell Pl. G75: E Kil 4E **157**
Russell Pl. G76: Busby 4E **139**
Russell Pl. PA3: Lin 5F **79**
Russell Rd. G81: Dun 6A **24**
Russell St. ML2: Wis 1G **165**
Russell St. ML3: Ham 4D **144**
Russell St. ML4: Moss 2F **131**
Russell St. ML6: Chap 3E **117**
Russell St. PA3: Pais 4H **81**
Russell St. PA5: John 2G **99**
Rutherford Av. G61: Bear 5B **26**

Rutherford Av. G66: Kirkin	1H **53**
Rutherford Ct. G81: Clyd	5C **44**
Rutherford Dr. G66: Lenz	2F **53**
Rutherford Grange G66: Lenz	1C **52**
Rutherford La. G75: E Kil	3H **157**
Rutherford Rd. G66: Lenz	2F **53**
Rutherford Sq. G75: E Kil	3G **157**
RUTHERGLEN	5C **108**
Rutherglen Bri.	2B **108**
Rutherglen Ind. Est. G73: Ruth	4B **108**
....(not continuous)	
Rutherglen Links G73: Ruth	4D **108**
Rutherglen Mus.	5D **108**
Rutherglen Rd. G73: Ruth	3A **108**
Rutherglen Station (Rail)	5D **108**
Rutherglen Swimming Pool	6C **108**
Ruthven Av. G46: Giff	6B **122**
Ruthven La. G12: Glas	6A **64**
Ruthven La. ML5: Glenb	3G **71**
Ruthven Pl. G64: B'rig	1E **67**
Ruthven St. G12: Glas	6B **64**
Rutland Ct. G51: Glas	5C **86**
....(off Govan Rd.)	
Rutland Cres. G51: Glas	5C **86**
Rutland Pl. G51: Glas	5C **86**
Ryan Rd. G64: B'rig	6D **50**
Ryan Way G73: Ruth	4E **125**
Ryat Dr. G77: Newt M	3C **136**
Ryat Grn. G77: Newt M	3C **136**
....(not continuous)	
Ryat Linn PA8: Ersk	6D **42**
Rydal Gro. G75: E Kil	5B **156**
Rydal Pl. G75: E Kil	5B **156**
Ryden Mains Rd. ML6: Glenm	5F **73**
Ryde Rd. ML2: Wis	6A **150**
Ryebank Rd. G21: Glas	4E **67**
Rye Cres. G21: Glas	4D **66**
Ryecroft Dr. G69: Bail	6H **91**
Ryedale Pl. G15: Glas	3A **46**
Rye Dr. G21: Glas	4E **67**
Ryefield Av. ML5: Coat	4H **93**
Ryefield Av. PA5: John	4D **98**
Ryefield Pl. PA5: John	4D **98**
Ryefield Rd. G21: Glas	4D **66**
Ryehill Pl. G21: Glas	4E **67**
Ryehill Rd. G21: Glas	4E **67**
Ryemount Rd. G21: Glas	4E **67**
Rye Path ML5: Coat	1F **115**
Rye Rd. G21: Glas	4D **66**
Ryeside Rd. G21: Glas	4D **66**
Rye Way PA2: Pais	4C **100**
Ryewraes Rd. PA3: Lin	6H **79**
Rylands Dr. G32: Glas	1D **110**
Rylands Gdns. G32: Glas	1E **111**
Rylees Cres. G52: Glas	5G **83**
Rylees Pl. G52: Glas	5G **83**
Rylees Rd. G52: Glas	5G **83**
Rysland Av. G77: Newt M	4E **137**
Rysland Cres. G77: Newt M	4E **137**
Ryvra Rd. G13: Glas	3D **62**

S

Sachelcourt Av. PA7: B'ton	5H **41**
Sackville Av. G13: Glas	4F **63**
Sackville La. G13: Glas	4F **63**
Saddell Rd. G15: Glas	3B **46**
Sadlers Wells Ct. G74: E Kil	5B **142**
Saffron Cres. ML2: Wis	2D **164**
Saffronhall Cres. ML3: Ham	5H **145**
Saffronhall Gdns. ML3: Ham	5H **145**
Saffronhall La. ML3: Ham	5H **145**
St Abb's Dr. PA2: Pais	4E **101**
St Abbs Way ML6: Chap	5E **117**
St Aidan's Path ML2: Wis	3A **150**
St Andrew's Av. G64: B'rig	5A **50**
St Andrew's Av. PA3: Glas A	2G **81**
St Andrews Av. G71: Both	6E **129**
St Andrew's Brae G82: Dumb	1H **19**

St Andrew's Cl. G41: Glas	1D **106**
St Andrew's Ct. G75: E Kil	5E **157**
St Andrews Ct. ML1: Holy	1A **132**
St Andrews Ct. ML4: Bell	2D **130**
....(off Main St.)	
St Andrews Ct. ML8: Carl	3C **174**
St Andrew's Cres. G41: Glas	1C **106**
St Andrew's Cres. G82: Dumb	2H **19**
St Andrew's Cres. PA3: Glas A	2G **81**
St Andrew's Dr. G41: Glas	3A **106**
St Andrew's Dr. G68: Cumb	5B **16**
St Andrew's Dr. ML3: Ham	5B **144**
St Andrew's Dr. PA11: Bri W	4E **77**
St Andrew's Dr. PA3: Glas A	3H **81**
St Andrews Dr. G61: Bear	6D **26**
St Andrews Dr. ML5: Coat	5A **94**
St Andrews Dr. ML8: Law	5E **167**
St Andrew's Dr. W. PA3: Glas A	2G **81**
St Andrew's Gdns. ML6: Air	3B **96**
St Andrew's Ga. ML4: Bell	2B **130**
ST ANDREW'S HOSPICE	3A **96**
....(Airdrie)	
St Andrew's in the Square	5H **87**
St Andrew's La. G1: Glas	5H **87**
....(off Gallowgate)	
St Andrew's Oval PA3: Glas A	3G **81**
St Andrew's Parkway PA3: Glas A	3G **81**
St Andrew's Path ML9: Lark	4E **171**
....(off Blair Atholl Dr.)	
St Andrews Pl. G65: Kils	2G **13**
St Andrew's Rd. G41: Glas	1D **106**
St Andrew's Rd. PA4: Renf	6E **61**
St Andrew's Sq. G1: Glas	5H **87**
St Andrews St. G1: Glas	5H **87**
St Andrews St. ML1: Holy	2A **132**
St Andrew's Way ML2: Wis	3A **150**
St Andrew's Way PA3: Glas A	3H **81**
St Anne's Av. PA8: Ersk	1H **59**
St Anne's Ct. ML3: Ham	3H **161**
St Anne's Wynd PA8: Ersk	1H **59**
St Ann's Dr. G46: Giff	5A **122**
St Barchan's Rd. PA10: Kilba	3B **98**
St Blanes Dr. G73: Ruth	1A **124**
St Boswell's Cres. PA2: Pais	4E **101**
St Boswells Dr. ML5: Coat	1F **115**
St Bride's Av. G71: View	6G **113**
St Bride's Rd. G43: Glas	6B **106**
St Brides Way G71: Both	3E **129**
St Bryde La. G74: E Kil	1H **157**
St Bryde St. G74: E Kil	1H **157**
St Catherine's Rd. G46: Giff	5A **122**
St Clair Av. G46: Giff	4A **122**
St Clair St. G20: Glas	1D **86**
St Columba Dr. G66: Kirkin	6E **33**
St Cuthbert Way ML3: Ham	4D **144**
St Cyrus Gdns. G64: B'rig	6E **51**
St Cyrus Rd. G64: B'rig	6E **51**
St Davids Dr. ML6: Air	1C **116**
St David's Pl. ML9: Lark	2C **170**
St Denis Way ML5: Coat	3B **94**
St Edmund Ct. G53: Glas	4D **104**
St Edmunds Gro. G62: Miln	2G **27**
St Edmunds La. G62: Miln	2G **27**
St Enoch Av. G71: View	5G **113**
St Enoch Pl. G1: Glas	6C 6 (4F **87**)
St Enoch Shop. Cen.	6D 6 (5G **87**)
St Enoch Sq. G1: Glas	6C 6 (5F **87**)
....(off Howard St.)	
St Enoch Station (Subway)	6C 6 (5F **87**)
St Fillans Dr. PA6: Hous	1A **78**
St Fillans Rd. G33: Step	4C **68**
St Flanan Rd. G66: Kirkin	4B **34**
St Francis Pl. ML5: Coat	1E **115**
St Francis Rigg G5: Glas	1H **107**
ST GEORGE'S CROSS INTERCHANGE 1H 5 (2E **87**)	
St Georges Cross Station (Subway)	
....1H 5 (1E **87**)	
St George's Pl. G3: Glas	1H 5 (1E **87**)
....(off St George's Rd.)	

St George's Rd. G3: Glas	2G 5 (2D **86**)
St George's Ter. PA11: Bri W	3E **77**
....(off Horsewood Rd.)	
St Germains G61: Bear	3E **47**
St Giles Pk. ML3: Ham	1F **161**
St Giles Way ML3: Ham	1F **161**
St Helena Cres. G81: Hard	1E **45**
St Helens Gdns. G41: Glas	5D **106**
St Ives Rd. G69: Mood	4D **54**
St James Av. G74: E Kil	2A **156**
St James Av. PA3: Pais	4F **81**
St James Bus. Cen. PA1: Lin	1C **100**
St James Ct. G75: E Kil	2A **156**
St James Ct. ML5: Coat	1A **114**
ST JAMES EAST INTERCHANGE	3G **81**
St James Retail Cen.	2A **156**
St James Rd. G4: Glas	3F 7 (3H **87**)
St James' St. PA3: Pais	6A **82**
St James Way ML5: Coat	2A **114**
ST JAMES WEST INTERCHANGE	3F **81**
St John's Blvd. G71: Udd	1E **129**
St John's Ct. G41: Glas	1C **106**
St John's Quad. G41: Glas	1C **106**
St John's Rd. G41: Glas	2C **106**
St John St. ML5: Coat	4C **94**
St Johns Way G65: Twe	2D **34**
St Joseph's Ct. G21: Glas	2B **88**
St Joseph's Pl. G21: Glas	2B **88**
St Joseph's Vw. G21: Glas	2B **88**
St Kenneth Dr. G51: Glas	3D **84**
St Kilda Dr. G14: Glas	5E **63**
St Kilda Way ML2: Wis	4C **150**
St Lawrence Pk. G75: E Kil	2E **157**
ST LEONARDS	2C **158**
St Leonard's Dr. G46: Giff	4A **122**
St Leonards Rd. G74: E Kil	1B **158**
St Leonards Sq. G74: E Kil	2C **158**
St Leonards Wlk. ML5: Coat	2E **115**
St Lukes Av. ML8: Carl	5C **174**
St Lukes Bus. Cen. G5: Glas	6G **87**
....(off St Lukes Pl.)	
St Lukes Pl. G5: Glas	6G **87**
St Lukes Ter. G5: Glas	6G **87**
St Machan's Way G66: Len	2F **9**
St Machars Rd. PA11: Bri W	4G **77**
ST MARGARET OF SCOTLAND HOSPICE	2F **61**
St Margarets Av. PA3: Pais	4B **82**
St Margaret's Ct. ML4: Bell	2D **130**
....(off Dean St.)	
St Margarets Ct. PA3: Pais	4B **82**
St Margarets Dr. ML2: Wis	2E **165**
St Margaret's Pl. G1: Glas	5G **87**
....(off Jocelyn Sq.)	
St Mark Ct. G32: Glas	6G **89**
St Mark Gdns. G32: Glas	6H **89**
St Mark's Ct. ML2: Wis	3A **150**
St Mark St. G32: Glas	6G **89**
....(not continuous)	
St Marnock St. G40: Glas	6C **88**
St Martins Ga. ML5: Coat	1C **114**
St Mary's Ct. G2: Glas	5C 6 (4F **87**)
....(off Renfield St.)	
St Mary's Ct. ML2: Wis	1H **165**
St Mary's Cres. G78: Barr	5E **119**
St Mary's Gdns. G78: Barr	5E **119**
St Mary's La. G2: Glas	5C 6 (4F **87**)
....(off Renfield St.)	
St Mary's Rd. G64: B'rig	5A **50**
St Mary's Rd. ML4: Bell	2A **130**
St Mary's Way G82: Dumb	4F **19**
ST MAURICE'S RDBT.	4C **36**
St Michael Rd. ML2: Wis	2C **164**
St Michaels Ct. G31: Glas	6E **89**
St Michaels La. G31: Glas	6E **89**
St Michael's Way G82: Dumb	3D **18**
St Mirren FC	5G **81**
St Mirren Pk.	5G **81**
St Mirren's Rd. G65: Kils	3A **14**
St Mirren St. PA1: Pais	1A **102**

St Monance St. – School Rd.

St Monance St. G21: Glas 4B **66**
St Monicas Way ML5: Coat 1H **113**
St Mungo Av. G4: Glas 3E **7** (3G **87**)
St Mungo Ct. PA11: Bri W 3G **77**
St Mungo Mus. of Religious Life & Art 4H **7** (3A **88**)
St Mungo Pl. G4: Glas 3G **7** (3H **87**)
St Mungo Pl. ML3: Ham 5B **144**
St Mungo's Cres. ML1: Carf 5B **132**
St Mungo's Rd. G67: Cumb 4G **37**
St Mungo St. G64: B'rig 1B **66**
St Mungo's Wlk. G67: Cumb 3H **37**
St Ninian's Cres. PA2: Pais 3B **102**
St Ninians Gro. ML2: Wis 3B **150**
St Ninian's Pl. ML3: Ham 6D **144**
St Ninian's Rd. ML3: Ham 6D **144**
St Ninian's Rd. PA2: Pais 3B **102**
St Ninian Ter. G5: Glas 6G **87**
St Oswald's Glebe G44: Glas 1A **124**
St Peters Cl. PA2: Pais 6G **101**
St Peters La. G2: Glas 5A **6** (4E **87**)
St Peter's Path G4: Glas 1E **87**
(off Unity Pl.)
St Peter's St. G4: Glas 1A **6** (1E **87**)
St Roberts Gdns. G53: Glas 2C **120**
St Rollox Brae G21: Glas 1A **88**
St Rollox Bus. & Retail Pk. 1B **88**
St Rollox Dr. G21: Glas 6H **65**
St Ronan's Dr. G41: Glas 4B **106**
St Ronan's Dr. ML3: Ham 3G **161**
St Ronans Dr. G73: Ruth 1E **125**
Saints St. PA3: Pais 5A **82**
St Stephen's Av. G73: Ruth 4F **125**
St Stephen's Ct. G81: Clyd 4B **44**
St Stephen's Cres. G73: Ruth 4G **125**
St Valentine Ter. G5: Glas 1H **107**
St Vigean's Av. G77: Newt M 6B **136**
(not continuous)
St Vigeans Pl. G77: Newt M 6C **136**
St Vincent Cres. G3: Glas 3C **4** (3B **86**)
St Vincent Cres. La. G3: Glas 3C **4** (3B **86**)
St Vincent La. G2: Glas 4A **6** (3E **87**)
St Vincent Pl. G1: Glas 5D **6** (4G **87**)
St Vincent Pl. G75: E Kil 3C **156**
St Vincent Pl. ML1: Moth 2G **147**
ST VINCENT'S HOSPICE 6B **98**
St Vincent St. G1: Glas 5C **6** (4F **87**)
St Vincent St. G2: Glas 4H **5** (3E **87**)
St Vincent St. G3: Glas 4F **5** (3D **86**)
St Vincent Ter. G3: Glas 4F **5** (3D **86**)
St Winifred's Way ML2: Wis 5G **149**
Salamanca St. G31: Glas 6F **89**
(not continuous)
Salasaig Ct. G33: Glas 4A **90**
Salen St. G52: Glas 6F **85**
Salford Pl. G66: Kirkin 4C **32**
(off New Lairdsland Rd.)
Saline St. ML6: Air 5F **95**
Salisbury G74: E Kil 5D **142**
Salisbury Cres. ML1: Moth 1D **146**
Salisbury Pl. G81: Clyd 2H **43**
Salisbury St. G5: Glas 1F **107**
Salkeld St. G5: Glas 1E **107**
Salmona St. G22: Glas 5F **65**
Salmon M. G66: Kirkin 6F **33**
Saltaire Av. G71: Udd 2E **129**
Salterland Rd. G53: Glas 2G **119**
Salterland Rd. G78: Barr 2G **119**
Saltire Cres. ML9: Lark 3E **171**
Saltmarket G1: Glas 5G **87**
Saltmarket Pl. G1: Glas 5G **87**
Saltmarsh Dr. G66: Lenz 1F **53**
Saltoun La. G12: Glas 6B **64**
Saltoun St. G12: Glas 6B **64**
Salvia St. G72: Camb 1H **125**
Samson Cres. ML8: Carl 5G **175**
Samuel Evans Av. PA2: Pais 3E **103**
Sandaig Rd. G33: Glas 6E **91**
Sandale Path G72: Blan 3A **144**
Sandalwood ML2: Wis 2D **164**
Sandalwood Av. G74: E Kil 5F **141**
Sandalwood Av. ML1: Carf 4C **132**
Sandalwood Ct. G74: E Kil 5F **141**
Sanda St. G20: Glas 5C **64**
Sanda Way PA2: Pais 6H **101**
Sandbank Av. G20: Glas 2B **64**
Sandbank Cres. G20: Glas 3B **64**
Sandbank Dr. G20: Glas 2B **64**
Sandbank St. G20: Glas 1B **64**
Sandbank Ter. G20: Glas 2B **64**
Sandend PA8: Ersk 4E **43**
Sandend Rd. G53: Glas 6A **104**
Sanderling Parkway PA3: Glas A 3G **81**
Sanderling Parkway PA3: Pais 3G **81**
Sanderling Pl. G75: E Kil 6C **156**
Sanderling Pl. PA5: John 6D **98**
Sanderling Rd. PA3: Glas A 3H **81**
Sanderson Av. G71: View 1H **129**
Sandfield Av. G62: Miln 2G **27**
Sandfield St. G20: Glas 4C **64**
Sandford Gdns. G69: Bail 6H **91**
Sandgate Av. G32: Glas 2D **110**
Sandhaven Pl. G53: Glas 6A **104**
Sandhaven Rd. G53: Glas 6A **104**
Sandhead Cres. ML6: Chap 4E **117**
Sandhead Ter. G72: Blan 1B **160**
Sandholes Rd. PA5: Brkfld 6C **78**
Sandholes Rd. PA6: C'lee 4C **78**
Sandholes St. PA1: Pais 1G **101**
Sandholm Pl. G14: Glas 4H **61**
Sandholm Ter. G14: Glas 4H **61**
Sandiefield Rd. G5: Glas 1G **107**
Sandielands Av. PA8: Ersk 2H **59**
Sandilands Cres. ML1: Moth 4D **146**
Sandilands St. G32: Glas 6B **90**
Sandmartin Gro. G66: Lenz 1F **53**
Sandmill St. G21: Glas 2C **88**
Sandpiper Cres. ML5: Coat 2F **115**
Sandpiper Dr. G75: E Kil 6C **156**
Sandpiper Pl. G75: E Kil 6C **156**
Sandpiper Way ML4: Bell 5A **114**
Sandra Rd. G64: B'rig 5E **51**
Sandringham Av. G77: Newt M 3G **137**
Sandringham Ct. G77: Newt M 4G **137**
Sandringham Dr. PA5: Eld 4H **99**
Sandringham La. G12: Glas 6B **64**
(off Kersland St.)
Sandwood G52: Glas 6A **84**
Sandwood Cres. G52: Glas 6A **84**
Sandwood Path G52: Glas 6A **84**
Sandwood Rd. G52: Glas 6A **84**
Sandyfaulds St. G5: Glas 1H **107**
Sandyford Av. ML1: N'hse 5D **116**
Sandyford Pl. G3: Glas 3E **5** (3C **86**)
Sandyford Pl. ML1: N'hse 6D **116**
Sandyford Pl. La. G3: Glas 3E **5** (3C **86**)
Sandyford Rd. ML1: N'hse 6D **116**
Sandyford Rd. PA3: Pais 3C **82**
Sandyford St. G3: Glas 3A **4** (3A **86**)
SANDYHILLS 1D **110**
Sandyhills Cres. G32: Glas 2B **110**
Sandyhills Dr. G32: Glas 2B **110**
Sandyhills Golf Course 2C **110**
Sandyhills Gro. G32: Glas 3B **110**
Sandyhills Pl. G32: Glas 2B **110**
Sandyhills Rd. G32: Glas 2B **110**
Sandyknowes Rd. G67: Cumb 5H **37**
Sandy La. G11: Glas 1G **85**
Sandy Rd. G11: Glas 1G **85**
Sandy Rd. ML8: Carl 3D **174**
Sandy Rd. PA4: Renf 2E **83**
Sannox Dr. ML1: Moth 2D **146**
Sannox Gdns. G31: Glas 3D **88**
Sannox Pl. G75: E Kil 1B **168**
Sanquhar Dr. G53: Glas 5A **104**
Sanquhar Gdns. G53: Glas 5A **104**
Sanquhar Gdns. G72: Blan 5H **127**
Sanquhar Pl. G53: Glas 5A **104**
Sanquhar Rd. G53: Glas 5A **104**
Sanson La. ML8: Carl 5G **175**
Sapphire Rd. ML4: Bell 4C **130**
Saracen Head La. G1: Glas 5A **88**
Saracen Pk. 4H **65**
Saracen St. G22: Glas 6G **65**
Saramago St. G66: Kirkin 6D **32**
Sarazen Ct. ML1: Cle 1E **149**
Sardinia La. G12: Glas 6B **64**
Saskatoon Pl. G75: E Kil 2D **156**
Saturn Av. PA1: Pais 1C **100**
Saucel Cres. PA1: Pais 1A **102**
Saucelhill Ter. PA2: Pais 2A **102**
Saucel Pl. PA1: Pais 1A **102**
Saucel St. PA1: Pais 1A **102**
Sauchenhall Path G69: Mood 4E **55**
Sauchiehall Cen. 3B **6** (3F **87**)
(off Sauchiehall St.)
Sauchiehall La. G2: Glas 3H **5** (3E **87**)
(not continuous)
Sauchiehall St. G2: Glas 3B **6** (3F **87**)
Sauchiehall St. G3: Glas 2C **4** (2B **86**)
Sauchiesmoor Rd. ML8: Carl 5E **175**
Saughs Av. G33: Glas 3H **67**
Saughs Dr. G33: Glas 3H **67**
Saughs Ga. G33: Glas 3H **67**
Saughs Pl. G33: Glas 3H **67**
Saughton St. G32: Glas 4G **89**
Saunders Ct. G78: Barr 4D **118**
Savoy Cen. 3B **6** (3F **87**)
Savoy St. G40: Glas 1B **108**
Sawmillfield St. G4: Glas 1F **87**
Sawmill Rd. G11: Glas 1F **85**
Saxon Rd. G13: Glas 2D **62**
Scadlock Rd. PA3: Pais 6F **81**
Scalloway La. G72: Camb 4H **125**
Scalloway Rd. G69: G'csh 5C **70**
Scalloway Rd. G72: Camb 4G **125**
Scalpay G74: E Kil 2C **158**
Scalpay Pass G22: Glas 2H **65**
Scalpay Pl. G22: Glas 2H **65**
Scalpay St. G22: Glas 2G **65**
Scapa St. G23: Glas 1C **64**
Scapa Way G33: Step 3E **69**
Scapesland Ter. G82: Dumb 3G **19**
Scaraway Dr. G22: Glas 1H **65**
Scaraway Pl. G22: Glas 1H **65**
Scaraway St. G22: Glas 1G **65**
Scaraway Ter. G22: Glas 1H **65**
Scarba Dr. G43: Glas 2H **121**
Scarba Quad. ML2: Wis 2E **165**
Scarffe Av. PA3: Lin 6F **79**
Scarhill Av. ML6: Air 6H **95**
Scarhill La. ML6: Air 6A **96**
Scarhill St. ML1: Cle 5H **133**
Scarhill St. ML5: Coat 2B **114**
Scarrel Dr. G45: Glas 3C **124**
Scarrel Gdns. G45: Glas 3C **124**
Scarrel Rd. G45: Glas 3C **124**
Scarrel Ter. G45: Glas 3C **124**
Scavaig Cres. G15: Glas 3G **45**
Schaw Ct. G61: Bear 1E **47**
Schaw Dr. G61: Bear 1E **47**
Schaw Dr. G81: Faif 6G **25**
Schaw Rd. PA3: Pais 5C **82**
Scholar's Ga. G75: E Kil 5F **157**
Scholars Wynd ML3: Ham 1E **161**
School Av. G72: Camb 2B **126**
School Dr. G13: Glas 4D **62**
School Ho. PA11: Quarr V 1A **76**
Schoolhouse La. G72: Blan 3A **144**
School La. G66: Len 3F **9**
School La. G66: Milt C 5C **10**
School La. G71: Both 6F **129**
School La. G72: Flem 3E **127**
School La. G82: Dumb 3D **18**
School La. ML8: Carl 4C **174**
School Quad. ML6: Air 1H **95**
School Rd. ML2: Newm 5E **151**
(Main St.)

School Rd. – Sheldrake Pl.

School Rd. ML2: Newm 6F **151**
(*Morningside Rd.*)
School Rd. G33: Step 3E **69**
School Rd. G64: Torr 4E **31**
School Rd. G77: Newt M 5D **136**
School Rd. PA1: Pais 6G **83**
School St. ML3: Ham 2H **161**
School St. ML5: Coat 1C **114**
School St. ML6: Chap 3D **116**
School Vw. ML1: Moth 4G **147**
School Wynd PA1: Pais 6A **82**
School Wynd PA11: Quarr V 1A **76**
Scioncroft Av. G73: Ruth 6E **109**
Scone Pl. G74: E Kil 6F **141**
Scone Pl. G77: Newt M 5H **137**
Scone St. G21: Glas 6G **65**
Scone Wlk. G69: Bail 2G **111**
Sconser PA8: Ersk 2G **59**
Sconser St. G23: Glas 6C **48**
Scorton Gdns. G69: Bail 1F **111**
Scotia Cres. ML9: Lark 4C **170**
Scotia Gdns. ML3: Ham 4G **161**
Scotia St. ML1: Moth 2E **147**
Scotkart Indoor Kart Racing **1C 126**
(*Cambuslang*)
Scotkart Indoor Kart Racing **1E 61**
(*Clydebank*)
Scotland St. G5: Glas 6D **86**
Scotland Street School Mus. **6D 86**
Scotland St. W. G41: Glas 6B **86**
Scotsblair Av. G66: Kirkin 1C **52**
Scotsburn Pl. G21: Glas 5E **67**
Scotsburn Rd. G21: Glas 5E **67**
SCOTSTOUN 5B 62
Scotstoun Athletic Track **5C 62**
SCOTSTOUNHILL 3B 62
Scotstounhill Station (Rail) 4B 62
Scotstoun Leisure Cen. **5D 62**
Scotstoun St. G14: Glas 6C **62**
Scotstoun Way ML5: Coat 6E **95**
Scott Av. G60: Bowl 5B **22**
Scott Av. G66: Milt C 5C **10**
Scott Av. PA5: John 5E **99**
Scott Cres. G67: Cumb 6F **37**
Scott Dr. G61: Bear 1C **46**
Scott Dr. G67: Cumb 6F **37**
Scott Dr. ML8: Law 5E **167**
Scott Gro. ML3: Ham 1H **161**
Scott Hill G74: E Kil 6A **142**
Scott Ho. G67: Cumb 2A **38**
Scottish Ent. Technology Pk. G75: E Kil 4A **158**
Scottish Event Campus **5C 4 (3B 86)**
Scottish Mask & Puppet Theatre **4A 64**
Scottish Nat. Football Mus. **6F 107**
Scott Pl. ML4: Bell 6D **114**
Scott Pl. PA5: John 5E **99**
Scott Rd. G52: Hill E 3H **83**
Scott's Pl. ML6: Air 3B **96**
Scott's Rd. PA2: Pais 2D **102**
Scott St. G3: Glas 3A **6** (3E **87**)
Scott St. G4: Glas 1A **6** (2E **87**)
Scott St. G69: Bail 1H **111**
Scott St. G81: Clyd 3A **44**
Scott St. ML1: Moth 2G **147**
Scott St. ML3: Ham 2H **161**
Scott St. ML9: Lark 3D **170**
Scott Wynd G66: Kirkin 5E **33**
Scoular Ha Pl. ML8: Carl 3B **174**
SEAFAR 3G 37
Seafar Rd. G67: Cumb 5G **37**
SEAFAR RDBT. 5G **37**
Seafield Av. G61: Bear 6F **27**
Seafield Cres. G68: Cumb 4A **36**
Seafield Dr. G73: Ruth 4F **125**
Seaforth Cres. G78: Barr 2D **118**
Seaforth La. G69: Mood 5E **55**
Seaforth Pl. ML4: Bell 4B **130**
Seaforth Rd. G52: Hill E 4A **84**
Seaforth Rd. G81: Clyd 6D **44**
Seaforth Rd. Nth. G52: Hill E 4A **84**
Seaforth Rd. Sth. G52: Hill E 4A **84**
Seagrove St. G32: Glas 5F **89**
Seamill Gdns. G74: E Kil 1F **157**
Seamill Path G53: Glas 2H **119**
Seamill St. G53: Glas 2H **119**
Seamill Way ML5: Coat 6B **94**
Seamore St. G20: Glas 1D **86**
Seath Av. ML6: Air 4G **95**
Seath Rd. G73: Ruth 4C **108**
Seath St. G42: Glas 3G **107**
Seaton Ter. ML3: Ham 5E **145**
Seaward La. G41: Glas 5C **86**
Seaward Pl. G41: Glas 6D **86**
Seaward St. G41: Glas 6C **86**
(not continuous)
SEAWARD STREET INTERCHANGE 6C **86**
Second Av. G33: Mille 4B **68**
Second Av. G44: Glas 1F **123**
Second Av. G61: Bear 4G **47**
Second Av. G66: A'loch 6C **52**
Second Av. G71: Tann 4C **112**
Second Av. G81: Clyd 4B **44**
Second Av. G82: Dumb 3C **20**
Second Av. PA4: Renf 2E **83**
Second Av. La. G44: Glas 6F **107**
Second Gdns. G41: Glas 1G **105**
Second Rd. G72: Blan 4C **144**
Second St. G71: Tann 5D **112**
Seedhill PA1: Pais 1B **102**
SEEDHILL 1C 102
Seedhill Rd. PA1: Pais 1B **102**
Seggielea La. G13: Glas 3D **62**
Seggielea Rd. G13: Glas 3D **62**
Seil Dr. G44: Glas 3F **123**
Selborne Pl. G13: Glas 4E **63**
Selborne Pl. La. G13: Glas 4E **63**
Selborne Rd. G13: Glas 4E **63**
Selby Gdns. G32: Glas 6D **90**
Selby Pl. ML5: Coat 1H **93**
Selby St. ML5: Coat 1H **93**
Selkirk Av. G52: Glas 1C **104**
Selkirk Av. PA2: Pais 4E **101**
Selkirk Dr. G73: Ruth 6E **109**
Selkirk Pl. G74: E Kil 6D **142**
Selkirk Pl. ML3: Ham 1A **162**
Selkirk St. G72: Blan 2B **144**
Selkirk St. ML2: Wis 4A **150**
Selkirk St. ML3: Ham 1A **162**
Selkirk Way ML4: Bell 6D **114**
Selkirk Way ML5: Coat 2G **115**
Sella Rd. G64: B'rig 5F **51**
Selvieland Rd. G52: Glas 6H **83**
Semphill Gdns. G74: E Kil 1B **158**
Sempie St. ML3: Ham 5D **144**
Sempill Av. PA8: Ersk 5D **42**
Semple Av. PA7: B'ton 4H **41**
Semple Pl. PA3: Lin 4H **79**
Senate Pl. ML1: Moth 6E **131**
Senga Cres. ML4: Bell 6C **114**
Seres Ct. G76: Clar 1B **138**
Seres Dr. G76: Clar 1B **138**
Seres Rd. G76: Clar 1B **138**
Service St. G66: Len 2E **9**
Seton Ter. G31: Glas 4B **88**
Settle Gdns. G69: Bail 1F **111**
Seven Sisters G66: Lenz 2E **53**
Seventh Av. G71: Tann 5D **112**
Seventh Rd. G72: Blan 4C **144**
Severn Rd. G75: E Kil 4B **156**
Seymour Grn. G75: E Kil 3D **156**
Seyton Av. G46: Giff 6A **122**
Seyton Ct. G46: Giff 6A **122**
Seyton La. G74: E Kil 6G **141**
Shackleton Dr. G74: E Kil 5H **141**
Shaftesbury Ct. G74: E Kil 4C **142**
Shaftesbury La. G3: Glas 5G **5** (4D **86**)
Shaftesbury St. G3: Glas 4G **5** (3D **86**)
Shaftesbury St. G81: Clyd 5B **44**
Shafton Pl. G13: Glas 1E **63**
Shafton Rd. G13: Glas 1E **63**
Shaftsbury Cres. ML1: N'hill 4D **132**
Shakespeare Av. G81: Clyd 3B **44**
Shakespeare St. G20: Glas 4C **64**
Shamrock St. G4: Glas 1A **6** (2E **87**)
Shamrock St. G66: Kirkin 5D **32**
Shand La. ML8: Carl 2D **174**
Shandon Cres. ML4: Bell 6C **114**
Shandon Ter. ML3: Ham 6D **144**
Shand Pl. ML8: Carl 2D **174**
Shand St. ML2: Wis 6H **149**
Shandwick Sq. G34: Glas 3G **91**
Shandwick St. G34: Glas 3G **91**
Shankly Dr. ML2: Newm 6F **151**
Shanks Av. G78: Barr 5E **119**
Shanks Bus. Pk. G78: Barr 3E **119**
Shanks Cres. PA5: John 3E **99**
Shanks St. G20: Glas 4C **64**
Shanks St. ML6: Air 2A **96**
Shanks Way G78: Barr 2E **119**
Shannon St. G20: Glas 4D **64**
Shapinsay St. G22: Glas 1H **65**
Sharp Av. ML5: Coat 1G **113**
Sharp St. ML1: Moth 2D **146**
Shaw Av. PA7: B'ton 4A **42**
Shawbridge Arc. G43: Glas 5A **106**
Shawbridge Ind. Est. G43: Glas 6H **105**
Shawbridge St. G43: Glas 6H **105**
Shawburn Cres. ML3: Ham 5F **145**
Shawburn St. ML3: Ham 5F **145**
Shaw Ct. G77: Newt M 5F **137**
Shaw Ct. PA8: Ersk 4D **42**
Shaw Cres. ML2: Wis 2D **164**
SHAWFIELD 3B 108
Shawfield Cres. ML8: Law 6D **166**
Shawfield Dr. G5: Glas 3A **108**
Shawfield Rd. G73: Ruth 3B **108**
Shawfield Stadium **3A 108**
Shawgill Ct. ML8: Law 1F **173**
SHAWHEAD 2B 114
Shawhead Av. ML5: Coat 1D **114**
Shawhead Cotts. ML5: Coat 3D **114**
Shawhead Ind. Est. ML5: Coat 2E **115**
Shawhill Cres. G77: Newt M 6E **137**
Shawhill Pk. **5A 106**
Shawhill Rd. G41: Glas 5B **106**
Shawhill Rd. G43: Glas 5B **106**
Shawholm Cres. G43: Glas 6H **105**
(not continuous)
SHAWLANDS 5B 106
Shawlands Arc. G41: Glas 5B **106**
Shawlands Station (Rail) 5B 106
Shawmoss Rd. G41: Glas 4A **106**
Shawpark Ct. G20: Glas 3C **64**
Shawpark St. G20: Glas 3C **64**
Shaw Pl. PA3: Lin 6H **79**
Shawrigg Rd. ML9: Lark 3E **171**
Shaw Rd. G62: Miln 5G **27**
Shaw Rd. G77: Newt M 5E **137**
SHAWSBURN 3G 171
Shawsgate ML9: Shaw 4G **171**
Shaws Rd. ML9: B'haw 6D **170**
Shaws Rd. ML9: Lark 6D **170**
Shaw St. G51: Glas 3G **85**
Shaw St. ML9: Lark 5D **170**
Shawwood Cres. G77: Newt M 6E **137**
Shearer Av. ML3: Fern 1E **163**
Shearer Dr. ML3: Ham 4G **161**
Shearers La. PA4: Renf 6F **61**
Shearer St. G5: Glas 5E **87**
(*off Springfield Quay*)
Sheddens Pl. G32: Glas 6G **89**
Sheepburn Rd. G71: Udd 6C **112**
Sheepburn Wynd G71: Udd 6C **112**
Sheila St. G33: Glas 5G **67**
Sheiling Hill ML3: Ham 5A **146**
Sheldrake Pl. PA5: John 6D **98**

Shelley Ct. – Slatefield

Shelley Ct. G12: Glas 4G **63**
Shelley Dr. G71: Both 4F **129**
Shelley Dr. G81: Clyd 3C **44**
Shelley Rd. G12: Glas 4F **63**
Shells Rd. G66: Kirkin 4E **33**
Shepford Pl. ML5: Coat 4H **93**
Shepherds Way G72: Newt 1F **127**
Sherbrooke Av. G41: Glas 2A **106**
Sherbrooke Dr. G41: Glas 1A **106**
Sherbrooke Gdns. G41: Glas 2A **106**
Sherbrooke Pl. G75: E Kil 2E **157**
Sherburn Gdns. G69: Bail 2F **111**
Sherdale Av. ML6: Chap 3D **116**
Sheriff Court **4F 19** *(Dumbarton)*
Sheriff Court **5G 87** *(Glasgow)*
Sheriff Court **5H 145** *(Hamilton)*
Sheriff Court **6A 82** *(Paisley)*
Sheriff Pk. Av. G73: Ruth 6C **108**
Sherry Av. ML1: Holy 2H **131**
Sherry Dr. ML3: Ham 2E **161**
Sherry Hgts. G72: Camb 1A **126**
Sherwood Av. G71: Udd 2E **129**
Sherwood Av. PA1: Pais 5C **82**
Sherwood Dr. G46: T'bnk 4G **121**
Sherwood Pl. G15: Glas 4B **46**
Sherwood Rd. ML5: Glenb 3B **72**
Shetland Dr. G44: Glas 3F **123**
SHETTLESTON **6B 90**
SHETTLESTON DAY HOSPITAL **1H 109**
Shettleston Rd. G31: Glas 5E **89**
Shettleston Rd. G32: Glas 6G **89**
Shettleston Station (Rail) **6B 90**
Shiel Av. G74: E Kil 6H **141**
Shielbridge Gdns. G23: Glas 6C **48**
Shiel Ct. G78: Barr 2D **118**
Shieldaig Dr. G73: Ruth 3D **124**
Shieldaig Rd. G22: Glas 1F **65**
Shieldburn Rd. G51: Glas 4C **84**
SHIELDHALL **3C 84**
Shieldhall Gdns. G51: Glas 4C **84**
Shieldhall Rd. G51: Glas 3B **84**
Shieldhill G75: E Kil 4H **157**
Shieldhill Ct. ML8: Carl 4D **174**
Shieldhill Rd. ML8: Carl 5C **174**
SHIELDMUIR **5D 148**
Shieldmuir Station (Rail) **5C 148**
Shieldmuir St. ML2: Wis 5C **148**
Shiel Dr. ML9: Lark 6H **163**
Shields Ct. G53: Glas 2D **120**
Shields Ct. ML1: Moth 6B **148**
Shields Dr. ML1: Moth 6B **148**
Shields Rd. G41: Glas 6D **86**
Shields Rd. ML1: Moth 5A **148**
Shields Road Park & Ride **6D 86**
Shields Road Station (Subway) **6D 86**
Shields Twr. ML1: Moth 6B **148**
Shiel Pl. G74: E Kil 6H **141**
Shiel Pl. ML5: Coat 6F **95**
Shiel Rd. G64: B'rig 6D **50**
Shiel Ter. ML2: Newm 3D **150**
Shilford Av. G13: Glas 2A **62**
Shillay St. G22: Glas 1A **66**
Shillingworth Pl. PA11: Bri W 5F **77**
Shilton Dr. G53: Glas 2C **120**
Shilton La. PA7: B'ton 3C **42**
Shinwell Av. G81: Clyd 6F **45**
Shipbank La. G1: Glas 5G **87** *(off Clyde St.)*
Shira Av. G69: G'csh 3E **71**
Shira Ter. G74: E Kil 2B **158**
Shirley Quad. ML1: Moth 6F **147**
SHIRREL **6C 114**
Shirrel Av. ML4: Bell 6C **114**
Shirrel Rd. ML1: Holy 3A **132**
Shiskine Dr. G20: Glas 2A **64**
Shiskine Pl. G20: Glas 1A **64**
Shiskine St. G20: Glas 1A **64**
Sholto Cres. ML4: Bell 6H **113**
Shore St. G40: Glas 3B **108**
Shortridge St. G20: Glas 4C **64**
SHORTROODS **4A 82**
Shortroods Rd. PA3: Pais 4H **81**
Shott Dr. G72: Blan 3H **143**
Shotts St. G33: Glas 3D **90**
Showcase Cinema **1F 113** *(Glasgow)*
Showcase Cinema **6C 80** *(Paisley)*
Shuna Cres. G20: Glas 4C **64**
Shuna Gdns. G20: Glas 4C **64**
Shuna Pl. G20: Glas 4C **64**
Shuna Pl. G77: Newt M 3B **136**
Shuna St. G20: Glas 3C **64**
Shuttle St. G1: Glas 6F **7** (4H **87**)
Shuttle St. G65: Kils 3H **13**
Shuttle St. PA1: Pais 1A **102**
Shuttle St. PA10: Kilba 1A **98**
Siding La. G5: Glas 3G **107**
Sidland Rd. G21: Glas 4E **67**
Sidlaw Av. G78: Barr 6E **119**
Sidlaw Av. ML3: Ham 1D **160**
Sidlaw Ct. ML5: Coat 2E **115**
Sidlaw Dr. ML2: Wis 6F **149**
Sidlaw Rd. G61: Bear 1B **46**
Sidlaw Way ML6: Chap 4F **117**
Sidlaw Way ML9: Lark 6H **163**
Sielga Pl. G34: Glas 3G **91**
Siemens Pl. G21: Glas 1D **88**
Siemens St. G21: Glas 1D **88**
Sievewright St. G73: Ruth 4E **109**
SIGHTHILL **1A 88**
Sighthill Av. G21: Glas 1H **87**
Sighthill Circus G4: Glas 1F **7** (1H **87**)
Sighthill Loan ML9: Lark 1D **170** *(off Muirshot Rd.)*
Sighthill Pk. **1H 87**
Sighthill Stone Circ. G21: Glas **1G 7 (2H 87)**
SIKESIDE **6F 95**
Sikeside Pl. ML5: Coat 6F **95**
Sikeside St. ML5: Coat 6F **95**
Silkin Av. G81: Clyd 6F **45**
Silk St. PA1: Pais 6B **82**
Silvan Pl. G76: Busby 4E **139**
SILVERBANK **1G 125**
Silverbanks Ct. G72: Camb 6G **109**
Silverbanks Gait G72: Camb 1G **125**
Silverbanks Rd. G72: Camb 1G **125**
Silver Birch Dr. G51: Glas 4D **84**
Silver Birch Gdns. G51: Glas 4D **84**
Silverburn Cres. ML1: N'hill 4D **132**
Silverburn Shopping Cen. **6C 104**
Silverburn St. G33: Glas 3G **89**
Silverdale G74: E Kil 6E **141**
Silverdale St. G31: Glas 1E **109**
Silverdale Ter. ML6: Plain 6F **75**
Silverfir Ct. G5: Glas 1H **107**
Silver Firs ML1: N'hill 4C **132**
Silverfir St. G5: Glas 2H **107**
Silver Glade G52: Glas 1B **104**
Silvergrove St. G40: Glas 1A **108**
SILVERTON **3G 19**
Silverton Av. G82: Dumb 4H **19**
SILVERTONHILL **1B 162**
Silvertonhill Av. ML3: Ham 3A **162**
Silvertonhill La. G82: Dumb 4H **19**
Silvertonhill Pl. ML3: Ham 4H **161**
Silverwells G71: Both 6F **129**
SILVERWELLS **6E 129**
Silverwells Ct. G71: Both 6E **129**
Silverwells Cres. G71: Both 6E **129**
Silverwells Dr. G71: Both 6E **129**
Silverwood Ct. G71: Both 6F **129**
Simons Cres. PA4: Renf 4F **61**
Simpson Ct. G71: Udd 1D **128**
Simpson Ct. G81: Clyd 5C **44**
Simpson Dr. G75: E Kil 4F **157**
Simpson Gdns. G78: Barr 5D **118**
Simpson Hgts. G4: Glas 6H **7** (4A **88**) *(off Drygate)*
Simpson Pl. G75: E Kil 4F **157**
Simpson St. G20: Glas 6D **64**
Simpson Way ML4: Bell 6E **115**
Simshill Rd. G44: Glas 4F **123**
Sinclair Av. G61: Bear 1E **47**
Sinclair Dr. G42: Glas 6D **106**
Sinclair Dr. ML5: Coat 4H **93**
Sinclair Gdns. G64: B'rig 1D **66**
Sinclair Gro. ML4: Bell 5B **130**
Sinclair Pk. G75: E Kil 3H **157**
Sinclair Pl. G75: E Kil 3H **157**
Sinclair St. G62: Miln 3G **27**
Sinclair St. G81: Clyd 1F **61**
Singer Rd. G75: E Kil 5H **157**
Singer Rd. G81: Clyd 4B **44**
Singer Station (Rail) **5D 44**
Singer St. G81: Clyd 4D **44**
Sir Chris Hoy Velodrome **1D 108**
Sir James Black Ct. G71: Udd 2E **129**
Sir Matt Busby Sports Complex **2B 130**
Sir Michael Pl. PA1: Pais 1H **101**
Sir Thomas Lipton Way G72: Camb 1H **125**
Sir Walter Scott's Statue **5D 6 (4G 87)**
Siskin Way G68: Cumb 5A **36**
Siskin Way ML5: Coat 2F **115**
Sixth Av. PA4: Renf 2E **83**
Sixth St. G71: Tann 4C **112**
Skaethorn Rd. G20: Glas 2H **63**
Skara Wlk. ML2: Newm 2D **150** *(off Murdostoun Vw.)*
Skaterigg Dr. G13: Glas 4F **63**
Skaterigg Gdns. G13: Glas 4F **63**
Skaterigg La. G13: Glas 4E **63**
Skelbo Path G34: Glas 2B **92**
Skelbo Pl. G34: Glas 2B **92**
Skellyton Cres. ML9: Lark 3D **170**
Skene Rd. G51: Glas 6H **85**
Skerne Gro. G75: E Kil 5B **156**
Skerray Quad. G22: Glas 1G **65**
Skerray St. G22: Glas 1G **65**
Skerryvore Pl. G33: Glas 3B **90**
Skerryvore Rd. G33: Glas 3B **90**
Skibo La. G46: T'bnk 4E **121**
Skibo Pl. G69: G'csh 5C **70**
Skimmers Hill G66: Milt C 1B **32**
Skipness Av. ML8: Carl 5E **175**
Skipness Dr. G51: Glas 4D **84**
Skipness Rd. G69: G'csh 4C **70**
Skirsa Ct. G23: Glas 1E **65**
Skirsa Pl. G23: Glas 2D **64**
Skirsa Sq. G23: Glas 2E **65**
Skirsa St. G23: Glas 1D **64**
Skirving St. G41: Glas 5C **106**
Skovlunde Way G75: E Kil 5G **157**
Skye G74: E Kil 2C **158**
Skye Av. PA4: Renf 2E **83**
Skye Ct. G67: Cumb 5F **37**
Skye Cres. G60: Old K 2G **43**
Skye Cres. PA2: Pais 6H **101**
Skye Dr. G60: Old K 2G **43**
Skye Dr. G67: Cumb 5F **37**
Skye Gdns. G61: Bear 1B **46**
Skye Pl. G67: Cumb 5F **37**
Skye Pl. ML6: Air 5D **96**
Skye Quad. ML2: Wis 4C **150**
Skye Rd. G67: Cumb 5F **37**
Skye Rd. G73: Ruth 4F **125**
Skye Wynd ML3: Ham 2D **160**
Skylands Gro. ML3: Ham 3E **161**
Skylands Pl. ML3: Ham 4E **161**
Skylands Ri. ML3: Ham 3E **161**
Skylark Wynd ML1: Moth 1C **148**
Slakiewood Av. G69: G'csh 2C **70**
Slatefield G66: Len 3F **9**

272 A–Z Glasgow

Slatefield Ct. – Speyburn Pl.

Slatefield Ct. G31: Glas ... 5C 88
... (off Slatefield St.)
Slatefield St. G31: Glas ... 5C 88
Slateford Rd. PA7: B'ton ... 3E 41
Sleaford Av. ML1: Moth ... 5F 147
Slenavon Av. G73: Ruth ... 4F 125
Slessor Dr. G75: E Kil ... 4G 157
Slioch Sq. ML1: N'hill ... 3C 132
Sloy St. G22: Glas ... 5H 65
Sloy St. ML2: Wis ... 2G 165
Small Cres. G72: Blan ... 2B 144
Sma' Shot Cottages ... 1A 102
Smeaton Av. G64: Torr ... 5D 30
Smeaton Dr. G64: B'rig ... 3C 50
Smeaton Gro. G20: Glas ... 3D 64
Smeaton St. G20: Glas ... 3D 64
Smethurst Dr. G69: Chry ... 3H 69
Smith Av. ML2: Wis ... 4G 165
Smith Cl. G64: B'rig ... 1F 67
Smith Cres. G81: Hard ... 2D 44
Smith Gdns. G64: B'rig ... 1F 67
Smith Gro. G64: B'rig ... 1F 67
Smithhills St. PA1: Pais ... 6A 82
Smith Quad. ML5: Coat ... 4E 95
Smith's La. PA3: Pais ... 5A 82
SMITHSTONE ... 3B 36
Smithstone Cres. G65: Croy ... 6A 14
Smithstone Rd. G68: Cumb ... 3B 36
Smith St. G14: Glas ... 1E 85
... (not continuous)
Smith Ter. G73: Ruth ... 4D 108
Smithview ML2: Over ... 4H 165
Smith Way G64: B'rig ... 1F 67
Smithycroft ML3: Ham ... 1C 162
Smithycroft Ct. G33: Glas ... 3G 89
Smithycroft Rd. G33: Glas ... 3F 89
Smithycroft Way G72: Blan ... 3H 143
Smithyends G67: Cumb ... 6B 16
Smollett Rd. G82: Dumb ... 4H 19
Snaefell Av. G73: Ruth ... 3E 125
Snaefell Cres. G73: Ruth ... 3E 125
Snead Vw. ML1: Cle ... 6E 133
Sneddon Av. ML2: Wis ... 2A 166
Sneddon St. ML3: Ham ... 3D 144
Sneddon Ter. ML3: Ham ... 3D 144
Snowdon Pl. G5: Glas ... 1H 107
Snowdon St. G5: Glas ... 1H 107
Snowdrop Gdns. G33: Mille ... 3A 68
Snowdrop Path G33: Mille ... 4A 68
Snuff Mill Rd. G44: Glas ... 2E 123
Soccerworld ... 2B 90
... (Glasgow)
Society St. G31: Glas ... 6D 88
Solar Ct. ML9: Lark ... 5D 170
Sollas Pl. G13: Glas ... 1G 61
Solsgirth Gdns. G66: Kirkin ... 4H 33
Solway Ct. ML3: Ham ... 3F 161
Solway Pl. G69: Chry ... 6B 54
Solway Rd. G64: B'rig ... 5F 51
Solway St. G40: Glas ... 3B 108
Somerford Rd. G61: Bear ... 6F 47
Somerled Av. PA3: Pais ... 2B 82
Somerset Av. ML3: Ham ... 5F 145
Somerset Pl. G3: Glas ... 2F 5 (2D 86)
Somerset Pl. M. G3: Glas ... 2F 5 (2D 86)
... (off Clifton St.)
Somervell St. G72: Camb ... 1H 125
Somerville Dr. G42: Glas ... 5F 107
Somerville Dr. G75: E Kil ... 4G 157
Somerville La. G75: E Kil ... 4H 157
Somerville Ter. G75: E Kil ... 4G 157
Sommerville Pl. ML2: Wis ... 1A 166
Sorby St. G31: Glas ... 6F 89
Sorley St. G11: Glas ... 1F 85
Sorn St. G40: Glas ... 2D 108
Souter Gdns. ML5: Coat ... 1E 115
Souterhouse Path ML5: Coat ... 6B 94
Souterhouse Rd. ML5: Coat ... 6B 94
Southampton Dr. G12: Glas ... 3H 63
Southampton La. G12: Glas ... 3H 63
... (off Southampton Dr.)
South Annandale St. G42: Glas ... 3F 107
South Av. G72: Blan ... 4B 144
South Av. G81: Clyd ... 5C 44
South Av. ML8: Carl ... 4C 174
South Av. PA2: Pais ... 5B 102
South Av. PA4: Renf ... 6F 61
Southbank Bus. Pk. G66: Kirkin ... 6C 32
Southbank Dr. G66: Kirkin ... 5C 32
Southbank Rd. G66: Kirkin ... 6B 32
... (not continuous)
Southbank St. G31: Glas ... 6F 89
South Bank St. G81: Clyd ... 2E 61
SOUTHBAR ... 1E 59
Southbar Av. G13: Glas ... 2A 62
Southbar Rd. PA4: Inch ... 3E 59
SOUTH BARRWOOD ... 4A 14
South Barrwood Rd. G65: Kils ... 4A 14
South Biggar Rd. ML6: Air ... 4B 96
South Brae G66: Len ... 5E 9
Southbrae Av. PA11: Bri W ... 4D 76
Southbrae Dr. G13: Glas ... 4C 62
Southbrae Gdns. G13: Glas ... 4D 62
Southbrae La. G13: Glas ... 4E 63
South Bri. St. ML6: Air ... 3A 96
Southburn Rd. ML6: Air ... 4F 95
South Caldeen Rd. ML5: Coat ... 6D 94
South Calder ML1: Moth ... 1H 147
South Calder Way ML2: Newm ... 3F 151
South Campbell St. PA2: Pais ... 2A 102
South Carbrain Rd. G67: Cumb ... 5H 37
SOUTH CARDONALD ... 1C 104
South Cathkin Cotts. G73: Ruth ... 1E 141
South Chester St. G32: Glas ... 6A 90
South Circular Rd. ML5: Coat ... 4C 94
South Claremont La. G62: Miln ... 4G 27
South Commonhead Av. ML6: Air ... 2H 95
Southcroft Rd. G73: Ruth ... 4A 108
Southcroft St. G51: Glas ... 4H 85
South Crosshill Rd. G64: B'rig ... 6C 50
South Dean Pk. Av. G71: Both ... 5E 129
Southdeen Av. G15: Glas ... 4A 46
Southdeen Gro. G15: Glas ... 4B 46
Southdeen Rd. G15: Glas ... 4A 46
South Douglas St. G81: Clyd ... 1E 61
South Dr. PA3: Lin ... 5H 79
South Dumbreck Rd. G65: Kils ... 3F 13
South Elgin Pl. G81: Clyd ... 2E 61
South Elgin St. G81: Clyd ... 2E 61
Southend Pl. ML4: Bell ... 3B 130
Southend Rd. G81: Hard ... 2D 44
Southern Av. G73: Ruth ... 2D 124
Southerness Dr. G68: Cumb ... 6A 16
SOUTHERN GENERAL HOSPITAL ... 3D 84
South Erskine Pk. G61: Bear ... 2D 46
Southesk Av. G64: B'rig ... 4B 50
Southesk Gdns. G64: B'rig ... 4B 50
South Exchange Ct. G1: Glas ... 6D 6 (4G 87)
... (off Queen St.)
Southfield Av. PA2: Pais ... 5A 102
Southfield Cres. G53: Glas ... 5C 104
Southfield Cres. ML5: Coat ... 6E 95
Southfield Ho. G77: Newt M ... 2E 153
Southfield Rd. G68: Cumb ... 4E 37
South Frederick St. G1: Glas ... 5E 7 (4G 87)
Southgate G62: Miln ... 4G 27
Southgate G74: E Kil ... 2G 157
... (within East Kilbride Shop. Cen.)
South Glassford St. G62: Miln ... 4H 27
South Hallhill Rd. G32: Glas ... 6B 90
Southhill Av. G73: Ruth ... 1E 125
Southinch Av. G14: Glas ... 3G 61
South Lanarkshire Crematorium ... 5H 143
South Lanarkshire Lifestyles Leisure Cen.
... 6G 109
Southlea Av. G46: T'bnk ... 4G 121
South Line Vw. ML2: Wis ... 1E 165
South Loan G69: Chry ... 1B 70
Southloch Gdns. G21: Glas ... 6B 66
Southloch St. G21: Glas ... 6B 66
South Mains Rd. G62: Miln ... 4F 27
South Medrox St. ML5: Glenb ... 2G 71
South Moraine La. G15: Glas ... 5C 46
South Mound PA6: Hous ... 1A 78
South Muirhead Ct. G67: Cumb ... 3A 38
South Muirhead Rd. G67: Cumb ... 3A 38
Southmuir Pl. G20: Glas ... 4B 64
South Nimmo St. ML6: Air ... 4B 96
SOUTH NITSHILL ... 3A 120
South Pk. Av. G78: Barr ... 4D 118
Southpark Av. G12: Glas ... 1B 86
South Pk. Dr. PA2: Pais ... 3A 102
South Pk. Gro. ML3: Ham ... 6H 145
South Pk. La. G12: Glas ... 1C 86
South Pk. Rd. ML3: Ham ... 1H 161
Southpark Ter. G12: Glas ... 1C 86
SOUTHPARK VILLAGE G53: Glas ... 5C 120
South Pl. ML4: Bell ... 3B 130
South Portland St. G5: Glas ... 6F 87
... (not continuous)
South Rd. G76: Busby ... 4E 139
South Robertson Pl. ML6: Air ... 4G 95
South Scott St. G69: Bail ... 1H 111
Southside Cres. G5: Glas ... 1G 107
South Speirs Wharf G4: Glas ... 1F 87
South St. G11: Glas ... 1E 85
South St. G14: Glas ... 5A 62
South St. PA4: Inch ... 5F 59
South St. PA6: Hous ... 1A 78
South Vesalius St. G32: Glas ... 6A 90
South Vw. G72: Blan ... 6A 128
South Vw. G81: Clyd ... 4B 44
South Vw. ML4: Bell ... 3A 130
Southview Av. G76: Busby ... 4D 138
Southview Ct. G64: B'rig ... 2B 66
Southview Cres. PA11: Bri W ... 2F 77
Southview Dr. G61: Bear ... 2C 46
Southview Gro. G61: Bear ... 2C 46
Southview Pl. G69: G'csh ... 3C 70
Southview Ter. G64: B'rig ... 2B 66
South William St. PA5: John ... 3F 99
Southwold Rd. PA1: Pais ... 6G 83
Southwood Ct. G77: Newt M ... 1D 152
Southwood Dr. G44: Glas ... 2G 123
Southwood Pl. G77: Newt M ... 1D 152
South Woodside Rd. G20: Glas ... 6D 64
South Woodside Rd. G4: Glas ... 1C 86
Soutra Pl. G33: Glas ... 3B 90
Spairdrum Rd. G67: Cumb ... 3H 57
Spalehall Dr. ML1: N'hill ... 4F 133
Spangler Cres. G72: Camb ... 6H 109
SPATESTON ... 6D 98
Spateston Rd. PA5: John ... 6C 98
Spean Av. G74: E Kil ... 2B 158
Spean St. G44: Glas ... 6E 107
Spectrum Ho. G81: Clyd ... 5D 44
Speirsfield Ct. PA2: Pais ... 2H 101
Speirsfield Gdns. PA2: Pais ... 2A 102
Speirs Gait ML8: Law ... 6E 167
Speirshall Cl. G14: Glas ... 4H 61
Speirshall Ter. G14: Glas ... 3G 61
Speirs Rd. G61: Bear ... 4G 47
Speirs Rd. PA5: John ... 2H 99
Speirs Rd. PA6: Hous ... 1B 78
Speirs Wharf G4: Glas ... 1F 87
Spence Ct. G75: E Kil ... 2E 157
Spencer Cl. PA2: Pais ... 5C 100
Spencer Dr. PA2: Pais ... 5B 100
Spencerfield Gdns. ML3: Ham ... 6B 146
Spencer Pl. PA2: Pais ... 5C 100
Spencer St. G13: Glas ... 2F 63
Spencer St. G81: Clyd ... 4C 44
Spencer Vennel PA2: Pais ... 5C 100
Spence St. G20: Glas ... 1A 64
Spey Av. PA2: Pais ... 5C 100
Speyburn Pl. G33: Step ... 3E 69
Speyburn Pl. ML6: Air ... 6A 74

A–Z Glasgow 273

Station Rd. G65: Kils	2H **13**
Station Rd. G66: Len	3F **9**
Station Rd. G66: Lenz	3C **52**
Station Rd. G68: C'cry	2F **17**
Station Rd. G69: Bail	1A **112**
Station Rd. G69: Muirh	2A **70**
Station Rd. G71: Both	5E **129**
Station Rd. G71: Udd	1C **128**
Station Rd. G72: Blan	1C **144**
Station Rd. G76: Busby	4E **139**
Station Rd. G78: Neil	2D **134**
Station Rd. G82: Dumb	3E **19**
Station Rd. ML1: Cle	6H **133**
Station Rd. ML1: New S	4B **132**
Station Rd. ML2: Wis	1G **165**
Station Rd. ML6: Air	3E **97**
Station Rd. ML6: Plain	1H **97**
Station Rd. ML8: Carl	5B **174**
Station Rd. ML8: Law	6D **166**
Station Rd. ML9: Lark	1D **170**
Station Rd. PA1: Pais	2E **101**
Station Rd. PA11: Bri W	4G **77**
Station Rd. PA4: Renf	5F **61**
Station Rd. PA7: B'ton	5H **41**
Station Row ML8: Law	5E **167**
Station Way G71: Udd	1D **128**
Station Wynd PA10: Kilba	3B **98**
Staybrae Dr. G53: Glas	4H **103**
Staybrae Gro. G53: Glas	4H **103**
Steading, The ML2: Wis	4H **149**
Steel Pl. ML2: Wis	1F **165**
Steel St. G1: Glas	5H **87**
Steel St. ML2: Wis	1H **165**
Steeple Sq. PA10: Kilba	2A **98**
Steeple St. PA10: Kilba	2A **98**
Stein Pl. ML2: Newm	6G **151**
Stein Ter. ML3: Fern	1E **163**
Stemac La. ML6: Plain	1G **97**
Stenhouse Av. G69: Muirh	2A **70**
Stenton Cres. ML2: Wis	2D **164**
Stenton Pl. ML2: Wis	2D **164**
Stenton St. G32: Glas	4G **89**
Stenzel Pl. G33: Step	4F **69**
Stepford Path G33: Glas	4G **91**
Stepford Pl. G33: Glas	4F **91**
Stepford Rd. G33: Glas	4F **91**
Stepford Sports Pk.	5G **91**
Stephen Cres. G69: Bail	6F **91**
Stephenson Pl. G72: Blan	4H **143**
Stephenson Pl. G75: E Kil	3F **157**
Stephenson Sq. G75: E Kil	3F **157**
Stephenson St. G52: Hill E	3G **83**
Stephenson Ter. G75: E Kil	3F **157**
STEPPS	4C **68**
Stepps Rd. G33: Glas	2C **90**
Stepps Rd. G66: A'loch	5E **53**
STEPPS ROAD INTERCHANGE	2C **90**
Stepps Station (Rail)	4E **69**
Stevens La. ML1: New S	4A **132**
Stevenson Pl. ML4: Bell	6D **114**
Stevenson St. G40: Glas	5A **88**
	(not continuous)
Stevenson St. G81: Clyd	3B **44**
Stevenson St. ML8: Carl	3C **174**
Stevenson St. PA2: Pais	2A **102**
Stevenston Ct. ML1: New S	3A **132**
Stevenston St. ML1: Holy	3A **132**
Stevenston St. ML1: New S	3A **132**
Stewart Av. G72: Blan	2A **144**
Stewart Av. G77: Newt M	3E **137**
Stewart Av. ML3: Ham	3D **160**
Stewart Av. PA4: Renf	2D **82**
Stewart Ct. G73: Ruth	6E **109**
Stewart Ct. G78: Barr	3E **119**
Stewart Ct. ML5: Coat	5E **95**
	(off Clifton Pl.)
Stewart Cres. G78: Barr	3F **119**
Stewart Cres. ML2: Newm	3E **151**
Stewart Dr. G69: Barg	5F **93**

Stewart Dr. G76: Clar	1B **138**
Stewart Dr. G81: Hard	1D **44**
STEWARTFIELD	5E **141**
Stewartfield Cres. G74: E Kil	5E **141**
Stewartfield Dr. G74: E Kil	5F **141**
Stewartfield Gdns. G74: E Kil	5E **141**
Stewartfield Gro. G74: E Kil	5D **140**
Stewartfield Rd. G74: E Kil	6E **141**
Stewartfield Way G74: E Kil	6B **140**
Stewartgill Pl. ML9: Ashg	4H **171**
Stewarton Dr. G72: Camb	2G **125**
Stewarton Ho. ML2: Wis	1H **165**
	(off Stewarton St.)
Stewarton Rd. G46: T'bnk	1D **136**
Stewarton Rd. G77: Newt M	4A **136**
Stewarton St. ML2: Wis	1H **165**
Stewarton Ter. ML2: Wis	1H **165**
Stewart Pl. G78: Barr	3F **119**
Stewart Pl. ML8: Carl	3D **174**
Stewart Quad. ML1: Holy	1B **132**
Stewart Rd. PA2: Pais	5B **102**
Stewarts La. ML2: Wis	6A **150**
Stewart St. G4: Glas	1C **6** (2F **87**)
Stewart St. G62: Miln	4G **27**
Stewart St. G78: Barr	3F **119**
Stewart St. G81: Clyd	4A **44**
Stewart St. ML3: Ham	4E **145**
	(not continuous)
Stewart St. ML4: Moss	2E **131**
Stewart St. ML5: Coat	3C **94**
Stewart St. ML8: Carl	2C **174**
Stewartville St. G11: Glas	1H **85**
Stirling Av. G61: Bear	5E **47**
Stirling Dr. G61: Bear	1D **46**
Stirling Dr. G64: B'rig	4A **50**
Stirling Dr. G73: Ruth	2D **124**
Stirling Dr. G74: E Kil	6A **142**
Stirling Dr. ML3: Ham	5C **144**
Stirling Dr. PA3: Lin	6F **79**
Stirling Dr. PA5: John	3D **98**
Stirlingfauld Pl. G5: Glas	6F **87**
Stirling Gdns. G64: B'rig	4A **50**
Stirling Ga. PA3: Lin	5G **79**
Stirling Ho. G81: Clyd	5D **44**
Stirling M. G66: Milt C	5B **10**
Stirling Pl. G66: Len	3G **9**
Stirling Rd. G4: Glas	4G **7** (3H **87**)
Stirling Rd. G65: Kils	2A **14**
Stirling Rd. G67: Cumb	6A **38**
Stirling Rd. G82: Dumb	1G **19**
Stirling Rd. G82: Mil	1G **19**
Stirling Rd. ML6: Chap	1D **116**
Stirling Rd. ML8: Carl	1C **174**
Stirling Rd. Ind. Est. ML6: Air	1B **96**
Stirling St. G67: Cumb	1B **38**
Stirling St. ML1: Moth	5B **148**
Stirling St. ML5: Coat	1H **113**
Stirling St. ML6: Air	4H **95**
Stirling Way G69: Bail	1G **111**
Stirling Way PA4: Renf	2F **83**
Stirrat Cres. PA3: Pais	5G **81**
Stirrat Pl. G20: Glas	3B **64**
Stirrat St. G20: Glas	3A **64**
Stirrat St. PA3: Pais	4F **81**
Stobcross Bus. Pk. G3: Glas	4D **4** (3C **86**)
	(off Minerva Way)
Stobcross Rd. G3: Glas	4A **4** (3A **86**)
Stobcross St. G3: Glas	5F **5** (4C **86**)
Stobcross St. ML5: Coat	5C **94**
Stobcross Wynd G3: Glas	5B **4** (4B **86**)
Stobhill Cotts. G21: Glas	2C **66**
STOBHILL HOSPITAL	3C **66**
Stobhill Rd. G21: Glas	2B **66**
Stobo G74: E Kil	5C **142**
Stobo Ct. G74: E Kil	5C **142**
Stobo St. ML2: Wis	4A **150**
Stobs Dr. G78: Barr	2D **118**
Stobs Pl. G34: Glas	2A **92**
Stock Av. PA2: Pais	2A **102**

Stock Exchange	5D **6** (4F **87**)
	(Glasgow)
	(off St Vincent St.)
Stockholm Cres. PA2: Pais	2A **102**
Stockiemuir Av. G61: Bear	6D **26**
Stockiemuir Ct. G61: Bear	6E **27**
Stockiemuir Rd. G61: Bear	1D **46**
Stockiemuir Rd. G62: Miln	3C **26**
Stocks Rd. ML1: Cle	1D **150**
Stock St. PA2: Pais	3A **102**
Stockwell Pl. G1: Glas	5G **87**
Stockwell St. G1: Glas	5G **87**
Stoddard Sq. PA5: Eld	2B **100**
Stonebank Gro. G45: Glas	4H **123**
Stonebyres Ct. ML3: Ham	6E **145**
Stonecraig Rd. ML2: Wis	1H **165**
Stonedyke Cres. ML8: Carl	2E **175**
Stonedyke Gro. G15: Glas	5B **46**
Stonedyke Rd. ML8: Carl	2E **175**
STONEFIELD	1B **144**
Stonefield Av. G12: Glas	3A **64**
Stonefield Av. PA2: Pais	4B **102**
Stonefield Cres. G72: Blan	3A **144**
Stonefield Cres. G76: Clar	1A **138**
Stonefield Cres. PA2: Pais	4B **102**
Stonefield Dr. PA2: Pais	4B **102**
Stonefield Gdns. ML8: Carl	2D **174**
Stonefield Gdns. PA2: Pais	4B **102**
Stonefield Grn. PA2: Pais	4A **102**
Stonefield Gro. PA2: Pais	4A **102**
Stonefield Pk. PA2: Pais	5A **102**
Stonefield Pk. Gdns. G72: Blan	1C **144**
Stonefield Pl. G72: Blan	3H **143**
Stonefield Rd. G72: Blan	2A **144**
Stonefield St. ML6: Air	2A **96**
Stonehall Av. ML3: Ham	1F **161**
Stonehaven Cres. ML6: Air	6G **95**
Stonelaw Community Sports Cen.	1E **125**
Stonelaw Ct. G73: Ruth	6D **108**
Stonelaw Dr. G73: Ruth	6D **108**
Stonelaw Rd. G73: Ruth	6D **108**
Stonelaw Towers G73: Ruth	1E **125**
Stoneside Dr. G43: Glas	1G **121**
Stoneside Sq. G43: Glas	1G **121**
Stoney Brae PA2: Pais	5A **102**
Stoneyetts Dr. G66: Lenz	1F **53**
Stoneyetts Rd. G69: Mood	4D **54**
Stoneyflatt Av. G82: Dumb	2H **19**
Stoneyflatt Ct. G82: Dumb	2H **19**
Stoneyflatt Gdns. G82: Dumb	2H **19**
Stoneyflatt Rd. G82: Dumb	2H **19**
Stoneymeadow Rd. G72: Blan	3E **143**
Stoneymeadow Rd. G74: E Kil	5B **142**
Stony Brae PA1: Pais	6A **82**
Stonyhurst St. G22: Glas	5F **65**
	(not continuous)
Stonylee Rd. G67: Cumb	4A **38**
Storie St. PA1: Pais	1A **102**
Stormyland Way G78: Barr	5E **119**
Stornoway Cres. ML2: Wis	4C **150**
Stornoway St. G22: Glas	1G **65**
Stow Brae PA1: Pais	1A **102**
Stow St. PA1: Pais	1A **102**
Strachan Pl. G72: Blan	6B **144**
Strachan St. ML4: Bell	3C **130**
Strachur Cres. G22: Glas	2E **65**
Strachur Gdns. G22: Glas	2E **65**
Strachur Gro. G22: Glas	2E **65**
Strachur Pl. G22: Glas	2E **65**
Strachur St. G22: Glas	2E **65**
Strain Cres. ML6: Air	5B **96**
Straiton Dr. ML3: Ham	1B **160**
Straiton Pl. G72: Blan	1B **144**
Straiton St. G32: Glas	4G **89**
Stranka Av. PA2: Pais	2G **101**
Stranraer Dr. G15: Glas	5C **46**
Stratford G74: E Kil	4D **142**
Stratford St. G20: Glas	4B **64**
Strathallan Av. G75: E Kil	2B **156**

Strathallan Cres. – Sundale Av.

Strathallan Cres. ML6: Air 6A **74**
Strathallan Gdns. G66: Kirkin 5D **32**
(off Willowbank Gdns.)
Strathallan Ga. G75: E Kil 2B **156**
Strathallan Wynd G75: E Kil 2B **156**
Strathallon Pl. G73: Ruth 4F **125**
(off Ranald Gdns.)
Strathaven Rd. G75: E Kil 3A **158**
Strathavon Cres. ML6: Air 1A **96**
Strathbeg Ct. ML6: Air 4H **95**
Strathblane Ct. G13: Glas 1E **63**
Strathblane Cres. ML6: Air 6A **74**
Strathblane Dr. G75: E Kil 3A **156**
Strathblane Gdns. G13: Glas 1E **63**
Strathblane Rd. G62: Miln 3H **27**
Strathblane Rd. G66: Cam G 1A **8**
Strathbran St. G31: Glas 1F **109**
Strath Brennig Rd. G68: Cumb 3B **36**
STRATHBUNGO 3D **106**
Strathcairn Cres. ML6: Air 6A **74**
Strath Carron ML8: Law 5E **167**
Strathcarron Cres. PA2: Pais 5D **102**
Strathcarron Dr. PA2: Pais 4D **102**
Strathcarron Grn. PA2: Pais 4D **102**
Strathcarron Pl. G20: Glas 3B **64**
Strathcarron Pl. PA2: Pais 5D **102**
Strathcarron Rd. PA2: Pais 5D **102**
Strathcarron Way PA2: Pais 4D **102**
Strathcarron Wynd PA2: Pais 4D **102**
Strathclyde Bus. Cen. G72: Flem 4E **127**
(off Strathclyde Gdns.)
Strathclyde Bus. Cen. ML1: New S 3H **131**
Strathclyde Bus. Pk. ML4: Bell 5A **114**
Strathclyde Country Pk. **6A 130**
Strathclyde Country Pk. Vis. Cen. **6H 129**
Strathclyde Dr. G73: Ruth 6C **108**
Strathclyde Gdns. G72: Flem 4E **127**
Strathclyde Loch Water Sports Cen. **3C 146**
Strathclyde Pk. Golf Course **4A 146**
Strathclyde Path G71: Udd 1C **128**
Strathclyde Rd. G82: Dumb 2G **19**
Strathclyde Rd. ML1: Moth 3D **146**
Strathclyde St. G40: Glas 3C **108**
Strathclyde Vw. G71: Both 6F **129**
Strathclyde Way ML4: Bell 6E **115**
Strathcona Dr. G13: Glas 2F **63**
Strathcona Gdns. G13: Glas 2G **63**
Strathcona La. G75: E Kil 4G **157**
Strathcona Pl. G73: Ruth 3F **125**
Strathcona Pl. G75: E Kil 4G **157**
Strathcona St. G13: Glas 3F **63**
Strathconon Gdns. G75: E Kil 2A **156**
(off Strathnairn Dr.)
Strath Dearn ML8: Law 6E **167**
Strathdearn Gro. G75: E Kil 3A **156**
Strathdee Av. G81: Hard 2D **44**
Strathdee Rd. G44: Neth 5C **122**
Strathdon Av. G44: Neth 5C **122**
Strathdon Av. PA2: Pais 3G **101**
Strathdon Dr. G44: Neth 5D **122**
Strathdon Pl. G75: E Kil 3A **156**
(off Strathnairn Dr.)
Strathearn Dr. ML6: Plain 6F **75**
Strathearn Gro. G66: Kirkin 4H **33**
Strathearn Rd. G76: Clar 3C **138**
Strath Elgin ML8: Law 6D **166**
Strathendrick Dr. G44: Glas 3C **122**
Strathfillan Rd. G74: E Kil 1F **157**
Strathgoil Cres. ML6: Air 6A **74**
Strathgryffe Cres. PA11: Bri W 2E **77**
Strath Halladale ML8: Law 6E **167**
Strathhalladale Ct. G75: E Kil 3A **156**
(off Strathmore Gro.)
Strathisla Way ML1: Carf 5B **132**
Strathkelvin Av. G64: B'rig 2B **66**
Strathkelvin La. G75: E Kil 3A **156**
Strathkelvin Pl. G66: Kirkin 6C **32**
Strathkelvin Retail Pk. 2E **51**
Strathlachlan Av. ML8: Carl 4E **175**
Strathleven Pl. G82: Dumb 4F **19**
Strathmiglo Ct. G75: E Kil 3A **156**
(off Strathspey Av.)
Strathmore Av. G72: Blan 6A **128**
Strathmore Av. PA1: Pais 1F **103**
Strathmore Cres. ML6: Air 1A **96**
Strathmore Gdns. G73: Ruth 3F **125**
Strathmore Gro. G75: E Kil 3A **156**
Strathmore Ho. G74: E Kil 2G **157**
(off Cornwall St.)
Strathmore Pl. ML5: Coat 6F **95**
Strathmore Rd. G22: Glas 2F **65**
Strathmore Rd. ML3: Ham 6A **146**
Strathmore Wlk. ML5: Coat 6F **95**
Strathmungo Cres. ML6: Air 1H **95**
Strath Nairn ML8: Law 6E **167**
Strathnairn Av. G75: E Kil 3A **156**
Strathnairn Ct. G75: E Kil 3A **156**
Strathnairn Dr. G75: E Kil 3A **156**
Strathnairn Way G75: E Kil 3A **156**
Strath Naver ML8: Law 6E **167**
Strathnaver Cres. ML6: Air 6A **74**
Strathnaver Gdns. G75: E Kil 3A **156**
Strathord Pl. G69: Mood 3E **55**
Strathord St. G32: Glas 2A **110**
Strath Peffer ML8: Law 6D **166**
Strathpeffer Cres. ML6: Air 1A **96**
Strathpeffer Dr. G75: E Kil 3A **156**
(off Strathnairn Dr.)
Strathrannoch Way G75: E Kil 3A **156**
Strathspey Av. G75: E Kil 3A **156**
Strathspey Cres. ML6: Air 6A **74**
Strathtay Av. G44: Neth 5C **122**
Strathtay Av. G75: E Kil 3A **156**
Strathtummel Cres. ML6: Air 6A **74**
Strathview Gro. G44: Neth 5C **122**
Strathview Pk. G44: Neth 5C **122**
Strathview Rd. ML4: Bell 4A **130**
Strathvithie Gro. G75: E Kil 3A **156**
Strathwhillan Ct. G75: E Kil 3B **156**
Strathwhillan Dr. G75: E Kil 3B **156**
Strathy Pl. G20: Glas 3B **64**
Strathyre Ct. G75: E Kil 3A **156**
Strathyre Gdns. G61: Bear 2H **47**
Strathyre Gdns. G69: Mood 4E **55**
Strathyre Gdns. G75: E Kil 3A **156**
Strathyre Gdns. ML6: Glenm 4H **73**
Strathyre Rd. G72: Blan 3D **144**
Strathyre St. G41: Glas 5C **106**
Stratton Dr. G46: Giff 5H **121**
Strauss Av. G81: Clyd 6G **45**
Stravaig Path PA2: Pais 6E **101**
Stravaig Wlk. PA2: Pais 6E **101**
Stravanan Av. G45: Glas 5H **123**
Stravanan Ct. G45: Glas 5A **124**
Stravanan Gdns. G45: Glas 5H **123**
Stravanan Pl. G45: Glas 5H **123**
Stravanan Rd. G45: Glas 6H **123**
Stravanan St. G45: Glas 5H **123**
Stravanan Ter. G45: Glas 5H **123**
Stravenhouse Rd. ML8: Law 1E **173**
Strawberry Fld. Rd. PA6: C'lee 2B **78**
Strawhill Ct. G76: Busby 2D **138**
Strawhill Rd. G76: Clar 2C **138**
Streamfield Gdns. G33: Glas 2G **67**
Streamfield Ga. G33: Glas 2F **67**
Streamfield Lea G33: Glas 1G **67**
Streamfield Pl. G33: Glas 2G **67**
Strenabey Av. G73: Ruth 3F **125**
Striven Ct. ML5: Coat 2D **114**
Striven Cres. ML2: Wis 2G **165**
Striven Gdns. G20: Glas 6D **64**
Striven Ter. ML3: Ham 2E **161**
Stroma St. G21: Glas 1D **88**
Stromness St. G5: Glas 1E **107**
Strone Gdns. G65: Kils 3F **13**
Stronend St. G22: Glas 4F **65**
Strone Path ML5: Glenb 3G **71**
Strone Pl. ML6: Air 6C **96**
(off Minch Way)
Strone Rd. G33: Glas 4B **90**
Stronsay Pl. G64: B'rig 5F **51**
Stronsay St. G21: Glas 1D **88**
Stronvar Dr. G14: Glas 5B **62**
Stronvar La. G14: Glas 5B **62**
Stroud Rd. G75: E Kil 6E **157**
Strowan Cres. G32: Glas 1B **110**
Strowan's Rd. G82: Dumb 2C **20**
Strowan St. G32: Glas 1B **110**
Strowan's Well Rd. G82: Dumb 2C **20**
Struan Av. G46: Giff 4A **122**
Struan Gdns. G44: Glas 2E **123**
Struan Rd. G44: Glas 2E **123**
Struie St. G34: Glas 3G **91**
Struma Dr. G76: Clar 1A **138**
Struther & Swinhill Rd. ML9: Lark 6E **171**
Strutherhill ML9: Lark 4D **170**
STRUTHERHILL 5D **170**
Strutherhill Ind. Est. ML9: Lark 5E **171**
Struthers Cres. G74: E Kil 5B **142**
Struther St. ML9: Lark 5D **170**
Stuart Av. G60: Old K 2F **43**
Stuart Av. G73: Ruth 2D **124**
Stuart Dr. G64: B'rig 1A **66**
Stuart Dr. ML9: Lark 4E **171**
Stuart Ho. G67: Cumb 2B **38**
Stuarton Pk. G74: E Kil 1G **157**
Stuart Quad. ML2: Wis 2E **165**
Stuart Rd. G76: Crmck 1H **139**
Stuart Rd. G82: Dumb 1C **20**
Stuart Rd. PA7: B'ton 3H **41**
Stuart St. G60: Old K 2F **43**
Stuart St. G74: E Kil 1H **157**
Stuartville ML5: Coat 4D **94**
Studio Dr. G82: Dumb 2G **19**
STV Studios **6D 4 (5C 86)**
Succoth St. G13: Glas 2F **63**
Sudbury Cres. G75: E Kil 2D **156**
Suffolk St. G40: Glas 5H **87**
Sugworth Av. G69: Bail 6H **91**
Suisnish PA8: Ersk 2G **59**
Sumburgh St. G33: Glas 4H **89**
Summerfield Cotts. G14: Glas 1E **85**
Summerfield Rd. G40: Glas 2D **108**
Summerfield Rd. G67: Cumb 1C **56**
Summerfield St. G40: Glas 2D **108**
Summerhill & Garngibbock Rd. G67: Cumb 5E **57**
Summerhill Av. ML9: Lark 3C **170**
Summerhill Dr. G15: Glas 3B **46**
Summerhill Gdns. G15: Glas 3B **46**
Summerhill Pl. G15: Glas 3B **46**
Summerhill Rd. G15: Glas 3A **46**
Summerhill Rd. G76: Busby 2D **138**
Summerhill Way ML4: Bell 3B **130**
Summerlea Rd. G46: T'bnk 3F **121**
SUMMERLEE 3B **94**
Summerlee Cotts. ML5: Coat 4B **94**
Summerlee Mus. of Scottish Industrial Life **3B 94**
Summerlee Raceway Larkhall **5A 164**
Summerlee Rd. ML2: Wis 5C **148**
Summerlee Rd. ML9: Lark 6H **163**
Summerlee St. G33: Glas 3C **90**
Summerlee St. ML5: Coat 4B **94**
SUMMERSTON 6B **48**
Summerston Station (Rail) **1B 64**
Summer St. G40: Glas 6B **88**
Summertown Path G51: Glas 4H **85**
Summertown Rd. G51: Glas 4H **85**
Sunart Av. PA4: Renf 5D **60**
Sunart Ct. ML3: Ham 2E **161**
Sunart Gdns. G64: B'rig 6E **51**
Sunart Rd. G52: Glas 6E **85**
Sunart Rd. G64: B'rig 6E **51**
Sunart St. ML2: Wis 2G **165**
Sunbury Av. G76: Clar 2A **138**
Sundale Av. G76: Clar 3B **138**

Sunderland Av. G82: Dumb	3C **18**
Sundrum Ct. ML6: Air	5H **95**
Sunflower Gdns. ML1: Moth	1F **147**
Sunlight Cotts. G11: Glas	1B **4** (1B **86**)
Sunningdale Av. G77: Newt M	4F **137**
Sunningdale Dr. PA11: Bri W	5E **77**
Sunningdale Rd. G23: Glas	1B **64**
Sunningdale Wynd G71: Both	4C **128**
Sunnybank Dr. G76: Clar	3B **138**
Sunnybank Gro. G76: Clar	3B **138**
Sunnyhill G65: Twe	2D **34**
Sunnylaw Dr. PA2: Pais	3F **101**
Sunnylaw Pl. G22: Glas	4F **65**
Sunnylaw St. G22: Glas	5F **65**
SUNNYSIDE	3C **94**
Sunnyside Av. G71: Udd	2D **128**
Sunnyside Av. ML1: Holy	2B **132**
Sunnyside Cres. ML1: Holy	2A **132**
Sunnyside Dr. G15: Glas	6A **46**
Sunnyside Dr. G69: Barg	6D **92**
Sunnyside Dr. G76: Clar	1B **138**
Sunnyside Ga. ML1: Holy	2A **132**
Sunnyside Oval PA2: Pais	4A **102**
Sunnyside Pl. G15: Glas	6A **46**
Sunnyside Pl. G78: Barr	5D **118**
Sunnyside Pl. ML1: Holy	2A **132**
Sunnyside Rd. ML1: Cle	1H **149**
Sunnyside Rd. ML5: Coat	4C **94**
Sunnyside Rd. PA2: Pais	4H **101**
Sunnyside St. ML9: Lark	1B **170**
Sunnyside Ter. ML1: Holy	2A **132**
Suntroy Gro. G75: T'hall	3G **155**
Suntroy La. G75: T'hall	3G **155**
SUREHAVEN GLASGOW	5B **46**
Surrey La. G5: Glas	1F **107**
Surrey St. G5: Glas	1F **107**
Sussex St. G41: Glas	6C **86**
Sutcliffe Ct. G13: Glas	2E **63**
Sutcliffe Rd. G13: Glas	2E **63**
Sutherland Av. G41: Glas	2H **105**
Sutherland Av. G61: Bear	6E **27**
Sutherland Ct. G41: Glas	1C **106**
Sutherland Cres. ML3: Ham	5E **145**
Sutherland Dr. G46: Giff	6B **122**
Sutherland Dr. G82: Dumb	2C **20**
Sutherland Dr. ML6: Air	6G **95**
Sutherland La. G12: Glas	1B **86**
Sutherland Pl. ML4: Bell	5B **130**
Sutherland Rd. G81: Clyd	5D **44**
Sutherland St. G72: Blan	4A **144**
Sutherland St. PA1: Pais	6H **81**
Sutherland Way G74: E Kil	6C **142**
Sutherness Dr. G33: Glas	4A **90**
Swaledale G74: E Kil	6E **141**
Swallow Dr. PA5: John	6C **98**
Swallow Gdns. G13: Glas	2H **61**
Swallow Rd. G81: Faif	6F **25**
(not continuous)
Swallow Rd. ML2: Wis	5H **149**
Swan Pl. PA5: John	6C **98**
Swanston St. G40: Glas	3C **108**
Swan St. G4: Glas	1E **7** (2G **87**)
Swan St. G81: Clyd	4B **44**
Swan Way ML8: Law	1F **173**
Sween Av. G44: Glas	3E **123**
Sween Dr. ML3: Ham	2E **161**
Sween Path ML4: Bell	4E **131**
(off Millbank Av.)
Sweethill Ter. ML5: Coat	2F **115**
Sweethill Wlk. ML4: Bell	6E **115**
Sweethope Gdns. G71: Both	5F **129**
Sweethope Pl. G71: Both	4E **129**
Sweet Thorn Dr. G75: E Kil	1B **168**
Swift Bank ML3: Ham	2C **160**
Swift Cl. ML2: Wis	6H **149**
Swift Cres. G13: Glas	1H **61**
Swift Pl. G75: E Kil	5A **156**
Swift Pl. PA5: John	6D **98**
Swinburne Av. G72: Blan	2H **143**

Swindon St. G81: Clyd	4A **44**
SWINHILL	6E **171**
Swinstie Rd. ML1: Cle	1A **150**
SWINTON	5G **91**
Swinton Av. G69: Bail	6A **92**
Swinton Cres. G69: Bail	6A **92**
Swinton Cres. ML5: Coat	1F **113**
Swinton Dr. G52: Glas	6B **84**
Swinton Gdns. G69: Bail	6B **92**
Swinton Path G69: Bail	6B **92**
Swinton Pl. G52: Glas	6B **84**
Swinton Pl. ML5: Coat	1F **113**
(off Swinton Cres.)
Swinton Rd. G69: Bail	6A **92**
Swinton Vw. G69: Bail	6B **92**
Swisscot Av. ML3: Ham	3F **161**
Swisscot Wlk. ML3: Ham	3F **161**
Switchback Rd. G61: Bear	5F **47**
Swordale Path G34: Glas	3G **91**
(off Kildermorie Rd.)
Swordale Pl. G34: Glas	3G **91**
Sword St. G31: Glas	5B **88**
(not continuous)
Sword St. ML6: Air	4H **95**
Sycamore Av. G66: Lenz	2D **52**
Sycamore Av. G71: View	6G **113**
Sycamore Av. PA5: John	4G **99**
Sycamore Ct. G75: E Kil	5F **157**
Sycamore Cres. G75: E Kil	5E **157**
Sycamore Cres. ML6: Air	5D **96**
Sycamore Dr. G81: Clyd	3C **44**
Sycamore Dr. ML3: Ham	1B **162**
Sycamore Dr. ML6: Air	5D **96**
Sycamore Gro. G72: Blan	1A **144**
Sycamore Pl. G75: E Kil	5F **157**
Sycamore Pl. ML1: N'hill	4C **132**
Sycamore Way G66: Milt C	6C **10**
Sycamore Way G72: Flem	3F **127**
Sycamore Way G76: Crmck	2H **139**
Sydenham Ct. G12: Glas	5H **63**
(off Kingsborough Gdns.)
Sydenham La. G12: Glas	6A **64**
Sydenham Rd. G12: Glas	6A **64**
Sydes Brae G72: Blan	5H **143**
Sydney Cres. G40: Glas	3D **108**
Sydney Dr. G75: E Kil	4E **157**
Sydney Pl. G75: E Kil	3E **157**
Sydney St. G31: Glas	5A **88**
(not continuous)
Sydney St. G81: Clyd	3H **43**
Sykehead Av. ML4: Bell	2D **130**
Sykeside Rd. ML6: Air	1G **115**
Sykes Ter. G78: Neil	2F **135**
Sylvania Way G81: Clyd	5D **44**
Sylvania Way Sth. G81: Clyd	6D **44**
Symington Dr. G81: Clyd	5C **44**
Symington Sq. G75: E Kil	3H **157**
Syriam Gdns. G21: Glas	4B **66**
Syriam Pl. G21: Glas	5B **66**
Syriam St. G21: Glas	4B **66**

T

Tabard Pl. G13: Glas	1C **62**
Tabard Rd. G13: Glas	1C **62**
Tabernacle La. G72: Camb	2A **126**
Tabernacle St. G72: Camb	2A **126**
Taggart Rd. G65: Croy	2B **36**
Taig Gdns. G66: Kirkin	6H **33**
Taig Rd. G66: Kirkin	6H **33**
Tain Av. PA7: B'ton	5F **41**
Tain Ter. G72: Blan	6A **144**
Tait Av. G78: Barr	3F **119**
Tait Circ. PA2: Pais	3E **103**
Talbot G74: E Kil	5C **142**
Talbot Ct. G13: Glas	4B **62**
Talbot Cres. ML5: Coat	1A **114**
Talbot Dr. G13: Glas	4B **62**
Talbot Pl. G13: Glas	4B **62**

Talbot Ter. G13: Glas	4B **62**
Talbot Ter. G71: Tann	5C **112**
Talisker Cres. ML6: Air	6B **74**
Talisman G81: Clyd	6F **45**
Talisman Av. G82: Dumb	3C **18**
Talisman Rd. ML1: Moth	5F **131**
Talisman Rd. G13: Glas	3C **62**
Talisman Rd. PA2: Pais	6C **100**
Tallant Rd. G15: Glas	4B **46**
Tallant Ter. G15: Glas	4C **46**
Talla Rd. G52: Glas	5A **84**
Tall Ship at Riverside, The	3H **85**
Tamarack Cres. G71: View	4G **113**
Tamar Dr. G75: E Kil	5B **156**
Tambowie G62: Miln	1B **26**
Tambowie Av. G62: Miln	3F **27**
Tambowie Cres. G62: Miln	3F **27**
Tambowie St. G13: Glas	1E **63**
Tamrawer Row G65: Kils	2B **14**
Tamshill St. G20: Glas	3D **64**
Tanar Av. PA4: Renf	2G **83**
Tanar Way PA4: Renf	1G **83**
TANDLEHILL	3C **98**
Tandlehill Rd. PA10: Kilba	4A **98**
Tanera Av. G44: Glas	2G **123**
Tanfield Pl. G32: Glas	4C **90**
Tanfield St. G32: Glas	4C **90**
Tankerland Rd. G44: Glas	1E **123**
Tannadice Av. G52: Glas	2C **104**
Tannadice Path G52: Glas	1C **104**
(off Tannadice Av.)
Tanna Dr. G52: Glas	2F **105**
Tannahill Cen.	5E **81**
Tannahill Cres. PA5: John	4E **99**
Tannahill Dr. G74: E Kil	6C **142**
Tannahill Rd. G43: Glas	1D **122**
Tannahill Rd. PA3: Pais	5F **81**
Tannahill's Cottage	1G **101**
Tannahill Ter. PA3: Pais	5F **81**
Tannin Cres. G75: E Kil	1A **168**
Tannoch Dr. G62: Miln	2G **27**
Tannoch Dr. G67: Cumb	6H **37**
Tannoch Pl. G67: Cumb	6H **37**
TANNOCHSIDE	4F **113**
Tannochside Dr. G71: Tann	4E **113**
Tannochside Pk. G71: Tann	4F **113**
Tannock St. G22: Glas	5F **65**
Tantallon Ct. ML8: Carl	2C **174**
Tantallon Dr. ML5: Coat	2G **93**
Tantallon Dr. PA2: Pais	4E **101**
Tantallon Pk. G74: E Kil	1F **157**
Tantallon Rd. G41: Glas	5C **106**
Tantallon Rd. G69: Bail	2G **111**
Tantallon Rd. G71: Both	4F **129**
Tanzieknowe Av. G72: Camb	4B **126**
Tanzieknowe Dr. G72: Camb	4B **126**
Tanzieknowe Pl. G72: Camb	4A **126**
Tanzieknowe Rd. G72: Camb	4A **126**
Taransay St. G51: Glas	3G **85**
Tarbert Av. G72: Blan	5A **128**
Tarbert Av. ML2: Wis	2G **165**
Tarbert Ct. ML3: Ham	2E **161**
Tarbert Pl. ML8: Carl	4E **175**
Tarbert Way ML5: Coat	1A **114**
Tarbolton G74: E Kil	6D **142**
Tarbolton Cres. ML6: Chap	4D **116**
Tarbolton Dr. G81: Clyd	4E **45**
Tarbolton Path ML9: Lark	2B **170**
Tarbolton Rd. G43: Glas	1B **122**
Tarbolton Rd. G67: Cumb	3B **38**
Tarbolton Sq. G81: Clyd	4E **45**
Tarbrax Way ML3: Ham	6E **145**
Tarff Av. G76: Eag	6C **154**
Tarfside Av. G52: Glas	1C **104**
Tarfside Gdns. G52: Glas	1D **104**
Tarfside Oval G52: Glas	1D **104**
Target Cres. G53: Glas	5C **120**
Target Rd. ML6: Air	5B **96**
Tarland St. G51: Glas	5F **85**

Tarn Gro. G33: Glas	1G 67
Tarquin Pl. ML1: Moth	1E 147
Tarras Dr. PA4: Renf	2G 83
Tarras Pl. G72: Camb	2D 126
Tasman Dr. G75: E Kil	4D 156
Tasmania Quad. ML2: Wis	6C 150
Tassie Pl. G74: E Kil	1A 158
Tassie St. G41: Glas	5B 106
Tattershall Rd. G33: Glas	1C 90
Tavistock Dr. G43: Glas	2B 122
Tay Av. PA4: Renf	6G 61
Tay Ct. G75: E Kil	4A 156
Taycourt G69: Mood	5D 54
(off Heathfield Av.)	
Tay Cres. G33: Glas	2G 89
Tay Cres. G64: B'rig	6D 50
Tay Gdns. ML3: Ham	3F 161
Tay Gro. G75: E Kil	4A 156
Tayinloan Dr. ML8: Carl	5F 175
Tay La. ML2: Newm	4E 151
Tay Loan ML1: Holy	2A 132
(off Windsor Rd.)	
Taylor Av. ML1: Carf	5D 132
Taylor Av. PA10: Kilba	2A 98
Taylor Bowls Vis. Cen.	1D 108
Taylor Pl. G4: Glas	3G 7 (3H 87)
Taylor St. G4: Glas	4G 7 (3H 87)
Taylor St. G81: Clyd	1E 61
Taymouth St. G32: Glas	2B 110
Taynish Dr. G44: Glas	3F 123
Tay Pl. G75: E Kil	4A 156
Tay Pl. G82: Dumb	1H 19
Tay Pl. ML9: Lark	5C 170
Tay Pl. PA5: John	5C 98
Tay Rd. G61: Bear	5D 46
Tay Rd. G64: B'rig	6D 50
Tayside ML6: Air	2H 95
Tay St. ML5: Coat	2G 93
Tay Ter. G75: E Kil	3A 156
Tay Wlk. G67: Cumb	4H 37
(within The Cumbernauld Shop. Cen.)	
Teacher Ct. G13: Glas	4D 62
Teacher St. ML3: Ham	1E 161
Teak Pl. G71: View	4H 113
Teal Ct. ML4: Bell	5A 114
Teal Cres. G75: E Kil	6B 156
Teal Dr. G13: Glas	2A 62
Tealing Av. G52: Glas	1C 104
Tealing Cres. G52: Glas	1C 104
Teasel Av. G53: Glas	4B 120
Teawell Rd. G77: Newt M	4D 136
Technology Av. G72: Blan	5A 144
Teesdale G74: E Kil	6E 141
Teign Gro. G75: E Kil	5B 156
Teith Av. PA4: Renf	1H 83
Teith Dr. G61: Bear	4D 46
Teith Pl. G72: Camb	2D 126
Teith St. G33: Glas	2G 89
Telephone La. G12: Glas	1A 86
(off Highburgh Rd.)	
Telfer Ct. ML9: Lark	2A 172
Telford Av. ML9: Lark	5E 171
Telford Ct. G81: Clyd	5C 44
Telford Pl. G67: Cumb	5A 38
Telford Rd. G67: Cumb	5A 38
Telford Rd. G75: E Kil	3F 157
Telford St. ML4: Bell	1C 130
Telford Ter. G75: E Kil	3H 157
(off Telford Rd.)	
Teme Pl. G75: E Kil	4B 156
Templar Av. G13: Glas	6D 46
TEMPLE	2F 63
Temple Cotts. G67: Cumb	6D 36
(off Dalshannon Rd.)	
Temple Ct. ML8: Law	5E 167
Temple Gdns. G13: Glas	2F 63
Templegill Cres. ML2: Wis	5H 149
Templeland Rd. G53: Glas	3C 104
Temple Locks Ct. G13: Glas	2G 63

Temple Locks Pl. G13: Glas	2F 63
Temple Rd. G13: Glas	2G 63
Templeton Bus. Cen. G40: Glas	6A 88
Templeton Ct. G40: Glas	6A 88
Templeton St. G40: Glas	6A 88
Tenement House	2H 5 (2E 87)
(Glasgow)	
Tennant Av. G74: E Kil	1C 156
Tennant Complex, The G74: E Kil	1C 156
Tennant St. PA4: Renf	5F 61
Tennant Wynd ML4: Bell	5C 114
Tennent St. ML5: Coat	6D 94
Tennyson Dr. G31: Glas	1G 109
Tennyson Gdns. G72: Blan	2A 144
Tenters Way PA2: Pais	2F 101
Tern Pl. PA5: John	6D 98
Tern Way ML5: Coat	2G 115
Terregles Av. G41: Glas	3H 105
Terregles Cres. G41: Glas	3A 106
Terregles Dr. G41: Glas	3A 106
Tesla Pl. ML1: Moth	5G 147
Teviot Av. G64: B'rig	4C 50
Teviot Av. PA2: Pais	5C 100
Teviot Cres. G61: Bear	5D 46
Teviotdale G74: E Kil	1F 157
(off Cadzow Grn.)	
Teviotdale G77: Newt M	4H 137
Teviot Dr. PA7: B'ton	5A 42
Teviot Pl. G72: Camb	2E 127
Teviot Sq. G67: Cumb	3H 37
(within The Cumbernauld Shop. Cen.)	
Teviot St. G3: Glas	3A 4 (3A 86)
Teviot St. ML5: Coat	1H 93
Teviot Ter. PA5: John	5C 98
Teviot Wlk. G67: Cumb	3H 37
(within The Cumbernauld Shop. Cen.)	
Teviot Way G72: Blan	2A 144
Tewkesbury Rd. G74: E Kil	4D 142
Thane Rd. G13: Glas	3C 62
Thanes Ga. G71: Both	2C 128
Thankerton Av. ML1: Holy	2H 131
Thankerton Rd. ML9: Lark	4D 170
Tharsis St. G21: Glas	2B 88
Theatre Royal	3C 6 (3F 87)
(Glasgow)	
Thetford Gro. ML5: Glenb	3B 72
Third Av. G33: Mille	4B 68
Third Av. G44: Glas	6F 107
Third Av. G66: A'loch	5D 52
Third Av. G82: Dumb	3C 20
Third Av. PA4: Renf	1E 83
Third Av. La. G44: Glas	6F 107
Third Gdns. G41: Glas	1G 105
Third Part Cres. G13: Glas	2G 61
Third Rd. G72: Blan	4C 144
Third St. G71: Tann	5D 112
Thirlmere G75: E Kil	6B 156
Thistle Av. G77: Newt M	2C 136
Thistle Bank G66: Lenz	3D 52
Thistlebank PA11: Bri W	2E 77
Thistlebank Gdns. ML5: Coat	2A 114
Thistle Cres. ML9: Lark	3D 170
Thistledown Dr. G72: Newt	6F 111
(not continuous)	
Thistledown Gro. ML5: Coat	5E 95
Thistle Gdns. ML1: Holy	2A 132
Thistleneuk G60: Old K	6E 23
Thistle Pl. G74: E Kil	6G 141
Thistle Quad. ML6: Air	2B 96
Thistle Rd. ML1: New S	3A 132
Thistle St. G5: Glas	6G 87
Thistle St. G66: Kirkin	5D 32
Thistle St. ML1: Cle	6H 133
Thistle St. ML6: Air	2B 96
Thistle St. PA2: Pais	3G 101
Thistle Ter. G5: Glas	1G 107
Thomas Campbell Ct. G4: Glas	5G 7 (4H 87)
(off Rottenrow East)	
Thomas Muir Av. G64: B'rig	1C 66

Thomas Muir Mus.	6C 50
Thomas St. PA1: Pais	1F 101
Thomas Tunnock Gro. G71: Udd	2E 129
Thompson Brae PA1: Pais	2A 102
Thompson Pl. G81: Hard	1E 45
Thomson Av. G66: Kirkin	5E 33
Thomson Av. ML2: Wis	2D 164
Thomson Av. PA5: John	2E 99
Thomson Ct. G73: Ruth	6B 108
Thomson Dr. G61: Bear	1F 47
Thomson Dr. ML1: Moth	4F 147
Thomson Dr. ML4: Bell	2H 129
Thomson Dr. ML6: Air	5H 95
Thomson Gro. G72: Camb	6A 110
Thomson St. G31: Glas	5C 88
Thomson St. ML8: Carl	3D 174
Thomson St. PA4: Renf	1E 83
Thomson St. PA5: John	3E 99
Thorn Av. G72: Blan	6B 144
Thorn Av. G74: T'hall	6G 139
Thornbank St. G3: Glas	3A 4 (3A 86)
Thorn Brae PA5: John	2G 99
Thornbridge Av. G12: Glas	4A 64
Thornbridge Av. G69: Bail	6H 91
Thornbridge Gdns. G69: Bail	6G 91
Thornbridge Rd. G69: Bail	6G 91
Thorncliffe Gdns. G41: Glas	3C 106
Thorncliffe La. G41: Glas	3C 106
(off Vennard Gdns.)	
Thorn Ct. PA5: John	3H 99
Thorncroft Dr. G44: Glas	3H 123
Thorndale Gdns. FK4: Alla	1H 17
Thorndean Av. ML4: Bell	3D 130
Thorndean Cres. ML4: Bell	3D 130
Thorndene PA5: Eld	2H 99
Thorndene Av. ML1: Carf	5C 132
Thornden La. G14: Glas	5A 62
Thorn Dr. G61: Bear	1D 46
Thorn Dr. G73: Ruth	3E 125
Thorndyke G74: E Kil	4C 142
Thorn Hgts. G61: Bear	3C 46
Thornhill Av. G72: Blan	1B 144
Thornhill Av. PA5: Eld	3H 99
Thornhill Dr. PA5: Eld	3H 99
Thornhill Gdns. G77: Newt M	1D 152
Thornhill Gdns. PA5: John	2G 99
Thornhill La. G71: Both	4F 129
Thornhill Path G31: Glas	6F 89
Thornhill Rd. ML3: Ham	5C 144
Thornhill Way ML5: Coat	2F 115
Thorniecroft Dr. G67: Cumb	1E 57
Thorniecroft Pl. G67: Cumb	1E 57
Thornielee G74: E Kil	1B 158
Thorniewood Gdns. G71: Tann	6E 113
Thorniewood Rd. G71: Tann	5D 112
Thornkip Pl. ML5: Coat	6F 95
Thornlea Dr. G46: Giff	3B 122
Thornlea Gdns. ML6: Air	2A 96
Thornlea St. ML8: Carl	5E 175
Thornley Av. G13: Glas	3B 62
THORNLIEBANK	4F 121
Thornliebank Ind. Est. G46: T'bnk	4E 121
Thornliebank Rd. G43: Glas	1H 121
Thornliebank Rd. G46: T'bnk	3G 121
Thornliebank Station (Rail)	3G 121
Thornlie Gill ML2: Wis	1H 165
THORNLY PK.	5B 102
Thornly Pk. Av. PA2: Pais	5B 102
Thornly Pk. Dr. PA2: Pais	5B 102
Thornly Pk. Gdns. PA2: Pais	4B 102
Thornly Pk. Rd. PA2: Pais	4A 102
Thorn Pk. G72: Blan	6B 144
Thorn Rd. G61: Bear	2C 46
Thorn Rd. ML4: Bell	2D 130
Thornside Rd. PA5: John	2G 99
THORNTONHALL	6G 139
Thorntonhall Station (Rail)	6F 139
Thornton La. G20: Glas	2C 64

Thornton Pl. ML3: Ham	5H **161**	
Thornton Rd. G74: E Kil	6G **139**	
Thornton Rd. G74: T'hall	6G **139**	
Thornton St. G20: Glas	2B **64**	
Thornton St. ML5: Coat	1H **93**	
Thorntree Av. ML3: Ham	4D **144**	
Thorntree Dr. ML5: Coat	6A **94**	
Thorntree Way G71: Both	4F **129**	
Thornwood Av. G11: Glas	1G **85**	
Thornwood Av. G66: Lenz	2A **52**	
Thornwood Cres. G11: Glas	6F **63**	
Thornwood Dr. G11: Glas	1F **85**	
(not continuous)		
Thornwood Dr. PA11: Bri W	4D **76**	
Thornwood Dr. PA2: Pais	3F **101**	
Thornwood Gdns. G11: Glas	1F **85**	
Thornwood Pl. G11: Glas	6F **63**	
(not continuous)		
Thornwood Quad. G11: Glas	6F **63**	
Thornwood Rd. G11: Glas	1F **85**	
Thornwood Ter. G11: Glas	1F **85**	
Thornyburn Dr. G69: Bail	1B **112**	
Thornyburn Pl. G69: Bail	1A **112**	
Thorny Pk. Ct. PA2: Pais	5A **102**	
Thornyview Dr. G71: Bail	2B **112**	
THRASHBUSH	**1A 96**	
Thrashbush Av. ML2: Wis	5B **150**	
Thrashbush Cres. ML2: Wis	5B **150**	
Thrashbush La. ML6: Air	1B **96**	
Thrashbush Quad. ML6: Air	1A **96**	
Thrashbush Rd. ML2: Wis	6B **150**	
Thrashbush Rd. ML6: Air	1A **96**	
Thread Mill Mus.	**1C 102**	
(Paisley)		
Thread St. PA1: Pais	2B **102**	
Threave Ct. ML8: Carl	2C **174**	
Threave Pl. G69: G'csh	5C **70**	
Threave Pl. G77: Newt M	4B **136**	
Three Queens Sq. G81: Clyd	6D **44**	
Three Rivers Wlk. G75: E Kil	3D **156**	
Threestonehill Av. G32: Glas	5B **90**	
Threshold G74: E Kil	1A **158**	
Threshold Pk. G74: E Kil	1A **158**	
Thriplee Rd. PA11: Bri W	3E **77**	
Thrums G74: E Kil	4D **142**	
Thrums Av. G64: B'rig	6E **51**	
Thrums Gdns. G64: B'rig	6E **51**	
Thrushcraig Cres. PA2: Pais	3B **102**	
Thrush Pl. PA5: John	6D **98**	
Thurso Cres. PA7: B'ton	5F **41**	
Thurso St. G11: Glas	1A **4** (2A **86**)	
Thurston Rd. G52: Glas	6A **84**	
Thyme Sq. ML1: Moth	1G **147**	
Tianavaig PA8: Ersk	2G **59**	
Tibbermore Rd. G11: Glas	6G **63**	
Tiber Av. ML1: Moth	6E **131**	
Tighnasheen Way G72: Blan	1B **144**	
Tillanburn Rd. ML1: N'hill	4F **133**	
Tillet Oval PA3: Pais	4H **81**	
Tillie St. G20: Glas	6D **64**	
Till St. ML2: Wis	3H **149**	
Tillycairn Av. G33: Glas	1D **90**	
Tillycairn Dr. G33: Glas	1D **90**	
Tillycairn Pl. G33: Glas	1E **91**	
Tillycairn Rd. G33: Glas	1D **90**	
Tillycairn St. G33: Glas	1E **91**	
Tilt Rd. ML2: Newm	3D **150**	
Tilt St. G33: Glas	1G **89**	
Time Capsule	**5B 94**	
(Coatbridge)		
Timmons Gro. ML4: Moss	2F **131**	
Timmons Ter. ML6: Chap	4D **116**	
Tinker's La. ML1: Moth	3E **147**	
Tintagel Gdns. G69: Mood	4D **54**	
TINTOCK	**3A 34**	
Tintock Dr. G66: Kirkin	4F **33**	
Tintock Pl. G68: Dull	5F **15**	
Tintock Rd. G66: Kirkin	3H **33**	
Tinto Ct. ML5: Coat	2E **115**	

Tinto Cres. ML2: Wis	1A **166**	
Tinto Dr. G68: Cumb	3F **37**	
Tinto Dr. G78: Barr	6D **118**	
Tinto Gro. G69: Barg	5F **93**	
Tinto Rd. G43: Glas	2A **122**	
Tinto Rd. G61: Bear	1B **46**	
Tinto Rd. G64: B'rig	6F **51**	
Tinto Rd. ML6: Air	5B **96**	
Tinto Sq. PA4: Renf	2D **82**	
Tinto St. ML2: Wis	1A **166**	
Tinto Vw. ML3: Ham	3A **162**	
Tinto Vw. Rd. ML9: Shaw	6F **171**	
Tinto Way G75: E Kil	6D **156**	
Tinto Way ML1: Cle	5H **133**	
Tinwald Path G52: Glas	6A **84**	
Tiree G74: E Kil	4C **158**	
Tiree Av. PA2: Pais	6H **101**	
Tiree Av. PA4: Renf	3E **83**	
Tiree Ct. G67: Cumb	5F **37**	
Tiree Cres. ML2: Newm	2D **150**	
Tiree Dr. G67: Cumb	5F **37**	
Tiree Gdns. G60: Old K	1G **43**	
Tiree Gdns. G61: Bear	1B **46**	
Tiree Gdns. ML6: Glenm	4H **73**	
Tiree Grange ML3: Ham	2D **160**	
Tiree Pl. G60: Old K	1G **43**	
Tiree Pl. G77: Newt M	4B **136**	
Tiree Pl. ML5: Coat	1H **113**	
Tiree Rd. G67: Cumb	5F **37**	
Tiree St. G21: Glas	1E **89**	
Tiree Way G72: Camb	4H **125**	
Tirry Av. PA4: Renf	1H **83**	
Tirry Way PA4: Renf	1H **83**	
Titan Crane	**1C 60**	
(Clydebank)		
Titwood Rd. G41: Glas	3A **106**	
(not continuous)		
Titwood Rd. G77: Newt M	2D **152**	
Tiverton Av. G32: Glas	2D **110**	
Tivoli Ct. G75: E Kil	5G **157**	
Tobago Pl. G40: Glas	6B **88**	
Tobago Pl. G75: E Kil	2C **156**	
Tobago St. G40: Glas	6A **88**	
Tobermory Gdns. ML6: Air	6A **74**	
Tobermory Rd. G73: Ruth	4F **125**	
Todburn Dr. PA2: Pais	6B **102**	
Todd Pl. G31: Glas	4E **89**	
Todd St. G31: Glas	4E **89**	
Todhills G75: E Kil	3H **157**	
(off Todhills Sth.)		
Todhills Nth. G75: E Kil	3H **157**	
Todhills Sth. G75: E Kil	3H **157**	
Todholm Cres. PA2: Pais	3D **102**	
Todholm Rd. PA2: Pais	3D **102**	
Todholm Ter. PA2: Pais	3D **102**	
Tofthill Av. G64: B'rig	5B **50**	
Tofthill Gdns. G64: B'rig	5B **50**	
Toll, The G76: Clar	1C **138**	
Tollbrae Av. ML6: Air	4B **96**	
TOLLCROSS	**2A 110**	
Tollcross International Swimming Cen.		
	1H **109**	
Tollcross Pk. Gdns. G32: Glas	2G **109**	
(off Tollcross Rd.)		
Tollcross Pk. Gro. G32: Glas	2H **109**	
Tollcross Pk. Leisure Cen.	2H **109**	
Tollcross Pk. Vw. G32: Glas	2G **109**	
Tollcross Rd. G31: Glas	6F **89**	
Tollcross Rd. G32: Glas	1G **109**	
Toll Ga., The G51: Glas	5C **86**	
(off Marine Cres.)		
Tollhouse Gdns. ML4: Bell	4E **131**	
Toll La. G51: Glas	5C **86**	
Tollpark Cres. ML2: Newm	4E **151**	
Tollpark Pl. G68: Cumb	3E **17**	
Tollpark Rd. G68: Cumb	3D **16**	
Toll St. ML1: Moth	4H **147**	
Toll Wynd ML3: Ham	4G **161**	
Tolmount Cres. ML1: Moth	6D **148**	

Tolsta St. G23: Glas	6C **48**	
Tom Johnston Ho. G66: Kirkin	6C **32**	
Tom Johnston Way G66: Kirkin	1F **53**	
Tom McCabe Gdns. ML3: Ham	5A **146**	
Tomtain Brae G68: Cumb	6B **36**	
Tomtain Ct. G68: Cumb	6B **36**	
Toner Gdns. ML2: Over	4H **165**	
Tontine La. G1: Glas	6F **7** (5H **87**)	
Tontine Pl. G73: Ruth	3G **125**	
Topaz Ter. ML4: Bell	4C **130**	
Toppersfield PA10: Kilba	3C **98**	
Torbeg Gdns. G75: E Kil	1B **168**	
Torbreck St. G52: Glas	6F **85**	
Torbrex Rd. G67: Cumb	4A **38**	
Torburn Av. G46: Giff	3H **121**	
TORBUSH	**5F 151**	
Tordene Path G68: Cumb	2F **37**	
Torgyle St. G23: Glas	6B **48**	
Tormeadow Rd. G77: Newt M	4D **136**	
Tormore Ct. G33: Step	3E **69**	
Tormore St. G51: Glas	5D **84**	
Tormusk Dr. G45: Glas	3C **124**	
Tormusk Gdns. G45: Glas	3C **124**	
Tormusk Gro. G45: Glas	3C **124**	
Tormusk Pl. G45: Glas	4C **124**	
Tormusk Rd. G45: Glas	3B **124**	
Torness St. G11: Glas	1A **4** (1A **86**)	
Torogay Pl. G22: Glas	1A **66**	
Torogay St. G22: Glas	2G **65**	
Torogay Ter. G22: Glas	1G **65**	
Toronto Wlk. G32: Carm	5C **110**	
Torphin Cres. G32: Glas	5A **90**	
Torphin Wlk. G32: Glas	5B **90**	
TORRANCE	**5D 30**	
Torrance Av. G75: E Kil	6B **158**	
Torrance Av. ML6: Air	4D **96**	
Torrance Ct. G75: E Kil	1H **169**	
Torrance Gait G75: E Kil	1H **169**	
Torrance House Golf Course	5C **158**	
Torrance La. G75: E Kil	1H **169**	
Torrance Pk. Golf Course	2D **132**	
Torrance Rd. G64: B'rig	5D **30**	
Torrance Rd. G64: Torr	5D **30**	
Torrance Rd. G74: E Kil	1G **157**	
TORRANCE RDBT.	6B **158**	
Torrance Wynd G75: E Kil	1H **169**	
Torran Dr. PA8: Ersk	2A **60**	
Torran Rd. G33: Glas	4F **91**	
Torranyard Ter. ML3: Ham	2C **160**	
Torr Av. PA11: Quarr V	1A **76**	
Torr Gdns. G22: Glas	5H **65**	
Torriden Ct. ML5: Coat	6A **94**	
(off Torriden St.)		
Torriden Pl. ML5: Coat	6A **94**	
Torriden St. ML5: Coat	6A **94**	
Torridon Av. G41: Glas	2G **105**	
Torridon Av. ML1: N'hill	4D **132**	
Torridon Ct. G20: Glas	1E **87**	
(off Cedar St.)		
Torridon Dr. PA4: Renf	1G **83**	
Torridon Gdns. G61: Bear	6D **26**	
Torridon Gdns. G77: Newt M	5H **137**	
Torridon Path G41: Glas	2G **105**	
(off Dumbreck Pl.)		
Torrington Av. G46: Giff	1G **137**	
Torrington Cres. G32: Glas	2D **110**	
Torrin Rd. G23: Glas	6B **48**	
Torrisdale Pl. ML5: Coat	4A **94**	
Torrisdale St. G42: Glas	3D **106**	
Torrisdale St. ML5: Coat	4A **94**	
Torr La. PA11: Quarr V	1A **76**	
Torr Pl. G22: Glas	5H **65**	
Torr Rd. G64: B'rig	6F **51**	
Torr Rd. PA11: Bri W	2C **76**	
Torr St. G22: Glas	5H **65**	
Torryburn Cl. G21: Glas	5E **67**	
Torryburn Rd. G21: Glas	5E **67**	
Torwood Brae ML3: Ham	1D **160**	
Torwood La. G69: Mood	5E **55**	

TORYGLEN – Uist Way

TORYGLEN 5A 108
Toryglen Regional Football Cen. 5G 107
Toryglen Rd. G73: Ruth 5B 108
Toryglen St. G5: Glas 3A 108
Toul Gdns. ML1: Moth 6C 148
Tourmaline Ter. ML4: Bell 4D 130
Tournai Path G72: Blan 2B 144
Toward Ct. G72: Blan 6C 128
Toward Rd. G33: Glas 4C 90
Toward Way PA2: Pais 6H 101
Tower Av. G78: Barr 3F 119
Tower Ga. G66: Kirkin 1G 53
Towerhill Rd. G13: Glas 6C 46
Tower Pl. G20: Glas 3B 64
Tower Pl. G62: Miln 3H 27
Tower Pl. PA5: John 4G 99
Tower Rais G78: Barr 4G 119
Tower Rd. G62: Bald 2D 28
Tower Rd. G64: Balm 2G 29
Tower Rd. G64: Torr 2G 29
Tower Rd. G67: Cumb 1H 57
Tower Rd. PA5: John 4F 99
Towerside Cres. G53: Glas 3A 104
Towerside Rd. G53: Glas 3A 104
Towers Pl. ML6: Air 4F 97
Towers Rd. ML6: Air 3E 97
Tower St. G41: Glas 6C 86
Tower Ter. PA1: Pais 1H 101
Tower Vw. G53: Glas 3H 103
Towie Pl. G71: Udd 1D 128
Town Cen. G67: Cumb 4H 37
TOWNEND 2F 19
Townend Rd. G82: Dumb 3F 19
TOWNHEAD G1 6E 7 (4G 87)
TOWNHEAD G66 5C 32
TOWNHEAD ML5 2H 93
Townhead G66: Kirkin 5D 32
Townhead Av. ML1: Holy 5G 115
Townhead Dr. ML1: N'hill 4F 133
TOWNHEAD INTERCHANGE 3H 7 (3A 88)
(M8, Junction 15)
Townhead Pl. G71: Tann 5E 113
Townhead Rd. G77: Newt M 5C 136
Townhead Rd. ML5: Coat 1E 93
Townhead St. G65: Kils 3H 13
Townhead St. ML3: Ham 6B 146
(not continuous)
Townhead Ter. PA1: Pais 1H 101
Townhill Rd. ML3: Ham 6B 144
Townhill Ter. ML3: Ham 6C 144
Townmill Rd. G31: Glas 3B 88
Townsend St. G4: Glas 1D 6 (1G 87)
Track Dr. G71: Tann 5F 113
(not continuous)
Trades Hall 6E 7 (4G 87)
(Glasgow)
(off Glassford St.)
TRADESTON 6E 87
Tradeston Ind. Est. G5: Glas 1D 106
Tradeston St. G5: Glas 6E 87
Trafalgar Ct. G68: Dull 5F 15
Trafalgar St. G81: Clyd 4B 44
Trainard Av. G32: Glas 1H 109
Training Dr. G13: Glas 4D 62
Training Pl. G13: Glas 4D 62
Tramway 2E 107
Tranent Pl. G33: Glas 3G 89
Tranent Pl. ML1: Cle 5H 133
Traquair Av. ML2: Wis 4A 150
Traquair Av. PA2: Pais 5C 100
Traquair Dr. G52: Glas 1B 104
Traquair Gdns. G77: Newt M 6A 136
Traquair Wynd G72: Blan 2A 144
(off Winton Cres.)
Treeburn Av. G46: Giff 4H 121
Treemain Rd. G46: Giff 1G 137
Trees Pk. Av. G78: Barr 3D 118
Trees Pk. Gdns. G78: Barr 3D 118
Trefoil Av. G41: Glas 5B 106
Trefoil Pl. PA6: Hous 1B 78
Trench Dr. G53: Glas 5C 120
Trent Pl. G75: E Kil 5A 156
Trent St. ML5: Coat 1H 93
Trequair Ct. G20: Glas 6D 64
(off Wilton St.)
Tresta Rd. G23: Glas 1C 64
Triangle, The G64: B'rig 6C 50
Triangle Shop. Cen., The 6C 50
Tribboch St. ML9: Lark 2B 170
Trident Ho. PA3: Pais 3C 82
(off Renfrew Rd.)
Trident Way PA4: Renf 2E 83
Trinidad Grn. G75: E Kil 2C 156
Trinidad Way G75: E Kil 2C 156
Trinity Av. G52: Glas 1C 104
Trinity Dr. G71: Udd 2D 128
Trinity Dr. G72: Camb 4C 126
Trinity Gdns. ML6: Air 2D 96
Trinity Way ML9: Lark 4E 171
Trinley Rd. G13: Glas 6D 46
Triton Pl. ML4: Moss 2H 131
Trondra Path G34: Glas 3F 91
Trondra Pl. G34: Glas 4F 91
Trongate G1: Glas 6E 7 (5G 87)
Trongate 103 5G 87
(off King St.)
Tron Theatre 5H 87
Troon Av. G75: E Kil 5C 156
Troon Ct. G75: E Kil 5D 156
Troon Dr. PA11: Bri W 4E 77
Troon Gdns. G68: Cumb 5H 15
Troon Pl. G77: Newt M 5G 137
Troon St. G40: Glas 2D 108
Trossachs Av. ML1: Holy 2A 132
Trossachs Ct. G20: Glas 6E 65
Trossachs Rd. G73: Ruth 5F 125
(not continuous)
Trossachs St. G20: Glas 6E 65
Troubridge Av. PA10: Kilba 4B 98
Troubridge Cres. PA10: Kilba 3B 98
Trovaig PA8: Ersk 2G 59
Trows Rd. ML2: Over 5H 165
Truce Rd. G13: Glas 1B 62
Truro Av. G69: Mood 4D 54
Tryst Rd. G67: Cumb 4H 37
Tryst Sports Cen. 3A 38
Tryst Wlk. G67: Cumb 4H 37
Tudor La. Sth. G14: Glas 6E 63
Tudor Rd. G14: Glas 6E 63
Tudor St. G69: Bail 2F 111
Tula Way G69: G'csh 4D 70
Tulip Dr. G77: Newt M 2C 136
Tulley Wynd ML1: Moth 5F 131
Tulliallan Pl. G74: E Kil 3A 158
Tullis Ct. G40: Glas 1A 108
Tullis Gdns. G40: Glas 1B 108
Tullis St. G40: Glas 1A 108
Tulloch-Ard Pl. G73: Ruth 4F 125
Tulloch Gdns. ML1: Moth 5B 148
Tulloch St. G44: Glas 1E 123
Tullymet Rd. ML3: Ham 3H 161
Tummel Dr. ML6: Air 1H 95
Tummel Grn. G74: E Kil 6G 141
Tummell Way PA2: Pais 4D 100
Tummel St. G33: Glas 1G 89
Tummel Way G67: Cumb 3H 37
(within The Cumbernauld Shop. Cen.)
Tunnel St. G3: Glas 6D 4 (4C 86)
Tuphall Rd. ML3: Ham 1H 161
Tureen St. G40: Glas 5A 88
(off Millroad Dr.)
Turnberry Av. G11: Glas 6H 63
Turnberry Cres. ML5: Coat 1A 114
Turnberry Cres. ML6: Chap 4E 117
Turnberry Dr. G73: Ruth 2B 124
Turnberry Dr. G77: Newt M 5G 137
Turnberry Dr. ML3: Ham 1B 160
Turnberry Dr. PA11: Bri W 5E 77
Turnberry Gdns. G68: Cumb 6H 15
Turnberry Pl. G73: Ruth 2B 124
Turnberry Pl. G75: E Kil 5D 156
Turnberry Pl. G82: Dumb 3C 18
Turnberry Rd. G11: Glas 6G 63
Turnberry Wynd G71: Both 4C 128
Turnbull St. G1: Glas 5H 87
Turner Rd. G21: Glas 1B 88
Turner Rd. PA3: Pais 3B 82
Turners Av. PA1: Pais 2F 101
Turner St. ML5: Coat 5B 94
Turnhill Av. PA8: Ersk 2F 59
Turnhill Cres. PA8: Ersk 2F 59
Turnhill Dr. PA8: Ersk 1F 59
Turnhill Gdns. PA8: Ersk 2F 59
Turnhill Rd. G65: Twe 2D 34
Turnlaw G75: E Kil 6F 157
Turnlaw Farm G72: Camb 6A 126
Turnlaw Rd. G72: Camb 6A 126
Turnlaw St. G5: Glas 1H 107
Turnyland Mdws. PA8: Ersk 2F 59
Turnyland Way PA8: Ersk 2F 59
Turquoise Ter. ML4: Bell 4D 130
Turret Cres. G13: Glas 1C 62
Turret Rd. G13: Glas 6C 46
Turriff St. G5: Glas 1F 107
TWECHAR 2D 34
Twechar Ent. Pk. G65: Twe 1D 34
Twechar Recreation Cen. 2D 34
Tweed Av. PA2: Pais 3D 100
Tweed Ct. ML6: Air 6C 96
Tweed Cres. G33: Glas 2F 89
Tweed Cres. ML2: Wis 4A 150
Tweed Cres. PA4: Renf 6G 61
Tweed Dr. G61: Bear 4D 46
Tweed La. ML1: Holy 2B 132
Tweedmuir Pl. ML5: Coat 2F 115
Tweed Pl. PA5: John 5C 98
Tweedsmuir G64: B'rig 5E 51
Tweedsmuir Cres. G61: Bear 6E 27
Tweedsmuir Pk. ML3: Ham 3G 161
Tweedsmuir Rd. G52: Glas 1B 104
Tweed St. G75: E Kil 4B 156
Tweed St. ML5: Coat 2D 114
Tweed St. ML9: Lark 4C 170
Tweedvale Av. G14: Glas 3G 61
Tweedvale Pl. G14: Glas 3G 61
Tweed Wlk. G67: Cumb 4H 37
(within The Cumbernauld Shop. Cen.)
Twinlaw St. G34: Glas 2B 92
Tylney Rd. PA1: Pais 6F 83
Tyndrum Rd. G61: Bear 2H 47
Tyndrum St. G4: Glas 1D 6 (2G 87)
Tyne Av. G75: E Kil 1C 168
Tynecastle Cres. G32: Glas 4B 90
Tynecastle Path G32: Glas 4B 90
Tynecastle Pl. G32: Glas 4B 90
Tynecastle St. G32: Glas 4B 90
Tyne Pl. G75: E Kil 5A 156
Tyne Pl. ML5: Coat 2A 114
Tynron Ct. ML3: Ham 2C 160
Tynwald Av. G73: Ruth 3F 125

U

UDDINGSTON 2D 128
Uddingston Park & Ride 1C 128
Uddingston Rd. G71: Both 4D 128
Uddingston Station (Rail) 1C 128
UDSTON 5D 144
UDSTON HOSPITAL 5D 144
Udston Rd. ML3: Ham 5C 144
Udston Ter. ML3: Ham 4D 144
Uig Pl. G33: Glas 6E 91
Uist Cres. G33: Step 5E 69
Uist Dr. G66: Kirkin 5G 33
Uist Pl. ML6: Air 5D 96
Uist St. G51: Glas 4F 85
Uist Way ML2: Wis 4C 150

280 A–Z Glasgow

Ullapool Gro. – Vigilant Ho.

Ullapool Gro. PA7: B'ton 5F **41**
Ullswater G75: E Kil 6B **156**
Ulundi Rd. PA5: John 3D **98**
Ulva St. G52: Glas 6F **85**
Ulverston Ter. ML3: Ham 5H **161**
Umachan PA8: Ersk 2G **59**
Underwood Ct. PA3: Pais 6H **81**
Underwood Dr. ML2: Newm 2E **151**
Underwood La. PA1: Pais 6H **81**
Underwood Rd. G73: Ruth 1E **125**
Underwood Rd. PA3: Pais 6G **81**
Underwood St. G41: Glas 5C **106**
Union Ct. PA2: Pais 3A **102**
Union Pl. G1: Glas 5C **6** (4F **87**)
Union St. G1: Glas 5C **6** (4F **87**)
Union St. G66: Kirkin 5C **32**
Union St. ML1: New S 3A **132**
Union St. ML3: Ham 5G **145**
Union St. ML8: Carl 4D **174**
Union St. ML9: Lark 2C **170**
Union St. PA2: Pais 3A **102**
Union Way G71: Tann 5F **113**
Unitas Cres. ML8: Carl 4C **174**
Unitas Rd. ML4: Moss 2E **131**
Unity Pl. G4: Glas 1E **87**
University Av. G12: Glas 1B **86**
University Gdns. G12: Glas 1B **86**
University of Glasgow **6G 47**
(Garscube Campus)
University of Glasgow **1B 86**
(Gilmorehill Campus)
University of Glasgow **2F 63**
(Netherton Rd.)
University of Glasgow **1C 86**
(Park Drive)
University of Glasgow **6F 47**
(Switchback Road)
University of Glasgow **1G 63**
(University Veterinary Hospital)
University of Glasgow Vis. Cen. **1B 86**
University of Strathclyde **5F 7 (4H 87)**
(John Anderson Campus)
University of the West of Scotland **5H 145**
(Hamilton Campus)
University of the West of Scotland **1H 101**
(Paisley Campus)
University Pl. G12: Glas 1A **86**
(not continuous)
Unsted Pl. PA1: Pais 1C **102**
Unst La. G72: Camb 5G **125**
Unthank Rd. ML4: Moss 2E **131**
Uphall Pl. G33: Glas 4G **89**
Upland La. G14: Glas 5C **62**
(off Danes La. Nth.)
Upland Rd. G14: Glas 5C **62**
UP La. G65: Kils 3H **13**
Upper Bourtree Ct. G73: Ruth 3E **125**
Upper Bourtree Dr. G73: Ruth 3D **124**
Upper Glenburn Rd. G61: Bear 2C **46**
Upper Mill St. ML6: Air 3A **96**
UP Rd. G65: Kils 3H **13**
Urquhart Cres. PA4: Renf 1E **83**
Urquhart Dr. G74: E Kil 6A **142**
Urquhart Pl. G69: G'csh 5C **70**
Urrdale Rd. G41: Glas 6H **85**
Urwin La. G75: E Kil 3D **156**
Usmore Pl. G33: Glas 6E **91**

V

Vaila La. G72: Camb 4H **125**
Vaila Pl. G23: Glas 2E **65**
Vaila St. G23: Glas 1D **64**
Valence Twr. G71: Both 3B **128**
Valerio Ct. G72: Blan 1B **144**
Valetta Pl. G81: Clyd 4H **43**
Valeview Ter. G42: Glas 5E **107**
Valeview Ter. G82: Dumb 1G **19**
Vale Wlk. G64: B'rig 1E **67**
Vallance Wynd PA5: Eld 4A **100**
Vallantine Cres. G71: Tann 5E **113**
Vallay St. G22: Glas 1H **65**
Valleybank G65: Bant 1F **15**
Valley Ct. ML3: Ham 1G **161**
Valleyfield G66: Milt C 5A **10**
Valleyfield G75: E Kil 2F **157**
Valleyfield Av. ML3: Fern 2E **163**
Valleyfield Cres. ML3: Fern 2E **163**
Valleyfield Dr. G68: Cumb 4A **36**
Valleyfield St. G21: Glas 6A **66**
Valley Vw. ML1: Moth 6B **148**
Vancouver Ct. G75: E Kil 2D **156**
Vancouver Dr. G75: E Kil 2D **156**
Vancouver La. G14: Glas 5D **62**
(Norse La. Nth.)
(off Norse La. Nth.)
Vancouver La. G14: Glas 5C **62**
(Norse La. Sth.)
(off Norse La. Sth.)
Vancouver Pl. G81: Clyd 4H **43**
Vancouver Rd. G14: Glas 5C **62**
Vancouver Way G40: Glas 3D **108**
Vanguard St. G81: Clyd 5E **45**
Vanguard Way PA4: Renf 2E **83**
Vardar Av. G76: Clar 1A **138**
Vardon Lea ML1: Cle 6E **133**
Varna La. G14: Glas 6E **63**
Varna Rd. G14: Glas 5E **63**
Varnsdorf Way ML6: Air 5D **96**
Vasart Pl. G20: Glas 5D **64**
Veir Ter. G82: Dumb 4E **19**
Veitches Ct. G81: Dun 1C **44**
Veitch Pl. G66: Len 3F **9**
Vennacher Rd. PA4: Renf 5C **60**
Vennard Gdns. G41: Glas 3C **106**
Vermont Av. G73: Ruth 6C **108**
Vermont St. G41: Glas 6B **86**
Vernon Bank G74: E Kil 6G **141**
Vernon Dr. PA3: Lin 5G **79**
Verona Av. G14: Glas 5C **62**
Verona Gdns. G14: Glas 5C **62**
Verona La. G14: Glas 5C **62**
Vesalius St. G32: Glas 6A **90**
Vesuvius Dr. ML1: Moth 5B **148**
Veteran's Cotts. PA7: B'ton 2D **42**
Viaduct Rd. G76: Busby 2D **138**
Vicarfield Pl. G51: Glas 4H **85**
Vicarfield St. G51: Glas 4H **85**
VICARLAND **2A 126**
Vicarland Pl. G72: Camb 3A **126**
Vicarland Rd. G72: Camb 2A **126**
Vicars Wlk. G72: Camb 2B **126**
Vickers St. ML1: Moth 1D **146**
Victoria Av. G78: Barr 3D **118**
Victoria Av. ML8: Carl 4C **174**
Victoria Bowling Green **4E 31**
Victoria Bri. 5G **87**
Victoria Cir. G12: Glas 6A **64**
Victoria Ct. G77: Newt M 1D **152**
Victoria Ct. ML9: Lark 1C **170**
Victoria Cres. G65: Kils 3F **13**
Victoria Cres. G76: Busby 2D **138**
Victoria Cres. G78: Barr 3D **118**
Victoria Cres. ML2: Wis 5D **148**
Victoria Cres. ML6: Air 5G **95**
Victoria Cres. La. G12: Glas 6A **64**
Victoria Cres. Pl. G12: Glas 6A **64**
Victoria Cres. Rd. G12: Glas 6A **64**
Victoria Cross G42: Glas 3E **107**
Victoria Dr. G78: Barr 3D **118**
Victoria Dr. E. PA4: Renf 1E **83**
Victoria Dr. W. PA4: Renf 6D **60**
Victoria Gdns. G78: Barr 3D **118**
Victoria Gdns. ML6: Air 4H **95**
Victoria Gdns. PA2: Pais 3G **101**
Victoria Glade G68: Dull 5F **15**
Victoria Gro. G78: Barr 3D **118**
Victoria La. G77: Newt M 1D **152**
Victoria Loan G40: Glas 2D **108**
VICTORIA MEMORIAL COTTAGE HOSPITAL **3F 13**
Victoria Pk. G65: Kils 3F **13**
Victoria Pk. Cnr. G14: Glas 6D **62**
Victoria Pk. Dr. Nth. G14: Glas 5D **62**
Victoria Pk. Dr. Sth. G14: Glas 6D **62**
(not continuous)
Victoria Pk. Gdns. Nth. G11: Glas 6F **63**
Victoria Pk. Gdns. Sth. G11: Glas 6F **63**
Victoria Pk. La. Nth. G14: Glas 6D **62**
Victoria Pk. St. G14: Glas 6D **62**
Victoria Pl. G62: Miln 4H **27**
Victoria Pl. G65: Kils 3G **13**
Victoria Pl. G73: Ruth 5C **108**
(off King St.)
Victoria Pl. G78: Barr 3E **119**
Victoria Pl. G81: Hard 1D **44**
Victoria Pl. ML4: Bell 3B **130**
Victoria Pl. ML6: Air 5G **95**
Victoria Quad. ML1: Holy 2H **131**
Victoria Rd. G33: Step 4C **68**
Victoria Rd. G42: Glas 4E **107**
Victoria Rd. G66: Lenz 3C **52**
Victoria Rd. G68: Dull 5F **15**
Victoria Rd. G73: Ruth 1D **124**
Victoria Rd. G78: Barr 3D **118**
Victoria Rd. PA2: Pais 3G **101**
Victoria Rd. PA5: Brkfld 6D **78**
Victoria Sq. G77: Newt M 1D **152**
Victoria St. G66: Kirkin 5C **32**
Victoria St. G72: Blan 3B **144**
Victoria St. G73: Ruth 5C **108**
Victoria St. G82: Dumb 5G **19**
Victoria St. ML2: Newm 5E **151**
Victoria St. ML3: Ham 3F **145**
Victoria St. ML9: Lark 2C **170**
Victoria Ter. G68: Dull 5F **15**
Victor St. ML6: Plain 1G **97**
Victory Baths **5F 61**
Victory Dr. PA10: Kilba 1A **98**
VICTORY GARDENS **1E 83**
Victory Way G69: Bail 1H **111**
Viewbank G46: T'bnk 4G **121**
Viewbank Av. ML6: C'bnk 3B **116**
Viewbank St. ML5: Glenb 4B **72**
Viewfield G69: Mood 3C **54**
VIEWFIELD **4B 130**
Viewfield ML6: Air 4G **95**
Viewfield Av. G64: B'rig 1A **66**
Viewfield Av. G66: Lenz 2C **52**
Viewfield Av. G66: Milt C 6B **10**
Viewfield Av. G69: Bail 6F **91**
Viewfield Av. G72: Blan 6C **128**
Viewfield Dr. G64: B'rig 1A **66**
Viewfield Dr. G69: Bail 6F **91**
Viewfield Gdns. G74: Ners 2A **142**
Viewfield La. G12: Glas 1C **86**
Viewfield Rd. FK4: Bank 1D **16**
Viewfield Rd. G64: B'rig 1A **66**
Viewfield Rd. ML4: Bell 4B **130**
Viewfield Rd. ML5: Coat 1F **113**
Viewglen Ct. G45: Glas 6H **123**
Viewglen Ga. G45: Glas 6H **123**
Viewmount Dr. G20: Glas 2B **64**
Viewmount Vs. G20: Glas 2B **64**
Viewpark G62: Miln 4H **27**
VIEWPARK **6G 113**
Viewpark Av. G31: Glas 3D **88**
Viewpark Ct. G73: Ruth 1E **125**
Viewpark Dr. G73: Ruth 1D **124**
Viewpark Gdns. **1F 129**
Viewpark Gdns. PA4: Renf 1D **82**
Viewpark Pl. ML1: Moth 3E **147**
Viewpark Rd. ML1: Moth 3E **147**
Viewpark Shop. Cen. **1H 129**
Viewpoint Ga. G21: Glas 3B **66**
Viewpoint Pl. G21: Glas 3B **66**
Viewpoint Rd. G21: Glas 3B **66**
Vigilant Ho. PA3: Pais 4A **82**

A–Z Glasgow 281

W

Willow Pl. – Woodlands Ct.

Willow Pl. PA5: John 3G **99**
Willows, The G76: Crmck 1H **139**
Willow St. G13: Glas 2F **63**
Willow Tea Rooms 3B **6** (3F **87**)
(off Sauchiehall St.)
Willowtree Way ML1: Carf 4C **132**
Willow Way ML3: Ham 2A **162**
Willox Pk. G82: Dumb 2G **19**
Willwood Rd. ML2: Wis 2A **150**
Wilmot Rd. G13: Glas 3D **62**
Wilsgait St. ML1: Cle 5H **133**
Wilson Av. PA3: Lin 5G **79**
Wilson Ct. ML4: Bell 2B **130**
Wilson Pl. G74: E Kil 5A **142**
Wilson Pl. G77: Newt M 5C **136**
Wilson St. G1: Glas 6E **7** (4G **87**)
Wilson St. ML1: Moth 2H **147**
Wilson St. ML3: Ham 4E **145**
Wilson St. ML5: Coat 4E **95**
Wilson St. ML6: Air 2H **95**
Wilson St. ML9: Lark 4D **170**
Wilson St. PA1: Pais 1G **101**
Wilson St. PA4: Renf 5F **61**
Wiltonburn Pl. G53: Glas 3A **120**
Wiltonburn Rd. G53: Glas 3A **120**
Wilton Ct. G20: Glas 5C **64**
(off Kelvinside Gdns. La.)
Wilton Cres. La. G20: Glas 6D **64**
Wilton Dr. G20: Glas 6D **64**
Wilton Gro. PA5: Eld 4A **100**
Wilton Rd. ML8: Carl 5E **175**
Wilton St. G20: Glas 5C **64**
Wilton St. ML5: Coat 1H **93**
Wilverton Rd. G13: Glas 1E **63**
Winburne Cres. ML3: Ham 5F **145**
Winchester Dr. G12: Glas 3H **63**
Windermere G75: E Kil 6B **156**
Windermere Gdns. ML3: Ham 5G **161**
Windermere St. ML4: Bell 3B **130**
Windhill Cres. G43: Glas 2H **121**
Windhill Pk. G76: Wfoot 1C **154**
Windhill Pl. G43: Glas 2A **122**
Windhill Rd. G43: Glas 2H **121**
Windlaw Ct. G45: Glas 5H **123**
Windlaw Gdns. G44: Neth 3D **122**
Windlaw Pk. Gdns. G44: Neth 3D **122**
Windlaw Rd. G76: Crmck 6H **123**
Windmill Ct. ML1: Moth 4H **147**
Windmill Ct. ML3: Ham 5H **145**
Windmillcroft Quay G5: Glas 5E **87**
Windmill Gdns. ML8: Carl 3D **174**
Windmillhill St. ML1: Moth 3H **147**
Windmill Rd. ML3: Ham 5H **145**
Windrow Ter. ML2: Wis 2A **150**
Windsor Av. G77: Newt M 4F **137**
Windsor Ct. ML8: Carl 3D **174**
Windsor Cres. G81: Clyd 4C **44**
Windsor Cres. PA1: Pais 5C **82**
Windsor Cres. PA5: Eld 4H **99**
Windsor Cres. La. G81: Clyd 4C **44**
Windsor Dr. ML6: Glenm 5H **73**
Windsor Gdns. ML3: Ham 4E **145**
Windsor Path G69: Barg 5D **92**
(off Park Rd.)
Windsor Path ML9: Lark 3E **171**
(off Carrick St.)
Windsor Pl. PA11: Bri W 3F **77**
(off Main Rd.)
Windsor Quad. ML8: Carl 3D **174**
Windsor Rd. ML1: Holy 2A **132**
Windsor Rd. PA4: Renf 1E **83**
Windsor St. G20: Glas 1E **87**
Windsor St. G32: Glas 5C **90**
Windsor St. ML5: Coat 2A **114**
Windsor Ter. G20: Glas 1E **87**
Windsor Wlk. G71: View 6F **113**
Windward Rd. G75: E Kil 2C **156**
Windyedge Cres. G13: Glas 4C **62**
Windyedge Pl. G13: Glas 4C **62**
Windyedge Rd. ML1: Cle 4H **133**
Windyhill Cres. PA5: John 6D **78**
Windyhill Golf Course **5A 26**
Windyridge ML3: Ham 2A **162**
Windyridge Pl. G72: Blan 2A **144**
Windy Yetts G65: Twe 2D **34**
Wingate Cres. G74: E Kil 5C **142**
Wingate Dr. G74: E Kil 5C **142**
Wingate Pk. G74: E Kil 5C **142**
Wingate St. ML2: Wis 5D **148**
Wingfield Gdns. G71: Both 6F **129**
Winifred St. G33: Glas 5F **67**
Winning Ct. G72: Blan 6C **128**
Winning Quad. ML2: Wis 6D **148**
Winning Row G31: Glas 6F **89**
Winnipeg Dr. G75: E Kil 3D **156**
Winston Cres. G66: Len 3F **9**
Wintergreen Ct. G74: E Kil 5F **141**
Wintergreen Dr. G74: E Kil 5F **141**
Winton Av. G46: Giff 5A **122**
Winton Cres. G72: Blan 2A **144**
Winton Dr. G12: Glas 4A **64**
Winton Gdns. G71: Tann 6D **112**
Winton La. G12: Glas 4A **64**
Winton Pk. G75: E Kil 2C **156**
Wirran Pl. G13: Glas 1G **61**
Wisham Golf Course **5G 149**
Wishart La. ML8: Law 6E **167**
Wishart St. G31: Glas 5H **7** (4A **88**)
WISHAW **6G 149**
WISHAW GENERAL HOSPITAL **6E 149**
Wishaw High Rd. ML1: Cle 1H **149**
WISHAWHILL **5F 149**
Wishawhill St. ML2: Wis 6F **149**
Wishaw Low Rd. ML1: Cle 3G **149**
Wishaw Rd. ML2: Newm 2B **166**
Wishaw Rd. ML2: Wis 2B **166**
Wishaw Sports Cen. **1F 165**
Wishaw Station (Rail) **1G 165**
Wisner Ct. G46: T'bnk 3F **121**
Wisteria La. ML8: Carl 5D **174**
Wiston St. G72: Camb 2E **127**
Witchwood Ct. ML5: Coat 1H **93**
Witchwood Gro. G77: Newt M 1C **136**
Witcutt Way ML2: Wis 2E **165**
Woddrop St. G40: Glas 3D **108**
Wolcott Dr. G72: Blan 1B **144**
Wolfe Av. G77: Newt M 2C **136**
Wolfson Hall G20: Glas 6H **47**
Wolseley Dr. G5: Glas 2H **107**
Wolseley St. G5: Glas 2H **107**
Wolseley Ter. G5: Glas 3H **107**
Women's Library **5G 87**
(off Parnie St.)
Wood Aven Dr. G74: E Kil 5F **141**
Woodbank Cres. G76: Clar 3C **138**
Woodbank Cres. PA5: John 3F **99**
Woodburn Av. G72: Blan 1C **144**
Woodburn Av. G76: Clar 3C **138**
Woodburn Av. ML6: Air 5H **95**
Woodburn Ct. G73: Ruth 1D **124**
Woodburn Gro. ML3: Ham 6H **145**
Woodburn Pk. **1D 124**
Woodburn Pk. ML3: Ham 6A **146**
Woodburn Pl. PA6: C'lee 4E **79**
Woodburn Rd. G43: Glas 2B **122**
Woodburn Rd. ML1: N'hse 6D **116**
Woodburn St. ML1: Moth 1G **147**
Woodburn Ter. ML9: Lark 3E **171**
Woodburn Way G62: Miln 4G **27**
Woodburn Way G68: Cumb 3E **37**
Wood Cres. ML1: Moth 6G **131**
Woodcroft Av. G11: Glas 6F **63**
Woodcroft Dr. G66: Lenz 1E **53**
Wooddale ML1: Moth 5F **147**
Woodend G72: Blan 3B **144**
Woodend Ct. G32: Glas 3E **111**
Woodend Dr. G13: Glas 4E **63**
Woodend Dr. ML6: Air 2C **96**
Woodend Dr. PA1: Pais 1F **103**
Woodend Gdns. G32: Glas 3D **110**
Woodend La. G13: Glas 4E **63**
Woodend La. ML9: Lark 4E **171**
(off Keir Hardie Rd.)
Woodend Pl. PA5: Eld 3H **99**
Woodend Rd. G32: Glas 3D **110**
Woodend Rd. G73: Ruth 3C **124**
Woodend Rd. ML8: Carl 3E **175**
Woodfarm Rd. G46: T'bnk 5G **121**
Woodfield G71: View 1G **129**
Woodfield Av. G64: B'rig 6D **50**
Woodfoot Cres. G53: Glas 3A **120**
Woodfoot Path G53: Glas 3B **120**
Woodfoot Quad. G53: Glas 3A **120**
Woodfoot Rd. ML3: Ham 1E **161**
Woodford Pl. PA3: Lin 5G **79**
Woodford St. G41: Glas 6C **106**
Woodgreen Av. G44: Glas 1F **123**
Woodgreen Ct. ML2: Wis 3G **165**
Woodhall ML1: Holy 5A **116**
Woodhall Av. ML1: Holy 2H **131**
Woodhall Av. ML3: Ham 5F **145**
Woodhall Av. ML5: Coat 2A **114**
Woodhall Av. ML6: C'bnk 3B **116**
Woodhall Cott. Rd. ML6: C'bnk 4C **116**
Woodhall Est. ML6: C'bnk 4B **116**
Woodhall Mill Rd. ML6: C'bnk 4B **116**
Woodhall Mill Rd. ML6: Chap 4B **116**
Woodhall Pl. ML5: Coat 2B **114**
Woodhall Rd. ML2: Newm 5D **150**
Woodhall Rd. ML2: Wis 5D **150**
Woodhall Rd. ML6: C'bnk 3B **116**
Woodhall St. G40: Glas 3C **108**
Woodhall St. ML6: Chap 4D **116**
Woodhead Av. G66: Kirkin 6D **32**
Woodhead Av. G68: Cumb 6B **36**
Woodhead Av. G71: Both 1F **145**
Woodhead Ct. G68: Cumb 6B **36**
Woodhead Cres. G71: Tann 6D **112**
Woodhead Cres. ML3: Ham 3E **161**
Woodhead Cres. ML6: Glenm 6G **73**
Woodhead Gdns. G71: Both 1F **145**
Woodhead Grn. ML3: Ham 3F **161**
Woodhead Gro. G68: Cumb 6B **36**
Woodhead Ind. Est. G69: Chry 3H **69**
Woodhead La. ML3: Ham 3F **161**
Woodhead Path G53: Glas 2A **120**
Woodhead Pl. G68: Cumb 6B **36**
Woodhead Rd. G53: Glas 2H **119**
Woodhead Rd. G68: Cumb 6B **36**
Woodhead Rd. G69: Chry 3H **69**
Woodhead Ter. G69: Chry 2H **69**
Woodhead Vw. G68: Cumb 6B **36**
Woodhill Rd. G21: Glas 3D **66**
Woodhill Rd. G64: B'rig 6E **51**
Woodholm Av. G44: Glas 1G **123**
Woodhouse Ct. G76: Busby 4E **139**
Woodhouse St. G13: Glas 2E **63**
Woodilee Cotts. G66: Lenz 1E **53**
Woodilee Ct. G66: Lenz 1F **53**
Woodilee Ind. Est. G66: Lenz 1E **53**
Woodilee Rd. G66: Kirkin 6E **33**
Woodilee Rd. G66: Lenz 2E **53**
Woodilee Rd. G66: Lenz 6E **33**
Woodilee Rd. ML1: N'hill 3E **133**
Woodland Av. G66: Kirkin 5B **32**
Woodland Av. ML6: Air 1C **116**
Woodland Av. PA2: Pais 5A **102**
Woodland Cres. G72: Camb 3B **126**
Woodland Cres. G76: Eag 6B **154**
Woodland Gdns. G76: Crmck 2H **139**
Woodland Gdns. ML3: Ham 1B **162**
Woodlands, The ML4: Bell 4F **131**
Woodlands Av. G69: G'csh 2C **70**
Woodlands Av. G71: Both 4E **129**
Woodlands Av. ML8: Law 5D **166**
Woodlands Ct. G46: T'bnk 5F **121**
Woodlands Ct. G60: Old K 2F **43**

Published by Geographers' A-Z Map Company Limited
An imprint of HarperCollins Publishers
Westerhill Road
Bishopbriggs
Glasgow
G64 2QT

www.az.co.uk
a-z.maps@harpercollins.co.uk

HarperCollinsPublishers
Macken House, 39/40 Mayor Street Upper, Dublin 1, D01 C9W8, Ireland

7th edition 2023

A catalogue record for this book is available from the British Library.

ISBN 978-0-00-856043-0

10 9 8 7 6 5 4 3 2 1

Printed in India

This book is produced from independently certified FSC™ paper
to ensure responsible forest management.

For more information visit: www.harpercollins.co.uk/green